BOLLINGEN SERIES LX

SAMOTHRACE

EXCAVATIONS

CONDUCTED BY THE INSTITUTE OF FINE ARTS

OF NEW YORK UNIVERSITY

KARL LEHMANN

PHYLLIS WILLIAMS LEHMANN

Editors

Volume 5

Detail of the frieze of dancing maidens from the Propylon. Samothrace Museum.

SAMOTHRACE

THE TEMENOS

BY

PHYLLIS WILLIAMS LEHMANN

AND

DENYS SPITTLE

WITH CONTRIBUTIONS BY

KARL LEHMANN

ELSBETH B. DUSENBERY, MARTHA LEEB HADZI, MARY B. MOORE,
AND STUART M. SHAW

Text

BOLLINGEN SERIES LX · 5

PRINCETON UNIVERSITY PRESS

Published by Princeton University Press, Princeton, New Jersey
In the United Kingdom: Princeton University Press, Guildford, Surrey

Library of Congress Cataloging in Publication Data will be found on the last printed page of this volume.

THIS IS PART ONE OF THE FIFTH VOLUME
IN A PUBLICATION ON SAMOTHRACE
CONSTITUTING NUMBER LX IN BOLLINGEN SERIES,
SPONSORED BY BOLLINGEN FOUNDATION

This book has been composed in Linotype Caledonia.
It is based on a design by Andor Braun.
Clothbound editions of Princeton University Press books are printed on acid-free paper, and binding materials are chosen for strength and durability.
Composed by Princeton University Press, Princeton, N.J.
Printed by the Meriden Gravure Company, Meriden, Conn.

In Memory of

KARL LEHMANN

PREFACE

WHEN Karl Lehmann died in December 1960, he had published three preliminary reports in *Hesperia* which both recorded the excavation of the Propylon and the Temenos in 1949 and 1950, and presented his initial interpretation of the building, the precinct, and the remarkable ceramics discovered in the depths of the precinct. In the later fifties, he assembled an immense quantity of notes dealing, in particular, with the architecture of the Propylon and its relationship to major buildings of the fourth century B.C. These notes and reports proved essential to me when I inherited the task of preparing the final publication of an area of the Sanctuary in which I had not been previously active. It was not until late summer, 1970, that I could finally undertake this task. In the meantime, Professor Lehmann had selected Denys Spittle, a professional architect and member of the Royal Commission on Historical Monuments (England) with whom he had previously collaborated in the publication of *Samothrace*, Volume 4, part II, *The Altar Court*, to again collaborate in the final reconstruction of the Propylon. It has been my great good fortune to have him as a faithful colleague in working out this final reconstruction.

In view of these circumstances, I found it essential to reexamine every scrap of evidence connected with the excavation of this area. It was especially important inasmuch as additional blocks or fragments of the Propylon had been recovered out-of-context, as so often happens in ongoing excavations, in the years following Professor Lehmann's death. Some had been reused in a post-antique Byzantine fortification built of blocks plundered from the destroyed Sanctuary; others, including one crucial coffer lid, had been assembled to be burned in a limekiln but happily escaped that fate. As a result, the present reconstruction of the Propylon differs markedly from the previous preliminary reconstructions of the building, as does my own interpretation of the history of the Temenos. I am confident that Karl Lehmann would have welcomed this new evidence and the opportunity it has afforded to correct his preliminary statements. I can only hope that he would have agreed with my present far-reaching conclusions. The responsibility for them is wholly mine; the guiding presence behind them, as always, his.

Plates I-III, the plan and sections of the extant Temenos, Propylon and terrace, and Plates XV, XVI, the capital of the Propylon and Fig. 71, a detail of the bolster pattern, are the work of Stuart M. Shaw. Plates I and III have been slightly emended by Nicholas D. Ohly on the basis of observations made in Samothrace in 1970 and 1977. These, and the remaining plates (IV-XIV and XVII-LX), by Denys Spittle, have formed the basis of Mr. Spittle's description and reconstruction of the Propylon in Chapter I and of my own discussions in Chapters I and II. I remain grateful to Professor Lehmann for having chosen Martha Leeb Hadzi in 1952 to prepare the final publication of the frieze of dancing maidens. Her sensitive eye has made our collaboration on Chapter III a pleasure. Mrs. Hadzi has also dealt with the few fragmentary sculptures that were found in the area of the terrace. I am greatly indebted, too, to Mary B.

Moore for having obliged me by undertaking to prepare the Catalogue of Ceramic Finds and for producing it in record time, and to Elsbeth B. Dusenbery for contributing an item to the Catalogue of Finds. It is a special pleasure to record my indebtedness both to Mrs. Dusenbery and to James R. McCredie for the many, long hours we have spent in Samothrace, in the Museum, and in the field, discussing the intricate problems posed by this volume. Mrs. Dusenbery's knowledge of terracottas, in particular, and Mr. McCredie's skill as an excavator have been an enormous asset to me. I am especially indebted, too, to another member of the Samothracian staff, Ioannis K. Akamatis, whose knowledge of Samothrace and the Sanctuary I have found invaluable. Finally, I would like to thank John Kurtich, long-time architect in Samothrace, for drawings and sections of the Sanctuary that have aided me in my work, and Madelaine De Huszar Bullwinkel, who drew the great majority of the ceramic profiles published in the Catalogue. Additional ceramic profiles were drawn by Mary Dabney and Leslie Simon in the summer of 1975.

It is a pleasure to acknowledge the generous collaboration of Anna Wachsmann and Alison Frantz, many of whose splendid photographs appear in this volume. The remainder of the unacknowledged photographs of the excavation and of Samothracian monuments were taken by members of the staff. I am indebted, again, to Mr. McCredie for rephotographing a large portion of the fragments and fragmentary blocks of the frieze of the Propylon and the miscellaneous sculptures published in this volume, and to Miss Moore to whose photographic skill we owe the illustrations of the Catalogue of Ceramics.

We are, as always, especially indebted to the successive directors of the Antikenabteilung of the Kunsthistorisches Museum in Vienna—to the late Fritz Eichler, to Rudolf Noll and, in particular, to Wolfgang Oberleitner—for providing us with every facility and courtesy during our repeated stays in Vienna to examine and, in 1970, to allow Mr. Spittle and me to reexamine the architectural and sculptural fragments of the Propylon in the storerooms of the Museum. In this volume, as in all the other volumes of our publication in which evidence recorded by our Austrian predecessors in Samothrace is reconsidered, and where certain of the blocks and sculptures of a building are housed in Vienna, we are partially dependent on access to that material in the possession of the Kunsthistorisches Museum. That such access is always at our disposal has been indispensable to our work.

Now, as this volume goes to press, a new museum, the Ephesos-Museum, is being opened in Vienna in which the architectural and sculptural fragments of the Propylon originally stored in the Kunsthistorisches Museum will be exhibited. I am greatly indebted to Kurt Gschwantler of the Antikensammlung, who has been in charge of the new installation, for his care and courtesy in informing me about the specific fragments that will be on exhibition in the new museum.

I owe a special debt of gratitude to Jiří Frel, who made available to me in Prague, in the summer of 1967, the series of precious drawings drawn by J. Nepomucký recording the drum, capital, and column fragments first discovered by A. Salač in his excavation in the *Ruinenviereck* in 1926-27. Dr. Frel, at the time the successor to Salač as Professor of Archaeology at the Charles University, generously provided me with the photographs of the drawings reproduced in Chapter I that reveal the superior preservation of the blocks in the twenties of the century. Several important features of these weathered and important blocks thereby became intelligible.

During the autumn semesters of 1970 and 1976, I was Research Fellow at the American School of Classical Studies in Athens, where I had the daily opportunity to use the splendid Library of the School. I am most grateful to the Director, Professor McCredie, for appointing me to this post, and take pleasure in thanking the librarians, Mrs. Philippides and Miss Winter, and the staff of the School for the use of its facilities and for its warm hospitality. The Library and Photograph Collection of the Deutsches Archäologisches Institut in Athens and of the William Allen Neilson and Art Libraries of Smith College have, as always, proved helpful. It is a pleasure, too, to express my gratitude to D.E.L. Haynes and Brian F. Cook for putting the facilities of the Department of Greek and Roman Antiquities in the British Museum at my disposal.

In the spring semester of 1977, I was Mary Flexner Lecturer at Bryn Mawr College. One of my public lectures, "New Light on Skopas," was not separately published inasmuch as large sections of it were to appear as portions of Chapters III and IV of this volume. I am grateful to Mary Patterson McPherson and members of the Departments of Classical and Near Eastern Archaeology and of the History of Art for their willingness to allow me to incorporate this material in these chapters.

Finally, I am indebted to a host of additional friends and colleagues for sharing opinions and information with me and for providing photographs for this volume. Their individual contributions are for the most part indicated in relevant footnotes, but I would like gratefully to acknowledge their assistance here: Stylianos Alexiou, François Baratte, Peter H. von Blanckenhagen, Nancy Bookidis, Dietrich von Bothmer, Jan Bouzek, Bruce Barker-Benfield, Edwin Colbert, Luigi D'Amore, Necati Dolunay, G. Dontis, Alfred K. Frazer, Kurt Gschwantler, Wolf-Dieter Heilmeyer, Wolfram Hoepfner, V. G. Kallipolitis, Semni Karouzou, E. La Rocca, Judith A. Lerner, Elaine P. Loeffler, Iris C. Love, Michael Maass, Lawrence Majewski, Ira S. Mark, Margo Marshall, Antonietta Morandini, Elizabeth Papagiorgiou, Anneliese Peschlow, Photios M. Petsas, Barbara Philippaki, Graham Pollard, Edith Porada, Frederick H. Pough, Irene Fraley Preston, Elisabeth Rohde, H.-D. Schultz, Andrew F. Stewart, the late Donald Strong, Thomas Todd, Nancy M. Waggoner, Franz Willemsen, Charles K. Williams II, Nicholas Yalouris and L. C. Zoreda.

Special thanks go to the editorial and production departments of the Princeton University Press for their care and skill in coping with this volume, and to Erna G. Huber for typing the manuscript. I remain permanently indebted to Mrs. Huber for her continuing readiness to help me in innumerable ways.

We dedicate this volume to the memory of Karl Lehmann. Under his direction, the Propylon and the Temenos were excavated. His preliminary drawings, his records, notes, and reports have been essential to Mr. Spittle, to Mrs. Hadzi, to Miss Moore and to me. Without them, the present volume would have been impossible.

Haydenville, Massachusetts
April, 1978

PHYLLIS WILLIAMS LEHMANN

CONTENTS

CATALOGUE OF FINDS

The Plates are bound separately.

ABBREVIATIONS

AA	*Archäologischer Anzeiger.*
AAA	*Athens Annals of Archaeology.*
Agora XII	Brian Sparkes and Lucy Talcott, *Black and Plain Ware of the Sixth, Fifth, and Fourth Centuries B.C.* (*The Athenian Agora*, XII). Princeton, 1970.
AJA	*American Journal of Archaeology.*
Annuario	*Annuario della (Regia) Scuola Archeologica di Atene.*
Antikes Traufleisten-Ornament	Martin Schede. *Antikes Traufleisten-Ornament.* Strassburg, 1909.
ArchEph	Ἀρχαιολογικὴ Ἐφημερίς.
Arias	Paolo Enrico Arias. *Skopas* (*Quaderni e guide di archeologia,* I). Rome, 1952.
Ashmole	Bernard Ashmole. *Architect and Sculptor in Classical Greece.* New York, 1972.
AthMitt	*Mitteilungen des deutschen archäologischen Instituts, Athenische Abteilung.*
AZ	*Archäologische Zeitung.*
BCH	*Bulletin de correspondance hellénique.*
BdA	*Bollettino d'arte.*
Berl. Ber.	Preussischen Akademie der Wissenschaften. Berlin. *Monatsberichte.*
Berve-Gruben-Hirmer	Helmut Berve, Gottfried Gruben, and Max Hirmer. *Greek Temples, Theaters and Shrines.* New York, 1963.
BonnJbb	Bonner Jahrbücher.
BSA	*Annual of the British School at Athens.*
BullComm	*Bullettino della Commissione Archeologica Comunale di Roma.*
Chapouthier	Fernand Chapouthier. *Les Dioscures au service d'une déesse* (Bibliothèque des Ecoles françaises d'Athènes et de Rome, 137). Paris, 1935.
CIG	*Corpus Inscriptionum Graecarum.*
CIL	*Corpus Inscriptionum Latinarum.*
Cook-Plommer	J. M. Cook and W. H. Plommer. *The Sanctuary of Hemithea at Kastabos.* Cambridge, 1966.
Corinth	Results of Excavations Conducted by the American School of Classical Studies at Athens. *Corinth,* Princeton, 1929–
Coupel-Demargne	Pierre Coupel and Pierre Demargne. *Fouilles de Xanthos,* III, *Le Monument des Néréides, L'architecture.* Paris, 1969.
Courby-Picard	Fernand Courby and Charles Picard, *Recherches archéologiques à Stratos.* Paris, 1924.
CRAI	*Comptes rendus de l'Académie des inscriptions et belles lettres.*
CVA	*Corpus Vasorum Antiquorum.*
Délos	Ecole française d'Athènes. *Exploration archéologique de Délos.* Paris, 1909–
Deltion	Ἀρχαιολογικὸν Δελτίον.

Demangel	R. Demangel. *La Frise ionique* (Bibliothèque des Ecoles françaises d'Athènes et de Rome, 136). Paris, 1932.
Deville-Coquart	G. Deville and E. Coquart. "Rapport sur une mission dans l'île de Samothrace," *Archives des missions scientifiques et littéraires.* 2nd ser., 4 (1867), pp. 254 ff.
Didyma	Theodor Wiegand, ed. *Didyma.* Berlin, 1941– .
Dinsmoor	William Bell Dinsmoor. *The Architecture of Ancient Greece.* London and New York, 1950.
Dörpfeld	William Dörpfeld. *Troja und Ilion: Ergebnisse der Ausgrabungen in der vorhistorischen und historischen Schichten von Ilion, 1870-1894.* Athens, 1902.
Dugas	Charles Dugas, Jules Berchmans, Mogen Clemmensen, *Le Sanctuaire d'Aléa Athéna à Tégée au IVe siècle.* Paris, 1924.
Etudes thasiennes	Ecole française d'Athènes. *Etudes thasiennes.* Paris, 1944– .
FdDelphes	Ecole française d'Athènes. *Fouilles de Delphes.* Paris, 1909– .
FGrHist	F. Jacoby. *Die Fragmente der griechischen Historiker.* Berlin and Leiden, 1923– .
Frankfort	Henri Frankfort. *The Art and Architecture of the Ancient Orient.* Baltimore, 1954.
Fuchs	Werner Fuchs. *Die Vorbilder der Neu-attischen Reliefs. JdI-EH,* 20 (1959).
Furtwängler-Reichhold	Adolf Furtwängler and Karl Reichhold. *Griechische Vasenmalerei,* ser. I-III. Munich, 1904-32.
Gruben	Gottfried Gruben. *Die Tempel der Griechen.* Munich, 1966.
Guide	Karl Lehmann. *Samothrace. A Guide to the Excavations and the Museum.* New York, 1955.
Guide[2]	Idem. 2nd edn., revised. Locust Valley, New York, 1960.
Guide[3]	Idem. 3rd edn., revised. Locust Valley, New York, 1966.
Guide[4]	Idem. 4th edn., revised and enlarged. Locust Valley, New York, 1975.
Harrison	Evelyn B. Harrison. *Archaic and Archaistic Sculpture* (*The Athenian Agora,* XI). Princeton, 1965.
Hemberg	Bengt Hemberg. *Die Kabiren.* Uppsala, 1950.
Hoepfner	Wolfram Hoepfner. *Das Pompeion und seine Nachfolgenbauten* (Deutsches Archäologisches Institut, *Kerameikos,* X). Berlin, 1976.
IG	*Inscriptiones Graecae.*
IstMitt	*Istanbuler Mitteilungen.*
Jacobstahl	Paul Jacobstahl. *Die Ornamente griechischer Vasen.* Berlin, 1927.
JdI	*Jahrbuch des deutschen archäologischen Instituts.*
JHS	*Journal of Hellenic Studies.*
JPKS	*Jahrbuch des preussischen Kunstsammlungen.*
JRIBA	*Journal of the Royal Institute of British Architects.*
JRS	*Journal of Roman Studies.*
JWarb	*Journal of the Warburg and Courtauld Institutes.*
Kabirenheiligtum	P. Wolters et al. *Das Kabirenheiligtum bei Theben.* Berlin, 1939– .

Karouzou	S. Karouzou. *National Archaeological Museum, Collection of Sculpture, A Catalogue.* Athens, 1968.
Koldewey	Robert Koldewey. *Die antiken Baureste der Insel Lesbos.* Berlin, 1890.
Labraunda	Kristian Jeppesen. *Labraunda* I, 1, *The Propylaea* (*Skrifter Utgivna av Svenska Institutet i Athen* 4°, V, 1:1). Lund, 1955.
Lacroix	Léon Lacroix. *Les Reproductions de statues sur les monnaies grecques* (Bibliothèque de la Faculté de Philosophie et Lettres de l'Université de Liège, fasc. 116). Liège, 1949.
Lawrence	A. W. Lawrence. *Greek Architecture.* Baltimore, 1957.
Lethaby	W. R. Lethaby. *Greek Buildings Represented by Fragments in the British Museum.* London, 1908.
Lindos	C. Blinkenberg et al. *Lindos. Fouilles et recherches, 1902-1914.* Berlin, 1931– .
Martin	Roland Martin. *L'Agora* (*Etudes thasiennes*, VI, 1). Paris, 1959.
Milet	Theodor Wiegand, ed. *Milet.* Berlin, 1906– .
Neandria	Robert Koldeway. *Neandria* (*51. Programm zum Winckelmannsfeste*). Berlin, 1891.
Nemea	Bert Hodge Hill and Charles Kaufman Williams II. *The Temple of Zeus at Nemea.* Princeton, 1966.
Nilsson	Martin P. Nilsson. *Geschichte der griechischen Religion.* Munich, 1941, 1950.
NSc	*Notizie degli Scavi di Antichità.*
ÖJh	*Jahreshefte des österreichischen archäologischen Institutes in Wien.*
Olympia	E. Curtius and F. Adler. *Olympia.* Berlin, 1890-97.
Olynthus	D. M. Robinson et al. *Excavations at Olynthus.* Baltimore, 1929-52.
Paton-Stevens	J. M. Paton, G. P. Stevens et al. *The Erechtheum.* Cambridge, 1927.
Pedimental Sculptures	Phyllis Williams Lehmann. *The Pedimental Sculptures of the Hieron in Samothrace.* Locust Valley, New York, 1962.
Pergamon	Königliche (Staatliche) Museen zu Berlin. *Altertümer von Pergamon.* Berlin, 1885– .
Pettazzoni	Raffaele Pettazzoni, "Una rappresentazione romana dei Kabiri di Samotracia," *Ausonia*, 3 (1908), pp. 79-90.
Praktika	Πρακτικὰ τῆς ἐν Ἀθήναις Ἀρχαιολογικῆς Ἑταιρίας.
Priene	T. Wiegand and H. Schrader. *Priene. Ergebnisse der Ausgrabungen und Untersuchungen in den Jahren 1895-1898.* Berlin, 1904.
RA	*Revue archéologique.*
RE	G. Wissowa et al. *Paulys Real-Encyclopädie der classischen Altertumswissenschaft.* Stuttgart, 1894– .
Reise	Alexander Conze. *Reise auf den Inseln des thrakischen Meeres.* Hannover, 1860.
RhM	*Rheinisches Museum für Philologie.*
Ridgway	Brunilde S. Ridgway. "Notes on the Development of the Greek Frieze," *Hesperia*, 35 (1960), pp. 180 ff.
Robertson	Martin Robertson. *A History of Greek Art.* Cambridge, 1975.
RömMitt	*Mitteilungen des deutschen archäologischen Instituts, Römische Abteilung.*

Roscher	W. H. Roscher. *Ausführliches Lexikon der griechischen und römischen Mythologie.* Leipzig, 1884-1937.
Roux	Georges Roux. *L'Architecture de l'Argolide aux IVe et IIIe siècles avant J.-C.* Paris, 1961.
Rubensohn	Otto Rubensohn. *Die Mysterienheiligtümer in Eleusis und Samothrake.* Berlin, 1892.
S,*I*	A. Conze, A. Hauser, and G. Niemann. *Archäologische Untersuchungen auf Samothrake.* Vienna, 1875.
S,*II*	A. Conze, A. Hauser, and O. Benndorf. *Neue archäologische Untersuchungen auf Samothrake.* Vienna, 1880.
Samothracian Reflections	Phyllis Williams Lehmann and Karl Lehmann. *Samothracian Reflections, Aspects of the Revival of the Antique* (Bollingen Series, XCII). Princeton, 1973.
Sardis	Howard Crosby Butler. *The Temple of Artemis* (*Sardis,* II, 1). Leyden, 1925.
Schede	Martin Schede. *Die Ruinen von Priene.* 2nd edn., by G. Kleiner and W. Kleiss, Berlin, 1964.
Schleif-Zschietzschmann	H. Schleif and W. Zschietzschmann. *Olympische Forschungen,* I. Berlin, 1944.
Schmidt	Eduard Schmidt. *Archaistische Kunst in Griechenland und Rom.* Munich, 1922.
Shoe	Lucy T. Shoe. *Profiles of Greek Mouldings.* Cambridge, 1963.
Skopas in Samothrace	Phyllis Williams Lehmann. *Skopas in Samothrace.* Smith College, Northampton, Mass., 1973.
Stewart	Andrew F. Stewart. *Skopas of Paros.* Park Ridge, New Jersey, 1977.
Thieme-Becker	Ulrich Thieme, Felix Becker, et al. *Allgemeines Lexikon der bildenden Künstler von der Antike bis zur Gegenwart.* vol. 31, Leipzig, 1937.
Travlos	John Travlos. *Pictorial Dictionary of Ancient Athens.* London, 1971.
Troy	Carl Blegen, Cedric Boulter, John Caskey, Marion Rawson. *Troy, Settlements VIIa, VIIb, and VIII,* Vol. IV. Princeton, 1958.

LIST OF TEXT FIGURES

SAMOTHRACE:

THE TEMENOS

Text

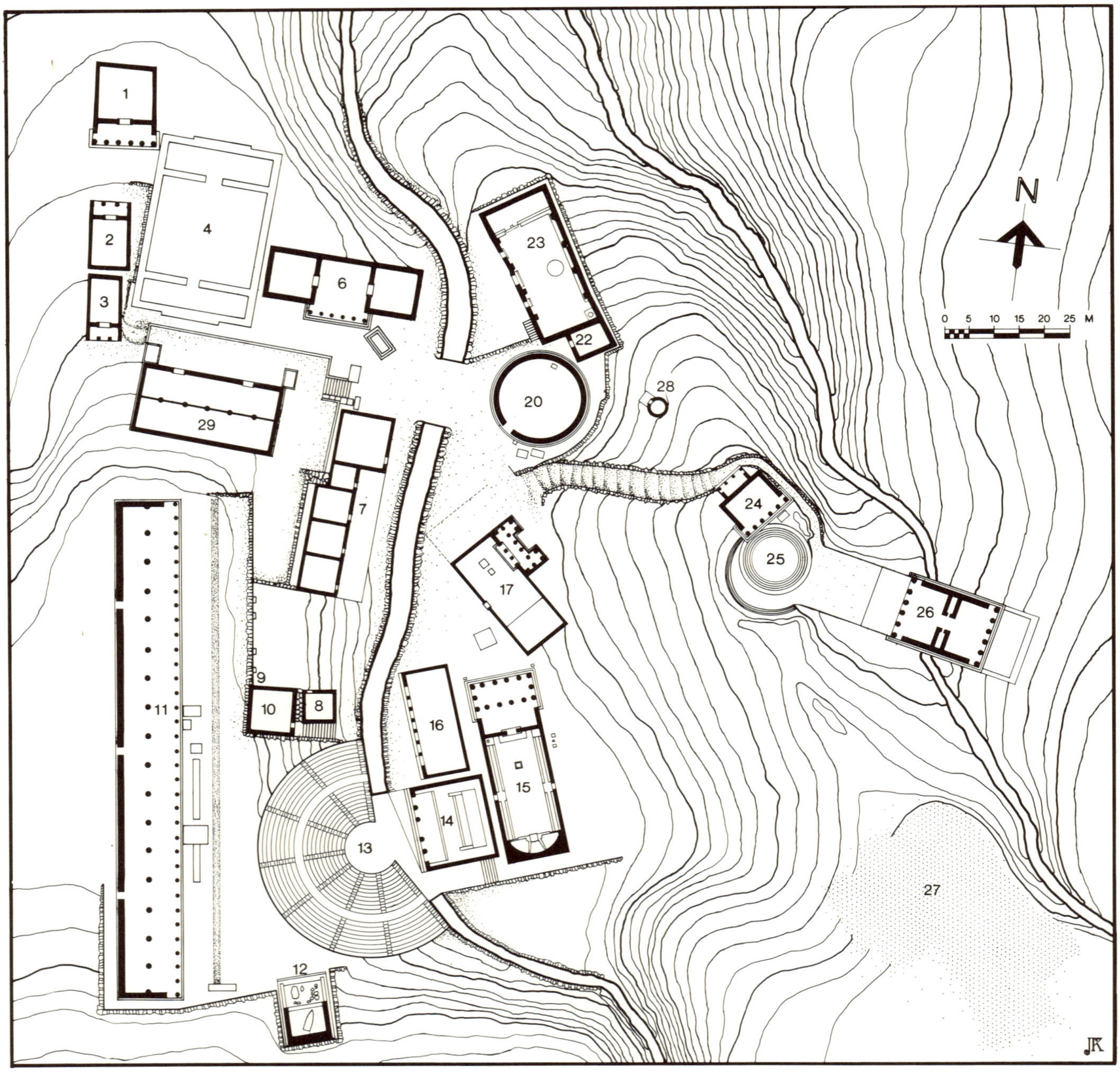

1. Restored sketch plan of the Sanctuary of the Great Gods. (First Century A.D.). Buildings 1, 2, 3. Unidentified late Hellenistic buildings. 4. Unfinished early Hellenistic building. (5. Byzantine fortifications lying above building 4 omitted on the drawing.) 6. Milesian Dedication. 7. Dining rooms. 8. Unidentified room. 9. Archaistic niche. 10. Unidentified room. 11. Stoa. 12. Nike Fountain. 13. Theater. 14. Altar Court. 15. Hieron. 16. Hall of Votive Gifts. 17. Temenos. (18, 19. Altar and Sacred Rock omitted on drawing.) 20. Rotunda of Arsinoe II. (21. Double Precinct omitted on drawing.) 22. Sacristy. 23. Anaktoron. 24. Dedication of Philip III and Alexander IV. 25. Theatral area. 26. Propylon of Ptolemy II. 27. Nekropolis. 28. Heroon (?). 29. Unidentified Hellenistic building.

2. View of Palaiopolis, with the Gattilusi citadel in the foreground.

Introduction

On October 2, 1444, Cyriacus of Ancona set sail for Samothrace from nearby Imbros. The brief account of his short stay on the island, the earliest extant report on the destroyed ancient sanctuary and city, is preserved in an eloquent, if fragmentary, extract from his lost journal in the Vatican Library.[1] The most influential and remarkable of all visitors to the island in modern times, he approached the island in characteristic fashion —responsive, above all, to its antiquities and self-taught to interpret what he saw and recorded through hard-won knowledge of ancient history and literature.[2]

1. Cod. Vat. lat. 5250, fols. 13^v-14^v. For this manuscript, see E. Jacobs, "Die Thasiaca des Cyriacus von Ancona im Codex Vaticanus 5250," *Ath Mitt*, 22 (1897), pp. 113 ff.

2. For Cyriacus' visit to Samothrace, see *Samothracian Reflections*, pp. 3-56, 100-108, 111-115, and the additional references cited on p. 3, n. 2; and *Cyriacus of Ancona's Journeys in the Propontis and the Northern Aegean 1444-1445* (edited by Edward W. Bodnar, S.J., and Charles Mitchell), Philadelphia, 1976, pp. 2 ff., 37 ff., figs. 7-10, 13-15, 17-24.

3. Detail of Palamede Gattilusio's citadel, showing reused ancient blocks.

On October 4, Cyriacus went from the modern village of Chora to Palaiopolis in the company of John Laskaris, governor of Samothrace on behalf of Palamede Gattilusio. As he traversed the southern limits of the ancient sanctuary, he noted "the huge remains" of the Doric Hieron,[3] but the ruins of the nearby Temenos and its small Propylon, flung deep in

3. *Samothrace*, Vol. 3, *The Hieron* (Bollingen Series, LX.3), Princeton, 1969.

the ravine to its north (fig. 1) lay buried from sight. Passing through a gateway or breach in the city wall, Laskaris and his guest proceeded to the new citadel built by Palamede in the ancient city, that romantic keep, perched above the ancient harbor, which commanded the western part of the northern coast (fig. 2). Its towers, then as now, were encrusted with marble blocks, spoils from the ancient city and sanctuary—a miscellany of building blocks, sculptures, and inscriptions that Cyriacus did not fail to note (fig. 3). In fact, he paused there long enough both to record and to sketch—to record and sketch, among other antiquities, two blocks from the frieze of the Propylon that had been plundered from the destroyed and deserted sanctuary and reused to adorn one of the towers of the citadel.

Among the miscellaneous extracts from Cyriacus' journals preserved in a codex in Treviso, the following passage occurs:

> From here [i.e., the Sanctuary], after we came to the new citadel built by Prince Palamede, there were seen in a tower many old marbles constructed with painstaking skill, on which we noticed several sculptured dancing nymphs; and we found here and there very many extraordinary monuments of antiquity of this great city and some excellent old inscriptions with Greek lettering and also with our own.[4]

This account of Cyriacus' visit to Samothrace is unillustrated; but in two other manuscripts, in the Bodleian Library in Oxford and the Laurentian Library in Florence, illustrations accompany a briefer text:

> On the citadel of ancient Samothrace, the city which today they call Palaiopolis, on a very old marble frieze sculptured with exceptional skill set as an ornament in the wall of a tower.[5]

4. In the Biblioteca Capitolare, Ms. I, 138, fol. 192^{v}. *Et inde postq(uam) ad novam a palamade principe condita(m) arcem venimus ad turrim ipsam pleraq(ue) vetusta arte elaborata marmora vident(ur) composita ubi plerasq(ue) nymphar(um) choreas consculptas inspeximus et alia q(uam) plurima hinc inde veternitatis tantae urbis eximia monume(n)ta co(m)p(er)imus et nobilia atq(ue) veterima graecis ac et(iam) nostra(tu)m litt(eris) epigrammata.* This text is an amplified form of the last paragraph of the Vatican text, fol. 14^{v}.

I owe the translations of Cyriacus' reports printed in this chapter to the kindness of Edward W. Bodnar, S.J.

For the Samothracian texts in this manuscript, see Erich Ziebarth, "Cyriacus von Ancona in Samothrake," *AthMitt*, 31 (1906), pp. 405-414. Ziebarth assumed that the sole reference to the dancing nymphs occurred in this passage in the Codex Tarvisimus. As mentioned above, it also appears on fol. 14^{v} of the Vatican manuscript which Ziebarth, himself, had not seen and knew only from the text printed by Alexander Conze et al., S,*I*, p. 1, n. 1. He miscopied the text in Conze's note and omitted several lines, including Cyriacus' reference to the dancing Nymphs. Cf. his article, pp. 407 f.

5. Bodleian Ms. Lat. Misc. d. 85, fol. 137; Biblioteca Medicea-Laurenziana: Laurentianus Ashburnensis 1174, fol. 123^{v}. *Ad arcem antiquae samothraciae urbem quam hodie παλαιόπολιν vocitant ad antiquissimam listam marmoream insigni arte persculptam ad turrisque parientem ornamento positam.*

ΕΡΑΤΩ
ΘΑΛΕΙΑ

ΠΟΛVΜΝΙΑ
ΟVΡΑΝΙΑ
ΚΑΛΙΟΠΙ

ΕΡΑΤΩ
ΘΑΛΕΙΑ
ΠΟΛVΜΝΙΑ
ΟVΡΑΝΙΑ
ΚΑΛΙΟΠΙ

4. Ms. Lat. Misc. d. 85. A. Fol. 137^{v}. B. Fol. 138^{r}. C. Fol. 138^{v}. Oxford, Bodleian Library.

5. Ms. Ashb. 1174. A, B. Fols. 123^{v}, 124^{r}. C. Fol. 125^{r}. Florence, Biblioteca Medicea-Laurenziana.

6. Samothrace Museum. Frieze of dancing maidens. *F(S)10, 11.*

These drawings (figs. 4, 5),[6] copies of Cyriacus' lost originals, record two blocks from the frieze of the Propylon which were taken to the Louvre in 1863 but, since 1955, have been on permanent loan in the Samothrace Museum (fig. 6).[7] They show a band of nine dancing female figures followed by a tenth, a musician holding a tympanum. On the actual blocks, thirteen figures appear. Cyriacus' original drawing must have included another three figures, since on the copies, the names of six of the nine Muses are inscribed in bold, majuscule letters above the heads of the dancers, the remaining figures being identified as the Samothracian Nymphs. Whether the sheet on which he recorded the now missing figures was lost before the extant copies of his other sheets were made or the latter were derived from another, defective, copy cannot be determined.[8]

6. Bodleian Ms. Lat. Misc. d. 85, fols. 137^{v}-138^{v}. Pen and wash drawings on vellum. Text and original Greek names written in pale red ink; Italian names and defacements added in black ink. The ill-written Italian transcriptions above the Greek names are a later addition, presumably the work of a person who further defaced the drawing by adding a beard and mustache to Ourania's features and reinforced the contours of this group of figures. The ground lines inserted between the figures are a similar addition. Ignoring the Greek text labeling the last four figures as Samothracian Nymphs, or unable to read it, the defacer struggled to supply these figures with the names of the missing Muses. His difficulties are reflected in the mistranslated or altered identifications over the figures of Cyriacus' Muses and the repetition and canceling of the Muses' names applied to his Nymphs. Apart from these later blemishes, the quality of the Bodleian drawing is superior to that of the Laurentian. R. M. Hunt, former Keeper of Western Manuscripts in the Bodleian Library, has kindly informed me that the Italian additions to fols. 137^{v}-138^{r} are "perhaps 17th or 18th century in date."

For this manuscript, see Fritz Saxl, "The Classical Inscription in Renaissance Art and Politics," *JWarb*, 4 (1940-41), pp. 21 ff., and for these drawings, *Samothracian Reflections*, pp. 100 ff. In Saxl's illustration of these pages, pl. 7b, the sequence of Muses is incorrect, fol. 138^{r} appearing before instead of after 137^{v}, the triad beginning with Erato.

Laurentianus Ashburnensis 1174, fols. 123^{v}, 124^{r}, 125^{r}. Pen drawings in sepia ink and wash, except for the names, which are written in red ink. Previously illustrated and discussed by Ziebarth, *op. cit.*, pp. 408 ff., and in *Samothracian Reflections*, pp. 100 ff. (Ziebarth had evidently not seen the manuscript himself, hence his misconception that all six Muses occur on fol. 123^{v}.)

7. A. Héron de Villefosse, *Catalogue sommaire des marbres antiques* (Musée du Louvre, Département des antiquités grecques et romaines), Paris [1896], p. 39, nos. 698, 699; *Guide*^{4}, p. 100. See below, pp. 183 ff.

8. In the Laurentian codex, the verso of 124 is blank—an indication that the copyist was aware that three figures were missing in his archetype, whereas

When Cyriacus drew these blocks, they already must have been severely weathered. He cannot be blamed for having misunderstood the indecipherable traces of some object on the heads of his "Muses," which he interpreted as crowns of laurel rather than the low poloi that the well-preserved recently discovered blocks show them to have worn (figs. 147, 148, 195, 210). Nor did he detect the characteristic zigzag, swallowtail folds of the scarfs of these archaistic figures. But he did catch their narrow-shouldered, flaring contours, the turn of their heads, the prominent vertical folds of drapery between their legs, and the presence of strands of material fluttering between each pair of figures. He did not realize that these were elegant shawls worn by alternate figures, seeing them, instead, as fillet-like objects which he interpreted, reasonably enough, as occasional connectives between the figures. Nor were his garments authentic but a cross between a girdled peplos and a sleeved chiton.

All in all, Cyriacus' transcription of this damaged relief was a creditable performance for an amateur. That the frieze was archaistic rather than classicistic as he unwittingly made it, that it represented neither Muses nor Samothracian Nymphs but a section of a long procession of ritual dancers, he could not know. But this very interpretation was a characteristic aspect of his humanistic mentality. Confronted with a relief representing dancing maidens and recalling descriptions of the Muses as figures dancing to Apollo's lyre,[9] he interpreted the first nine as Muses and, in his learned fashion, assumed that the remaining four figures must be local nymphs, ΑΙ ΤΩΝ ΣΑΜΟΘΡΑΚΩΝ ΝΥΜΦΑΙ—a conclusion he probably drew from a passage in one of his favorite authors, Strabo.[10] Hence he added to

---

the extant figures in the Bodleian manuscript occur on three successive pages.

9. E.g., the Homeric Hymns to Pythian Apollo and to Artemis (3.189 ff., 27.13 ff.): *Hesiod, The Homeric Hymns and Homerica*, ed. by Hugh G. Evelyn-White, Loeb edn., London and Cambridge, 1936, pp. 338, 452; and Pausanias, 5.18.4. The marginal notes to 3.8 ff. on fol. 58r of his copy of the *Fasti* (Vat. lat. 10672, the oldest known codex in Cyriacus' hand, finished in May 1427, for which see Domenico Fava, "La scrittura libraria di Ciriaco d'Ancona," *Scritti di paleografia e diplomatica in onore di Vincenzo Federici*, Florence, 1944, pp. 295 ff.) indicate his interest in the Muses, Pegasus, and the Castalian Spring as does his letter to his friend Pietro Donato in which he reports having seen in Thessaloniki the inscribed base of a tripod dedicated to the Muses. His interest in this inscription, which he linked with a passage in Aulus Gellius (3.11.3 f.), illustrates the fashion in which he constantly sought to relate the monuments he encountered with the information he had gained through reading ancient literature. For this letter on fol. 81ᵛ of Ham. Ms. 254 in the Deutsche Staatsbibliothek in Berlin, see Theodor Mommsen, "Über die Berliner-Excerptenhandschrift des Petrus Donatus," *JPKS*, 4 (1883), especially pp. 77 ff., and pl. A (the old manuscript number, 458, is no longer correct); and Helmet Boese, *Die lateinischen Handschriften der Sammlung Hamilton zu Berlin*, Wiesbaden, 1966, pp. 125 ff.

10. 10.3.21, where the author refers to nymphs called Cabirides in the context of a discussion on the Cabiri in Samothrace and elsewhere. For Cyriacus' annotated Strabo, see Richard Foerster, "Zur Handschriftenkunde und Geschichte der Philologie, IV," *RhM*, n. s. 51, (1896), pp. 481 ff., and Edward W. Bodnar, S.J., *Cyriacus of Ancona and Athens* (Collection Latomus, XLIII), Brussels-Berchem, 1960, pp. 118 f. Although he did not acquire this particular codex until 1447, there is every reason to assume that he had long been familiar with the author who, for example, was even translated by Guarino of Verona (J. E. Sandys, *A History of Classical Scholarship*, reprinted New York, 1958, II, p. 50).

7. Frieze of dancing maidens, after Blau and Schlottmann.

this drawing of an uninscribed relief the names of the Muses and Samothracian Nymphs in large letters having the character of an inscription.[11]

The fragmentary record of Cyriacus' brief visit to Samothrace reflects his customary interest in historical documents, in the eloquent "stones" of the past, in architecture, and in sculpture. It reveals his continuous effort to interpret the scattered physical remains of antiquity in the light of ancient literature, his reintegration of the legendary, the historical, and the monumental into an ever-expanding picture of the ancient world.[12]

Cyriacus was followed, nearly four centuries later, by another breed of learned traveler-explorer. More limited than he in intellectual approach, they were content to record their observations in less speculative terms. But they, too, were drawn to Palamede's citadel and noted, and sometimes drew, the reliefs of the dancing maidens. In mid-June 1816, the youthful O. F. von Richter visited the ancient city.[13] Observing blocks in the Doric order reused in the towers, he concluded that they came from a small temple and that the reliefs showing a procession of female figures also embedded there had once adorned its interior. His phraseology—"drei bis vier ziemlich verstümmelte Fragmente desselben Basreliefs"[14]—suggests that more than the two blocks drawn by Cyriacus and subsequently taken to the Louvre once existed. This implication is further supported by the block that Blau and Schlottmann noted and drew (fig. 7) which was located in the same central tower of the triad as the blocks later transported to the Louvre. Although they did not publish this drawing in their official report on their visit to Samothrace in the summer of

11. For the influence of Cyriacus' drawing of this seemingly inscribed relief on Mantegna's *Parnassus*, see *Samothracian Reflections*, pp. 99 ff.

A second time during his brief stay in Samothrace, he drew an uninscribed marble bust which he interpreted as Aristotle and inscribed in similar majuscule letters, in that instance, providing the basis for later incorrect Renaissance representations of the great philosopher. *Ibid.*, pp. 15 ff.

12. For further comment on and analysis of Cyriacus' mentality, see *ibid.*, pp. 3 ff.

13. *Wallfahrten im Morganlande*, Aus seinem Tagebüchern und Briefen dargestellt (ed. by J.P.G. Ewers), Berlin, 1822, pp. 440 ff.

14. *Ibid.*, p. 443.

8. Frieze of dancing maidens, after Conze.

1854,[15] the drawing was reproduced by Eduard Gerhard in 1856.[16] As Mrs. Hadzi has pointed out in Chapter III,[17] this drawing is not simply an amateur recording of one of the blocks taken to the Louvre but a document of a different variety of frieze block from any of the other extant blocks. The existence of this block seems to be confirmed by Major Sir Grenville Temple, who had visited Samothrace early in April 1834. He noted the "many pieces of sculptured marble" reused in the towers and called attention to "the fragment of a bas-relief, representing seven draperied female figures, probably some Muses."[18] Thus this now vanished block has shed some light on the reconstruction of the missing central scene in the frieze of the Propylon.[19]

Blau and Schlottmann had characterized the dancers on their block as female initiates.[20] Alexander Conze, when he first visited Samothrace in June 1858,[21] once again recorded the blocks seen by Cyriacus (fig. 8).[22] Like Cyriacus, he failed to detect the maid-

15. "Altertümer von Samothrake und Imbros," *Berl. Ber.*, 1855, pp. 601 ff.

16. "Alterthümer von Samothrake," *AZ*, 14 (1856), pl. XCV, fig. 8.

17. See below, pp. 199, 203 ff.

18. *Travels in Greece and Turkey*, London, 1843, vol. I, p. 111. I am indebted to Ioannis Akamatis for having brought this report on Samothrace to my attention.

19. See below, pp. 205 f.

20. *Op. cit.*, p. 622: μύστιδες. They described the block as having six figures; Gerhard, *op. cit.*, col. 244, as depicting seven. The drawing shows six and one-half figures, the end figure at the left being completed on the adjacent block.

21. *Reise*, pp. 46 ff. In *S,I*, p. 3, Conze mistakenly reported the year 1857 as the year of his visit to Samothrace—hence my own mistake in citing that fact in *Samothrace*, Vol. 3, text I, p. 4. In *Reise*, pp. 3, 46, the correct date is given.

22. *Ibid.*, pl. XII.

ens' poloi, seeing the few preserved heads as bound by a fillet. Understandably, he misunderstood the weathered hand and scarf on the dancer before the tympanist, providing her with a wreath. Nor was he clear about the sex of this musician. He, too, was an amateur draughtsman, but he did catch the proportions, the archaism of the dancing figures. Most extraordinarily, in his own learned fashion, he deduced from these battered blocks a number of astonishing and correct conclusions: the parallel between the hieratic style of the figures and the retention of an autochthonous language in the ritual as Diodorus 5.47.3 had reported in his account of the Samothracian religion; the fact that women took part in the mysteries; that the musician played a tympanum, hence that this was a cult of Kybele and Demeter, whom the ancients had named as Samothracian goddesses; and finally, on the importance of dancing in the cult.[23] His form of scholarship was as characteristic of the nineteenth century as Cyriacus' Renaissance humanism was of the fifteenth. He concluded his report on the antiquities of Samothrace with an ardent statement on the desirability of excavating the Sanctuary.[24]

Before he himself organized the first major excavation of the site in 1873, both Charles Champoiseau, French Consul at Adrianople, and Gustave Deville and Ernest Coquart, two members of the Ecole française d'Athènes inaugurated brief excavations in the Sanctuary. Among the marbles sent to the Louvre by Champoiseau in 1863 were not only the famous Victory[25] but also the two weathered blocks first drawn by Cyriacus[26] in Palamede's citadel that he, like Conze, assumed represented a dance of priestesses of Kybele. Champoiseau's investigations determined the mission of Deville and Coquart in the summer of 1866.[27] Now, for the first time, there was reference both in plan (fig. 9) and text to the area of the Temenos-terrace. They linked this region with that of the Doric Hieron and regarded it as "un ilôt bas." In their sketch plan, they showed the central river of the Sanctuary sharply bent to the southeast to form a ravine north of the terrace wall and south of the Rotunda of Arsinoe.[28] At the extremity of this islet, they noted "une plate-forme, élevée d'environs 2 mètres," and saw it as "un ancien sanctuaire."[29] The walls which supported this platform, built of irregular blocks, they characterized as very thick and well

23. *Ibid.*, p. 62.

24. *Ibid.*, pp. 73 f.

25. Charles Champoiseau, "La Victoire de Samothrace," *RA*, n.s. 39 (1880), pp. 11-17; *S,I*, pp. 3 f.; *S,II*, p. 55.

26. In the report cited in n. 25, Champoiseau stated, p. 11, that his first care (in March 1863) had been "d'enlever tous les marbres dignes d'attention, encastrés soit dans les murs des constructions élevées au moyen âge par les Gatelusio, seigneurs souverains du pays, soit dans ceux des maisons du village moderne bâti à l'intérieur de l'île sur la pente du mont Phingari. Ce sont des *bas-reliefs, dont l'un, représentant une danse de prêtresses de Cybèle, est placé au Louvre* (italics mine) dans la même salle que les beaux marbres rapportés de Thasos par M. Miller."

27. Deville-Coquart, pp. 254 ff.

28. *Ibid.*, pp. 259, 262 f., 276.

29. *Ibid.*, p. 276. See, too, the brief reference by Ernest Coquart, *Académie des inscriptions et belles-lettres, Comptes rendus*, 1873, p. 260, reprinted as "A Monsieur le Président de l'Académie des inscriptions et belles-lettres," *RA*, 2nd ser., 27 (1874), p. 25, where, among the drawings listed, there is reference to: "Soubassement d'une area (construction cyclopéenne au fond du ravin, 1er sanctuaire?)."

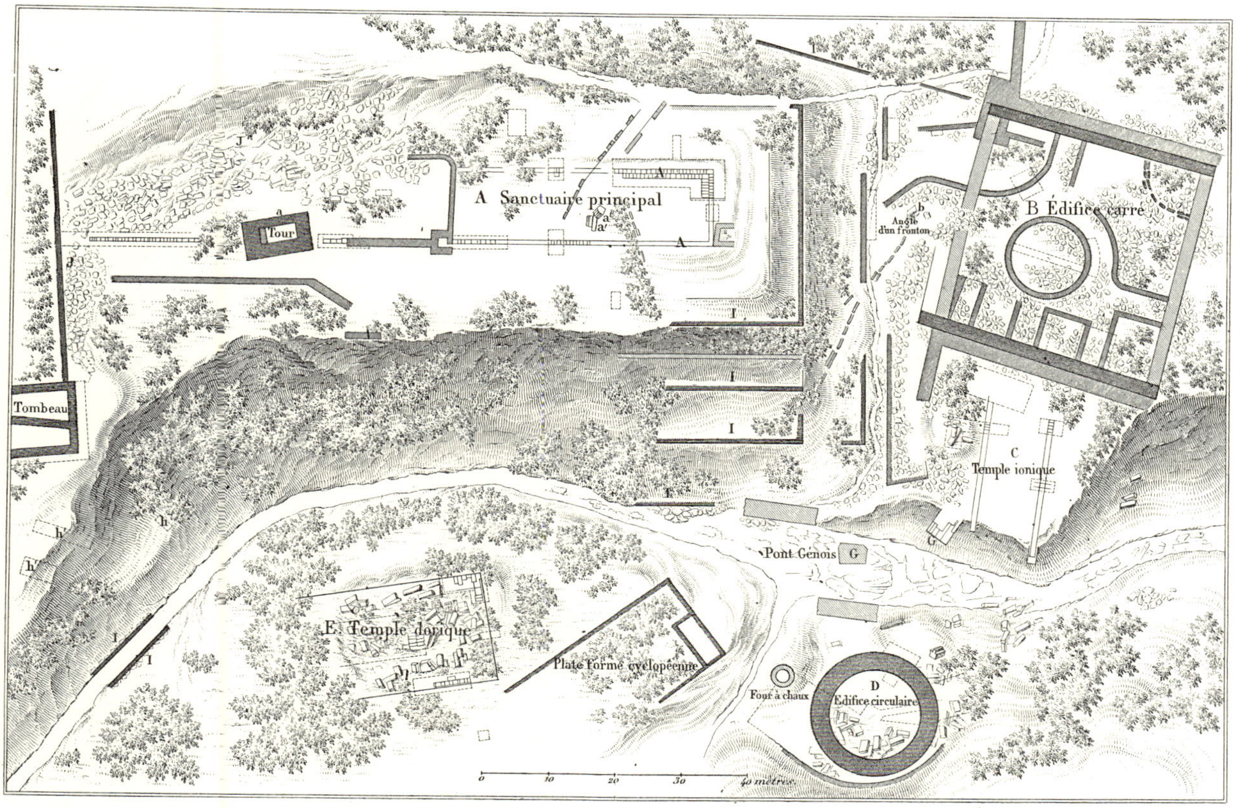

9. Coquart's plan of the Sanctuary after the French excavation of 1866.

constructed, and contemporary with the walls of the ancient city—that is, "cyclopéenne."[30] On this platform, they had found a tiny fragment of the frieze of dancing maidens, and they queried whether the area simply contained an altar.[31] Finally, they noted that olive trees, brambles, and boxwood completely covered this platform which had long been abandoned.[32] They emphasized the appalling devastation of the site not simply by violent earthquakes but by men who, for centuries, had used this area for a quarry, and they drew attention to two large limekilns still in use.[33]

It was not until their second campaign, in 1875, that Conze and Alois Hauser explored the area of the Temenos-terrace.[34] Disappointed that he had not discovered the oldest "temple" in the Sanctuary in 1873, Conze returned for another season. Like Deville and Coquart, he had believed that the enormous limestone ruin on the Western Hill was its oldest temple. Restrictions of time and money had forced him to postpone its excavation

30. *Ibid.*, p. 268.

31. *Ibid.*, p. 273: "Il y avant là peut-être seulement un autel. Nous y avons trouvé un tout petit fragment de bas-relief; la jambe d'une danseuse avec quelques plis flottants de sa robe." See below, p. 200, *Fβ*.

32. *Ibid.*

33. *Ibid.*, pp. 254, 276.

34. *S,II*, pp. 1-17 (Conze); 21-27, 31 f. (Conze and Hauser); pp. 97 ff. (Benndorf).

10. View of the terrace wall in 1875.

in 1873. But early in the second campaign, it became apparent that this vast structure was a stoa, and that he must look elsewhere for this "uralt Haupttempel," since the Doric Temple discovered in the previous campaign was Hellenistic. Hauser had observed, in 1873, a foundation course at the northeastern corner of the Doric building,[35] part of Coquart's "plate-forme," a platform that the two Frenchmen had never excavated, as its vegetation indicated. Tracing the long southwestern line of the precinct wall to its juncture with the polygonal terrace wall (fig. 10), the Austrians assumed that this foundation had been added to an older terrace wall. Recalling the discovery, in 1873, at the same northeastern corner of the Doric building, of a beautiful corner geison-sima block, a sima fragment (figs. 11, 51, 52, 104; Pls. XXXII, XXVIII.1), and an antefix (figs. 12, 113), they were struck by the seeming contrast between the antiquity of the terrace wall and the elegance of this corner block and the character of the foundation. Two periods, two structures must be implied, they concluded.

35. *Ibid.*, p. 13. The German text actually says *south*east and exemplifies the frequent errors in defining the geographical location of blocks in these volumes.

Discussion in *S,I* of blocks or issues that later proved related to the excavation of 1875 occurs on pp. 10 f., 28, 31, 49 and fig. 15, pls. XLIX, LI.

11. Corner geison-sima block and sima fragment, after Hauser.

12. Fragmentary antefix, after Hauser.

In excavating the platform, they discovered a worn block of the frieze of dancing maidens which they immediately identified as identical in type with the two archaistic blocks taken to the Louvre by Champoiseau. They recalled that they had found two fragments of this relief north of the Doric Temple in 1873, as Deville and Coquart had found one on the platform, and soon they discovered another three blocks of the frieze on the same platform.[36] They had also found north of the "temple" dentils and, to its east, two coffer lids.[37] Now they discovered many more dentils, fragments of the sima, and a fragmentary coffer lid.[38] They concluded that these blocks and fragments belonged to an Ionic building adorned with a frieze of festive dancers that once stood on this platform—as, indeed, it did. They commented on the scant traces of the superstructure of this building (not realizing that the greatest part of its marble blocks had crashed to the bottom of the polygonal terrace wall in the final earthquake), and emphasized, more than once, that no other area they had excavated had been so severely devastated because of the presence, nearby, of two large limekilns—doubtless, those mentioned by Deville and Coquart.

It is important for the history of the excavation and the present reconstruction of the Propylon to again emphasize these facts. Clearly, the blocks and fragments of its marbles, whether architectural or sculptural, had been assembled in this area to be reduced to lime.[39] A prime proof of this point is provided by the corner geison-sima block (Pl. XXXII; figs. 11, 51, 52, 104[40]) found *against* the northeast corner of the foundation of the Doric "temple"—obviously, intentionally placed there by a would-be lime burner. I suspect that the Austrians' apparent "discovery" of this block near the southwest corner of the adjacent foundation played a significant role in their later assumption that the renewed Old Temple stood on the entire foundation of what we, today, regard as a foundation for a precinct wall.

Within the southwestern corner of this foundation,[41] the Austrians uncovered several marble paving slabs and numerous blocks of "soft" stone—presumably porous limestone or tufa—of the underpavement (fig. 13). Having found the extant remnants of the entire foundation (even then, lacking at the southeast and northeast), they concluded that they had laid bare the inner marble pavement of a rectangular building, but they lacked evidence of its ground plan and could not determine whether it included a pronaos or an

36. See the Catalogue of the frieze below, p. 200 $F\gamma,\delta,\epsilon$.

37. See the Catalogue of coffers below, pp. 151 ff. *C(V)1, 2*; S,*I*, pl. LI. Hauser had correctly recognized that these elements did not belong to the Doric Hieron.

38. See below, pp. 153 f. *C(V)3*.

39. We have repeatedly encountered a similar situation in excavating the numerous limekilns found throughout the Sanctuary since 1948.

40. S,*I*, p. 11, pl. XLIV; S,*II*, p. 13. The sima fragment also drawn in S,*I*, pl. XLIV, was later joined to another fragment preserving a lion's head waterspout shown in a photograph in pl. XXX. A third fragment was added to the photograph in S,*II*, pl. X, where another lion's head (now missing) and an antefix appear.

41. It is stated in S,*I*, p. 49, and S,*II*, p. 24, that the material of the eastern blocks of the southwestern corner of the foundation (shown in a schematic diagram, fig. 15) is marble. Actually, they are of porous limestone.

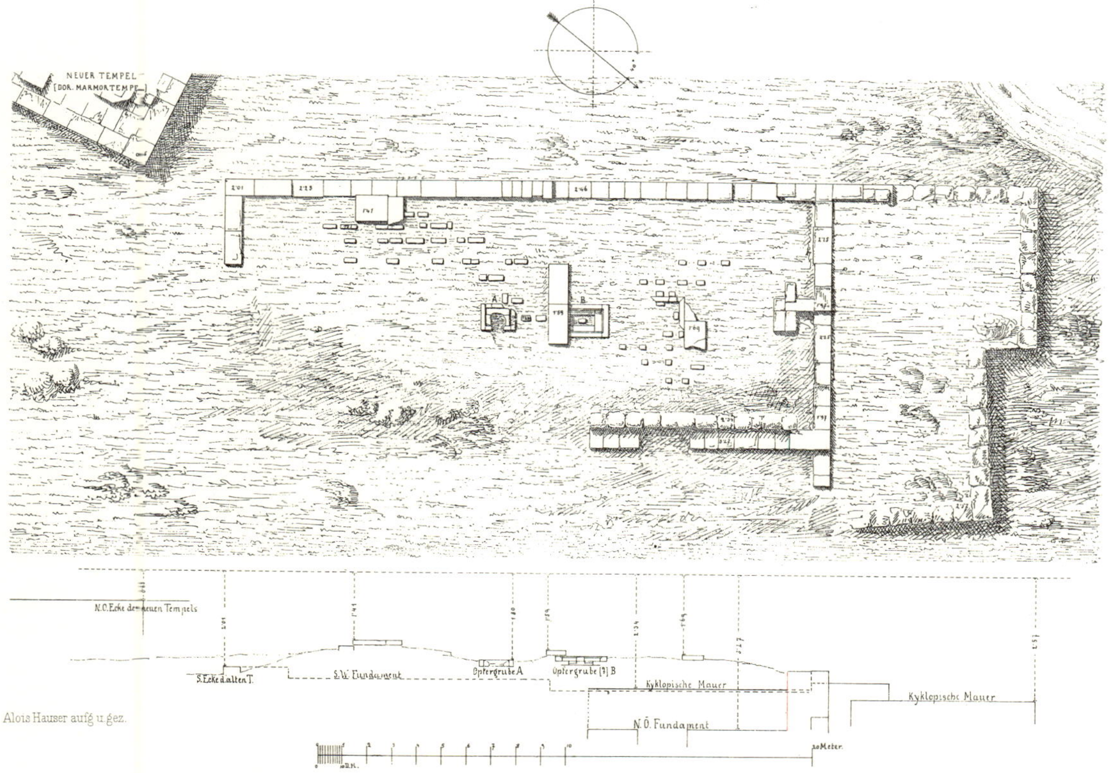

13. Hauser's plan of the Temenos after the Austrian excavation of 1875.

external colonnade.[42] Within this structure, they discovered *Opfergrube* A and B (figs. 14-16), two bothroi, they believed, both covered by the marble pavement. To the north, they uncovered two sides of another marble frame surrounded by—and at the level of—the marble paving, for which they offered no explanation.[43]

Although they worked until the last day of their second campaign in this area,[44] the Austrians were saddened to consider that they had not completed its excavation. In the depths, evidently south of *Opfergrube* A, they had discovered two fragments of an archaic Doric geison (fig. 17), and they regretted being unable to dig further at this lower level.

This solitary fragmentary tufa block was to prove of paramount importance to Conze's and Hauser's theory. They associated it with *Opfergrube A* and the polygonal terrace wall and regarded it as evidence that the original "Old Temple" was an archaic Doric building. It was replaced by a larger, more costly marble building in the Ionic order (fig. 18), which they dated no later than the first half of the fourth century B.C. in view of the style of its sima and lion's head waterspouts. To the walls of this Ionic building, they attributed a series of marble inscriptions recording the initiation of *theoroi* to the Samothracian festi-

42. *S,II*, p. 21.
43. For explanation of these ritual installations, see below, p. 271, Pls. LVI-LIX.
44. September 21, 1875.

14. A, B. Views of the eschara in the Temenos after the excavation of 1875.

15. View of the bothros in the Temenos after the excavation of 1875.

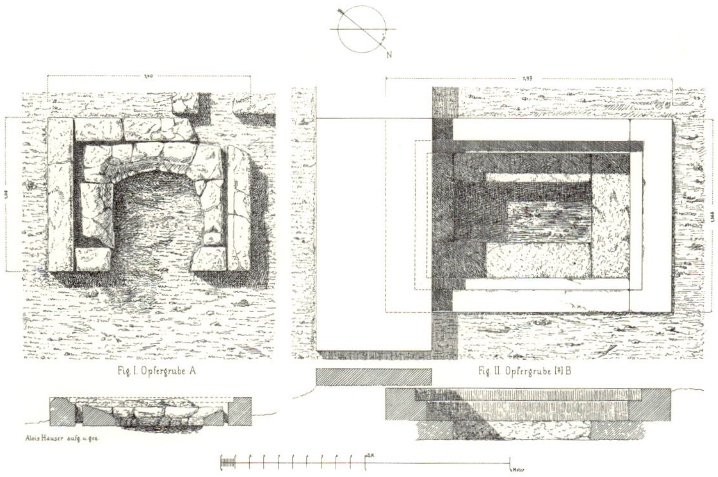

16. Plan and section of the eschara and bothros after the excavation of 1875.

vals found in the Gattilusi towers in the ancient city, among them a Doric architrave,[45] with the thought that this Doric element in an Ionic building was an echo of the original Old Temple.[46] With the "discovery" of the Old Temple, whether in its original or renewed form, the original name of the "temple" excavated in 1873 was changed from the Doric Temple to the New Temple. For virtually a century, these terms persisted in archaeological literature. Finally, it was thought, the Old Temple did not cease to function when the New Temple was built but both continued to serve for worship of the same chthonic divinities. Unfortunately, for this singular theory, the solitary archaic Doric geison fragment has proved to be the solitary fragment of the superstructure of the archaic Doric Hieron,[47] and the Ionic architrave blocks of this Ionic building, found with additional frieze blocks in our excavation of 1949,[48] fit each other precisely.[49]

45. *S,II*, pp. 23, 97 ff.; *IG*, XII, 8, nos. 160-177. These inscribed blocks have a height of 0.34-0.36 m. (see *S,II*, pp. 97 f.). Hence they are far too low for the walls of the Propylon whose marble blocks have a height of 0.554-0.558 m. See below, pp. 56 f. Nor did these marble blocks fit the stuccoed porous limestone walls of the precinct, for which see below, pp. 44 f. Two of the three additional lists of *theoroi* found or recovered in our excavations (Vol. 2, pt. I, **23**, **24**) have the same height as those earlier published and evidently belonged to the same structure. **23** was again found near the Gattilusi towers; **24** came from Chora—i.e., out of context.

46. *Ibid.*, p. 101. In using the Parthenon as an example of this scheme, Conze neglected to state that, on the Parthenon, the frieze appears on the cella wall not in the entablature of the *exterior* of the building.

47. Vol. 3, text II, pp. 52 f., fig. 364.

48. See below, pp. 64 f.

49. See below, pp. 65 f. Before the discovery of these Ionic architrave blocks, scholars had continued to accept Conze's and Benndorf's theory that the *theoroi* inscriptions, including the Doric architrave, supported the entablature of the Ionic Old Temple (e.g.: Rubensohn, pp. 135, 140; Demangel, p. 323, n. 2; Arnold Schober, "Der neue Tempel von Samothrake," *ÖJh*, 29, [1935], p. 2. Rubensohn, however, pp. 142, 215, n. 44, assumed that this hypothetical building was colonnaded and queried the date of *Opfergrube* B).

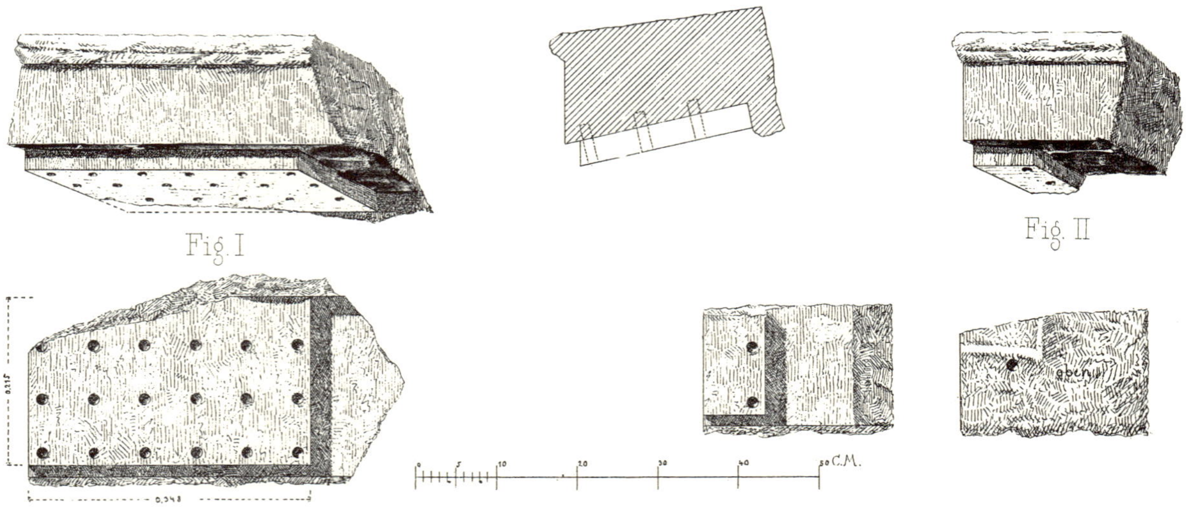

17. Fragmentary Doric geison block. A. After Hauser. B, C. Vienna, Ephesos-Museum.

18. Hauser's partial reconstruction of the entablature of the Propylon.

A second time, between 1923 and 1927, two members of the Ecole française d'Athènes, Antoine Salač and Fernand Chapouthier, excavated in the Sanctuary of the Great Gods. Although there is no statement in their brief official reports[50] that they dug in the area of the Temenos-terrace, there was physical proof that one of them had.[51] But they did report on their work in the *Ruinenviereck*[52]—the tenth-century Byzantine fort on the terrace north of the Stoa[53]—a structure in which a number of key blocks of the Propylon had been reused.[54]

Ten years later, in 1937, before the actual resumption of excavation in the Sanctuary by the Archaeological Research Fund of New York University in 1938, Professor Lehmann dug a trial trench in the southwest part of the "Old Temple" as part of his brief preliminary

50. "Chronique des fouilles," *BCH*, 47 (1923), pp. 540-1; 48 (1924), p. 504; 49 (1925), p. 466; 50 (1926), p. 567; 51 (1927), pp. 490-492. No final excavation report on these campaigns was ever published, although A. Salač, "Griechen und Hethiter," *Archiv Orientální*, 1 (1929), p. 348, n. 1, announced that the excavations "können jetzt (nach der Kampagne von 1927) als abgeschlossen gelten," and Chapouthier, p. 162, n. 6, stated: "La publication de ces dernières campagnes est en preparation."

51. See below, p. 26. Unfortunately, the two official colleagues were unable to work together, as even a careful reading of their reports indicates. Hence they came to excavate at different seasons. This frank admission was made by Chapouthier in Paris many years ago.

52. "Chronique des fouilles," *BCH*, 50 (1926), p. 567; 51 (1927), pp. 490-492.

53. *Guide*⁴, pp. 20, 81.

54. See below, pp. 25, 34 f., 37.

19. View of the excavation in 1950. Foreground: terrace wall; middle ground: northern wall of the precinct.

investigation of the site.[55] He concluded that the "archaic building" had had the same size as its marble replacement and that it had been destroyed by earthquake ca. 400 B.C.—conclusions that were to be corrected when this region of the Sanctuary was fully excavated in subsequent years.

On June 16, 1949, we began to remove overgrowth from the area south and southwest of the Rotunda of Arsinoe and north of the polygonal terrace wall of the Old Temple—as we still assumed it was. On June 23, we found a sizable fragment of the frieze of dancing maidens lying to the north of the wall.[56] When we began to excavate on the 24th, only the upper section of the wall shown in the Austrians' plan and photograph was visible (figs. 10, 13). Presumably, the eastern stretch of this wall had been hidden in the ground at the time of the Austrians' excavation. Soon we traced the line of this grey crystalline porphyry

55. See "Observations in Samothrace," *AJA*, 42 (1938), p. 126, for the brief statement on the trial trenches made that season and reported at the General Meeting of the A.I.A. in Philadelphia in 1937. From the plan made by Professor Lehmann that summer, it is clear that he dug a trench 4.50 m. wide and 2 m. long 5.50-7.50 m. north of the southwest corner of the precinct. Naturally, he used Hauser's plan and levels (fig. 13). Other aspects of his activity in 1937, including a trench 2 m. long and 10 m. wide east of the porch of the Hieron that shed light on the post-antique destruction of the southeastern part of the "Old Temple"—i.e., the Temenos—were referred to in his first excavation report, "Excavations in Samothrace," *AJA*, 44 (1939), pp. 140 f.

56. Acc. No. 49.1043C; Catalogue of the frieze: *F(S)12*.

20. Discovery of frieze block *(S)1A*, Karl Lehmann as observer.

wall[57] to a length of 15.50 m. and found that it rested on bedrock which descended toward the riverbed roughly from east to west (fig. 19; Pls. I-II). It was clear that both Coquart's and Hauser's plans of this wall were incorrect. Coquart's schematic diagram was, in a sense, more correct, although both had regarded an inner line of rock packing as an actual line of wall, as we discovered the following year.

Already on the first day of excavation, we began to find to the northwest of this wall an accumulation of blocks—marble orthostates, ceiling beams, euthynteria and geison-sima blocks, and a fragmentary threshold as well as polygonal stones from the wall and porous limestone blocks of what proved later to be the Temenos wall.[58] On the next day, ca. 8.50-9.50 m. east of the western corner of the wall and ca. 2 m. north of its face, a fine fragmentary block of the frieze of dancing maidens appeared,[59] and on the following day, a joining section of the block (fig. 20).[60] The same day, other blocks—additional euthynteria, ceiling beam and geison-sima blocks, and another fragmentary threshold block as well as steps and an architrave—were found. It was now clear that these blocks belonged to an Ionic building (in view of the recovery of small fragments of Ionic flutes) and that the frieze of dancing maidens had adorned it. It was clear, too, that this building had once

57. We are indebted to Dr. Frederick Pough of the American Museum of Natural History for this identification.

58. The marble blocks found in 1949 were given + numbers; those found in 1950, ++ numbers; length, height and thickness of each porous limestone block were recorded in the daily diary, as was the specific provenance of each block, whether marble or limestone.

59. Acc. No. 49.1043 B: *F(S)1*, right.

60. Acc. No. 49.1043 A: *F(S)1*, left.

21. Necking-drum: 49.985. Samothrace Museum.

stood somewhere on the upper terrace, and that in the final, fearful earthquake that shook the Sanctuary,[61] its blocks crashed down to the bottom of the wall and toward the riverbed. In little more than a week, additional crucial blocks were uncovered in this area: epistyles and a columnar architrave block, step blocks, wall blocks, and the solitary well-preserved monolithic columnar shaft. Three meters below the lowest line of the terrace wall, there lay the sole intact paving slab of the building. Here, too, the largest numbers of fragments and fragmentary blocks of the frieze were excavated.[62] Among these marbles, a fragmentary coffer lid was found,[63] identical in scheme and dimensions with those found by the Austrians, indicating that they, too, decorated the building. Next we discovered the lower courses of a limestone foundation set on bedrock that had later sheathed the polygonal wall to support monuments (figs. 19, 33, 35, 37; Pls. I, II.1, 2)[64] and, to its east, the porphyry base of a monument.[65] On July 7, we struck ground water ca. 1.40 m. below the surface of this porphyry base and, with that, the excavation before the terrace wall was terminated.

For the next fortnight, we excavated the enormous late antique and post-antique limekiln built in the ravine south of the Rotunda, which, at one point, came within 1.50 m. of the northeastern corner of the polygonal wall.[66] But already, on July 18, Professor Lehmann concluded in the excavation diary that the building that had once stood on the terrace—of which more than one hundred marble blocks or fragments of blocks had been recovered—in no way resembled the Austrians' hypothetical Old Temple. Material, dimensions, technical features indicated that the blocks belonged to a small Ionic building.

On August 1, Mr. B. Kallipolitis, at the time representative of the Greek Archaeological Service to the excavations in Samothrace, brought to the Musuem an unusual and beau-

61. See *Hesperia*, 19 (1950), pp. 21 f.

62. See the Catalogue of frieze blocks: *F(S)1, 2, 12, 13, 15, 19, 20, 21.*

63. See pp. 155 f., *C(S)2*, Acc. No. 49.355.

64. See below, Chap. IV, pp. 296 f.

65. *Ibid.*, pp. 292 f.

66. See *ibid.*, pp. 299 f. for discussion of the several periods of this limekiln.

tiful necking-drum that he had discovered in the garden of a house in Chora (figs. 21, 42, 70, 81).[67] It proved to fit the monolithic Ionic shaft previously excavated north of the terrace wall (Pl. XIII). And to this drum, in turn, two fragments of an Ionic capital recovered from a collection once housed in the Church of Hagios Demetrios in Chora could be fitted (figs. 42, 47, 62, 63; Pls. XIV, XV, XVI).[68] Nor was this surprising, since all three of these pieces had been reused in the *Ruinenviereck*, the Byzantine fort, where Salač had excavated in 1927.[69] These handsome, ornamental blocks had been carried off to Chora since, until our arrival in Samothrace in 1938, no guard existed in the Sanctuary. Years later, when I visited Prague in 1967, I was given access to notes, photographs, and drawings formerly in the possession of Professor Salač through the kindness of his successor, Jiří Frel, then Professor of Classical Archaeology at the Charles University.[70] Among the drawings of this Ionic order made by Salač's architect, J. Nepomucký, were numerous drawings of precisely these blocks (figs. 41, 43, 44, 47, 48). Although these drawing are not altogether reliable in style or spacing, they reveal features, especially of the drum and shaft, that supplement the evidence of the actual blocks which, in the meantime, have become more weathered.[71]

Throughout the summer, Professor Lehmann measured and recorded the blocks of this Ionic building, his drawings yielding its first provisional reconstruction. Even then, it was evident from the inner corner step block (+24), the columnar architrave blocks (+12, +35) and the geison-sima block (+18), that the building had projecting wings. He proposed, in his first preliminary report on the structure,[72] that it was probably a propylon leading into a sacred precinct (as a result of evidence provided by the Austrians), and, on the basis of the frieze, that dances and ritual actions were performed there in connection with the dramatic performance known to have taken place at the annual festivals, which was concerned with the legendary Wedding of Kadmos and Harmonia. What proved later to be a flaw in the proposed restoration was the location of the frieze. Given the presence of lewis holes normally found on the blocks of this building wherever they had to be lifted into a high position and the absence of this feature on the one most complete frieze block (Pl. XXIII.1), he concluded that the frieze did not belong in the entablature but should be placed above the orthostates, at eye level. Inasmuch as the figures of the frieze moved in two directions, he assumed that it should be placed within the colonnade of the building, and that its figures converged on a single door.[73]

67. Acc. No. 49.985.

68. Acc. No. 49.414 A, B. The drum and capital fragments are mounted on the column shaft +33 and +28 in Hall B of the Museum. See *Guide*[4], p. 99, fig. 46.

69. In "Chronique des fouilles," *BCH*, 51 (1927), p. 492, it is stated that: "Au mois d'août et de septembre, M. A. Salač a repris les recherches sur le même emplacement [i.e., the *Ruinenviereck*] et a dégagé tous les morceaux antiques contenus dans les murs récents."

70. Professor Salač died in 1960. These documents record his activity in Samothrace from 1923 to 1927.

71. See pp. 37, 59 for a precise statement on the differences between the drawings and the blocks.

72. *Hesperia*, 20 (1951), p. 18.

73. *Ibid.*, p. 17. Another error, later to be

The following season, we attacked the area south of the polygonal wall—the region of the terrace and precinct. We discovered to our dismay that local vandals had destroyed the sparse elements of the interior installations found by our Austrian predecessors.[74] Faulty and schematic as Hauser's plan of the precinct foundations was to prove (cf. fig. 13 and Pl. I),[75] the record of the few marble paving slabs and their underpavement, of their *Opfergrube* A and B, and the rectangular frame sunk in the floor to the north (that actually proved to be an eschara and bothros below the marble floor, and a second fragmentary eschara contemporary with it) was essential to our understanding of this area. Olive and pear trees had long been planted here and had now wholly eradicated any trace of its original appearance. Our work was further hampered by the existence of two dumps and two large funnel-shaped holes dug in the terrace and, to its south, in the northern section of the precinct. Presumably, this activity should be attributed to the French-Czech mission of 1923-27, since there is no record of any other excavators at work in the Sanctuary in the years between the Austrian expedition and our own.[76] The hole on the terrace proved a major obstacle to the proper excavation of this area. Within it, traces of a wall, the northwest wall of the precinct, were visible.[77]

In excavating the terrace, we left a section at its southwest undug to allow for any future exploration of this area (see Pl. I). Already in excavating the terrace we began to find black, burned fill which proved to come from a section behind the northwestern precinct wall (fig. 221; Pls. I, II). It consisted of a dense accumulation of burned bones and ceramic fragments which ranged from fine, wheelmade sub-geometric kantharoi of the first half of the seventh century B.C. to coarse, handmade vessels.[78] Excavation of the northwest wall of the precinct, carried down to bedrock on the terrace, indicated that it was composed of two sections: an earlier limestone foundation toward the west and, at the east, a later, sloppily built foundation of coarser limestone that overlapped it (figs. 30, 224; Pl. III.3). The construction of these two sections of wall, it soon became clear, had cut through the black layer that we were to find on the other side of the wall in the precinct itself. This burned, black fill came from a shallow pit into which

corrected, was the statement that the spiral-rinceau sima with which the Austrians had provided their sima blocks was incorrect and did not fit the geison-sima blocks visible in the excavation. Actually, they do. Cf. pp. 33 f.

74. We had encountered a similar scene of destruction, a year earlier, in the excavation of the Hieron: Vol. 3, text I, pp. 21 f. Henry Fanshawe Tozer, *The Islands of the Aegean* Oxford, 1890, p. 329, reported that in April 1889, the *Opfergruben* were "concealed under mounds of earth," and Otto Kern, reporting on his visit to Samothrace in July 1892 (*Nord-griechische Skizzen*, Berlin, 1912, p. 92), commented that they had been buried to prevent their subjection to destruction.

75. A situation analogous, again, to our experience in excavating the Hieron: Vol. 3, text I, pp. 8 f.

76. Throughout the excavation diary for 1950, these holes were referred to as "Salač's holes." It is conceivable that in his candid conversation with Professor Lehmann in Paris some years earlier, M. Chapouthier had reported this fact. The contrast between the funnel-shaped holes in the terrace and precinct and Chapouthier's own trench in the cella of the Hieron (Vol. 3, text I, pp. 13 ff.) would, in any case, imply such.

77. This hole was 3 m. wide, 2.50 m. long and 1.75 m. deep. The hole in the precinct was 5 m. in diameter and 2.0 m. deep.

78. See the Catalogue of Ceramics, **1-82.**

the debris of sacrifices had been thrown and, beneath this pit, we found a primitive hearth. Earth, ashes, fragments of charcoal and a few burned bones of pigs and lambs were found on its floor. This hearth, itself undatable, appears to reflect the earliest activity in the Sanctuary.[79]

Proceeding southward in the precinct, we uncovered the area of the Austrians "bothroi," finding the whole region disturbed, doubtless as a result of earlier excavation and limekilns. Here, too, we excavated the Austrians' dumps, one to the east and one to the west of the southern region of the precinct, and one within its southeast corner.

In the meantime, we had recovered the sparse traces of the Propylon's sub-foundation (fig. 39; Pls. I, II.3). It consisted of an incompletely preserved short extension of the northwestern precinct foundation, a remnant of the northern foundation of the northern wing of the building and, at a right angle to that foundation, the short, preserved portion of foundation that had supported the rear wall of the building. The foundation of the building was set on bedrock that had been dressed down to receive it. Excavation of the terrace had indicated that no foundations existed there for however small a building. Soon we discovered that the foundations of virtually all the rear wall and the long northeastern wall of the precinct had been swept away in post-antique times and that, at the same time, the foundation of the entire southern wing of the building must have been destroyed together with missing sections of the foundation for the rear wall and the northern wing. Discovery, later in the season, of a large number of marble blocks from the Propylon that had been flung into the ravine to the northeast of this foundation supported the attaching of the building to this northeast section of the precinct wall.[80] Years later, the discovery of the processional road leading across the Eastern Hill of the Sanctuary and descending toward the façade of the Propylon confirmed this location (fig. 1).[81]

We continued to uncover the foundations of the precinct, finding large sections of the southeast and northeast foundations destroyed, as previously mentioned. But we did find rock cuttings for the now vanished southeastern corner of the precinct (Pl. I). To the east of the precinct, we found evidence of the post-antique history of this damaged quarter of the Sanctuary.[82] Here, too, roughly parallel with the northeastern corner of the polygonal terrace wall, we unearthed a rock altar.[83] Earlier, we had discovered the short, lateral face of the limestone sheath for the terrace wall at its opposite western corner (figs. 19, 33, 35, 37; Pl. I, II.1, 2).

In the course of this campaign, we had recovered many additional blocks of the Propylon and the precinct walls. This year only one block was found north of the polygonal terrace wall—a wall architrave block, discovered beneath the western corner of the wall (Pl. XXI). On the terrace itself, there lay a stereobate block, an orthostate, and a wall

79. For further details and facts about the pre-fourth-century B.C. precinct, see below, Chap. IV, pp. 267 ff.

80. See below, p. 39, pp. 50 ff., and n. 27.

81. For this stepped ramp, see James R. McCredie, "Samothrace: Preliminary Report on the Campaigns of 1965-67," *Hesperia*, 37 (1968), p. 231.

82. See below, Chap. IV, pp. 299 f.

83. *Ibid.*, pp. 293 ff.

block of the precinct wall, a geison-sima block and coffer fragment of the Propylon as well as a small fragment of the frieze of dancing maidens. In front of the foundation for the building, that is, to the east, we discovered a euthynteria block and a fragmentary step block. In the eastern part of the precinct, too, we found a stereobate block and wall block of the precinct wall. A group of three geison-sima blocks appeared in the northeast corner of the precinct. They were not in fallen position but seemingly had been placed there by previous excavators. A large group of marble blocks was found outside the eastern end of the terrace above the level of the rock altar,[84] as previously stated. It included three euthynteria blocks, a step block, a whole and a fragmentary geison-sima block, coffer fragments, a fragment of the shaft of a column in addition to a fragmentary step and wall block of the precinct wall, and a marble container for one of the bench supports originally present on the terrace.[85] A second sizable group of blocks (two orthostates and four geison-sima blocks)[86] came from the southern part of the precinct or outside its southwest corner, where evidently it had been assembled by would-be modern lime-burners, since some of the blocks had been found leaning against the stumps of pear trees. Numerous fragments of the frieze were recovered from the Austrian dumps; and dentils were excavated in the northern part of the precinct, although they were not recognized as such at the time.[87] Finally, what was construed to be an unusual variety of frieze block was found in the riverbed some distance southwest of the terrace wall (fig. 22 A, B).[88]

In his report on the campaign of 1950,[89] Professor Lehmann published a first tentative reconstruction of the Propylon, based on his own preliminary drawings, which later appeared in both the first and second editions of the *Guide*.[90] It showed an Ionic building entered by a single door in its rear wall (fig. 23 A). Two projecting wings flanked the structure. Both the wings and the central section of the building were topped by shallow pediments. Four columns supported the central section, a column and a hypothetical anta and anta wall each wing. The wings rested on two single-recess steps and a euthynteria. The frieze in the entablature was based on the so-called frieze block illustrated in figure 22. This solitary block is characterized by small, round dowel holes and traces of what must have been applied decoration that has been pried off. Evidently, this ornament was of bronze. The damaged surfaces on the block seemed to imply that it was adorned with implements not figures—hence the paterae, bucranes, and other motifs restored to it. Like the other blocks in the uppermost courses of the Propylon, it had a lewis hole on its top surface. Thus it seemed to confirm the earlier suggestion that the frieze of dancing

84. This altar had been buried from early in the third century B.C. on. See below, Chap. IV, p. 296.

85. See below, *ibid.*, p. 290 and n. 83, for this container now used to hold the support exhibited in the Museum in the center of Hall C.

86. One of the geison-sima blocks was ++5 illustrated on Pl. XXVII.

87. See the singular statement in *Hesperia*, 21 (1952), p. 42.

88. Found 9 m. southwest of the western corner of the terrace wall.

89. *Hesperia*, 21 (1952), pp. 26 ff., and fig. 2.

90. *Samothrace. A Guide to the Excavations and the Museum*, New York, 1955, p. 57, fig. 30; 2nd edn., *ibid.* The actual drawing was made by Stuart M. Shaw.

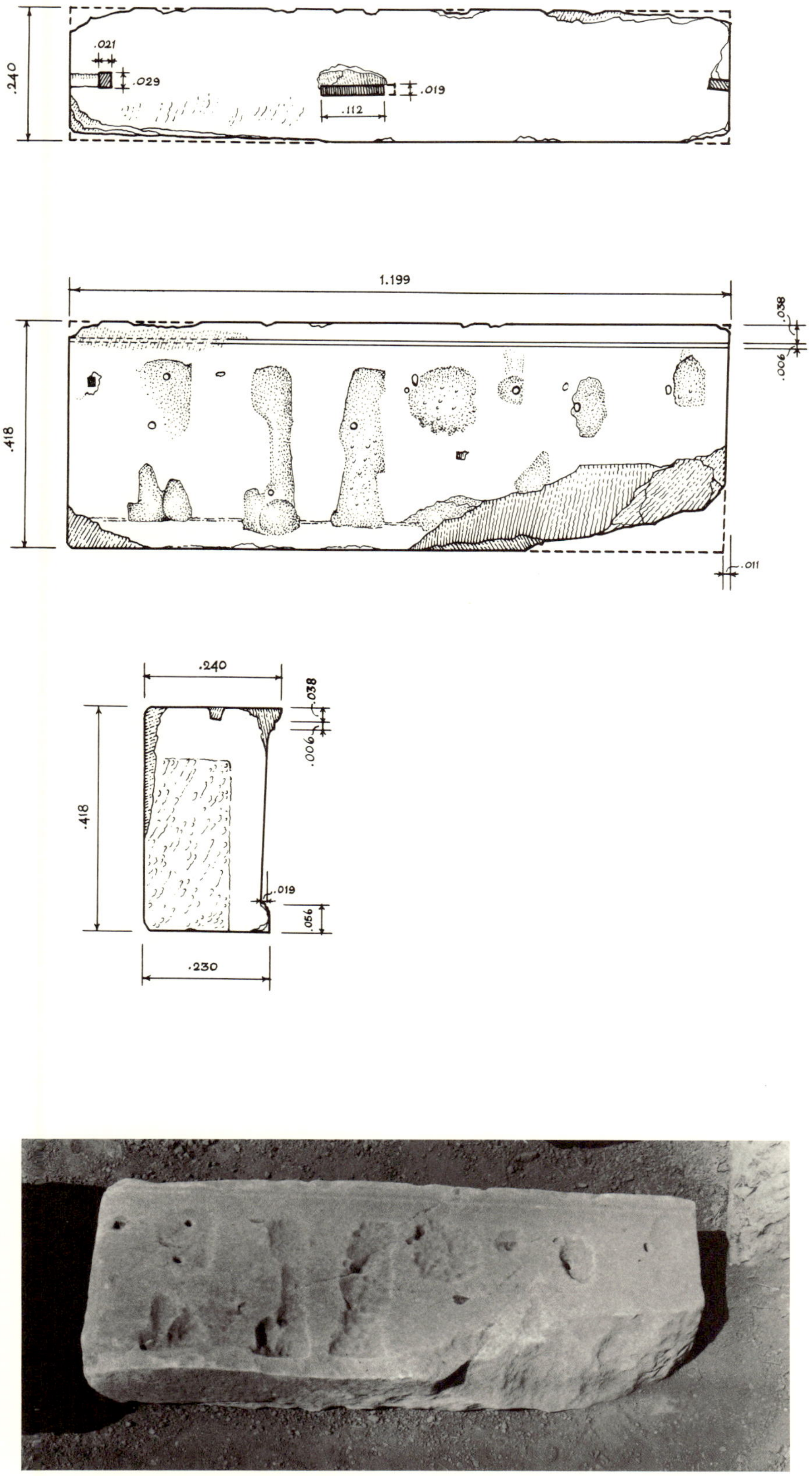

22. Frieze block from an unknown monument. A. Drawn by Denys Spittle. B. View.

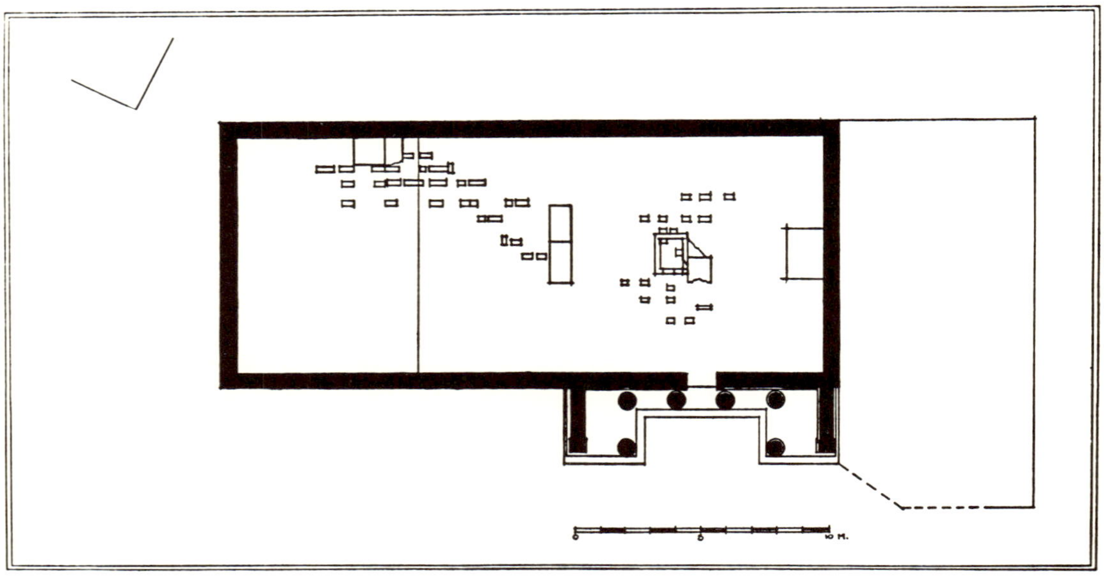

23. A. First tentative reconstruction of the Propylon. B. First tentative plan of the fourth-century B.C. Propylon and Temenos.

maidens—the longest block of which lacks a lewis hole—should be placed above the orthostates and converge on the doorway as it does in this reconstruction. Finally, the so characteristic feature of the Propylon, its beautiful sima, had not yet been recognized as belonging to the geison-sima blocks, which were provided with simple, separately attached bronze cylinders as waterspouts.[91] Such were the major features of this first tentative reconstruction of the Propylon.[92] The initial date proposed for the restored Propylon was ca. 320 B.C.[93]

The tentative restored plan of the Propylon and Temenos published in this same report (fig. 23 B)[94] was a curious mixture of reconstruction and the precise retaining of elements known from the Austrian's plan—that is, their incompletely preserved but extant paving slabs and underpavement. But the fourth-century eschara was restored and adjacent to the northwestern wall of the precinct stood a restored statue base—the presumed base of Skopas' lost group of Aphrodite and Pothos. Its genesis was the discovery of a fieldstone foundation for such a base, it was believed, adjacent to the wall.[95]

The campaign of 1950 in the Temenos has proved of unique importance in our excavations in the Sanctuary. Through the discovery of the primitive hearth in its depths and, above it, the shallow pit containing the debris of sacrifices, hence the recovering of the earliest ceramic vessels found in the Sanctuary,[96] its history has been led back to the first half of the seventh century B.C.

The last of the marble blocks belonging to the Temenos and Propylon were recovered the following season in 1951. Two orthostates and a small fragment of the stringcourse of the precinct wall were found to the east of the precinct and terrace in the region of the rock altar. Here, we excavated to the bedrock. Further evidence was obtained, too, regarding the post-antique limekiln south-southeast of the Rotunda.[97] And a third fragment of a capital of the Propylon[98] was discovered in the Church of Hagios Ioannis, southwest of Palaiopolis by Andreas Vavritsos, at the time, representative to the excavations of the Greek Archaeological Service.

In 1953, we cleaned the lines of the missing southeastern and northeastern foundation of the precinct and then placed miscellaneous limestone blocks in these lines to indicate the original dimensions of the precinct (fig. 24). The varied character of these blocks and the fact that they were laid on earth, not bedrock, should suggest to the visitor that they were not found *in situ*. A little stairway built in the line of the northeastern foundation

91. This is the source of the error in the statement by Brunilde S. Ridgway regarding the survival of metal decorations in architecture till the fourth century B.C. (Ridgway, pp. 190 f., 203, n. 65).

92. Other discrepancies exist between our final reconstruction, Pls. XLVIII-LI, and this first attempt —e.g. the hypothetical base moulding on the wall. Final examination of all the blocks has yielded a building of different plan and dimensions from those stated in *Hesperia*, 21 (1952), p. 27.

93. *Ibid.*, p. 22.

94. *Ibid.*, p. 23, fig. 1.

95. *Ibid.*, p. 29. See below, Chap. IV, p. 287.

96. See the Catalogue of Ceramics, pp. 317 ff., **1-82**.

97. See Chap. IV, pp. 299 f.

98. Acc. No. 51.909. On exhibition in Hall B. See *Guide*[4], p. 99.

24. View of the Temenos in 1953, showing the modern limestone foundations for its southern and southeastern foundations.

should also aid the visitor to reach the precinct.[99] The following year, we assembled within the precinct, all the marble blocks or fragments belonging either to it or to the Propylon[100] save for the blocks or fragments of the Propylon on exhibition or in storage in the Museum (fig. 25). That same summer, we installed in Hall B of the Museum the monolithic column shaft, placing on it the best preserved drum and capital fragments, as well as another more fragmentary drum and additional capital fragments, and the two best preserved frieze blocks.[101] At the same time, the late Hellenistic bench support was also placed in its marble container and installed in the center of Hall B.[102] In the summer of 1955, the Musée du Louvre generously consented to return to the Museum in Samothrace, as a permanent

99. We also filled in earth to the level of the modern northeastern foundation on its exterior face as we did in the inner northern corner of the precinct, where we had dug deeply, in order to make access to the precinct and altar easier for visitors. See *Archaeology*, 7 (1954), pp. 94 f.

In 1955, it was necessary to alter the original appearance of the terrace wall in two respects: a Π-shaped support of Decauville rails was placed beneath two blocks of the terrace wall, which overhung the shaling bedrock and were in danger of falling; and the large boulder at the northern corner of the wall was set in cement for the same reason.

100. A few fragments and porous limestone blocks were placed in the narrow area to the southeast of the precinct. It proved desirable to add a second course to the modern foundations of the precinct in connection with this work.

101. Capital shaft +33 and +28; drum 49.985; capital fragments 49.414 A, B; a more fragmentary drum, 52.215, recovered from the Church of Hagios Stephanos in Chora; 51.909 and a second capital fragment. The precise procedure followed in installing these blocks is reported in Diary I, pp. 86 f., for 1954. The two joining frieze blocks are *F(S)1*. See *Guide*[4], pp. 99 f.

102. See below, Chap. IV, p. 290. This support has provisionally been transferred to Hall C (see *Guide*[4], p. 109). Its original position is now occupied by a plaster restoration of a Corinthian column from the western porch of the Propylon of Ptolemy II (see *Guide*[4], p. 99) which, it is hoped, will ultimately be shifted to Hall D, when the partial reconstruction of other buildings in the Sanctuary, including the Propylon of Ptolemy II, can be arranged.

25. View of the Temenos in 1954.

loan, the two fragmentary blocks that had been reused in the Gattilusi towers and recorded by Cyriacus.[103] They, too, were installed in Hall B along with another fragmentary block of the frieze.[104]

Between 1950 and 1952, Stuart M. Shaw completed the plan of the Temenos, the elevation of its northern wall, and began to prepare the sections of the Temenos-terrace, the final sections not being finished until the campaign of 1961 (Pls. I-III).[105]

In 1955, Professor Lehmann appointed Denys Spittle of the Royal Commission on Historical Monuments (England), a professional architect, who, for some years, had already been a member of our Samothracian staff, to aid him in remeasuring and recording the blocks of the Propylon and in working out its final reconstruction. Within a few weeks of this reinvestigation, Mr. Spittle had established the fact that, contrary to previous statements, the corner geison-sima block in Vienna (Pl. XXXII) did, in fact, belong to the

103. *F(S)10, 11.* These blocks are the front elevation of blocks that were sawed off, presumably to be transported to the Louvre (see *Guide*[4], p. 100). At the same time, the Louvre also sent on permanent loan an anta capital from the western porch of the Propylon of Ptolemy II, now in Hall B, and a fragment of the marble finial of the roof of the Rotunda of Arsinoe (now in Hall A) in exchange for the right hand and other fragments of the Victory of Samothrace (see Jean Charbonneaux, "La main droite de la Victoire de Samothrace," *Hesperia*, 21 [1952], pp. 44 ff).

104. *F(S)12.* Heavy winter-spring rains the following year washed earth away from the trunk of the single tree that we had left in the center of the Temenos (see fig. 25) revealing not only a number of shapeless marbles from destruction debris of the Propylon but also the forepart of a lion's head waterspout, Acc. No. 55.148.

105. He was aided in 1954 by Martin R. Jones, who made the plan of the porphyry base abutting the terrace wall and of the wall itself. In 1960, the capital previously installed in Hall B of the Museum was lowered to allow Mr. Shaw to make the drawings reproduced as Pls. XV-XVI.

Propylon; that all the extant geison-sima blocks were so badly damaged and broken at the sima that the original impression that this member lacked sculptured ornament was incorrect, since both the dimensions and profiles of the spiral-tendril sima fitted the geison-sima blocks precisely. The Vienna antefix (Pl. XXXIII) also proved to fit this sima. He noted, too, that so many geison-sima blocks existed as to indicate that the central pediment proposed in the first tentative restoration of the Propylon (fig. 23 A) was incorrect, the pediments being present only above the wings. Professor Lehmann immediately accepted these revisions to the first tentative reconstruction. Although the text of the second edition of the *Guide* was emended and adjusted to the revised geison-sima blocks, the first tentative reconstruction was unfortunately retained.[106] It was not until the third edition of the *Guide* that an improved version of the reconstruction of the building was published (fig. 26).[107] Now the central pediment has been eliminated and the pediments themselves are larger and steeper. The correct sculptured sima and antefixes have been introduced along with hypothetical akroteria and ridge antefixes. An additional pair of Ionic columns has replaced the previous deep antae walls, which have been shortened and aligned with the interior colonnade.[108] The building stands on three steps above a continuous euthynteria. In this second tentative construction, the faulty "frieze" block (fig. 22) has been retained as has been the position of the frieze of dancing maidens.

In 1970, a decade after Professor Lehmann's death, I was, at last, able to turn to the problem of the final publication of the Temenos and its Propylon, and, with Mr. Spittle, to reexamine and reconsider the reconstruction of both the building and the precinct. We rechecked the blocks of the Propylon in the Kunsthistorisches Museum in Vienna in the autumn of that year, and spent the better part of June and July 1971 reexamining the blocks of the Propylon and Temenos in Samothrace. In the previous decade, long after the excavations of 1949-50, a number of new blocks or fragments of blocks had been discovered in other parts of the Sanctuary, particularly in the *Ruinenviereck*,[109] the Byzantine fort north of the Stoa (fig. 1), in which so many blocks from the destroyed buildings in the Sanctuary had been reused, and in a vast limekiln on the Eastern Hill. None was so important as a fragmentary corner block of the frieze of dancing maidens found in the excavation conducted in the *Ruinenviereck* in 1967 (figs. 151-153).[110] Reexamination of the solitary so-called "frieze" block (fig. 22) and of the many blocks of the frieze of dancing maidens had already indicated that while the former did not fit the adjacent blocks

106. *Guide*[2], pp. 57 f., fig. 30. In a letter to Mr. Spittle written on December 12, 1959, Professor Lehmann reported his regret that a new reconstruction of the building had not been agreed upon in time for the second edition and that it was necessary, therefore, to republish "the old illustration, faulty and unsatisfactory as it is." In the revised text, the singular notion that the sculptured lions' heads were provided with bronze waterspouts was retained from the original reconstruction.

107. *Guide*[3], pp. 57 ff., fig. 29.

108. Not visible in the previous fig. 29 but present in other reconstruction drawings of this phase of work on the Propylon.

109. See James R. McCredie, "Samothrace: Preliminary Report on the Campaigns of 1965-1967," *Hesperia*, 37 (1968), pp. 204 ff.

110. *F(S)4*. In 1971, Mrs. Hadzi discovered that a tiny fragment of the frieze, Acc. No. 65.99, fitted side B of the corner block, 67.32. It, too, came from surface cleaning of the *Ruinenviereck*.

26. Second tentative reconstruction of the Propylon, 1966.

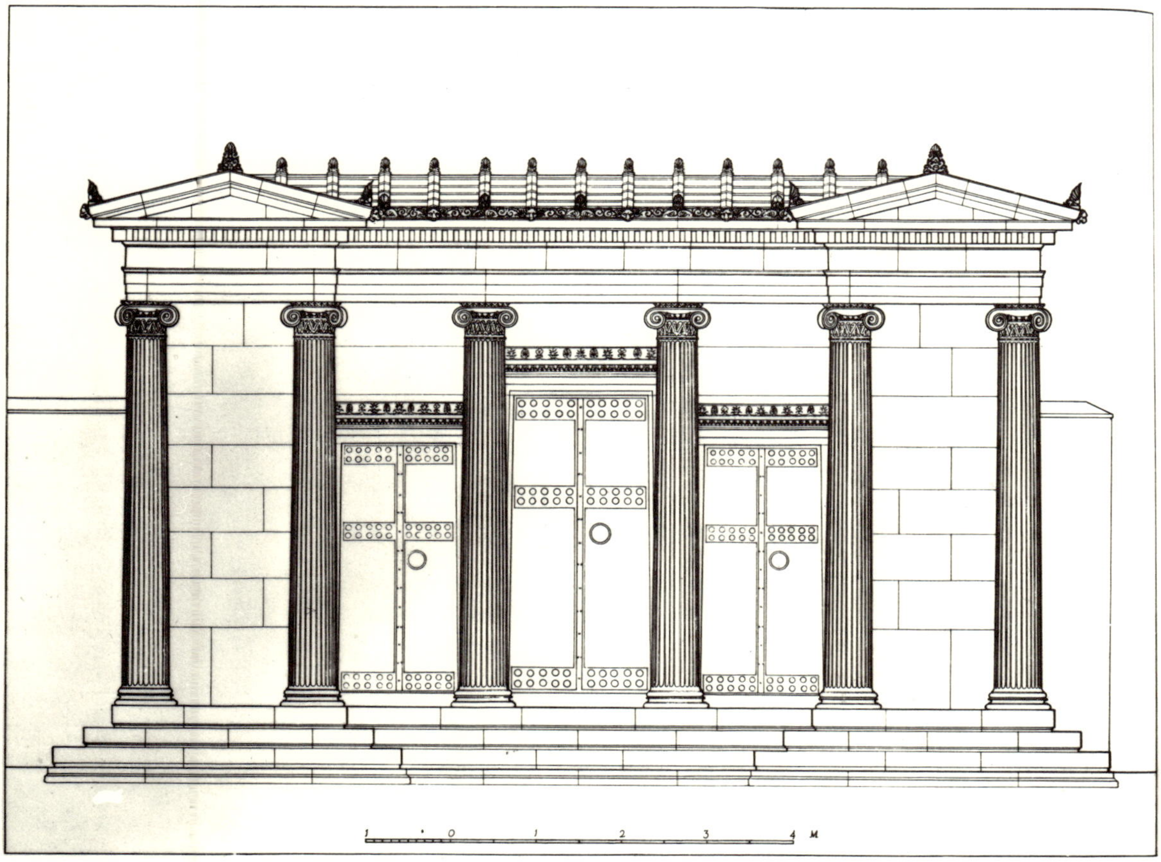

27. Restored elevation of the Propylon, 1972.

of the entablature precisely (and, in view of its provenance, doubtless belonged to a monument or structure in the vicinity),[111] the latter category of block fitted into the

111. Found, it will be recalled, in the riverbed, 9 m. southwest of the western corner of the terrace wall.

28. Tourist Pavilion, Gelibolu: drum from the Propylon.

entablature exactly (see Pls. XLVIII-LI). The new corner frieze block clinched this solution, since it was an *exterior* corner block—a block for which there was no place in the previous preliminary reconstructions of the Propylon (figs. 23 A, 26).

In reexamining the smaller marble fragments from the Propylon and Temenos in 1971, we discovered that we had fragments of two thresholds, not one, and that the solitary over-lintel block was appropriate in size for a lateral door but too small for the main door of the Propylon[112]—hence that the building had three doors, not the single door with which it had been provided in the earlier provisional reconstruction drawings and descriptions.[113] We also observed the previously unrecognized blocks that had framed the fourth-century bothros in the Temenos which indicated that, in the fourth century, too, the ritual installations of the past, the eschara and the bothros, had both been retained.[114] These observations led to a new reconstruction of the plan of the Propylon and the Temenos (Pl. LIX), and a third restored elevation of the Propylon published in the fourth edition of the *Guide* (fig. 27) and in a preliminary study for this volume.[115] These drawings are our final reconstructions of the Propylon and the Temenos and, as such, their presentation constitutes the content of the text and plates of this volume.

Among the most illuminating fragments of the Propylon recovered in the sixties was a coffer lid found in the previously mentioned limekiln on the Eastern Hill (figs. 130, 142),[116] along with a tiny fragment of the frieze of dancing maidens. [117] Noted in 1970, it provided the initial clue that Skopas of Paros might prove to be the designing architect-sculptor of the Propylon.

112. See Pls. XLI, XLII.

113. *Hesperia*, 21 (1952), pp. 23, 28; *Guide*[1,2], pp. 57 f.; *Guide*[3], p. 59.

114. See below, pp. 44 and 271 and Pls. LVII-LIX. I should point out that, in this respect, as in others, the plan of the Propylon and Temenos published in Vol. 3, text II, p. 57, fig. 369, is incorrect.

115. *Guide*[4], pp. 62 ff., fig. 29, Plan III; *Skopas in Samothrace*, pp. 4 ff., figs. 3, 8, 15, 29.

116. *C(S)3*. See below, pp. 156 f., 170.

117. *F(S)3*.

Last of the blocks of the Propylon to have come to light, in 1977, is a fourth example of the palmette drum that once embellished its columns (fig. 28). The sculptured motifs of this drum are sharper and more complete than the best of the previously known examples (figs. 21, 42, 43, 70, 81), although the drum itself is more incomplete as a block.[118] It preserves the elements recorded by Nepomucký earlier in the century still more visibly (figs. 41, 43, 44): the bead and reel crowning molding; the leafy calices framing the top volutes, and the ribbing of the stems and, especially, the upright acanthus leaves at the base, which appear to mark both the junction of the lyre-shaped frames of the hanging palmettes and the base of the upright palmettes, although this element was not noted in Nepomucký's drawings. The presence of a bronze peg in the center of one of the upper volutes implies that the volutes contained inserted gilded eyes. Discovered in the garden of the Tourist Pavilion at the harbor of Gelibolu in Turkey, the former Gallipoli, it is a vivid reminder of the Austrians' determined effort to salvage marbles that would doubtless be destroyed in Samothrace by transporting them either to Vienna or Gallipoli.[119] Almost none of the blocks intended for the Ottoman Museum in Constantinople reached that city;[120] the remainder must have languished on the shore in Gallipoli, and, apart from this solitary drum, seem to have vanished. Although there is no reference to this drum in the Austrians' publication, Conze stated his intention to deposit a selection of finds from the excavations in Samothrace at Gallipoli for their presumed transport to Constantinople.[121] Since the Austrians also excavated briefly in the *Ruinenviereck*, [122] the source of this drum is clear—it, too, like the three other drums, must have been reused in the Byzantine fort.

118. Published by Anneliese Peschlow-Bindokat, "Ein hellenistische Saulenhalsstück in Gelibolu," *Festschrift für Frank Brommer*, Mainz/Rhein, 1977, pp. 237-240, and pl. 64. The diagram on p. 237, fig. 1, shows a drum identical with the Samothracian examples in height but slightly greater in diameter—a conceivable variation for a specific column.

I am most grateful to Dr. Peschlow for having taken the trouble to reinvestigate this drum. It proves to have a round dowel hole on both the top and bottom surfaces as well as a lewis hole on the top surface as do the Samothracian examples, although the presence of the upper dowel hole was not indicated in the diagram on p. 237.

On p. 238, Dr. Peschlow originally interpreted the drill holes at the base of the drum and in the volutes at the top as an indication that gilded bronze attachments were applied to it. Recent examination of the drum has shown that the shallow drill holes at its base reflect the carving of the acanthus leaves shown in Nepomucký's drawings (figs. 43, 44). In drawing far-reaching conclusions about the use and importance of bronze attachments on the Propylon, Dr. Peschlow has been influenced by Professor Lehmann's errors in his first two reports in *Hesperia*, in which he assumed the use of metal attachments for the so-called frieze block (fig. 22), and for the waterspouts of the sima—both of which have been shown to be incorrect. There is no trace of metal application on any block from the Propylon in Samothrace but the better preservation of the Turkish drum indicates that, at least on the drums, bronze attachments were applied. Dr. Peschlow's date, "Hellenistic," reflects Professor Lehmann's first date for the building in *Hesperia*, 20 (1951), p. 15, which he soon abandoned as all the editions of the *Guide* attest.

I am grateful to Ira S. Mark for originally having alerted me to this important article. In the meantime, Dr. Peschlow has not only checked on the drum in Gelibolu but also provided the excellent photographs that are illustrated in figs. 28, 46, 82.

119. *S,II*, pp. 16 f.

120. See Gustave Mendel, *Catalogue des sculptures grecques, romaines et byzantines* (Musées impériaux ottomans), Constantinople, III, 1914, p. 431.

121. *S,II*, p. 17.

122. *Ibid.*, p. 7, pls. LXV, LXVI.

Professor Lehmann had entrusted Martha Leeb Hadzi, who had taken part in the excavation of the Temenos, with the publication of the frieze of dancing maidens. In 1974, I selected Mary B. Moore to study and publish the ceramic finds from the Temenos and terrace that appear in the Catalogue of Finds.[123] Another long-time member of the staff, Elsbeth B. Dusenbery, has contributed to this Catalogue.

As is clear from this introductory chapter, the Temenos and its Propylon have been repeatedly discussed in our preliminary reports, *Guides*, and miscellaneous articles. These are superseded by the present volume, in which the results of our long investigation of this remarkable building are, at last, presented.[124]

123. Iris C. Love had originally been assigned this task by Professor Lehmann in 1956. Her later obligations as director of the excavations in Knidos prevented her from completing it.

124. I have incorporated in the notes to this volume all previously published statements and opinions wherever they are at variance with the conclusions presented in this final study in order to correct any factual errors and to explain every re-evaluation of evidence.

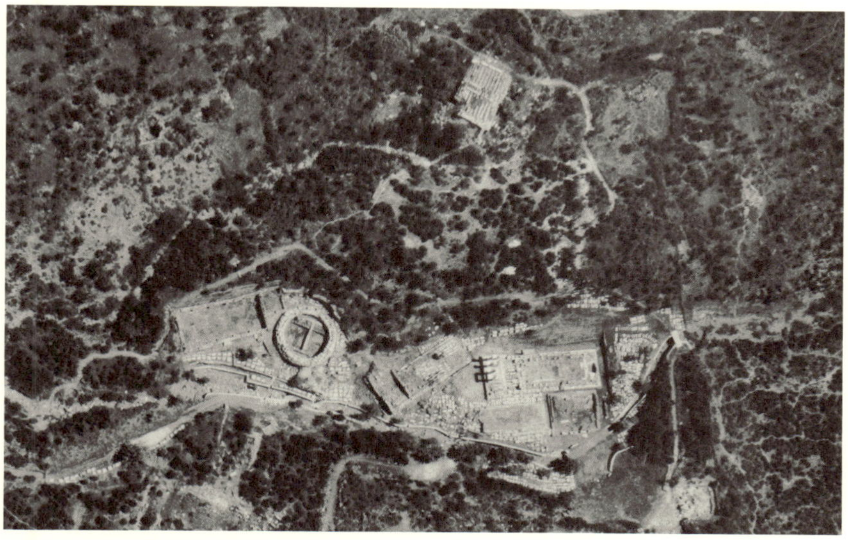

29. Air view of the Sanctuary, 1957.

I. Description and Reconstruction of the Temenos and the Propylon

THE TEMENOS

THE Temenos,[1] an open precinct in which ceremonies performed during the annual Samothracian festival appear to have been celebrated,[2] is located in the center of the Sanctuary (fig. 1). It and the adjacent terrace were oriented toward the northwest, having a deviation to the west of north of 48°. The Propylon, which gave access to the Temenos, faced toward the northeast in the direction of the processional road.

When the Propylon and Temenos were built ca. 340 B.C., their nearest neighbors in the southern part of the Sanctuary were the archaic Hall of Votive Gifts and the early classical *epopteion*, the hall for initiation into the higher degree of the Samothracian mysteries, which was presumably identical in size and location with the present, early

1. For the use of this term, see Chap. II, n. 1.
2. See below, pp. 288 f.

30. View of the northern wall of the Temenos.

Hellenistic Hieron.[3] As yet, the Altar Court had not replaced the venerable rock altar. The triad of the Temenos-Propylon-terrace, lying directly athwart this pair of earlier buildings, rose boldly above the central river of the Sanctuary to its northwest, seeming to form a promontory above the river. The bedrock on which the southern portion of the Temenos rests drops steeply to the north and west, and to the northeast a ravine separates this complex from the Eastern Hill of the Sanctuary.

The external dimension of the Temenos, walls included, has a length of 24.78 m. northwest-southeast and a width of 10.45 m. southwest-northeast, the internal length being 23.78 m. and the internal width 9.40 m. For convenience in the present description of the foundations of the Temenos, the short northwestern foundation will be termed "north"; the short southeastern foundation "south"; the long northeastern foundation "east"; and the long southwest foundation "west."

The earliest portion of the Temenos foundations is a short section of the northern foundation near its western end (Pl. III.3; fig. 30). Built of porous limestone blocks, it is six courses in height. The courses are of irregular length (ca. 3.10 m. at the third course) and decrease markedly in height from the top course downward. At the approximate center of this section of the foundation, it is ca. 2.10 m. in height. It is one block thick and laid irregularly of headers and stretchers. It appears to be a fragment of a foundation that once extended farther to the northeast.[4] When the fourth-century Temenos was built, this fragment was included in the new northern foundation of the precinct, and its courses were overlapped by a section of grey conglomerate blocks. For the most part, they are

3. Vol. 3, text I, p. 36, text II, pp. 58, 69.
4. See, too, p. 50.

larger and more irregular both in size and coursing (Pl. III.3; fig. 30). Technically, this and the other extant "foundations" of the Temenos are sub-foundations, since only at the southwest corner are three clamped blocks *in situ* of the type of clamped blocks that evidently served as the actual foundation of the wall proper.

Apart from this northern sub-foundation, only the long western sub-foundation of the Temenos and an adjacent block of the foundation at the southwest corner, and a portion of the sub-foundation of the Propylon itself are preserved, the remainder of the eastern and southern foundations having been washed away in post-antique times (Pl. I; figs. 31, 32).[5] But at the southeastern corner of the Temenos, the dressed-down bedrock that once supported that corner is visible, and at the southwestern corner, it is also present. To the north, on this western side of the precinct, the bedrock drops down speedily, and as it descends, the single course of the porous limestone sub-foundation is supported by an increasing height of fieldstone boulders. Toward the north of this western line of the precinct, only such boulders are extant but the limestone course is preserved ca. 9 m. north of the southwestern corner (Pl. I; figs. 32, 33). In the vicinity of the corner, where the irregular limestone blocks rest directly on bedrock, they are laid alternately as headers separated by a pair of stretchers (the inner "stretcher" several times being made up of more than one block). The remainder of this course, now resting on an increasing height of fieldstones above the descending bedrock, was laid as headers or binders which have frequently been dressed down to receive the next course—the actual, clamped foundation course. Three blocks of this course, as previously mentioned, are extant. Each block was linked with its neighbor by a single Π-clamp set in lead (Pl. I; fig. 31). Thus the foundations of the entire precinct rested on bedrock or a combination of bedrock and fieldstone boulders.

In linking the short northern sub-foundation with the long western sub-foundation of the Temenos, five low courses, ranging from two to three blocks per course, were stuffed into the interval between the two sub-foundations (Pl. III.3; fig. 30). These blocks are spoils[6] and differ both in material and size. They have been adjusted to the higher courses of the older portion of the northern sub-foundation from which they project as much as 0.10 m. Both the retention of the older section of this northern sub-foundation and this sloppy device are unexpected in view of the quality of the precinct wall itself.

The older section of this northern sub-foundation is undatable. Earlier than the fourth-century Temenos and later than the seventh-century ceramic deposit found in the depths of the precinct, it probably should be associated with *Opfergrube* A and B found by the Austrians below the level of the fourth-century marble floor of the enclosure.[7] Very likely, its line determined the northern line and the orientation of the fourth-century Temenos

5. See below, pp. 299 f.

6. These blocks differ in material. Technical features such as dowel and pry holes appear where they are useless—e.g., the western block in course three has a dowel hole at the western end, where it abuts a fieldstone; the top course has a pry hole on its northern, outer face.

7. See below, p. 44.

31. View of the western sub-foundation and south-western corner of the foundation of the Temenos.

32. A. View of the western sub-foundation of the Temenos, looking toward south. B. Detail of southern section of A.

33. View of the excavation in 1950, showing the northwest corner of the terrace wall seen from the west.

as *Opfergrube* A and B, an eschara and a bothros,[8] were the ritual predecessors of the eschara and bothros in the later precinct.

The sparse but invaluable evidence regarding the interior installation of the Temenos recovered by the Austrians in 1875 had vanished by 1950.[9] Within the precinct, only earth, stray boulders, and a packing of fieldstones were uncovered as Plate I indicates. The line of fieldstone boulders was especially clear behind the sub-foundation of the Propylon (for which see below) and parallel to the southern section of the western sub-foundation. Here, it is markedly higher than the top surface of that sub-foundation (fig. 31) and it implies that the level of the rock packing in the rear portion of the Temenos was higher than that in the remainder of the precinct. The levels recorded by the Austrians in this region of the precinct[10] indicate that this area was, indeed, higher. Hence, in the restored plan of the Temenos (Pl. LIX), a broad step the full width of the precinct and 6.60 m. long has been added to the marble floor in the remainder of the precinct.

8. *Opfergrube* A is illustrated in *S,II*, pls. II, IV, 1, V, VI; *Opfergrube* B, on pls. II, IV, 2, VII. They are described on pp. 21 f. *Opfergrube* A was clearly an eschara. A porous rectangular frame enclosed what seemingly was a fire-resistant stone resting on earth. The latter stone appears cracked and shows traces of burning (cf. the related eschara found in the Hieron: Vol. 3, text I, pp. 128 f.). *Opfergrube* B was a bothros.

9. See above, pp. 26 f.

10. *S,II*, pp. 21 f., pl. II.

The marble floor, itself, was attested by the Austrian plan (fig. 13). Scattered marble paving slabs occurred throughout the enclosure. They rested on an underpavement of "soft" material, presumably tufa or porous limestone of the variety found elsewhere in the Sanctuary.[11] To the north of *Opfergrube* A and B, the Austrians uncovered two sides of a rectangular marble frame (fig. 13).[12] Mitred at each corner, they were let into the marble floor of the fourth-century precinct. These fragmentary blocks (Pl. LVIII.1, 2), together with a fragmentary paving slab that had abutted this frame to its north (Pl. LVIII.3) were recovered in our excavation in 1950. We also discovered three additional marble blocks that framed a second enclosure (Pls. LVI, LVII.1, 2).[13] One block abuts another and the under surfaces of these thin blocks are wider than the upper surfaces. Like *Opfergrube* B, they were cut with a rebate for a lid. They, too, are larger than the mitred blocks found by the Austrians and later recovered by ourselves, as *Opfergrube* B was larger than *Opfergrube* A. Clearly, they are the fourth-century counterparts to the earlier eschara and bothros discovered by the Austrians. In the restored plan, Plate LIX, the relationship between the fourth-century eschara and bothros has been determined by the known position of the eschara frame and the abutting paving slabs to the north recorded by the Austrians and the placing of the newly found blocks of the bothros adjacent to those paving slabs.

The Temenos walls were largely built of stuccoed porous limestone blocks. Scores of these blocks were found intermingled with the marble blocks in this area. They were connected with Π-clamps at each end, one or two, according to the thickness of the block. The lengths, heights, and thicknesses of these blocks varied.[14] These variations in dimensions were of no consequence inasmuch as the individual blocks were concealed by their stucco coating. On the interior of the precinct, the marble orthostates rested on a marble stereobate provided with a single recess and they were topped with a marble stringcourse that penetrated the thickness of the wall. Above the stringcourse, the walls of the Temenos were of stuccoed porous limestone. The fact that the exterior face of the stringcourse was not dressed indicates that it, too, was stuccoed. The marble orthostates had limesone backers. Hence from the exterior the precinct walls appeared to be built solely of stuccoed limestone.

11. E.g., in the porch of the Hieron: Vol. 3, text I, pp. 94 f., Pl. I. Too few marble pavement slabs were found and recorded by the Austrians to allow us to indicate the specific sizes of these blocks. Hence, the restored plan of the Temenos (and of the terrace, for which see below) lacks any subdivision in the marble floor.

12. *S,II*, p. 22, pl. II.

13. They differ in dimension from the marble blocks of which *Opfergrube* B was composed and are better preserved than the latter blocks as *S,II*, pl. VII indicates.

Although we are uncertain of the precise function and location of the block shown as PL. LVII.3, it has been included because of its seeming relationship to the other blocks shown on Pls. LVI, LVII.

14. The dimensions of these porous blocks recorded in the daily diary in terms of preserved length, height, and thickness are confusing, since it is clear that many of these blocks were fragmentary. Hence I find it futile and misleading to report specific figures for them. Unfortunately, these blocks were not numbered, as were the marble blocks, and inasmuch as they were later frequently reused to build modern retaining walls, it has proven impossible to check on them. The essential point is that above the marble stringcourse, the walls of the Temenos were built of blocks of stuccoed porous limestone.

Only one fragmentary stereobate block attributable to the walls of the precinct exists (Pl. LII.2). Identical in height with the adjacent stereobate course of the rear elevation of the Propylon (Pl. VII.2), it was provided with a single recess to differentiate it from the double-recessed stereobate of the building. No trace of dowel or clamp holes is preserved on this fragmentary block.

Six orthostate blocks from the wall exist (Pl. LII.1). They are 0.65 m. high (far lower than the orthostates of the Propylon, hence easily identified). Their average length is 1.15 m., but one block, +4, is exceptionally long: 1.64 m. They were doweled to the stereobate and stringcourse blocks. A single Π-clamp at either end connected each block with the two adjacent to it. The rear, slightly L-shaped section of the block was left undressed to adjust it to its porous backer. No such backer is preserved, but the width and dowel holes on the lower face of the stringcourse confirm their existence.

Two entire and one fragmentary block of the stringcourse are preserved (Pls. LIII.1, 2, LIV.1). The length of the fully preserved blocks varies slightly (1.14 and 1.168 m.) as does their height (0.225-0.227 m.) and thickness (0.554-0.555 m.). Two dowel holes on their lower surfaces attached each block to the marble orthostate and porous backer on which it rested A pair of Π-clamps at each end attached the block to the two blocks adjacent to it. A single dowel hole on the upper surface connected each of the preserved blocks with the lowest course of the limestone blocks of which the remainder of the wall consisted. The fragmentary stringcourse block (Pl. LIV.1) is of interest in confirming the fact that the northern sub-foundation of the precinct was wider than the other three: its width is 0.703 m.

The precinct walls must have had some form of coping, but none has been preserved. Nor is there any certain evidence of their height. Hence the reconstruction of these two elements is hypothetical.

Both the northern wall and the northern sub-foundation of the Temenos are wider than the other three walls.[15] This reflects the careful adjustment of the Propylon to the enclosure, since the width of the northern wall fits the width of the crepidoma on the rear of the building (Pls. XLVII.A, XLIX, LIX). As a building, the Propylon is clearly distinguished from the Temenos—one abuts the other. Had the northern wall of the precinct overlapped the northern wing of the Propylon, the effect to a spectator standing within the precinct would have appeared unarticulated and ungainly. At the same time, the northern wall extends up to the anta wall and is equivalent in width to the treads of the second and third steps of the Propylon and the narrow strip of the stylobate not occupied by the anta wall.

Two fragmentary blocks best explained as belonging to the jambs of a door were recovered among the marble blocks belonging to the Propylon and the precinct wall (Pl. LV). They do not fit the Propylon itself;[16] hence they have been used to provide a door

15. Attested, as has been mentioned, by the difference between the northern and adjacent stringcourse blocks: ca. 0.70 m. and 0.55 m.

16. For the doors of the Propylon, see below, pp. 76 ff.

34. View of the central Sanctuary showing the terrace wall and northern wall of the Temenos, with the Hieron in the background.

in the long western wall of the Temenos, where access to the triangular area leading to early classical *epopteion*, the Hall of Votive Gifts, and the archaic rock altar that preceded the Altar Court was highly desirable. The fragmentary block reproduced on Plate LV.2, was provided with a dowel and lewis hole on the top. It preserves four small circular holes on one side that presumably imply the existence of a grille. Its full width has not been preserved, hence a rebate has been conjectured for the door. The second, still more fragmentary block characterized by a recessed margin, Plate LV.1, was later inscribed with a list of initiates on the external face of the jamb.[17] The precise location of this door is hypothetical (fig. 1). Its present position would allow the visitor to enter this region of the Sanctuary a reasonable distance north of the altar situated before the *epopteion* and midway between the ritual installations and the step within the Temenos itself (Pl. LIX).

THE TERRACE

A broad terrace 16.60 m. wide and 8.0 m. long lay directly to the north of the Propylon and the Temenos. Its width was approximately that of the combined building and enclosure and it could be entered solely from the northern wing of the Propylon whose northern steps led onto it (Pls. I, LIX). Its restored level was equivalent to the stereobate of the Propylon (Pl. XLVIII) and it must have been ca. 0.50 m. lower than the precinct (Pl. LX).

The terrace was retained at the north by a strong wall preserved to a height of ca. 3.20 m. at the northwest corner (Pls. I, II; fig. 33). Built of blocks and boulders of grey, crystalline porphyry, it rested directly on bedrock which descends from the northeastern corner of the wall to the river valley (figs. 34, 35, 237). A massive boulder serves as the cornerstone of this end of the wall (fig. 36). At the western corner, on both the northern and western faces, the blocks have been shaped in a roughly ashlar fashion.[18] Elsewhere, they are polygonal (fig. 37). Both the blocks and the boulders vary greatly in size and the interstices between the large stones are stuffed with smaller fragments. The wall is a hybrid. Much of it is constructed of irregularly cut and assembled polygonal boulders of varying size laid in almost regular courses. The number of such courses increases from east to west, reflecting the descending bedrock on which the terrace wall is founded.

Close to the western corner of the wall, on its northern face, the letters Γ ΓΙΙ are carved (fig. 38).[19] Their meaning is uncertain.[20]

17. Dated "Imperial" by Fraser, Vol. 2, pt. I, **45**, p. 98, Pl. XIX. Text: Ἀγαθῇ τύ[χῃ].
[μύστ]ạ[ι εὐσεβεῖς]

18. The present top stone on the west corner had fallen out of place and was later put back in position.

19. *Hesperia*, 20 (1951), p. 13, pl. 4, fig. f.; Vol. 2, pt. I, **86**, Pl. XXIX. Height of letters: 0.038-

35. View of the terrace wall.

36. View of the northeast corner of the terrace wall, showing the bedrock on which it rests.

37. View of the terrace wall, showing the limestone sheathing.

38. Detail of the northwestern corner of the terrace wall.

A solitary porous limestone block marks the eastern line of the terrace (Pl. I). The bedrock has been cut to receive this block, which has been set as a stretcher, and at one end, the top surface of the block is level with the rock. Presumably, it reflects the firmly founded lowest course of the sub-foundation.

At the west, the technique characteristic of the western sub-foundation of the Temenos continues: as the bedrock descends to the river valley, the height of the wall is built up of fieldstone boulders. No upper course is preserved. The northern subfoundation of the Temenos, whose eastern portion is set on bedrock, constitutes the southern termination of the terrace. Both the Temenos and the terrace are contemporary as the ceramic finds recovered in the fill of the terrace and the precinct indicate.[21]

Early in the third century B.C., when the Rotunda of Arsinoe was built, the western section and the corner of the terrace wall were provided with a limestone sheathing (Pls.

0.04m. Fraser's statement regarding the later screening of the polygonal wall by a limestone face and his assumption, therefore, that the inscription antedated the completion of the Temenos is incorrect. For this limestone sheathing see, in particular, Chap. IV, pp. 296 f. In theory, the inscription could postdate the wall, it must antedate the erection of the limestone screen associated with the gigantic earth fill added to this area of the Sanctuary in connection with the building of the Rotunda of Arsinoe. In all likelihood, the inscription was contemporary with the Temenos and its Propylon.

20. Originally, *Hesperia*, 20 (1951), p. 13, Professor Lehmann assumed that these letters were a mason's mark. Later, in Vol. 2, pt. II, p. 103, he noted the relationship between these letters and the combination of Π and another letter in ceramic inscriptions found on pottery in the Sanctuary, and suggested that such letters must have been a meaningful abbreviation whose specific content he did not know. Fraser, *loc. cit.*, made no attempt to explain them but was content to record them.

21. See the Catalogue of Finds, pp. 383 ff.

I, II.1, 2; figs. 35, 37). It reflects the introduction into the area between the Rotunda, the Eastern Hill, the terrace, and the adjacent retaining walls of the central river of the Sanctuary of an enormous earth fill required to conceal the gigantic limestone foundation of the Rotunda. No longer was it possible to found monuments (like the monument once supported on a porphyry base adjacent to the terrace wall)[22] on bedrock—the normal procedure in the Sanctuary. The limestone sheathing placed directly on bedrock at the front of the terrace wall and attached to its surface below the present uppermost blocks provided a relatively solid basis for the erection—or reerection—of monuments in the vicinity of the terrace wall.[23]

The interior of the terrace contained a packing of field stones and boulders set on earth. An intentionally unexcavated section of roughly triangular packing in the northwest corner of the terrace is visible in Plate I.[24] This packing, and possibly a true underpavement, must have supported the marble floor of the terrace which is implied by marble bench supports once present on the open terrace. These supports were inserted in thin marble containers that have been dressed to be inserted into a marble floor (Pl. LIV.2).[25] It is conceivable that the marble pavement was restricted to a certain area or border within the terrace and that a second form of flooring complemented it. Lacking any evidence regarding such a combination of materials, we have restored a plain marble floor to the terrace.

Finally, although there must have been some form of parapet above the terrace wall, we have omitted it in the restored elevation (Pl. LX), since there is no evidence regarding its nature or height.

THE PROPYLON

FOUNDATION (Pls. I, II.3; Fig. 39)

Only sparse traces of the sub-foundation of the Propylon exist. They consist of a line of porous limestone blocks 7.85 m. long that underlay a large section of the rear wall of the building and a short section of the north sub-foundation of the northern wing of the building, ca. 2.55 m. long, that actually is an extension of the north sub-foundation of the precinct. All trace of the foundation of the southern wing, the remainder of the northern wing, and of the porch proper have disappeared as a result of the post-antique circumstances in this region of the Sanctuary.[26]

The sub-foundation of the Propylon rests on bedrock which has been dressed down to receive it (fig. 39). The blocks are laid as headers or binders save for a solitary, fragmen-

22. For this monument, see below, Chap. IV, pp. 292 f.

23. For a specific description and further details about this limestone sheathing, itself part of the later history of the terrace, see below, Chap. IV, pp. 296 f.

24. We are at a loss to explain the irregular interval ranging from ca. 0.95 m. to ca. 1.30 m. in width which separates the irregular inner line of the terrace wall and the packing of the terrace.

25. See below, Chap. IV, pp. 289 ff. for a description of these bench supports and containers.

26. See below, Chap. IV, pp. 299 f.

39. View of the sub-foundation of the rear wall of the Propylon seen from the east.

tary stretcher at the south. They are irregular in length and have a height of ca. 0.28 m. At the north, two blocks of a second course approximately level with the top preserved course of the extension of the precinct wall are extant. At least three courses must be predicated above the lower preserved course. Directly behind this fragmentary sub-foundation, the fieldstone packing that underlay the marble floor of the precinct rises above it (cf. Pl. II.3; fig 39).[27]

Proof that these scant traces are to be ascribed to the sub-foundation of the Propylon rests on three factors: one negative, two positive. The marble blocks of the Propylon can be restored to a building marked by two projecting wings of precise dimensions, as will now be demonstrated. That building fits precisely into the proposed location, where it is attached to—or is one with—the northern section of the eastern precinct wall, and where its wings extend the precise additional width of the terrace that lies to the east of the Temenos. No foundation exists for this building on the terrace itself—a location theoretically conceivable given the discovery of many of its marble blocks below the terrace wall. But marble blocks of the Propylon were also found in the ravine to the east of the terrace.[28] Given the northerly direction in which blocks were thrown in the last earthquake in the Sanctuary,[29] this circumstance was to be expected. The rock-cuttings to the east of the

27. It is interesting to note that, simply on the basis of Hauser's plan in *S,II*, pl. II, both Fernand Chapouthier, *Le Sanctuaire des dieux de Samothrace* (*Exploration archéologique de Délos*, XVI), Paris, 1935, p. 80 and n. 9, and René Vallois, *L'Architecture hellénique et hellénistique à Délos* (Bibliothèque des Ecoles françaises d'Athènes et de Rome, fasc. 157), Paris, 1944, pp. 138 f., suggested that some sort of façade indicated especially by the northern extension of the north wall of the precinct, should be predicated at this point and that the façade would have faced toward the Eastern Hill.

28. See above, p. 27.

29. E.g., the Hieron: Vol. 3, text I, pp. 18 f.; text II, p. 130.

Temenos and to the south of the terrace attest some structure. Finally, the later discovery of the processional road traversing the Eastern Hill to a point where it could lead to the *façade* of the Propylon was a welcome confirmation of the location that has always been proposed for the building (fig. 1).[30]

P.W.L.

In the foregoing description of the existing foundations of the Temenos reference has been made to the ⊓-shaped plan of the Propylon. Before describing, in detail, the various blocks associated with the building, it may be appropriate to give a general account of some of the crucial blocks which show that the plan took this form.

At an early stage in the study of the marble blocks, it became apparent that the building was an elegant Ionic structure built of Thasian marble. It was also clear that it was integral and contemporaneous with the precinct wall, and consequently was the earliest marble structure in the Sanctuary. Two large blocks were fundamental in demonstrating the plan and form of the Propylon: a step block and a geison-sima block both having moldings which returned as re-entrant angles. The building, therefore, either had a portico standing forward of the main part or it had a ⊓-shaped plan; the former was disproved for various reasons but, particularly, because the beams, most of which remain, could not have been associated with such a plan. As the analysis of the blocks continued, many architectural elements confirmed conclusively the ⊓-shaped plan. This was largely due to the fortunate survival of the variety, rather than the quantity, of blocks. Only one element of the entablature (fig. 90), other than certain decorative blocks, is not represented among the surviving marbles: the inner block behind the frieze. In restoring the building with wings, it should be pointed out that such a plan presupposes a hipped roof at the back. Whereas surviving blocks indicate pediments on the fronts of the wings, the sub-foundation shows that the rear wall was continuous without provision for short wings on the precinct side, which would have been necessary if the roofs of the wings had ended there, too, in pediments.

It should be emphasized that the building was a small one. With columns 4.90 m. high, it may be contrasted with the north porch of the Erechtheum with columns that measure 7.64 m.; the Temple of Athena Nike, which has columns 4.05 m. high, may portray broadly the scale of the Propylon. The plan measured ca. 12.30 m. by 6.20 m.

One further factor governed the general restoration of the Propylon. Although the fortunate survival of well-preserved blocks of the architrave indicates the intercolumniation of those bays associated with the wings, the spacing of the central pair of columns in the façade depended on the calculated length of an architrave block, now missing, based on the measurements of the extant geison-sima blocks; restored with two standard geison-sima blocks, the spacing was shown to be slightly greater than that between the other pairs of columns which, because of the adjustment necessary where the architrave returned at

30. See above, p. 27, and below, p. 296, for indication of the levels required for the road leading into this central area of the Sanctuary.

right angles, did not relate rigidly to the regular sequence of lions' heads on the geison-sima course.

EUTHYNTERIA (Pl. IV)

Three large blocks and a small fragment which formed the euthynteria have survived. Of these, two have lower rusticated projections along their lengths, and one has the projection on its shorter end. The first type is represented by a well-preserved block (+26; Pl. IV.2) which was set as a stretcher and secured by two Π-clamps at each end. A second category is a large block which is slightly wedge-shaped (+14; Pl. IV.1). Two dowel holes in the lower edge of one side show the method of fixing it to the limestone foundation. On the top surface are twin and single Π-clamps, a dowel hole, and pry holes. A double setting line exists 0.078 m. from the front face indicating the position of the lowest, single-recess step block, and the sides have anathyrosis of different patterns implying that one of the neighboring blocks was a stretcher. It is not possible to say where each type of euthynteria block was originally placed, but the single dowel hole on block +14 (Pl. IV.1) suggests a comparatively narrow step block in the course above. The second block in the first category is similar to that illustrated on Plate IV.2, and constructional features of the same type are repeated. A smaller fragment with rustication exists, and may belong to either category. In the restoration drawings (Pls. XLVIII-LI), the earth level has been shown so that the rustication is covered, the upper vertical face and the margin on the top surface remaining visible. The heights of the euthynteria blocks vary between 0.173 m. and 0.209 m.

STEPS, STYLOBATE, STEREOBATE, AND PAVING SLAB (Pls. V, VI, VII, VIII, IX, X; Fig. 40)

The step blocks of which there are numerous examples fall into two categories: those with a single recess along the lower edge and those with a double recess. As was standard practice, the single recess variety came from the lowest course in the flight.[31] The steps with double recesses have, therefore, been allocated to the second and top courses.

The lowest step with a single recess is represented by three blocks (++55, +22; Pl. V.1, 2; and +15; Pl. VI.1) and by another more fragmentary piece. They have heights varying between 0.225 m. and 0.239 m.; the tops of the recesses are slightly concave. The thicknesses of these blocks (i.e., from front to back) vary; block ++55 (Pl. V.1) was a stretcher with a thickness of 0.520 m., but block +15 (Pl. VI.1) measures over a meter and was possibly a header. The stretcher block ++55 (Pl. V.1) has a Π-clamp at the back edge, and doubtless was attached to a limestone backer; near this clamp is a dowel hole implying a large block on the course above with end dowels in it. The other block (+15; Pl. VI.1) has, on the other hand, a Π-clamp at the side, apparently relating to an adjacent step block of lesser thickness; its dowel hole might indicate a block in the next course of similar thickness to block ++55. Both these blocks and the third (+22; Pl. V.2) have the

31. See below, Chap. II nn. 32-36.

40. Inner corner step block +24.

surface of the tread very slightly raised above the part at the rear on which the next step rested. None of the extant blocks retains dowel holes in the under surfaces, but holes in the euthynteria show that such was the normal method of attachment.

The middle course of steps having double recesses is represented by a long block now in two pieces (+43 and +46; Pl. VI.2) and by a well-preserved block (+23; Pl. VII.1). With the exception of the inner corner step block that is described below, these are the only surviving blocks that have been attributed to this course; they have practically the same height (average 0.237 m.) and both show that they had an additional step above them. The length of +43 (Pl. VI.2) is known approximately (the central break makes complete accuracy impossible), and this dimension is only slightly less than the intercolumniation of the columns on the wings. This block has, therefore, been restored to the center of the wings; a similarly long block has been conjectured for the center of the façade.

The L-shaped step block (+24; Pl. VIII) must have been located in this same course, having both the same height (0.236 m.) and double recesses as those already described. This block, which is fundamental to the restoration of the building, has at one corner a re-entrant angle around which the double recesses are well preserved. Both the tread and the L-shaped dressed surface for the top course of steps are clearly visible, and on the formerly hidden part are Π-clamp holes, one for attachment to an adjacent step and two others to a backing block, possibly of the limestone foundation. There is anathyrosis for the adjacent steps, but one side is cut at a slightly obtuse angle. The dowel holes with their pry holes indicate that the top course of steps consisted of three rectangular blocks, placed in L-formation, rather than another block with a re-entrant angle. It is interesting to note that this block was provided with a lewis hole showing that large marbles were moved and lifted by a lewis even if they were destined for a low level in the construction. This step block may have come from either the northern or southern return between a wing and the façade.

Only one stylobate block remains (+21; Pl. IX), but its good state of preservation indicates clearly the arrangement at this level. Having a double recess and a total height of 0.254 m., it belongs to a course about one and a half centimeters higher than those of both courses below. Such a progression from lower to higher risers has parallels elsewhere.[32] On the bottom, there are two dowel holes at one end only, and the sides have anathyrosis. In the restored plan (Pl. XLVII A), stylobate blocks of this size have been placed between both the front columns of the wings and the similarly spaced side columns of the wings.

Of the same height as the stylobate and having a double recess is a small fragment that has setting lines on the top surface showing it to be a fragmentary stereobate block (+32; Pl. X.1). The setting lines, at different distances from the front and side, have been interpreted as the marks of the rectangular base of the anta. Originally, it was probably secured by two dowels, but only one such cutting remains.

The stylobate was completed by paving slabs of which only one has survived (+120; Pl. X.2). Its height relates it to the stylobate and stereobate blocks, and it has anathyrosis on all sides and is moderately well preserved. This is a large slab and has, therefore, been placed in the restored plan (Pl. XLVII A) in the center of the central bay of the building.

ORTHOSTATE (Pl. XI)

Remaining on the site of the Temenos are several orthostate blocks. They are of two sizes. The larger have been attributed to the wall of the Propylon and were seemingly placed back to back. One (++15; Pl. XI) measures 1.050 m. in height as does another unillustrated example, ++31, that has the same height and constructional features. The smaller orthostates, ca. 0.650 m. high, have been ascribed to the surrounding walls of the precinct.[33] Two of the larger variety are in a good state of preservation; a third, of which only the lower half is preserved, probably also belongs to the larger category. The orthostate illustrated on Plate XI, ++15, has features common to others: a ridge on the roughly cut back separates the thicker lower part from the thinner upper part; presumably this ledge acted as a key for limestone fillers between two such blocks placed back to back. The blocks were secured at the base by dowels at one end only, and connected by Π-clamps to adjacent orthostates. The example shown on Plate XI is slightly wider at the top than at the bottom, a fact which can be explained by the sloping jamb of the doorway against which it was placed. The orthostates were attached to the wall blocks above by dowels, and it is assumed that such blocks were binders linking the interior and exterior orthostates. One dowel was provided in the top of each orthostate for this purpose. The or-

32. See above, n. 31.

33. See above, p. 45, Pl. LII.1.

thostates which faced toward the precinct are thought to have been of the same variety as those on the side of the Propylon, but to have been placed on a stereobate to allow for the difference in levels on either side of the wall. Such a stereobate has survived (+100; Pl. VII.2). Its height of 0.272 m. is slightly more than that of the stereobate of the Propylon but the double recesses are similar. As already stated in connection with the precinct wall,[34] these stereobate blocks have the same height as those under the lower orthostates of the Temenos wall. Π-clamps attached this stereobate block to its neighbors at the sides and back. The faint line of a dressed surface along the front suggests that the top surface of the stereobate was slightly in advance of the main wall face, a fact confirmed by the location of the dowel holes in the bottom of the orthostates and on the top of the stereobate.

As shown in the restoration drawings (Pls. L, LX), there would have been space on either side of the doorways, both internally and externally, for two orthostates, but adjacent to these blocks and to the antae walls, there would have been two blocks less wide than the others.

WALL BLOCKS (Pl. XII)

Several fragments of marble wall blocks have survived but only four are sufficiently well preserved to afford any indication of the construction of the wall of the Propylon. Of these four blocks, two (+45, +53; Pl. XII) show the range of heights of courses as 0.554 m. and 0.558 m. respectively. The other two, not illustrated, have comparable dimensions. One is 1.184 m. long, 0.558 m. high, and 0.347 m. thick; the other is 1.160 m. long, more than 0.550 m. high, and of unknown thickness. A multiple of seven courses based on these blocks, and placed directly above the large orthostates, provides an isodomic wall equivalent to the height of the column, so far as that element could be reconstructed.[35] However, there is an insufficient quantity of complete blocks, or blocks with constructional details, to say precisely where each of the surviving blocks was originally located. No header blocks remain, but a binding course has been restored over the back-to-back orthostates as a means of connecting these blocks. A similar course of binders has been conjectured at the top of the wall for the sake of rigidity. The remaining courses have been reconstructed as alternately longer and shorter blocks, the longer dimensions being taken from three of the blocks mentioned above. Nevertheless, the three doorways of the Propylon (for which see below) limited the area of walling in which a regular system of masonry could be employed. In the restored longitudinal section (Pl. L) large wall blocks have been placed above the door lintels on the exterior of the building, but the over-lintel (Pl. XLI) provides some evidence for restoring two blocks on the side facing the precinct.

The blocks were secured by dowels at the bottom and top surfaces; the recess at the top end of +53 (Pl. XII.1) is unexplained. No Π-clamps are preserved. Lacking surviving headers, the thickness of the wall can only be determined by calculation, although an approximate dimension is obtained by doubling the thickness of the extant blocks. A calcula-

34. See above, p. 45.
35. See below, p. 57.

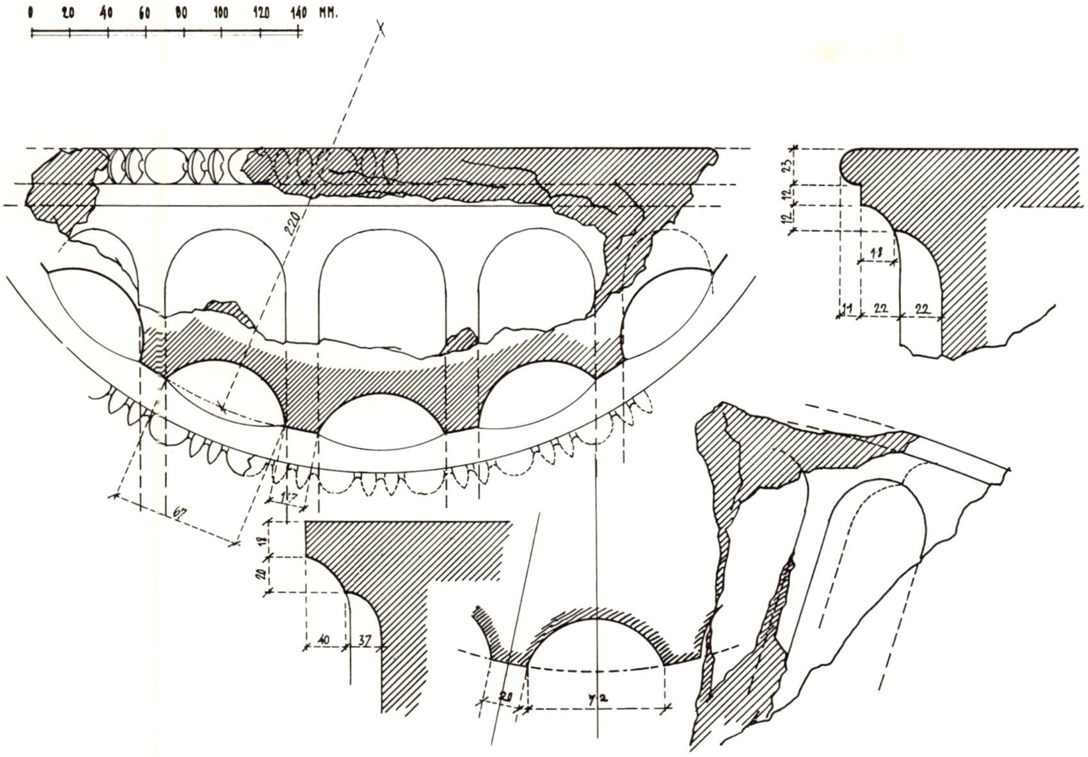

41. Lost fragment of column drawn by Nepomucký.

tion may be based on a comparison between the interior and exterior measurements of the building; the former measurement is determined by the length of the beams which spanned from the façade to the wall, and the latter by relating the wall to the entablature, precise details of which are known. The reconstruction of the system of coffers contributed to the discussion on the lengths of the beams which are sufficiently preserved to give only an approximate figure. The resultant figure for the thickness of the wall is ca. 0.70 m., a measurement that would accommodate two wall blocks.[36]

COLUMN (Pl. XIII; Fig. 41)

Two column shafts, preserved in a comparatively complete state, and two smaller fragments have survived. One, now re-erected in the Museum (+33, +28; Pl. XIII) lacks the lower part of the shaft, but in the top, which remains, there is a dowel hole and a lewis hole. Although the fillets of the flutes have been mutilated, entasis could be measured from the hollows of the flutes and is recorded on the diagram (Pl. XIII.1); no attempt has been made to indicate the broken fillets on that diagram. At the top of the shaft is an astragal. Although this element is now worn, a short length of bead and reel remained on fragments recorded by Nepomucký during the French-Czech excavation (fig. 41).[37] The total height of the shaft, excluding the missing base, has been restored as 4.490 m.

36. For discussion of the beams, coffers, and the entablature, see below.

37. For this excavation see above, pp. 21, 25.

42. Fragmentary capital 49.414 and drum 49.985.

43. Drum 49.985 as drawn by Nepomucký.

44. Detail of drum 49.985 as drawn by Nepomucký.

45. A, B. Fragmentary drum 52.215.

The other column shaft lies north of the terrace and measures 0.840 m. in height, but both ends are broken and only part of the complete diameter remains. The diameter measures 0.450 m., probably indicating that it belonged to the lower end of the shaft, but it is very waterworn. Another fragment exists (+25) having a height of 0.261 m. and a maximum diameter in the hollows of the flutes of 0.455 m. and a minimum of 0.405 m. There is also a small fragment of a column, 0.350 m. high, of which only seven flutes remain.

No base for these shafts was recovered. The restoration drawings have, therefore, included a conjectural element modeled on the bases of the Ionic columns of the Propylon of Ptolemy II.[38]

DRUM (Pl. XIV.2, 3; Figs. 21, 28, 42-46, 63, 70, 81-82)

Above the shafts were drums of which four have been recovered.[39] Two of the three remaining in Samothrace are shown on Plate XIV.2, 3 (70.939 and 49.985). The third, 52.215, appears in figure 45. Figures 21, 42, 63, 70, 81 illustrate 49.985. Each has a lewis hole and a round dowel hole in the top surface, and a similar round dowel secured it to the shaft. The height of the drums varies slightly, as does the diameter, but the average height is 0.250 m. The drums are enriched by alternate upright and pendant palmettes carved in relief, each separated by S-shaped stems from which the palmettes spring. At the base, where the stems meet and also below the upright palmettes were small acanthus leaves more visible in Nepomucký's day (figs. 42-44). The top of the drum was crowned by an astragal as recorded by Nepomucký. Only traces of this molding are visible on the blocks remaining on Samothrace, but it is confirmed on the drum recently discovered in Gelibolu (figs. 28, 46, 82).[40] This drum is important in indicating that

38. See *Samothrace*, Vol. 10, forthcoming.

39. See above, pp. 24 f., and below, pp. 106 ff., for a full description and discussion of these blocks.

40. For this drum see above, Introduction, nn. 118 ff.

46. A. Tourist Pavilion, Gelibolu: drum from the Propylon.
B. Detail of the drum.

gilded bronze eyes were inserted into the upper volutes. Traces of a bronze pin are preserved in the central volute in the detail illustrated in figure 46 B. This drum, therefore, offers the solitary indication among the extant marble blocks that bronze attachments were applied to the Propylon.

CAPITAL (Pls. XIV, XV, XVI, XVII; Figs. 42, 47, 48, 62, 63, 70, 71)

In the Propylon, there were ten capitals of which six were corner or angle capitals, placed either at an external or an inner angle. Of these capitals only two remain, both incomplete and of the normal, not angle, variety.[41] The larger piece (49.414 A, B; Pls. XIV.1, XV, XVI, XVII) is that recorded by Nepomucký (figs. 47, 48), when the volute existed to a somewhat greater extent. However, sufficient remains to provide evidence for a restoration (Pl. XVII).

This elegant capital rested directly on the carved drum with its decorated band of bead and reel on the astragal. The egg and dart of the echinus has been severely damaged but there are vestiges of the half palmette which hung above the volute and overlapped the carved echinus. A reconstruction of the missing part of the capital shows that the eye, with a diameter of 0.026 m., was aligned with the bottom of the block and with the sides of the drum; the centers of the eyes are 0.214 m. apart. The volute scrolls consist of ovolos with small fillets on each side. The outer molding, now totally destroyed, was perhaps completed as an ovolo and a fillet, as seen from the side of the bolster.[42] The lower line of the canalis sags gracefully over the center of the capital and continues with two and a half turns to die into the eye. The surfaces between the scrolls are slightly hollow. The square abacus is carved with a Lesbian cymation which is damaged, but a repetition of the leaf forms can be discerned; in the restoration drawing, the uninscribed hanging palmettes at the corners are based on those from the Temple of Athena at Priene[43] since this part of the abacus has entirely disappeared. The bolster is enriched by a wide band of decoration composed of repetitive scroll and palmette forms similar, in vein, to the pattern on the drum. The band is edged by a bead and reel molding (figs. 42, 47 B, C, 48 A, 62 B, 71).

Constructional features show that the capital was attached to the drum by a central round dowel and on its upper surface there are two dowel holes; doubtless there were originally four. In the center, there is a lewis hole, and the whole surface is dressed to provide an octagonal area on which the ends of the architraves rested (Pl. XIV.1).

41. Both fragmentary capitals are in the Museum: 49.414 A, B placed on the drum 49.985 and shaft +28 and +33, and 51.909 on the drum 52.215. See *Guide*[4], p. 99.

42. An ovolo and fillet has been conjectured on the analogy of a capital from Olympia. See F. Adler *et al.*, *Die Baudenkmäler von Olympia*, Berlin, 1896, pl. LXXXIX, although other variations cannot be dismissed.

43. See below, Chap. II, n. 61.

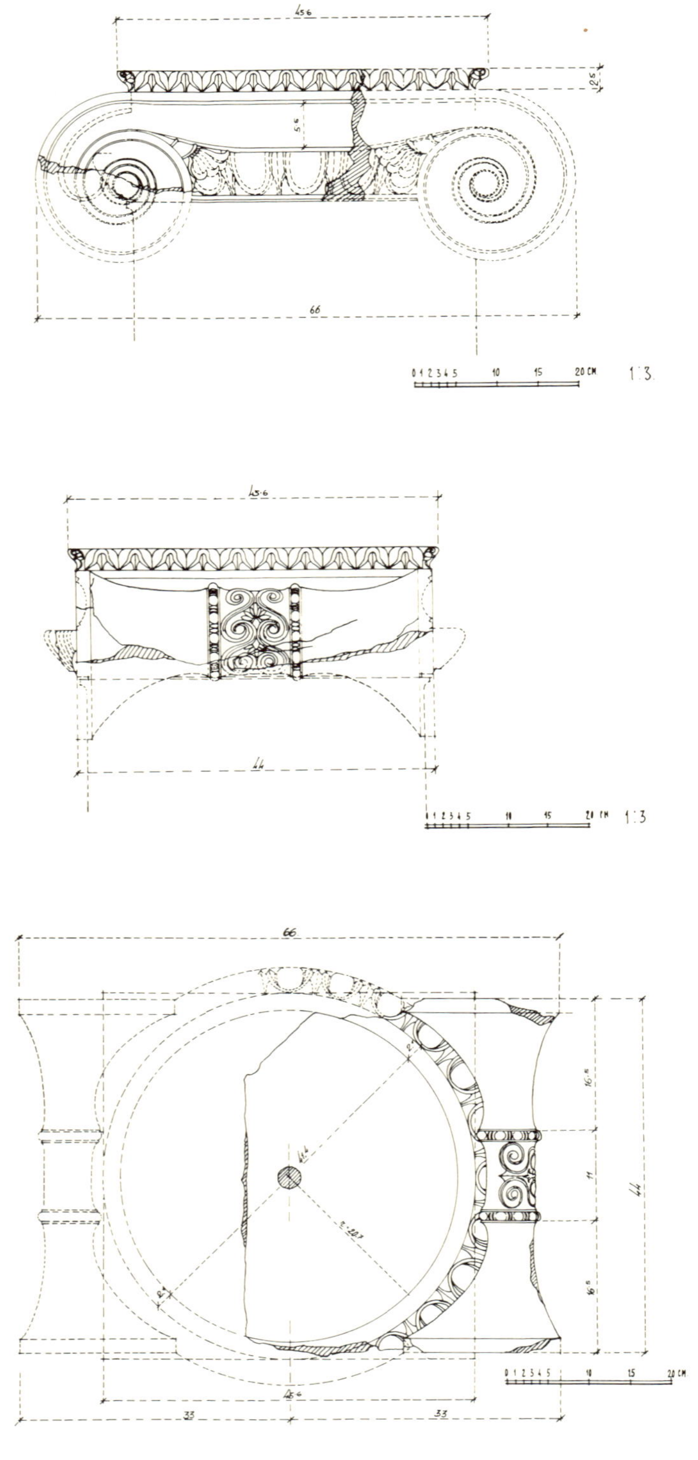

47. Fragmentary capital 49.414 as drawn by Nepomucký. A. Side. B. Bolster. C. Bottom.

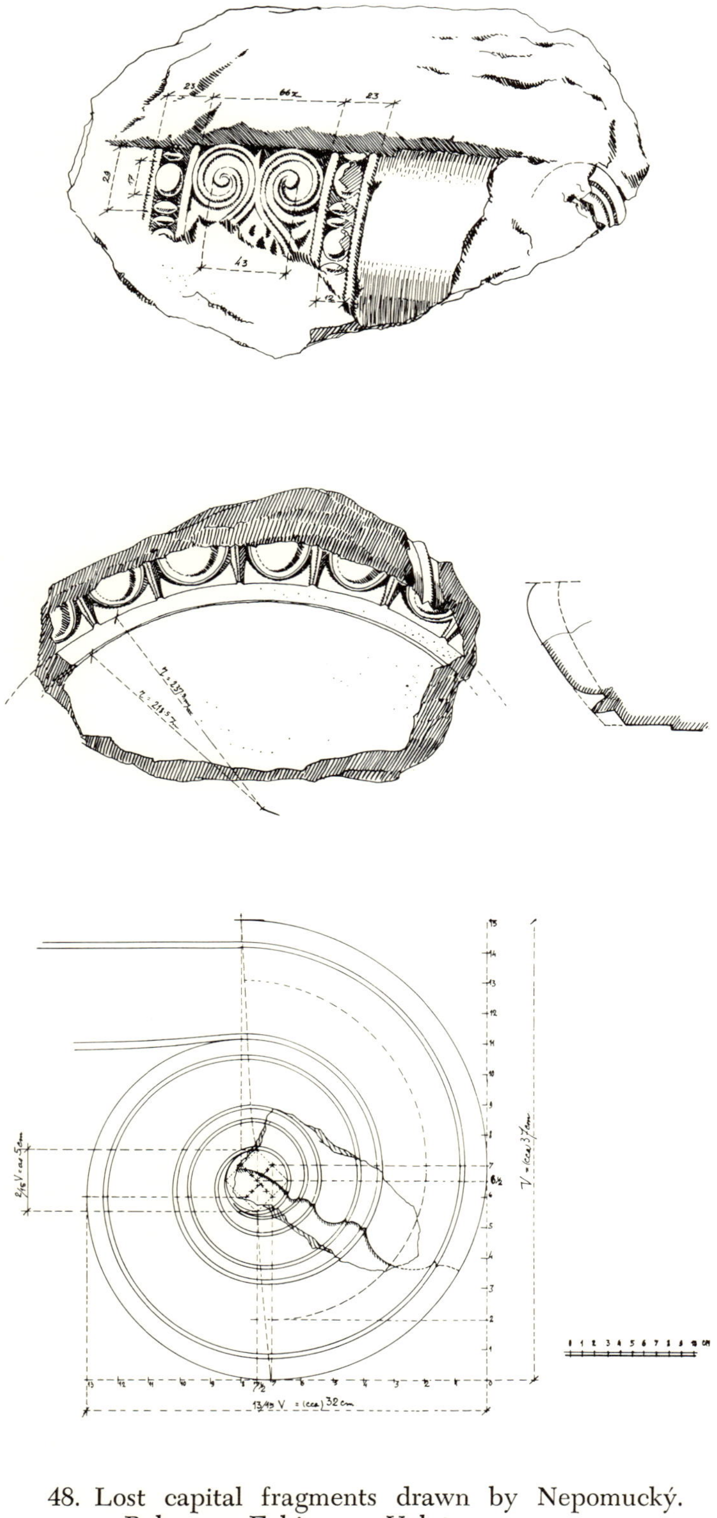

48. Lost capital fragments drawn by Nepomucký.
A. Bolster. B. Echinus. C. Volute.

COLUMNAR AND WALL ARCHITRAVE (Pls. XVIII, XIX, XX, XXI, XXII, XLIV.1)

The fortunate survival of three architrave blocks from the epistyle is added proof of the plan as we have restored it. In particular, it demonstrates the scheme of intercolumniation on which the system of the entablature and the roofing depended. Two well-preserved blocks (+12, +35; Pls. XVIII and XIX) have moldings on their outer and inner faces, comprising three plain fasciae and a crowning molding on the outer side, and two fasciae, a midway molding, a fascia, and a crowning molding on the inner side. The soffits of the architrave blocks are fair-faced with no constructional features except at the ends, indicating their columnar position. The significant difference between the two blocks is that architrave block +12 has a wide chamfer across the left corner of its exterior face, and architrave block +35 is chamfered across the interior corner. The other ends are square-cut, indicating a straight continuation with the next block. In the Propylon, there is only one place where each of these architrave blocks could have been placed: block +12 would have spanned the left, or southern, side bay of the central façade; block +35 would have fitted over the southern side of the south wing. As there are no alternatives to these locations in the entablature, valuable evidence is gained for determining the intercolumniation of the building as a whole. This intercolumniation is shown to be 1.994 m. on the evidence of the architraves alone. Since the chamfered ends are damaged, it is not possible to say how the architrave blocks were keyed together where they met at right angles, but it is probably that one block extended beyond the chamfer by about 0.230 m. as a "spur," about half the width of the block; the end of the adjacent block, at right angles, would have been partly chamfered and would not have had a "spur." Assuming that the architrave blocks over the sides of both wings were similar to +35, then the two blocks on the fronts of the wings would have had partly chamfered ends which would have been keyed into blocks at right angles, thus providing a symmetrical system of jointing on the façade.[44] In the surviving blocks, there are Π-clamp holes placed diagonally across the chamfered cutting, but at the standard ends, architrave block +35 has two Π-clamps and +12 has none. In conformity with the dowel holes in the top surface of the capital, there are end dowel holes at only one end of the architrave; curiously, block +35 appears to have no end dowels, but both blocks have lewis holes, pry holes, and dowel holes for attaching the frieze blocks in the next course. The top surface is dressed to receive these frieze blocks, but no settings for the marble beams which would come at the ends of the architrave blocks has been noted, nor indeed, any dowel for attaching them. Both these architrave blocks have similar dimensions: a height of 0.384 m., and a thickness at the soffit of 0.466 m. and 0.468 m., measurements which show that the abacus of the capital projected very slightly beyond the lowest fascia of the architrave. A conventional arrangement for attaching the architrave to the capital is exemplified by block +114 (Pl. XX) which retains twin dowel holes. Dressing on the undersurface for its seating on the capital

44. A similar system of chamfered blocks at right angles, one with a "spur," is fully preserved on the Nereid Monument. See Coupel-Demargne, pl. LXXXVII.

is faintly visible, but the dressed surfaces for the frieze and the blocks behind it are pronounced. These are the only three epistyle blocks remaining.

Examples of the architrave blocks from the wall are sparsely represented, but two blocks indicate clearly the arrangement. One block (++47; Pl. XXI) has a molding on the exterior face only, the back being roughly cut. It has a fully preserved length of 1.143 m. and its thickness is 0.366 m., measured at the bottom. In the top surface, there is a large sinking for a dowel, but no other signs of attachments to adjacent blocks. Another block (+5; Pl. XXII) is slightly shorter, but on one side are the scant remains of a molding clearly of an inner architrave block. On the back, there is an unexplained ledge along the top edge. It has a roughly picked back surface and a thickness, taken at the bottom, of 0.570 m. On the top, there is a lewis hole, twin Π-clamp holes, and the underside is roughly dressed. Whereas block ++47 would occupy almost exactly half the width of the wall as calculated, block +5 would require a comparatively thin slab, of 0.130 m. thickness, to carry the exterior architrave molding. The enigmatic ledge is perhaps a method of holding in position an exterior block of L-shaped section.

FRIEZE (Pls. XXIII, XXIV, XXV, XLIV.3, 4; Figs. 6, 147-177, 195, 210)

The sculpture on the frieze is discussed fully in Chapter III. Hence only the architectural and constructional details will be described in this section. Suffice it to say here that the frieze is carved with dancing maidens some of whom moved from left to right and some from right to left. One large block (49.1043 A, B; Pl. XXIII), and a large number of smaller pieces of this important frieze have survived.[45] The large block (Pl. XXIII) is destroyed at the right end, but is otherwise well preserved. Its front face slopes slightly back from the vertical so that the upper parts of the sculptured figures are in higher relief than the lower (see the profile of the fragmentary block, 49.1043 C, shown on Pl. XLIV.3). At the top of the face there is a hollow below a crowning molding comprising an ovolo, a half round, and a small fillet. It is now 1.651 m. long; the thickness at the base is 0.309 m., and the height is 0.324 m. On the top, which is roughly dressed except for a smooth margin along the front edge, there are two dowel holes indicating a block in the course above (i.e., a dentil course *q.v.*) of almost one meter in length. Also remaining is a recess at the preserved end which appears to be another dowel hole, although a Π-clamp would have been more normal. The preserved end also has anathyrosis, but a break at the bottom may have once contained a lower end dowel hole. Another large block *F(S)10* (formerly Louvre MA 698; fig. 157), on permanent loan from the Louvre, has a length of 0.890 m., but it is broken at the left end and its original thickness is unknown since the sculptured face was detached from the block in the last century leaving extant no constructional features. The frieze block (*F(S)11*; fig. 158) against which *F(S)10* was once erroneously mounted was mutilated in the same way. Some of the fragmentary blocks illustrate standard constructional methods. They show end Π-clamps and dowel holes

45. See Chap. III, pp. 172 ff.

in the lower end (49.1043 C, 50.378; Pl. XXIV.1, 2). The heights of the blocks vary slightly but 0.320 m. is an average height; the thicknesses vary only slightly, between 0.290 m. and 0.313 m., measured from the surface of the block to the roughly cut rear face.

It will be seen that these measurements of thicknesses coincide with the dressed areas in the top surfaces of the architrave blocks (e.g., block +12). The centers of the dowel holes in the lower ends of the frieze blocks also agree well with those in the architrave blocks; for example, in the frieze blocks last mentioned (Pl. XXIV.1, 2), the dowel holes coincide with the holes in architrave block +12 (Pl. XVIII), taking into account the setting line on the architrave block. It is not implied, of course, that these particular blocks were associated together, but the inference regarding the relation between the frieze blocks and architrave blocks is clear. Finally, the distances between the dowel holes in the architrave blocks are ca. 0.900 m., indicating the lengths of a category of frieze block. It may be noted that the Louvre block (*F(S)10*), now measuring 0.890 m. long, may belong to this group, and that it has been only slightly shortened by breakage. It may, too, suggest that the long block (Pl. XXIII) originally had a length of about twice that of the shorter variety of frieze block. Similar features are visible on architrave block +35 (Pl. XIX), but the fact that there is only one dowel hole may suggest that a long frieze block rested on this block.

In Chapter III it is argued that the figures on the frieze over the wall moved from right to left, with the start of the sequence at the southwest corner of the building.[46] The large block (49.1043 A, B) of 1.651 m. length, therefore, did not come from the wall but possibly from the southern side of the south wing over, or mostly over, architrave block +35, which has already been shown to have been in this location. This suggestion is hypothetical, but this long block probably did not come from the north side of this wing since the preserved left end does not imply a junction at a corner. Likewise, it certainly did not come from the southern bay of the central façade where architrave block +12 is known to have been placed. Dowel holes in this block show that the frieze blocks were of the shorter variety. In the restoration of the north elevation (Pl. LI), a long block, comparable with 49.1043 A, B, has been placed near the center for the reasons argued above, but the figures would have moved in the opposite direction, that is from right to left.

Two exceptional blocks of the frieze (65.99, 67.32; Pl. XXV) have been recently discovered and identified. These pieces, retrieved at different times, were found to fit together and to be a fragment of an external corner block. Only the lower part of the figures has survived, hence no constructional features remain. From which corner of the building they might have come is discussed in Chapter III.[47]

The blocks backing on to the frieze are discussed below in the account of the marble beams.

46. See below, p. 201.
47. See below, pp. 206 f.

DENTILS (Pl. XXVI.4,5)

The dentil course above the frieze is represented by sixteen detached dentils (eight of which are in the Museum), but the parent slab to which they were attached has entirely disappeared. The dentils attributable to the Propylon have a height of 0.143 m., a width of 0.067 m. and a projection of 0.136 m.; the distance between the dentils was probably 0.035 m. on the evidence of one dentil fragment which extends sufficiently for the vestiges of an adjacent dentil to remain. There is no indication of the size, from front to back, of the parent slab, but it presumably extended at least as far back as did the geison-sima blocks. The width of each slab may have been about one meter, to judge from the spacing of the dowels on a frieze block. Setting lines demonstrate that the backs of the dentils proper were set 0.046 m. from the front of the crowning molding of the frieze. A smooth surface on the underside of the geison-sima blocks, about 0.20 m. wide, is presumably to allow a fair soffit to be visible between the dentils. There was no molding or other member above the dentil slabs.

Apart from the archaeological significance of the inclusion of dentils in this entablature, there is also a structural implication: without this course, the wooden roof members would have interfered with the marble coffers. An Attic system without dentils, or, for that matter, an Asiatic scheme without a frieze, would have been impossible, if only on constructional grounds.

GEISON-SIMA (Pls. XXVII, XXVIII, XXIX, XXX, XXXI, XXXII, XLIII, XLV; Figs. 49, 50, 51, 52, 104, 120)

Of the nine standard geison-sima blocks which have remained, some are fragmentary and none has retained the carved sima.[48] Many blocks in this category have the same constructional features, but there are varieties in the measurement from the front of the bed-mold to the back of the block. This measurement varies from 0.583 m. to 0.703 m., with two examples measuring 0.630 m. There are also small variations in the widths of the blocks, the maximum difference being 0.30 m.

Two well-preserved standard geison-sima blocks are illustrated on Plates XXVII, XXVIII.2 (++5 and ++14), and it will be seen that the top surface has a roughly dressed area at the back, at a flatter pitch than the front part, which was exposed and is marked by rainwater grooves. The angles of the slopes in the different blocks are also inconsistent, the lower, exposed slopes varying between 12° and 14° and the upper between 8° 45′ and 9° 45′. A relationship between these recordings and the thickness of the block, from front to rear, could not be found for certain, although there seemed to be a tendency for the larger blocks to have the upper part at a lesser pitch. The larger geison-sima blocks are believed to have come from the wall of the Propylon which is thicker than the entablature

48. Fragments of additional blocks, that is, portions of the sima exist—e.g., 49.42, 50.20, 50.72, and 50.638, the latter on exhibition in Case 3 of Hall B, as is a detached lion's head waterspout 54.203. See *Guide*[4], p. 105. A second fragmentary lion's head, 55.148, is in storage.

49. Geison-sima block ++14 (bottom).

50. Geison-sima block ++14 (top).

over the colonnade. The relationship between wall thickness and slope on the block was to be expected in view of the slightly lower pitch of the main roof compared with that over the wings. The pitch of the upper slope, of course, relates to the pitch of each stroter and not to the pitch of the roof as a whole. The roof pitch appears to be reflected in the steeper pitch of the lower slope of the geison-sima blocks.

The upper surface of these blocks is carefully dressed to receive the stroters, and at the sides of the lower exposed part there are lips which were covered by kalypters that terminated as antefixes. The geison-sima blocks have lewis holes which are located centrally toward the sima, and well away from the center of gravity. In line with the lewis hole is a rectangular shallow sinking, roughly cut to take the end of the kalypter. These blocks show a dowel hole diagonally placed in the under surface, which is characteristic of them; unfortunately, the comparable diagonal dowel holes cannot be verified in the course below since this part of the dentil block has not survived. These dowels were the only anchors between the geison-sima blocks.

The delicate cymation has not remained attached to a single block still in Samothrace, but a large part of a carved sima is preserved in Vienna (I, 424 B, Pl. XXVIII.1; figs. 11, 51, 95).[49] Several detached fragments exist both in Vienna and Samothrace (fig. 109), and they provide sufficient grounds for appreciating the elegant carving discussed fully in Chapter II.[50] It is, therefore, sufficient to say here that each geison-sima block was enriched with a lion's head waterspout emerging from a calyx of acanthus leaves which was flanked by three rinceaux scrolls on either side, the final ones ending as spiral tendrils.

49. The detached lion's head waterspout illustrated in *S,II*, pl. X, apparently no longer exists in the storerooms of the Antikensammlung in Vienna. In Pl. XXVIII.1, the first loop of the spiral tendril should be ribbed like the other two loops, not V-shaped as it has been drawn.

50. See below, pp. 124 ff.

51 Fragmentary lateral sima block I, 424 B. Vienna, Ephesos-Museum.

These blocks lack the customary low crowning fillet. Indeed, their thickness is no more than 0.040 m., the top edge diminishing to a single edge, which implies that the top of the rinceaux scrollwork was allowed to advance slightly beyond the field, producing the effect of a "chéneau à silhouette."[51] A tendril from the final scroll continued beyond the sima to form one of the volutes at the base of the antefix. The lions' heads have entirely disappeared from the geison-sima blocks in Samothrace, and the present smooth hollow on blocks ++5 and ++14 can only be explained as subsequent cutting away of the damaged jaws leaving a cuplike channel for rain water which was allowed to run down the face of the corona.[52]

In addition to these features, the geison-sima blocks have large cuttings and recesses which vary among different blocks. They indicate to a considerable degree the relationship between the geison-sima blocks, the marble beams, and the construction of the wooden roof. Cut into the top back edge are three rectangular recesses, one in the center and two others, of half the width, at the sides. These recesses received the ends of the wooden tie-beams which would have measured about 0.160 m. in width and 0.150 m. in height, and been placed at intervals of ca. 0.570 m. The recesses are only about 0.05 m. to 0.070 m. deep, indicating the small area on which the beams rested. Also at the back of the blocks are some much larger and more roughly cut recesses. They are usually triangular in form and at the lower back edge of the block. Some occur at the sides of the block (e.g., ++14; Pl. XXVIII.2), others in the center (e.g., +11; Pl. XXIX). These substantial cuttings were necessary so that the back of the blocks would not impinge against the higher part of the marble beams spanning the building. The roughness of the workmanship would suggest that these cuttings were executed at a late stage in the construction without anticipating where the offending parts of the beams might come. Besides the triangular cuttings, some blocks had the whole corner (++5; Pl. XXVII) or a large central area cut away (+67; Pl. XXXI.2). In this latter instance, the cutting has one side at a sharp angle, perhaps indicating that during the construction the block was swung round into position after the beams had been installed. It was noted that the smaller variety of blocks, referred to above, also had similar but smaller cuttings for the marble beams, which might imply that they came from the entablature above the colonnade

51. Roux's term, for which see below, Chap. II, n. 141.

52. See below, Chap. IV, p. 297.

52. Corner geison-sima block I, 424 A. Vienna, Ephesos-Museum.
A. Front. B. Top. C. Side.

rather than from the thicker wall; the ends of the beams on the columnar side were not so high as those over the wall, and would, therefore, not impinge on the geison-sima course to such a great extent (e.g., ++14; Pl. XXVIII.2, and +67; Pl. XXXI.2).

Attention should also be drawn to the slightly wedge-shaped geison-sima blocks (++5; Pl. XXVII) and the distinctly trapezoidal block (+67; Pl. XXXI.2). Whether this peculiarity had some special significance for stability, or was, perhaps, a method of placing the blocks in position is not known.

A geison block crucial to the restoration of the building should now be described. This block (+18; Pls. XXX, XXXI.1) is a large marble with a short length of bed-mold which returns in a re-entrant angle. Its upper surface has the exceptional feature of the exposed area being dished in a diagonal direction. We have, therefore, one of the two inner angle geison blocks which existed between the main portion of the Propylon and the wings. As with the other geison-sima blocks, it was provided with a lewis hole, but the L-shaped "hidden" area has a less pronounced slope than on the standard geison-sima blocks. A large cutting in one rear face was doubtless contrived to avoid a high part of a marble beam, and one side is not at right angles with the front edge, perhaps for the reasons advanced above. On the other, rear face, there is a wide recess for a tie beam. The small length of molding, returning in a re-entrant angle on the underside, is a fortunate survival, since it indicates how the adjacent geison-sima blocks met in this corner of the building. Enough remains to show that this block was the corona of a geison block and lacked a sima: reconstruction indicates that one adjacent block had a sima which returned at right angles with a mason's mitre, and that the other adjacent block was a standard geison-sima block. The large cutting for a marble beam may imply that this corner block came from the northern inner angle of the building. The particularly wide recess for a wooden tie beam may be due to the necessity for a more substantial beam at a point where the wing joined the main section of the Propylon.

The second important geison-sima block is now in Vienna (I, 424 A, Pls. XXXII, XLV.1; figs. 11, 52, 104, 120). It is a corner block, the only extant block which contains elements of a pediment, in this case, a lower left end. It has a pitch of 14° 30′. The block is preserved to its full width, but it is broken along the back. The block must have been considerably longer, given the existence of a lewis hole visible at its broken rear end. The top surface has a raised rib associated with the final row of kalypters, and a dressed area with dowel holes to receive a corner akroterion. A channel and a rib along the highest side allowed for the attachment of the next block of the raking geison-sima. The surviving area of the tympanum is small and shallow; also, the raking geison-sima is higher than the lateral geison-sima. In the corner of the tympanum is a dowel hole, set diagonally. An explanation for these atypical features has been advanced in Chapter II;[53] it has been suggested that a thin marble slab with carving was applied to this small area. The raking sima is unsculptured and its top lip is considerably stouter than that of the horizontal sima.

53. See below, pp. 262 ff.

Although damaged, the carved lateral sima of this block is of particular significance. Instead of the normal sequence of three scrolls, this tendril has two scrolls and its ribbed stem grows from the customary acanthus calyx toward the end of the block. Adjacent to this acanthus leaf is a roughly cut boss. It has been restored as a half palmette rather than a lion's head, in view of both its size and position so close to the corner[54] and the fact that normally such a half palmette emerges from the acanthus leaf (see Pl. XXVIII.1; fig. 51). This length of sima, with its individual scheme of carving, has provided valuable evidence concerning the form that the decoration took at other corners, particularly at the rear of the building. The carved lateral sima on this block is the only instance of the sima remaining attached to an extant geison-sima block. Nevertheless, this adaptation from the normal sequence of lions' heads and scrolls points to a difficulty in the arrangement for the whole length of the lateral geison-sima blocks, whether on the north and south of the building or on the inward-facing sides of the wings. It is evident that a regular sequence of lions' heads could not be coordinated here with the intercolumniation of the building.

Two further fragments come from the pediment. One (+102; Pl. XLV.2) is a piece of a raking sima broken at the back and on one side. On the preserved side there is anathyrosis. Its profile accords with the raking sima of the pedimental geison block. Another small fragment (+27; Pl. XLIII), represents the horizontal geison and crown-molding of the tympanum; the molding of the geison agrees with the details of the standard geison-sima blocks (++5; Pl. XXVII). Both these fragments would indicate a comparatively normal depth for the tympanum, but as remarked above, the pedimental block suggests the opposite.

ROOF CONSTRUCTION (Pls. XLIX, L)

The recesses for timber beams on the back edge of the geison-sima blocks imply a simple roof for both the main section and the wings consisting of tie beams, principal rafters, ridge pieces, short king posts and, doubtless, boarding. The pitch of the roof over the wings was 14° 30′ as dictated by the pediment, but over the main area the pitch was slightly less (12° 20′) because of the longer span and the necessity to preserve a constant ridge line. The hipped roof at the rear of the building and at the valleys next to the wings at the front would have required rafters on the diagonal. No cuttings in the geison-sima blocks have these features, perhaps suggesting that the feet of the diagonal rafters rested on the tie beams.

STROTER, KALYPTER, AND ANTEFIX (Pls. XXVI.1, 2, 3, XXXIII, XLVIII-LI; Figs. 12, 113, 114, 245)

It has been assumed that the few surviving marble stroters found on and around the site came from the Propylon, and that they were used in conjunction with marble kalypters and antefixes. All the stroters are fragmentary but those illustrated (Pl. XXVI.1, 2, 3) are

54. S,*I*, pl. XLIX (here fig. 11). The restoration, in perspective, shows a lion's head at this point.

ca. 0.03 m. deep with a raised lip along the edge giving a maximum height of 0.45 m. One fragment (50.540; Pl. XXVI.3) has the lip returning round two adjacent sides; one lip would have come under the fillet at the bottom edge of the stroter belonging to the row above, and the other would fit under the kalypter. The restored size of each standard stroter, over the main area, has been calculated as 0.50 m. wide and 0.420 m. from back to front, but those over the wings would have measured about 0.10 m. less in width. Special stroters would have been required for the hips and valleys. Close analogies for "bonnet" stroters necessary for hipped roofs are provided by those found at Olympia,[55] and other dish-shaped tiles from the same site indicate that the problems associated with the tiling of abnormal roofs were ingeniously overcome. At the hip, the kalypters would have continued to meet those on the adjacent side of the roof. There would have been no ridge kalypters on the hip, but instead bonnet tiles would have covered the junction over the hip rafter.

No complete kalypter remains,[56] but the form is indicated by the rear part of an antefix (49.347; Pl. XXXIII.2). The block has a roughly picked concave under surface which would have bridged the lips of the stroters. The gabled tops are slightly hollowed. No ridge kalypters have remained, but those belonging to the Nereid Monument provide a suitable pattern.[57]

The sculptured faces of the gracefully executed antefix now in Vienna (I, 423 A: figs. 113, 114) and its replacement (I, 423 B: Pl. XXXIII.1; fig. 245) are discussed fully in Chapters II and IV.[58] The better preserved example, 423 B, runs into a kalypter of similar section to kalypter 49.347. It has a roughly picked hollow underneath to fit over the lips at the sides of the geison-sima blocks. It is sufficient to say here that there is no base molding or plinth below the palmette, the volute rising directly from the scrolls on the sima.

No ridge antefix remains, but in the restoration drawings, a design that is a variation on the normal antefixes has been adopted, a solution found on other contemporary buildings.[59] Hence the ridge antefixes have been restored with flame palmettes as a foil to the drooping petals on the regular antefixes. At the junction of the ridges of the roof of the main part and a wing, coupled with the fact that the hipped roof and the valleys also met at this point, an antefix with a complicated base would have been required. As far as the antefix at this point is concerned, the restoration drawings (Pls. XLIX-LI, LX) have included one based on that from the Nereid Monument which had an antefix, square on plan, with palmettes on each face.[60]

55. Adler *et al.*, *op. cit.*, pl. LXXXXIX. I am grateful to Dr. Hugh Plommer for this reference.

56. The Austrians, however, reported that they had found marble kalypters north of the Hieron—i.e., adjacent to the Temenos (*S,I*, p. 10). Presumably, they belonged to the Propylon, since the Hieron had a tile roof.

57. Coupel-Demargne, pl. LXXXVII.

58. See below, pp. 133 ff., 298 f.

59. E.g., the Hieron and the Temple of Athena Aléa at Tegea: Vol. 3, text I, pp. 80 ff., 180 ff.; Dugas, pp. 24 ff., pls. XV-XVII, XLVI, XLVII.

60. Coupel-Demargne, pl. LXXXVII.

BEAMS (Pls. XXXIV, XXXV, XXXVI, XXXVII, XXXVIII, XLIV.2)

Although not preserved at their ends, the surviving marble beams give an indication of the distance of the façade of the building from the wall. Of the four which originally existed, three remain.[61] The largest (+60; Pl. XXXIV) now measures 2.550 m. long, and, in common with the other examples, it originally had on both sides two fasciae below an ovolo and fillet crowning molding above a higher fillet (Pl. XLIV.2); the soffit is enriched with a long channel framed by a cyma reversa molding. The total thickness at the soffit is ca. 0.430 m. A characteristic feature of these beams is the long sloping "spine," 0.275 m. thick, which tapers toward one end; at the highest point the spine reaches 0.540 m. above the molding. It may be assumed that this strengthening spine had the higher end over the wall, with the tapered end over the epistyle. The spine is not precisely triangular, flattening off at the top of the higher end. The second of these large beams (+72; Pl. XXXV), although not complete, shows clearly the termination of the soffit channel: the return is mutilated by rough-picking, and one may assume that these ends of the channel were obscured by the crowning molding of the architrave. The end of the channel on a beam of a smaller variety (+9; Pl. XXXVII) has been cut away in a similar way. The third large beam (+48; Pl. XXXVI) is very damaged but serves to illustrate the shallower end of beams in this category. The end has been damaged, but the sloping spine apparently did not end as an acute angle. A cutting in the top of the spine was probably made to accommodate the back of a geison-sima block, a difficulty usually solved by cutting triangular recesses in the geison-sima blocks. It is of interest to note that the distance between the bottom of this cutting and the top of the molding of the beam is almost exactly the same as the height of the dentil course, confirming the relationship between the beams and the entablature.

One other beam exists in a remarkably good state (+9; Pl. XXXVII). The fully preserved soffit channel demonstrates that the block is practically complete in length; it measures 1.860 m. long at present, considerably less than those in the category described above. It also has no spine, presumably because extra strength was not required over a shorter span. A beam of this length coincides with the span dictated by the regular column spacing. Hence it has been restored at the junction of a wing with the main body of the building, at right angles with one of the larger beams. A particularly interesting feature in this block is the mitred return of the molding; the molding at right angles would be on a block placed behind the frieze, but none of these backing blocks has survived. It will be observed, however, that the total height of beam +9, including the slightly raised area in the center, is the same as that of the frieze blocks. The circular cutting in the end of this beam has not been explained.

61. A fragment (+16), 0.680 m. long, also exists. It has a paneled soffit and a "spine" but it is not possible to say whether it is part of a fourth beam or was formerly attached to one of the surviving, short fragments.

In this second category of smaller beams is a rather damaged block which also illustrates the chamfered return of the moldings (+82; Pl. XXXVIII). A clamp hole shows that one return block was attached with a diagonally placed Π-clamp, but the other return block was attached by a standard clamp. This fragment is from the companion beam to +9, but it is not possible to say whether it came from the northern or southern wing. It is possible, however, that the beam did not extend much further into the wall beyond the Π-clamps; otherwise, there would be insufficient space for the frieze blocks on the outside of the wall.

COFFERS (Pls. XXXIX, XL, XLVI, XLVII B; Figs. 125-131, 142, 227)

Numerous fragments of coffers have been found but although incomplete in length, they have been largely preserved in height, thus illustrating a variety of moldings and other details. There are two basic categories of coffer fragments: one with a wide overhang, averaging 0.089 m., beneath the lid, and one with a smaller overhang having an average measurement of 0.050 m. (see Pl. XXXIX). However, all the pieces have moldings of the same profile with two fasciae, crowned by a cyma reversa between fillets; those with the greater overhang or corona have a wider and flatter cyma. The soffits of the blocks are cut with channels or panels, one side of which is cut vertically, while the other is chamfered. Although fragmentary, one piece (+44; Pl. XXXIX.1) has an overhang of the smaller variety with a width of 0.330 m., and near the center there is a hole drilled for securing a coffer lid. This block, therefore, indicates the existence of one variety with a coffer lid opening of about 0.330 m. Another block (+ 61; Pl. XXXIX.2) with an overhang of the larger variety is broken in such a way as to permit a calculation to be made of the original minimum size of the coffer lid; it proved to be 0.392 m. Those fragments of coffers without drilled holes give a less clear indication of the size of the lids with which they were associated. However, the survival of seven coffer lids of the same small size allows a scheme of coffering to be reconstructed. The lids have a visible soffit area of ca. 0.170 m. square; the drilled holes, on opposite sides, are 0.180 m. apart (e.g., *C(V)2*; Pl. XL.2). In one coffer lid, there are drilled holes on adjacent sides (*C(S)1*; Pl. XL.3). The lids are carved with various male and female heads set in rebated surrounds. The curved tops of the lids are roughly cut. The five best preserved of these lids are illustrated on Plate XL and fully discussed in Chapter III.[62] There are also two lesser fragments in this group.[63]

The evidence provided by these lids and the coffer fragments demonstrates that there were originally two sizes or lengths of coffering slabs and three sizes of coffers and coffer lids. By placing one of the existing coffer lids on a coffer with the larger overhang, it can be shown that one pair of such a unit fits precisely in the two outer bays of the porch of the Propylon proper, but not in the central bay. In the other dimension (east and west), three of these units fit between the wall and the façade. It is, therefore, suggested that the four bays flanking the central door were covered by four units of coffering, each unit

62. See below, pp. 148 ff.
63. *C(V)3 and C(S)2*; see below, pp. 153 f., 155 f.

containing six coffers. Likewise, coffer fragment +44, with a smaller-sized overhang, had a coffer lid of ca. 0.330 m. square, as demonstrated above. An arrangement of two pairs of these double units fits the square area of the projecting wings. Similarly, coffer +61, which has an overhang of the larger variety, is known, as shown above, to have been associated with large coffer lids; the lids would have measured at least 0.392 m. in one direction. The wide central bay of the building could receive two pairs of coffers of this category with large rectangular lids. The final arrangement, based on these arguments, is given on Plate XLVII B.

In spite of the lack of large pieces of coffering, the surviving fragments contain a variety of details which provide evidence of their location. The channels in the soffits are arranged in five different ways (Pl. XLVI): (a) with a complete channel placed almost centrally in the soffit; (b) with the channel cut toward one edge of the soffit; (c) with the channel at the back lower edge of the block so that one side of the channel is lacking; (d) with a chamfer at the back lower edge; (e) without any cutting at the back edge.[64] Types (a) and (b) are assumed to be from the channels which ran as a margin round a group of coffers; type (a) would have been at the ends of each unit so that part of the soffit could carry the load on the beams, but type (b), which has an insufficient area to carry such a load, would be along one side adjacent to the epistyle or the wall. Types (c) and (d) indicate a system of coffers placed back to back so that the channel is recessed in one block (c), but is provided with a "closing" side by the adjacent block (d) or (e). It will be seen, however, that the complete channels have one side vertical and the other chamfered, and it would appear that the vertical side went around the outside edge of the margin and that the chamfered side was toward the center. The channels which divided each coffer would, therefore, have been chamfered on both sides as implied by the combining of types (c) and (d).

DOORWAYS (Pls. XLI, XLII, XLVII A, XLVIII-LI)

Two elements of the doorways have remained: a large block that has been interpreted as an over-lintel (+64; Pl. XLI) and two fragmentary threshold blocks, each of which has a sinking for a door pan (+2, +13; Pl. XLII.1.2).

The over-lintel is practically complete except for its fragmentary front molding and is instrumental in the reconstruction of the doorways in general. The threshold blocks were associated with doorways of two different sizes, implying, for a propylon, the original presence of three doorways.[65] The over-lintel has a length of almost two meters and a front to back measurement of 0.719 m., a size appropriate for the lateral doors. The top surface has a hollowed out area along the length of the block indicating that it was built into the wall by at least 0.554 m. A molded overhanging cornice projects beyond this assumed wall face by 0.117 m., a difference accounted for by the lintel of the door. This molded cornice is incom-

64. The numbers of blocks in these categories, illustrated on Pl. XLVI, are: No. 1, +44; No. 2, +61 and one other fragment; No. 3, +58; No. 4, +56 and four other fragments; No. 5, +59 and three other fragments.

65. See below, Chap. II, n. 40, for parallels.

53. Restored longitudinal section of the South Propylaea at Labraunda.

plete but it is probably a bed-mold for a more pronounced, projecting element. On the top surface there are Π-clamp holes showing that a wall course ran through at this level. One Π-clamp placed at the back of the block is at a slight angle, presumably to harness the over-lintel to a large block for which a corner of the over-lintel had been removed. The other corner at the back has also been cut away but no Π-clamp hole is visible. In the center, there is a lewis hole, but no attachment for wall blocks, although a pry hole implies two blocks above. Underneath, there is an end dowel hole. The back surface is roughly cut and a block ca. 0.150 m. high would have been placed against it. The hollowed-out upper surface implies exposure to the weather and the block has been restored, therefore, to the precinct side. On the main Propylon side, the lintels having three fasciae crowned by a cornice composed of an ovolo and astragal below a sima-like molding enriched with floral forms are hypothetical. Our reconstruction is based on the simple, fascied door frames employed on the South Propylaea at Labraunda (fig. 53) and the Temple of Athena at Priene (fig. 54), and, in view of the ornamental character of the order, on the carved crown of the north door of the Erechtheum.[66] The pattern on the crown is based on the pattern of the raking sima of the Hieron (see below, fig. 239), in view of the relationship between such door crowns and sima profiles. All three doorways have been restored with the same details but those on the central doorway are at a proportionally larger scale.

The two remaining blocks from the thresholds are very worn (+2, +13; Pl. XLII.1.2), but both have similar circular sinkings for door pans. However, these sinkings are at different distances from the sides, implying that the two fragments came from different

66. For further discussion of these restored elements, see Chap. II, pp. 90 f.

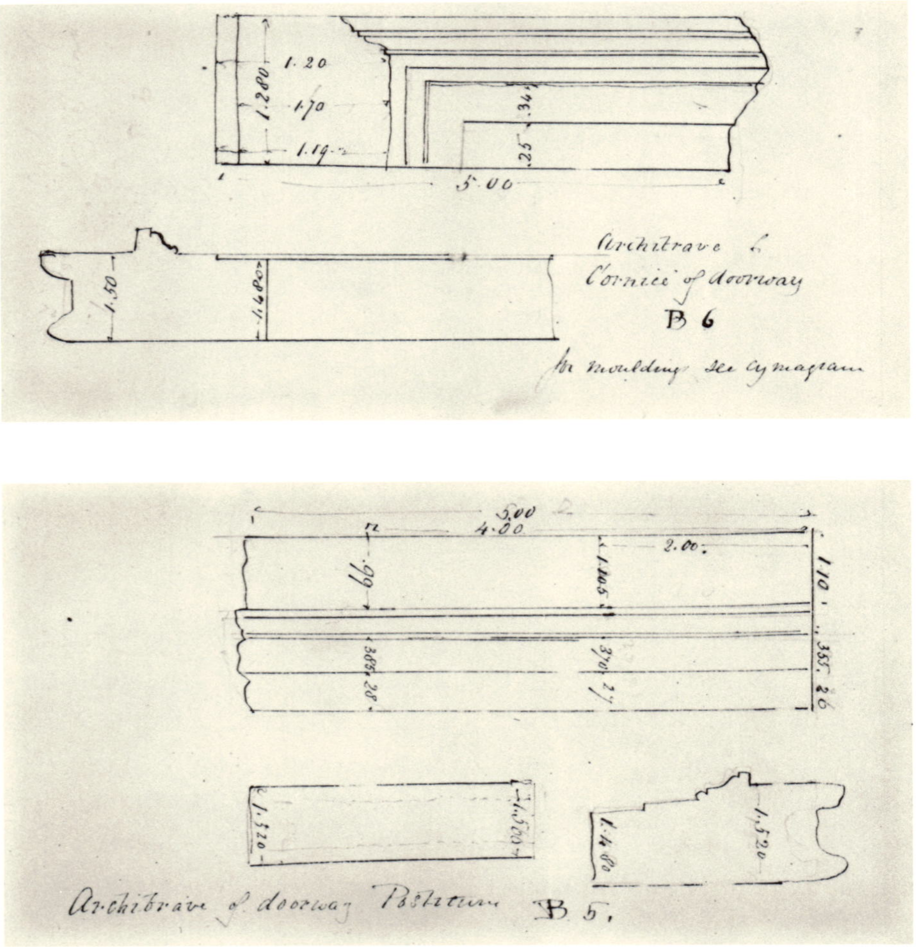

54. Drawings of the door frame of the Temple of Athena at Priene by R. P. Pullan.

thresholds. The position of the door pan in threshold fragment +2 suggests that it is part of a larger block which would have been required by the central doorway. As shown in the sections through these blocks, the top surfaces have been entirely destroyed, thus removing any sign of a ledge or door stop. On the analogy of a well-preserved lateral threshold of the Hieron,[67] such a ledge has been introduced, a decision supported by the discovery of a block with a ledge of similar character (+52; Pl. XLII.3). This piece is now fragmentary and has no structural features.

It has been assumed that the thresholds continued as a platform in the precinct in order to accommodate the doors when swung open. Below these thresholds in the precinct, one course of steps of the same height as the stereobate of the wall would allow the level of the Temenos to be reached (Pls. XLVII A, XLIX, LI).

67. Vol. 3, Pl. XXXII.

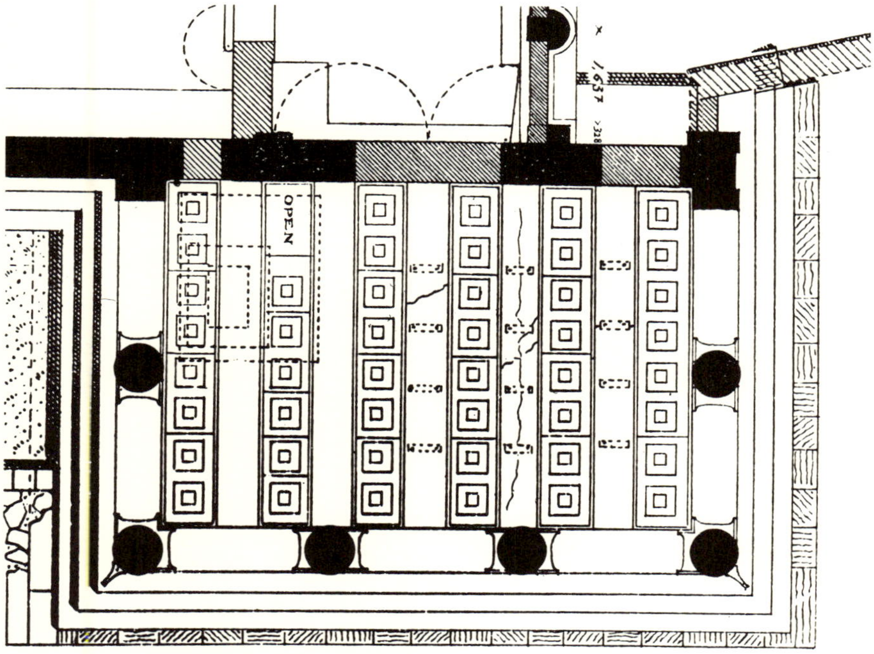

55. Plan of the north porch of the Erechtheum.

HYPOTHETICAL ELEMENTS OF THE RESTORATION (Pls. XLVII-LI)

In order to complete the restoration, certain architectural elements for which we have no evidence have been included, based, for the most part, on contemporary analogies.

Plan. No block of the antae walls has survived, but, since the ground plan of the Propylon is porchlike in character and it was necessary to allow convenient access to the adjacent terrace, we have assumed that these walls are midway between normal antae walls and strongly projecting pilasters or pierlike returns on the analogy of the plan of the north porch of the Erechtheum (fig. 55).[68]

Elevation. The courses of the antae walls have been assumed to coincide with each alternate wall course, thus allowing each anta wall to consist of four blocks of almost equal height. Only a small fragment of a stereobate block shows marks which could have related to the rectangular base of an anta. The molding of the base has been taken from that of the hypothetical column base, and the capital has been modeled on the anta capitals of the South Propylaea at Labraunda (see fig. 85 below).[69] The wooden doors have been restored on the basis of the doors of the Hieron for which ample comparative material was available.[70] The remaining restored elements, that is, the base of the column, the backers for the frieze, the door frames, and the ridge antefix have already been reported in the previous discussion of these parts of the building.

68. Paton-Stevens, detail of pl. I.

69. *Labraunda,* pls. IV, VII, 7, 8. For a more detailed description of this restored capital, see Chap. II, n. 91.

70. Vol. 3, text I, pp. 56, 189 ff., and below, Chap. II, n. 46.

The hypothetical sculptures attributed to the Propylon—the theme and style of the central portion of the frieze, the pedimental reliefs and akroteria—are discussed in Chapter III.[71]

TECHNICAL FEATURES

The marble blocks of the Propylon were secured by Π-clamps and dowels were employed throughout. In two instances only has any of the metal remained (orthostate blocks +90, +94). The size of the Π-clamps implies that the total length of the clamp was ca. 0.200 m., the metal measuring 0.020 m. square. The diagonally placed Π-clamps which linked architrave blocks at right angles should be noted. Beams in a comparable position were also harnessed with diagonal clamps (Pl. XXXVIII). A similar diagonal Π-clamp secured the over-lintel to a wall block in a course further back in the wall, perhaps because of the abnormal arrangements of blocks around the lintels.

Dowel holes indicate dowels of about 0.055 m. by 0.020 m. and 0.060 m. in length, although there are many variations including those of square section (e.g., wall block +45; Pl. XII.2). They are placed longitudinally in the block, and nearby are, normally, the telltale pry holes which indicate clearly the direction in which the blocks were levered into position. In addition, lewis holes (ca. 0.110 m. by 0.020 m. at the top) with one sloping side are found in most of the blocks, including one at a very low level in the building (inner corner step block +24; Pl. VIII), but this appears exceptional. The normal arrangement was to have two Π-clamps and two dowels, but again, there are many blocks where only one such attachment was used. In such tall, comparatively thin, blocks as the orthostates a single dowel was employed at the top and another at the bottom; the width of the block allowed for only one Π-clamp at each end. Curiously, the orthostate blocks were not provided with clamp holes at the back, but perhaps a binding course, doweled firmly to the orthostate blocks served the same purpose. The surviving wall blocks indicate that dowels rather than Π-clamps were favored.

One further characteristic should be mentioned, relating to the method of harnessing the geison-sima blocks to the dentil course. The dowel used for this purpose is set at a pronounced angle; each block has one such dowel only, placed at one side. This may have been a particularly firm method of doweling the blocks together; the slightly tapering sides of these blocks may be deliberate and for the same reason.

Very few blocks have dowel holes with lead-pouring channels. The column shaft, the drum, and the capital have round dowel holes of 0.022 m. in diameter in contrast with the normal squarish dowels. The top surface of the architrave block +12 (Pl. XVIII) illustrates typical structural features found in the building.

The ends of most of the marble blocks have anathyrosis, and setting lines on the tops and bottoms define fair-faced surfaces against which adjacent blocks could fit closely.

D. S.

71. Below, pp. 232 f., 262 ff.

II. Structure and Style of the Temenos and the Propylon

THOSE who entered the Ionic Propylon to the Temenos[1] passed through a building tightly interrelated with the enclosing wall of an open, rectangular precinct (Pl. LIX). From it, one stepped into the marble-paved enclosure.[2] Before it, there lay an eschara and a bothros, ritual installations that had also been present in the earlier precinct that appears to have preceded the Temenos.[3] But the Propylon itself, and the broad marble-paved terrace that looked northwest to the sea, to which it also gave access, were the new elements in this ensemble.

1. The term Temenos is used here in the sense of "a piece of land marked off from common uses and dedicated to a god, a precinct" (see *s.v.* τέμενος, Henry George Liddell and Robert Scott, *A Greek-English Lexicon*, rev. edn., Oxford, 1968).

The so-called Temenos dedicated to Demeter, Persephone, and other underworld divinities at Knidos, a rectangular, unroofed, enclosed precinct containing important sculptures, offers a contemporary analogy to the Samothracian enclosure (C. T. Newton, *A History of Discoveries at Halicarnassus, Cnidus, and Branchidae*, London, 1862, Chap. XV, pl. LIII).

The term τέμενος was used by Pausanias 6.25.1 to describe the precinct of Aphrodite Pandemos in Elis in precisely the fashion in which it applies to the Samothracian precinct. It was "a temenos surrounded by a wall," περιέχεται . . . τὸ τέμενος θριγκῷ. It contained a bronze statue by Skopas—a point that will prove of interest in the course of this volume (see below, pp. 283 f.)—of Aphrodite mounted on a goat. The fact that Pausanias uses similar words to describe the Hippodameion at Olympia, 6.20.7, χωρίον περιεχόμενον θριγκῷ, implies that this precinct in the Altis could have been called a temenos, again an analogy to the Temenos in the Samothracian Sanctuary. The term τέμενος occurs in the *Anthologia Palatina* 9.189 and Schol. AD to *Iliad* I, 129, to characterize the precinct of Hera at Lesbos, a precinct in which women dance in honor of the goddess as they appear to have done in the Samothracian Temenos (see below, pp. 230 f., 288 f.).

For a non-literary reference, see the Temenos of Zeus at Neandria, where at least six inscriptions carved on the rock surrounding a sacred area repeat the formula ΤΕΜΕΝΟΣ ΔΙΟΣ (*Neandria*, pp. 13 f.)

2. Hauser's plan, *S,II*, pl. 2, shows beneath the marble floor of the precinct an underpavement of narrow rails of "soft" stone of the variety encountered, too, in the Hieron (*ibid.*, p. 21), presumably, therefore, of porous limestone or tufa. No trace of these blocks was recovered in our excavation. They appear to be related to the underpavement west of the *Edifice* or *Monument à abside* and south of the Kératôn in Delos. If this pavement and underpavement belong to the period of the later building—a point that I have been unable to ascertain—they would be contemporary with the lost pavement and underpavement of the Temenos. See René Vallois, *Les Constructions antiques de Délos. Documents* (Bibliothèque des Ecoles françaises d'Athènes et de Rome, fasc. 157 bis), Paris, 1953, pl. III, and Philippe Bruneau and Jean Ducat, *Guide de Délos*, Paris, 1965, pp. 96 ff., plan I.

3. For discussion of these earlier installations, see Chap. IV, p. 271 f.

Like the early Hellenistic Hieron, the Temenos was provided at its southern end with a platform,[4] in this case, one step higher than the floor of the remainder of the precinct. On the interior, the walls of the precinct were built of stuccoed porous limestone blocks above a marble dado composed of a course of orthostates topped by a stringcourse, a form of construction employed for the precinct wall of the Pompeion at Athens built ca. 400 B.C.[5] The walls of the Temenos stood on a stereobate treated like the double-recessed stereobate of the Propylon which it abutted (Pls. LII.2, LX). Identical in height, the two stereobates were differentiated from each other by the use of a single recess beneath the orthostates of the enclosure. On the exterior, the precinct walls were built of stuccoed porous limestone blocks except for the marble stringcourse, but, inasmuch as the latter was not dressed to be visible, the entire wall appeared to be of stuccoed limestone.

Asymmetrically located behind the central and northern doors of the Propylon and let into the floor of the precinct were an eschara, or hearth, probably for sacrifices to Aëtion, the hero-founder of the Samothracian mysteries,[6] and, to the north, a bothros or pit for liquid libations to the gods (Pls. LVI-LVIII, LIX). Such ritual installations occur almost exclusively in the archaic and pre-archaic times[7] and their presence in this late classical precinct reflects, as we have seen, their similar presence in its forebear. Here, as elsewhere in this traditional Sanctuary, the retention of such installations and even of their specific location is evidence of a characteristic religious conservatism.[8]

4. See Vol. 3, Pls. CIV-CV. There, too, one stepped down into the cella from the threshold of the door.

5. Hoepfner, pp. 43 ff. For the date, between 404 and 392 B.C., pp. 112 f.

6. See Vol. 3, text II, p. 30 and nn. 133-139 for this explanation.

7. *Ibid.*, text I, p. 158, n. 9, for examples of archaic escharai. For examples of other pre-archaic and archaic escharai found not in buildings but, like the eschara in the Temenos, out-of-doors, either adjacent to a temple or in a precinct, see the naos at Tinos (N. Kondoleon, "Ἀνασκαφὴ ἐν Τήνῳ," *Praktika*, 1952, pp. 259 ff.); the Temple of Apollo at Neandria (*Neandria* pp. 28 f., fig. 58); one in the Agora of Thasos (F. Salviat, "Chronique des fouilles en 1955," *BCH*, 80 [1956], pp. 418 ff., figs. 25 a, b; *Guide de Thasos*, Paris, 1968, p. 39); in the Sanctuary of Hera on Mt. Cynthus in Delos (André Plassart, *Les Sanctuaires et les cultes du Mont Cynthe* [*Délos*, XI], Paris, 1928, p. 210, figs. 154, 172); outside the Peribolos of the Twelve Gods in the Agora of Athens (Homer A. Thompson and R. E. Wycherley, *The Agora of Athens* [*The Athenian Agora*, XIV], Princeton, 1972, p. 132, pl. 4); and the later examples in the Sanctuary of Demeter and Kore at Iasos (Doro Levi, "Gli scavi di Iasos," *Annuario*, n. 5., 29-30 [1967-68], pp. 569 ff.), and at Nisos on Corfu (Heinrich Bulle, "Ausgrabungen bei Aphiona auf Korfu," *AthMitt*, 59 [1934], pp. 202 f. and Beilage XV, 6, 7).

For early Hellenistic out-of-door bothroi, see the examples behind the Kabeirion at Thebes (Gerda Bruns, *Das Kabirenheiligtum bei Theben*, Berlin, 1940, p. 15, fig. 4); in the precinct of Demeter at Priene (Theodor Wiegand and Hans Schrader, *Priene*, Berlin, 1904, pp. 148 ff., figs. 119, 123; Schede, pp. 90 ff., figs. 103, 107, 110), and in the forecourt of the precinct of Demeter at Pergamon (Wilhelm Dörpfeld and H. Hepding, "Die Arbeiten zu Pergamon 1908-1909," *AthMitt*, 35 [1910], pp. 356, 441).

For a general discussion on escharai and bothroi, see Fernand Robert, *Thymélè* (Bibliothèque des Ecoles françaises d'Athènes et de Rome, fasc. 147), Paris, 1939, pp. 43, 143, 151, 161 ff., 312, 340, 363, 415, 417, 424.

8. For the bothroi in the southern section of the Double Precinct beneath the Arsinoeion and the southeastern corner of the Anaktoron, see *Hesperia*, 19 (1950), pp. 11 f., pl. 9; *Guide*, *Guide*^{2}, *Guide*^{3}, pp. 54 f., *Guide*^{4}, p. 59, for the former and, for the latter, *AJA*, 44 (1940), p. 334 and fig. 11; *Guide*, *Guide*^{2}, pp. 47 f., *Guide*^{4}, p. 51. Our current rein-

Within the precinct, convenient access to the triangular area before the *epopteion*, leading also to the Hall of Votive Gifts and the archaic rock altar that preceded the Altar Court of Arrhidaios was provided by a door in the long western wall of the Temenos (fig. 1). At least one jamb of this door was later inscribed with a list of initiates (Pl. LV.1),[9] as had occurred previously in the Stoa, a building that also was not restricted to initiates.[10]

The most important new feature in this ensemble was the Propylon. An elegant entrance to a venerable area, it alluded, via its rich sculptural decoration, to the antiquity of the rites performed within the precinct and their life-giving nature.[11] In all probability, it reflects, too, the desire of the donor to make a conspicuous gift to the Sanctuary.[12]

The eccentric position of the Propylon, its off-center location before the northeastern section of the Temenos, was obviously dictated by its relationship to the processional road that led from the city across the eastern river and the eastern hill of the Sanctuary into its very heart (fig. 1). Presumably, this road was always located where it now is, coming at least to the western edge of the hill, from which it must have turned sharply to the southeast, and either wound down into the lower, archaic and classical levels of the Sanctuary or led to a stairway giving access to that lower level. From the early third century B.C. on, the road descended the eastern hill to a point opposite the terrace and level with it and the Propylon, thereby giving direct access both to the Propylon and the Rotonda of Arsinoe, buildings especially associated with the annual festivals.[13]

Such an eccentric position is by no means unusual for a propylon. It is characteristic of a number of entrance buildings leading into sanctuaries, markets, or precincts,[14] a par-

---

vestigation of both the Double Precinct and the Anaktoron indicates that these structures are later than we once believed. But the bothros in the Double Precinct, in any case, is earlier than the fourth-century eschara and bothros in the Temenos.

9. Vol. 2, p. 92, **45**. This fragmentary inscribed block which is clearly part of a door jamb, as mentioned in Chap. I, p. 47, is too large for the Propylon doors. It was found among blocks belonging to the Propylon. We consider it evidence of a door in the Temenos and have placed it arbitrarily in the long western wall both to provide a necessary exit from the precinct to those nearby buildings and, within the precinct, between the ritual installations and the rear platform. The inscription itself, judged by Fraser to be "Imperial," was added to the jamb long after the door was built. It is impossible to tell whether the badly damaged fragment, *ibid.*, **57**, belonged to this block.

10. See James R. McCredie, "Samothrace: Preliminary Report on the Campaigns of 1962-64," *Hesperia*, 34 (1965), pp. 108 f.; *Guide*[3], p. 75, *Guide*[4], p. 83.

11. Cf. Chap. III, pp. 265 f. and n. 270.

12. Cf. Chap. IV, pp. 273 f.

13. Cf. Chap. IV, p. 296. It is interesting to note that, although they naturally used the old terminology, both Rubensohn, p. 189 and note, and Arnold Schober, "Der neue Tempel von Samothrake," *ÖJh*, 29 (1935), p. 3, have pointed out that the Propylon of Ptolemy II and the processional road led directly to the "Old Temple" and the Rotunda.

14. For example, at Aegina (Gabriel Welter, *Aigina*, Berlin, 1938, p. 65, fig. 56; C. A. Doxiadis, *Architectural Space in Ancient Greece*, Cambridge, 1972, figs. 18-20); Sounion (William B. Dinsmoor, Jr., *Sounion*, Athens, 1971, p. 9; Doxiadis, *op. cit.*, figs. 52, 53); the later Olympieion at Athens (Ida Thallon Hill, *The Ancient City of Athens*, Cambridge, 1953, pp. 211 f., and Travlos, pp. 402 ff., fig. 524); the west gate of the Agora at Ephesos (*Forschungen in Ephesos* III, Vienna, 1923, p. 5, fig. 4, pl. I, and, particularly, Hans Hörmann, "Das Westtor der Agora in Ephesos," *ÖJh*, 25 [1929], pp. 22 ff.); and the Roman gate to the South Market at Miletos (Hubert Knackfuss, *Der Südmarkt und die benachbarten Bauanlagen* [*Milet*, I, 7], Berlin,

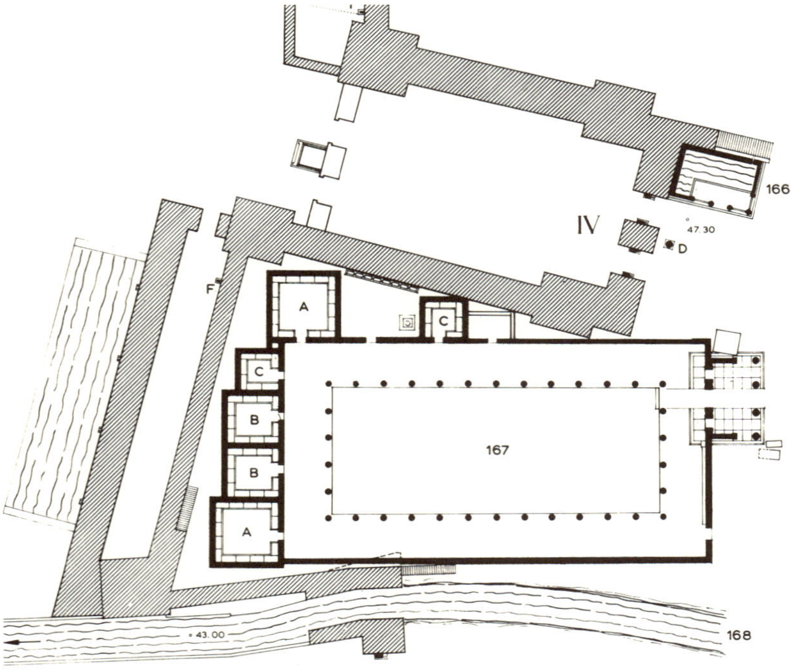

56. Plan of the Pompeion.

ticularly relevant example being the Ionic propylon to the Pompeian in Athens (fig. 56),[15] built ca. 400 B.C., whence festal processions set forth to the Panathenaic Way that led across the Agora to the Akropolis. In each case, the specific position was determined by the avenue of approach.

Unlike the wide doorway of the great later Propylon of Ptolemy II leading from the city to the Sanctuary,[16] the doors of this small propylon were triple in number, the central one being taller and wider than the lateral pair. Again, the three doors of the propylon to the Pompeion, the five doors of the Mnesiklean Propylaea, the triple doors of the South Propylaea at Labraunda (fig. 57), a dedication of Idrieus, who reigned from 351 to 344 B.C., not to mention the great later gateways at Lindos, Ephesos, and Miletos, offer analogies to this scheme.[17]

Therefore, in location and in this feature of its plan, the Propylon was not unorthodox.

1924, fig. 1; Gerhard Kleiner, *Die Ruinen von Milet*, Berlin, 1968, pp. 64 ff., general plan). Although the propylon of the Temple of Athena at Priene falls in this same category, it was not built until the Augustan period. Nevertheless, location of the propylon was determined by the street that had always led to this fourth-century temple (Schede, pp. 26, 39, fig. 27).

15. Hoepfner, p. 36, pls. 15, 30; Travlos, pp. 477 ff., figs. 602-605.

16. *Samothrace*, Vol. 10, *The Propylon of Ptolemy II* by Alfred K. Frazer, forthcoming. *Guide*[4], fig. 40.

17. For the Pompeion (Hoepfner, pp. 47 f., 55 f., pls. 15, 24, 25, 28, 30); the Mnesiklean Propylaea (Travlos, pp. 482 ff., figs. 612-614); Labraunda, (*Labraunda*, pls. XXI, XXII A); Lindos (Ejnar Dygge, *Lindos, Fouilles de l'Acropole*, 1902-1914 et 1952, III, 1, *Le Sanctuaire d'Athana Lindia et l'architecture lindienne*, Berlin, 1960, pp. 155 ff., pls. V, K, L, M); Ephesos (*op cit.*, fig. 4, pl. I); Miletos (Knackfuss, *op. cit.*, fig. 65).

57. Restored façade of the South Propylaea at Labraunda.

But in building type, there is no exact analogy to this Propylon among either earlier or contemporary propylaea. It is neither a conventional entrance building to a sanctuary, as at Aegina, nor to an area within a sanctuary, as at Labraunda. It is not a normal propylon, that is, a door preceded and followed by a porch with a continuous façade, whether in antis or prostyle, like the later Propylon of Ptolemy II. On the contrary, the most unusual feature of its plan is that it is essentially a porch with projecting wings, the rear wall of the entire building being one with a portion of the precinct wall (Pls. XLVII A, LIX).[18]

One of the sources of this ground plan was the Π-shaped building with projecting wings and a columnar façade. Although different in function, the Stoa of Zeus in the Athenian Agora illustrates this type.[19] A two-aisled building lacking doors in its original state, it has been suggested that this structure reflects the influence of the Mnesiklean Propylaea on stoa design and that it dates, therefore, in the last third of the fifth century B.C.[20] An influential building type, it was followed, at a number of other places, for buildings of

18. In this respect, again, it was akin to the propylon of the Pompeion. There, too, the inner steps were located within the colonnade (Hoepfner, p. 23, pls. 15, 24, 25, 27, 30).

19. Homer A. Thompson, "Buildings on the West Side of the Agora," *Hesperia*, 6 (1937), pp. 5 ff.; Roland Martin, "Le Stoa basileios, portiques à ailes et lieux d'assemblée," *BCH*, 66-67 (1942-43), pp. 274 ff.; R. E. Wycherley, "The North-West Stoa of the Athenian Agora," *JHS*, 68 (1948), pp. 152 ff.; Thompson and Wycherley, *The Agora of Athens*, pp. 96 ff. With the discovery of the actual Royal Stoa in the Agora, it is no longer necessary to argue whether that name should be applied to the Stoa of Zeus. See T. Leslie Shear, Jr., "The Athenian Agora: Excavations of 1970," *Hesperia*, 40 (1971), pp. 243 ff.; Thompson and Wycherley, *op. cit.*, pp. 83 ff.

20. Thompson, *op. cit.*, p. 53.

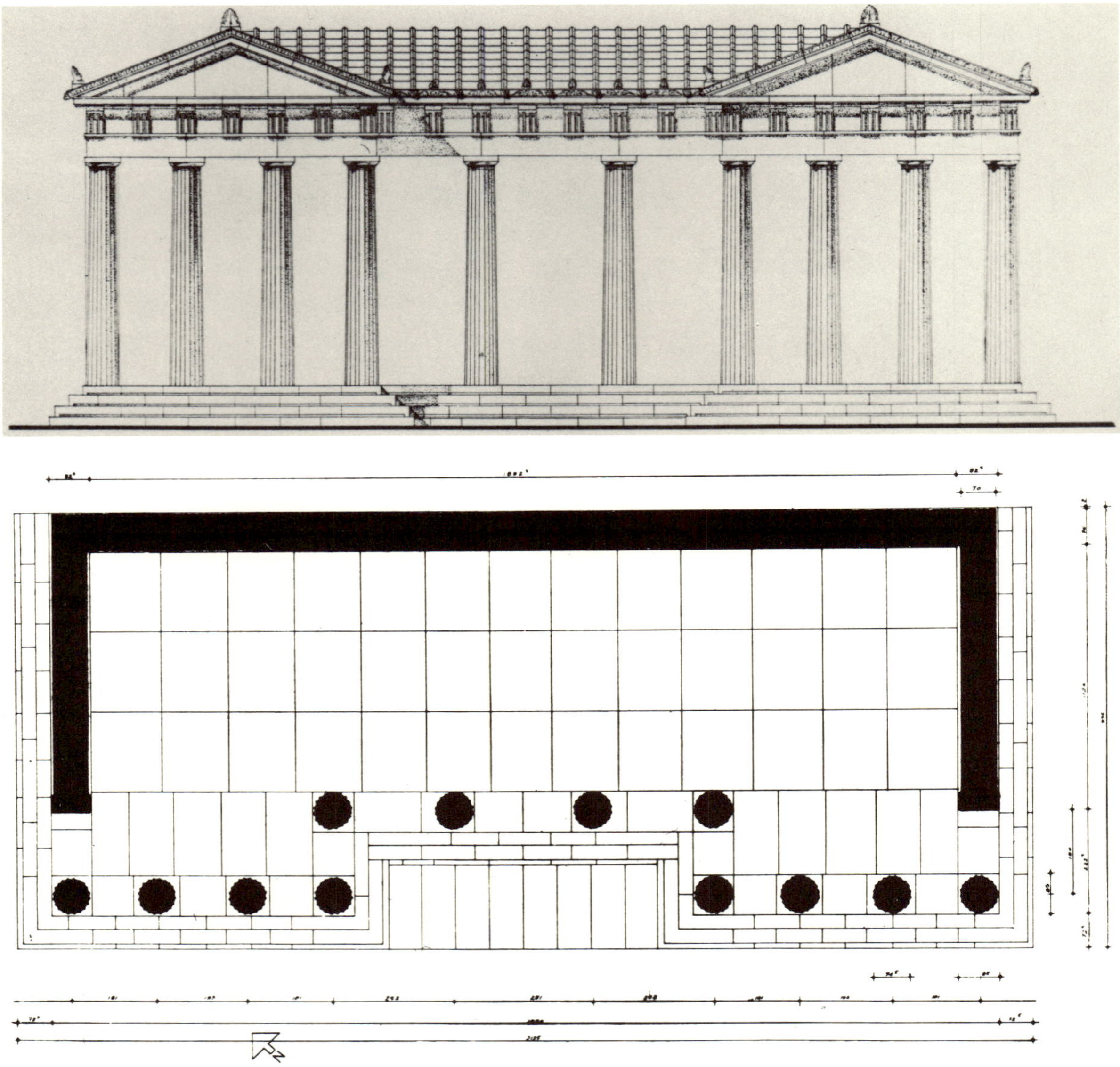

58. Restored façade and plan of the *Edifice à paraskénia* at Thasos.

varied or enigmatic purpose,[21] among them, the *Edifice à paraskénia* at Thasos dating from the second half of the fourth century B.C. (fig. 58).[22]

Very likely, the suggestion that this group of buildings ultimately reflects the influence of the Mnesiklean Propylaea is correct.[23] In any case, the use of wings for a propylon and the creation thereby of a shallow forecourt framed by columns and steps in this conspicuous building was surely another ingredient in the application of the Π-shaped plan to a propylon.

Insofar as the ground plan of the Propylon is porchlike in character and its antae walls

21. For convenience, see the list in Martin, *op. cit.*, pp. 288 ff.

22. Martin, "L'édifice à paraskénia," pp. 59 ff., pls. J, K; *Guide de Thasos*, ed. François Salviat, Paris, 1968, pp. 25 ff., figs. 8, 9.

23. Noted, too, by Claudio Tiberi, *Mnesicle l'architetto dei Propilei*, Rome, 1964, p. 176.

reduced to rudimentary members that are midway between normal antae walls and strongly projecting pilasters or pierlike returns, the plan of the north porch of the Erechtheum (see above, fig. 55), another exceptional and inventive building on the Akropolis, may have influenced the architect of the Propylon in designing his plan, as it clearly did in the still more significant matter of his columnar order.[24] These abbreviated antae walls made access to the terrace easy and convenient, and created a lightness and openness of architectural form in character with the grace and elegance of this Ionic building (cf. Pls. XLVIII-LI).

Far closer to the Propylon in both plan and elevation than any extant building or ruin is the representation of a theater building on a fragmentary Gnathian kalyx-krater from Tarento in Würzburg (cf. Pls. XLVII A, XLVIII and figs. 59, 60).[25] Dating from the mid-fourth century B.C., it shows an Ionic structure with projecting wings, again, a porch attached to a wall pierced by doors. Connoisseurs of the ancient theater have long assumed that this sherd reflects the appearance of the contemporary wooden stage building.[26] In Athens, too, the drama was performed before just such a structure, whether the permanent stone stage building completed in the time of Lykourgos, ca. 340-330,[27] or its wooden forebear. For both were evidently provided with precisely such shallow projecting wings or *paraskenia*.

24. Paton-Stevens, pl. II, begun in 421 B.C. For discussion of the order, see pp. 107, 112. It is worth noting that the porch of the Serapeion in Miletos preserves a very similar solution to this problem (*Milet, loc. cit.*, p. 203).

25. In the Martin von Wagner-Museum of the University. See Heinrich Bulle, "Eine Skenographie," *94. Berliner Winckelmannsprogramm*, Berlin, 1934, pp. 3 ff. (Fig. 5 and pl. II show a restoration of the building in which the inner columns are engaged. But neither the wall, the antae nor the pilasters are shown. I do not see why the inner columns may not have been free-standing, before the door wall, like the columns of the Propylon.) For more recent discussions of this frequently published fragment, see Maurizio Borda, *Ceramiche apule*, Bergamo, 1966, pp. 55, 110, pl. XIX; Lidia Forti, *La ceramica di Gnathia* (Monumenti antichi della Magna Grecia, II), Naples, 1965, pp. 15, 98, pl. XIII, C; and A. D. Trendall and T.B.L. Webster, *Illustrations of Greek Drama*, London, 1971, p. 101. Once published as Apulian, it has now been attributed to the workshop of the Konnakis Painter.

The general relationship between the ground plans of the Propylon and of both the Mnesiklean Propylaea and the *paraskenia* of the theater was observed by Karl Lehmann in *Hesperia*, 21 (1952), p. 28.

26. For example, A. W. Pickard-Cambridge, *The Theatre of Dionysus in Athens*, Oxford, 1946, pp. 170 f., figs. 55, 56; Margarete Bieber, *The History of the Greek and Roman Theater*, 2nd edn., Princeton, 1961, p. 68, fig. 266. Recently, however, Erika Simon and Brinna Otto, "Eine neue Rekonstruktion der Würzburger Skenographie," *JdI*, 88 (1973), pp. 121 ff., have denied this assumption and interpret the sherd not as a representation of a building but as *skenographia*, as scene painting applied to the wall of the stage building. I find this unorthodox interpretation and the arguments on which it is predicated wholly unpersuasive. On p. 122, n. 1, the authors indicate that Professor Trendall, who had previously published this fragment as a bell krater by the Konnakis Painter (above, n. 25), had later agreed with Bulle that it was a sherd from a calyx krater and to be attributed to the workshop of the Konnakis Painter not to the painter himself. The varying interpretations by Bulle, Webster, and Simon-Otto of the actual play performed on this sherd are of no concern in the context of the present discussion.

27. For brief statements on the Lykourgan theater, see Dinsmoor, pp. 208 ff.; Bieber, *op. cit.*, pp. 60 ff.; Berve-Gruben-Hirmer, pp. 120 ff. See, too, the sound comments of Wycherley, *op. cit.*, pp. 153 ff., regarding the genesis of the stage building with *paraskenia* in criticism of Carlo Anti, *Teatri greci arcaici*, Padua, 1947, pp. 277 ff.

59. Fragmentary Gnathian kalyx-krater from Tarento. Würzburg, Martin von Wagner-Museum of the University.

60. Reconstruction of stage building on figure 59 by Heinrich Bulle.

Faced with the problem of providing a propylon to an old ritual area within which liturgical actions and choral dancing were evidently performed,[28] our architect appears to have been particularly influenced by the contemporary stage building, in this case, using it to give access to a precinct within which liturgical dances were presumably performed rather than as a theatrical backdrop for choral dancing and the drama—a novel solution for this particular propylon through which one entered an enclosed festal area.[29]

A creative architect familiar with fourth-century Athens, as we shall see, with the use of the Π-shaped plan for both the temporary stage building of the Theater of Dionysos and the Stoa of Zeus, with the great entrance to the Akropolis, and the Erechtheum, with the Pompeian and the functional location of its propylon in relation to the processional way could well have drawn on his knowledge of these prime Athenian monuments when commissioned to design a new building, a propylon without previous precedent, for the Samothracian Sanctuary.

This is the most plausible explanation of the various features of the plan of the Propylon, all of which emanate from Athenian architecture of the late fifth and early fourth centuries B.C. It is a type at once novel and appropriate for a propylon, a type rich in architectural overtones and the creative use of visual sources—which, as will become evident, is characteristic of the architect of the Propylon.[30]

It will be recalled that the greater part of the foundations of the Propylon and of the northeastern and southeastern precinct walls were largely destroyed by the stream that swept through this quarter of the Sanctuary in post-antique times.[31] Only a portion of the subfoundation of the door wall and a fragment of the sub-foundation of the north wall of the northern wing exists (Pls. I, II.3). For the most part, these limestone blocks are laid as binders; but one fragmentary stretcher appears at the southern end of the foundation of the door wall, and the short portion of the foundation for the wing was also laid with stretchers. The bedrock has been cut down to receive these foundations. Too little of the foundation is preserved to make it useful to compare it with other foundations in Samothrace or elsewhere.

Built of Thasian marble, the Propylon is the first of the buildings erected in the Sanc-

28. For comment on this point, see Chap. IV, p. 288.

29. It it worth quoting Martin's remark in *BCH*, 66-67 (1942-43), p. 294, in a discussion on the interrelationship between agoras and theaters, Π-shaped stoas and the stage building with projecting wings, that "le plan en Π, qui répond au besoin naturel de concentrer l'attention d'une assemblée, a des origines lointaines; il reçut de multiples applications, scènes et théâtres, portiques d'agoras, salles d'assemblée, répondant toujours aux mêmes préoccupations"; and in *L'Agora*, p. 87; "Il est notable en effet, que tous les édifices de même plan se trouvent en bordure de places d'assemblées politiques ou religieuses."

30. It is interesting to note that the late second-century B.C. west gate to he Agora in Ephesos appears to be a descendant of our Propylon in plan, in the fact that it, too, is embedded in the enframing stoa (the counterpart to the precinct), in its Ionic order, and in its off-center location (*loc. cit.*). Apart from its different order, the Antonine gate to the South Market at Miletos also follows this tradition, in addition to having a coffered ceiling (*loc. cit.*).

31. See above, Introduction, p. 27, and Chap. I, p. 41.

tuary to have been constructed of marble, hence it is the ancestor of a series of splendid Hellenistic buildings, for the most part, built of that same Thasian marble.

The crepidoma of the Propylon consists of three steps resting on a euthynteria only the upper portion of which is dressed to be visible (Pls. IV-X, XLVIII-LI). The upper two steps are provided with two recesses, the lowest with one, and the stereobate on the interior of the door wall with two in conformity with the stylobate (Pls. V-X).[32] They are identical in system of recesses with the steps of the Temple of Zeus at Stratos, dated ca. 330 B.C.[33] and the Temple of Hemithea at Kastabos, dated at about the same time,[34] and, in their lowness, close to the steps of the early fourth-century Temple of Asklepios at Epidauros and the Amphiaraion at Oropos.[35] Low steps are a feature of fourth-century architecture. They are not restricted to mainland Greece but also occur in Asia Minor, for example, on the South Propylaea at Labraunda.[36] But the steps of that building are typical of the region in lacking the recesses commonly found in the Peloponnesos and, to a lesser extent, in northwest Greece and Attica. Finally, in profile, the steps of the Propylon are related to the stereobate of the slightly later Hieron.[37]

Above the orthostates, the wall of the Propylon is isodomic (Pls. XI, XII, XLVIII-LI, LX). It lacks base molding, stringcourse, and epikranitis. There appears to be no exact parallel for this system.[38] But it is a simple classical scheme, a foil and backdrop to the ornamental richness of the order and the entablature in contrast with the drafted-margin masonry inaugurated in Samothrace by the architect of the Doric Hieron, ca. 325 B.C., and used, too, early in the third century B.C., for the Ionic Propylon of Ptolemy II.

It will be recalled that although neither the jambs nor the lintels of the Propylon's doors are preserved, there is evidence that they were three in number, the central one being the higher, and that they were grouped together in the door wall.[39] A practical scheme for a small propylon, lack of space precluded the use of the normal Ionic door with a cornice resting on brackets. In this respect, it was analogous to the triple doors of the propylon of the Pompeion at Athens and of the South Propylaea at Labraunda,[40] and our

32. Stylobate: 0.254 m. high, with two recesses. Second step: 0.237 m. high, with two recesses. Lowest step: ca. 0.238 m. high, with one recess. Stereobate: 0.277 m. high, with two recesses.

33. Courby-Picard, pl. VII, pp. 85 ff.

34. Cook-Plommer, pp. 79 f., fig. 14, and pl. XIII, 2. The south side of the crepidoma is *in situ*, as pl. XIII, 2 indicates. It is curious, therefore, that the second step is slightly higher than the stylobate, judging by fig. 14. On the whole, the authors prefer a date ca. 335 B.C. (p. 168).

35. For these and other figures, see W. Zschietzschmann in *Schleif-Zschietzschmann*, I, pp. 26 ff.

36. *Labraunda*, p. 30.

37. Cf. Pls. VI-VIII and Vol. 3, Pl. XCV.3, 4.

38. E.g., the walls of the Erechtheum and Temple of Athena Nike on the Akropolis, the Hephaisteion, the Tholoi at Delphi and Epidauros, the Temple at Tegea, the naiskos at Didyma, and, in Samothrace, the Propylon of Ptolemy II are isodomic, but the latter has drafted-margin masonry and the others either have a base molding, a stringcourse, or an epikranitis. The South Propylaea at Labraunda is reported to have an orthostate course, but the few other wall blocks are almost as high as the so-called orthostate course and, therefore, produce a different effect from the wall of the Propylon. See *Labraunda*, pp. 10 f., pl. XVI.

39. See Chap. I, pp. 76 ff.

40. Hoepfner, p. 23, figs. 6, 17; *Labraunda*, pls. XIX, XXI (above, figs. 56, 57).

reconstruction is based both on the simple, fascied door frames crowned by molded cornices employed there and at the Temple of Athena at Priene (cf. figs. 53, 54),[41] which also lacked the customary Ionic door known from the Lycian tombs[42] and the Temple of Artemis at Sardis.[43] In view of the ornamental character of the order, we have followed the analogy of the north door of the Erechtheum and restored a carved cornice over all three doors on the main side of the building[44] (Pls. XLVIII, L) and, given the sima-like profile of such a member, provided it with the sequence of sculptured motifs found on the raking sima of the Hieron[45] inasmuch as the raking simas of the Propylon were painted.

On the rear side of the building, the lintels were evidently provided with a projecting, overhanging cornice to judge by the appearance of one such over-lintel (Pls. XLI, XLIX) —a practical arrangement since the doors were not protected by a porch on that side. The broken profile of this block shows a fragmentary hawk's beak above a cyma reversa terminating in a fillet. On that side of the building, one step led down into the precinct and was double-recessed like the stereobate of the Propylon's wall (Pls. XLVII A, XLIX, LI).

The doors proper, implied by the cuttings for door pans on two fragmentary thresholds, have been restored on the basis of the standard doors known from a number of Macedonian tombs.[46]

Ionic was the order chosen for his building by the architect of the Propylon as it had been chosen for the propylon to the Pompeion in Athens and the South Propylaea in Labraunda in Caria,[47] places within the ancient world with which he must have been familiar, as we shall see.

The columns have been reconstructed from fragmentarily preserved capitals and shafts and necking blocks, one of which is fully preserved (Pls. XIII-XVI). No base is preserved. Inasmuch as the slighter later Ionic porch of the dedication of Philip Arrhidaios and Alexander IV and of the Propylon of Ptolemy II[48] both had unadorned Attic-Ionic bases, and in view of the strength of local architectural tradition in Samothrace, we have restored this form to the order.

41. Drawing from R. P. Pullan's unpublished field Notebook V in the Department of Greek and Roman Antiquities of the British Museum. W. R. Lethaby, *Antiquities of Ionia*, London, 1915, p. 27, reported that the outer molding was carved with a leaf and dart molding, a precedent that we have followed.

42. Ekrem Akurgal, *Die Kunst Anatoliens von Homer bis Alexander*, Berlin, 1961, p. 130, figs. 81, 82, 110.

43. Howard Crosby Butler, *The Temple of Artemis* (*Sardis II*, 1), Leyden, 1925, pp. 39 ff., 55 ff., Atlas, pls. III, IV, for this Roman replica of the original door. For confirmation of the date of this door, see Gottfried Gruben, "Beobachtungen zum Artemis-Tempel von Sardis," *AthMitt*, 76 (1961), pp. 159 f.

44. Paton-Stevens, pl. XXV.

45. Vol. 3, text I, p. 77, fig. 131.

46. For convenience, cf. the examples quoted, *ibid.*, pp. 189 ff., figs. 149-151. The recently discovered painted tomb at Lefkadia offers still another example of this kind of door. Katerina Rhomiopoulou, "A New Monumental Chamber Tomb with Paintings of the Hellenistic Period near Lefkadia (West Macedonia)," *AAA*, 6 (1973), pp. 87-92.

47. Hoepfner, pp. 83 ff., pls. 26-29; *Labraunda*, pl. XXI, above, fig. 57. See the comments on the use of the Ionic order in the Argolid at this time in Roux, pp. 355, 407 f., in which he stresses its use primarily for small, secular buildings.

48. See *Samothrace*, Vols. 9, 10 forthcoming.

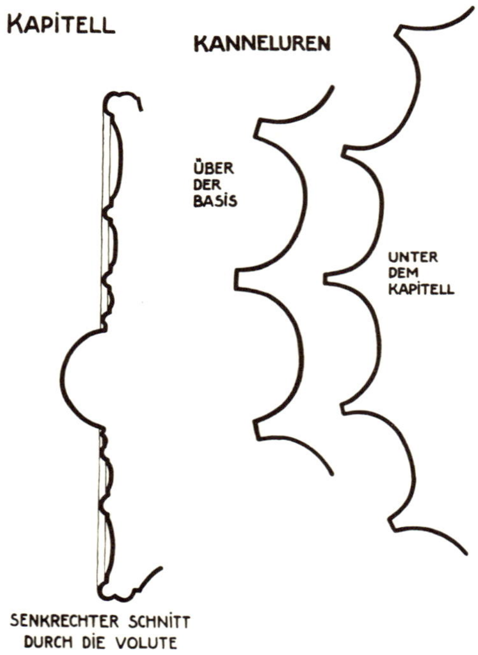

61. Section of the flutes of the shaft and the volute of the capital of the Philippeion at Olympia.

The shafts are monolithic, composed of twenty-four flutes of nearly semicircular section, with a carved astragal at the top (Pl. XIII). Monolithic shafts were used for the Temple of Athena Nike on the Akropolis, dated ca. 425 B.C.,[49] and for the Nereid Monument at Xanthos, now dated ca. 380-370 B.C.,[50] doubtless reflecting the small size of these buildings.

From the mid-fifth century B.C. on, twenty-four flutes were standard for Ionic buildings both in Attica and Asia Minor[51] in contrast with the regular use of twenty in the Peloponnesos.[52] The section of the flutes is paralleled by those of the Philippeion at Olympia built ca. 338 B.C. (Pl. XIII.3, fig. 61).[53] The upper astragal carved with a bead and reel pattern is found in Asia Minor on the Temples of Athena at Priene, erected between 350 and 330 B.C., of Hemithea at Kastabos, dating ca. 335 B.C., of Artemis at Ephesos,

49. See, for example, A. K. Orlandos, "Nouvelles observations sur la construction du temple d'Athéna Niké," *BCH*, 71-72 (1947-48), pp. 22 ff.

50. Coupel-Demargne, pp. 73 ff., pl. XXVII. Dated 380-370 B.C. by William A. P. Childs, "Prolegomena to a Lycian Chronology: The Nereid Monument from Xanthos," *Opuscula Romana* (Skrifter Utgivna av Svenska Institutet i Rom, 4°, XXXIII), 9 (1973), p. 115. This date contrasts with the old dates ca. 420 B.C. of Walter H. Schuchhardt, "Die Friese des Nereiden-Monumentes von Xanthos," *Ath Mitt*, 52 (1927), p. 147, and ca. 410-400 B.C. of Dinsmoor, p. 256.

51. With the exception of the Nereid Monument, which has only twenty, possibly because of the size of the shafts. See Coupel-Demargne, p. 75.

52. Roux, pp. 334 ff.

53. *Schleif-Zschietzschmann*, I, Atlas, pl. 5. According to Pausanias 5.20.10, the Philippeion was built after the Battle of Chaeroneia in 338 B.C. It must have been begun, i.e., designed, between 338 and 336 B.C., when Philip II was murdered. Therefore, I do not understand Dinsmoor's statement, p. 236, that it was begun in 339 B.C.

completed before the end of the fourth century B.C., and of Artemis at Sardis, begun at the end of the fourth century B.C.[54] The shafts of the Propylon are characterized by entasis, like those of the Mausoleum of Halikarnassos[55] begun in 353 B.C.,[56] of the Temple of Athena at Priene[57] and the Philippeion at Olympia.[58] Therefore, as a whole, the shafts of the Propylon are equally connected with Attic Ionic and the tradition of Asia Minor.

The restored capital has a scamillus but no plinth (Pls. XIV-XVII; figs. 42, 47, 48, 62, 63).[59] Its square abacus is carved with a Lesbian cymation terminating, at the corners, in uninscribed hanging palmettes; half of each palmette is visible from the front, half from the side.[60] The lower line of the canalis sags gently toward the center of the capital. The volutes appear to turn quickly toward the eye, which was not inserted, to judge by the earlier Czech drawing (figs. 47 A, 48 C). The center of the eye appears to have been level with the bottom line of the echinus and to lie just outside the outer line of the shaft. The profile of the canalis volute is relatively shallow. The echinus was evidently carved with five eggs and accompanying darts, of which the outer two eggs and darts are overlapped by two half-palmettes that, in turn, slightly overlap the upper margin of the echinus.

54. For Priene: Theodor Wiegand and Hans Schrader, *Priene*, Berlin, 1904, pp. 90, fig. 57; 92, 105, fig. 74, and H. Riemann, *RE*, Stuttgart, 1963, *s.v. Pytheos*, cols. 459 ff.; for Kastabos: Cook-Plommer, p. 88, fig. 24, pl. XIV, 2; for Ephesos: A. H. Smith, *A Catalogue of Sculpture in the Department of Greek and Roman Antiquities, British Museum*, II, London, 1900, no. 1222, and Anton Bammer, *Die Architektur des jüngeren Artemision von Ephesos*, Wiesbaden, 1972, pp. 20 f., figs. 16, 17, 19, 20, pls. 4a, 5b, 6a,c,d; for Sardis: Butler *op. cit.*, p. 46, Atlas, pls. VIII, IX. For the date of Ephesos, see Wilhelm Alzinger, "Alt-Ephesos," *Das Altertum*, 13 (1967), p. 41, and Bammer, *op. cit.*, p. 42, who consider that the huge temple had been completed by 300 B.C. For an earlier date, cf. Fritz Krischen, "Das Artemision von Ephesos," *Wilhelm Dorpfeld, Festschrift zum 80. Geburtstag*, Berlin, 1933, p. 73. For the date of Sardis, Gottfried Gruben, "Zum Artemis-tempel von Sardis," *AthMitt*, 76 (1961), pp. 155 ff.

55. For this fact, see William B. Dinsmoor, "The Mausoleum at Halicarnassus," *AJA*, 12 (1908), p. 10. In this article, pp. 15 ff., and as late as *The Architecture of Ancient Greece*, pp. 257 ff., and pl. 63b, Dinsmoor still maintained that the Mausoleum had a frieze in its entablature, although the order had long been correctly restored in the British Museum (see *A Guide to the Department of Greek and Roman Antiquities in the British Museum*, 6th edn., London, 1928, pl. 6). For a recent clear statement on the fact that the Mausoleum was a characteristically friezeless Asiatic Ionic building, see Kristian Jeppesen, *Paradeigmata*, Aarhus, 1958, pp. 32 f.

56. See Dinsmoor, pp. 257 f. Abundant new evidence regarding the architecture and sculpture of the Mausoleum has been found in the recent Danish excavations, for which see Kristian Jeppesen and Ian Zahle, "The Site of the Mausoleum at Halikarnassus Reexcavated," *AJA*, 77 (1973), pp. 336-338; *idem*, "Investigations on the Site of the Mausoleum 1970/1973," *ibid.*, 79 (1975), pp. 67-79. In the latter report, p. 79, the authors conclude that work on the monument continued for more than a decade and was finally suspended ca. 340 B.C.

57. Wiegand-Schrader, *op. cit.*, p. 92.

58. Schleif in *Schleif-Zschietzschmann*, I, p. 8.

59. For the use of a scamillus, see, e.g., the Temple of Athena at Priene, Wiegand-Schrader, *op. cit.*, p. 92. See Zschietzschmann in Schleif-Zschietzschmann, I, p. 30, for examples of the use of the plinth on Ionic capitals from the Philippeion on. It was rarely used in the fourth century but common in the Hellenistic age. However, examples are also known from the archaic age. Cf. Heinrich Drerup, "Pytheos und Satyros," *JdI*, 69 (1954), p. 26.

60. Its profile is too damaged to allow for any precise comparisons, but it was certainly a cyma reversa. Lucy T. Shoe (Shoe, p. 81) says that the earliest cyma reversa of all comes from the abacus of the archaic Temple of Artemis at Ephesos, that it was revived for that member in the mid-fourth century B.C. in Asia Minor and, p. 172, that both the ovolo and cyma reversa abacus types were used in the fourth century B.C.

62. Fragmentary capital 49.414 A, B. A. Side. B. Bolster. C. Bottom.

63. Fragmentary capital and drum: 49.414 A, B and 49.985.

64. Capital and top of shaft from the Mausoleum at Halikarnassos. London, The British Museum.

65. Architrave, capital, and top of shaft from the Mausoleum at Halikarnassos. London, The British Museum.

The abacus, with its carved Lesbian cymation and corner palmettes, is closely related to the abaci of the Mausoleum of Halikarnassos and the Temple of Athena at Priene (figs. 64-66).[61] It differs from the Attic tradition of a painted cymation[62] or a carved ovolo.[63]

61. For the capitals of the Mausoleum: Lethaby, especially, pp. 57 ff.; of the Temple at Priene, Wiegand-Schrader, *loc. cit.*; Schede, pp. 30 ff.; but note certain corrections in connection with the corner capital: Otto Bauer, "Vorläufiger Bericht über die Neubearbeitung des Athenatempels zu Priene in der Jahren 1965/66," *Istanbuler Forschungen*, 28 (1968), pp. 215 ff., and *idem*, "Beobachtungen am Athenatempel in Priene bei den Bestandsaufnahmen 1965 und 1966," *BJb*, 169 (1969), pp. 117 ff. For the capitals of both the Mausoleum and Priene, see Drerup, *op. cit.*, pp. 1 ff. He points out, p. 26, that in the fourth century, on the Greek mainland, there is not a single case known of an Ionic capital with a sculptured echinus. See, too, Carl Weickert, *Das lesbische Kymation*, Leipzig, 1913, p. 30, fig. 3, no. 4, for the profile of the abacus on the Temple of Athena at Priene, and pl. V f, for the elevation of the abacus on the Mausoleum.

62. E.g., the Temple on the Ilissos, the Propylaea, the Temple of Athena Nike. See Iona Mylonas Shear, "Kallikrates," *Hesperia*, 32 (1963), pp. 375-424.

63. See Paton-Stevens, pls. XXII, XXIII. This carved ovolo abacus also occurs in Asia Minor on the Temples of Artemis at Ephesos (Lethaby, pp. 19 f.) and Sardis (Butler, *op. cit.*, pp. 119 ff.).

66. A. Capital and top of shaft from the Temple of Athena at Priene. B. Oblique view of capital and top of shaft from the Mausoleum at Halikarnassos.

Judging by our damaged leaf and dart pattern, it, too, is close to the Mausoleum and the Temple at Priene in their elegant curving lines.

The form and motifs of the canalis and echinus appear to be close to the capitals of the Mausoleum and the Temple at Priene[64] but they have been modified, probably under Attic influence; that is, the curve of the canalis is more graceful than the curves on the

64. See Drerup, *loc. cit.* A quickly turning volute would be closer to the Mausoleum than to Priene. In this connection, note a related fragmentary capital from Larisa am Hermos, found out-of-context and dating in the fourth century, on exhibition in the Izmir Archaeological Museum. See Johannes Boehlau and Karl Schefold, *Larisa am Hermos*, I: *Die Bauten*, Berlin, 1940, pp. 120, 125 f., pls. 20, 21.

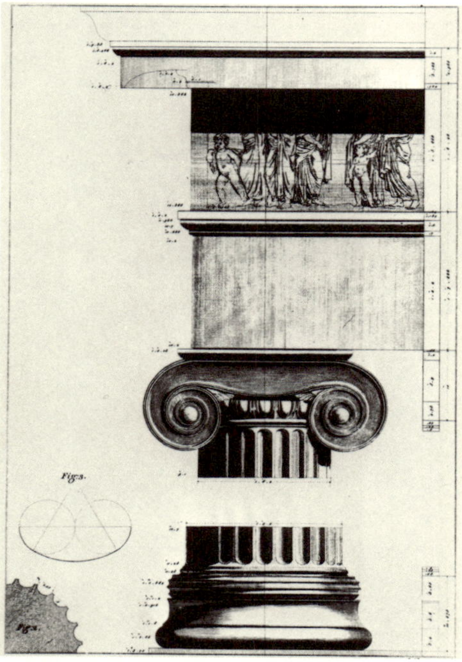

67. Capital and top of shaft of the Temple on the Ilissos.

68. Portion of the Ionic order of the Propylaea at Athens.

69. Rear View of the Temple of Athena Nike.

capitals from the Mausoleum and Priene and related to the capitals of the Temple on the Ilissos, the Propylaea, and the Temple of Athena Nike (figs. 66-69) and, like them, the capital of the Propylon has eyes that are carved rather than separately inserted.[65] Both the position of the eye and the shallow, molded profile running through the canalis and volute are close to the Philippeion (fig. 61).[66] The present damaged condition of the echinus reveals traces of its carved egg and dart pattern but they are not sufficient to allow precise comparisons.

65. Shear, *loc. cit.* On the Mausoleum, at Ephesos, and at Priene, the eyes are inserted. See Lethaby, p. 58.

66. Zschietzschmann in Schleif-Zschietzschmann, I, pp. 31 ff., Atlas, pls. 1, 4, 5. The patterns on the capitals of the Philippeion were painted (*ibid.*, p. 29), hence it is impossible to compare them, in most respects, with those of the Propylon.

70. Fragmentary capital 49.414 and drum 49.985.

71. Pattern on bolster of capital 49.414.

The upper and lower contours of the bolster of the Propylon's capital are differentiated, the lower being the more arching, as is true of the capitals of the Mausoleum and the Temple at Priene (Pl. XV.2; figs. 47, 62 B). The bolster is ornamented by a central band bordered by carved astragals set on the edges of the band (figs. 47 B, 62 B, 70, 71). Within

72. Capital and shaft of the Mausoleum at Halikarnassos. London, The British Museum.

73. Portion of the Ionic order of the Propylaea at Athens.

the astragals, there are flame palmettes, each supported by a pair of tendrils, from which another pair of tendrils rises to frame each palmette, and each pair of tendrils, in turn, sends down lateral hanging half-palmettes—forming a complicated pattern of parallel upright and hanging forms separated by fluent, enframing tendrils grooved into a V-shaped section. Three such units evidently unfolded on each bolster. Each palmette is composed of a singular central petal that extends between the paired tendrils to form a second upper tip and it is flanked, on each side, by two drooping petals above an upturned petal.

This pattern is a hitherto unknown variant on the rich and varied schemes of bolster decoration in earlier and contemporary Ionic architecture. It represents a fusion and reshaping of earlier systems.

One such system, exemplified by the Mausoleum and the Temple at Priene, was the use of a central panel on the bolster containing carved ornament bordered on each side by a molding (figs. 65, 66 B, 72). There the ornament consisted of a band of laurel leaves arranged in scale pattern. This scheme may reflect the painted bolsters of the Mnesiklean Propylaea (figs. 68, 73) which, it is reported, had a central band of laurel leaves framed by bead and reel moldings flanked by luxuriant acanthus tendrils spreading out to occupy the lateral fields of the bolster.[67]

67. Schaubert in A. F. von Quast, *Mittheilungen uber Alt- und Neu-Athen*, Berlin, 1834, p. 8: "die Seiten wiederum auf das Zierlichste bemalt. Zwischen gemalten Perlenstäbchen legt sich die bekannte

74. Detail of corner column and entablature of the north porch of the Erechtheum at Athens.

Such a scheme is in contrast with the subdivision of the entire bolster into flutes separated by moldings either enriched, as on the Erechtheum, with carved astragals (fig. 74), or plain,[68] or by the use of palmettes at the very base of the bolster visible only from below, as on the Artemision at Ephesos.[69]

Schuppenverzierung, gleichfalls nur gemalt, um die dünneren Mittelteile der Seitenvolute, während eine reiche Akanthusranke sich bis an den breiteren Rand hinauf windet."

This type was repeated in sculptured form on the capitals of the late Hellenistic propylon to the Temple of Athena at Priene. Cf. Wiegand-Schrader, *op. cit.*, p. 135, fig. 105.

For other Attic forerunners of this type, including bolsters with sculptured floral motifs on the central band, see Hans Mobius, "Attische Architekturstudien," *AthMitt*, 52 (1927), pp. 167 ff. Beilage XVIII, figs. 6, 8. See new, joining fragments fitting fig. 8 published by Wolfgang Züchner, "Fragmente auf der Akropolis und im Asklepieion zu Athen," *AA*, 51 (1936), cols. 329 ff., figs. 18-20.

This form of capital was also used on capitals II-IV of the later Asklepieion in Athens. See R. Martin, "Chapiteaux ioniques de l'Asklepieion d'Athènes," *BCH*, 68-69 (1944-45), pp. 342 ff., pls. XXVII-XXIX. See Martin's comments, pp. 371 ff., on Mnesikles's capitals as having come out of the local background, that is, that he rejuvenated old Attic forms. Martin also emphasizes that the contracting of volutes happened more quickly in Greece than in Asia Minor.

68. See Wilhelm Alzinger, "Ionische Kapitelle aus Ephesos I," *ÖJh*, 46 (1961-63), pp. 105 ff.

69. E.g., British Museum no. 1224, Lethaby, p. 20; Bammer, *op. cit.*, p. 22, fig. 22, pl. 5 b. See, too, the later examples from Sardis, e.g., Butler, *op. cit.*, capitals C, D, pp. 65 ff., Atlas, pl. XVII, XVIII.

On the bolster of the Propylon, this Attic-rooted scheme in which the ornament was confined to a central panel was now coupled with or influenced by another tradition in which floral forms, often of palmettes, lotus flowers, and tendrils, were carved across the entire bolster or a band the full width of the bolster. An example of this variety appeared on Polykrates' huge dipteral Temple of Hera at Samos, begun ca. 530 B.C., on which work was still going on in the fourth century B.C. (fig. 75).[70] Here, the lower half of the bolster was carved with alternate palmettes and lotus flowers resting on pairs of tendrils. Small palmettes hung from these tendrils and they, in turn, curved down to enclose additional upright palmettes. A very similar capital is known from Syracuse (fig. 76).[71] There the entire surface of the bolster has been carved and framed by an egg and dart at the top and meanders at the sides. A related Ionic capital from the Temple of Zeus at Labraunda, another dedication of Idrieus, combines hanging palmettes and lotus flowers in a scheme that reverses and updates the motifs of the earlier Samian capital (fig. 77).[72]

On the bolster of the Propylon, this exuberance of pattern is restrained. Its ornament is confined to a central band. The detail of the pattern is contemporary. For example, the use of a palmette within lyre-shaped tendrils from which half-palmettes drop is related to the pattern in the similarly narrow fields in the painted viae of the Temple of Asklepios at Epidauros (fig. 78).[73] Related systems of painted decoration also occur on vases, for

70. This very fragmentary capital was restored by Oscar Reuther, *Der Heratempel von Samos*, Berlin, 1957, pp. 41, 52 ff., 60, figs. 245-47. See, too, Gruben, pp. 315 ff.

71. A sporadic capital found in the nekropolis of the city: *NSc.*, 1943, pp. 79 ff., figs. 37, 38, evidently part of a small column that supported another object (Paolino Mingazzini, "Archäologische Grabungen und Funde in Italien," *AA*, 65-66 [1950-51], cols. 255-257). See, too, a capital from Selinus in the Museo Nazionale, Palermo, *ibid.*, p. 82, fig. 39, on which the bolster is entirely covered with carved laurel leaves. For another example, see a colossal archaic capital in Marseilles that has on its bolster an applied bronze ornament consisting of two half-palmettes and a pair of lotus flowers. It also has carved acanthus leaves in the spandrels between the volutes and the echinus. See Fernand Benoit, "Le chapiteau ionique de Marseilles," *CRAI*, 1953, p. 221 and, in greater detail, *RA*, 43 (1954), pp. 17 ff. The author (*CRAI*, p. 220, and *RA*, p. 21), refers to the two preceding examples as archaizing and gives a good photograph of the Syracuse capital on p. 37, fig. 15.

72. Pending final publication of this building, see *Labraunda*, p. 16, fig. 11. Axel Persson, "Swedish Excavations at Labranda (sic) 1948," *Årsberattelse* (Lund), 1948-49, III, p. 26, ascribes the Temple to Pytheos in the interval between his work on the Mausoleum and at Priene. Alfred Laumonier, *Les Cultes indigènes en Carie* (Bibliothèque des Ecoles françaises d'Athènes et de Rome, fasc. 188), Paris, 1958, p. 50, has accepted this attribution. On the subject of bolster patterns, see, too, Alzinger, *op. cit.*, pp. 127 ff., 135. He emphasizes, p. 128, the experimental character of Ionian architecture in the first half of the fourth century B.C.

Among the several analogies that the pseudodipteral Ionic Temple to Aphrodite at Messa bears to the Propylon is the presence of varied floral designs on the sculptured panels of its bolsters. The date of the building is debated. The excavator, Robert Koldewey, dated it in the first half of the fourth century B.C. (Koldewey, pp. 58 f.). However, Vitruvius, 3.3.8., reports that Hermogenes was the first to use the pseudodipteral plan and, 3.3.2., that he used it for the Temple of Artemis at Magnesia—a building that is probably second century in date. Vitruvius does not mention the Lesbian temple, but presumably it was not earlier than the temple at Magnesia. Dinsmoor dated the temple at Messa ca. 280 B.C., evidently a compromise between the fourth century and the period of Hermogenes (Dinsmoor, p. 272, n. 1). In all likelihood, the temple was Hellenistic, whatever its century. For the sculptured bolsters, Koldewey, pl. 25.

73. Alphonse Defrasse and Henri Lechat, *Épidaure*, Paris, 1895, p. 58.

75. Drawing of bolster of the Temple of Hera at Samos.

76. Drawing of bolster of a capital from the nekropolis of Syracuse.

77. Capital and shafts from the Temple of Zeus at Labraunda.

78. Painted viae from the Temple of Asklepios at Epidauros.

example, as a vertical ornamental panel on an Apulian "amphora" in Munich dating from the mid-fourth century (fig. 79).[74] They attest the interrelationship between these varied media. Thus the bolster scheme of the Propylon is a variation on the types used at the Mausoleum and Priene, themselves dependent on Attic tradition, and on the decorative system derived from the archaic Ionic tradition in Asia Minor. In Samothrace, this form led to the still more elaborate bolster pattern of the early Hellenistic Propylon of Ptolemy II (fig. 80).[75]

Taken as a whole, the capitals of the Propylon are closely related to the capitals of the Mausoleum and the Temple of Athena at Priene and follow the traditions of Asia Minor. They also reflect the influence of both the older Heraion at Samos and the contemporary Temple of Zeus at Labraunda. They offer a highly individual synthesis and may well imply, in addition, the direct experience of Attic monuments.[76]

Unfortunately, no examples of the obviously widespread use of painted ornament in the architecture of this period survive. But it is clear that the patterns on contemporary vases often mirror those on architecture. For examples, cf. nn. 74, 84, 85, 87, 156, 157.

74. Paul Jacobstahl, *Die Ornamente griechischer Vasen*, Berlin, 1927, pl. 107b. I cite only one of many such examples.

75. Now in the Ephesos-Museum, Vienna. See Vol. 10 forthcoming and, in the meantime, *S,II*, pls. XXVI, XXVII.

76. In this connection, see below, pp. 107 ff. As reported above, Chap. I, p. 61, among the three fragments of the Propylon's capitals extant, none is from a corner capital. But we have restored such capitals for the four outer columns of the wings and the two inner columns between the porch and the wings inasmuch as, by this time, such corner capitals were common to the traditions of both the mainland and Asia Minor.

79. Detail from an Apulian amphora. Munich, Staatliche Antikensammlungen.

80. Bolster from the Ionic porch of the Propylon of Ptolemy II. Vienna, Ephesos-Museum.

81. Drum 49.985.

82. Tourist Pavilion, Gelibolu. Drum from the Propylon.

Unfortunately, the severely damaged profiles of the capitals, and the impossibility of determining with sufficient precision either the shape of the volute or the lower diameter of the incomplete monolithic shafts make it futile to compare the profiles or proportions of this capital with those of other Ionic capitals.

A richly carved drum crowned by an astragal lay between the capital and the shaft of the Propylon's columns (figs. 28, 42, 43, 44, 46, 63, 70, 81, 82). It was decorated by a band of palmettes, alternately upright and hanging, framed by lyre-shaped stems that spring from and link the volutes from which each palmette grows. At the base, which the upright palmettes abut, there is a series of upright acanthus leaves. The upright palmettes form a ring around the lower portion of the drum; the hanging ones, about its upper section; and together they interlace in a tight circle of abutting lyre-shaped units. The palmettes themselves are composed of a central petal flanked on each side by three drooping petals above an upturned flame petal—an elaboration of the palmettes on the bolster. Like the tendrils of the bolster, these tendrils are ribbed, and the upper tendrils, themselves, each spring from a pair of leafy calyxes. The presence of upright and hanging palmettes of related type within bold, curvilinear frames links the designs of the bolster and the drum.

The use of an ornamental necking in Ionic architecture is documented from the archaic age on.[77] In the fifth century, the most conspicuous example of its appearance was on the columns of the north and east porches of the Erechtheum (fig. 74).[78] But the ornamental drum of the Propylon is closer in type and ornament to examples known from Asia Minor than it is to this tradition. It is closer by far, to a mid-fourth-century drum of unknown provenance from Halikarnassos now in the British Museum (fig. 83).[79] The top molding of this drum is battered. Conceivably, it, too, was an astragal. The drum is adorned with a band of alternating flame palmettes and lotus flowers supported by volutes emerging from lyre-shaped tendrils that curl into lower volutes each of which supports a small leaf.

The basic concept of such a separate drum is identical with ours and certain details are strikingly similar: the lower motif of lyre-shaped tendrils curling into volutes at both top and bottom and containing a leaf, the leaf, itself, being similar to the motif originally present at the base of our drum. It is as though the designer of the Propylon's drum, under the influence of the collarlike band on the columns of the Erechtheum had taken the lower half of this Halikarnassos drum (eliminating the upright static palmettes and lotus flowers of the upper zone), replaced each leaf by an upright palmette and introduced a hanging

77. For example, the Temple of Apollo at Naukratis. See Dinsmoor, pp. 125 f.

78. Paton-Stevens, pls. XVI, XIX, XXII, XXIII. For other very similar columns from Delphi, see the discussion by Karl Lehmann, "Samothrace: Fourth Preliminary Report," *Hesperia*, 20 (1951), p. 15, n. 48, and Drerup's comment, *op. cit.*, p. 26, n. 69.

Another fifth-century example is the so-called New Temple at Locri. See Robert Koldewey and Otto Puchstein, *Die griechischen Tempel in Unteritalien und Sicilien*, I, Berlin, 1899, pp. 7 f., fig. 5. Dated, according to the authors, in the first half of the fifth century B.C.; by Dinsmoor, p. 138, ca. 450; by Alfonso de Franciscis, "Gli acroteri marmorei del tempio Marasà a Locri Epizefirii," *RömMitt*, 67 (1960), p. 23, between 450 and 425 B.C.; by Leonard von Matt-Umberto Zanotti-Bianco, *Grossgriechland*, Zürich, 1961, p. 131, 430-425 B.C. It is painful that in his reference to this temple, A. W. Lawrence mentions "old drawings of one [i.e. a temple] at Athens which was destroyed in 1778" (Lawrence, p. 140), dating apparently from the mid-fifth century and, therefore, in the background of the Erechtheum, without citing any reference for this information.

It has been suggested that the Temple of Athena at Miletos also had such an ornamental collar at the top of its columns: Theodor Wiegand, *Milet*, I, 8 (Armin von Gerkan, *Kalabaktepe, Athenatempel und Umgebung*), Berlin, 1925, pp. 65 ff., fig. 37. But as Dinsmoor has said (Dinsmoor, p. 136, n. 2), there is no evidence for this suggestion.

79. Found in the Castle. Smith, *op. cit.*, pp. 88 f., no. 999. Ht.: 0.572 m. I am grateful to Denys E. L. Haynes and Brian F. Cook for having allowed me to examine this drum in January 1971. Evidently Dinsmoor refers to this piece, p. 223, and ascribes it to the Temple of Ares at Halikarnassos. If so, it clearly does not imply "Athenian influence in Asia Minor" as the present discussion should make clear, since the tradition behind this drum is dependent not on the Erechtheum but on the Heraion at Samos. Mr. Cook has recently informed me that the attribution of this drum to the Temple of Ares was earlier suggested by W. L. Lethaby, *The Builder*, 1929, p. 1019.

palmette into the empty adjacent units, and transposed their leaves to the base of his slightly expanded one-zone system. The result was a decorative system related to the upright and hanging palmettes on the bolster of the capital, in which the static forms of earlier classical neckings were replaced by bold, undulating units.

The Halikarnassos drum is itself the outgrowth of a local tradition. It is an updated, fourth-century version of the necking restored to the late archaic Temple of Hera at Samos (fig. 84).[80] In motif, if not in date, it is even closer to the Propylon's drum than the Halikarnassos drum. For within the curling tendrils in the lower zone, there are both upright and pendant leaves. On our drum, the leaves have simply been replaced by upright and pendant palmettes—the latter closely related to the lyre-shaped hanging palmettes that constitute the central motif of the lateral faces of the anta capitals on the South Propylaea at Labraunda (fig. 85).[81] Our architect has reduced the double-tiered scheme of this Samian necking to a single tier or, to put it differently, he has increased the size of the lower tier of the Samian necking and eliminated its upper tier. It is tempting to assume that this gigantic temple must have been known to him. The bolster of the Propylon's capital has already proved to have affinities with the capital of this temple.

Another fragmentary drum of unknown provenance walled into a mosque in Halikarnassos offers a variation on the double-tiered Samian scheme (fig. 86).[82] Actually, the pattern is composed of a series of independent, contiguous palmettes each supported by the coiling extensions of its own pair of volutes. No pattern occupies the blank spaces within the curvilinear stalks. Again, the top of the drum is battered and conceivably it, too, may have had a carved moulding. This necking crowns the top of the irregularly broken shaft. It appears to be a late fifth century in date.

80. Gruben, pp. 315 ff.; Berve-Gruben-Hirmer, pp. 448, fig. 112, 455. According to Dinsmoor, some of the shafts of the archaic Temple of Artemis at Ephesos were also provided with neckings carved with "lotus-and-palmette bands of varying designs" (Dinsmoor, p. 131 and n. 1). Mr. D.E.L. Haynes confirms the fact that they have never been illustrated.

In his recent publication of the fourth-century Temple of Artemis, Bammer, *op. cit.*, pp. 21 ff. and fig. 6, has restored the sculptured drums normally placed below the shafts of the column to their tops, directly beneath the capitals. Quite apart from faulty calculation of the diameters of the drums and shafts that would force the drums to overhang the shafts markedly, the very notion of placing sculptured, *figural* drums at the top of the shafts of a gigantic building where they would have been virtually invisible is preposterous. The analogies adduced for this high position (e.g., the Erechtheum, the archaic temples at Samos, Naukratis, and Locri) are all floral and ornamental, creating a wholly different aesthetic effect. Such a restoration ignores the crucial evidence of the coins, which clearly indicate the location of the drums at the base of the shafts (see Bluma L. Trell, *The Temple of Artemis at Ephesos* [Numismatic Notes and Monographs, no. 107], New York, 1945). Ironically enough, Bammer accepts coin evidence for doors in the pediment (p. 16). The entire volume has been harshly and, in my view, properly reviewed by Hugh Plommer in *JHS*, 94 (1974), pp. 249 ff.

81. See *Labraunda*, pl. VII, 8.

82. Diameter: ca. 0.55 m.; height: ca. 0.35 m. I owe knowledge of this marble drum and the photograph illustrated above to Dr. Annaliese Peschlow, who has suggested that I include it among the ornamental drums discussed here.

83. Drum from Halikarnassos. London, The British Museum.

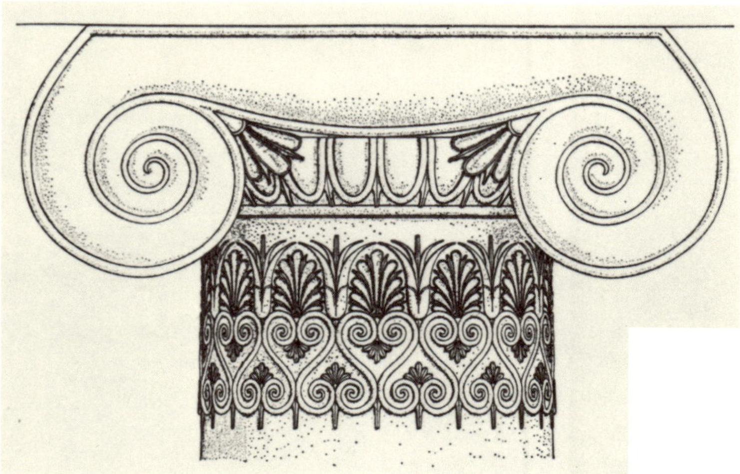

84. Drawing of capital and drum from the Temple of Hera at Samos.

85. Lateral faces of anta capitals from the South Propylaea at Labraunda.

86. Drum-shaft from Halikarnassos. Provenance unknown.

87. Drum-shaft from Thessaloniki. Paris, Musée du Louvre.

88. Detail from the neck of an Apulian krater from Ruvo. Naples, Museo Nazionale.

Yet another ornamental drum from an unknown structure in Thessaloniki, now in the Louvre, is united with the upper section of its Ionic shaft (fig. 87).[83] The design of the necking is single-tiered, as on the Erechtheum, and consists of two parallel, abutting palmettes, an upright, flame palmette and a hanging, drooped-petal palmette. They are linked and framed by curvilinear stems that emerge from each volute. Linear and classicistic in execution, this incomplete shaft must date from a later time, whether in the later Hellenistic or Roman periods.

Closest of all to the ornamental pattern of our drum is the border crowning the neck on a colossal Apulian krater in Naples on which the Pyre of Patroklos is represented (fig. 88).[84] Here hanging white palmettes in lyre-shaped frames alternate with upright red palmettes of identical shape. Even the form of the palmette itself, with its elongated, arrow-tipped central petal, is analogous to the palmettes on our drum.[85] Only the absence of the acanthus leaves at the base of the drum and the slightly variant form of the palmette differentiates the otherwise strikingly similar pattern on a vessel dated ca. 330 B.C. Like many other patterns on South Italian vases, it evidently reflects contemporary architectural ornament. It is especially interesting in view of the multiplicity of Ionic buildings represented on fourth-century Apulian vases that show an upright palmette on a necking—clearly an abbreviated rendering of such an ornamental drum—and suggests that this architectural form, rare in Greece, was popular in southern Italy.[86]

The use of boldly framed juxtaposed palmettes so characteristic of our drum has an interesting forebear in the related, if by no means, identical terracotta lateral akroterion attributed to Pheidias' workshop at Olympia dated ca. 430 B.C. (fig. 89).[87] The form of the

83. MA 3391. Height: 0.77 m.; upper diameter: 0.555 m.; diameter of shaft: 0.52 m.; Lewis hole on top surface. According to the Louvre inventory, this drum-shaft came 'de la fontaine de Banja, près de Monastir."

84. Museo Nazionale, Heydemann no. 3254. Attributed to the Master of the Dareios Krater by Anna Rocco, "Il Pittore del Vaso dei Persani," *Archeologia Classica*, 5 (1953), pp. 175 ff., pl. LXXXV, 2, and dated, p. 184, n. 1, shortly after 350 B.C. A. D. Trendall, *Vasi antichi dipinti del Vaticano. Vasi italioti ed etruschi a figure rosse*, Vatican City, I, 1953, p. 70, placed the Dareios Painter in the last third of the fourth century B.C., a date followed by Margot Schmidt, *Der Dareiosmaler und sein Umkreis* (Orbis Antiquus, 15), Münster, 1960, p. 72 (ca. 330-320 B.C.), and Maurizio Borda, *op. cit.*, p. 102 (specifically 330-325 B.C.), who also accepted attribution of this krater to the Dareios Painter, p. 51, fig. 38.

85. The Apulian vase in Munich illustrated as fig. 79 shows the same variety of palmette, a variety typical also of the bolster palmette. This type of palmette recurs constantly on Apulian ware, on vessels coming from the third or fourth quarter of the fourth century. For a few additional examples, see Trendall, *Vasi . . . del Vaticano*, II, pls. LII a, b, LIII d, and Jacobsthal, *op. cit.*, pls. 108a, 113a,b.

Returning to architectural analogies, the lateral faces of the anta capitals at the South Propylaea at Labraunda are carved with a palmette almost identical, in number of mostly drooping petals and the length of the central arrow-tipped petal, with those of our drum. See *Labraunda*, pl. VII, 8.

86. For a few characteristic examples, see Lehmann, *op. cit.*, p. 15, n. 48; A. D. Trendall, *Frühitaliotische Vasen*, Leipzig, 1938, pl. 29; *idem*, *Early South Italian Vase-Painting*, Mainz, 1974, pl. 29; Borda, *op. cit.*, p. 45, fig. 36; Fürtwangler-Reichhold, ser. I, p. 301, pl. 60; ser. III, pp. 362 ff., pls. 179, 180, 3.

87. Alfred Mattwitz and Wolfgang Schiering, *Die Werkstatt des Pheidias in Olympia* (*Olympische Forschungen*, 5), Berlin, 1964, pp. 119, 124 ff., pls. 18, 50, 51. Ht.: 0.245 m. Hand made. For another related decorative scheme see the ornament on an Apulian volute krater in Munich. Jacobstahl *op. cit.*, pl. 113 b.

89. Terracotta lateral akroterion. Olympia Museum.

central palmette, in particular, its prominent arrow-tipped central petal flanked by three gently drooping petals on each side above an upturned leaf hanging from the volutes appears to be an earlier version of the type of palmette on the drum. It is of interest, too, that this design was used on an actual architectural piece.

Finally, the painted pattern on the soffit of the marble ceiling beams of the later naiskos at Didyma shows a scheme related to the carved pattern on both the bolster of the Propylon's capital and its drum.[88] Again, a series of palmettes supported by volutes is framed by boldly curving oval shapes.

The primary sources of this drum lie in western Anatolia, although the use of a single zone for the design rather than a double tier probably reflects the influence of the necking of the Erechtheum. Lost terracotta architectural forms from the Greek mainland may also have conditioned its aesthetic direction. The parallels in Apulian vase painting show the contemporary nature of this ornamental vocabulary and, as suggested, doubtless reflect the forms of monumental decorative art.

The capital and ornamental drum of this elegant Ionic column imply that the architect of the Propylon drew primarily on the traditions of Asia Minor, modifying them somewhat on the basis of his knowledge of mainland currents. It is already clear that his style was a highly personal one involving a marked taste for rich sculptural design.

Neither the height of the column nor the lower diameter is certain inasmuch as the shaft is not quite complete and the base has been restored. If we estimate that the lower

88. *Didyma*, p. 111, Z.538, 50-51, pl. 192, F722, 722a. Walter Voigtländer, *Der jüngste Apollontemple von Didyma* (*IstMitt*, Beiheft 14), Tübingen, 1975, p. 55, pl. 8, 4, has remarked this connection.

diameter (taken from flute to flute above the lower apophyge which is actually missing) was 0.55 m. and that the height of the column was 4.90 m., the proportion of lower diameter to the height of the columns is 1:8.9. This is very close to the parallel figure for the Temple of Athena at Priene (1:8.8)[89] and precisely the proportion of the later Propylon of Ptolemy II.[90] Inasmuch as these figures for the Propylon's column are hypothetical, it is unwise to make further comparisons.

The relationship between the lower diameter (not altogether certain) and the normal intercolumniation (that is, not the slighter wider central one) is 1:3.67. It is not surprising that this relationship is close to the proportion of the north porch of the Erechtheum: 1:3.79.[91]

As a discussion of the date of the Propylon will ultimately establish,[92] this is the first example in the history of Greek architecture of the use of an entablature containing an architrave, frieze, dentils, and geison-sima (Pls. XLVIII, LI, LX; fig. 90).

Earlier Ionic buildings in mainland Greece always combine a banded architrave with a frieze, the frieze, itself, being sculptured.[93] A characteristic example of this scheme is the late fifth-century Temple of Athena Nike on the Akropolis (fig. 91).[94] In Asia Minor, the frieze was not used; on the contrary, dentils, a feature not used on the mainland, rest directly on the banded architrave as may be seen in the typical Temple of Athena at Priene (fig. 92).[95] Normally, in this region, no sculpture is present in the entablatures. The Nereid

89. Dinsmoor, p. 223. The comparable relation for the Erechtheum is ca. 1:9.5.

The fact that it is seldom clear where the lower diameters of Ionic columns have been measured makes it exceedingly difficult to use the charts of proportions given by many scholars. In any case, the size and position of a building may be more important factors with regard to its proportions than its purely theoretical comparative proportions as a basis for determining its date.

90. This may be the result of local tradition.

91. Cf. Dinsmoor, Chronological List of Greek Temples. As reported in Chap. I, p. 79, no anta capitals are preserved. We have restored them on the basis of the anta capitals of the South Propylaea at Labraunda. On the front face of these capitals, a fillet is succeeded by an egg-and-dart followed by a row of hanging palmettes and darts, in turn succeeded by a leaf-and-dart moulding above a bead-and-reel—a pattern identical with the front face of both the anta capital of the Temple of Athena at Priene and the comparable face of the anta capital of the Propylon of Ptolemy II, although the single motifs of the latter are each separated by an astragal. (See *Labraunda*, pls. IV, VII; Wiegand-Schrader, *op. cit.*, p. 96, fig. 64; Schede, p. 34, fig. 37; and *S,II*, pls. XXVIII, XXIX. In *Labraunda*, pl. IV, the second motif has been restored as a series of alternately hanging palmettes and lotus flowers. I wonder whether it, like the capitals at Priene and the large Propylon at Samothrace, is not a series of hanging palmettes and darts.) On the lateral face, there is a jagged-leaved acanthus calyx from the center of which a hanging palmette emerges. It is flanked by two tendrils, the upper one terminating in a backward half-palmette and a shooting flower. The flowers and character of the acanthus leaves in the sima of the Propylon are so close to these elements of the lateral face of the anta pilaster at Labraunda, and the hanging palmette of the latter is so related to the hanging palmettes of the drum as to suggest that this was an appropriate model to use for this restored capital. For the sima of the Propylon, see below, pp. 124 ff., figs. 51, 52, 95.

92. See below, pp. 143 f. and Chap. IV, pp. 273 ff.

93. An exception being the atypical south porch of the Erechtheum, a porch rather than a building, with its banded architrave and dentils. See Paton-Stevens, pp. 113 f., pl. VI.

94. For convenience, see Berve-Gruben-Hirmer, pp. 384 ff., fig. 30; Travlos, pp. 148 ff., figs. 203-206.

95. Berve-Gruben-Hirmer, pp. 475 ff., figs. 140-142. For a definitive article on this topic, see Armin von Gerkan, "Zum Gebälk des Athenatempels in Priene," *AthMitt*, 43 (1918), pp. 165 ff. and p. 169, fig. 2.

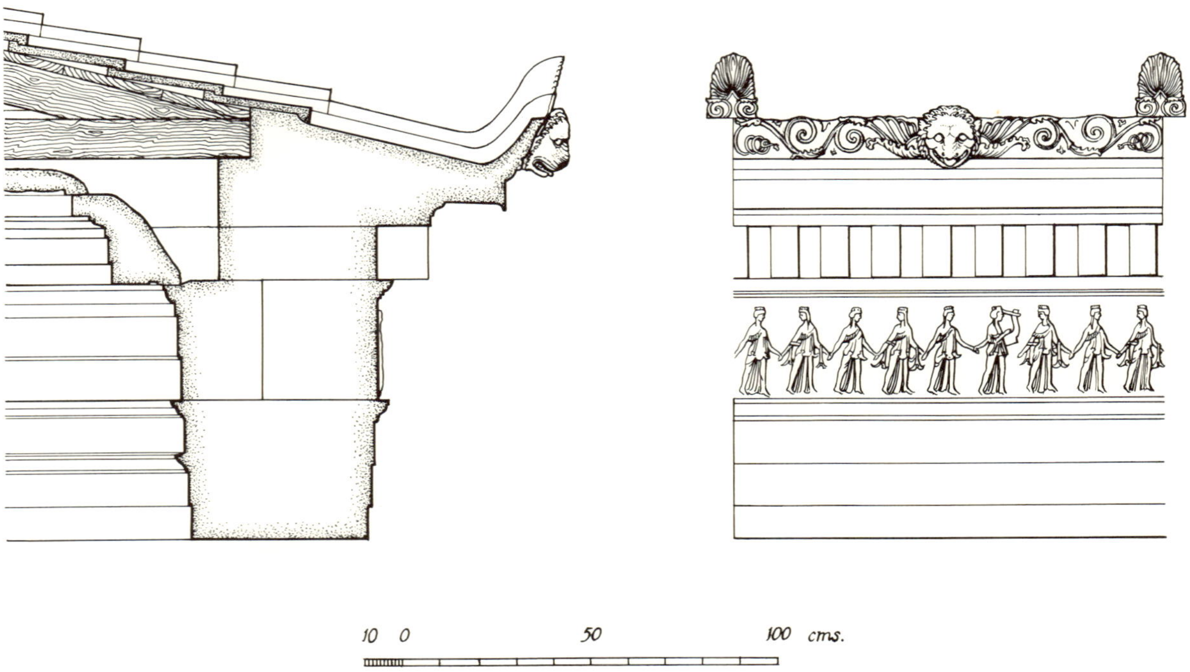

90. Details of the restored entablature of the Propylon. Left: section. Right: elevation.

Monument at Xanthos presents the exception, with a course of dentils resting on a sculptured architrave (fig. 93).[96] The presence or absence of a frieze is clearly tied up with the use of sculptured decoration. To one facing this tomb, it appears to lack an architrave, to be composed of a sculptured frieze beneath a course of dentils. How many other Ionic entablatures of this type once existed? In any case, the architect of the Propylon has combined the sculptured frieze and banded architrave of the mainland with the course of dentils customary in Asia Minor, a scheme destined to become standard in later Ionic and Corinthian architecture. Can he have been acquainted with the Nereid Monument (or some other similar but now lost monument)[97] and have coupled its scheme with the

---

A general discussion of the lack of friezes in this area will be found in Demangel, pp. 258 ff.

96. See Coupel-Demargne, pl. XCVIII. Two other exceptions are the archaic Doric temple at Assos and the archaic Ionic Temple of Apollo at Didyma, since there is evidence that it, too, had a sculptured architrave: *Didyma*, I, text I, pp. 125 f. For Assos, see F. H. Bacon, J. T. Clarke, and Robert Koldewey, *Investigations at Assos*, Cambridge, 1902-21, pp. 145, 165 f.; and particularly, F. Sartiaux, *Les Sculptures et la reconstruction de temple d'Assos en Troade*, Paris, 1915. Gottfried Gruben, "Das archaische Didymaion," *JdI*, 78 (1963), p. 176, is of the opinion that a sculptured architrave may have been the rule in archaic Ionic buildings.

97. See below, p. 141 f., for another link between the Propylon and the Nereid Monument.

91. View of the Temple of Athena Nike in Athens.

92. Detail of the entablature and columns of the Temple of Athena at Priene. Berlin, Staatliche Museen.

93. Restored façade of the Nereid Monument at Xanthos.

94. Detail of the Monument of Lysikrates in Athens.

banded architrave any Greek architect would consider aesthetically essential? Clearly, the entablature of the Propylon was designed by an architect familiar with the Ionic traditions of both the mainland and Asia Minor who wanted—or was commissioned—to provide it with a sculptured frieze. Even at this point in our discussion, it is tempting to speculate on whether this architect was an architect-sculptor.

Soon after its appearance in Samothrace, this new scheme was adopted for the Corinthian Monument of Lysikrates in Athens, dedicated in 334 B.C. (fig. 94).[98] Indeed, this Corinthian monument and our Ionic Propylon are the last two buildings, or reflection of a building, on which a figural frieze was used until the revival of classical norms in the second century B.C. at Teos, Alabanda, the Smintheion, Magnesia, and Lagina.[99] Atypical

98. Heinrich Bauer, "Lysikratesdenkmal, Baubestand und Rekonstruktion," *AthMitt*, 92 (1977), pp. 197 ff.; for convenience, Travlos, pp. 348 ff., figs. 450-452. In discussing the Philippeion at Olympia, Lawrence, p. 186, and Roux, p. 355, assumed that this dynastic memorial was the first structure in which the dentils of Asia Minor and the mainland frieze were combined. Dinsmoor was closer to the mark in allowing for the possibility that frieze and dentils had been combined "slightly earlier at Samothrace." (Dinsmoor, p. 236) in what he assumed to have been (p. 231) a marble temple "built shortly before the middle of the fourth century." So was Robertson, in cautiously suggesting in a footnote that "the oldest example is perhaps the rebuilt form of the old Cabirion of Samothrace" (Robertson, p. 145, n. 1), i.e., the Propylon. Actually, the low, unsculptured fascia-like frieze of the Philippeion, resting, as it does, on a double rather than a triple-fasciaed architrave, creates the impression of a triple-banded architrave subdivided by a molding between the upper two fasciae and crowned by a course of dentils—a highly unorthodox effect that is, in a sense, a variation on the Asiatic Ionic tradition. Note, too, the hybrid Attic-Asiatic base with its plinth. See Schleif-Zschietzschmann, p. 36, pl. 8 and Atlas, pl. 1. Alfred Mallwitz, *Olympia und seine Bauten*, Darmstadt, 1972, pp. 132 f., also refers to this member as a frieze. Stella Grobel Miller, in her persuasive article, "The Philippeion and Macedonian Hellenistic Architecture," *AthMitt*, 88 (1973), pp. 189 ff., in which she has suggested the likelihood that the architect of the building was a Macedonian rather than one coming from Attica, as the authors of *Olympische Forschungen*, I, had believed, still assumed, pp. 203 ff., that this low, fascia-like frieze was a genuine frieze. On p. 203, n. 66, Mrs. Miller indicated that the date of the Propylon to the Temenos and the question which Greek building first combined a frieze with dentils must await the present publication.

The late fourth-century naiskos at Didyma presents a related problem. Between the dentils and the banded architrave, there was a low, floral "frieze" that is less a frieze than a rich moulding. Again, it is another variation on the Asiatic-Ionic tradition. See Knackfuss, *Didyma*, pp. 113 ff., Z.597, 598, pl. 202, F548, F548 A. Friedrich Krauss, "Die Höhe der Säulen des Naiskos im Tempel von Didyma," *IstMitt*, 11 (1961), p. 128, still maintained that this was a genuine frieze. For the chronology of Didyma, see the short summary in Vol. 3, text I, p. 162, n. 24.

The Ionic temple at Messa has been said to have an undecorated frieze. (Koldewey, pl. 20, 1). But Demangel, pp. 252 f., n. 4, 330, maintained that the "frieze" has been misplaced in the building and that the temple followed the normal Asiatic tradition. Fritz Krischen, "Der Aufbau des Nereidenmonumentes von Xanthos," *AthMitt*, 47 (1923), pp. 72 f., fig. 2, had earlier taken the same position. See above, n. 72, for the problem of its date.

Courby and Picard have restored to the interior of the Temple of Zeus at Nemea an Ionic order with architrave, frieze, and geison to which a tiny dentil course is attached, although no example of the capital was found (Courby-Picard, pp. 73 ff., fig. 55, pl. XV). Roux doubts that the frieze was ever executed (Roux, p. 45).

It should be remarked that the seventh-century B.C. Temple A at Prinias has been restored with a frieze in its entablature (see Luigi Pernier, "New Elements for the Study of the Archaic Temple of Prinias," *AJA*, 39 [1934], pp. 175 ff., pls. XVII, XIX. W. B. Dinsmoor, preferred to place the frieze as a parapet bordering the roof, a form of sima (Dinsmoor, pp. 46 f. and n. 1]). In any case, this interesting building is not Ionic; it lacks any order.

99. See Vol. 3, text I, pp. 235, 315 f., 387.

as a figural frieze, as we shall see,[100] and composed of two types of figures that alternate with each other, they produce, in figural terms, something akin to the use of alternate abstract or inanimate motifs like the bucranes and rosette-pateras on the early Hellenistic Propylon of Ptolemy II (e.g., fig. 215). That is, in basic design, the frieze of the Propylon moves away from the classical figural frieze and anticipates the direction soon to be taken in architectural sculpture.

Therefore, one of the most original and influential features of the building was its entablature.

The columnar architrave or epistyle blocks are only very slightly narrower than the abacus of the capitals.[101]

The outer face of the epistyle has the normal triple fasciae decreasing in height from the top downward and tapering inward, a trait characteristic of the architraves of Asia Minor (Pls. XVIII-XXII).[102] It is crowned by a fillet, a cyma reversa, and a half-round; the inner face is subdivided into two sections, the lower presumably intended to follow an analogous system.[103] This lower section is crowned, again, by a similar sequence of moldings of modified, less vigorous profile; the upper fascia slopes backward and is topped by a larger and smaller ovolo above a tiny fillet.

This combination of moldings is very unorthodox, the normal Ionic epistyle crown in the fourth century being an ovolo.[104] In fact, the upper fascia of the inner face is crowned by a molding related to the ovolo of the frieze (cf. Pl. XLIV.1 and 3) and the lower crown on this inner face is a variation on the crown of the outer face of the architrave. Evidently, there is an intentional contrast between the ovolo-cyma reversa relationships in the frieze (Pls. XXIII-XXV) and epistyle. The specific combinations here appear to be unique[105] and in character, therefore, with the atypical nature of the entire entablature.

It should be noted, too, that the moldings on the entablature of the Propylon were not carved—the normal scheme in the fourth century in Asia Minor—but painted. In this respect, our architect has followed the tradition of painted moldings used on the earlier Temple on the Ilissos and the Temple of Athena Nike in Athens,[106] and also on the Philippeion at Olympia. The Propylon, like the Philippeion, also lacks the customary molded panel on the soffit of the architrave.[107]

The crowning molding of the frieze (Pl. XLIV.3) is equally individual: an ovolo, a half-round, and a tiny fillet. The only conceivable parallel to the strong, simple arc of

100. See below, Chap. III, pp. 261 f.

101. Ca. 0.005 m. The precise width of the abacus, it will be recalled, is based on a theoretical calculation.

102. Roux, p. 353, and in the more recently published Temple of Hemithea at Kastabos, Cook-Plommer, pp. 96 f.

103. Cf. block +35. But +12 actually has a slightly lower upper fascia.

104. Shoe, pp. 170 f.

105. So far as I am aware, only the geison soffit of the naiskos at Didyma and a molding conjecturally attributed to its epikranitis offer any parallel to these forms (Shoe, pls. XXX, 46; XXVIII, 14).

Mrs. Shear, *op. cit.*, pp. 398 f., makes a similar comment about the originality of Kallikrates' moldings on the Temple on the Ilissos.

106. *Ibid.*, p. 421.

107. Schleif in *Schleif-Zschietzschmann*, I, p. 37, pl. 8.

the crowning ovolo and fillet is found on the capital of the inner order of the Leonideion at Olympia.[108] But Ionic friezes often have no crowning molding and, if they do, the molding is the reverse of the epistyle crown—that is, if an ovolo is used for the frieze, a cyma reversa will be used for the architrave[109]—which is precisely the case on the Propylon.

No dentil blocks exist from the Propylon but actual dentils, snapped off from the blocks themselves, do (Pl. XXVI.4, 5). It is clear that this was a separate course as at the Nereid Monument, the Mausoleum, Priene, and the East Propylaea at Labraunda,[110] unlike the technique on the Philippeion, where the dentils and the geison were combined in a single block.[111] The dentils were virtually square (that is, their height in relation to their depth) as at the Mausoleum and the East Propylaea at Labraunda unlike the oblong shape used at the Temple of Athena at Priene.[112] Inasmuch as no actual dentil blocks exist, it is uncertain what the interval between the dentils was. We have restored seventeen to the central intercolumniation of the building and fifteen to the others (the Philippeion having sixteen; the Propylon of Ptolemy II seventeen).[113]

Normally, the geison and sima courses are separate. On the Propylon, these two courses have been combined into one, to my knowledge for the first time, perhaps because of the small scale of the building (Pls. XXVII-XXXII). The scheme recurs on the early Hellenistic Temple of Zeus at Priene and the third-century building in Samothrace dedicated by a Milesian lady.[114]

108. Post mid-fourth century B.C. Shoe, *op. cit.*, p. 98, pl. XLVIII, 4. The author, referring to the entire profile of this capital, calls it unique.

109. *Ibid.*, p. 170.

110. See Coupel-Demargne, pp. 82 f., pl. 37 and XXXVI; Jeppesen, *Paradeigmata*, pp. 32 f.; Wiegand and Schrader, *op. cit.*, p. 102; *Labraunda*, p. 38, pl. X, fig. 9. Jeppesen, in *Labraunda*, pp. 42 ff., dates the East Propylaea slightly later than the South Propylaea, possibly in the last quarter of the fourth century B.C. Portions of this course on the naiskos at Didyma were also separately made. See Knackfuss, *Didyma*, pp. 114 f., Z.547, 9, 10, pl. 75, pl. 194, F555.

111. Schleif in *Schleif-Zschietzschmann*, p. 38, pl. 9.

112. In a recent article on dentils by Paavo Roos, "Observations on the Internal Proportions of the Ionic Dentil in the Aegean," *RA*, 1976, pp. 103 ff., the author states, p. 110, that the proportions of dentils should never be used as a definitive criterion in dating a building.

According to the definition on pp. 104 f., the squares on his chart (p. 105) mean that a dentil has the same height as its depth—i.e., the dentil of the Propylon should have been a square. But 35, representing our Propylon, is shown as a rectangle inasmuch as it was derived from S, *II*, pl. VIII, 3, where only the elevation is shown and neither on the plate nor in the text, p. 23, is any comment made about the depth of the dentils. Fortunately, Roos' comparisons fit those of the text above, that is, the Mausoleum and East Propylaea at Labraunda, 47 and 44, are shown as squares, and the Temple of Athena at Priene, 9, is oblong.

113. *Schleif-Zschietzschmann*, Atlas, pl. I; *Samothrace*, Vol. 10 forthcoming.

114. Wiegand-Schrader, *op. cit.*, pp. 143 f.; *Samothrace*, Vol. 8, pt. II, forthcoming. For the latter see, for the time being, James R. McCredie, "Samothrace: Preliminary Report on the Campaigns of 1965-1967," *Hesperia*, 37 (1968), p. 208. Kyle M. Phillips, Jr., "Subject and Technique in Hellenistic-Roman Mosaics: A Ganymede Mosaic from Sicily," *The Art Bulletin*, 42 (1960), p. 248, has quoted Lucy T. Shoe, *Profiles of Western Greek Mouldings*, Rome, 1952, p. 27, for proposing the idea that the combining of geison and sima blocks was a Sicilian invention of the third century B.C. The existence of this type of block in fourth-century Samothrace disproves this statement.

This results in a block in which the slope for the roof is provided by the sima rather than the geison, and doubtless established the tradition of flat geison and sloping sima blocks used in Samothrace on the Hieron and the Propylon of Ptolemy II.[115] At Ephesos and Priene, too, the sima blocks of the Temples of Artemis and Athena provide the slope for the roof.[116] At Priene, these blocks were given a similar broad strip across the rear upper surface to receive the lowest tier of stroters. This scheme was later followed on the naiskos at Didyma.[117]

From the fifth century on, both the Doric and Ionic geison soffits terminate in a cyma reversa and, from the fourth century on, it was used for both horizontal and raking geisa.[118] In the fourth century, too, the depth of the cyma reversa is greater than its height and its upper curve is less than its lower—a type of profile that is almost never used thereafter.[119] These criteria apply to the horizontal and raking geisa of the Propylon. Among non-Samothracian buildings, the closest in profile and proportion to the Propylon is the Temple of Athena at Delphi and the Philippeion at Olympia.[120] But the raking geison soffit of the Hieron is still closer because of the taper of the base fillet.[121]

As on the Philippeion, the drip evidently ended in line with the bottom of the cymation[122] and the profile from the drip proper to the cymation is similar to it, if gentler in slope and, in this respect, recalls the geison profile of the Temple of Athena Nike in Athens.[123]

No close parallel exists for the ovolo corona and the base fillet of the sima because of the unique character of this block. The nearest general analogy, however dissimilar the contour, appears on the combined geison-sima blocks of the later Temple of Zeus at Priene[124] and other later Hellenistic buildings because of the use of a similarly combined block.[125] The cyma recta profile of the sima, fully preserved only on the raking sima of the corner block (Pl. XLV.2), is related to the simas of the fourth-century Altar Court and the Hieron in Samothrace but is gentler in profile.[126]

Since the whole scheme of the entablature is new, comparative statistics reporting the proportions of other Ionic entablatures in the classical period, whether on the main-

115. Vol. 3, Pls. LII-LVI. Pending vol. 10, see S,*II*, pl. XLI.

116. Weigand-Schrader, *op. cit.*, p. 104, figs. 68, 72; Armin von Gerkan, "Zum Gebälk des Athenatempels in Priene," p. 169, fig. 2 Mr. D.E.L. Haynes very kindly informs me that the fragmentary sima block from the Artemision in the British Museum implies a block similar in character to the sima blocks from Priene.

117. *Didyma*, p. 118 f., Z.573, 17-18, pl. 78.

118. Shoe, pp. 168 f.

119. *Ibid.*, p. 70.

120. *Ibid.*, pls. XXX, 21 (the Temple of Athena, dated ca. 350 B.C.) and XXXI, 19 (the Philippeion).

121. Vol. 3, Pl. XCVIII.3.

122. All such blocks are broken at this point. For the Philippeion: *Schleif-Zschietzschmann*, Atlas, pl. 7.

123. Shoe, *op. cit.*, p. 160, pl. LXXIV, 30.

124. *Ibid.*, pl. XLII, 5, here called the Temple of Asklepios.

125. E.g., the Sanctuary of the Syrian Gods in Delos, *ibid.*, pl. XLIV, 6. The author points out, p. 165, that in the second century B.C., a cyma recta sima is regularly carved on the same block as the geison and that a fascia sometimes separates the standard ovolo of the geison crown from the cyma recta sima.

126. Vol. 4, Pt. II, pp. 84 f., Pl. XXXVIII, 8; Vol. 3, text I, p. 176, Pl. XCIX.1.

land or in Asia Minor, is neither relevant nor meaningful, inasmuch as one or the other ingredient—either the dentils or the frieze—is always lacking.[127] But consideration of the entablature in terms of the number of its courses, the types of its blocks and moldings, reveals strikingly original features: the concept of including both frieze and dentils in the entablature (that is, of fusing the established traditions of the mainland and of Asia Minor); the design for a combined geison-sima block; and for a series of moldings that are individual and without exact parallel, although within the general vocabulary of the fourth century B.C.

The long lateral sima, present on all sides of this Π-shaped building, save over its two small pedimented wings, is one of its most characteristic and inventive features (figs. 95, 109). Its carved ornament established the basic scheme followed on subsequent Samothracian simas. The character of the decoration on the raking sima, which was not carved but painted is unknown (fig. 52 A). The same scheme of painted decoration on the raking sima and carved rinceaux on the lateral sima was used on both the earlier fourth-century Temple of Asklepios at Epidauros[128] and, slightly later on, on the Temple of Athena Alea at Tegea.[129]

As at the Mausoleum and Priene and also on the Philippeion,[130] the waterspouts did not fall over the columns (Pls. XLVIII, LI).[131] In type, these tranquil, almost sombre lion's head waterspouts (figs. 95-97) are closest to the waterspouts of the Temple of Asklepios at Epidauros (fig. 98 A, B)[132] and, especially, to the lions of the Temple of Zeus at Nemea (fig. 99).[133] The broad, low, slightly arched brows of the lions from the Propylon and Nemea, the shape of their wide, emphatically outlined eyes, their prominent cheek-

127. In any case, Von Gerkan's old comment ("Zum Gebälk des Athenatempels in Priene," p. 175), that buildings of different size have different proportions remains a sensible approach.

128. See Roux, p. 104, pl. 31, figs. 2, 3.

129. Dugas, pl. LI. For the date of this temple, ca. 360 B.C., see below, n. 207.

130. Smith, *op. cit.*, pl. 15; Wiegand-Schrader, *op. cit.*, pp. 104 f. and Schede, p. 31; Schleif-Zschietzschmann, Atlas, pl. 1. F. Krischen, "Ionische Bauten Kleinasiens und der Aufbau des Mausoleums von Halikarnass," *BonnJbb*, 128 (1923), p. 9, insists that on the Mausoleum there is a lion's head waterspout over each column and two between each pair of columns. A. E. Henderson, "The Temple of Diana at Ephesus," *JRIBA*, 40 (1932-33), p. 770, states that the waterspouts on that temple did not fall over the columns. Yet on the model illustrated on p. 771, they do.

131. Save the waterspouts over the front columns of the wings (Pls. XLIX, LI).

132. As Martin Schede, *Antikes Traufleisten-Ornament*, Strasburg, 1909, p. 87, long ago remarked. His date for our sima, pp. 86 ff., in the second quarter of the fourth century B.C. is, however, too early. See below, pp. 143 f. for the date. On the other hand, Franz Willemsen, *Die Löwenkopf-Wasserspeier vom Dach des Zeustempels* (*Olympische Forschungen* IV), Berlin, 1959, pp. 58, 127, dates the waterspouts of the Propylon too late, at the end of the fourth century B.C., because of his (mistaken) view that the ornament of the sima cannot be dated earlier. For illustration and reference to the lions of the Temple at Epidauros, see Willemsen, pp. 58 f., 126, pl. 49.

Unfortunately, it is difficult either to see or photograph the lions in the local museum at Tegea, given their position on the wall. They would be of interest in view of my opinion regarding the architect of the Propylon, for which see below, pp. 144 ff.

133. Bert Hodge Hill and Charles Kaufman Williams II, *The Temple of Zeus at Nemea*, Princeton, 1966, p. 17, fig. 25. For the date, pp. 44 ff. A waterspout from an apparently unidentified building in Knidos is related to the Propylon's lions and probably similar in date. See Iris Cornelia Love, "A Preliminary Report of the Excavations at Knidos, 1970," *AJA*, 76 (1972), pp. 70, 71, fig. 6, pl. 18, fig. 21.

95. Fragmentary lateral sima block I, 424 B, 1. Vienna, Ephesos-Museum.

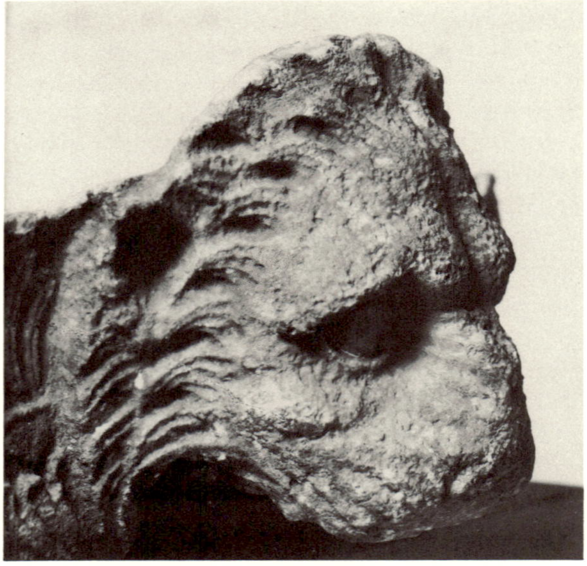

96A, B. Lion's head waterspout from block I, 424 B, 1. Vienna, Ephesos-Museum.

97. Lion's head waterspout 54.203.

98.A, B. Lion's head waterspout from the Temple of Asklepios at Epidauros. Athens, National Archaeological Museum.

99. Lion's head waterspout from the Temple of Zeus at Nemea.

100. Lion's head waterspout from sima block 52.493 of the Hieron in Samothrace.

bones and lean, broad, short muzzles, their broad, blunt noses slashed with rippled flesh, their nostrils, and the shape and ribbing of the double rows of the mane are remarkably similar. Both of these types derive, it seems, from the quiet lions of Epidauros. The peaked ears, adopted, like the ring of mane and the arched brow by the master who designed the sima of the Hieron, are without precise parallel. In general, these lions differ from the dramatic, emotional, boldly stylized waterspouts of the Hieron (fig. 100) and their close relatives on the Tholos at Epidauros.[134]

The waterspouts at the center of each block (fig. 95; Pl. XXVIII.1) emerge from a calyx of two long, low jagged acanthus leaves, their tips seen in perspective, from which grow, on each side of the lion's head a half-palmette of grooved flame petals and a rinceau of tendrils and flowers. The ribbed stalks of the tendrils are subdivided three times by smaller, similarly jagged or toothed acanthus leaves and from these leaves and lesser calyxes spring tendrils, the outermost pair again ribbed, the central one V-shaped in section. The outer tendrils coil in a counterclockwise spring; the inner follow a clockwise rhythm. The outermost tendrils of each block curl into a triple spiral of overlapping loops, again shown in perspective, that terminates in a shooting flower. Between each pair of tendrils a flower of varied form occupies the center of the field. In view of the presence of similar flowers on the anta capital of the Temple of Athena at Priene (figs. 101, 102),[135] on the anta and pilaster capitals of the Temple of Apollo at Didyma,[136] in the border of the Stag Hunt mosaic from Pella (fig. 103),[137] and on innumerable Apulian vases (figs. 110, 111), it is reasonable to assume that these now floating flowers were once provided with painted stems—as the entire sima must surely have been painted.[138] As the corner block in Vienna attests (figs. 52 C, 104),[139] the lateral simas terminated at each end in a half-palmette, that is, the lion has been eliminated from the central motif. One long acanthus leaf and the half-palmette springing from it have been retained and, at this point, the standard triple rhythm of the lateral sima has been reduced to two tendrils because of the atypical length of the corner blocks.[140]

Unlike most simas, which terminate at the top with a low fillet, the sima of the Propylon lacks a crowning border. Instead, the undulating forms of its tendrils and the petals of its half-palmettes define its upper margin as the lions' heads rise pronouncedly above it. This loose, free form is characteristic of a group of Argive simas, having originated

134. Vol. 3, text I, pp. 174 ff., figs. 122-130.

135. Wiegand-Schrader, *op. cit.*, p. 96, fig 64; Schede, *op. cit.*, p. 34, fig. 37.

136. *Didyma*, pl. 106, F207-209; pl. 114, F271, 278; pl. 116, F291; pl. 118, F272, 282; pl. 119, F273, etc.

137. P. M. Petsas, "Mosaics from Pella," *La Mosaique gréco-romaine* (Colloques internationaux du Centre national de la recherche scientifique, Paris, 29 août-3 septembre 1963), Paris, 1964, pp. 49 f., fig. 7.

138. As Schede realized in his discussion of this sima, *Antikes Traufleisten-Ornament*, pp. 83 ff. See Roux, pp. 107 f., on the painted sculptured sima of the Temple of Asklepios at Epidauros. For traces of paint on the sculptured sima of the naiskos at Didyma, see *Didyma, op. cit.*, p. 118.

139. See above, Chap. I, p. 72.

140. At Tegea, too, the corner sima block is atypically long and its ornamental pattern has been adjusted to it. See Dugas, p. 25, pls. XV-XVII, and Roux, p. 106.

101. Drawing of the anta capital of the Temple of Athena at Priene by R. P. Pullan.

102. Fragmentary side of anta capital from the Temple of Athena at Priene. London, The British Museum.

103. Stag Hunt Mosaic from Pella.

104. Side of corner geison-sima block I, 424 A. Vienna, Ephesos-Museum.

toward 370 B.C. on the Temple of Asklepios at Epidauros (fig. 105) and on the contemporary Tholos at Delphi.[141] This Epidaurian scheme is the source, too, of that major innovation in architectural design in the fourth century B.C.—the use of luxuriant rinceaux of acanthus to adorn the sima.[142]

However different in rhythm and composition, a variation of this essentially Argive scheme occurs on the Temple of Athena at Priene (fig. 106).[143] There, the lion's head waterspouts emerge from acanthus calyxes and they are flanked by ribbed acanthus stalks. From each major stalk three lesser ribbed stalks grow, and from their smaller acanthus calyxes three tendrils spring, the outer pair also sprouting a flame half-palmette. Here, too, the tendrils are V-shaped in section. Two of the three tendrils are placed almost vertically and coil toward the lion; the third again coils backward and its half-palmette also turns toward the lion creating a tight, closed composition from block to block. The total effect of each block, with its strong vertical accents differs completely in rhythm and composition from the fluent, horizontal rinceaux of the Epidaurian tradition. But the fact remains that here in Asia Minor, where one would not expect a sima to be adorned with acanthus tendrils, such a type exists.[144]

It was to the normal Epidaurian tradition that the architect of the Propylon turned in designing his sima. He has retained the ribbed acanthus rinceau but expanded what continued to remain the standard two-tendril scheme into a triple-tendril, triple-stalk system, thereby inaugurating the scheme found on subsequent simas in Samothrace.[145] He has also

141. *Ibid.*, pp. 105 f., 328 f. Roux's so-called "chéneau à silhouette" or "tableau decoupé." On p. 414 f., he lists the buildings, including the Temple of Zeus at Nemea, having this variety of sima.

142. *Ibid.*, pp. 106, 328 ff.

143. See Schede, *Antikes Traufleisten-Ornament*, pp. 76 ff., and Martin Schede, "Heiligtümer in Priene," *JdI*, 49 (1934), pp. 100 f., figs. 5, 7, 12.

144. W. R. Lethaby, "The Sculptures of the Later Temple of Artemis at Ephesus," *JHS*, 33 (1913), pp. 94 ff., states that the Priene sima copied the motifs at Ephesos and that fragments of the latter exist in a storeroom of the British Museum. He suggested that this sima might have been derived from Epidauros (the drawing of the Ephesian sima in Josef Durm, *Die Baukunst der Griechen*, 3rd edn., Leipzig, 1910, p. 338, fig. 324a implies that this is true). Regarding this point, see below, n. 208. Krischen, too, "Das Artemision von Ephesos," p. 73, insists that the Temple at Priene corresponds so closely to the forms of the Artemisium that it might be called an exact copy. The previously mentioned sima from Knidos (above, n. 133) also follows the Epidaurian scheme.

Other exceptions come from Xanthos in Lycia. See two sima blocks, one from Temple A, the other from Building E, presumably dating in the second-half of the fourth century B.C., decorated with a normal Argive-type two-tendril rinceau, a flower, and windblown acanthus leaves similar in form to the calyx on the Propylon. Henri Metzger, "Fouilles du Létoon de Xanthos (1962-1965)," *RA*, n.s. 1966, p. 105, fig. 4, and *idem*, "Fouilles de Létoon de Xanthos (1966-1969)," *RA*, n.s., 1970, p. 311, fig. 5, respectively. It should be noted that the sima of the (probably later) Temple at Messa appears to follow the Argive system, with the addition of the terminal half-palmettes found at Priene, although certain of its motifs are hypothetical. Koldewey, pp. 55 f., pl. 21.

145. Roux, p. 331, mentions this Samothracian variation on the basic Peloponnesian type and queries its origin. If, as I shall try to establish, the architect of the Propylon was an eminent artist, this circumstance would be easily understood.

The suggestion made by G. Daux and A. Laumonier, "Fouilles de Thasos (1921-1922)," *BCH*, 47 (1923), p. 320, n. 2, that this form of sima was transmitted from the mainland to the northeastern Aegean via the early third-century Arsinoeion is, of course, incorrect.

Outside Samothrace, the triple-tendril sima has been found only in neighboring Thasos, in the Northwest Stoa and the *Edifice à paraskénia* in the Agora

added to the elongated buds between the tendrils on the Epidaurian sima (fig. 105), two other floral types, one a ragged-petaled blossom, the other a bell-shaped flower seen in perspective like the spiral tendril from which it grows.

Related bell-shaped flowers occur on a fine terracotta sima fragment from Olympia (fig. 107),[146] and are coupled with almost identical, toothed acanthus leaves on the lateral faces of the anta capitals of the South Propylaea at Labraunda, whose lyre-shaped pendant palmettes have already proved closely related to the palmettes on the drum (fig. 85),[147] to cite but a few early examples of a floral motif that became extremely popular in all media in the later fourth and the third centuries B.C.[148] The ragged blossom is also ever present at this time.[149] And all three of the sima's flowers, emanating from a similar toothed acanthus calyx, appear on the lateral face of the anta capital of the Temple of Athena at Priene (figs. 101, 102).[150] Finally, the narrow, foliate band on the epikranitis of the Temple at Tegea (fig. 108) is very analogous, even as a type, to the Propylon's sima.[151] Here, too, there are jagged acanthus leaves, ribbed stalks, tendrils of V-shaped section, and flowers.

The most unusual motif on the Propylon's sima is the spiral tendril at the ends of each block (figs. 95, 109). Seen in perspective[152] and coiling into three diminishing circles, the last of which sends forth a terminal bell-shaped flower, this spiral tendril appears to be the earliest example in monumental art—certainly in sima design—of a motif that gained

---

(Martin, p. 49, pls. 10, fig. 1, 26, fig. 1; and p. 74, pl. 22, fig. 5, respectively) and at Avlakia (*Guide de Thasos*, p. 97, fig. 40). All three are said to be fourth century in date, the Northwest Stoa being dated in the late fourth century B.C. Both the sima of the Northwest Stoa and the sima at Avlakia contain flowers related to those on the Propylon. The seemingly floating flowers of the former are evidence that they were, of course, painted.

146. Ernst Curtius and Friedrich Adler, *Olympia* (II, *Die Baudenkmäler*), Berlin, 1892, p. 199, pl. CXXIII, 2. Dated by R. Borrmann in the second half of the fourth century B.C. It is not known to which building this sima belonged. A similar flower also appears on another fragmentary terracotta sima from Naoussa. See "Chroniques des fouilles en 1965," *BCH*, 90 (1966), p. 870, fig. 12. Evidently a bell flower also appears on the terracotta sima of the Thersilion at Megalopolis (E. A. Gardner *et al.*, *Excavations at Megalopolis 1890-1891* [Society for the Promotion of Hellenic Studies, Supp. Papers, I]), London, 1892, pl. XII, to judge by a poor drawing.

Bell-shaped flowers seen in perspective also occur on antefixes from Olynthos (see D. M. Robinson *et al.*, *Excavations at Olynthos*, II, Baltimore, 1930, pp. 60 f., figs. 163, 164) and early in the fourth century B.C., on grave stelai (e.g., Karouzou, no. 2744, p. 79).

147. *Labraunda*, pl. VII, 8.

148. For random examples, e.g., pilaster capitals from Didyma (*Didyma*, pl. 106, F207-209; pl. 190, F530, 531; pl. 191, F533); a mosaic pavement in Tholos A at Pella ("Chroniques des fouilles en 1965," *BCH*, 90 [1966], pp. 871, 875, fig. 5); and, for the Attic background of this type of flower, see the akroteria on certain grave stelai (Hans Möbius, *Die Ornamente der griechischen Grabstelen klassischer und nachklassischer Zeit*, Berlin, 1929, p. 20, pls. 7b, 10a, 11a, 16b).

149. E.g., on the rear raking sima of the Hieron (Vol. 3, text I, p. 178, fig. 131); on pilaster capitals at the Didymaion (*Didyma*, pl. 106, F207, F209, for example); on the painted frieze on the façade of the Tomb at Vergina (K. A. Rhomaios, Ὁ Μακε*δονικὸς τάφος τῆς βεργίνας* [Μακεδονικὴ *βιβλιοθήκη* 14] Athens, 1951, p. 19, fig. 6, pl. B), to cite but three of many examples.

150. Schede, "Heiligtümer in Priene," p. 98, fig. 1.

151. Dugas, pl. XCIII.

152. Schede, *Antikes Traufleisten-Ornament*, p. 87, stated that only one of the triad of tendrils is shown in perspective, the others being flat. Evidently, he had no opportunity to examine the actual fragments in Vienna or see good photographs of this detail. All three are shown in perspective.

105. Sima and antefixes of the Temple of Asklepios at Epidauros.

106. Restored entablature of the Temple of Athena at Priene. London, The British Museum.

107. Terracotta sima from Olympia.

108. Epikranitis from the Temple of Athena Alea at Tegea.

109. Fragments from the sima of the Propylon I, 424 B, 2-4.
A. Vienna, Ephesos-Museum. B. Samothrace Museum.

110. Detail of an Apulian neck-amphora from Ruvo. Naples, Museo Nazionale.

immense popularity.[153] It reached an exuberant culmination in the spiral tendrils of the jagged acanthus plants that frame the early third-century Stag Hunt pebble mosaic signed by Gnosis at Pella[154]—a border filled with elaborations of the basic forms of the earlier floral motifs (fig. 103).[155] How many other and earlier examples of the use of these motifs in monumental art must have existed we may only speculate from their enormous popularity on Apulian vases of the mid- and second half of the fourth century B.C. Two examples (figs. 110, 111), a neck-amphora in Naples,[156] and a volute krater in Munich[157] must suffice to suggest both the close parallelism between sima decoration and the use of narrow bands of ornament on vases (here, at the top of the neck on the krater and encircling the body of the amphora) and the appearance on such vases of all the basic forms of our sima, including the toothed acanthus.[158] Again, the degree to which such vases reflect architectural ornament is evident if one observes the egg-and-dart and leaf-and-dart patterns below the lip of the Munich krater.[159]

153. The sinuous single-looped floral terminations of the acanthus rinceaux growing in the narrow spandrels between the coffers in the cella of the Tholos at Epidauros may lie in the background of this new ornamental form. Roux, pl. 51, fig. 2.

A fragmentary marble relief (part of a sima block?) walled into the Monastery at Kaisariani shows the tip of a rinceau having two such spiral tendrils. This terminal is freer and still more elaborate than the sima of the Propylon and probably later. It evidently belonged to a piece now in Berlin that Schede, *Antikes Traufleisten-Ornament*, p. 88, dated late in the fourth century B.C.

For two second-century architectural examples, see the frieze of an entablature block found near the lower market in Pergamon (Franz Winter and Jakob Schrammen, *Altertümer von Pergamon*, VII², Berlin, 1908, pp. 382 f., XXX) and the frieze of the actual altar of the Great Altar at Pergamon (*loc. cit.*, III¹, Berlin, 1906, pp. 68, 71, pl. XVIII, fig. 2).

Note, too, the spiral tendrils and flowers on the painted frieze on the façade of the Great Tomb at Lefkadia dated by the excavator at the beginning of the third century B.C. (P. M. Petsas, *Ὁ τάφος τῶν Λευκαδίων*, Athens, 1966, p. 179, pl. *β*, 3; I, 1; 33*β*).

154. Ph. Petsas, "Mosaics from Pella," *La Mosaïque gréco-romaine*, Paris, 1965, pp. 49 f., figs. 7-10.

155. See, also, the related and contemporary pebble mosaic in Room E of the palace at Palatitza (M. Andronikos, Ch. Makaronas, N. Montsopoulos, G. Bakalakis, *Τό ἀνάκτορο τῆς βεργίνας*, Athens, 1961, pp. 21 f., pls. XVI, XVII).

For a second-century B.C. version of spiral tendrils in mosaic technique, note the floral border of the mosaic from the northwest room of Palace V in Pergamon (*Pergamon*, V¹, Berlin, 1930, pp. 63 ff., pls. XVI-XVIII).

156. In the Museo Nazionale (Heydemann 3218). Rocco, *op. cit.*, pp. 182 ff., pl. LXXXIX, 1; Borda, *op. cit.*, pp. 44, 100, fig. 34. Dated in the last quarter of the fourth century B.C.

157. Munich, no. 3297. Otto Jahn, *Beschreibung der Vasensammlung König Ludwigs in der Pinakothek zu München*, Munich, 1854, pp. 273 f., **849**; Furtwängler-Reichhold, II, pp. 139 f., pl. 10; Schmidt, *Der Dareiosmaler*, pp. 22, 38, 40 n. 54, 42, 48 n. 76, 54, 58. Attributed to the Underworld Painter (scene A on this vase) in the workshop of the Dareios Painter and dated ca. 330 B.C.

158. Otto Rubensohn, long ago drew attention to the relationship between our sima and Apulian vases (Rubensohn, p. 141). Schede, too, *Antikes Traufleisten-Ornament*, p. 87, has noted the relationship between the spiral tendril on our sima and South Italian vases, as has Möbius, *op. cit.*, p. 69, remarking, too, that the spiral tendril supposedly never occurs in Attica. But the example now at Kaisariani should alter this conclusion (see n. 153 above). It should be noted that the spiral tendril is not peculiar to South Italian vases. It occurs, for example, on the body of an amphora from Alexandria dating from the last quarter of the fourth century B.C. See Ernst Buschor, *Griechische Vasen*, Munich, 1969, pp. 256 f., fig. 271, who has remarked on its relationship to South Italian vases.

159. See, for example, the sandstone reliefs from Taranto adorned with spiral tendrils seen in perspective, flowers, and acanthus plants, dating from the second half of the fourth century B.C. published by Bernard Neutsch, "Archäologische Grabungen und Funde in Unteritalien 1949-1955," *AA*, 1956, cols. 203 f., fig. 5, 249 f., fig. 38.

111. A-D. Details from an Apulian volute krater. Munich, Staatliche Antikensammlungen.

112. Detail of the sima of the Argive Heraion. Athens, National Archaeological Museum.

Apart from the spiral tendril, the ornamental tradition behind the sima is rooted in Argive architecture of the second quarter and the middle of the fourth century B.C. Even the half-palmettes flanking the lion's head waterspout occurred on the earlier Argive Heraion (fig. 112).[160]

The solitary fragmentary antefix that may be attributed to the original building period of the Propylon (figs. 113, 114)[161] consists of a palmette composed of eleven petals, the central one slightly taller than the others, flanked by five petals that thicken toward their

160. Charles Waldstein, *The Argive Heraeum*, Boston and New York, 1902, I, pp. 117 ff., and Schede, *Antikes Traufleisten-Ornament*, pl. III, 18.

The use of one half-palmette to terminate the motifs of the lateral sima on the corner blocks suggests that a second matching half-palmette occurred at the ends of the painted raking sima. Cf. the similar solution on the Temple of Athena at Priene and the naiskos at Didyma where, however, both the raking and the lateral simas are carved, Schede, "Heiligtümer in Priene," p. 101, fig. 6; *Didyma*, Z.597, pl. 67.

The terracotta sima attributed to the Metroon at Olympia, now possibly to be connected with Pheidias' workshop, also has a pair of half-palmettes as the last motifs of the corner sima block. See *Olympische Forschungen*, 5, pp. 127 f., fig. 43, pl. 52.

161. See above, Chap. I, p. 73. I am greatly indebted to Dr. Kurt Gschwantler of the Antikensammlung for having rediscovered this antefix and for the photograph reproduced as fig. 113. In 1970, when Mr. Spittle and I worked in the storerooms of the Antikensammlung, we were unable to find it. It was associated with the building by Hauser in *S,I*, pp. 49, 76, and illustrated by him on pl. XXXI, fig. II (here fig. 114), and later mentioned and illustrated in *S,II*, pp. 14, 23, pl. X. Preserved height: 0.165 m.; preserved width: 0.102 m.; estimated restored lower width: 0.144 m.

In *S,II*, pl. VIII, fig. III (above, fig. 18), in his partial reconstruction of the entablature of the *Alter Tempel*, Hauser provided this antefix with a nonexistent plinth and placed it on a sima provided, again, with a nonexistent upper moulding, evidently being unaware of the unusual open silhouette of that course.

It is interesting to note that this antefix is related to the antefix belonging to the dedication of Philip III and Alexander IV. See *Hesperia*, 37 (1968), pl. 69d.

113. Antefix I, 423 A. Vienna, Ephesos-Museum.

tips and droop gently. They rise from an arrow-shaped sheath on which traces of a floral element are faintly discernible, in turn supported by a pair of ribbed stalks each provided with a long, overhanging leaf, seen in perspective, from which a tendril coils. Severely weathered like the once ribbed stalks, they were probably once V-shaped.[162] On this particular antefix, at least, the tendrils must have been completed on the sima.

The ribbed stalks on the antefix curl upward from the same calyx on the sima as the ones from which the spiral tendrils hang[163]—a scheme not unrelated to that on the Tholos

162. Alhough it is not visible in Hauser's drawing in *S,I*, pl. XXXI, fig. II, Dr. Gschwantler reports that the stalks of the volutes that support this antefix are, in fact, ribbed. Hauser's drawing also shows two additional petals flanking the central petal that are, again, nonexistent. See fig. 113.

163. Contrary to the statement made by Schede, *Antikes Traufleisten-Ornament*, p. 83, that no connec-

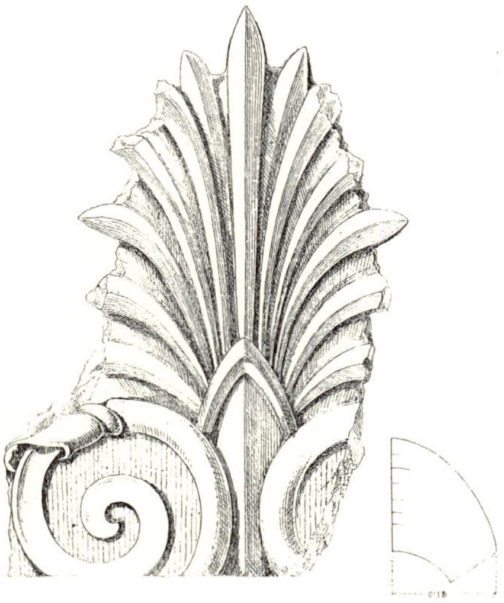

114. Drawing of antefix I, 423 A, by Hauser.

of Delphi (fig. 115),[164] where the tendrils that support the antefix emanate from the subcalyx from which a larger tendril drops. Both the spiral tendrils of the sima and the volute tendrils of the antefix are ribbed. The palmette has thus become a flower growing from the rinceaux of the sima.

This antefix belongs generically to the class of antefixes that are organically related to the sima rather than dissociated from it and made into an independent member by being provided with a plinth—like the antefixes of the Hieron and the Altar Court in Samothrace.[165] But it is neither let into the sima, as at Tegea and Nemea (figs. 116, 117),[166] nor is it an independent palmette-faced kalypter supported by tendrils contained within the sima, as on the Temple of Asklepios at Epidauros and the Tholos at Delphi (figs. 105, 115);[167] nor is it like the palmette antefixes on the Temple of Apollo at Delphi,[168] which consist of abutting half-palmettes issuing from the projecting calyxes of stalks on the sima. It is related to the ridge antefixes of the Temple of Asklepios at Epidauros (fig. 118) and the Temple of Athena Alea at Tegea which are identical in type.[169] Although the style of our antefix differs from the style of these two ridge antefixes, having slender, slightly convex, ridged petals rather than fat, markedly convex ones, the number of the petals is identical, and all three are supported by tendrils that emerge either from acanthus leaves on the actual ridge kalypters or from the sima. However, for a standard antefix as opposed to

---

tion is made between the sima and the antefix. Karl Lehmann was the first to observe the unusual relationship between the antefix and the sima in Vienna in August 1955.

164. *Ibid.*, pp. 54 ff., pl. V, fig. 30.

165. Vol. 3, text I, pp. 180 ff., figs. 134, 135. For a discussion of Samothracian antefixes, see Vol. 4, pt. II, pp. 86 ff., 96 f.

166. Dugas, pp. 24 ff., pls. XLVI, LXXXVI; Hill-Williams, *op. cit.*, pp. 17 ff., pl. XVII.

167. Roux, pl. 34, fig. 1; Schede, *op. cit.*, pl. V, fig. 30.

168. *Ibid.*, pl. 5, fig. 33.

169. Roux, pl. 34, fig. 3; Dugas, *op. cit.*, pl. XLVII.

115. Partial reconstruction of the Tholos of Delphi. Delphi Museum.

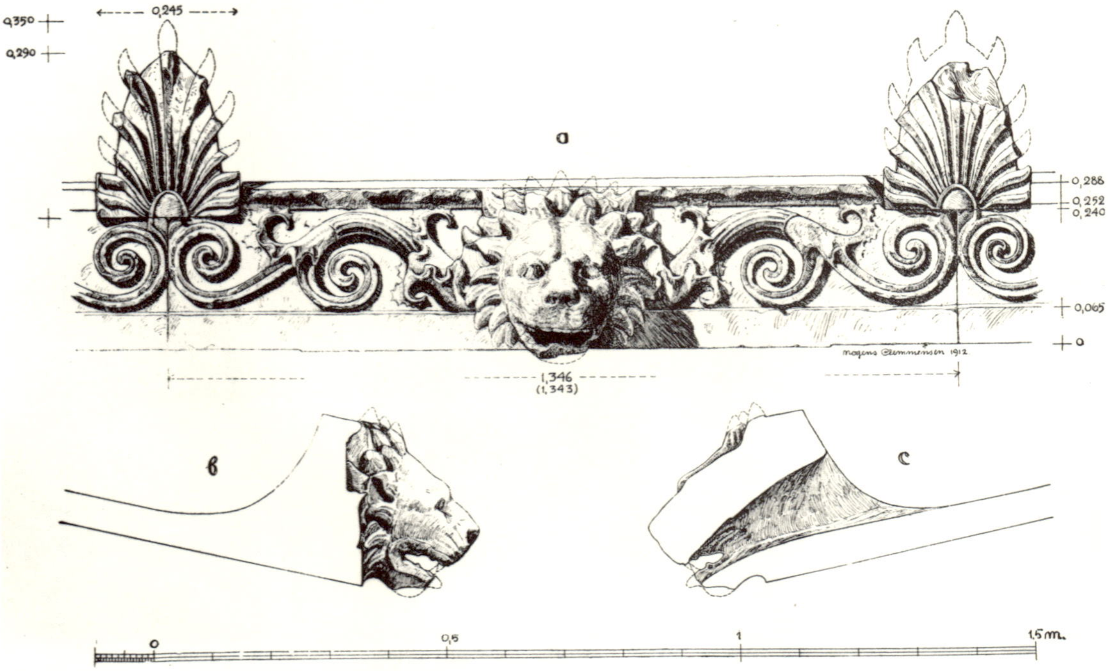

116. Sima and antefixes from the Temple of Athena Alea at Tegea.

117. Sima and antefix from the Temple of Zeus at Nemea. Nemea Museum.

118. Ridge antefix from the Temple of Asklepios at Epidauros.

119. Terracotta antefix 61.186.

a ridge antefix, this type appears to be without parallel. In the number of its petals, and in the form of its volutes, it is not unrelated to the antefix that has been ascribed to the early classical Hieron in Samothrace (fig. 119).[170] That antefix, however, is separated from the sima by a plinth. Discarding the plinth, the architect of the Propylon has intensified the interrelationship between the antefix and the sima, causing the antefix to grow directly from the sima. Thus the crowning elements of the entablature, the antefixes and the sima, are powerfully linked.[171] Doubtless, the use of an open silhouette on the sima rather than a crowning fillet was dictated by the desire to achieve precisely this interrelationship.[172]

The kalypters to which these antefixes belonged were of the Corinthian type (Pl. XXXIII.2), a type used both on the mainland and in Asia Minor.[173] The roof tiles of this

170. Vol. 3, text I, p. 184, fig. 140; text II, pp. 61 f.

171. For additional comment on the interrelationship of the sima and the antefix of the Propylon, see Vol. 4, pt. II, pp. 88 ff.

172. How careful the architect was to interrelate the details of his ornamental design is evident from the fact that the curiously shaped, elongated leaves that overhang the volutes of the antefix reappear on the drum of the column, where the upper volutes emerge from the same kind of elongated leaves.

For the restored ridge antefix, see above, Chap. I, p. 73.

173. E.g., at Tegea and on the Nereid Monument (Dugas, pls. IX, XLVII B, C.; Coupel-Demargne, pls. LXXXV-LXXXVII).

120. Front of corner geison-sima block I, 424 A. Vienna, Ephesos-Museum.

small building were of marble[174]—a practice found, again, both on the mainland and in Asia Minor.[175]

Because of their small scale, the pediments were constructed in such a fashion as to include the tips of the tympanum wall in the corner geison-sima blocks (figs. 52 A, 120; PL. XXXII). A similar structural device was used on the small Temple of Athena Nike in Athens and on the Nereid Monument at Xanthos.[176] Presumably, three additional blocks of ascending height sufficed to complete the tympanum wall—an orthodox solution for a pediment.

With an angle of 14° 30′, the pediment has a pitch of 1:3.9, a proportion close to the classical norm of 1:4[177] and identical with the slope of the late fourth-century cella of the Hieron.[178]

174. See above, Chapter I, pp. 72 f. and Pl. XXVI.1, 2, 3 for fragments of the marble stroters that fit beneath the marble kalypters. The Austrians had found marble kalypters north of the Hieron (*S,I*, p. 10). Inasmuch as the tiles of the Hieron were of terracotta apart from the antefix-kalypters, these tiles probably came from the Propylon.

175. E.g., on the Erechtheum, the Argive Heraion, at Tegea (Paton-Stevens, p. 79, pl. XVII, 2; Waldstein, *op. cit.*, p. 123 f.; Dugas, p. 25); on the Nereid Monument, at Ephesos, and at Sardis (Coupel-Demargne, pl. 62; Smith, *op. cit.*, p. 184, no. 1236; Gruben, "Zum Artemis-tempel von Sardis," p. 174).

It will be recalled that no ridge kalypters were recovered. They have been restored as flame palmettes related to the flame half-palmettes of the sima.

176. A. K. Orlandos, "Nouvelles observations sur la construction du temple d'Athéna Niké," pp. 26 f., fig. 18; Coupel-Demargne, pp. 146 f., pls. XXXVI, LXXIX.

177. For comparative figures, cf. A. K. Orlandos, "Τὸ ἀέτωμα τοῦ ἐν Σουνίῳ ναοῦ τοῦ Ποσειδῶνος," *ArchDelt*, 1 (1915), p. 3, n. 4; and Etiénne Lapalus, *Le Fronton sculpté en Grèce des origines à la fin du IV*[e] *siècle* (Bibliothèque des Ecoles françaises d'Athènes et de Rome, 165), Paris, 1947, pp. 234 f. The classical buildings for which such figures are available range from 1:4.031 to 1:4.210.

178. Vol. 3, text I, p. 188.

The narrow dowel hole in the corner of the corner geison-sima block directly in front of the tympanum wall (fig. 120) indicates that something was attached to that wall—obviously, decoration, whether in the form of another set of thin carved blocks,[179] that is, relief sculpture, or separately applied decoration. Inasmuch as the greatest height of the tympanum wall is less than that of the frieze (0.28 m. as compared with 0.324 m.), it is inconceivable that this decoration was figural. On the contrary, it was doubtless floral, whether its material was of bronze or marble.

There is documentation for this form of pedimental decoration in the same circle of South Italian vases that has afforded other striking analogies to the ornamental features of the Propylon. Such vases have preserved faithful representations of architectural forms not otherwise extant. Note, for example, the pedimental decoration on the fragmentary Gnathian krater discussed above (fig. 59). That a floral, foliate motif must have been used in the pediments of the Propylon is implied, too, by a group of sarcophagi from the royal nekropolis at Sidon, where each lid is in the form of an architectural roof and entablature, and each pediment is occupied by floral and foliate forms.[180] But it will be best to postpone until the next chapter further consideration of the sculptural decoration of the pediments.

The dowel holes and dressing on the upper surface of the corner geison-sima block in Vienna indicate that it bore a lateral akroterion (fig. 52 B). There were, therefore, akroteria on the two pediments. No trace of them has been preserved. Hence, we have restored conventional floral akroteria to the building. Again, it will be best to delay until the next chapter further discussion of such sculptural features.

The marble coffered ceiling rested on marble beams (Pls. XXXIV-XXXVIII, XLVII B), in turn, supported by the architrave. The longer of the two varieties of beams (Pls. XXXIV-XXXVI), those that ran from the colonnade of the porch to the wall of the building, were provided with a sloping projection or spine that fitted into cuttings at the back of the geison-sima blocks, doubtless to strengthen them and counteract strain. This rare system was also used on the Mausoleum[181] and later elaborated for the great pronaos beams of the Late Hellenistic porch of the Hieron.[182]

Double-fascied and crowned by an ovolo moulding beneath a low and above a high fillet, the beams were given profiles and proportions suitable for blocks resting on the inner face of the architrave (Pl. XLIV.2).[183] They were also provided with a paneled soffit—a feature lacking on the architrave. A narrow, shallow panel, it is bordered by a cyma reversa molding similar to the crown of the outer face of the architrave. Such paneled soffits on beams were normally not used on the mainland,[184] but they are a regular feature of Asiatic-

179. See Chap. I, pp. 71 f., for a detailed description of this block and its implications.

180. O. Hamdy Bey and Théodore Reinach, *Une Nécropole royale à Sidon*, Paris, 1892, pp. 48 ff., pl. XL, nos. 4-6. See below, pp. 262 ff.

181. Jeppesen, *Paradeigmata*, p. 31, fig. 18.

182. Vol. 3, text I, pp. 110 f.; pls. LXXVII-LXXX.

183. I know of no precise parallel to these moldings, although an oval ovolo was regularly used on Ionic ceiling beams (see Shoe, p. 176). The curve of the ovolo is not unrelated to the profile of the ceiling beams of the Temple of Athena at Priene (*ibid.*, pl. XXI, 30).

184. An exception being the Temple at Tegea. Dugas, pls. LIII A, LXXXVII B.

Ionic buildings occurring, for example, on the Mausoleum, at Priene, and on the naiskos at Didyma.[185] But the carved moldings customary in this region were omitted on the beams, as they had been in the entablature.[186]

The moldings of the coffers are a variation on those of the beams (Pls. XXXIX, XLVI). Two fascias, the upper again higher than the lower, are crowned by a cyma reversa molding between fillets—the cyma reversa being a characteristic molding on fourth-century coffers.[187] The coffers were provided with a smoothly dressed overhang of varying projection to which their separately worked lids were pinned by small, circular dowels—a system analogous to that used on the Mausoleum.[188] Again, their soffits were cut to produce a simple chamfered panel that frames each field. The invisible upper surfaces of the coffers have been sheared off to reduce weight.

The fragmentarily preserved coffers have been shown to come from three sets of coffers of differing size.[189] The smaller two are square, the largest rectangular (Pl. XLVII B). The latter belonged to the intercolumniation preceding the central door, the smallest to the four remaining intercolumniations of the porch proper, the intermediate size to the projecting wings of the building. Thus each section of the building—its wider central intercolumniation and main doorway, the remaining bays of the porch, and the wings—was given its own articulation in the design of the ceiling.

The use of multiple coffers in a single intercolumination was the norm on the mainland and is also found in Asia Minor.[190] Normally, too, coffers are square in a given building or portion of a building, whether they are of uniform size or of several sizes.[191] But on the Mnesiklean Propylaea, the differing sizes of the spaces roofed are reflected in the use of both square and rectangular coffers.[192] The unusual aspect of the Propylon's coffering is

185. Newton, *A History of Discoveries*, pl. 27; Wiegand-Schrader, *op. cit.*, p. 109; Knackfuss, *Didyma*, p. 111 f., Z.538, 18, 19, pl. 74. Paneled soffits were also used on the beams of the late Hellenistic porch of the Hieron (Vol. 3, *loc. cit.*).

186. See above, p. 118.

187. Shoe, p. 177.

188. Jeppesen, *Paradeigmata, loc. cit.*

189. Above, Chap. I, pp. 75 f.

190. E.g., on the Nereid Monument and at Didyma. Two notable exceptions being the Mausoleum and the Temple of Athena at Priene with their single coffers per intercolumniation. See Krischen, "Ionische Bauten Kleinasiens," pp. 13 ff., figs. 4, 5, pl. 1, and Von Gerkan, "Zum Gebälk des Athenatempels in Priene," p. 170, fig. 2. Nothing seems to be known about the ceiling of the Temple of Artemis at Ephesos. But Krischen, "Das Artemision von Ephesos," pl. 3, appears to have restored the ceiling with single coffers per intercolumniation—doubtless on the basis of the Mausoleum and Priene.

191. On the Nereid Monument, there are square coffers of three sizes. Coupel-Demargne, pp. 93, pls. XXXVIII-XLII.

192. Charles Picard, *L'Acropole*, Paris, n.d., pl. 52. To a limited extent, this is true of the Mausoleum, where the coffers are oblong except for the square corner fields. Krischen, "Ionische Bauten Kleinasiens," *loc. cit.*

On the Hephaisteion, the number of the coffers differs in the two porches and in the lateral colonnades. See Herbert Koch, *Studien zum Theseustempel in Athen* (*Abhandlungen der sächsischen Akademie der Wissenschaften zu Leipzig*, Phil.-hist. Klasse, 47, pt. 2), Berlin, 1955, pp. 62 ff., figs. 49, 57, pl. 42.

On the Antonine gate to the South Market at Miletos, four different sizes and shapes, both square and rectangular, were used for the coffers (Knackfuss, *Der Südmarkt*, fig. 99). A closer analogy with the system on the Propylon is offered by the porch of the third-century A.D. Serapeion at Miletos, where the coffers before the door are rectangular, the others square (*ibid.*, pp. 197 ff., fig. 213).

the presence of varied sizes and shapes of coffers within one architectural unit.[193] Doubtless, this diversity of size and shape also reflects the decorative system of the ceiling, a matter that will be considered in the following chapter.

The coffers were all provided with separately made lids, although the only extant lids come from the smallest of the coffers, those occupying four of the five bays of the porch proper (figs. 125-131; Pl. XL). This technique was especially convenient when, as here, the lids were sculptured, but it was not restricted to this form of lid.[194]

The earliest sculptured coffer lids come from the Mausoleum (fig. 123),[195] and Pytheos probably also planned to use them on the Temple of Athena at Priene.[196] In each case, these lids were carved with figural scenes. Still earlier in the fourth century, the wooden coffered ceiling of the Temple of Asklepios at Epidauros was decorated with either painted or applied metal πρόσωπα (faces or countenances), as the building inscriptions for the temple attest,[197] and painted heads also adorned the marble coffers of the

193. In its variety of size and shape, the coffered ceiling of the Propylon seems to be without parallel before the second-century porch-pronaos ceiling of the Hieron which was obviously dependent upon it (*Samothrace*, Vol. 3, text I, pp. 232 ff., 245 f., Pls. LXXXI-LXXXV).

194. Separate lids of this unsculptured variety occur, e.g., on the Hephaisteion; those conjectured for the Temple of the Athenians at Delos; on the naiskos at Didyma, among others (Koch, *op. cit.*, fig. 50, pls. 14, 15; Fernand Courby, *Les Temples d'Apollon* [*Délos*, XII], p. 139; *Didyma*, p. 112, Z.538, 23 ff., pl. 74, Z.561, pl. 76 respectively).

195. For description of these fragmentary reliefs in the British Museum, see A. H. Smith, *op. cit.*, vol. II, pp. 121 f., nos. 1038-42. The partially restored coffer illustrated below in fig. 123 is reproduced from an address by A. S. Murray, "The Mausoleum at Halikarnassos," *Transactions of the Glasgow Archaeological Society*, n.s., 2 (1894), p. 296, pl. 3.

196. The reliefs in the British Museum (Smith, *op. cit.*, pp. 156 f., nos. 1165-76), later attributed to the great altar before the temple, were convincingly re-identified as coffer lids by C. Praschniker, "Die Gigantomachie-Reliefs von Priene," *ÖJh*, 30 (1936/37), pp. 45-49. (It is astonishing that in the revised edition of Martin Schede, *Die Ruinen von Priene* by G. Kleiner and W. Kleiss, Berlin, 1964, these sculptures still appear on the base of the altar: p. 37 and figs. 33, 45-47.) See also H. Riemann, *s.v. Pytheos*, *RE*, XXIV, cols. 487 ff. Inasmuch as Pytheos had used sculptured coffers on the Mausoleum, it is more than likely that the Gigantomachy and Amazonomachy carved on the coffered ceiling of the peristasis of the Temple at Priene had been projected in his original fourth-century plan, whenever the temple was actually completed. Further fragments of these sculptured lids have recently been recovered: see Bauer, "Beobachtungen am Athenatempel in Priene" (above, n. 61), p. 124, figs. 15-16. It has recently been proposed that these coffers antedate the frieze of the Great Altar at Pergamon—which for nearly a century they had been thought to postdate—and conceivably were executed in the third century B.C. For this proposal and detailed bibliography on these coffers, see Joseph C. Carter, "The Date of the Sculptured Coffer Lids from the Temple of Athena Polias at Priene," *Studies in Classical Art and Archaeology*, Locust Valley, N.Y., 1979, pp. 139-151.

For Pytheos, in general, see Riemann, *op. cit.*, cols. 371-513, and for his role at Halikarnassos and Priene, in particular, G. Kleiner, *s.v. Priene*, *RE*, supplement vol. IX, Stuttgart, 1962, col. 1193.

197. Alison Burford, *The Greek Temple Builders at Epidauros*, Toronto, 1969, pp. 57, 214 f., A I, 54-57, 65-66, B I, 74-76, 82-84, p. 219, B II, 202, 270 ff.; Roux, pp. 127 f., 170. Burford, pp. 57, 202 assumes that the πρόσωπα καλυμμάτων of this wooden ceiling were "gorgons, lions or something of the kind" and painted. In view of the extant monumental evidence, I agree with Roux that these πρόσωπα were more likely divine or human faces, and that the coffer decorations were attachments made of gilded metal. They were of two, possibly three, types—heads, rosettes or stars, and, conceivably, acanthus plants, although A, 49-50, may refer to the sima.

Nereid Monument at Xanthos (fig. 121).[198] But the coffers of the Propylon provide the earliest example of *sculptured* heads—a motif that was to become popular in the ceiling decoration of later centuries. Nor is this surprising in view of the richness of the building's sculptural ornament. Shown full-face, in profile, and in three-quarter view (figs. 125-131), these heads occupy virtually the entire square field and each field was framed by a narrow, flat border. Like other ornamental details of the building, these heads and their backgrounds must have been painted or picked out with color.[199]

In construction and design, the ceiling of the Propylon reflects architectural practice common to both the mainland and Asia Minor. But its ornamental features—its paneled beam soffits and sculptured coffer lids decorated with heads—reveal knowledge of Ionic buildings in Asia Minor and, very likely, of the Temple of Asklepios at Epidauros.

Invisible above the marble coffered ceiling were the timbers of the roof (Pls. XLIX, L). They are implied, as has been shown,[200] by the shape of the geison-sima blocks which housed beams, rafters, and boarding. A ridge pole and short kingposts were probably also employed. Although the span of the Propylon's roof was small, unlike the mighty span of the Hieron's roof, the principle of the truss has again been used in this somewhat earlier building.[201] It suggests the likelihood that the truss had already been used in the forebears of the Hieron and that this form of roof was a traditional one in Samothrace.

Certain features of the Propylon imply a knowledge of Athenian architecture of the later fifth and early fourth centuries B.C.: all the ingredients of the plan; elements of the bolster and necking design; the dentil-less Ionic entablature provided with a sculptured frieze, in particular.

Others are dependent on non-Attic, Peloponnesian or Argive-Epidaurian practice of the second and third quarters of the fourth century B.C.: low, recessed steps; the type and basic ornamental system of the sima and antefix, as well as the style of the waterspouts.

Still others reflect the traditions and forms of Ionic architecture in Asia Minor, indicating knowledge, it would seem, of the Mausoleum, the Temple of Athena at Priene, the dedications of Idrieus at Labraunda in the mid-fourth century and the immediately succeeding years, of the late archaic Temple of Hera at Samos, and, possibly, of a building like the Nereid Monument, if not the monument itself—knowledge of the Asiatic-Ionic

198. One is preserved in the British Museum: Smith, *op. cit.*, no. 934 (3). Almost all the details shown in the drawing of this coffer published by J. Six, "Pausias," *JdI*, 20 (1905), p. 157, fig. 3, are still discernible, as I had an opportunity to see in January 1971 (see the photograph, fig. 121). I do not, therefore, agree with the skeptical phrasing of Coupel-Demargne, p. 94, that this three-quarter-view head is no longer visible. For description of the ceiling system, see *ibid.*, pp. 93 ff., and for illustration of the painted floral patterns decorating other lids, fig. 1.

199. See Chap. III, pp. 148 ff., for discussion of the sculptures themselves, for further discussion of the tradition behind the use of heads to decorate coffers, for the other motifs presumably present in the ceiling, and for the formal arrangement of the coffers within the entire ceiling.

200. See above, p. 72.

201. See Vol. 3, text I, pp. 78 f., 198 ff., for discussion of the roof of the Hieron and the use of the truss.

entablature, of bolster and drum-necking design, of details such as the treatment of beam soffits.

Apart from the sources of the plan and the character of the steps and sima, which are either without parallel in Asia Minor or, if present there, in incipient form that clearly reflects Peloponnesian influence, the majority of the forms of the Propylon reveal a conscious fusion of mainland and Asiatic elements: for example, the order, with its twenty-four flutes common to Attica and Asia Minor, or the modification of Asiatic forms through the influence of Attic monuments evident in the design of the bolster and necking ornament; the fusion of Argive and Asiatic practice in the motif and design of the coffered ceiling; and, most striking and important of all, the fusion of the long-established mainland and Asiatic entablatures.

This knowledge of widely varying regional practices and traditions has allowed the architect of the Propylon to design a building of the utmost originality. He has produced a propylon unique among propylaea in its ground plan, an order also without exact parallel. He has devised a new form of Ionic entablature destined to become a standard formula in later architecture; he has established a type of ceiling decoration that persisted for centuries; and he has created architectural sculpture of remarkable originality, as we shall see. For however possible it has proved to detect the sources of his architectural style, to become aware of the special impact that certain buildings appear to have made upon him, his work is not eclectic in the normal sense of the word, but the product of what must have been an artist of exceptional capacity to respond to new visual experiences, to absorb them into his creative imagination, and to transmute them into new, highly individual artistic forms.

This building, the first of a long line of remarkable and atypical buildings donated to the Sanctuary by a series of royal benefactors,[202] the first marble building to be constructed in the Sanctuary, betrays no sign of drawing on local architectural tradition. Only in the all-important realm of ritual installation, in the retention of the eschara and bothros from the previous period in the enclosure and of the open precinct itself, is there a firm link with earlier Samothracian tradition. Strictly architecturally, the propylon is the work of an outsider, a man familiar with an exceptional range of Greek architecture and sculpture on the mainland and in Asia Minor. His use of the fullest range of architectural sculpture possible on this building, in particular his coupling of the sculptured frieze of the mainland with Asiatic forms, imply an unusual interest in sculpture. Was he one of the architect-sculptors of the fourth century B.C.?

Apart from our architect's obvious knowledge and use of Attic models of the later fifth century B.C. and doubtless, too, of older structures in Asia Minor, his stylistic and technical connections link him with a group of buildings dating between ca. 370 and 330

202. The Altar Court, a dedication of Arrhidaios before he succeeded to Alexander the Great's throne; the Hieron, possibly another dedication of Arrhidaios (see Vol. 3, text II, pp. 74 f.); another Doric building dedicated by Arrhidaios as Philip III, co-ruler with the infant Alexander IV; the Rotunda of Arsinoe; and the Propylon of Ptolemy II.

B.C. They range from the Temple of Asklepios at Epidauros (ca. 370 B.C.), the Philippeion at Olympia (ca. 338 B.C.), and the Temple of Zeus at Nemea (ca. 330 B.C.) on the mainland to, in Asia Minor, the Mausoleum at Halikarnassos (begun in 353 B.C.), the Temple of Athena at Priene (finished ca. 330 B.C.), and the dedications of Idrieus at Labraunda (351-344 B.C.), to cite only the most precisely datable monuments.

It seems reasonable to conclude that the Propylon was built in the second half of this broad period—that is, within the decades 350-330 B.C. or, preferably, soon after the buildings commissioned by Maussollos and Idrieus, and certainly no later than the Temple at Nemea.[203]

The testimony of the ceramic material found in the relevant fills of the Temenos and the terrace confirms this date, since none of the easily datable Attic plain ware is later than the third quarter of the fourth century.[204] As we shall see, the sculptures of the coffered ceiling, to leave aside the unorthodox frieze, again confirm this general conclusion based on architectural comparisons only.[205]

Can this date be made more precise? Are there historical circumstances that help to define it?

It is evident from the previous analysis that the architect of the Propylon was a man who must have been acquainted with the architecture of the mid-fourth century B.C. and the following decade or so, both on the mainland and in Asia Minor. Either he was a native of Asia Minor, trained in its Asiatic-Ionic traditions, who modified them in both large and small respects through his knowledge of contemporary architecture found on the mainland, or he was a man who, wherever he was born, had lived and worked on the mainland, both in the Peloponnesos and in Athens, as well as in Asia Minor. No historical personality is known who fits the former alternative. But an historical personality does exist whose activity and career coincide exactly with the latter alternative, who is known to have worked at or near every building or site with which the Propylon has tangible connections: Skopas of Paros.[206]

As a sculptor, Skopas is known to have executed commissions for Megara, Sikyon, and Argos (hence he can hardly have been unfamiliar with the Temple at Epidauros), for Elis, Gortyn in Arcadia, Thebes, and Athens—quite apart from having served as architect-

203. Architectural detail reflected on Apulian vases dated 350-330 B.C. confirms this date, as we have seen.

204. Cf. the Catalogue, **83-107**. Actually, only five sherds date in this quarter of the century, the remainder dating no later than the mid-century. It is, of course, impossible to date plain ware to the decade within a specific quarter century. Two fragments of late Hellenistic conical bowls were found in the extensive fill of the precinct and the terrace. Inasmuch as they both had marble pavements, it is reasonable to assume that these potsherds come from a repair to the pavement.

205. See Chapter III, pp. 170 ff.

206. For Skopas' career and the ancient sources documenting his activity, see Margarete Bieber, *s.v. Skopas* in Thieme-Becker, vol. 31, Leipzig, 1937, pp. 115-19; Paolo Enrico Arias, *Skopas* (*Quaderni e guide di archeologia*, I), Rome, 1952, and *idem*, "Skopas," *Enciclopedia dell'arte antica, classica e orientale*, Rome, 1966, VII, pp. 364-369; Bernard Ashmole, "Skopas," *Encyclopedia of World Art*, XIII, New York, Toronto, London, 1967, cols. 57-62; and the recent excellent volume of Andrew F. Stewart, *Skopas of Paros*, Park Ridge, New Jersey, 1977.

sculptor of another highly original building, the Temple of Athena Alea at Tegea.[207] He is known to have worked with his compatriot, Satyros, on the Mausoleum at Halikarnassos, along with Pytheos, architect, too, of the Temple of Athena at Priene[208] (thus he can hardly have been unfamiliar with the dedications at Labraunda erected by Maussollos' successor, Idrieus), as well as elsewhere in Anatolia, at Ephesos, at Knidos, and, to the north, in the Troad. Around 350 B.C., he was working at Halikarnassos.

What is more, we know from the Elder Pliny that Skopas created for the Samothracian Sanctuary a celebrated group of Aphrodite and Pothos which was worshiped with the

207. Pausanias 8.45.5 reports that Skopas was the architect at Tegea without attributing to him the temple's sculptures. But the fact that he was one of the most celebrated sculptors of the fourth century and that the style of the Tegea sculptures corresponds precisely with the style of the other sculptures that have been attributed to him makes it reasonable to assume that he served both as architect and designing sculptor at Tegea, whether or not he personally executed its figures—indeed, any discussion of Skopas' sculptural style must rest primarily on his work at Tegea. For this accepted position see, recently, Ashmole, col. 58, and Stewart, p. 3.

I agree with, among others, Bieber, *op. cit.*, p. 115, Shoe, *passim*, Roux, pp. 404, 413, 415, 417, and Stewart, pp. 68 f., in dating the completion of the Temple at Tegea ca. 360 B.C., that is, before the Mausoleum. Andreas Linfert, *Von Polyklet zu Lysipp. Polyklets Schule und ihr Verhaltnis zu Skopas von Paros*, Giessen, 1966, pp. 29, 44, assumes that work on the Temple began after 370/69 and that by that time sketches or models for the sculptures may have been available, although the actual period of construction may have been a lengthy one (for further discussion of this issue, see Chap. III, pp. 170 ff.). Ernst Pfuhl, "Bemerkungen zur Kunst des vierten Jahrhunderts," *JdI*, 43 (1928), p. 31, Dinsmoor, p. 220, Ernst Buschor, *Maussollos und Alexander*, Munich, 1950, pp. 11 ff., 18 ff., 46, Charles Picard, *Manuel d'archéologie grecque, La sculpture*, Paris, 1954, IV, 1, pp. 75 f., Arias, pp. 116 f., and most recently Steven Lattimore, "Two Statues of Herakles," *The J. Paul Getty Museum Journal*, 2 (1975), p. 17, n. 8, among others, date the Temple after the Mausoleum largely because a votive relief found near the Temple and now in the British Museum shows Idrieus and Ada, the successors of Maussollos and Artemisia, honoring Zeus Stratios, on the assumption that the dedicator was a person who had earlier worked with Skopas on the Mausoleum before he undertook his work at Tegea. As Karl Lehmann has pointed out in Vol. 4, pt. II, p. 74, n. 57, one can as easily assume that the dedicator was an Arcadian craftsman who had assisted Skopas at Tegea and whom the latter took with him to work on the Mausoleum, and that, after his safe return from Anatolia, he dedicated this relief in his native land. Martin Robertson (I, p. 458) and Stewart (p. 68) have made the same comment. In any case, it makes far more sense to assume that Skopas, among other eminent sculptors and architects, was called to work on the Mausoleum and elsewhere in Asia Minor after he had established a personal reputation as an architect-sculptor.

In dating the Temple at Tegea mid-fourth century, Alzinger, *op. cit.*, p. 120, and Willemsen, *op. cit.*, p. 49, do not seem to have taken a stand on this issue. Recently, Stewart (pp. 81 f.) has suggested that during his years in Asia Minor, Skopas may have returned to Tegea at intervals to check on work there, possibly, too, to supervise the architectural sculpture, and ultimately to carve the cult statues.

The relationship between the temples at Tegea and Nemea is marked. In fact on April 17, 1957, Bert Hodge Hill remarked to my husband and me that he considered the Temple at Nemea to be the work of a pupil of Skopas, post-Tegea in date, and built by local workmen, including some of the same workmen who had earlier worked at Tegea. This is not the position that Williams himself ultimately adopted (*op. cit.*, p. 19).

208. Schrader in Wiegand-Schrader, *op. cit.*, p. 104, has pointed out the relationship between the simas at Tegea and Priene. There is also the evident fact that the sima at Priene was dependent on that at Ephesos (see above, n. 144). One wonders whether it was via Skopas that this Argive form of sima decoration was introduced into these two major temples. Was it also through the agency of Skopas that Pytheos adopted a bolster pattern on the Mausoleum and at Priene related in scheme to that on the Mnesiklean Propylaea?

most sacred ceremonies.[209] In fact, it is the first work of Skopas mentioned by Pliny in his thumbnail sketch of the master.

The professional itinerary of Skopas, then, is in complete accord with the suggestion that he was the architect-sculptor responsible for the design of the Propylon.

Little opportunity is afforded for comparison between an Ionic propylon and Skopas' only documented architectural work, the Doric Temple of Athena Alea at Tegea. Yet they do share certain technical and stylistic features: the use of recessed steps; of paneled soffits on the beams; comparable details on the sima of the Propylon and the inner epikranitis at Tegea;[210] the presence of a carved lateral sima but a painted raking sima; the basic design of the antefix of the former and the ridge antefix of the latter; the use of marble roof tiles. That is, no architectural feature of the Temple at Tegea precludes attribution to Skopas of the Propylon. When one turns from architecture to sculpture, it is precisely with the sparsely preserved pedimental sculptures from Tegea that a telltale coffer lid of the Propylon offers striking confirmation of this suggestion.[211]

That Skopas, trained in the Doric traditions of the Peloponnesos, familiar with the Ionic buildings on the Akropolis of Athens, famous enough to be called to Asia Minor to participate in a number of prime undertakings, and encountering there the overwhelming Asiatic-Ionic tradition, would be moved to adopt basic features of that tradition when designing an Ionic building is easily imagined. That he would bring to this task an artistic point of view conditioned by his Athenian experience and by the desire or need to incorporate in this building a sculptured frieze, thereby joining the tradition of the mainland with that of Asia Minor, is an entirely credible hypothesis. Sculptor as well as architect, he created a building exceptional in the richness and originality of its sculptured decoration.

In sum, all that is known of Skopas' activity permits the hypothetical attribution to him of the design for the Propylon. Confirmation of this hypothesis must derive from the style of the sculptures of that building,[212] and from the historical fact that Skopas worked in Samothrace.

209. *Naturalis historia* 36.5.25: *Is fecit Venerem et Pothon qui Samothrace sanctissimis caerimoniis coluntur.* "He [Skopas] made the [statues of] Venus and Pothos that are worshiped at Samothrace with the most sacred ceremonies." (The translation of Naphtali Lewis, *Samothrace*, Vol. 1, no. **160**. I question whether [statues of] might be [group of].)

For further discussion of this group, see Chap. IV, pp. 276 ff.

210. A point acknowledged by Stewart, p. 171, n. 40. I do not agree with certain of the author's own architectural comparisons for the Propylon on pp. 107 f. However, acquainted only with the earlier, brief study, *Skopas in Samothrace*, he has emphasized its provisional character and reserved judgment on my attribution of the architecture of the building to Skopas until the publication of the present volume. For his acceptance of Skopas' role in its coffered ceiling, see below, p. 170, n. 49.

Roux, pp. 365 ff., has pointed out that the definitive form of the Corinthian capital at Tegea, especially the naturalistic character of its leafy forms and cauliculi, is Skopas' creation. Luxuriant plant forms are the common denominator between the capitals at Tegea and the sima of the Propylon.

See Pfuhl, *op. cit.*, pp. 27 ff., for an interesting analysis and appreciation of the design of the interior of the Temple as well as for an effort to link Skopas' architectural and sculptural styles.

211. See below, Chap. III, p. 170.

212. *Ibid.*, pp. 170 ff.

The further suggestion that the Propylon was built ca. 340 B.C. as a donation to the Samothracian gods by Philip II of Macedon must, again, await consideration of Philip's well-known interest in the Samothracian Sanctuary.[213]

213. See below, Chap. IV, pp. 273 ff. On the extraordinary assumption that the well-known anta capital carved with a relief of griffons devouring a stag belonged to *this* Propylon, Voigtländer, *op. cit.*, pp. 56 f., has pronounced that the building dates from early in the third century B.C. and was added to the earlier Temenos. Although the fourth edition of the *Guide*, where on pp. 106, fig. 48, this anta capital is stated to belong to the Propylon of Ptolemy II was not available to the author, at no time has it been suggested in print that this anta capital belonged to the Propylon to the Temenos.

III. The Sculptures of the Propylon

THE extant sculptures of the Propylon come from its coffered ceiling and its frieze. But there is evidence that its pediments were sculptured and that they were crowned by akroteria.

THE COFFERED CEILING

The ceiling of the Propylon has been shown to be composed of three sets of coffers of differing size.[1] The smaller two are square, the largest rectangular (Pl. XLVII B). The extant sculptures are fragmentary lids that belonged to the smallest variety, four of the five bays of the porch proper.

Inasmuch as these lids are carved with heads, it is unlikely that the other two varieties—the four large coffers before the central door and the coffers in the wings—were figural. Larger scale heads in the two other categories would have been inharmonious and painful. Nor would figural compositions have been preferable. In all probability, the coffers of the central bay and the wings were nonfigural, whether floral or foliate in design, especially in view of the character of the ornamental drums and the sima.[2]

Earlier in the century, the painted coffers of the Nereid Monument at Xanthos in Lycia included both heads and floral forms (figs. 121, 122),[3] and the building inscriptions

1. For reconstruction and description of the ceiling, see above, pp. 75 f.

2. Roux, p. 128, too, assumed that the nonfigural coffers in the Temple of Asklepios at Epidauros were larger than the coffers decorated with πρόσωπα.

It is worth recalling that sculptured coffers in the late Hellenistic porch of the Hieron were also both figural and nonfigural, and that they, too, differed in size, although in this later monument, it was the nonfigural reliefs that were the smaller. See *Samothrace*, Vol. 3, text I, pp. 237-244, pls. LXXXI-LXXXV.

3. For the Nereid Monument, see above, Chap. II, nn. 190, 191, 198. For its date, Chap. II, n. 50.

According to Pliny, *Naturalis historia* 35.40. 124, Pausias of Sikyon first introduced the painting of coffers: *idem et lacunaria primus pingere instituit, nec cameras ante eum taliter adornari mos fuit.* His precise date is disputed. Cf. J. Six, "Pausias," *JdI*, 20 (1905), pp. 155 ff. (377-368 B.C.); P. Cavvadias, "La Tholos d'Epidaure et le peintre Pausias," *Mélanges Nicole*, Geneva, 1905, p. 613 (toward the middle of the fourth century B.C.); G. Lippold, *RE*, XVIII, Stuttgart, 1949, cols. 2417 ff., *s.v. Pausias* (*ca.* 372-360 B.C.); Roux, p. 128 (*ca.* 370 B.C.). It is not inconceivable that this "invention" antedated the Nereid Monument.

121. Painted coffer from the Nereid Monument at Xanthos. London, The British Museum.

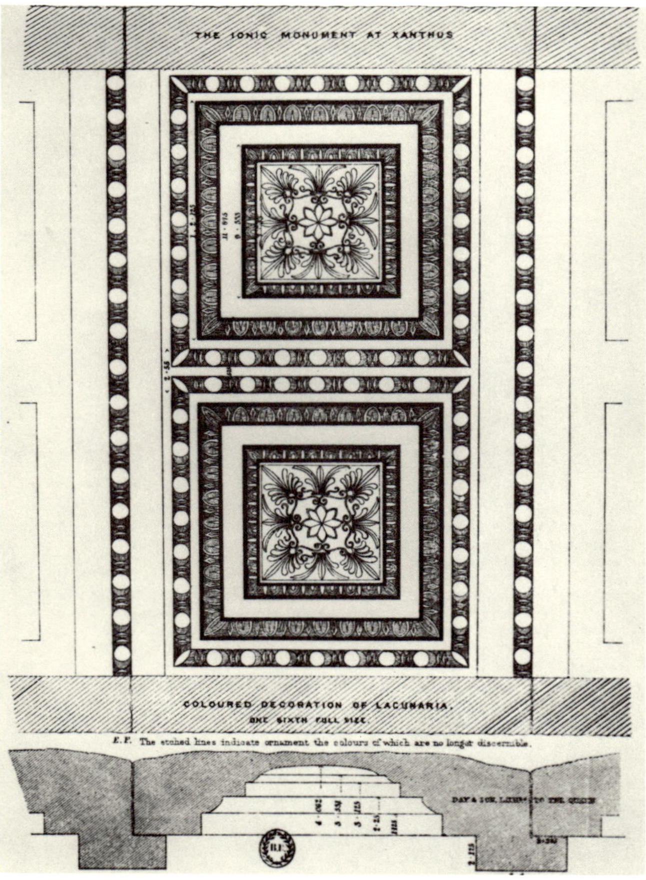

122. Painted coffers from the Nereid Monument at Xanthos.

123. Fragmentary coffer from the Mausoleum at Halikarnassos.

124. Fragmentary coffer lid from the Temple of Athena at Priene, no. 1171. London, The British Museum.

for the Temple of Asklepios at Epidauros indicate that πρόσωπα, 'faces or countenances, were combined with stars or rosettes and, possibly, acanthus plants in the wooden coffers of the temple, all three varieties evidently in the form of gilded metal attachments.[4] The use of three sizes of coffers in the Propylon and the likelihood that three different motifs were employed to decorate them emphasized the clear articulation in the design of the ceiling into three units: the central intercolumniation and main door, the remaining bays of the porch proper, and the wings.[5]

The earliest sculptured coffer lids come from the Mausoleum at Halikarnassos, as we have seen,[6] where Skopas is known to have worked,[7] and Pytheos probably intended to use them for the peristasis of the Temple of Athena at Priene.[8] But the coffers of both these monuments were decorated with mythological scenes, the latter, with a Gigantomachy (figs. 123, 124).

On the contrary, the coffers of the Propylon were carved with heads, and appear to reflect the architect-sculptor's fusion of Peloponnesian and Ionic tradition in the first half of the fourth century B.C. The extant fragments belong to seven lids, three in Vienna and four in Samothrace.[9]

The Vienna pieces include:

C(V)1. Inv. No. I, 676. Ephesos-Museum. (Fig. 125.)
S,I, pp. 11, 28, pl. 51, right; *S,II*, p. 68, n. 1; Heinrich Heydemann, "Marmorkopf Riccardi," *Dreizehntes Hallisches Winckelmannsprogramm*, Halle, 1888, p. 12; Otto Kern, "Die boiothischen Kabiren," *Hermes*, 25 (1890), p. 13 and n. 2; Rubensohn, p. 141; Otto Kern, *RE*, *s.v. Kabeiros und Kabeiroi*, X, col. 1426; Pettazzoni, p. 87; Arnold Schober, "Der neue Tempel von Samothrake," *ÖJh*, 29 (1935), p. 14; Chapouthier, pp. 177 f., fig. 18; *Hesperia*, 20 (1951), p. 16; *Skopas in Samothrace*, pp. 9, 28, n. 56, fig. 34; Stewart, pp. 107, 171, n. 38; *Funde aus Ephesos und Samothrake*, Vienna, 1978, no. 219.

Fragmentary coffer lid broken on all sides. Head of a bearded man seen full-face. Hair parted in the center and falling in waves on each side of the skull until it merges with a

4. For discussion of these coffers, see above, Chap. II, nn. 197, 198.

5. In connection with the specific character of these nonfigural, ornamental designs, the acanthus rinceaux in the triangular fields separating the floral coffers in the cella ceiling of the Tholos of Epidauros are of interest. See Roux, pl. 51, figs. 1, 2.

6. For the coffers of the Mausoleum, see above, Chap. II, nn. 190 192.

7. Skopas' much-discussed role at Halikarnassos rests on the testimony of Pliny, *Naturalis historia* 36.30-31, and Vitruvius, *De architectura*, 7, Preface, 12-13.

8. For the reliefs from Priene, see above, Chap. II, n. 196. It is a singular fact that H. Riemann, in his discussion of painted and sculptured coffer lids, *s.v. Pytheos*, *RE*, XXIV, cols. 487 ff., *passim*, omits any reference to the coffers of the Propylon.

9. The extant sculptures of the Propylon, being actual building blocks, are of the same Thasian marble employed for the building itself.

full, bushy beard. Drooping moustache reveals full lower lip. Eyes originally deep-set and double-lidded with pouches above the outer corners. Broad, low brow; damaged but triangular nose; fleshy cheeks. Powerful, short, thick neck. Hair worn but seemingly loose and free.

Field framed by a dressed rectangle, 0.015 m. high, within a second, once dressed but now badly battered, outer frame 0.02 m. in height. Both frames only preserved at upper right of the relief. Rear roughly picked and rounded at sides.

Height of field: ca. 0.135.

Found on the "platform" east or northeast of the Hieron, i.e., the Temenos.

125. *C(V)1.*

C(V)2. Inv. No. I, 675. Ephesos-Museum. (Fig. 126.)

S,*I*, pp. 11, 28, pl. 51 left; S,*II*, pp. 14, 68, n. 1; Heydemann, *op. cit.*, pp. 3, 12 f., and n. 45; Kern, *Hermes*, 25 (1890), p. 13, n. 2; Rubensohn, p. 141; Kern, *RE*, *loc. cit.*; Pettazzoni, p. 87; Schober, *loc. cit.*; Chapouthier, pp. 177 f., fig. 18; *Hesperia*, 20 (1951), p. 16; *Skopas in Samothrace*, pp. 9, 28, n. 56, fig. 51; Stewart, pp. 107 ff., 171, n. 44; *Funde aus Ephesos und Samothrake*, Vienna, 1978, No. 218.

Fragmentary coffer lid broken at upper and lower left and at the left, and chipped at lower right. Youthful male head facing right. Luxuriant mass of hair falls below line of chin, conceals the ear, and projects beyond the brow. Regular, forceful features; large nose, full lips, firm, rounded chin, full cheeks. Lips slightly upturned. Eyes deep-set;

prominent double outline on upper lid.[10] Hair worn; background discolored (from water or lichen?).

Inner frame 0.01 m. high; outer frame 0.02 m. high.[11] Broken pinhole at top; plugged-up pinhole on lower border. The former seemingly 0.014 m. deep and 0.005 m. in diameter. Roughly picked on back and flat.

Height of field: 0.144; width: ca. 0.144.

Found on the "platform" east or northeast of the Hieron, i.e., the Temenos.

126. *C(V)2.*

C(V)3. Inv. No. I, 1702. Kunsthistorisches Museum; storeroom of the Antikensammlung. (Fig. 127.)

S,II, p. 14, fig. 3; Heydemann, *op. cit.*, p. 12; Kern, *Hermes*, 25 (1890), p. 13, n. 2; *idem*, *RE*, *loc. cit.*; Pettazzoni, p. 88; Schober, *loc. cit.*; Chapouthier, pp. 178 f.; *Hesperia*, 20 (1951), p. 16; *Skopas in Samothrace*, p. 28, n. 56; Stewart, pp. 107, 171, n. 38.

Fragmentary coffer lid. Only left lower corner preserved. Neck of a head facing right? Badly worn.

10. A detail not visible in fig. 126.

11. It is clear from *(V)2*, *(V)3*, and *(S)1* that the outer border was smoothly dressed in order to fit the upper surface of the coffer.

Inner frame 0.008 m. high; outer frame 0.026 m. high.

Preserved height of fragment: 0.076; preserved width: 0.108; preserved height of neck: 0.045.

No specific provenance but presumably found with V 1, 2.

127. *C(V)3.*

The pieces in Samothrace consist of:

C(S)1. 55.149. Samothrace Museum; on exhibition. (Fig. 128.)
Chapouthier, pp. 178 f., and p. 179, n. 1, fig. 18; *Hesperia*, 20 (1951), p. 16, n. 52; *Samothrace*, Vol. 3, text I, pp. 232 f., fig. 185; *Skopas in Samothrace*, pp. 9, 28 f., nn. 56, 60, fig. 33; Stewart, pp. 107, 171, n. 38.

Fragmentary coffer lid. Irregularly broken and lacking the left lower corner and a portion of the left center frames. Edges chipped save at upper left of coffer and along the greater part of the right side. Youthful female head facing right. Surface worn but traces of a melon hairdress visible. Hair may have continued below break. Originally deep-set, large, heavy-lidded eye; double outline on upper lid. Large, regular nose, full lips, and rounded (now broken) chin; full cheeks; traces of small ear.

Inner frame: 0.015 m. high; outer frame: 0.02 m. high. Trace of a pinhole at top center and a complete hole at center of right side. Rear roughly picked and slightly rounded at sides.

Height of field: 0.143; width of field: 0.152.

Recovered by Chapouthier, who reported (p. 179, n. 1): "Le paysan chez qui je me le suis procuré l'aurait découvert sur le site de la ville antique (probablement remployé)."[12]

12. Presumably it was Chapouthier who took this lid to the National Archaeological Museum, where it was inventoried as no. 3632 (Chapouthier, p. 179, n. 1). It was returned to the Samothrace Museum in 1955. On pp. 178 f., Chapouthier suggested that *(V)3* might be the missing lower left cor-

128. *C(S)1.*

129. *C(S)2.*

C(S)2. 49.355. Samothrace Museum; on exhibition. (Fig. 129.)

Hesperia, 20 (1951), p. 16, pl. 6d; *Skopas in Samothrace,* p. 28, n. 56.

Fragmentary coffer lid. Only a portion of the bottom and lower left of the relief is pre-

ner of this lid. The dimensions of its frames and the position of the neck indicate that the two fragments do not fit together.

served. Irregularly broken at top and at sides. Male head facing right. Neck and beginning of shoulder preserved; heavy mass of hair falling onto the nape of the neck and seemingly curling up into a spiral above the shoulder. Simple, unmodelled columnar neck related to *(S)1* in style and scale.

Inner frame: 0.015 m. high; outer frame: 0.024 m. high.

Preserved height of field: 0.117; preserved width of field: 0.165.

Found north of the terrace wall at the lowest level of its limestone facing.

C(S)3. 66.611. Samothrace Museum; on exhibition. (Figs. 130, 142.)
Hesperia, 37 (1968), pp. 229f., pl. 70 c; *Deltion,* 23 (1968), p. 368, Pl. 320 b; *Skopas in Samothrace,* pp. 9 f., 28 f., nn. 56, 60 f., figs. 35, 37, Stewart, pp. 107, 171, n. 38.

Fragmentary coffer lid. Youthful male head looking toward the spectator's right, seen in a three-quarter view. Short, curly hair above low, indented brow; deep-set eyes, with pouches overhanging the outer corners and double outline defining the lids. Broad, short face with prominent cheekbones. Shapely, small ear. Only the upper portion of the double frame is partially preserved over the head; the nose is damaged, and from the upper lip down, the face is missing.

Inner frame: 0.15 m. high; outer frame: ca. 0.12 m. high.

130. *C(S)3.*

Preserved height of fragment: 0.142; preserved width: 0.135; width of head: 0.11; height from crown to mouth: 0.085. Rear roughly picked and rounded at sides.

Found in a dump on the Eastern Hill.[13]

C(S)4. 70.848. Samothrace Museum; on exhibition. (Fig. 131.)

Deltion, 26 (1971), p. 443, Pl. 438 a; *Skopas in Samothrace*, pp. 9, 28, n. 56, fig. 36, Stewart, pp. 107, 171, n. 38.

Fragmentary coffer lid. Broken on all sides save for a small section of the double frame above the head. Youthful female head looking toward the spectators left, seen in a three-quarter view. Apart from the broken tip of the nose and the broken, severely weathered back of the head, the head is well preserved, if weathered. The hair, worn in a melon coiffure, frames a low, broad forehead. The eye is deep set and its heavy lids are double outlined. Nose originally large and regular; full, articulated lips; rounded, prominent chin;

131. *C(S)4.*

13. The previous year, *F(S)3*, a fragmentary figure from the frieze, and 65.31, a small fragment of the lateral sima were found there. Evidently, these fragments formed part of a collection of marbles from the destroyed Sanctuary that had been assembled in the vicinity of a large limekiln; indeed, 65.31 was actually found in the kiln (see *Hesperia*, 37 [1968], p. 234; *Deltion*, 23 [1967], p. 368, pl. 320 b). In these preliminary reports, Professor McCredie attributed this fragmentary coffer and other fragmentary coffers decorated with rosettes to a Doric building and connecting Ionic porch dedicated by Philip III Arrhidaios and Alexander IV (*ibid.*, p. 230). But the fragments carved with rosettes differ from No. 66.611 in scale and technical details. In view of the exact correspondence in material and all comparable dimensions between No. 66.611 and the other coffer lids known to have come from the Propylon, and of its unstratified provenance, Professor McCredie agrees with me that this lid should be attributed to the Propylon.

broad, short face with prominent cheekbones. The upper portion of the field to the left of the head is strongly weathered.

Inner frame: 0.013 m. high; outer frame: 0.018 m. high.

Preserved height of fragment: 0.155; preserved width: ca. 0.148. Rear roughly picked and rounded at sides.

Found outside the southernmost dining room in the complex of dining rooms below the Stoa in a late antique fill containing architectural fragments from other buildings in the Sanctuary.

132. Fragmentary lost coffer from Larissa.

Although the specific form of the πρόσωπα in the Temple of Asklepios at Epidauros is unknown, that is, whether they were shown full-face, in profile, or in three-quarter view, the faintly visible painted head from the Nereid Monument now in the British Museum is shown from a three-quarter angle facing toward the spectator's left (fig. 121). This female head was surely not unique. Other such heads, doubtless some in the reverse pose facing toward the right, must have existed.[14] A fragmentary lost coffer from a presumably fourth-century Thessalian monument in Larissa contained two images, a frontal head interpreted as Medusa and a profile head of Hermes or Perseus framed by an ivy tendril (fig. 132).[15]

14. A painted bust of Demeter or Kore appears in a coffer from the ceiling of a tomb at Bolshaja-Blisnitza dating late in the fourth century B.C.: M. Rostovtzeff, *Ancient Decorative Painting in South Russia* (in Russian), St. Petersburg, 1913, pls. 7 (fig. 2), 8. For reference to this monument, see Karl Lehmann, "The Dome of Heaven," *The Art Bulletin*, 27 (1945), p. 4. My old comments regarding what are clearly certain coffers from the Propylon (not the Hieron) cited in n. 23 on this page have proved to be wholly incorrect.

15. H. Brunn, "Nordgriechische Sculpturen," *AthMitt*, 8 (1883), pp. 96 ff.; Paul Wolters, "Zwei thessalische Grabstein," *ibid.*, 12 (1887), p. 80; R. Heberdey, "Reliefs aus Thessalien," *ibid.*, 15 (1890), pp. 200, 206; Frank Brommer, "Neue thessalische Bildwerke vorklassischer Zeit," *ibid.*, 65 (1940), p. 113, n. 1; Riemann, *RE*, vol. 47, *s.v.*, *Pytheos*, cols. 510 f.

133. Block from the coffered ceiling of the Façade of the Colossal Figures in Corinth. Corinth Museum.

134. Detail of Helios from the coffered ceiling of the Façade of the Colossal Figures in Corinth. Corinth Museum.

Here the coffer fields were rectangular. Two other Roman fragments are of interest. A block from the coffered ceiling of the Façade of the Colossal Figures in Corinth preserving two busts of Selene and Helios shown in three-quarter view facing each other, along with a third coffer carved with a rosette, all three coffers framed by tendrils (figs. 133, 134);[16]

16. Franklin P. Johnson, *Sculpture, 1896-1923* (*Corinth*, IX), Cambridge, 1931, pp. 105 f. Dated by Cornelius C. Vermeule, *Roman Imperial Art in Greece and Asia Minor*, Cambridge, 1968, pp. 83 ff., in the early third century A.D. I am grateful to Charles K. Williams for having called to my attention this new date.

135. Fragmentary coffer. Brussels, Musées Royaux du Cinquantenaire.

136. Coffered ceiling of the porch to the Serapeion in Miletos.

and a fragmentary relief in Brussels showing a female head crowned with flowers seen *en face* surrounded by smaller fields filled with rosettes (fig. 135).[17]

Of particular interest, however, is the coffered ceiling of the porch to the Serapeion in Miletos, in spite of its date in the second half of the third century A.D. (fig. 136).[18] Here the porch is divided into bays, the central one wider than the lateral pair, hence the coffers in the central bay are rectangular, those in the lateral bays square. Each bay is roofed by three units of two coffers, that is, six coffers occupy each bay. The central bay is adorned with frontal busts of divinities, the lateral with busts of the Muses and another triad,

17. Franz Cumont, *Catalogue des sculptures et inscriptions antiques des Musées Royaux du Cinquantenaire*, Brussels, 1913, p. 135, no. 116.

18. Hubert Knackfuss, *Der Südmarkt und die benachbarten Bauanlagen* (*Milet* I, 7), Berlin, 1924, pp. 197-205.

possibly the Graces. It has been suggested that the major divinities worshipped in Miletos were represented in the central bay. Again, it is of special interest that the bust of Apollo reflects the cult image at Didyma. Traces of color and a painted inscription identifying Ourania are reported.[19]

Sparse though they are and differing widely in chronology, these analogies in form and content are valuable. They offer parallels for the use of square and rectangular coffers in the same ceiling; for the use of full-face, profile, and three-quarter views of the head in coffers; and, at least in the last instance, for a meaningful content.

The existence of seven fragmentary coffer lids indicates that at least two bays sculptured with heads were present in the ceiling of the Propylon. Theoretically, they might have been confined to the area above the two lateral doors. But the difficulty of combining these heads into two satisfactory compositions in view of the varied angles from which they are presented makes it likely that actually they were distributed in the four bays of the porch proper. This accords, in fact, with the implications of the restriction of the sculptured heads to the smallest size of the coffers.[20]

Until recently, only the Vienna lids and *(S)1* were known. Hence few scholars have tried to interpret them. Conze assumed that *(V)1* was a representation of Zeus.[21] He made no effort to interpret *(V)2* or *3*. Heydemann saw in *(V)1* and *2* Hades and Eubouleus;[22] Kern assumed that *(V)2* was Kadmilos, and *(V)1*, the elder Kabeiros, Axiokersos-Hades.[23] In a remarkable article on the Tomb of the Haterii,[24] Raffaele Pettazzoni interpreted *(V)1* as Hades-Axiokersos, *(V)2* as Hermes-Kadmilos, and *(V)3* as one of the two female members of the Great Gods. Unaware of this article, Chapouthier, having found *(S)1*, assumed that *(V)1* and *2* and *(S)1* were Zeus, Hermes, and Cybele, and that they belonged to the porch of the Hieron.[25] But even when *(V)1* and *2* were first discovered, Hauser had reported quite correctly that they were too small for that building and belonged to the building on the "platform."[26] Most recently, Karl Lehmann tentatively proposed that

19. See, too, the funerary tower of Elahbēl at Palmyra, where the ceiling is carved with square coffers filled with rosettes and, in the center, quadruple-sized coffers are carved with frontal busts. Doubtless this is a descendant of painted Roman ceilings. *Palmyra, Ergebnisse der Expeditionen von 1902 und 1917* (ed. Theodor Wiegand), Berlin, 1932, p. 40, pl. 30.

Related forms exist in Etruria. Elaine P. Loeffler has drawn my attention to a stuccoed coffer with a frontal demonic head (Charon?) in the late fourth-century B.C. Tomba François at Vulci. See F. Messerschmidt and Armin von Gerkan, *Nekropolen von Vulci* (*JdI, Ergänzungsheft*, 12), pp. 114 f., fig. 88.

20. The minute differences in the frames of the lids (always less than 0.01 m. in sculptures to be seen at a distance), hence in the size of the original actual field appear to provide no clue to their arrangement.

21. *S,I*, p. 28.

22. Heinrich Heydemann, "Marmorkopf Riccardi," *Dreizehntes Hallische Winckelmannsprogramm*, Halle, 1888, pp. 3, 12 and n. 45, 13. He made no attempt to interpret *(V)3* and was uncertain of the function of the reliefs. On p. 3, *(V)2* appears in a crude line drawing made after a cast in the Halle Museum.

23. Otto Kern, "Die boiotischen Kabiren," *Hermes*, 25 (1890), pp. 13 and n. 2, 14, and *idem*, *RE, s.v. Kabeiros und Kabeiroi*, X, col. 1426. Again, he did not interpret *(V)3*.

24. "Una rappresentazione romana dei Kabiri di Samotracia," *Ausonia*, 3 (1908), pp. 79-90, specifically pp. 87 f.

25. Chapouthier, p. 177, n. 1.

26. S,*I*, p. 28, *II*, p. 14.

137. Lintel from the Tomb of the Haterii. Rome, Lateran Collection of the Vatican.

(V)1 and *2* and *(S)1* and *2* might represent Axiokersos, Kadmilos, Axieros, and Axiokersa, although *(V)2* might be one of the Kabeiroi-Dioskouroi.[27]

These fragmentary reliefs, lacking attributes as they do, are extremely difficult, not to say almost impossible, to interpret. The suggestions proposed here are hypothetical. Yet it may be well to try to make some sense of these fragments, given the exceptional quality of the building.

It was Pettazzoni's thesis that a lintel from the Tomb of the Haterii (fig. 137), today in the Lateran collection of the Vatican,[28] represented the Great Gods of Samothrace—the right pair being Pluto and Proserpina, the left pair Ceres and Mercury—and that one of the Haterii had been initiated in the Samothracian mysteries. Hence this initiate put the images of the Great Gods, known to the Greeks as Demeter, Hermes, Hades, and Persephone over the entrance to his sepulchral chamber as a testimony of his own faith, and as guardians of the peace of his last abode.[29]

27. *Hesperia*, 20 (1951), p. 16.

28. No. 1073. Wolfgang Helbig, *Führer durch die öffentlichen Sammlungen klassischer Altertümer in Rom*, 4th edn., rev. by Hermione Speier, Tübingen, I, 1963, pp. 774 f. Here dated Flavian. Pettazzoni's date, *op. cit.*, p. 87, was Trajanic. Unfortunately, this important article has been omitted from the bibliography of the fourth edition of this catalogue, although it was present in the third edition. Heinz Kähler, *Rom und seine Welt*, Munich, 1960, p. 249, pl. 158 above, has also omitted reference to Pettazzoni's interpretation. He dates the relief in the last quarter of the first century A.D.

29. Pettazzoni, p. 84. His interpretation of this relief has been accepted by another Samothracian student: Arnold Schober, "Der Neue Tempel von Samothrake," *ÖJh*, 29 (1935), p. 14.

138. Votive terracotta. Samothrace Museum.

I believe that this interpretation is correct and have used this relief to interpret the very fragmentary relief sculptures of the rear, south pediment of the Hieron,[30] which, again, appear to represent the Great Gods. In Samothracian terms, these divinities were known as Axieros, Kadmilos, Axiokersos, and Axiokersa.[31]

Apart from their stylistic differences, the relationship between the Axiokersos-Hades of the Trajanic relief and the elder head in Vienna is marked. Both are bearded and moustached, and their long curly hair, parted in the center, merges with their curly beards. The shape of the brow, the deep-set, unflinching eyes, the regular nose, full lips, and broad face with conspicuous cheekbones recur in both images and evoke the forbidding God of the Underworld.

It has already been suggested that the Axiokersos-Hades of the Lateran relief is related to a votive terracotta discovered in an early Imperial fill of the Hieron (fig. 138) and that it is a replica of a lost late Hellenistic cult image of the late second century B.C.[32] Although this terracotta lacks the central part in the hair of both the other heads, it, too, presents related features. Indeed, the drooping moustache and full beard of the terracotta are even closer to the coffer than is the Lateran relief and, again, the noses and cheekbones of the two are equally emphasized.

30. Vol. 3, text I, pp. 325 ff.

31. Scholia Laurentiana and Parisina to Apollonius Rhodius, *Argonautica*, line 917. See Naphtali Lewis, *Samothrace*, Vol. 1, **150, 150a**.

32. By Martha Leeb Hadzi, *Samothrace*, Vol. 3, text II, **177**. The implications of such a lost cult statue are considered on p. 170. It had earlier been assumed that this terracotta head represented Axiokersos-Hades. Cf. *Guide*[3], p. 24, fig. 11; *Guide*[4], p. 27, fig. 11.

If, then, the bearded head in Vienna is Axiokersos-Hades, is it possible to identify the other heads? What is the program of the ceiling? Surely, it must have been meaningful—such is the implication of the bearded head in Vienna—and appropriate for both initiates and those who had not been initiated to see.

In view of the almost hypnotic power of the Lateran relief, it is tempting to assume that all the heads combined with *(V)1* must have been frontal[33] and, since each bay includes six coffers, their attendant demons, the Kabeiroi-Dioskouroi, must have been included, and then they, too, must have been frontal.[34] This group of divinities, the most significant in the Samothracian cult, was doubtless placed in one of the two bays flanking the main door, that is, before one of the lateral doors. Presumably, then, the parallel bay before the other lateral door was similarly arranged, its coffers, too, provided with heads shown from the front. For arbitrary reasons, I shall place the Great Gods to the left of the main door. What was represented to the right of the main door?

Examination of the literary sources on the Samothracian cult indicates that three other groups are associated with it: another group of divinities, legendary figures that seem to constitute a paraphrase on the main group of Samothracian gods, and heroic, partially, divine initiates. The correlation between these four groups of divinities, legendary figures, and heroic initiates and the four bays of figural coffers that have emerged as a result of purely architectural, structural factors is significant and offers a welcome confirmation of the formal arrangement implicit in the program of the ceiling.

The additional divinities most frequently alluded to in the literary sources are Aphrodite and Hekate,[35] Rhea and Attis,[36] Athena, patron goddess of the city, as is known from her appearance on the obverse of the city's coins,[37] and Ares.[38] Let us assume that

33. Pettazzoni, pp. 87 f., naturally did not assume that other figural coffer lids would be discovered in later years, a fact that must be taken into consideration in working out the meaning of the ceiling. Purely formally, the extant coffer lids cannot be combined in one or two groups. Given the new formal types that have been found, I find it impossible to include *(V)2* and *3* in the same bay as the frontal *(V)1*. It is also not without interest that the fragment of a colossal head ascribed to the southern pediment of the Hieron, whether she be Axieros-Demeter or Axiokersa-Persephone, is a frontal bust (see *Samothrace*, Vol. 3, text I, pp. 318 f., *SP(V)1*), and that here, too, the Great Gods were shown *en face*.

34. For this major group, see in particular, the Scholia to Apollonius Rhodius, *Argonautica*, line 917, cited in n. 31, and Eusebius, *Praeparatio evangelica* 1.10, Damascius, *Vita Isidori* 302, by implication Orphic Hymn 38, Aristophanes, *Pax*, 276-286 and the Scholia to Aristophanes, *Pax*, 278; and Diodorus 4.43.1-2 (*Samothrace*, Vol. 1, **168**, **168b**, **217**, **226**, **226a**, **229b**).

35. Anon. *Paraphrasis antiquior Lycophronis* 72-78; Nonnus, *Dionysiaca* 4. 183-185, 213-214; Scholia to Nicander, *Theriaca* 1, 462; Stephanus Byzantius, Ethnica, *s.v.* ΖΗΡΥΝΘΟΣ; Suidas, *s.v.* ΖΗΡΥΝΘΙΑ; *Etymologicum Magnum*, *s.v.* ΖΗΡΥΝΘΙΑ; Scholia Vetera to Lycophron *Alexandra* 77; Pliny, *Naturalis historia* 36.5.25; Scholia to Aristophanes, *Pax*, 277 (*Samothrace*, Vol. 1, **53a**, **151**, **153-156**, **160**, **226a**).

36. Anon. *Paraphrasis antiquior Lycophronis* 78; Lucian, *de Dea Syria*, 15; Scholia to Clemens Alexandrinus *Protrepticus* 2.13:3; Hippolytus *Refutatio omnium haeresium* 5.9.7-9; Scholia (Tzetzes) to Lycophron *Alexandra* 78; Scholia to Aristides *Oratio* 13; *Etymologicum Gudianum*, *s.v.* Kabiroi (*Samothrace*, Vol. 1, **53a**, **144**, **146**, **148**, **157-159**).

37. See, for example, *Samothrace*, Vol. 3, text II, Catalogue of Finds **156-159**.

38. Nonnus, *Dionysiaca* 3.186 f. ("Samothrace, the Seat of Ares"); *Etymologicum Magnum*, *s.v.* ΖΗΡΥΝΘΙΑ (*Samothrace*, Vol. 1, **68**, **155a**).

139. Diagram of the coffered ceiling of the Propylon. A. Position of the heads. B. Proposed identification of the heads.

they were shown frontally before the right lateral door. And, again for arbitrary reasons, let us place the legendary figures—Elektra, Zeus, their children Aëtion, Dardanos, Harmonia and her spouse, Kadmos[39]—in the left bay of the porch, and the heroic initiates—

39. See, in particular, Diodorus, 5.48.4-50.1; Nonnus, *Dionysiaca* 3.124–4.246; Scholia Laurentiana and Parisina to Apollonius Rhodius, *Argonautica*, line 916; Scholia to Euripides *Phoenissae* 7 (*Samothrace*, Vol. 1, **142**, **67**, **70**, **70a**, **75**).

Agamemnon, Odysseus, Herakles, Jason, Orpheus and an unknown sixth, conceivably another Argonaut—in the right.[40]

Returning now to the formal arrangement of the coffer lids, *(V)2* and *3* and *(S)1* and *2* face to the right—which implies that other heads faced to the left—and some, *(S)3* and *4*, are shown in a three-quarter view, one facing toward the left, one toward the right. The paired three-quarter heads must be placed in the center of the six-part coffers in bays I and IV with confronting left and right profiles occupying the two other fields above and below (see the diagram, fig. 139 A). Such a formal arrangement of figural coffers emphasizes the clear articulation of the ceiling previously noted in the disposition of the figural and nonfigural units.

Let us try first to identify the heads seen in three-quarter views, *(S)3* and *4*. According to the scheme proposed here, *(S)4* will be restricted by bay I, since bay IV is occupied by male heroes. *(S)3*, the male head, might be any of the heroes, although he is less likely to have been one of the elder heroes, Agamemnon or Odysseus. As a three-quarter head, he also might have been paired with *(S)4*. But he bears a special relationship to a Herakles-type, as is evident if he is compared with the Lansdowne Herakles in the Getty Museum at Malibu (figs. 140, 141).[41] The tousled hair, the low brow, the deep-set eyes, the broad, short face, and the small ear are remarkably similar. Let us assume that *(S)3* is Herakles. If so, four of the other heroes must have been shown in profile and doubtless Agamemnon and Odysseus were paired. Otherwise, the specific location of the remaining Argonauts is, again, arbitrary.

According to this scheme, *(S)4* must be either Elektra or Harmonia, and in view of her greater youth, doubtless Harmonia. She must have been paired with her spouse, Kadmos, with her brothers Dardanos and Aëtion below, her parents Elektra and Zeus above, Elektra being to the left (see the diagram, fig. 139 B). For the only other female head that is not frontal (as the heads in bay III are) is that of Elektra, and she must, therefore, be *(S)1*, a profile head facing toward the right.[42]

(V)2, a male head facing to the right, is most likely one of the heroes and, given his youth, unlikely to have been Agamemnon or Odysseus. Can he have been Jason, leader of

40. Diodorus 5.50.1; 4.43.1-2; 4.48.5-7; Scholia Laurentiana and Parisina to Apollonius Rhodius, *Argonautica*, lines 917-918 (*Samothrace*, Vol. 1, **142**, **229b**, **c**, **g**, **h**).

Diodorus 5.49.6 explicitly includes the Dioskouroi among the ancient heroes and demigods who were initiated in the Samothracian mysteries along with Jason, Herakles, and Orpheus. Odysseus and Agamemnon are reported to have been initiates in the scholia to Apollonius Rhodius. Inasmuch as among the Greeks, the Dioskouroi were elsewhere equated with the Kabeiroi, I have preferred to eliminate them from this category lest they occur twice in the ceiling. Unfortunately, no other sixth hero is reported in the extant sources, although reference is made to "the Argonants" (*ibid.*, **229b-d**).

41. Cornelius Vermeule and Norman Neuerberg, *Catalogue of the Ancient Art in the J. Paul Getty Museum* [Malibu?], 1973, pp. 6 ff., no. 9; Seymour Howard, *The Lansdowne Herakles* (J. Paul Getty Museum, Publication No. 1), 1966, and for this comparison, figs. 1, 4; and, among discussions of Skopas' style, in general, the recent volume of Stewart, pp. 98 f., 142, 147 f., pl. 42a-c, and *passim*.

42. Lehmann, *Guide*[1], p. 83, *Guide*[2], p. 86, *Guide*[3], p. 90 suggested that this head might possibly be Harmonia—a reasonable suggestion at the time, before the discovery of *(S)4*.

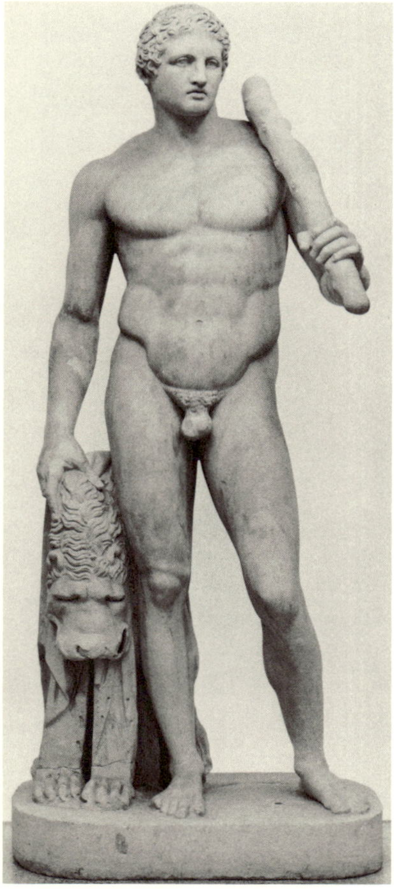

140. Lansdowne Herakles. Malibu, The J. Paul Getty Museum.

the Argonauts? It is tempting to think so, in view of the likelihood that this head may have been a portrait, but discussion of this problem is best postponed until the next chapter.[43]

Finally, there are the two fragments, *(V)3* and *(S)2*. *(V)3* was presumably a profile head facing to right. Hence this shattered fragment may have been one of the heroes, Agamemnon or Odysseus, or the legendary figures, Dardanos or Aëtion, depending on which of these paired heads faced left. *(S)2* must have been the other requisite male profile head facing left. His singular hairdo—a mass of hair falling on the nape of the neck and coiling up above the shoulder—is related to profile heads of Dionysos and Apollo on the coinage of Adramyteum in Mysia, where again, a mass of hair coils up into a spiral or bulbous S-shape at the back of the head.[44]

43. Chap. IV, pp. 274 ff.

44. Warwick Wroth, *Catalogue of the Greek Coins of Mysia*, London, 1892, p. 3, no. 7, pl. I, 8; H. von Fritze, "Die vorkaiserlichen Münzen von Adramytion," *Nomisma*, 5 (1910), p. 13, pl. I, 15, 16; 20, pl. I, 24. Von Fritze calls this hairdo a *Henkelfrisur*. I am indebted to Elsbeth B. Dusenbery for this comparison.

This fragmentary head was identified in *Hesperia*, 20 (1951), p. 16, as "evidently of a woman" presumably because of its long hair; but I am not aware of any analogous feminine coiffure. Had the head been more completely preserved, this feature might have helped to identify it.

141. Head of the Lansdowne Herakles. Malibu, The J. Paul Getty Museum.

143. Head from the east pediment of the Temple of Athena Alea at Tegea. Athens, National Archaeological Museum.

142. *C(S)3.*

144. Head from the east pediment of the Temple of Athena Alea at Tegea. Athens, National Archaeological Museum.

So much may be suggested for the program of the ceiling. With the exception of Axiokersos-Hades and possibly of Herakles, this proposal rests on pure theory or speculation; it cannot be proven.

An interesting problem emerges from these considerations. If the Great Gods were indeed represented on the ceiling of the Propylon, what does this imply about their reappearance on the rear pediment of the Hieron in the second century B.C., on the Tomb of the Haterii, and in an Early Imperial votive terracotta? Surely all three were not based on the coffered ceiling of the Propylon. Does a classical statuary group lie behind this tradition and was it quoted on the ceiling, too? Where could such a group have been exhibited, inasmuch as the Anaktoron and the Hieron were congregational buildings, not temples, hence lacked the cult images normally found in temples? Were they a group of busts carried in the procession in the annual festivals? Again, this is a matter for speculation.[45]

Among the better preserved lids, *(V)1* and *(S)1*, Axiokersos-Hades and Elektra, are severely worn and weathered. Yet all these lids have a number of features in common: low, rectangular brows; deep-set eyes with double-outlined lids, often with pouches over the outer corners; broad, short faces[46] in which the cheekbones are prominent; fleshy cheeks; regular features; full lips; rounded chins.

The most eloquent of these heads is *(S)3* (figs. 130, 142), the head that seems to represent Herakles. He bears a striking resemblance to one of the heads from the east pediment of Skopas' Temple of Athena Alea at Tegea (fig. 143, 144).[47] The same deep-set, heavily outlined eyes overhung by pouches; the same broad, short face in which the cheekbones are prominently visible beneath the fleshy cheeks; the same low, rectangular, horizontally indented brow; the same sketchily rendered hair and small ears recur. Herakles' damaged nose seems once to have had a similar form. Indeed, the relationship between these heads is so marked as to provide tangible visual proof that Skopas was associated with the Propylon as sculptor, and to confirm the earlier suggestion that he was its architect.[48] Here, as in Tegea, he must have been designing architect-sculptor.[49]

45. It will be recalled that the coffered ceiling of the porch of the Serapeion at Miletos (above, pp. 160 f.) involves a related problem in which at least one cult image was quoted.

46. Apart from *(V)2*, whose longer face reflects the fact that he is a specific individual not a general type. See below, Chap. IV, pp. 274 ff.

47. Today in the National Archaeological Museum, Athens, no. 179. Cf. Karouzou, p. 163; Dugas, no. 17, pp. 112 ff., pl. CII, B; Stewart, no. 9, pp. 16 ff., pls. 7, 8a,b, 38c,d, 52b,c, and *passim*.

I do not include here the extensive bibliography on Tegea since it will not clarify or contribute to an understanding of the interrelationships between that Temple and the Propylon. For Skopas' career and the ancient sources documenting his activity, see above, Chap. II, n. 206.

48. See above, pp. 144 ff.

49. This thesis has been accepted by Stewart, pp. 107, 171, n. 38. (On p. 107, Stewart mistakenly states that "only two of the seven heads are in frontal or profile views, the rest, as at Tegea, being shown in three-quarter view." Actually, the reverse is true—cf. the Catalogue, pp. 151 ff.; only two are shown in three-quarter view, four in profile, and one *en face*.)

See above, Chap. II, n. 207, for comment on the statement made by Pausanias 8.45.5 regarding Skopas' work at Tegea. To what extent the sculptures at Tegea or any other such architectural sculptures,

145. Head of an akroterion from the west pediment of the Temple of Athena Alea at Tegea. Piali Museum.

146. Head from the west pediment of the Temple of Athena Alea at Tegea. Athens, National Archaeological Museum.

A second coffer, the head of Harmonia (fig. 131), is also related to a fragmentary female head that has been attributed to one of the akroteria of the western pediment of the Temple (fig. 145).[50] Although the difference between Thasian and Doliana[51] marble is more apparent here than in the previous comparison, the heads share the same low, curving brow, the same deep-set strongly outlined eye, and a similarly shaped cheek and skull.

Other comparisons might be made with sculptures known to have been made by Skopas or attributed to him, although they are largely Roman copies. One, the Lansdowne

---

including those of the Propylon, were actually executed by the master is another matter. Doubtless, they were few. On this score, see the remarks of Alan J. B. Wace, "Design and Execution" *Annuario*, nos. 8-10 (1946-48), pp. 109 ff., and, regarding the Mausoleum at Halikarnassos, Ernst Buschor, *Maussollos und Alexander*, Munich, 1950, p. 10. This is the point of view of Stewart, *passim.*

Jean Charbonneaux, *La Sculpture grecque classique*, Paris, 1945, II, p. 84, comments that Skopas' shop was less good than Pheidias' and that the details executed by his shop were mechanically treated. This comment also applies to the sculptures of the Propylon.

50. Stewart, no. 4, pp. 12 ff., 48 f., 59 f., 64, 70, 76 f., pl. 4. This head is attributed to the recently discovered akroterion published in *Archaeological Reports for 1965-66*, p. 8, fig. 10, and "Chroniques des Fouilles," *BCH*, 92 (1968), pp. 806 ff., figs. 1-3, and now published by Stewart, no. 3, pp. 11 f., pl. 3. The head itself, now in the Apotheke of the Museum at Piali, has been previously published by Dugas, no. 106, pp. 124 f., pl. CXVI; Ernst Pfuhl, "Bemerkungen zur Kunst des vierten Jahrhunderts," *JdI*, 43 (1928), p. 35, fig. 11; and Charles Picard, *Manuel d'archéologie grecque, La sculpture*, IV, 1, Paris, 1954, p. 167, fig. 77.

51. Contrary to the statement in Bernard Ashmole "Skopas," *Encyclopedia of World Art*, XII, New York, Toronto, London, 1967, col. 58, that the sculptures at Tegea are of Parian marble, it is clear from Stewart's repeated comments, e.g., p. 39, that they were carved from marble from the nearby quarry at Doliana.

Herakles,[52] has already been adduced and bears out the assumption that Skopas was designing architect-sculptor of the Propylon. To multiply these comparisons is unnecessary. It is wiser to confine the argument to the prime monument associated with the master, the architectural sculptures for the Temple at Tegea,[53] completed in the decade 350-340 B.C.,[54] and to point out that other heads from Tegea, the head recently identified as Telephos, in particular,[55] and the helmeted head (fig. 146)[56] confirm this conclusion.[57]

P.W.L.

THE FRIEZE

The great majority of the surviving blocks and fragments described in the Catalogue that follows are today in the Samothrace Museum. Only five small fragments are known to exist elsewhere, two in the Antikensammlung of the Kunsthistorisches Museum and the Ephesos-Museum, Vienna, two in the storerooms of the Louvre, Paris, and one in the Archaeological Museum of the Charles University in Prague.[58] The frieze invites a listing divided into major categories based on the direction of the movement of the dancing girls, who seem to have been its principal subject matter (I and II); another substantial category (III) consists of missing blocks and fragments of which evidence is preserved in descriptions or drawings; and a lesser one (IV) of fragments of the crowning molding.

In the Catalogue, two kinds of directional indications are used; descriptions of blocks, including the classification according to the left-or-right movement of the dancers, are given with reference to the spectator's viewpoint, while descriptions of pose and gesture within the representations refer to the right and left sides of the figures.[59]

52. See the excellent discussions of Howard and Stewart, *loc. cit.*, on this statue. For a different point of view, see Steven Lattimore, "Two Statues of Herakles," *The J. Paul Getty Museum Journal*, 2 (1975), p. 26, where the author assumes that the statue was a Hadrianic pastiche: "The Lansdowne Herakles is—on the highest level—a pastiche, a new creation of imperial Roman sculpture." I owe knowledge of this reference to Jiří Frel.

In the recently published revised edition of *The Lansdowne Herakles*, 1978, pp. 30 f., Howard has altered his original attribution of the statue to Skopas and now suggests that it may have been a work by Euphranor. I do not find this suggestion persuasive.

53. See above, Chap. II, n. 207.

54. The pedimental and akroterial sculptures at Tegea, obviously, later than the building itself, were completed at this time. Cf. Stewart, pp. 69, 104, in particular.

55. Angelos Delivorrias, "ΣΚΟΠΑΔΙΚΑ (I)," *BCH*, 97 (1973), pp. 122 ff., figs. 2-4. Previously identified as Herakles: e.g., Dugas, no. 7, pp. 87 f., pls. XCIX A; C, A, B, C. See now, Stewart, no. 16, pp. 22 f., 53 ff., pls. 13, 14a,b, 52b,c, and *passim*.

56. Today in the National Archaeological Museum, Athens, no. 180, Karouzou, pp. 163 ff., no. 178; Dugas, pp. 89 f., pl. CII, A; Delivorrias, *op. cit.*, pp. 127 ff., figs. 6-8; and Stewart, no. 17, pp. 23 f., 55, pls. 14c,d, 15, 35c,d, 52a,c, and *passim*.

57. For consideration of the chronological implications of these connections, see below, p. 266.

Another Skopaic head found in the Sanctuary at Samothrace is discussed below, App. I, p. 303, fig. 247.

58. I am indebted to Dr. Jan Bouzek for informing me (by letter) that the Archaeological Museum of the Charles University in Prague possesses a small fragment of the frieze. The piece is not entered in this Catalogue because the promised photograph has not been received from Dr. Bouzek as Vol. V goes to the printer.

59. For assistance in the research on the frieze of the Propylon, I wish to thank Nina Longobardi

CATALOGUE

I. Frieze blocks and fragments with figures moving from left to right

F(S)1. 49.1043A-B. Samothrace Museum; on exhibition. "Victory on Samothrace," *Art News*, 48 (1949), p. 23; Ch[arles] P[icard], "Sur une frise samothracienne," *RA*, ser. 6, 36 (1950), pp. 157 ff.; *Hesperia*, 20 (1951), p. 16, pls. 8a, 9a, 10; *Hesperia*, 21 (1952), p. 25, n. 27; *Guide*[1], pp. 58-59, fig. 31, pp. 58 f., 81; W. Fuchs, *Die Vorbilder der Neuattischen Reliefs, JdI*, Ergänzungsheft 20 (1959), p. 52, n. 37, p. 55, n. 59; *Guide*[2], pp. 58-59, fig. 31, pp. 59, 84; C. M. Havelock, "Archaistic Reliefs of the Hellenistic Period," *AJA*, 68 (1964), pp. 50, 57, pl. 20, fig. 13; Harrison, p. 54, n. 93, p. 61; *Guide*[3], pp. 58-59, fig. 30, pp. 59, 88; Ridgway, p. 203; P. W. Lehmann, "An Antique Ornament Set in a Renaissance Tower," *RA*, n.s. 2 (1968), pp. 212 ff., figs. 9, 10; A. Liberman, *Greece: Gods and Art*, New York (1968), pl. 106; V. S. Scully, *The Earth, the Temple, and the Gods*, rev. edn., New York (1969), p. 204; *Skopas in Samothrace*, pp. 10 ff., figs. 39, 40; *Samothracian Reflections*, p. 107, figs. 31, 32; *Guide*[4], pp. 64-65, fig. 30, pp. 66, 99 f.; Werner Fuchs, *Die Skulpturen der Griechen*, Munich, 1969, p. 458,[60] fig. 538; Stewart, p. 107, n. 39. (Frontispiece, Figs. 147, 148, 195, 210; Pl. XXIII.1-3.)

This best preserved of all the surviving frieze blocks has been reconstituted out of two fragments of almost equal sizes (A, left, and B, right).[61] The crowning moulding, measuring 0.048 m. in height, and consisting of an ovolo, a half round, and a tiny fillet, is largely preserved on A, but damaged on B. The left end of the block, showing anathyrosis, is well preserved; the right end is broken. On the top surface there are, in the left-hand fragment (A), a broken clamp hole at the left end and a dowel hole placed obliquely 0.355 m. to the

---

and the staff of the Library of the American Academy in Rome, and Karin Einaudi of the Fototeca Unione; the Interlibrary Loan Department of the Williston Memorial Library at Mount Holyoke College; the staff of the Smith College Art Library. For their kind response to inquiries and requests: Edward W. Bodnar, S.J., Jan Bouzek, Brian F. Cook, Jiří Frel, Ulrich Gehrig, Kurt Gschwantler, Evelyn B. Harrison, Carol Harward, Antje Krug, Marina Moevs, Mary B. Moore, Alain Pasquier, Efie Sakellaris, J. Gy. Szilagyi, Bluma Trell, Emily Vermeule, Nicholas Yalouris. For the pleasures of friendly consultation: Blanche R. Brown, Phyllis Pray Bober, Elsbeth B. Dusenbery, Christine Mitchell Havelock, Elizabeth Papagiorgiou. I owe much to the notes on the frieze left by Karl Lehmann, and to the generous and painstaking collaboration of Phyllis Williams Lehmann.

60. Fuchs reproduces a detail of *F(S)1* which shows four dancers including the kithara player, and mistakenly identifies the block as one of those formerly in the Louvre, *F(S)10* and *F(S)11*.

61. Because of its exceptional length, high quality and good state of preservation, this block has been chosen for an initial, especially detailed description. Hereafter the Catalogue will rely on this description as having fundamental relevance to all subsequent blocks and fragments. The ensuing entries will thus be as brief as possible, placing emphasis upon such departures from the norm established by *F(S)1* as may be encountered in matters of physical condition, technique and subject matter.

147. *F(S)1.*

right of the left end of the block; in the top of the right-hand fragment (B), near the right end of the block, there are two dowel holes whose centers are 0.130 m. and 0.190 m. behind the front edge of the top surface; a dressing 0.045 m. in width extends the length of the block (cf. Pl. XXIII.2, 3).

Thirteen dancing girls including a kithara player (the sixth from the right) appear in the relief that adorns the face of the block. The figures are 0.246 m. in height, with slight variations, allowing an interval of approximately 0.015 m. between the tops of their poloi and the beginning of the crowning molding. Three have suffered extensive damage, the dancer at the extreme right being destroyed except for her right hand and lower forearm, while the first two figures at the opposite end of the block are preserved only from the hips up, the first of them surviving largely as a silhouette with head and arms intact. The accident which divided the original block into two fragments drove a vertical crack between the kithara player and the dancer to her rear, carrying away the latter's left foot.

The dancers glide on tiptoes against the undifferentiated background plane, and the bottom edge of the block provides the ground line upon which they place their feet. Moving uniformly toward the right, they are arranged in sets of facing pairs who dance *ἐπὶ καρπῷ*,[62] each dancer reaching her left hand forward to grasp the right wrist of her neighbor. This chain of repeated actions is interrupted by the kithara player, whose function prevents her from extending either arm; instead she looks ahead toward one companion, who faces her and extends her right arm toward her, while the dancer to her rear, also facing her, grasps a flounce of drapery between thumb and forefinger instead of holding her occupied right hand. In order that the latter figure may perform this action, her left arm reaches forward in a long curve which links her hand to the kitharist's flounce at a point somewhat higher than the other dancers' clasp of hand and wrist. Thus the kitharist's neighbors on both sides face her, forming with her a triad of figures which are related by gesture and glance. The rest of the dancers alternate in looking forward and backward; the dancer who follows the musician interrupts this pattern by looking forward, and thus is

62. See below, n. 140.

cast in the role of leader of a new set of dancers. This analysis accounts for all the figures' actions except that of the last dancer at the left end of the block. Her right hand is unengaged, so a design exactly consistent with the pattern already seen would place behind her a musician; however, the fact that she is looking forward excludes this.

The spacing of the figures is varied in such a manner that there is a greater distance, slight but measurable, between the facing dancers than between those whose heads turn away from each other. Within this basic system of alternation, exact regularity of spacing is eschewed in preference for a persistent variation (of millimeters) of the distances that separate all the figures from each other.

Excepting the musician, the figures are posed in such a way that the right leg and buttocks of each are raised as if in the act of shifting the body's weight over to the left leg, which is stiffened vertically to receive it. The transition from the profile representation of the legs to the quasifrontal position of the shoulders and arms is masked by the frontality of the upper drapery. Thus as a rule the frontal portrayal of the apoptygma contrasts abruptly with the profile view of the projecting buttocks; in the case of the kitharist, however, the apoptygma is foreshortened in obedience to the deviant position of the right arm. Slight variations in the shoulder contours accord with the alternating gestures of the figures, so that the downward slope of the right shoulder of each backward-turning dancer matches the slope of the opposite shoulder, while the right shoulder of the forward-turning figures is slightly raised.

Again, the poses of the heads alternate in agreement with gesture, the backward-turning heads tilting downward and projecting outward almost to a three-quarter view, while the backward-turning heads are carried more erectly and approximate more closely, if not exactly, the true profile view. The enlargement of a well-preserved head (fig. 148) reveals a face of ambiguous expressiveness, long and narrow in structure, with straight nose and full jaw and small eyes and mouth. The other heads are more damaged; however, a similar elongation seems to prevail among them, and the basic structure, including small eyes and mouths and long noses, is repeated. On the other hand, minor variations of detail impart a notable individuality to the faces that have survived: chins are sometimes pointed, sometimes heavy, noses sharp or straight.

Extreme height and slenderness of proportions characterize the figures as such. The heads are small, the shoulders narrow and the necks long. This attenuation is evident in the treatment of extremities, the legs and feet being elongated and the arms and hands exhibiting a linear fragility. The gestures of the hands are suggested by means of formulae abbreviating anatomy: the left hands which reach forward to grasp the adjoining figures' wrists are defined by the triangle of thumb and palm, while the inactive extended right hands show four well-defined fingers but no thumbs.

The dancers' costume consists, first of all, of a short-sleeved Ionic chiton, identifiable by means of the crinkled texture which marks the portion covering the upper arms and torso as well as the bottom edge emerging at the level of the feet. Their outer garment is a long mantle with overfall.[63] At the upper edge of the apoptygma there is a wide pleated border (diploidion) that descends from the left shoulder across the torso to a point below the right breast. The apoptygma terminates below at the level of the pelvis in a characteristic three-part pattern: this consists of lateral flaring clusters of vertical folds ending in a zigzag motif below, which enframe a central panel whose lower edge modulates from the broad pointed contour seen most clearly on the fourth dancer from the left, to the flat curve occurring on the figure that follows the kithara player. The mantle appears to be closed on the figure's right side; on the left side, it is open, as evidenced by the projecting curved flounce. The apoptygma, like the other representational features, follows a fundamentally unvarying pattern on all figures. Yet here, as elsewhere, modifications are introduced in agreement with the figures' alternating movements: the action of the backward-turning dancers is reflected (unmistakably in all but one instance) in a diagonal crease in the cloth crossing the abdomen. The lower part of the mantle clings to the legs, transparently exposing both knees and the entire length of the right leg, while the left leg is somewhat hidden by the intervening folds. Long, curving incised creases are visible on the right thighs of many of the figures. Between the legs the garment is disposed in one prominent vertical fold accompanied by narrower pleats, normally one on the side of the left leg and three on that of the right one.

An additional garment is worn by alternating dancers, those whose heads turn backward: this is a light scarf which is draped over the extended arms at the elbow, whence delicate folds descend to spread into a swallowtail double flounce with zigzag ornamentation. The scarf is represented as hanging behind the body, but its relationship to the arms varies insofar as it seems to hang sometimes in front of both arms, sometimes in front of the left arm but behind the right arm. This last arrangement is explicit in two cases, the sixth and eleventh figures from the left, where the horizontal upper edge of the scarf is seen to pass in front of the right arm just below elbow height.

The figures wear a low polos whose top surface slants slightly upward to meet the background plane. The coiffure upon which the polos rests provides a boldly projecting frame for the face. The straight rear profile of the head sometimes displays traces of a rounded projecting feature, quite certainly a bun (see fig. 148). The occurrence of the bun seems to be dependent upon the pose of the head: the heads shown in full profile re-

63. In Harrison, pp. 54 ff., the outer garment is identified as a mantle, and I have adopted this usage. However, in describing a naturalistic version of the costume which occurs on the Artemis of Gortyn (for which, see below, p. 211), G. E. Porro has used the term "peplo a diploidion" rather than mantle; he notes certain incongruities in its treatment, but suggests that these are to be explained by reference to the archaizing adoption of a form of dress unused for centuries past ("Il Pretorio di Gortina," *Bollettino d'arte*, VII, 1913, p. 359, fig. 10).

On this garment, see more recently Helga Herdejürgen (*Die thronende Göttin aus Tarent in Berlin*, Waldsassen-Bayern, 1968, pp. 63 ff.), who identifies it as a new form which had signalized the advent of an archaistic trend initiated ca. 480 B.C., in which the archaic "Schrägmantel" acquires certain features characteristic of the newly revived peplos: length, sleevelessness, overfall. The costume of the Samothracian dancers is discussed below (pp. 210 ff.) and in App. II (pp. 304 ff.).

148. Detail of *F(S)1.*

ceive it, while those turned outward toward the three-quarter view do not. The enlargements show that the hair is textured in a pattern of long roll-like curls that descend from beneath the polos toward the face, ending in round curls which border the forehead and temples. Careful scrutiny of the other illustrations will show, however, that this formula was sometimes varied with respect to both contours and texture. Thus the hair mass is sometimes angular in outline, sometimes rounded, and the roll-like and round units of surface pattern are not employed uniformly. Long strands of hair hang down upon the shoulders: in well-preserved examples, two strands normally are in evidence on the side opposite the facial profile, while one strand sometimes appears following the contour of the other shoulder.

The background relief plane slopes away from the vertical as it rises toward the crowning molding, with the result that the upper portions of the figures show a pronounced projection (the heads project 0.015-0.018 m.); this diminishes greatly in the descent toward the feet and edges of the lower drapery which are shown in very low relief.

Neatness and lightness of touch mark the execution of forms and textures throughout.

Preserved length 1.651; height (including molding) 0.322; thickness 0.313.

Both fragments were found ca. 2 m. north of the Terrace adjoining the Temenos.

F(S)2. 49.1043 E. Samothrace Museum; in storage. *Hesperia*, 20 (1951), p. 16. (Fig. 149.)

Small fragment in fair condition preserving a portion of the lower face of a block. The fragment forms a triangle with two long broken sides, based on a short side which constitutes a section of the lower edge of the block. The relief shows the lower half of one dancer, preserved from the waist down but lacking the left foot, and to the left, the left foot of a following dancer. The half figure is accompanied by swallowtail scarf-ends, permitting her reconstruction as a backward-turning dancer. Figure delicately proportioned; execution careful.

Preserved length 0.17; preserved height 0.164; preserved thickness 0.125.

Found ca. 2 m. north of the Terrace adjoining the Temenos.

149. *F(S)2.*

150. *F(S)3.*

F(S)3. 65.1146. Samothrace Museum; in storage. (Fig. 150.)
Weathered fragment, broken on all sides, partially preserving a single figure from the lower edge of the diagonal border of the apoptygma to the bottom of the skirt. The feet and bottom edges of chiton and mantle have been broken off, but the swallowtail scarf-ends remain to show that this was a dancer with head turned toward the rear. Figure boldly proportioned and loosely executed.

Preserved length 0.17; preserved height 0.16; preserved thickness 0.054.

Found in a dump on the Eastern Hill.

F(S)4. 67.32-65.99. Samothrace Museum; on exhibition. *Skopas in Samothrace*, pp. 4 f., figs. 11, 12, 13; Stewart, p. 107, n. 39. (Figs. 151, 152, 153; pl. XXV.)
Weathered fragmentary block, reconstituted from two fragments. The better preserved of two corner blocks of the frieze. The corner and portions of the two adjacent faces of the block are preserved to less than half their original height. The lower edge of the block is preserved; the block terminates above in a horizontal break and at the right and left ends of the two faces in vertical breaks. Side A (fig. 151) shows parts of two figures advancing to the right; side B (figs. 152, 153) whose surface is largely composed of the smaller, restored fragment, shows part of a single figure moving in the same direction.

The two dancers on A have been severed just below the waist. Swallowtail scarf-ends adjoin the left-hand figure, identifying her as a backward-turning dancer. These figures are exceptional in placing and proportions: the dancer at the right is pressed very close to the end of the block, in a position that barely allows for inclusion of her advancing left foot; the figure itself is compressed, moreover, so that the distance between the knees is measurably shorter than in the case of her companion. The end of the scarf that hangs between the two dancers almost touches the back of the corner figure's thigh, indicating a much closer spacing of these two than is found in the other preserved portions of the frieze. (Measured at the knees, these figures are in fact only 0.045 m. apart, while the closest of the figures on *F(S)11* [see fig. 158] are 0.06 m. apart at this point.) Just above this swallowtail there appears what must have been the extended left hand of the second dancer which almost touches her companion's buttocks. These details imply a pose on the part of the corner figure that would, again, be unprecedented in the preserved portions of the frieze: quite evidently the meeting of hand and wrist encountered elsewhere did not take place here, and some alternative action must have been performed by this dancer.

The smaller, split-off fragment of the recomposed block bears the left foot of the corner figure on A as well as a section of the corner itself and the major portion of the half-figure that occupies B. Like its neighbor around the corner, this dancer is narrower than normal; it, too, is placed very close to the end of the block. The proportions of the figures are gross, the execution clumsy.

151. *F(S)4.* Side A.

152. *F(S)4.* Side B.

153. *F(S)4.* Fragment of Side B.

A: preserved length 0.226; preserved height 0.15; B: preserved length 0.125; preserved height 0.153; greatest preserved thickness of restored block 0.135.

Both fragments were found on the Western Hill, south of the northern foundation of the Byzantine fortress.

F(S)5. 50.451. Samothrace Museum; in storage. *Hesperia*, 21 (1952), p. 25, n. 27. (Fig. 154.)

Minute relief fragment, broken on all sides, but with surface in excellent state of preservation, showing the characteristic cluster of drapery folds between a dancer's legs, adjoined by an unmistakable right knee and part of a left thigh. Precise execution.

Preserved length 0.054; preserved height 0.066; preserved thickness 0.015.

Found in an Austrian dump inside the Temenos.

154. *F(S)5.*

F(S)6. 50.507. Samothrace Museum; in storage. (Fig. 155.) Small worn fragment preserving a portion of the lower edge of the relief with, at the left side, the advancing lower left leg and part of the central drapery folds of a dancer moving to the right. The right side of the fragment is broken at the point where another dancer might be expected to have appeared; however, the outline of the break curves toward the first figure in a manner that suggests that it was not a dancer but some other compositional element, unprecedented among the surviving portions of the frieze, that stood here.

Preserved length 0.155; preserved height 0.077; preserved thickness 0.066.

Surface find inside the southeast corner of the Temenos.

155. *F(S)6.*

F(S)7. 39.515. Samothrace Museum; in storage. *AJA*, 44 (1940), p. 339. (Fig. 156.) Small weathered relief fragment, broken on all sides, preserving the lower torso and upper thighs of a dancer; normal drapery features are shown, including part of a swallowtail flounce to the right of the figure. The adjoining relief surface, further to the right, is worn away.[64]

64. This fragment was incorrectly mentioned in a preliminary report as part of a "rounded Monument" (*AJA*, 44 [1940], p. 339).

Preserved length 0.055; preserved height 0.039; preserved thickness 0.033.
Found among the debris on the surface of the Rotunda of Arsinoe.

156. *F(S)7.*

156A. *F(S)9.*

F(S)8. (A) 50.508, (B) 50.549. Samothrace Museum; in storage. (C) Paris, Louvre, Entry Cat. no. 1434; in storage.

Under this number are grouped three minute fragments showing insignificant parts or traces of single dancers moving from left to right. They offer no evidence concerning the frieze that is not better provided by the blocks and fragments of which detailed description is given in this Catalogue.

A was found on the surface inside the southeastern corner of the precinct; B near the northeast corner of the Hieron; provenance of C unknown.

F(S)9. 79.214. Samothrace Museum; in storage. (Fig. 156A.)

Fragment of relief without finished edges, showing the buttocks and part of the right leg and drapery of a dancer. An irregular horizontal break cuts through the leg above the ankle and through the lower drapery. The surface is badly worn.

Preserved length 0.08; preserved height 0.094; preserved thickness 0.03.

Found in the debris of a late Byzantine or post-Byzantine structure on the terrace between the Stoa and the Byzantine fortification.

II. Frieze blocks and fragments with figures moving from right to left

F(S)10. Louvre MA698. Samothrace Museum (on permanent loan from the Musée du Louvre); on exhibition. Cyriacus of Ancona (fifteenth-century copies after): Bodleian Ms. Lat. misc. d. 85, fol. 137v-138v; Laurentianus Ashburnensis 1174, fol. 123v, 124r, 125r;[65] O. F. von Richter, *Wallfahrten im Morgenland*, Berlin, 1882, p. 443; *Reise*, pp. 62 f., pl. 12 (center); *S,II*, pp. 13f., 23 f., pl. IX, fig. 2; Charles Champoiseau, "La Victoire de Samothrace," *RA*, n.s. 39 (1880), p. 11; E. Peterson, "Die dreigestaltige Hekate," *Archaeologisch-Epigraphische Mitteilungen aus Oesterreich*, 5 (1881), p. 12; Rubensohn, pp. 133 f.; A. Héron de Villefosse, *Catalogue sommaire des marbres antiques* (Musée du Louvre, Département des antiquités grecques et romaines), Paris [1896], p. 39, no. 698; Erich Ziebarth, "Cyriacus von Ancona in Samothrake," *AthMitt*, 31 (1906), p. 408; Martin Schede, *Antikes Traufleisten-Ornament*, Strassbourg, 1909, p. 87; Salomon Reinach, *Répertoire de reliefs grecs et romains*, II, Paris, 1909-12, p. 268, no. 3; Otto Kern, *RE, s.v., Kabeiros und Kabeiroi*, X, col. 1428; Schmidt, pp. 39 f.; August Brinckmann, "Altgriechische Mädchenriegen," *BonnJbb*, 130 (1925), pp. 134 f.; Camillo Praschniker, *Zur Geschichte des Akroters* (Schriften der philosophischen Fakultät der deutschen Universität in Prag, 5), Brünn-Prague-Leipzig-Vienna, 1929, p. 35; Hermann Thiersch, *Pro Samothrake*, Vienna and Leipzig, 1930, p. 6; Demangel, p. 442; Chapouthier, p. 157; M. Folman, *Introduction à l'étude de la sculpture archaïsante*, Montpelier, 1935, pp. 13, 66; Charles Picard, *Manuel d'archéologie grecque, La sculpture*, I, Paris, 1935, p. 393, n. 6; Fritz Saxl, "The Classical Inscription in Renaissance Art and Politics," *JWarb*, 4 (1940), pp. 34 f., 44, pl. 7b; Giovanni Becatti, "Lo stile arcaistico," *La Critica d'arte*, 6 (1941), p. 40; Karl Lehmann-Hartleben, "Cyriacus of Ancona, Aristotle and Teiresias in Samothrace," *Hesperia*, 12 (1943), pp. 115 ff., pl. IIb; André Dessenne, "Pyxis à figures noires du Musée d'Athènes," *RA*, ser. 6, 36 (1950), pp. 71 f.; C[harles] P[icard], "Sur une frise samothracienne," *ibid.*, pp. 157 ff.; *Hesperia*, 20 (1951), p. 16, pl. 8b; *Guide*[1], p. 81; W. Fuchs, *Die Vorbilder der Neuattischen Reliefs, JdI*, Ergänzungsheft 20 (1959), p. 52, n. 37, p. 55, n. 59; *Guide*[2], p. 84; *Guide*[3], p. 88; C. M. Havelock, "Archaistic Reliefs of the Hellenistic Period," *AJA*, 68 (1964), p. 50; Harrison, p. 54; Ridgway, p. 203; P. W. Lehmann, "An Antique Ornament Set in a Renaissance Tower," *RA*, n.s. 2 (1968), pp. 197 ff., 204, 212 ff., figs. 1, 11; *Samothracian Reflections*, pp. 18, 26, 56, 100, 105 ff., 108, n. 89, 115, n. 110, fig. 30; *Skopas in Samothrace*, pp. 4, 11, fig. 45; *Guide*[4], p. 100; Stewart, p. 107, n. 39. (Fig. 157).

65. See below, n. 81, on the possibility that Cyriacus of Ancona's drawings depend on the dancer type shown in *Fa* as well as that of *F(S)10* and *F(S)11*.

157. *F(S)10.*

One of two fragmentary blocks (see also *F(S)11*) evidently removed from the Sanctuary for reuse as decoration in one of three watchtowers which were erected by the Gattilusi during the fifteenth century in Palaiopolis and which are still partially intact. The French Consul Charles Champoiseau extracted these blocks from the tower in 1863 and transported them to the Louvre. With other Samothracian finds, they were returned to the Island in 1955 as the result of an exchange which brought to the Louvre the right hand and finger fragments of the Winged Victory (see J. Charbonneaux, "La main droite de la Victoire de Samothrace," *Hesperia*, 21 [1952], pp. 44 ff.).

The question whether these blocks were originally intended to be joined together has remained unresolved until very recently. When they were set in the Gattilusi tower, *F(S)10* was placed to the right of and joined to *F(S)11*, for so they are shown in the drawings by Cyriacus of Ancona. This initial reconstruction appears to have been invited by the vertical smoothness of the breaks terminating *F(S)10* on the left and *F(S)11* on the right. But these are, in fact, broken, not finished ends, so a joint between them cannot be assumed; accordingly, the Louvre authorities for many years exhibited the blocks detached, but in the order in which Cyriacus recorded them (*Hesperia*, 12 [1943], pl. IIb; P. W. Lehmann, "An Antique Ornament Set in a Renaissance Tower," *RA*, n.s. 2 [1968], pp. 198 f., fig. 1). However, each block does possess one finished end (the right on *F(S)10* and the left on *F(S)11*), and at some time, at least by the 1940s, the installation in the Louvre was changed in such a way that the two finished ends were joined and the tympanist took the central position among the total of thirteen figures which occupy the two blocks. In 1951 Karl Lehmann published the blocks in this manner (*Hesperia*, 20 [1951], p. 16, n. 53, pl. 8b), and so they have remained since that date, both in their installation in the Samothrace Museum and in all subsequent publications (see bibliography for all items after 1951). In July of 1975, however, Phyllis Williams Lehmann thoroughly reexamined the blocks and reached the conclusion that the by then long-accepted assumption that the blocks belonged together in this order as a joining pair was not tenable. This conclusion was based on the following observations: the right arm of the first figure at the left end of *F(S)11* is not high enough to reach the rear drapery flounce of the tympanist at the right end of *F(S)10* (compare figure following kitharist on *F(S)1*), and the backward-facing pose of the same dancer is not appropriate to a figure situated behind a musician, assuming that the pattern of poses seen clearly in *F(S)1* is obeyed throughout the frieze (see also *F(S)11* itself, where the dancer following the flutist quite certainly faces forward: this can be ascertained by touch, for the projecting bun found at the back of many of the dancers' heads is evident here to the hand, if not to the eye). Accordingly, blocks *F(S)10* and *F(S)11* have now been installed separately in the Samothrace Museum, and are published thus in this Catalogue.

F(S)10, like its companion from the Gattilusi tower *F(S)11*, has been sawed lengthwise (possibly in the process of extraction from the tower and transportation to France), and therefore preserves a thickness of only a few centimeters. The right end of the block was finished, since it shows anathyrosis; the left end terminates in an almost vertical break. The lower edge of the block, the sculptured frieze, and the crowning moulding survive, but their surfaces are extremely battered and weatherworn.

Seven dancers are represented, including a tympanist (the last figure to the right). The tympanist is preceded by a dancer with head turned back toward her, who initiates a new chain of pairs, of which two are complete. Of the last pair at the left end of the block only one figure survives: her right arm reaches forward to be severed by a vertical break which terminates the block at precisely the point where her hand would have met the succeeding dancer's wrist. Although the torsos of the other figures are shown in approximately frontal position, the tympanist is represented wholly in profile, as in the case of the kitharist of *F(S)1*. The heads are so much damaged that the alternation of forward and backward glances is not clearly apparent; only in two cases is the swallowtail scarf distinctly seen; the details of the apoptygma, in particular its diagonal upper edge, are lost; the precise manner in which the hands are joined cannot be determined; the vertical folds of the lower mantle are blunted and distorted. Among the preserved frieze figures, these dancers are exceptional for their height in relation to the height of the block: so tall are they that a negligible distance (0.005 m.) remains between the tops of their poloi and the molding above. (Contrast *F(S)1*, where the poloi are separated by 0.015 m. from the point where the curve of the moulding begins.) The condition of the surface forbids precise comment, but the figures appear loosely structured and the execution seems careless.

Preserved length 0.89; preserved height 0.328; preserved thickness 0.07 (as a result of the sawing off of the face of the block in the nineteenth century).

Found in a tower built by the Gattilusi in Palaiopolis.

F(S)11. Louvre MA699. Samothrace Museum (on permanent loan from the Musée du Louvre); on exhibition. Cyriacus of Ancona (fifteenth-century copies after): Bodleian Ms. Lat. misc. d. 85, fol. 137v-138r; Laurentianus Ashburnensis 1174, fol. 123v, 124r, 125r;[66] O. F. von Richter, *Wallfahrten im Morgenland*, Berlin, 1822, p. 443; *Reise*, pp. 62 f., pl. 12 (top); *S,II*, pp. 13 f., 23 f., pl. IX, fig. 1; Charles Champoiseau, "La Victoire de Samothrace," *RA*, n.s. 39 (1880), p. 11; E. Petersen, "Die dreigestaltige Hekate," *Archaeologisch-Epigraphische Mitteilungen aus Oesterreich*, 5 (1881), p. 12; Rubensohn, pp. 133 f.; A. Héron de Villefosse, *Catalogue sommaire des marbres antiques* (Musée du Louvre, Département des antiquités grecques et romaines), Paris [1896], p. 39, no. 699; Erich Ziebarth, "Cyriacus von Ancona in Samothrake," *AthMitt*, 31 (1906), p. 408; Martin Schede, *Antikes Traufleisten-Ornament*, Strassbourg, 1909, p. 87; Salomon Reinach, *Répertoire de reliefs grecs et romains*, II, Paris, 1909-12, p. 268, no. 2; Otto Kern, *RE, s.v. Kabeiros und Kabeiroi*, X, col. 1428; Schmidt, pp. 39 f., pl. XVII, 1; August Brinckmann, "Altgriechische Mädchenriegen," *BonnJbb*, 130 (1925), pp. 134 f.; Camillo Praschniker, *Zur Geschichte des Akroters* (Schriften der philosophischen Fakultät der deutschen Universität in Prag, 5), Brünn-Prague-Leipzig-Vienna, 1929, p. 35; Demangel, p. 442; Chapouthier, p. 157; M. Folman, *Introduction à l'étude de la sculpture archaïsante*, Montpelier, 1935, pp. 13, 66; Charles Picard, *Manuel d'archéologie grecque, La sculpture*, I, Paris, 1935, p. 393, n. 6; F. Saxl, "The Classical Inscription in Renaissance Art and Politics," *JWarb*, 4 (1940), pp. 34 f., 44, pl. 7b; Giovanni Becatti, "Lo stile arcaistico," *La Critica d'arte*, 6 (1941), p. 40; Karl Lehmann-Hartleben, "Cyriacus of Ancona, Aristotle and Teiresias in Samothrace," *Hesperia*, 12 (1943), pp. 115 ff., pl. IIb; André Dessenne, "Pyxis à figures noires du Musée d'Athènes," *RA*, ser. 6, 36 (1950), pp. 71 f.; C[harles] P[icard], "Sur une frise samothracienne," *ibid.*, pp. 157 ff.; *Hesperia*, 20 (1951), p. 16, pl. 8b; *Guide*[1], p. 81; W. Fuchs, *Die Vorbilder der Neuattischen Reliefs, JdI*, Ergänzungsheft 20 (1959), p. 52, n. 37, p. 55, n. 59; *Guide*[2], p. 84; *Guide*[3], p. 88; C. M. Havelock, "Archaistic Reliefs of the Hellenistic Period," *AJA*, 68 (1964), p. 50; Harrison, p. 54; Ridgway, p. 203; P. W. Lehmann, "An Antique Ornament Set in a Renaissance Tower," *RA*, n.s. 2 (1968), pp. 197 ff., 204, 212 ff., figs. 1, 11; *Samothracian Reflections*, pp. 18, 26, 56, 100, 105 ff., 108, n. 89, 115, n. 110, fig. 30; *Skopas in Samothrace*, pp. 4, 10, n. 62, 11, fig. 45; *Guide*[4], p. 100; Stewart, p. 107, n. 39. (Fig. 158.)

For the history of this block, see *F(S)10*. The relief surface is more damaged than that of its companion from the Gattilusi tower and the crowning molding is only intermittently preserved. The bottom edge and part of the finished left end are preserved. Six dancers appear, of which the last to the right has been partially carried away by a vertical splitting

66. See above, n. 65.

of the block. The preservation of the rest is sketchy, especially in the upper portions. The third figure from the right, to judge from the position of the arms, is an instrumentalist playing the double flute: in this case, as in *F(S)1* and *F(S)10*, an exception is made to the rule of frontal presentation of the upper body in order to accommodate the gesture of the musician, who is shown in profile. Parts of the background surface are so rough as to seem incompletely finished. The figures apparently agree with those of *F(S)10* in proportions and technique.

Preserved length 0.75; preserved height 0.328; preserved thickness 0.07 (as a result of the sawing off of the face of the block in the nineteenth century).

Found in a tower built by the Gattilusi in Palaiopolis.

158. *F(S)11.*

F(S)12. 49.1043 C. Samothrace Museum; on exhibition. *Hesperia*, 20 (1951), p. 16, pls. 9b, 14c; *Guide*[1], p. 81; Werner Fuchs, *Die Vorbilder der Neuattischen Reliefs, JdI*, Ergänzungsheft, 20 (1959), p. 52, n. 37, p. 55, n. 59; *Guide*[2], p. 84; Christine M. Havelock, "Archaistic Reliefs of the Hellenistic Period," *AJA*, 68 (1964), p. 50, n. 28; Harrison, p. 54, n. 37, p. 61, n. 93; *Guide*[3], p. 88; Ridgway, p. 203; P. W. Lehmann, "An Antique Ornament Set in a Renaissance Tower," *RA*, n.s. 2 (1968), p. 197, n. 3; *Samothracian Reflections*, p. 104, n. 85; *Guide*[4], p. 100; Stewart, p. 107, n. 39. (Figs. 159, 160; Pl. XXIV.1.)

Fragmentary block, recomposed out of two fragments; on the face, four dancers. The upper surface of the right end of the block is partly preserved, showing anathyrosis; the left end has been sheared away diagonally. Portions of the bottom and top surfaces are preserved, with much of the crowning molding. On the top near the preserved end there are a dowel hole and a Π-clamp hole; there is a dowel hole in the bottom surface at this end. In addition to a jagged break dividing the block into two pieces and running from its lower center toward its upper right corner, a conspicuous crack crosses the face of the

159. *F(S)12.*

160. Detail of *F(S)12.*

block from the upper left to the lower right side. The lower left corner has been sliced away, destroying the right arm and leg, the lower drapery and both feet of the first figure on the left, as well as the lower drapery and feet of her neighbor. The left dancer's head has disappeared leaving only the profile, turning right.

The second dancer from the left is otherwise the best preserved figure on the block, providing a detailed and refined version of the forward-looking dancer as described in *F(S)1* (see detail, fig. 148). The execution is precise, with particular attention given to the plastic definition of shapes and textures.

Here and in the dancer to the left a change in the arrangement of the mantle is clearly evident that must have been typical of the blocks showing left-moving figures: the diagonal upper border of the apoptygma now descends across the breast from left to right rather than from right to left.

The remaining figures are in very poor condition, the dancer at the extreme right surviving only in a very battered head with bun and sketchy indications of the right arm and lower drapery, and the next dancer to her right preserving a fragmentary polos and damaged portions of lower arms, legs, and drapery.

Preserved length 0.559; height 0.326; preserved thickness 0.348.

Found ca. 2 m. north of the Terrace adjoining the Temenos.

F(S)13. 50.378. Samothrace Museum; in storage. *Hesperia*, 21 (1952), p. 25, n. 27, (Fig. 161; Pl. XXIV.2.)

Battered block apparently preserved to its full length, with parts of the top and bottom surfaces also partially intact. The left end shows anathyrosis, and the rear lower corner of the right end seems original; however, neither end has fully preserved its angular contours and loss of all the corners of the right end has reduced it to a mere stump. The bottom and back of the block are roughly finished. In the back, at the upper left end, there is a rectangular cutting (0.26 m. x 0.24 m.) shaped irregularly but as if for the insertion of a beam, perhaps for a post-antique reuse of the block. The crowning molding has vanished entirely, as has the lower part of the relief surface, so that all the figures are cut off at the level of the knees. The remaining relief surface is severely damaged, but the outlines of three dancers are clearly discernible in the center of the block. The middle figure in this group can be reconstructed as a left-moving dancer given the pose of its right arm and the traces of drapery at its right hip; the shadow of a swallowtail flounce seems to hang over the lower right arm, allowing for the supposition that this figure turns its head to the rear, while its two companions should face ahead, in keeping with the pattern of actions seen in *F(S)1*. The length of the block would accommodate an additional dancer at the left end, of which, however, no trace remains; a half-figure, of which the extended right arm survives, must have occupied the right end.[67]

67. This appears to be the block that is mentioned, perhaps through a typographical error, as 50.371, in a preliminary report (*Hesperia*, 21 [1952], p. 25, n. 27), where Karl Lehmann suggests that it

Length 0.566; height 0.32; thickness 0.305.

Found on the surface ca. 5 m. outside the southwest corner of the Terrace adjoining the Temenos.

---

may be identical with $F\gamma$, a block described by Conze. However, since Conze stated that $F\gamma$ was long enough (about 0.87 m.) to contain seven figures, this identification seems to be mistaken. For $F\gamma$, see below, p. 200.

161. *F(S)13.*

162. *F(S)14.*

F(S)14. 50.620. Samothrace Museum; in storage. *Hesperia,* 21 (1952), p. 25, n. 27. (Fig. 162.)

Badly damaged fragmentary block, broken at both ends and at the bottom, preserving traces of the crowning molding, the roughly dressed rear surface and part of the finished right end. In the top surface near the right end there are a dowel hole, a pry hole and a Π-clamp hole. Two dancers can be dimly discerned on the front surface; a diagonal break, however, has removed the lower part of the left figure, from a point approximately at the lower edge of the apoptygma, and a somewhat larger portion of the right figure. Traces of the left arms of both dancers are visible, and the diagonal position of these arms indicates that the dancers move toward the left.

Preserved length 0.435; height 0.324; thickness 0.322.

Found in an Austrian dump 5 to 6 m. west of the southwest corner of the Temenos.

F(S)15. 49.1043d. Samothrace Museum; in storage. *Hesperia,* 21 (1952), p. 25, n. 27. (Fig. 163.)

Fragmentary, badly weathered block with broken right end and top, bottom and left end surfaces partially preserved, and the crowning molding worn away. Anathyrosis is visible on the left end, and a broken Π-clamp hole has survived near this end. Traces of two dancers, one of them situated close to the left end of the block, are discernible; the right end of the block is worn away on a diagonal line occurring where the profile of a third dancer would normally be found. The lower drapery and feet of both figures are lost. A fragment of swallowtail drapery adjoining the thigh of the left figure permits its reconstruction as a backward-turning dancer, while the closed rear silhouette of the other raises the question whether this may not be a musician with both arms extended forward, comparable to the flute player of *F(S)11*, or a dancer carrying some other attribute;[68] this figure in any case appears to face forward.

Preserved length 0.352; height 0.322; thickness 0.285.

Found ca. 2 m. north of the Terrace adjoining the Temenos.

68. See below, n. 74.

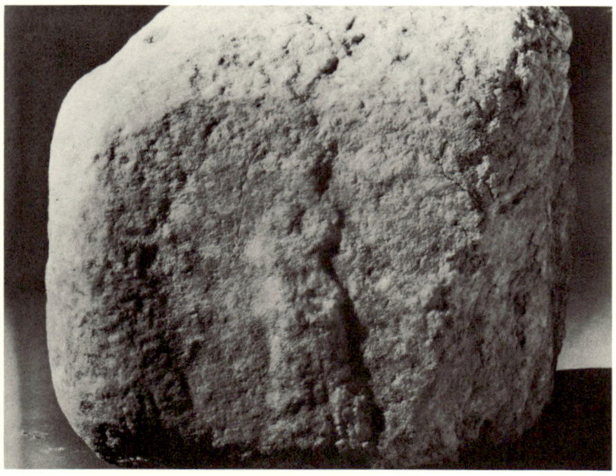

163. *F(S)15.*

164. *F(S)16.*

F(S)16. 63.144. Samothrace Museum; in storage. (Fig. 164; Pl. XXIV.3.) Battered, fragmentary block broken at the left end, but retaining the other surfaces in a state of partial preservation; the right end is roughly dressed and shows anathyrosis. A Π-clamp and a pry hole appear in the top surface at the right end. The outlines of three dancers are barely visible on the front of the block, evidently a normal trio, in which the middle figure wears the swallowtail scarf and looks backward.

Preserved length 0.387; height 0.324; thickness 0.29.

Found in the ruined chapel of Hagios Nikolaos in the region of Ano Meria, where it had been used as a support for the altar table.

165. *F(S)17.*

166. *F(S)18.*

167. *F(S)19.*

F(S)17. 54.214. Samothrace Museum; in storage. (Fig. 165.) Damaged, fragmentary block broken at the left end. Portions of the relief surface as well as of the bottom, top and right end are preserved; the right end is roughly dressed, showing anathyrosis. The crowning molding is completely worn away. A Π-clamp hole appears at the right end of the block. In spite of severe erosion of the relief surface, two dancers are clearly visible, the one adjoining the right end of the block lacking its head and much of its upper torso, and its neighbor surviving only fragmentarily in the central portion of the figure and thighs. Traces of the swallowtail scarf are evident adorning the right-hand dancer who, therefore, must have looked backward.

Preserved length 0.332; height 0.322; thickness 0.19.

Found on the hillside east of the Temenos.

F(S)18. 50.621. Samothrace Museum; in storage. (Fig. 166.)

Damaged fragmentary block, broken at both ends but retaining portions of its top, bottom, and front surfaces; crowning molding worn away. The torso and thighs of a figure occupy the small area of relief surface that survives. Details of drapery are not discernible, but the pose and traces of an extended right arm and scarf make the type of the frieze dancer and its left-to-right movement unmistakable.

Preserved length 0.400; height 0.326; preserved thickness 0.29.

Found 5 to 6 m. west of the southwest corner of the Temenos in an Austrian dump.

F(S)19. 49.1043f. Samothrace Museum; in storage. *Hesperia*, 20 (1951), p. 16, n. 55. (Fig. 167.)

Fragment broken on three sides but preserving a portion of the bottom of a frieze block with a section of the relief surface, which shows part of the right side of a dancer with lower right arm, a corner of the apoptygma, lower mantle, right foot; the swallowtail flounce indicates that the head turned backward.

Preserved length 0.135; preserved height 0.164; preserved thickness 0.06.

Found ca. 2 m. north of the Terrace adjoining the Temenos.

F(S)20. 50.481. Samothrace Museum; in storage. *Hesperia*, 21 (1952), p. 25, n. 27. (Fig. 168.)

Worn and irregularly shaped relief fragment, broken on all sides, showing the middle sections of two dancers. The torso and part of the skirt, with traces of the left arm, of the figure at the left are visible, and of the right-hand figure the torso, both arms and, to its right, a swallowtail drapery flounce.[69]

Preserved length 0.24; preserved height 0.145; preserved thickness 0.045.

Found in 1949 with other fragments of the frieze north of the Terrace adjoining the Temenos and later reaccessioned.

69. The preliminary report referred to in n. 67, above, mentions a fragmentary block with two figures as 50.481c (*sic*), identifying it, without evident reason, as being possibly part of *F(S)15*.

168. *F(S)20.*

F(S)21. 49.1043g. Samothrace Museum; in storage. *Hesperia,* 20 (1951), p. 16, n. 55. (Fig. 169.)

Fragment, broken on sides and bottom, preserving a small section of top surface, crowning molding and relief. A dancer's head with polos, facing left, appears; a loosely defined curving object seems to project from the back of the head.

Preserved length 0.15; preserved height 0.135; preserved thickness 0.10.

Found ca. 2 m. north of the Terrace adjoining the Temenos.

169. *F(S)21.*

170. *F(S)22.*

171. *F(S)23.*

172. *F(S)24.*

F(S)22. 50.570. Samothrace Museum; in storage. *Hesperia,* 21 (1952), p. 25, n. 25. (Fig. 170.)

Weathered fragment consisting of a portion of the bottom of a block, broken on other edges. Relief shows figure of a dancer from the knees to the feet. Right foot severed; lower chiton no longer visible.

Preserved length 0.084; preserved height 0.113; preserved thickness 0.05.

Found 15 m. west of the Terrace adjoining the Temenos.

F(S)23. 50.538. Samothrace Museum; in storage. (Fig. 171.)

Weathered chip from the lower front of a block, broken on three sides but preserving a portion of the bottom of the block. The relief shows faint traces of the legs and drapery of a dancer moving to the left.

Preserved length 0.148; preserved height 0.10; preserved thickness 0.03.

Found in an Austrian dump inside the Temenos.

F(S)24. 50.354. Samothrace Museum; in storage. (Fig. 172.)

Fragment broken on two sides but preserving, in weathered condition, portions of the bottom and left end of a block. The relief face shows a dancer's fragmentary right foot advancing to the left, part of the left foot and the lower parts of the mantle and chiton.

Preserved length 0.09; preserved height 0.063; preserved thickness 0.105.

Found in an Austrian dump inside the Temenos.

173. *F(S)25.*

174. *F(S)26.*

F(S)25. 50.26. Samothrace Museum; in storage. (Fig. 173.)
Worn fragment, broken on three sides, preserving a small portion of the bottom of a block The relief shows the left foot and part of lower drapery of a dancer moving to the left.

Preserved length 0.087; preserved height 0.066; preserved thickness 0.05.

Found north of the Hieron.

F(S)26. 50.60. Samothrace Museum; in storage. (Fig. 174.)
Minute fragment, broken on all sides, but with surface well preserved, coming from the lower central part of a dancer's drapery. It shows a section of the large vertical fold characteristic of the lower mantle, with four pleats adjoining it to the right; to the left are visible a thin pleat and a pair of creases curving to the left just below the knee (compare detail of *F(S)12*, fig. 160). Precise execution.

Preserved length 0.42; preserved height 0.029; preserved thickness 0.02.

Found on the Terrace adjoining the Temenos.

F(S)27. 50.450. Samothrace Museum; in storage. *Hesperia*, 21 (1952), p. 25, n. 27. (Fig. 175.)
Fragment, broken on all sides, bearing a portion of the upper thighs of a dancer with a damaged segment of the central drapery fold.

Preserved length 0.125; preserved height 0.06; preserved thickness 0.05.

Found in an Austrian dump inside the Temenos.

175. *F(S)27.*

175A. *F(S)29.*

F(S)28. (A) 49.1043h, (B) 50.569, (C) 53.605. Samothrace Museum; in storage. Under this number are grouped three fragments showing relatively small parts or traces of single dancers moving from right to left. They offer no evidence concerning the frieze that is not better provided by the blocks and fragments of which detailed description is given in this Catalogue.

A found ca. 2 m. north of the Terrace adjoining the Temenos; B found 13 m. west of the same Terrace; C found on slope opposite north corner of Propylon.

F(S)29. 79.151. Samothrace Museum; in storage. (Fig. 175A.) Fragment of relief without preserved edges, showing torso and upper thighs of a dancer, with traces of upper right arm. Surface badly worn.

Preserved length 0.074; preserved height 0.099; preserved thickness 0.051.

Found on the surface south of the Byzantine fortification.

F(P)30. Paris, Musée du Louvre (Entry Catalogue, no. 1435); in storage. Fragment recorded in a scale drawing in 1950 by Karl Lehmann, who noted that the thickness was not preserved and that both ends and the bottom surface were broken. Surviving are portions of the top surface, crowning moulding, and relief surface, where a dancer's head with polos who faces to the left is sketchily defined.

Preserved length 0.32; preserved height 0.251.

Provenance not recorded.

176. *F(V)31.*

177. *F(V)32.*

F(V)31. Inv. No. I, 1700. Vienna, Ephesos-Museum.
S,*I*, p. 10, fig. 2; S,*II*, p. 13; *Hesperia*, 20 (1951), p. 16, n. 55; ***Funde aus Ephesos und Samothrake***, Vienna, 1978, No. 217. (Fig. 176.)

Weathered fragment broken at right and top, preserving portions of the bottom and left end of a corner block. On the relief surface there appears the lower part of a dancer, from the knees down, with the advancing right foot and portions of both legs and of the chiton and mantle. Left face of block shows no trace of relief.

Preserved length 0.155; preserved height 0.017.

Found near the northeast corner of the Hieron.

F(V)32. Inv. No. I, 1701. Vienna, Kunsthistorisches Museum, Antikensammlung; in storage. S,*I*, p. 10, fig. 3; S,*II*, p. 13; *Hesperia*, 20 (1951), p. 16, n. 55. (Fig. 177.)

Small fragment, in poor state of preservation, broken on the top and sides, consisting of a portion of the bottom of a frieze block, showing on its front surface the lower legs and drapery, with parts of both feet, of a dancer advancing to the left.

Preserved length 0.099; preserved height 0.065.

Found near the northeast corner of the Hieron.

178. *Fa.*

III. Additional blocks and fragments of the frieze of which record is preserved but which are today missing.

Fa. O. F. von Richter, *Wallfahrten im Morgenland*, Berlin, 1822, p. 443; Major Sir Grenville Temple, *Travels in Greece and Turkey*, London, 1843, vol. 1, p. 111; Blau and Schlottmann, "Altertümer von Samothrake und Imbros," *Berl. Ber.*, 1855, p. 622; E. G[erhard], "Altertümer von Samothrake," *AZ*, 14 (1856), cols. 241 ff., pl. XCV, no. 8; *Reise*, p. 62, n. 1; *S,I*, p. 43; *S,II*, p. 12. (Fig. 178.)

In the report of Blau and Schlottmann's visit to Samothrace in 1854, they state, p. 622, that they saw a block representing six female figures. The block was not illustrated in this official report. However, the following year, in his brief paraphrase of their report in the *Archäologische Zeitung*, Gerhard published an illustration, evidently based on a sketch by one of the travelers, showing a relief on which six and one-half dancers are represented clasping hands, which he correctly characterized as having seven figures. All wear scarfs ending in swallowtails, and all are frontally posed, with heads turned slightly to the left. The feet are splayed outward, the right one in each case touching the lower edge of the block. They wear no poloi. Notable features of their hair arrangement are the thick tresses hanging on the left side of the face and the rounded knot (?) projecting from above the right forehead. Their costume is simpler than that normally found on the dancers of the frieze, and lacks its characteristic features. A single long garment is indicated, close fitted at the bust, girded, with curving neckline, sleeves undefined, and full gathered skirt.

Blau and Schlottmann, *op. cit.*, p. 622, state that they saw their block in the central tower. They give no measurements for it. An approximate length of 0.91 can be calculated for it on the basis of a unit of 0.14 which is the length occupied by one dancer on *F(S)10.*[70]

70. Temple mentions, among the ancient stones reused in the towers overlooking the sea, "one of the fragments of a bas-relief, representing seven draperied female figures probably some of the Muses." Although *Fa* in fact depicts six and one-half figures (see fig. 178), there can be little doubt that it is the block referred to. *F(S)10* (fig. 157), also from the towers, shows seven figures too, but we know from Cyriacus of Ancona's drawing (figs. 4, 5) that it adjoined a six-figure block, *F(S)11* (fig. 158); so it would hardly have been singled out for mention independent of its companion. It is so far inexplicable that, while Cyriacus' attention was primarily focused on *F(S)10* and *F(S)11*, the next series of visi-

Fβ. Deville-Coquart, p. 276; *S,I*, p. 10; *Hesperia*, 20 (1951), p. 16, n. 55.

Deville and Coquart mention "un tout petit fragment de bas-relief; la jambe d'une danseuse avec quelques plis flottants de sa robe . . ." which they considered might imply that an altar was situated on the platform which they characterized as "un îlot, au fond du ravin, 20 mètres environ plus bas que le sanctuaire principal"—i.e., the Stoa.

This provenance refers to the area of the Temenos-terrace. It was to the north of the terrace wall that many elements of the frieze came to light in 1949 and 1950. It is likely that the figures on this fragment moved from right to left.[71]

Fγ. *S,II*, p. 13, n. 1.1; *Hesperia*, 20 (1951), p. 16, n. 55; *Hesperia*, 21 (1952), p. 25, n. 27.

Conze mentions a "sehr ruinirter Block mit kaum mehr kenntlichen Resten von fünf Figuren; der Länge des Blockes nach (etwa 0.87 m.) können auf ihm sieben Figuren gewesen sein." On the direction in which the figures moved, see note 71.

Fδ. *S,II*, p. 13, n. 1.2; *Hesperia*, 20 (1951), p. 16, n. 55.

Conze mentions a "sehr ruinirter kleiner Block mit Resten von drei Figurein." On the direction in which the figures moved, see note 71.

Adopting the standard used for *Fa* an approximate length of 0.415 can be calculated for this fragment.

Found in cleaning the pronaos of the Hieron.

Fε. *S,II*, p. 13, n. 3.1.3,4.

Finally, in listing the known fragments of the frieze, Conze mentions two "kleine Bruckstücke, jedes mit dem Reste eines Kopfes einer Figur." See note 71.

Found in cleaning the pronaos of the Hieron.

IV. Fragments of the crowning molding of the frieze

Fourteen small fragments unmistakably recognizable as parts of the crowning molding are stored in the Samothrace Museum. Most of them were found in 1950, in the course of

---

tors (von Richter, Temple, and Blau and Schlottmann) took note only of the block represented by *Fa*. Perhaps, for reasons impossible to reconstruct, *F(S)10* and *F(S)11* were no longer as easily accessible as they had been in the fifteenth century, and the curiosity of nineteenth-century visitors was satisfied by a glimpse of the single block *Fa*. Greater accessibility would explain *Fa*'s ultimate disappearance (see text, below), as well as the survival of *F(S)10* and *F(S)11* into modern times. By the time Conze reached Samothrace, the original of the *Fa* must have vanished, for it was he who identified Blau and Schlottmann's drawing with *F(S)10* and *F(S)11* (see text, below).

71. In the Preliminary Report of 1951, Karl Lehmann argued that the figures on this block, *Fγ* and *Fδ* probably moved from right to left in view of the fact that Conze did not discriminate on this point between them and the "Louvre" blocks, *F(S)10* and *F(S)11*. The same might be said of the other fragments mentioned by Conze (*Fε*); see *Hesperia*, 20 (1951), p. 16, n. 55.

excavation of the Temenos and its adjoining Terrace. Two of them (50.93 and 50.541) have been mentioned in an annual report (*Hesperia*, 21 [1952], p. 25, n. 27). The other accession numbers are 49.1943i, 50.381, 50.509, 50.525ab, 50.526, 50.527, 50.574a-c, 50.618, 51.128.

By grouping the preserved blocks and fragments in accordance with the direction of the movement of the dancers depicted on them, the Catalogue affirms the most prominent characteristic of the frieze's design. A related fact indicates the way in which the frieze was adjusted to the building it adorned: the surviving left-moving figures are considerably the more numerous, their blocks measuring 8.141 m. in total length, while the blocks with right-moving figures measure 3.651 m. It is likely, therefore, that the two files of dancers, starting at the rear of the Propylon, converged upon the façade. The relative total lengths of the blocks bearing right- and left-moving dancers supply evidence that the starting point was the southwest corner of the building, following the model of the Parthenon in Athens.

The length of the frieze of the Propylon is 36.10 m. as reconstructed,[72] while the combined lengths of the blocks and fragments catalogued above make up 10.886 m.: somewhat less than one third of the frieze is thus preserved or known. However, it may be assumed, again with the model of the Parthenon frieze in mind, that a distinctive subject occupied the façade, forming the goal upon which the dancers converged: this would remove 5.77 m. (the length of the portion of the frieze framed by the lateral wings of the building) from consideration as a field for the representation of dancers alone, and increase the proportion of known blocks occupied by this subject matter to approximately one third.[73]

The figures depicted on the preserved sections of the frieze are all female.[74] Most are dancers; a few are musicians. Of the latter there are a kitharist among right-moving figures, on *F(S)1* (fig. 147), and, among the left-moving ones, a tympanist, on *F(S)10* (fig. 157), and a flutist, on *F(S)11* (fig. 158).[75] The figures on the surviving blocks uni-

72. Calculation of Mr. Spittle.

73. These measurements do not include the length estimated for F*a* (0.91 m.), which may have belonged to the section of the frieze that was situated between the lateral wings of the building; see below, pp. 205 f.

74. O. F. von Richter reports that the three or four frieze blocks which he saw in the medieval towers on Samothrace early in the nineteenth century bore representations of a procession of female figures led by a male (see n. 81 for a full quotation of von Richter's description). Did he misinterpret the sex of one of the familiar female dancers, or does he describe the subject matter of an additional portion of the frieze that has not survived? Hermes occurs as a frequent companion of the Nymphs, for example, on a relief in the Museo Barracco, Rome (fig. 250); however, he would not find an appropriate role in the iconographic context of the Samothracian frieze as it is interpreted here (see below, pp. 220 ff.). Conze was surely mistaken in questioning whether the tympanist *F(S)10* was bearded (*Reise*, p. 62).

75. *F(S)15* bears a damaged figure which, because it appears to have lacked the extended left arm of the typical leftward-moving dancer, could well have been a musician (flutist? compare *F(S)11*, fig. 158), or have carried some other attribute.

formly wear the polos and are costumed in a long mantle with diagonal diploidion crossing the breast, apoptygma with ornamental arrangement of folds and lower border, and chiton visible both above and below the other garment; alternating figures carry a light scarf which hangs from the elbows. Assuming that this procession occupied the entire frieze except for the front section, and assuming that the preserved portions resemble the missing ones at least with regard to basic content, we may reconstruct a troup of some 218 dancers and musicians processing along the back and wings of the building.[76] The blocks with left-moving figures have survived in lengths more than double (8.141 m.) those with right-moving figures (3.651 m.) and since there are two musicians among the first and one among the second they appear to be represented in something like a correct proportion.

The figures move toward their common goal with a staccato gait, silhouetted against the uniform background of the relief and pressing the tips of their toes against the ground line afforded by the bottom edge of the block. They are grouped in long sets (seven figures on *F(S)1*; fig. 147) of facing pairs with a forward-looking leader who follows the musician, who also looks forward; ahead of the musician, a new set of pairs begins with a backward-looking dancer. *F(S)1*, as well as *F(S)10* and *F(S)11* (figs. 147, 157, 158), seem to illustrate a compositional formula in which the gesture of clasping hands which normally knits the dancers into a continuous chain is replaced, necessarily, in the two dancers, who flank the musician: the rear one reaches forward to grasp the musician's rear drapery flounce between thumb and forefinger, while the forward one extends an empty hand.[77] Triads consisting of a musician and her two companions thus interrupt what appears to be an essentially repetitious series, rhythmically punctuating the tightly organized band of figures. A minor feature that creates a harmonizing repetition of accents is the scarf with swallowtail flounces that is worn by alternating dancers, those who look forward.

Can we deduce from the surviving material a constant numerical relationship between the dancers and the musicians appearing on the frieze? Turning to *F(S)10* (fig. 157), it will be observed that the set of six dancers moving ahead of the tympanist begins, as in *F(S)1* (fig. 147), with a dancer who turns back to face the musician. We would therefore expect that the next musician (whether on the same block or another adjoining it), will have been

76. To arrive at this estimate, the length of the section of the frieze adorning the center of the façade (5.77 m.), for which other subject matter is assumed (see below, p. 232), was subtracted from the total length of the reconstructed frieze (36.10 m.), and the resulting figure was divided by 0.14 m., which is the length occupied by a single dancer on *F(S)10*. The reliability of the estimate must be qualified by recognition that the content of the frieze may have been more varied than the surviving samples at first seem to indicate (see below, pp. 203 ff., especially n. 78), and by acknowledgment that additional dancers may have appeared within the central section of the frieze, as suggested below (see pp. 205 f.).

77. The flutist and neighboring figures on *F(S)11* are badly damaged, but the essential gestures of the group are discernible; the tympanist on *F(S)10* is without a following dancer, but does display the projecting rear flounce that presupposes the reaching hand which occurs on *F(S)1*.

followed by a facing dancer: the series would thus have to be extended by at least two additional figures, indicating that a total of eight dancers was the minimum number to be found in each of the sets separating the musicians.

It must be concluded, however, that, beyond the notation of this minimum, the disposition of dancers and musicians cannot be estimated with confidence. *F(S)1*, the longest block, and one that bears figures of both kinds, should be useful for this purpose, but the dancer at its left end (the seventh of those following the kitharist) is ambiguous in informing us what kind of figure appeared next to her on the right end of the adjoining block. Her right hand is unengaged, as if a musician might follow her, but she faces forward, disobeying the pattern set by the nearby kithara player and her companions. This figure may be read as evidence that the composition and iconography of the frieze may not have been quite as repetitious as the surviving blocks suggest at first glance, and may indeed have presented a variety of unexpected actions and groupings.[78]

Fa (fig. 178), the curious mid-nineteenth century drawing by Blau and Schlottmann, seems to afford further evidence of the same kind. Conze identified it with *F(S)10* and/or *F(S)11* (figs. 157, 158),[79] and one might concede that the fact that it differs from these blocks with regard to such features as the pose of the dancers, the hand-clasp, the uniform occurrence of the scarf and the absence of the polos could be explained by reference to the amateur character of the drawing on the one hand,[80] and, on the other, the extremely damaged condition of the blocks with which Conze associated it. But the incon-

78. The only other hints of such variety that are to be found among the surviving blocks and fragments are the traces on the right side of *F(S)6* (fig. 155) of a figure or other motif whose outline does not resemble the contours familiar from the better preserved portions of the frieze; the fragmentary corner block *F(S)4* (figs. 151 and 152), whose figures, because of their crowded arrangement, must have performed actions different from those seen elsewhere; and *Fa*, to be discussed below. (The crown that appears in the left hand of the dancer leading the tympanist in Conze's early drawing of *F(S)10* [*Reise*, p. 62 and pl. XII] is not taken for evidence of this kind because it seems to preserve a misreading of the worn surface of the relief.)

Some of the motifs lost from the Samothracian frieze may well be preserved through their imitation on the archaistic reliefs of dancing nymphs of Hellenistic and Roman date: for this material, see Havelock, *op. cit.*, pp. 43 ff.; Werner Fuchs, "Attische Nymphenreliefs," *AthMitt*, 77 (1962), pp. 242 ff.; Becatti, *op. cit.*, pp. 32 ff.; Schmidt, *passim*; see also the discussion of Fa, below, especially n. 83, as well as that of *F(S)4*, below. Similarly, a search among earlier reliefs of this kind, or the Hellenistic imitations of them, might result in the identification of models employed by the designer of the frieze of the Propylon. For example, the group of Neo-Attic reliefs with processing figures which has recently been associated by Harrison with late fifth-century prototypes (see Evelyn B. Harrison, "Alkamenes' Sculptures for the Hephaisteion," *AJA*, 81, 2 [1977], pp. 273 ff.) contains motifs that would seem to be imitated in the Samothracian frieze. These include the musician with follower grasping her rear drapery flounce (*ibid.*, fig. 22, p. 285), for which compare *F(S)1* (fig. 147). Again, a relief in Berlin (fig. 202; see Carl Blümel, *Katalog der Skulpturen der Staatlichen Museen*, III, Berlin, 1928, K83, pp. 59 f. and pl. 72), evidently of late fifth-century date, or reflecting a work of that period (Fuchs, *op. cit.*, pp. 243 ff.), offers classical precedent for the dance ἐπὶ καρπῷ (see p. 244, below).

79. *Reise*, p. 62.

80. Conze called it "eine Art von Abbildung" (*loc. cit.*) with justifiable scorn, but modest quality does not deny it archaeological value.

gruence in the total number of figures shown, including the presence at the left end of a figure which is divided precisely in the middle by the termination of the block, is not easily explained on either account, and should instead be seen as evidence that the drawing portrays a block not otherwise known. The similarities which unite it to the frieze—those of theme and composition, as well as the proportions of the block (no measurements are given) and the relation of the figures to the surface—also invite identification of the drawing as a document recording a lost portion of the frieze. It is interesting in this connection to note that O. F. von Richter, who visited Samothrace nearly forty years earlier than Blau and Schlottmann, reported that he saw in the two medieval towers not two but three or four blocks of a frieze which he assigned to the interior of a Doric temple.[81] It appears that *F(S)10* and *F(S)11* were not the only blocks of the frieze of the Propylon that were visible in the middle of the nineteenth century, and that Blau and Schlottmann saw and recorded another one. We may speculate that this piece may have been extracted from its setting in the medieval tower for reuse during the period of nearly ten years that ensued before the arrival of Champoiseau and the removal to France of *F(S)10* and *F(S)11*.[82]

Fa would thus seem to preserve not simply the mistakes of an unskilled draftsman but a valid if amateurish indication of the representation on the frieze of dancing figures differing from all the surviving examples. Similar hand-holding frontal dancers wearing a peplos with high-girt overfall occur on Attic archaistic votive reliefs of Hellenistic and later date (figs. 179, 250).[83] Their costume is sometimes adorned with the characteristically

81. Von Richter's account warrants full quotation: "Sichtbar sind diese beiden Thürme (aus den Zeiten der Genueser oder Byzantier; denn Inschrift finden sich nicht), sehr solid auf einem Schutthausen gebaut, der wohl von dem Fundamente der Mauer des alten Tempels herrühren mag, dessen zahlreiche Fragmente man in beiden Thürmen eingemauert erblickt. Aus demselben sah ich, dass der Tempel nur sehr klein gewesen ist; denn seine Saülen hatten kaum ein Paar Fuss im Durchmesser. Er war Dorischer Ordnung (wie sich aus den Triglyphen ergibt), mit cannelirten Säulen. Ich fand drei bis vier ziemlich verstümmelte Fragmente desselben Basreliefs, das wahrscheinlich das Innere zierte: eine Prozession weiblicher Figuren (wie es schien, wegen der langen Gewänder) darstellend, von einer männlichen gefürt" (*Wallfahrten im Morgenland*, Berlin, 1822, p. 443).

This indication that the two "Louvre" blocks, *F(S)10* and *F(S)11* (figs. 157, 158) were not the only parts of the frieze of the Propylon that decorated the Gattilusi towers may help to explain certain features of the drawings by Cyriacus of Ancona, long taken to represent them, although with improvisations thought to have been occasioned by the damaged condition of the originals (figs. 4, 5; see *Samothracian Reflections*, pp. 105 ff.). One wonders whether Cyriacus' procession of Muses may not instead bring together elements from all of the reliefs that were visible in the towers—the tympanist certainly being based on the figure in *F(S)11*, while the dancers' poses and costumes mingle features borrowed from the "normal" frieze type of *F(S)10* with *F(S)11* with others from the figures of *Fa* (fig. 178).

82. On Champoiseau's presence on Samothrace, see above, p. 12. The discovery of *F(S)16* (fig. 164) in a Samothracian chapel, where it served as a support for the altar table, testifies to one reuse among the many for which the Sanctuary's marbles must have been employed: the limekilns dotting the site bear witness to still others (see above, p. 16).

83. For National Archaeological Museum, Athens, no. 1966 (my fig. 179), see Dietrich Willers, "Zu den Anfängen der archaistischen Plastik in Griechenland," *AA*, Beiheft 4, Berlin, 1975, pp. 29 f., pl. 6, where it is placed in the late Hellenistic period. Frontal dancers also occur on a relief showing Hermes and Acheloos with Nymphs in the Metropolitan Museum of Art, New York, which is datable ca. 320-300 B.C.: see Gisela M. A. Richter, *Catalogue of Greek Sculptures in the Metropolitan Museum of Art*, Cambridge (Mass.), 1954, pp. 80 f.,

179. Nymphs Relief. Athens, National Archaeological Museum, no. 1966.

Attic swallowtail overfall, and it sometimes shows features such as the pronounced central fold of the peplos with chiton exposed below, which would seem to derive from the more familiar type of Samothracian dancer (fig. 147), but I would suggest that these are mere variations upon a type that reflects the influence of the dancers seen on *F*α.

One is tempted to assign *F*α to a particular place in the frieze of the Propylon, a position made appropriate by the figures' frontality and the sideways direction of their glance. They would be suitable spectators of the scene occupying the center of the façade, observing it from a lateral position within the area enframed by the projecting wings of the building, and they would quite certainly have been matched by corresponding figures on the other side. In this position, their frontality would serve to mediate between the profile

no. 143, pl. CVa. Here the Nymphs wear three distinct costumes, which seem to combine elements borrowed from both types of Samothracian dancers. In a Hellenistic relief of Apollo and the Nymphs in Treviso, the three frontal hand-holding dancing nymphs wear various late classical or Hellenistic garments, and one wears the costume seen on *F*α (see Friedrich Müthmann, "Weihrelief am Acheloos und Naturgottheiten," *Antike Kunst*, 1968, p. 33; Margherita Guarducci, "Antichità greche nel museo di Treviso," *Annuario*, 30-32, n.s. 14-16 [1952-54], pp. 184 ff., fig. 2, p. 185). Frontal dancers closely resembling those on *F*α appear on National Archaeological Museum, Athens, no. 1789, a round base showing the Muses dancing around an altar (Svoronos, *op. cit.*, pl. CXXXII, 1-3), and on a Nymphs relief in the National Archaeological Museum, Athens, no. 1448 (*ibid.*, pl. LXXIV); they are perpetuated in a group of reliefs from Thrace, evidently of Roman date: see V. Dobrusky, "Inscriptions et monuments figurés de la Thrace," *BCH*, 21 (1897), fig. 4, p. 122; fig. 10, p. 128; fig. 12, p. 130; fig. 13, p. 131; fig. 14, p. 133; fig. 15, p. 133; fig. 17, p. 138; fig. 18, p. 139. Several of these repeat the hand-holding pose, others are joined by placing hands on shoulders, still others stand frontally with arms at sides. (Schmidt refers to this material in a somewhat different context, *op. cit.*, note 22, p. 38). Fig. 250 is further discussed in App. II, p. 308.

180. Detail of an "Altar." Athens, National Archaeological Museum, no. 54.

poses and convergent flow of the normal figures of the frieze and the subject, probably symmetrical and static in composition, which is hypothesized for the center of the frieze.[84]

The better partially preserved corner block, *F(S)4* (figs. 151, 152), presents a puzzling problem in restoration. Here we again have unambiguous evidence of a departure from the norm of repetitive gestures that has been found on other portions of the frieze. The two figures appearing on Side A are too close together to have been portrayed ἐπὶ καρπῷ in the manner of the other dancers; nor would the space have permitted the end figures on Sides A and B to be linked together in this way. The figure on Side B (fig. 152) should perhaps be reconstructed as a musician. This would rationalize her isolation from her companions on the other face as well as the forward direction of both the profile of the head and the gesture of the arm, which is made obligatory by the narrowness of the field she occupies. The corner dancer on Side A (fig. 151), on the other hand, cannot easily

84. Mrs. Lehmann suggests the analogy of the east frieze of the Parthenon, where the cult scene is enframed not only by the seated divinities, but also by witnesses appearing on both sides (see Martin Robertson and Alison Frantz, *The Parthenon Frieze*, New York, 1975, East I, 1; II, 2-6; III, 7-19; IV, 20-22; VI, 42-48; VII, 49-56; VIII, 57-61; IX, 62-63). See below, pp. 231 ff.

have faced forward, and should probably be reconstructed as turning to face those who follow her—a similar pose, reversing the direction of the head to face toward the rear, being, of course, a normal feature of the frieze. Comparison with the Nymph (?) on an archaistic "altar" in Athens (fig. 180)[85] who turns back to confront Hermes advancing on the adjoining face, suggests that our corner figure might have twisted at the waist and raised her left hand to grasp a scarf held at shoulder level—although a somewhat different organization of the pose, adjusting it to the exiguous space at the corner of the block, would have been necessary to accommodate this gesture. The same gesture is used on later archaistic friezes, where it sometimes identifies Leto, although in these examples the turn of the body at the waist does not occur.[86] The second dancer on Side A is likely to have been a backward-facing figure too, to judge from the presence of the swallowtail scarf that hangs at her left side; a fragment of her left hand is to be seen, extended toward the buttock of her neighbor at the corner.

This block must have occupied one of the two corners of the southern wing of the Propylon, an option imposed by the left-to-right direction of the figures' movement.

The use of paint must not be neglected in a discussion of the reconstruction of missing elements of the frieze. For this *F(S)1* (fig. 147) offers the most unmistakable testimony, since the strings of the kithara must have been painted. Study of the same block tells us that the swallowtail scarfs worn by alternating dancers probably also received painted definition not supplied by the carving. An ambiguous relationship often apparent between scarfs and arms would perhaps have been clarified by this means and the painted form probably imitated the sculptured representation that is clear in the sixth and eleventh figures from the left, where the scarf winds in front of the right elbow and behind the left one.

The termination of *F(S)13* and *Fα* in such a way as to cut the end figure in half indicates that those frieze blocks which bear the procession of dancers and musicians, at least, were carved on the building (see figs. 161, 178).[87] Regarding the question of the technique by which the frieze was executed, the repetitious aspect of the design has invited the hypothesis that the dancing figures were copied mechanically, by means of "one pattern or car-

85. Svoronos (*op. cit.*, I, no. 54, pp. 97 ff., pl. XXII, 1, 2) suggested a date of ca. 480 B.C. for this work, and Becatti (*op. cit.*, p. 33) considered it to be a late archaic work; in Karouzou, p. 41, a date in the second half of the fifth century B.C. is suggested. I am inclined to place it near the end of the fourth century B.C. Herdejürgen refers to the female figure as a goddess (*op. cit.*, p. 80).

A related pose occurs in the marshall at the end of the northernmost block of the west frieze of the Parthenon, although in this case the raised hand holds a staff (see Robertson and Frantz, *op. cit.*, West I, 1).

86. It is to be found on one of the three "Parques" on the Altar of the Twelve Gods, Louvre no. 33347 (Photo Giraudon 1933), and on a relief with Apollo, Diana and Leto in the Louvre (no. 22538; *Encyclopédie photographique de l'art*, III, Paris, 1938, pl. 257B).

87. This evidence need not apply to the entire frieze: see Ashmole, pp. 125 ff., 141, on the carving of the Parthenon frieze, where the sections adorning both façades seem to have been prepared before installation, while those on the flanks must have been carved on the building.

toon."[88] But the blocks vary with respect to the heights of the figures as well as the lengths of the intervals separating them, as is evident if the dancers on *F(S)1* (fig. 147) are compared with those on *F(S)10* (fig. 157), for example. Thus the outlines of the same cartoon cannot have been transferred onto all blocks. Moreover, a variety of models must have been provided for the frieze's individual components. These include the two principle kinds of dancing figures, those looking backward and those looking forward; the modifications of these which depend upon the movement of the figures to right and left; such additional repeated types as may have been used (e.g. *Fa*; fig. 178); and variant actions such as those of the musicians and the end figure on Side A of *F(S)4* (see figs. 147, 151, 157, 158). It would seem that an extensive set of models was issued to craftsmen who then interpreted them with a certain degree of independence.[89]

The architectural function of the frieze, as well as the correctness of its placing in the entablature of the building rather than in a lower position, as was earlier supposed,[90] are confirmed by the treatment of the relief surface that is observable in *F(S)1* (figs. 147, 148): the background slopes away from the bottom edge of the block leaving the heads and poloi in substantially higher projection than the feet and lower drapery. By this means, the forms most distant from the spectator's eyes are given special prominence, compensating for the foreshortening that would have followed from the position of the frieze above eye level.[91] Having observed earlier that the figures are in general very tall and slender, we may now point out the extreme elongation of the necks and heads, which in the present context may be seen as a further device serving to compensate for the distortion which results from the spectator's standpoint below the frieze.

The designer has stressed the geometric nature of the frieze block by setting the figures out against the undifferentiated background so that they act as an abstract ornamental filigree articulating a two-dimensional plane. This again is best studied in *F(S)1* (fig. 147), where we see that the emphasis upon the surface of the block is enhanced by the carving

88. Havelock, *op. cit.*, p. 50. For criticism of Havelock's conclusions about the use of cartoons in archaistic reliefs, see Willers, *op. cit.*, pp. 29 ff.

Plastic models seem more likely to have been used for the execution of the frieze than linear cartoons, three-dimensional models being surely best adapted to the complexity of pose and gesture that underlies the apparent simplicity of the design (see pp. 237 ff.). If the models were less than full-scale, we would have an explanation for the variations in scale among the figures on the frieze blocks; the changing relations of size between figures and relief surface in this case would have resulted from decisions by different carvers in the absence of a pattern exact in this respect.

Stewart, p. 82, concludes that small terracotta models were probably used for the sculptures at Tegea and surveys recent discussion of the problem; however, his concern is not with relief sculpture.

89. See below, pp. 250 ff., for an analysis of the differences of style and skill found among the carvers of the frieze.

90. See above, pp. 28 ff.

91. See above, p. 178. Ashmole notes a similar compensatory slanting of the background surface in the Parthenon frieze (p. 118). However, an altogether singular awareness of the visual implications of the placing of architectural sculptures has recently been assigned to Skopas by Stewart (pp. 49 f.), a conclusion that is abundantly supported by our analysis of the sculptures of the Propylon; on the occurrence of foreshortening in the building's sima and antefix reliefs, see Chap. II, pp. 124 ff.; on its further use in the frieze, see below, pp. 235 ff.

of the figures in low relief, which varies from the slight projection of the heads and poloi, allowing the backward-turning heads to emerge almost imperceptibly toward the three-quarter view, to the shallow etching of the lower drapery and feet. Also, the figures insistently refer to the background plane through the linearism of the carving, while the pose restates it in profile views of heads and legs and in frontally displayed torsos. The horizontal dimension of the rectangle of the frieze block is reflected in the direction of the steps taken by the parading figures and is reiterated in the contours of the poloi, which remain constant in spite of the varying poses of the heads. The lively impression of onrushing forms, however carefully controlled, that is created by the Parthenon frieze is absent from this delicately adjusted design, where, indeed, such vitality would have overwhelmed the building itself. Instead, the main ingredients of the composition are dealt with in such a way as to create a final effect of virtual stasis, in which the human figure takes on something of the nature of the symbolic devices—bucrania, garlands, cult implements, weapons—that were presently to supplant it in the Ionic order.[92] The motionless pattern of vertical accents inherent in a colonnaded structure is echoed by the vertical contours of the advancing left legs and of the columns of drapery adjoining them. The fact that the figures are shown on tiptoes reinforces this denial of purposeful forward movement: their position is suspended between the forward impulse suggested by the extended rear leg and raised right buttock on the one hand and, on the other, the vertical of the left leg, tensed to accept the body's weight. This transitory and uncertain pose, together with the sketchy rendering of the anatomical structure of the legs, lends to the figures an effect of weightless immobility. In the upper zone of the design, arms extended to right and left reassert the theme of mutually cancelling opposed actions, while the exchange of glances between forward- and backward-turning heads again disrupts the implied unidirectional flow of the file with a regular internal rhythm of thrust and counterthrust. This alternation is repeated in the occurrences of the swallowtail scarf on backward-turning dancers only. The interruption and renewal of the procession of dancers through the introduction of musicians must have provided an additional rhythmic unit, something like a musical measure—difficult to assess precisely in its effect, since its exact length cannot be determined,[93] but certainly a significant ingredient of the frieze's composition. Altogether these stratagems disclose the designer's acutely sympathetic perception of the decorative requirements of the small Ionic building which carried the frieze.

Side A of the partially preserved corner block, *F(S)4* (fig. 151), reveals an especially purposeful expression of the frieze's architectonic function in the telescoping of the figures as well as of the intervals between them. The result is a dense filling of the relief surface at the corner, accompanied by a multiplication of vertical accents, which no doubt was

92. This development was initially outlined by Demangel; see also the observations of Karl Lehmann in a preliminary report (*Hesperia*, 20 [1951], p. 18), and of Harrison (p. 64). Brunilde S. Ridgway has dealt more searchingly with the evolution of the Greek frieze (Ridgway, pp. 188 ff., especially p. 203).

93. See above, pp. 202 f.

181. Statue of Artemis from Gortyn. Gortyn, Archaeological Museum.

intended to provide a visually satisfactory termination of the design comparable to the adjustment of the final triglyph in the Doric order.

In characterizing the treatment of drapery in the sculpture of the second half of the fourth century B.C., Hans Weber has drawn attention to the artist's objective of unifying the figure's total form on a stereometric basis.[94] The waist is no longer articulated, as in fifth-century art; instead a high girdle or a mantle accentuates the upper body in the region of the breast. Anatomical details are subordinated to the unity of the whole, and are at the same time isolated by the garments, which often combine the peplos and the chiton in layered arrangements. It is notable that, while classical art preferred the peplos alone, the elaboration of both garments that occurs in the later fourth century is paralleled only in archaic art. In this period, the classical harmony between the body and its clothing is

94. Hans Weber, "Griechische Frauentrachten im vierten Jahrhundert vor der Zeitwende," *Beiträge zür Trachtgeschichte Griechenlands,* Würzburg, 1938, pp. 139 ff.

thus disrupted in favor of a new kind of unity, of which we see a complex, mannered, and ornamental version in the dancers of the preserved portions of the frieze of the Propylon.

The forms and origin of the dress worn by these dancers will be considered closely, for this costume, with its special blend of archaic and contemporary features, will be seen to provide a key to an understanding at once of the creative procedures of the frieze's designer and of the development of archaistic art in the late classical period.[95] The costume's details are best studied by first looking ahead in time to compare the dress of the dancers on *F(S)1* and *F(S)12* (the best-preserved examples) with a monumental version appearing on the statue of Artemis from Gortyn, a Roman work following an original of Hellenistic or, possibly, fourth-century date (fig. 181).[96] Here all the familiar elements are present: the chiton visible on the upper torso and at the ankles; the mantle with apoptygma exhibiting the diagonal top border and vertical folds enframing a central panel with curving lower contour; the emphatic vertical folds which separate the legs. This costume, indeed, is distinguished from that of the dancers only by the naturalistic style in which it is presented—a style typified by the handling of the diagonal border of the apoptygma, which appears here as a pattern of loosely gathered folds, while the Samothracian examples show it as a stiff arrangement of vertical pleats.

This naturalistic version of the costume is quite common in Hellenistic sculpture of the eastern Aegean, being worn not only by Artemis but also by certain Tyche types, by the Muse Thyateira, and by the Charites among others.[97] Two bronze statuettes of eastern provenance and of late fourth-century or early Hellenistic date, one of which is illustrated here (fig. 182),[98] repeat the costume, adding a high polos. The statuettes seem to be related in content to the Charites and by the same token to the Samothracian dancers: they

95. I follow Harrison (p. 50) in using the terms archaizing and archaistic without chronological implication.

96. Harrison has drawn attention to the realistic representation of this costume in Hellenistic Asia Minor (p. 64). For the Artemis of Gortyn, see above, n. 63; see also R. Heidenreich ("Bupalos und Pergamon," *AA*, 50 [1936], col. 683 and fig. 8, col. 685), who assembles a large group of statues that are related to it in dress. The occurrence of the costume on a fourth-century bronze in the Louvre, which is discussed below (see pp. 212 f.), raises the question whether the original work upon which the statue from Gortyn is based may not have been at least this early in date.

97. For a numerous array of such statues, whose costumes differ from that of the Artemis of Gortyn only in the most trivial details, see Heidenreich, *ibid.*, cols. 693 ff. and figs. 6 ff. To them may be added a statue from Sardis of Hellenistic date (George M. A. Hanfmann, "Three Sculptures from Sardis in the Manisa Museum," *Anatolia*, 4 [1959], pp. 60 ff., pl. XIa,b) where the opening of the mantle is on the figure's left side and the diploidion is reversed (unless the photograph has been incorrectly reproduced); a Roman caryatid from the Theater at Miletus, which is in the Louvre (*Encyclopédie photographique*, *op. cit.*, pl. 249), where the central folds of the lower mantle continue those of the apoptygma; a Roman statue of Nemesis from the Gymnasium at Salamis, which is in the Cyprus Museum (Vassos Karageorghis, *Sculptures from Salamis*, I, Nicosia, 1964, pp. 12 ff.). It will be noted that these works typically are of eastern provenance.

98. The statuette shown in fig. 182 (Hermitage, Leningrad, Vas. 70) comes from a burial mound known as Vasyurina Mountain; it is reproduced with the kind permission of V. Suslov, the Director of the Hermitage Museum; see Heidenreich, *op. cit.*, fig. 6, col. 685, with bibliography. A similar statuette, found in Aidin (Turkey) is preserved in Berlin (Staatlichen Museen, Antiken-Sammlung no. 30895; *ibid.*, col. 687 and fig. 6, col. 685).

182. Statuette of a Dancer. Leningrad, The Hermitage Museum, Vas. 70.

are engaged in a stately dance or procession, and the costume, because of the provenances of the sculptures, no doubt identifies them as votaries of an eastern divinity.[99]

An earlier occurrence of this costume is found in a bronze statuette in the Louvre which is probably datable about 350 B.C. and seems to represent Leto (fig. 183).[100] In light

99. See below, pp. 221 ff. As will be shown below (App. II, p. 304), a costume closely dependent upon it is worn by the dancers encircling one of the types of the Hekataion occurring in the third century B.C.; this substantiates the identity of these statuettes as well as the Samothracian dancers as votaries of a goddess.

100. This statuette (Louvre Br. 4418) comes from Amrith, and was formerly in the De Clercq Collection (André H. P. de Ridder, *Collection de Clerq*, III, *Les Bronzes*, Paris, 1905, no. 139, pp. 94f., pl. 30), where it was identified as "Aphrodite ou femme se vêtant." Salomon Reinach had recognized it as Artemis (*Répertoire de la statuaire grecque et romaine, Paris*, IV, 1910, p. 188, No. 4), but the Louvre now calls it Nemesis. The gesture of the right hand, which is raised to touch the upper garment, is that of the figure of Leto in a fifth-century metope in the Villa Albani, Rome (Heinz Kähler, *Das griechische Metopenbild*, Munich, 1949, pl. 94; William Bell Dinsmoor, "Rhamnountine Fantasies," *Hesperia*, 30, 1961, pp. 199 ff.), and is closely related to the gesture of Leto as she appears in the archaistic relief previously cited (see above, n. 86). Herdejürgen includes it in a list of works exemplifying the use of the "Schrägmantel" in Hellenistic art (*op. cit.*, p. 88, e, 1). In proposing a date of ca. 350 B.C., I am guided by its pose primarily, which seems to signal a transitional point between the classical contrapposto, with its fluid interaction

183. Statuette of Leto. Paris, Musée du Louvre, Br. 4418.

of the continuous tradition that links this figure to the later examples cited above, the Samothracian dancers' costume may be understood as an archaized version of a type of dress that was current in the fourth century as the attribute of at least one divinity (Leto) and that was subsequently to be shared by other goddesses and their dancing votaries. The designer of the frieze of the Propylon, then, was not the inventor of this mode of dress; nor did he turn directly to archaic art itself for inspiration in composing it.[101] In-

of physical structure with drapery, and the unification of these elements on a new basis which took place in the second half of the fourth century (see below, pp. 238 f.). The statues marking this transition show openness of gesture and ambiguity of bodily movement, as if uncertain on which leg to place the body's weight, for which parallels are to be found in the portrait statues from Halikarnassos (see *The Mausoleum and Sculptures of Halicarnassos and Priene in the British Museum*, London, 1900, nos. 1001, 1003, pl. XVI). On the pose of Maussollos, see Blanche R. Brown, *Anticlassicism in Greek Sculpture of the Fourth Century B.C.*, New York, 1973, pp. 16 ff.

101. E. B. Harrison, the only authority who has examined the Samothracian dancers' costume attentively, has suggested that the mantle is derived from that worn by Apollo on an early classical relief from Thasos, and cites further examples from the same period (Harrison, p. 54). This connection is rather generalized, and affects only the mantle, while the costume of the statuette in the Louvre and other works dependent upon it resembles that of the dancers as a complete ensemble; it lacks only the archaizing aspect that must have directed Harrison's inquiry toward the earlier models.

184. Locrian pinax. Tarento, Museo Nazionale.

stead, he adapted to the special requirements of the Samothracian commission a costume already in use in contemporary sacred art, and he did this by stiffening and ornamentalizing its naturalistic forms in order to construct his own original, playfully archaic image.

We must now note that, although the costume we have been studying appears in numerous works of the fourth century and later that are naturalistic in *style*, even in these cases it in fact exhibits several features which are borrowed from archaic dress.[102] The upper termination of the apoptygma in a diagonal swathe of folds imitates the diploidion of the sixth-century himation.[103] The treatment of its lower edge, with two vertical pleats framing a central curved panel, occurs occasionally as a variant lower border of the late archaic himation,[104] and then appears in certain early classical works, where it is already an archaizing survival reserved for ritual subjects, as seen in the peploi of the dancers on a Locrian pinax (fig. 184).[105] Another archaic feature of the costume is, of course,

102. This was recognized by Porro (see above, n. 63).

103. The caryatids from the Siphnian Treasury at Delphi may be cited, among innumerable examples (see Gisela M. A. Richter, *Korai. Archaic Greek Maidens*, London, 1968, figs. 317-320).

104. This variant form of the himation occurs in small bronzes: for examples, see *ibid.*, figs. 435-438 (National Archaeological Museum, Athens) and fig. 656 (Mirror Support, Louvre), and a statuette in the British Museum, London (Henry B. Walters, *Catalogue of the Bronzes, Greek, Roman and Etruscan, in the Department of Greek and Roman Antiquities*, London, 1899, no. 241, p. 24).

105. For the Locrian pinax, see *Enciclopedia dell'arte antica*, Rome, 1958-73, *s.v. Locri*, fig. 803, p. 675. Another early classical example of the peplos treated in this manner is seen in the bronze statuette of a Girl Holding a Dove in the National Archaeological Museum, Athens, no. 540. (G.M.A. Richter, *Korai*, figs. 664-666). The himation also occurs in this form in early classical terracottas from Rhodes (see R. A. Higgins, *Catalogue of the Terracottas in the Department of Greek and Roman Antiquities, British Museum*, London, 1954, no. 111, pl. 21; no. 204, pl. 36).

the presence of emphatic vertical folds marking the center of the lower garment, which also occurs on the pinax but originated in Ionian archaic dress.[106] The low polos worn by the dancers is discussed elsewhere.[107] In connection with the evolution of archaism in the fourth century B.C., it is interesting, finally, to observe that the Louvre statuette (fig. 183) and its naturalistic successors exhibit a partial form of archaism which revives old-fashioned details of dress without, however, coming to terms with the archaic style that was their original vehicle. It was the designer of the frieze of the Propylon, then, who took a significant first step toward the recreation of the stylistic language of the archaic period as a totality. As we shall see,[108] he fashioned an ironic hybrid style, at once retrospective and up-to-date, still tied to the classical tradition in essential ways, but archaizing not only these details of dress, but also such basic features as pose, composition, and the representation of space. This designer also used motifs of what might be called pseudoarchaic character—motifs which lend his figures the air of being ancient without, in fact, being genuinely antiquarian. The swallowtail scarf-ends, for example, are especially effective in suggesting an ancient mode of dress; but the scarf itself, in this form, is not archaic but classical. It is a motif that probably occurred in statuary,[109] but for which more generous testimony is preserved in painting: one example, worn by Artemis on a fourth-century amphora in Ruvo di Puglia (fig. 185),[110] shows a naturalistic version of the scarf that is worn by the dancers on the Samothracian frieze. In spite of its archaizing stylizations, the dancers' scarf resembles this garment markedly in the volatility of its contours and in the manner

106. For archaic examples of the treatment of the lower garment closely resembling that of the Samothracian dancers, see the statue of a goddess in Delos (no. A4065) of ca. 500 B.C., and the Nereid Metope from the Heraion at the mouth of the River Sele in the Archaeological Museum, Paestum (Richter, *Korai*, fig. 548). Harrison has noted that the heavy central fold which was to become so common in archaistic works, is usual in the fifth century, less so in the archaic period itself (p. 62).

107. See below, p. 221.

108. See below, pp. 234 ff.

109. The two archaistic kouroi from the Agora, Athens, do in fact wear the small mantle draped across their backs and hanging down at their sides (Harrison, nos. 108, 109, pp. 67 f., pl. 22); however, damage prevents one from determining what the appearance of the hanging ends may have been: what remains indicates that they adhered closely to the statues' flanks, differing markedly from the Samothracian version. The statues are of late Hellenistic date, and, as Harrison suggests (p. 68), their drapery may be a translation into three dimensions of conventions developed in archaistic relief sculpture. On the other hand, the possible existence of archaistic statue types representing Athena with swallow-tail scarf is indicated by the various representations of the goddess on the Panathenaic amphorae of the fourth century B.C. (see below, n. 116). Mrs. Lehmann has recently suggested that the Athena appearing on the tetradrachms of Ptolemy I depicts the Athena Alkidemos of Pella (for reference, see n. 257, below).

110. See Giulio Emanuele Rizzo, "La base di Augusto," *BullComm.* 60 (1933), p. 70, fig. 10; Heinrich Heydemann, *Die Vasensammlung des Museo Nazionale zu Neapel*, Berlin, 1872, no. 3256. That the short scarf, usually worn suspended from both elbows, was ubiquitous in fourth-century art is suggested by the illustrations in A. D. Trendall and A. Campitoglu, *The Red-figured Vases of Apulia*, I, Oxford, 1978, *passim*, where it occurs on male as well as female figures, mostly in secular contexts. This garment has been referred to as a *chlaina* by Becatti (*op. cit.*, p. 36); however, the lack of evidence concerning the ancient use of this term has prompted me to prefer the more generic "scarf" (see *RE*, III, Stuttgart, 1899, *s.v.* χλαῖνα [cols. 2335 ff.]). Harrison calls it a small mantle, noting that the type with symmetrical swallow-tailed points does not appear before the end of the fifth century B.C. (Harrison, p. 61).

185. Detail from an Apulian amphora in the Jatta Collection in Ruvo.

in which it is worn. The archaized swallowtail scarf had already made a brief appearance on a Panathenaic amphora in the archonship of Charikleides (363/2 B.C.) (fig. 186).[111] However, there are notable differences between this example and the scarf worn by the Samothracian dancers, first of all in its bolder scale, but also with respect to precisely those characteristics which distinguish it from that of the Artemis in Ruvo (fig. 185): it has a rigid, symmetrical shape quite unlike the light, active outlines of the other, and, most strikingly, it is carried in front of Athena's torso and hangs behind her arms, while the scarf of

111. On this amphora, and a second example from the archonship of Charikleides, which were found recently in Eretria, see *Archaeological Reports for 1974-75*, no. 21, pp. 4f., p. 5, fig. 5; previously the amphorae of this archonship were known only through the fragmentary examples in Eleusis, illustrated by Becatti, *op. cit.*, pl. VII, 1-3.

186. Fragmentary Panathenaic Amphora. Athens, National Archaeological Museum.

our dancers twists behind the torso and behind one arm but in front of the other. The relationship is puzzling: one wonders whether fourth-century painting may not have offered two diverse prototypes, one of them on the order of the Artemis on the amphora in Ruvo, which inspired these differing versions of the "archaic" scarf.

The dancers' coiffure is an incongruous combination of contemporary and archaic details. The bun that appears on some of the heads is frequent in fourth-century statuary,[112] while the long strands of hair descending onto the shoulders occur typically on the korai

112. This feature recalls the hair arrangement of the Artemis of Dresden, for example, with its bound mass of projecting hair (see profile view in Charles Picard, *Manuel d'archéologie grecque, La Sculpture,* IV, 1, Paris, 1954, fig. 154, p. 357).

187. Herm of Artemis. Sparta, Archaeological Museum.

of the late archaic period.[113] The combination of such strands with curls clustered around the face is found in an archaistic image of Artemis which seems likely to have originated in the fourth century B.C. and, indeed, should perhaps be associated with Skopas. Comparison of a herm in Sparta (fig. 187)[114] with a detail of *F(S)1* (fig. 148) suggests that the de-

113. See, for example, Acropolis Museum, Athens, no. 675 (Richter, *Korai*, figs. 396, 397). Ilse Kleeman points out that in the classical period these shoulder locks, no longer in fashion, were to become emblems of maidenhood, as seen in the caryatids of the Erechtheum porch and the Athena Parthenos ("Eine Weihgeschenk an die Delische Artemis in Paros," *AthMitt*, 77 [1962], p. 215).

114. The herm in Sparta is no. 403 in M. N. Tod and A.J.B. Wace, *A Catalogue of the Sparta Museum*, Oxford, 1906. That it exhibits certain Skopaic characteristics has been noted by Sieveking (for reference, see *ibid.*, p. 173). The front view (Arndt-Amelung, *Einzelaufnahmen antiker Skulpturen*, no. 1315), exposing low eyebrows closely enframing the eyes, a full lower face and a small mouth, bears comparison with a head from Tegea (figs. 143, 144) and, by the same token, with the heads from the coffers of the Propylon (figs. 130, 142). For a speculative comment on Skopas' use of archaism in cult statues, see below, note 177; on his Apollo Smintheus, see below, pp. 258 ff.

A final observation about the treatment of the hair in the dancers of the frieze: the rounded curls clustered around the face, and the bold projection of the hair mass from the forehead and cheeks (see fig. 148), relate their coiffure to that of the only long-haired head among those on the preserved coffers of the Propylon, the one identified here as the youthful Alexander the Great (figs. 126, 228; see pp. 274 ff.).

188. Hekateion. Athens, The British School.

signer of the Samothracian figures may have imitated such a model. Careful examination of our profile view of the herm reveals that it could also have served as model for the pattern of roll-like curls descending toward the face which is a normal if not invariable feature of the dancers' heads.

The costume, to summarize, may be interpreted as an ingenious confection, in which major as well as minor features of contemporary origin, both archaizing and naturalistic in character, are imaginatively assembled and wittily flavored with authenticity through emphasis on a few genuinely archaic details. It is worth dwelling on the uniqueness and inventiveness of this costume by comparing it with the drapery employed in the archaistic figure types that had for some time been in vogue in Attica. The relevant Attic types are, of course, the Hekataia stemming from Alkamenes' invention (see fig. 188)[115] and the figure of Athena appearing on the earlier fourth-century Panathenaic amphorae.[116] These

115. See App. II, p. 304. The problem of Alkamenes' Hekataion has been reviewed most recently by Dietrich Willers (*op. cit.*, pp. 48 ff.), who concludes that the example in the British School in Athens (my fig. 188) most closely reflects the fifth-century monument. On the costume of the Hekataia, see Harrison, p. 53. On this sculpture, see Felix Eckstein, "Das Hekataion in der British School zu Athen," *Antike Plastik*, IV, pp. 27 ff., pls. 12-14.

116. On these types, see Jiří Frel, *Panathenaic Prize Amphoras*, Athens, 1973, with bibliography; see, too, pp. 216 f. and fig. 186.

figures wear the peplos with centrally divided overfall, and, except for the scarf, which, as just noted, is shared with one of the Athena types, their costume differs fundamentally from that of the Samothracian dancers. The sculptural comparisons adduced above make it clear, then, that the dancers' archaizing costume associates the frieze with an iconographic tradition of which no clear trace can be found in Attica during the preceding decades, and which, instead, is localized in the east Greek region. Our comparisons also suggest that it was a personal and highly original conception, doubtless inspired by the special circumstances of the Samothracian commission.[117]

If we are right in identifying *Fa* (fig. 178) as evidence for the occurrence of an alternative type of dancing figure on the frieze of the Propylon,[118] then we must also observe that these figures wore a costume that, for all the vagueness of its details, is easier to associate with classical than with archaic or archaizing prototypes. Only the scarfs hanging from their elbows relate them to the dancers on the preserved reliefs and recall their archaistic flavor; the costume otherwise seems to reflect the taste of the late fourth century B.C., in the high girdle and loosely draped skirt, perhaps colored by that of the nineteenth century A.D., in the treatment of the neckline and bodice. The upper portions of the figures must have been in very damaged condition when the drawing was made, for the hair arrangement also suggests a modern improvisation based on incompletely preserved traces in the model. Although *Fa* thus appears to be a pastiche of modern and original details, it does constitute evidence that the use of archaizing features within the frieze's file of dancers was inconsistent, and thereby helps to classify the frieze among a group of partially archaizing works that, as I will argue, typify the later fourth century B.C.[119]

M. L. H.

That the frieze of dancing maidens once adorned the entablature of the Propylon has been conclusively established.[120] As we have seen, its figures move in two directions.[121] Presumably, the two lines of antithetical figures converged on a lost central scene. How should this frieze be interpreted? Eduard Schmidt assumed that the figures were performing a cult dance.[122] Charles Picard believed that they were "les κοῦραι de Cybèle," "un *choros* bénéfique, un cortège de lustration perpétuelle."[123] André Dessenne considered that the figures might represent the dancing that occurred during the celebration of the myster-

117. See below, pp. 253 f.

118. See above, pp. 203 ff.

119. See App. II, pp. 309 ff.

120. See above, pp. 19, 23. Schmidt, p. 40, concerned over the lack of precedent for an archaistic frieze on a temple (the Austrian's assumption) and its visibility on such a building, tried to detach the fragments of the frieze from the sima block recovered with them and to propose that the frieze came from an altar or went "um den Rand der Opfergrube." This position was accepted by Camillo Praschniker, *Zur Geschichte des Akroters* (Schriften der philosophischen Fakultät der deutschen Universität in Prag, 5), Brünn-Prague-Leipzig-Vienna, 1929, p. 35. Charles Picard, "Sur une frise samothracienne," *RA*, ser. 6, 36 (1950), p. 158, and André Dessenne, "Pyxis à figures noires du Musée national d'Athènes," *ibid.*, pp. 71 ff., even after the discovery of the new blocks in 1949, still preferred to ascribe the frieze to an altar.

121. See above, pp. 201 f.

122. *Loc. cit.*

123. *Op. cit.*, p. 159.

ies.[124] Karl Lehmann thought that the frieze showed the choral dances of maidens in the Samothracian cult but not in the actual mysteries.[125]

Let us begin with the individual figures (see, for example, fig. 147). We have seen that each maiden wears a sleeved chiton beneath a long mantle characterized by an overfall with a diagonal ruffle at the top, a costume reserved for divinities and ceremonial occasions, a ceremonial dress, too, for musicians of whom there are three on the extant portion of the frieze (figs. 147, 157, 158).[126] Every other dancer wears a scarf ending in two swallowtails, a garment that Athena on Panathenaic vases wears over a peplos.[127] The use of an archaizing style for these maidens, particularly for the mantle and the shawl, in itself implies an allusion to the venerable past.[128]

Each of the maidens and the musicians wears a polos, the headgear reserved for divinity, especially the Great Goddess in her many forms, and for her mortal votaries. In profane life, mortal women are never shown wearing a polos[129] but, as participants in ritual actions, they become assimilated to divinity by wearing the garb that otherwise is restricted to the gods.[130] The low polos worn by these maidens is, ultimately, a Mycenaean type[131] and, among female divinities, worn by Aphrodite and Cybele, in particular.

That the Great Goddess worshiped in Samothrace—whether under the name of Axieros, Demeter, Cybele, or Aphrodite—wore such ritual headgear is attested by the Hellenistic coinage of Samothrace, where she appears on the reverse of bronze coins enthroned and attended by a lion (fig. 189).[132] A second Samothracian image wearing a low polos comes from the Sanctuary (fig. 190).[133] A veiled female head with long tresses like

124. *Op. cit.*, p. 73

125. *Hesperia*, 20 (1951), p. 18.

126. *Harrison*, pp. 54 f.

127. *Ibid.*

128. *Ibid.*, pp. 61 ff.

129. See Valentin Kurt Müller, *Der Polos, die griechische Götterkrone, Berlin*, 1915, pp. 21 f., 24, 35, 41, 45, 56 ff. 81 ff. (where the latter point is made), 88 ff.

130. Harrison, p. 64. She continues: Divinities and their worshipers constitute the subject matter of most archaistic art "to emphasize the venerability and permanence of existing institutions." Ilse Kleeman, *op. cit.*, pp. 224 ff., has also emphasized the religious content of the archaistic pictorial style of the fourth century B.C. in its combination of contemporary and older stylistic features. I owe this reference to Martha Leeb Hadzi. It is astonishing that so perceptive a scholar as Giovanni Becatti has branded the archaistic style as devoid of religious or cultural content, considering it to have "un puro valore ornamentale" ("Arcaistico, Stile," *Enciclopedia dell'arte antica classica e orientale*, Rome, 1958, I, p. 539).

131. For a very few obvious examples of figures wearing low poloi and of the sequence Mycenaean-archaic, see the Mycenaean goddess with a child, the geometric ivory statuette from the Dipylon, both in the National Archaeological Museum in Athens (A. Sakellariou-G. Papathanasopoulos, *National Archaeological Museum, Prehistoric Collections*, Athens, 1964, p. 27, no. 2493; Richter, *Korai*, p. 21, figs. 16-19); and the archaic Aphrodite of Lyon (Humfry Payne and G. M. Young, *Archaic Marble Sculpture from the Akropolis*, London, n.d., pp. 14 ff., 68, pls. 22-26. On p. 15, n. 2, Payne characterized this polos as "high." But cf. Müller, *passim*, for genuinely high poloi. The two other examples quoted by Payne, acc. nos. 669 and 696, seem to be wearing low poloi, too).

132. For brief comment on this type, *see Samothrace*, Vol. 3, text II, pp. 242 f., **159**.

133. Acc. No. 71.1113. Found in the fill of the Stoa, a building dated 300-250 B.C. Fourth century B.C.? Local workmanship. Only the front section of the hollow mold is preserved. Right side of face scorched. Preserved height: 0.0415 m. For further discussion of the head, see Chap. IV, pp. 282 f.

189. Reverse of a bronze coin of Samothrace. Samothrace Museum.

190. Terracotta head from the Sanctuary. Samothrace Museum.

the coin type and the dancing maidens, this fragmentary terracotta figure must be either the Goddess herself or a mortal votary like the figures on the frieze. But it is clear from this single example that this type of figure is a ritual one, whether divine or human.[134]

There appears to be no sculptural prototype for such a chorus of dancing maidens.[135]

134. Iris C. Love has very kindly informed me that Hellenistic female statuettes wearing low poloi, some seated, some standing, and including musicians who play the lyre, the kithara, and the double flutes have been found in a deposit in the Sanctuary of Aphrodite at Knidos.

135. A series of five metopes from the late sixth-century temple in the Sanctuary of Hera at the mouth of the Sele, each showing one or two female dancers, has been interpreted as a liturgical chorus or procession of dancing ἱεραὶ γυναῖκες (P. Zancani Montuoro and U. Zanotti-Bianco, *Heraion alla Foce del Sele*, Rome, 1951, I, pp. 123 ff., 136, 141 ff., pls. XLI-XLIV). The fact that they belonged to a Doric frieze rather than a continuous Ionic frieze, that is, that these dancers are not linked with each other in a long chain but are paired or single, differentiates them aesthetically from the Samothracian chorus. Thematically, however, they are of interest, for here, too, a chorus of dancing women appears to participate in the liturgy of the great goddess Hera. Yet inasmuch as there is no tangible proof in the form of costume that they must be liturgical figures, they cannot be used as certain evidence to establish the present point.

It has been suggested that a fragmentary, unfinished relief of dancing women from Karakeui, ancient Teichioussa, may have belonged to the sima of the archaic Temple of Apollo at Didyma (F. N. Pryce, *Catalogue of Sculpture in the Department of Greek and Roman Antiquities of the British Museum*, London, I, 1, 1928, pp. 116 f., pl. XVII; Picard, *Manuel*, I, Paris, 1935, p. 541). But this interpretation of its function is highly uncertain—it is not even mentioned, for example, in the definitive publication of Hubert Knackfuss, *Didyma*, I, *Die Baubeschreibung*, Berlin, 1941, text I, p. 126, where it is explicitly stated that the sima is not preserved, or in the later volume of Gruben, pp. 340 ff. If such a motif did occur on the continuous simas of buildings in this area, it would be of interest as conceivably indicating archaic architectural precedent for our frieze. Quite apart from the uncertain function of this fragment, it again differs markedly from the Samothracian frieze in that the double line of figures is composed of individual dancers who, unlike the choruses on ceramics now to be cited, are not linked to each other in an unbroken chain.

191. Early Corinthian pyxis. Berlin, Staatliche Museen, Antiken-Abteilung.

But they do occur frequently on late Geometric and Orientalizing pots.[136] Two will suffice to suggest the iconological and historical background for this theme. On an early Corinthian pyxis in Berlin (fig. 191),[137] a chain of draped female figures wearing low poloi and clasping hands faces to the right. Presumably they are dancing, static though the convention may be, and presumably they honor the Great Goddess, who emerges as a plastic head from the same upper zone and herself wears a low polos. Still more relevant is another early Corinthian vessel, an olpe in Madrid (figs. 192, 193),[138] where a file of sixteen draped female figures wearing low poloi and clasping hands encircles the upper zone of the pot preceded by a leader bearing a crown. Directly above, in the center of the neck, the Great Goddess wearing a similar polos is flanked by sphinxes and lions, the sphinxes

136. For random late geometric examples dating ca. 720 B.C., see J. N. Coldstream, *Greek Geometric Pottery*, London, 1968, pp. 63, 141, 331, pl. 11d, and Charles Waldstein, *The Argive Heraeum*, Boston and New York, 1905, II, p. 114, pl. LVII, 17. The majority of the linked figures in these scenes, whether geometric or orientalizing, lack poloi. This feature is essential for any consideration of the frieze of the Propylon. The examples discussed above include this crucial element.

137. Staatliche Museen, Antikenabteilung, no. 984. Adolf Furtwängler, *Staatliche Museen, Beschreibung der Vasensammlung im Antiquarium*, Berlin, 1885, I, No. 984; Müller, *op. cit.*, p. 82, pl. V, left.

138. Inv. No. 10788, from Vulci. J. K. Mélida, Musée Archéologique National, *CVA*, Spain I, Madrid I, Madrid, n.d., III C, pl. 4, fig. 7, pl. 5.

192. Early Corinthian olpe. Madrid, Museo Arqueológico Nacional.

193. Detail of Early Corinthian olpe. Madrid, Museo Arqueológico Nacional.

194. A, B. Fragments of bronze bowls from the Idaean Cave in Crete. Heraklion, Archaeological Museum.

also wearing poloi. Four zones of lions, sphinxes, and sirens follow. In the center of the next to the last zone, the Potnia Theron appears clasping a swan in each hand, again flanked by sphinxes and lions, and again goddess and sphinxes wear low poloi.

Related in motif and imagery are fragments of two bronze bowls from the Idaean Cave in Crete dating from the late eighth or early seventh century B.C. (fig. 194 A, B)[139] on which draped female figures wearing poloi dance. Like the dancing maidens on our

139. Emil Kunze, *Kretische Bronzereliefs*, Stuttgart, 1931, pp. 31, 212 ff., pl. 48, figs. 70 a-d; Fulvio Canciani, *Bronzi orientali e orientalizzanti a Creta nell' VIII e VII sec. A.C.* (Studia archaeologica, 12), Rome, 1970, pp. 27, **70**, **71**, 54, 113 f., 117, 123 ff., 145, 171, 190, pls. VIII, IX, 1. Now in the Archaeological Museum in Heraklion, inv. no. 32. Canciani, pp. 113, 124, describes this form of polos as a *tarbush*. I owe this reference to Paola Zancani.

195. Detail of *F(S)1*.

196. Restored amphora from Klazomenai. Tübingen University Museum.

197. Klazomenian pyxis. Munich, Staatliche Antikensammlungen.

198. Bronze bowl from Idalion in Crete. New York, The Metropolitan Museum of Art.

frieze (fig. 195), these tiny figures do not hold hands but clasp each other at the wrist—ἐπὶ καρπῷ, to use the Homeric phrase.[140] This detail, difficult to see on the bowls, is better visible on certain Klazomenian amphorae (fig. 196),[141] where, however, the figures lack

140. E.g.: *Iliad*, 18, lines 593-594. In connection with the previous bronze bowls, it is interesting to note that this passage occurs in the description of another object, the Shield of Achilles, as Kunze, *op. cit.*, p. 213, has noted. The phrase occurs elsewhere, e.g., the *Homeric Hymn to Apollo*, 3, lines 194-196, where Harmonia and Aphrodite take part in a dance in which the dancers hold each other at the wrist.

141. Tübingen University Museum, inv. 2656, restored amphora from Klazomenai. See Carl Watzinger, *Griechischen Vasen in Tübingen*, Reutlingen, 1924, p. 15, no. 9, pl. II; *CVA*, Deutschland, Tübingen, Antikensammlung des archäologischen Instituts der Universität, I, Munich, 1973, pp. 31 ff., pls. 13, 14. See, too, among others, *Antike Denkmäler*, II, Berlin, 1908, pp. 8 f., pl. 54, figs. 1 a, b; R. M. Cook, *CVA*, Great Britain, 13, British Museum, 8, London, 1954, p. 26, pls. 12, 2; 13, 3-4; J. M. Cook, "Old Smyrna: Ionic Black-Figure and Other Sixth-Century Figured Wares," *BSA*, 60 (1965), p. 130, no. 68. It is quite likely that the twenty-three female figures performing a ritual dance on an early Corinthian skyphos in the Bibliothèque Nationale in Paris also clasp each other by the wrist (*CVA*, Paris, Bibliothèque Nationale I, France, 7, Paris, 1928, pp. 13 f., pls. 15, no. 22, 16, no. 1). For this motif, see Renate Tölle, *Frühgriechische Reigentänze*, Waldsassen/Bayern, 1964, p. 56.

poloi. Indeed, on one such Klazomenian vessel, a pyxis in Munich (fig. 197), a flaming altar appears in the center of the dancers.[142] The ritual nature of the scene on one of the bronze bowls is also confirmed by a second fragment showing a procession of figures bearing offerings.

Particularly relevant is a seventh-century B.C. bronze bowl from Idalion in Cyprus now in the Metropolitan Museum of Art in New York (fig. 198).[143] On it, an enthroned goddess holding a lotus flower in her right hand and a round object (pomegranate?) in her left is preceded by a table on which a basket of offerings stands. To its left stands a priestess holding a fan and ladle; to her left, a second table supports an amphora and oinochoe. There follows a line of six draped female dancers wearing poloi[144] and clasping hands.[145] Behind the goddess, three female musicians wearing poloi play the double flute, what appears to be a form of kithara,[146] and a tympanum—precisely the instruments, soon to be mentioned, played by the musicians in the frieze of dancing maidens. Clearly, this is a cult scene; clearly, these dancers honor some form of the Great Goddess.

The ritual dancers on the Corinthian vessels and on these bronze bowls honor the Great Mother, by whatever name she was evoked. Surely the dancing maidens on the frieze of the Propylon perform a similar liturgy in the service of the Samothracian Great Goddess. Were these rites performed in the Temenos? It is tempting to think so.[147] Nor is

142. No. 570. Eleni Walter-Karydi, *CVA*, Deutschland, 28, Munich, Museum antiker Kleinkunst, 6, Munich, 1968, pp. 46 f., pls. 301-2. Fig. B is reproduced from the illustration in Johannes Sievieking and Rudolf Hackl, *Die königliche Vasensammlung zu München*, I, Munich, 1912, no. 570, pl. 20, showing a restored drawing of this damaged vessel.

This motif occurs on one of the recently discovered blocks of an Ionic frieze seemingly attributed to the late archaic Temple of Hera at Sybaris. (The author does not explain the presence of both a "triglyph frieze" and an "Ionic sculptured frieze" on the same building.) These blocks must have been subdivided horizontally when they were reused in a later building. One shows two dancing figures moving to the right, where one figure clasps her neighbor by the wrist; the other is a (female?) musician playing the double flutes. See Oliver C. Colburn, "A Return to Sybaris," *Expedition*, 18 (1976), p. 9 and fig. 4. I am indebted to Mrs. Hadzi for having drawn my attention to this article.

143. No. 535. Embossed and engraved. Gisela M. A. Richter, *The Metropolitan Museum of Art. Greek, Etruscan and Roman Bronzes*, New York, 1915, pp. 201 f.; John L. Myres, *Handbook of the Cesnola Collection of Antiquities from Cyprus*, New York, 1914, no. 4561, pp. 465 f.; *Cesnola Atlas*, III, pl. XXXIII, 2. The piece has been repeatedly discussed and illustrated. See Canciani, *op. cit.*, pp. 147 f., pl. XII, and Einar Gjerstad, "Bronze Decorated Metal Bowls from Cyprus," *Opuscula archaeologica*, 4 (1946), pp. 3 ff., pl. I.

See the related bronze bowl in the Louvre, no. A04702, presumably found near Sparta: R. Dussaud, "Coupe de bronze chyprophénicienne," *BSA*, 37 (1936-37), pp. 92-95, fig. 1; Gjerstad, *op. cit.*, p. 6, pl. II.

144. Myres, *op. cit.*, p. 465, describes this feature as hair piled on the head with one long plait hanging down—as, indeed, it does. But the rectangular objects on the heads with their regular horizontal lines are a form of headgear, as Gjerstad, *op. cit.*, p. 6, has observed, although he did not use the specific term "polos" to define it.

145. Between each pair of dancers, there stands either a lotus column (Myres) or a lotus tree (Gjerstad).

146. The characteristic straight bottom of the instrument is invisible. It has usually been called a lyre.

147. Again, it is worth recalling that there were dances performed by women in the Temenos of Hera at Lesbos. *Anthologia Palatina* 9.189; Scholia AD to *Iliad*, I, 129.

it without significance that the earliest pottery from the Temenos dates from the first half of the seventh century B.C.,[148] the very period reflected in these slightly later Corinthian pots, and to query whether such rites were not instituted at that time in the predecessor of the Temenos.[149] One wonders, too, whether this ritual garb, the polos and the ceremonial mantle, was still used in the fourth century B.C. If so, the choice and use of an archaistic style to depict this venerable rite would be understandable.

Among the dancers on the extant blocks of the frieze, three are musicians who play the kithara, the double flute, and the tympanum (figs. 147, 157, 158). Very likely, other musicians were once present, given the length of the frieze, and conceivably other instruments were also played—the lyre, the cymbals, and the krotala or castanets, all instruments mentioned in the literary sources on Samothrace in connection with its legends and cult.[150] Although these instruments occur in other contexts, both in literature and in works of art, it is worth pointing out that all three of the existing instruments, the kithara, the double flute, and the tympanum may be found in the circle of Kybele.[151]

Our dancing maidens appear to form a long procession at which varied hymns are sung in honor of divinity,[152] a *κίνησις ἀρχαϊκή*, to use the term of Athenaeus,[153] an ancient form of dance preserved over the centuries. Dancing was especially appropriate in the Sanctuary of the Great Gods, a mystery sanctuary, for as Lucian reports:

> I forbear to say that not a single ancient mystery-cult can be found that is without dancing, since they were established, of course, by Orpheus and Musaeus, the best dancers of that time, who included it in their prescriptions as something exceptionally beautiful to be initiated with rhythm and dancing. To prove that this is so, although it behooves me to observe silence about the rites on account of the uninitiate, nevertheless there is one thing everybody has heard; namely, that those who let out the mysteries in conversation are commonly said to "dance them out."[154]

148. Catalogue, **1-82.**

149. See below, pp. 271 ff.

150. E.g., *Samothrace*, Vol. 1, **142**, **214**, **215**, **219**, **220**.

151. It is needless to labor this point. For an example of the Great Goddess (here Kybele) wearing a singular, high polos and flanked by small musicians playing the double flutes and kithara, see the archaic statuary group from Boğazköy that was included in a covered niche in a gate in the city wall. See Kurt Bittel, "Ausgrabungen in Boğazköy," *Neue deutsche Ausgrabungen im Mittelmeergebiet und im vorderen Orient*, Berlin, 1959, pp. 115 ff.; Ekrem Akurgel, *Die Kunst Anatoliens*, Berlin, 1961, pp. 98 ff., figs. 56-59.

For the tympanum, the instrument most frequently connected with Kybele, see Charles Daremberg and Edmond Saglio, *Dictionnaire des antiquités grecques et romaines*, I, 2, Paris, 1887, *s.v. Cybèle*, pp. 1682 ff., especially 1687, and for a typical example, the tale reported by Herodotus, 4.76.

For musical instruments, see Max Wegner, *Das Musikleben der Griechen*, Berlin, 1949, pp. 28 ff.

152. See August Brinkmann, "Altgriechische Mädchenreigen," *BonnJbb*, 130 (1925), pp. 120 ff., and Tölle, *op. cit.*, pp. 54 ff., for discussion of liturgical dances performed by choruses of maidens and the ancient literary sources alluding to them.

153. 139 E.

154. Περὶ Ὀρχήσεως, 15 (tr. A. M. Harmon, Loeb edn., V, p. 229).

This is not to imply that, in Samothrace, where initiation took place in the Anaktoron and the Hieron that initiation itself took place in the Temenos, but that the maidens on the frieze dance in the liturgy of the Great Goddess as votaries, having donned her ritual garb. And if they danced in the Temenos, it was as votaries to the Great Mother in the form of Aphrodite Zerynthia.[155]

It is not impossible that the representation of dancing on the Propylon has more than one connotation. Not only did the gods take particular joy in dancing,[156] but also dancing was a standard feature of festivals in honor of heroes.[157] In the Temenos to which the Propylon gave access, there lay two ritual installations, a bothros and an eschara,[158] the latter customarily used for sacrifices in honor of a hero.[159] In Samothrace, it is likely that it was the hero-founder of the mysteries, Aëtion, he who was "reported to have been the first to celebrate the mysteries performed in Samothrace to Rhea,"[160] to whom sacrifice was made.[161] Is this yet another allusion implicit in the frieze?

Finally, dancing was a regular ingredient of weddings.[162] A fragment of Sappho gives a vivid picture of the maidens who sing holy songs to the sound of the flute, kithara, and krotala at the wedding of Hektor and Andromeda.[163] Can this nuptial practice provide a clue to the lost central portion of the frieze of the Propylon?

A key element in the Samothracian legend was the wedding of Kadmos and Harmonia. In the words of Diodorus:

> And after this Kadmos, the son of Agenor, came in the course of his quest for Europa to the Samothracians, and after having participated in the initiation he married Harmonia, who was the sister of Iasion. . . .[164] This wedding of Kadmos and Harmonia was the first, we are told, for which the gods provided the marriage feast, and Demeter (enamored of Iasion) presented the fruit of the grain, Hermes a lyre, Athena the renowned necklace and a robe and flutes, and Elektra the sacred rites of the Great Mother of the Gods, as she is called,

155. See below, p. 288. On the sacred nature of the ancient dance, see Mircea Eliade, *The Myth of the Eternal Return* (Bollingen Series XLVI), 1954, pp. 28 f.

156. Apuleius, *De deo Socratis*, 14 (Teubner edn., Leipzig, 1908, III, p. 22).

157. Walter Hahland, "Zu den Aufängen der attischen Malerei," *Corolla Ludwig Curtius*, Stuttgart, 1937, pp. 125 ff.

158. See above, pp. 81 f.

159. See Vol. 3 text II, p. 30 and nn. 133-139 for this practice.

160. Scholia to Clemens Alexandrinus *Protrepticus* 2.13.3 (*Samothrace*, Vol. 1, **146**).

161. For Aëtion in this capacity, see Vol. 3, text I, pp. 289 f.

162. For dancing as a regular feature of weddings, see Louis Séchan, *La Danse grecque antique*, Paris, 1930, pp. 218 ff.; *RE, s.v. Tanzkunst*, 2nd ser., IV, Stuttgart, 1931, cols. 2239 ff.

163. Frg. 66. Cf. too, the earlier seventh-century *Shield of Herakles*, ll. 272 ff., where maidens dance to the *φόρμιγξ* in connection with bridal festivities (*Hesiod, The Homeric Hymns and Homerica* [Loeb edn., ed. by Hugh G. Evelyn-White], pp. XXVI, 238 f.).

164. Also called Aëtion or Eëtion. Cf. Vol. 3, text I, p. 289, n. 67. Cf., too, Hesiod, *Theogony*, line 935.

> together with cymbals and kettledrums and the ecstatic revelers of her ritual; and Apollo played on the kithara and the Muses on their flutes, and the rest of the Gods spoke them fair and gave the pair their aid in the celebration of the wedding. . . .[165]

Indeed, it has already been suggested by Otto Rubensohn and Otto Kern that the frieze of the Propylon must represent the celebration of this legendary wedding on the basis of this very text.[166] It was implicit in Karl Lehmann's later suggestion that the dancing choruses of the frieze must "be connected with the story of the wedding of Kadmos and Harmonia."[167] If so, the logical position for a scene depicting the divinities present on that occasion would have been the central portion of the frieze above the façade proper. One may speculate on the nature of this scene. It would be rash to attempt to restore it. Lacking any precise notion of the character of this composition, we have preferred to omit any portion of the frieze in the restored elevation of the façade inasmuch as the central scene cannot be restored. In view of the likelihood that one function of the Temenos was to serve for the presentation of a sacred drama, the search for Harmonia who had been carried off by Kadmos,[168] it seems appropriate to suggest that the ensuing episode in the drama, the Wedding of Kadmos and Harmonia, was the theme of the frieze. Hypothetical though the suggestion may—and must—be, it is not implausible.[169]

165. 5.49.1 *Samothrace*, Vol. 1, **142**. In this account, Diodorus evidently drew on the fifth-century historian Hellanicus of Lesbos, in whose *Phoronis*, book I, a similar mythological account appears. See Lionel Pearson, *Early Ionian Historians*, Oxford, 1939, p. 164. See, too, Stephanus Byzantius *Ethnica*, *s.v.* ΔΑΡΔΑΝΟΣ *πόλις Τρωάδος*; Scholia Laurentiana and Parisina to Apollonius Rhodius *Argonautica* ll.915-16; Nonnus *Dionysiaca* 3.373-444; Scholia to Euripides *Phoenissae* 7 (**65**, **70**, **70a**, **74**, **75**).

166. Rubensohn, p. 133; Kern in *RE*, X, Stuttgart, 1919, *s.v. Kabeiros, Kabeiroi*, col. 1428 f.

Re: The wedding of Kadmos and Harmonia, see C. Kerényi, *The Heroes of the Greeks*, London, 1959, pp. 25 ff. On p. 19, Kerényi assumes that this wedding was "celebrated on Samothrace in the mysteries." There is no evidence whatever that this legendary event had anything to do with "the mysteries." On the contrary, it is probably a paraphrase of the *hieros gamos* of the mysteries.

167. *Hesperia*, 21 (1952), p. 30 and nn. 39 ff. And implicit, it seems, in the view of Dessenne, *op. cit.*, p. 73, and Hemberg, pp. 107 f.

168. For consideration of the rites performed in the Temenos, see Chap. IV, pp. 288 f.

169. Mary B. Moore has drawn my attention to two black-figured vases, a fragmentary oinochoe in Göttingen and an amphora in the Louvre on which the Wedding of Kadmos and Harmonia is depicted. On the latter, the inscribed figures stand in a chariot drawn by a lion and a boar in the presence of a kithara-playing Apollo. Such a group might well have been included in the central portion of the frieze along with the other divinities and the Muses present in Diodorus' text. On side B of the Louvre amphora Athena, Herakles, and Hermes are present. Athena and Hermes lack the attributes necessary for Diodorus' text and Herakles does not occur in it. Hence side B offers no useful parallels for the reconstruction of the missing figures (For these vases see Konrad Schauenburg, "Zu Darstellung aus der Sage des Admet und des Kadmos," *Gymnasium*, 64 [1957], 210 ff., pls. I, II).

The combination of divinities, Muses, and heroes required for this lost portion of the frieze also recalls the procession on an upper register of the François vase, where a similar cast of characters is present in connection with the marriage of Peleus and Thetis (see Furtwängler-Reichhold, ser. I, pp. 1-14, pls. I-III; Antonio Minto, *Il Vaso François* [Accademia toscana di scienze e lettere, Studi VI], Florence, 1960, pp. 21 f., 87-106). This scene does not lend itself to an appropriate solution of the formal problems inherent in the design of the central

If so, this theme is a singular medley of legend and liturgy. The Wedding of Kadmos and Harmonia was a cult legend. Yet within the tale, there is allusion to the fact that Elektra instituted the sacred rites of the Great Mother of the Gods, and of the cymbals and tympana used in her ritual, Elektra, mother of Aëtion, who first celebrated her mysteries. Thus the maidens dance at the wedding of Kadmos and Harmonia. In another sense, they perform a ritual dance in honor of the Great Goddess, possibly, too, of Aëtion, a dance that, it seems, may have been actually performed in the Sanctuary.[170] The concept of this theme is intricate and richly allusive in meaning.

Insofar as the chorus of dancing maidens appears to reflect an actual rite that was performed in the Sanctuary, insofar as the frieze depicts that rite, it recalls the Panathenaic frieze high up on the cella walls of the Parthenon, as has already been pointed out.[171] Indeed, the only precedent for representing a ceremonial action on the sculptured frieze of a building rather than decorating it with the normal varieties of mythological themes is provided by the frieze of the Parthenon.[172] Here, as we have seen,[173] the procession begins at the southwest corner of the temple, moves across the rear side, proceeds along both flanks, and culminates at the façade, where the two lines of mortal figures converge and, in this case, a ceremonial act takes place in the presence of the Olympian gods—an organization of the frieze that seems to have been echoed in the frieze of the Propylon. It is obvious that Skopas, who appears to have been the designing architect-sculptor of the Propylon was familiar with the Parthenon.[174] Hence it is not surprising that he employed a similar scheme in presenting his theme. And if we recall the original presence of the lost block *Fa* and the suggestion that it was one of at least a pair of such blocks flanking the missing central scene, its relatively quiet figures would constitute a further parallel with the quiet mortal figures flanking the gods on the east frieze of the Parthenon.

P. W. L.

On the basis of style, some authorities have assigned to the frieze a much later date than that which the archaeological evidence provides.[175] Moreover, the identification of Skopas

---

portion of the Propylon's frieze. But these vases, although they do not allow a precise graphic reconstruction of this portion of the frieze, suggest its general character.

170. Not in the actual mysteries. Initiation into the mysteries was individual and took place in the Anaktoron and the Hieron.

171. A. H. Smith, *The Sculptures of the Parthenon*, London, 1910, p. 50, fig. 96; Robertson and Frantz, *The Parthenon Frieze*, London, 1975.

172. As has long been apparent. Cf. Demangel, pp. 445 ff., who has referred to its theme as "sujet idéel à la fois et réel" and unique "dans la grande décoration de la Grèce."

The friezes attributed to the pronaos and cella walls of the late archaic Temple of Hera at Samos were devoted to miscellaneous mythological subjects. See Ernst Buschor, "Altsamische Bauschmuck," *AthMitt*, 72 (1957), pp. 12 ff., 26 ff., 30 ff.; Berve-Gruben-Hirmer, p. 455.

173. Above, p. 201.

174. For Skopas' biography, see above, Chap. II, nn. 206, 207.

175. Otto Rubensohn dated the frieze in the mid-fourth century B.C., (pp. 133 f.), but he incorrectly associated it with the "alter Tempel"; see also Introduction, p. 19, n. 49. Schmidt (pp. 39 f.) and Becatti (*op. cit.*, p. 40), who also knew the

as designing architect-sculptor of the Propylon[176] raises the question of the relation of the frieze to that artist's *oeuvre*. Hence one important task of the present discussion is to reconsider the problem of the frieze's style in the light of the archaeologically justified date of ca. 340 B.C.; another is to examine the monuments surely attributed to Skopas in search of clues linking them to the frieze. Its archaism cannot be taken as grounds for eliminating the frieze from Skopas' ambiance, as the case of the Apollo Smintheus demonstrates.[177] Yet the fact that no other securely datable archaizing work has actually survived from the immediate artistic environment of these reliefs must inhibit both efforts, unless we succeed in looking beyond those features which are borrowed from the past and in identifying such characteristics of the frieze as may connect its style with that of naturalistic works of appropriate date.

Close scrutiny of the dancers' most conspicuous archaizing trait, the pose that is employed for all preserved figures except the musicians, will validate this procedure. The ancient fractional view of the figure, introduced here for the first time in late classical art, is accentuated by juxtaposing the profile of the rear leg and buttock to the frontally drawn torso, in such a way that the two divergent views of the figure are not merely additively combined, as in archaic art, but are brought into vehement, caricaturistic collision (see, for example, *F(S)1*; fig. 195). It may be observed, moreover, that the actual components of the stylized, two-dimensional posture belong, not to archaic art, but to a sophisticated

---

frieze only on the basis of the damaged blocks then in the Louvre, *F(S)10* and *F(S)11* (figs. 157, 158), dated it respectively in the third century and "oltre." Havelock agreed with Becatti's late dating (*op. cit.*, p. 50; Mrs. Lehmann has commented on Havelock's opinion in *Skopas in Samothrace*, p. 14, n. 89), and Werner Fuchs has assigned to it a date around 300 B.C. (*Die Skulpturen der Griechen*, Munich, 1969, p. 458). Two observers writing since the publication of the Samothracian finds of the seasons of 1949 and 1950 (for which, see *Hesperia*, 20 [1951], pp. 16 ff., and 21 [1952], pp. 24 ff.) have accepted the excavator's conclusions about the date of the building and its sculptures (see Harrison, p. 54, and Ridgway, p. 202), but there has been no detailed consideration of the problem since Havelock's article of 1964, cited above.

176. On the attribution to Skopas, see above, pp. 144 ff., 170 ff.

177. On the Apollo Smintheus, see below, pp. 258 ff. Inasmuch as it has proved reasonable to attribute the Propylon to Skopas as designing architect-sculptor (see previous note), we should entertain the possibility that others among his commissions, in addition to that for the Apollo Smintheus at Chryse, may have led to the creation of archaistic statues. It would seem legitimate to speculate in this vein about the cult images attributed in the sources to Skopas, of which archaizing versions exist, whether their style is identifiably Skopaic or not. For example, the existence of the statuette of Artemis from Paros (fig. 251), for which a date in the first half of the fourth century B.C. has been suggested (Kleeman, *op. cit.*, pp. 221 ff.; see also App. II, below, p. 309), makes it likely that a major cult image of this kind had been made, and that, if Skopas was not indeed its creator, he may have followed such a pattern when he designed his image of Artemis at Thebes (Pausanias, 9. 17.1). For a Skopaic head of Artemis, see fig. 187 and n. 114, above. Again, Skopas could well have imitated the Hekataion by Alkamenes in the statue of Hekate which he made at the Sanctuary of Eilethyia in Argos (Pausanias 2. 22.7). Willers has correctly drawn attention to the Skopaic character of an archaistic Herm in the National Archaeological Museum, Athens, no. 106 ("Zum Hermes Propylaios des Alkamenes," *JdI*, 82 [1967], p. 97). Finally, Mrs. Lehmann has recently suggested not only that the Athena image on the tetradrachms of Ptolemy I depicts the Athena Alkidemos of Pella, but also that that image may have been the work of Skopas (see below, note 257).

realm of late classical style where gestures are delicately equilibrated for expressive effect, and are organized into complex interacting systems. In the more refined and better preserved figures, on *F(S)1* and *F(S)12* in particular (figs. 147, 148, 159, 195, 210), the forms of the upper body suggest a fluid almost sinuous action that contradicts the vertical rigidity of the major drapery lines: the detail of *F(S)12* (fig. 160) shows how deftly the leading right shoulder has been given plastic emphasis both by projection and by outlining with the chisel, while the opposite shoulder gently recedes toward the background plane, its contour sinking into continuity with the arm. That the arms are also conceived in spatial terms is clear not only from the subtlety of their form-defining outlines, but also from the absence of the thumb of the extended right hands—a lack that is surely to be explained, not as evidence of the carver's inadequate skill or knowledge, but as indicative of a foreshortening in which the thumb disappears behind the hand, and is thus concealed from view. The instinctive naturalism of the designer's style is nowhere more apparent than in the ready abandonment of the archaic conventional pose when required for the portrayal of spatially complex gestures such as those of the musicians, who are seen in full profile, with foreshortened torsos and with arms, now much damaged, which certainly extended forward to play their instruments; this is best visible in the kitharist of *F(S)1* (fig. 210). It is also evident that, even in the most convincingly archaized dancers, there occur in the modeling of the drapery devices that expose the habitual classical practice of the sculptor. For example, the diagonal crease which crosses the central panel of the apoptygma in the backward-turning figures, seen in *F(S)1* (figs. 148, 195) is only understandable as a reminiscence of the modeling of drapery that is appropriate, not to the fractional view, but to a naturalistic, spatially conceived figure, whose twisting torso generates diagonal tension in the overlying cloth.[178] Similarly, alongside the archaizing central folds and pleats of the lower mantle, slanting creases are to be seen crossing the thighs, which are normal elements of the representation of clothing stretched over limbs from the late fifth century onward (see fig. 210).[179] The tiptoe pose, too, never occurring in the archaic period, is emblematic of later fourth-century art, where quick, transitory movements suggestive of lightness and speed were first introduced, supplanting the ponderous, controlled and self-contained movements found in the fifth century and the stresses of the early fourth century.[180] A pelike by the Marsyas Painter showing Thetis carried off by Peleus (fig. 199), for example, presents two figures on tiptoes in a design that exemplifies well the new rhythms of the decades centering around 340 B.C.[181]

178. The use of this diagonal crease in the classical period is illustrated by the familiar relief showing the Nike adjusting her sandal from the parapet of the Nike Temple on the Acropolis, Athens (see Rhys Carpenter, *The Sculpture of the Nike Temple Parapet*, Cambridge [Mass.], 1929, pl. XXVII).

179. Stewart draws attention to the use of sharp-edged folds stretched across a thigh or toward a knee or breast as characteristic of the sculptures from the Temple of Athena Alea at Tegea (p. 77).

180. Brown has recently clarified the relationship between the sculpture of the fifth and that of the fourth century B.C., with some emphasis on the kinds of postures typically employed (*op. cit.*, pp. 9 ff).

181. British Museum no. 424; see Karl Schefold, *Kertscher Vasen*, Berlin, 1930, pls. 16a, 17. Figures moving on tiptoes also occur on such fourth-century

199. Pelike by the Marsyas Painter. London, The British Museum.

This pelike directs attention to a more subtle relationship that binds this phase of late classical art to that of the archaic period in the management of pose and space. It is evident here, especially in the female figures, that the freedom now felt in the designing of spatially complex poses, combined with a renewed appreciation of the compositional value of the two-dimensional plane, encouraged artists to so dispose the figure that the upper and lower parts of the body are opposed in 180° changes of direction.[182] The designer of the frieze of the Propylon would seem again to have caricatured this proclivity in his insistent reiteration of the alternating dancers who turn to look directly backward. I shall sug-

works as the Niinion Tablet in the Archaeological Museum at Eleusis—maenad at left center (see George Emanuel Mylonas, *Eleusis and the Eleusinian Mysteries,* Princeton, 1961, fig. 88); the Artemis Colonna in the Staatliche Museen, Berlin (see H. K. Süsserott, *Griechische Plastik des vierten Jahrhunderts vor Christus,* Frankfurt, 1938, pl. 30, 4, and p. 145, where the statue is dated ca. 370-360 B.C.); the mid-fourth century stele of Aristokles in the British Museum, London (Elgin Collection, no. 638).

182. In the Amazonomachy Frieze from the Mausoleum at Halikarnassos, the poses of several figures exhibit this reversal of direction or something approaching it (see Ashmole, figs. 206-208, pp. 178 f., especially the collapsing warrior on slab 1013).

gest below that in the decades following 350 B.C. there developed, especially in the composition of friezes, what may best be called an archaizing use of space, in which figures portrayed in naturalistic terms are spread out in a chainlike arrangement against a flat background, just as in the frieze of the Propylon.[183] Both the fractional pose and the pose that reverses the figure's direction lend themselves admirably to this compositional system.[184]

Before considering the more general topic of the chain composition, it will be useful to pursue our analysis of the typically fourth-century character of the designer's style by examining some further details of the frieze. Looking at the dancers' heads, for example, it may be remarked that the upward slope of the top surfaces of the poloi again betrays the intention to foreshorten, suggesting three-dimensional form and, at the same time, relating the figures spatially to the spectator at ground level.[185] Once more, in their positions, the heads seem constrained by archaism toward the profile view, but in fact they achieve it only intermittently because of the nuanced shifting of the glances, both in the downward and outward directions. These variations in the carriage of the head are underscored by the occurrences of the bun which projects from the back of some: the bun seems to have been omitted in those cases where the head's posture departs slightly from the full profile view, as if in exaggerated illustration of the effect of foreshortening (compare the treatment of the thumb noted above). May the designer not be using the frieze to comment wryly upon the conventions that accompany both naturalistic and archaic art?

The dancers' costume has already been analyzed closely with respect to the origin of the garments which compose it;[186] here, on the other hand, we may regard it as the expression of a particular style. One function of the tall and assertively columnar design of the drapery is to support the vivacious interchange of gesture and glance that dominates the upper zone of the frieze; its other function is to control and order the dissonant archaizing posture which it at once masks and exposes. For what particularly characterizes these figures as belonging to the period around 340 B.C. is the tension that exists between their active and expressive anatomical structure and the decorative carapace of drapery that encloses it, partly concealing and partly displaying its fluid forms. The fourth century was witness not only to the disintegration of the expressive harmony between the body and its clothing that typified the art of the fifth century B.C., but also to various modes of reintegrating these elements in order to express the new, intimate psychological values that are the sub-

183. See below, pp. 240 ff.

184. Another aspect of the use of pose in the frieze—that of the mirrored reversals that connect the two converging files of dancers—has recently been studied by Cornelius C. Vermeule III, who points out that, although the caryatids of the Erechtheum present the very first instance of mirrored poses, the earliest widespread use of the device occurred in precisely the period with which we are concerned (*Greek Sculpture and Roman Taste*, Ann Arbor [Mich.], 1977, pp. 4 f., 39).

185. On the visual adjustments occurring throughout the sculptural decoration of the Propylon, see above, p. 208, and note 91. For a discussion of the use of foreshortening in South Italian vase painting of the fourth century B.C., see John White, *The Birth and Rebirth of Pictorial Space*, New York, 1972, pp. 243 ff.

186. See above, pp. 211 ff.

ject matter of the primary art form of the period—the portrait.[187] This content is revealed by such expressive means as the tilt of the head in intense communion with a companion on a grave stele,[188] the lift of a shoulder,[189] the open gesticulation of a hand.[190] The bodies are caught in unsteady, transitory or undecided poses, which are not and cannot be integrated with the bold rhythms of the drapery of classical tradition. Our monument belongs to a period of crisis occasioned by the growth of these new artistic concerns, whose initial phase is represented by the portrait of Maussollos from Halikarnassos, to be dated ca. 350 B.C., where the conflicts generated by an unresolved pose are held in suspension by means of the bulky swathe of cloth that crosses and masks the lower torso;[191] the period is ushered out and the crisis is resolved in works such as the great stele from Rhamnous,[192] where drapery and body become one unified swaying stalk, simplified in order to bear the weight of expression that is concentrated in the arms, shoulders, and head. The figure is now extremely tall and its point of focus has moved up from the classical position at the solar plexus to a place above the waistline, as noted in our consideration of changes in the treatment of drapery in this period.[193]

187. In speaking of the portrait as the primary art form of this period, I mean to indicate, not that there were more portraits than works devoted to mythological or other subject matter (although the portrait was in process of emergence in a new sense now: see James Douglas Breckenridge, *Likeness*, Evanston [Ill.], 1968, pp. 115 ff.), but that the new perceptions embodied in all the art of the time were those proper to the portrait, arising from the close study of human emotion and its outward manifestations. This trend was bringing about the transformation of religious subject matter that is familiar especially in Praxiteles' works: one wonders in this context whether archaism may not in some cases be understood as a countermeasure intended to correct the "portrait"-like excesses of contemporary art (see M. Folman, *Introduction à l'étude de la sculpture archaïsante*, Montpelier, 1935, p. 64, for a similar view of the motivation of archaism in the fourth century B.C.; see also p. 261, below). The designer of the frieze of the Propylon, on the other hand, deals less seriously with archaism, as will be shown below (see p. 247 ff.), and, indeed, takes something like a portraitist's approach to several of the presumably anonymous faces of the dancers, as revealed in the firmly differentiated features and expressions shown in figs. 148, 160. For a survey of scholarly opinion about the meaning of the rise of archaistic art, see Willers, "Zu den Anfängen der archaistischen Plastik," pp. 21 ff.; see also Mrs. Lehmann's remarks, pp. 255 ff.

188. National Archaeological Museum, Athens, no. 833; Hans Diepolder, *Die attische Grabreliefs des 5. und 4. Jahrhunderts v. Chr.*, Berlin, 1931, p. 56, pl. 54.

189. The bronze Apollo in the British Museum, London (*Select Bronzes*, London, 1915, pl. XLII), is comparable to the dancers in its sinuously expressive pose; it is dated by Süsserott ca. 330 B.C. (*op. cit.*, p. 167).

190. See the Marathon Youth in the National Archaeological Museum, Athens (Robertson, pl. 126a) for the use of the open gesture in fourth-century statuary, but also for the more general characteristics of height, mannered grace, transitory pose that are found in the Samothracian figures. The statue is dated ca. 330 B.C. by Süsserott (*op. cit.*, p. 166).

191. Stewart summarizes recent investigation of the question and concludes that work on the Mausoleum may have occupied the period ca. 360-340 B.C. (pp. 101, 151). One might reasonably assume that the sculptures did not belong to the first phase of the work; hence a date around 350 B.C. seems appropriate for the Maussollos statue. See n. 100, above, for a reference to Brown's excellent analysis of the composition of the Maussollos and its expressive meaning.

192. For the stele from Rhamnous, see above, n. 188.

193. See above, p. 210.

If this reintegration of posture and drapery typifies the decade ca. 330-320 B.C., it is the style of the previous decade that appears in the Samothracian frieze, a style which accepts and, so to speak, deals openly with the conflicts that are muffled in the drapery of Maussollos. It employs mobile and complex postures and it relates drapery to these postures in a necessarily mannered and sometimes perverse way. It establishes a structural framework of clothing that is almost independent of the body's pose, and creates an interplay of active vertical and horizontal or diagonal accents which isolate and expose individual bodily forms—in the Samothracian dancers, it is the bust and rear leg and buttocks that are selected for display. Incorporating these varied stresses, the stance suggests a lurching uncertainty of movement, comparable, for example, with the indecisiveness in the placing of bodily weight that is seen in the contemporary Apollo Patrôos of Euphranor.[194] Implicit in this analysis is, of course, the assertion that the archaizing pose of the dancers is not a critical element of their style, but is simply an occasion for special exploitation of a disjointure that is found also in the naturalistic art of the period. The fractional view, then, releases for fuller and more entertaining elaboration a concept that is also present, for example, in the Muses of the Mantinea Base,[195] where the sinuous, animated postures are alternatingly opposed and exposed by a drapery structure that is, by turns, massive and angular or softly revealing. The final effect of this treatment, in the Mantinea Base as in the Samothracian frieze, is to diversify the foci of attention within the figure, so that these now include the body and its complex interaction with the garments in addition to the newly accentuated activities of arms and heads, which are engaged in busily communicative gesticulation.[196]

194. See Homer A. Thompson, "The Apollo Patrôos of Euphranor," *ArchEph.*, 1953/54, pp. 30 ff. and pls. I, II, where the statue is dated ca. 350-325 B.C.

195. National Archaeological Museum, Athens, nos. 215-217 (Svoronos, *op. cit.*, pls. XXX, XXXI). Democracy Crowning Athena, a decree relief from the archonship of Phrynikos (336 B.C.) in the Agora Museum, Athens (no. I6524), displays elements of the style of the Samothracian frieze in the enveloping drapery with its thick crossing folds above the waist and the strong line of the vertical fold at the right side of the figure.

196. The beautiful Roman version of a fourth-century Isis type in the Museo Nuovo of the Capitoline Museum, Rome (Domenico Mustilli, *Il Museo Mussolini*, Rome, 1939, pl. XLIII, no. 173), seems to reflect a work belonging to the same stylistic trend. Extremely tall, with an uncertainly swaying posture, and clothed in layer upon layer of richly textured garments, which at once mask and reveal the anatomical structure, this figure heightens the mannerism evident in the Samothracian dancers. A moderated expression of the same style is illustrated by the following statues in the National Archaeological Museum, Athens, which date from the second half of the fourth century B.C.; no. 709, a sepulchral statue of a woman; no. 1810, a statuette of Hygeia (Roman copy) from Epidauros. A fragmentary colossal statue of Themis in the Agora Museum, Athens (no. S2370), of the same period is related in style, as is a draped statue identified as a nymph (Roman copy) in the Archaeological Museum, Ostia (no. 15).

My analysis of the development of sculpture in the later fourth century B.C. owes much to the patient scrutiny of the votive reliefs by Hermione Speier ("Zweifiguren-Gruppen im fünften und vierten Jahrhunderts," *RömMitt*, 47 [1932], pp. 1 ff.) and Süsserott (*op. cit.*, *passim*, especially pp. 59 ff., 216 f.). See also Renate Kabus-Jahn, *Studien zu Frauenfiguren des vierten Jahrhunderts v. Chr.*, Darmstadt, 1963, pp. 2 ff., for a discussion of works of the decade ca. 340-330 B.C.

It is evident that the fourth century's exploration of new kinds of expressive content, and con-

An investigation of the relationship between the frieze of the Propylon regarded as relief sculpture and the art of the fourth century B.C. may begin with the observation that the basic format of its composition—a sequence of figures isolated against the background plane—is typical of frieze design in this period. Friezes of the classical age (including the early fourth century), on the contrary, normally engage the figures, whether narrative in content or processional, in interlocking actions that produce a dense overlapping of forms tending to eliminate from view the background plane. The friezes of the Parthenon in Athens[197] and the Temple of Apollo Epikourios at Bassae,[198] for all their dissimilarities, both show this effect, which is quite different from the sorting out and separation of figures that begins in the last decades of the fifth century B.C. (Erechtheum frieze[199] and Nike Temple balustrade[200]) and advances through the middle years of the fourth century, where it is illustrated, as Ridgway has pointed out, by the friezes of the Mausoleum at Halikarnassos (see figs. 204, 205).[201] It is as if slowly the seventh-century antithesis between the projecting figures and the wall-like surface that supports them (Prinias temple frieze)[202] had reemerged, but with a crucial difference—the contribution of the intervening classical experience—which is the psychological interaction of the figures, reticent in physical contact, but insistent in gesture and glance (Mantinea Base).[203] By reason of this content, the wall is not yet interpreted as a plane surface; at least at mid-century, it remains by implication a spatial continuum in which the psychological exchanges can occur.

Karl Lehmann, in his preliminary publication of the frieze of the Propylon, drew attention to the resemblance between it and the frieze of Erotes from a Sanctuary of Athena on the the north slope of the Akropolis at Athens, where winged male figures link hands in a

---

comitant search for new means for their communication through the human figure, gave rise to special problems in the integration of the figure with its drapery. The fact that we tend to think of the nude and seminude statues of the period as its greatest masterpieces may not be unrelated to this development. In these, the body alone, which after all is the most intimately expressive of sculptural motifs, could make its subtle statement without the necessarily mannered complication stemming from its interaction with clothing. It is perhaps enough to make a generalized reference to the major works of Praxiteles and Lysippos; by contrast, the bold, assured movements or the figures of the Pheidian school are enhanced and clarified by the forceful rhythms of their drapery.

My comments about the development of style in the later fourth century B.C. have been illustrated by major sculptures of diverse provenance because it is my understanding that, in the present state of our knowledge, local styles—even "mainland" as opposed to "east Greek"—cannot be defined. The movement of artists in this period may indeed make such a notion irrelevant, at least in the realm of "high" art. Qualitative inferiority or the intrusion of regional features in provincial monuments such as the Sarcophagus of the Mourning Women (Gustave Mendel, *Catalogue des sculptures grecques, romaines et byzantines* [Musées impériaux ottomans], Constantinople, 1912, vol. I, pp. 48 ff.) are another matter. So, too, is the localized evolution of iconographic types, as I have assumed in analyzing the costume of the Samothracian dancers (see pp. 211 ff., above).

197. See Robertson and Frantz, *op. cit.*, figs., *passim.*

198. See Charline Hofkes-Brukker and Alfred Mallwitz, *Der Bassai-Fries*, Munich, 1975, pp. 50-91.

199. See Stanley Casson, *Catalogue of the Acropolis Museum*, Cambridge, vol. 2, 1921, pp. 174 ff.

200. See *ibid.*, no. 12, pp. 156 ff.

201. Pp. 202 f.

202. See Robertson, pl. 9e.

203. See above, n. 195.

200 Frieze of Erotes. Athens, National Archaeological Museum no. 1451.

continuous band (fig. 200).[204] This example has been dated in the later fourth century B.C., and it presents no features indicating a date earlier than 340; I think it should be regarded as a follower rather than as a precursor of the Samothracian work.[205] In either case, it belongs to a cluster of related sculptures, including two additional representations of male dancers, which resemble the Samothracian frieze in presenting rows of similar or identical figures in a format that may be called a "chain" composition.[206] These works exemplify an archaizing return to the design format exposing the planar surface of the relief ground that was referred to above, but, less enterprising than the sculptor of the Samothracian frieze, their designers combine the spatial archaism described above with naturalistic figures of classical pedigree. The clearest case serving to identify and define this kind of hybrid archaism is not sculptural, but is found on those fourth-century Panathenaic amphorae which display, on the side opposite the familiar archaistic Athena, friezes, normally naturalistically drawn, showing foot racers linked by overlapping arms and legs in "chain" compositions for which the indubitable late archaic models are ready to hand (fig. 201).[207] These panels of racers date from 336 B.C. and later. Altogether, it seems not unlikely that the Propylon helped to create a favorable climate, if it did not, indeed, provide inspiration for the archaism that is exhibited in varying ways in the group of frieze designs under review.

204. National Archaeological Museum, Athens, nos. 1451, 1452; Svoronos, *op. cit.*, pl. CII, 2, 3. See the Preliminary Report in which Karl Lehmann presented his principal published examination of the frieze: *Hesperia*, 20 (1951), pp. 16 ff., especially p. 18, where he referred to the frieze of Erotes as "slightly earlier" than the frieze of the Propylon. Subsequently, Havelock noted the relationship between the two friezes, but proposed a date not earlier than the middle of the second century B.C. for both works (*op. cit.*, p. 51, n. 28). For the frieze of Erotes, see Oscar Broneer, "Excavations on the North Slope of the Acropolis," *Hesperia*, 4 (1935), pp. 143 ff. and figs. 33, 34.

205. Broneer suggested a date in the second half of the fourth century B.C. (*ibid.*, p. 147).

206. One of these is the "Atarbos" relief in the Acropolis Museum, Athens (no. 1338), for which a date in the last quarter of the fourth century B.C. has been suggested by J. Miltiades (*Guide sommaire du Musée de l'Acropole*, Athens, 1968, p. 12); another is the related composition showing Pyrrhic dancers. For the latter, see Fuchs, pp. 41 ff., who lists all the surviving replicas and cites the evidence dating the original in the second half of the fourth century.

207. The late fourth-century version of the footracers "chain" composition is seen in *CVA*, Great Britain, fasc. I, Br. Mus. III Hf, pl. 3, 2b (dated 336 B.C.) and Hf, pl. 4, 1b (dated 328): the first of these archaizes the figures of the runners, while the other presents them in naturalistic style, as in my fig. 201. For an illustration of the late sixth-century model of this motif, see *ibid.*, III He, pl. 4, 1b.

201. Detail from a Panathenaic amphora. London, The British Museum.

202. Nymphs Relief. Berlin, Staatliche Museen, K83.

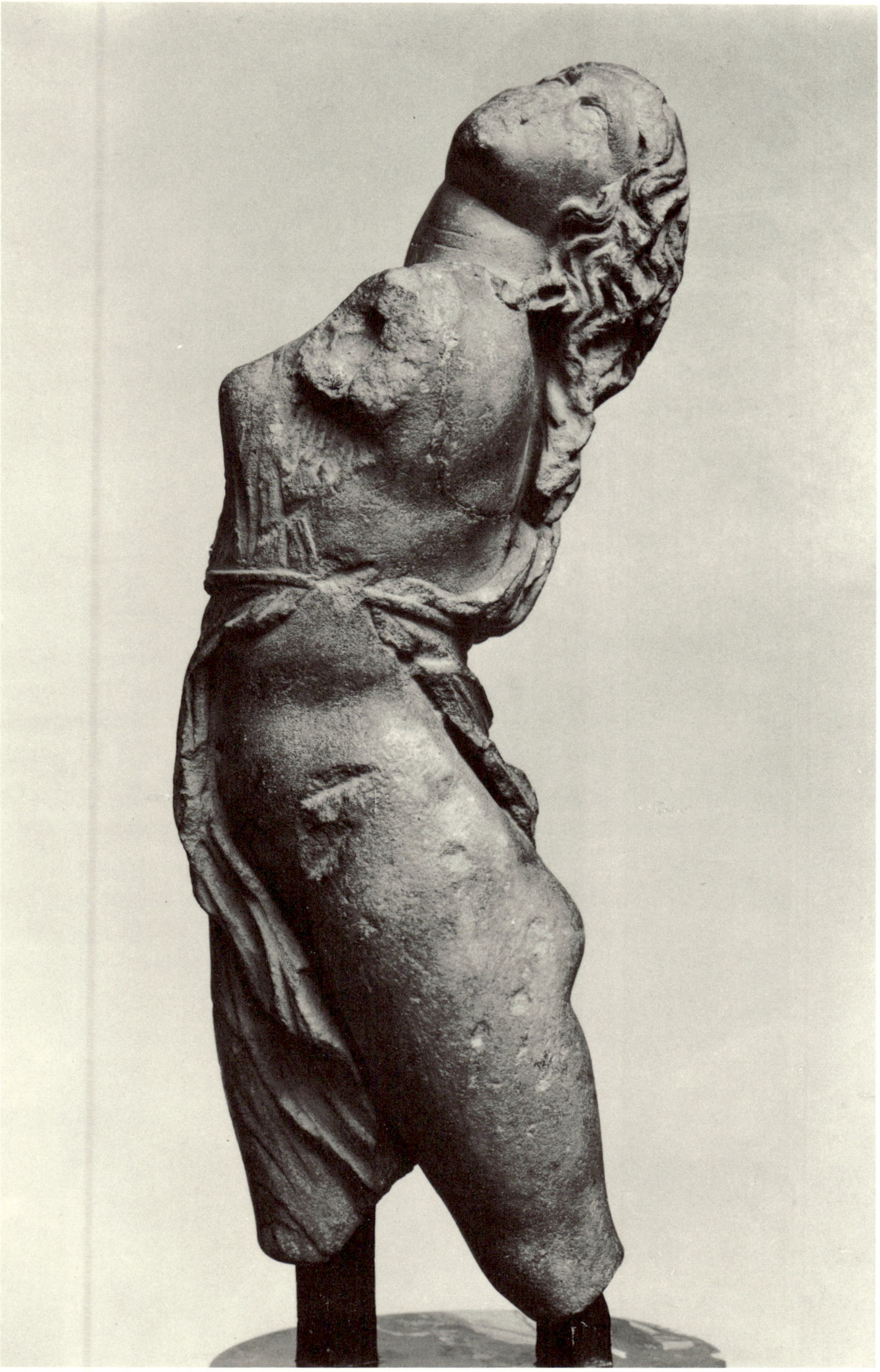

203. Maenad by Skopas. Dresden Museum.

Although nymphs dancing ἐπὶ καρπῷ had made an appearance in a type of votive relief originating in the late fifth century B.C. (fig. 202),[208] no friezes of dancers have survived from the mid-fourth century; however, the Maenad in Dresden (fig. 203) may serve to indicate the kind of movement such a composition would have employed.[209] The existence of the Maenad also underscores the deliberateness of the choice that was made by the designer of the frieze of the Propylon when he extended his files of linked dancers in a "chain" composition. This chain of dancers, like that of the racing men on the Panathenaic amphorae, is derived from a model of preclassical origin. For the representation of dancers clasping wrists, the Nymphs relief in Berlin (fig. 202) is certainly the closest prototype; however, for the discrete placing of the dancers against their background plane, with the linkage through outstretched arms, an older model must be sought. Closer to the Samothracian composition in this respect, is a frieze found on a charming white ground phiale in the Museum of Fine Arts, Boston, which is datable in the early fifth century B.C. (fig. 208).[210] Here, two files of dancers, thought to be participants in a ritual of the cult of Artemis, converge on an altar.[211] The reappearance in the fourth-century monument of this "archaic" composition, with its ritual associations, testifies to the designer's explicit selection of the earlier version of the motif as appropriate to the antiquity of the Samothracian rites.[212]

On the other hand, the relief sculpture of the decade or so immediately preceding the date assigned to the Samothracian frieze reveals a new tendency that anticipates its more explicit archaism. It is in that monumental compendium of mid-fourth century sculpture, the Mausoleum at Halikarnassos,[213] I think, that we can observe the artistic experience that stood directly behind the creation of the "chain" composition of the frieze of the Propylon. In examining a selection of the reliefs from Halikarnassos, I shall emphasize the "chain"-like aspect of their design, and shall also lay stress upon certain differences between two basic styles encountered among them that encompass a shift from relative naturalism to a planar organization of the design that is close to the style of the Samothracian frieze. The

208. On this relief, see n. 78 above, and App. II, p. 306. Fuchs considers it to be a reflection of an important monument of late fifth-century date, and notes that this was in its turn dependent on the late archaic so-called Socrates-relief of the Charites, Acropolis Museum, Athens, no. 702 ("Attische Nymphenreliefs," pp. 243 ff.).

209. On the Maenad, see below, p. 248. Fuchs has assigned a fourth-century date to the original of the relief in the Museo Barracco, Rome (no. 124), showing a maenad of "type 30" (pp. 83 f. and pl. 19b). A mirror case in the Louvre also illustrates the kind of complex action displayed by the naturalistically portrayed dancer of the fourth century B.C. (see Ernst Pfuhl, *Masterpieces of Greek Drawing and Painting*, New York, 1926, fig. 112). Fuchs points to the Nymphs relief in Berlin (fig. 202) as the late fifth-century B.C. prototype upon which the entire subsequent series of representations of the dancing nymphs depends (for references, see n. 78, above; see also App. II, below, p. 306).

210. Museum of Fine Arts, Boston (acc. no. 65.908); see Penelope Truitt, "Attic White-ground Pyxis and Phiale, ca. 450 B.C.," *Boston Museum Bulletin*, 67, no. 348 (1969), pp. 72 ff. See below, p. 253 and nn. 232-234.

211. *Ibid.*, pp. 86 ff.

212. See above, pp. 253 f.

213. On the date of the sculptures from Halikarnassos, see n. 191, above. For recent discussion of Skopas' part in the designing of the friezes, see Stewart, pp. 96 ff.

204. Blocks from the Amazonomachy frieze of the Mausoleum at Halikarnassos. London, The British Museum, nos. 1011, 1012.

205. Block from the Centauromachy frieze of the Mausoleum at Halikarnassos. London, The British Museum, no. 1032.

Amazonomachy slabs, BM 1011-1012 (fig. 204),[214] show a series of violently interacting two- and three-figure groups of combatants who, disposed in varied bending and twisting postures, do not at first glance resemble the dancers of the Propylon; however, it will be noted that it is by means of linkages created by overlapping extremities, weapons and flying drapery, that continuity is achieved among the fighting groups. Thus the essen-

214. My selection among the Amazonomachy slabs of British Museum 1011 and 1012 denotes agreement with Stewart's attribution of them to Skopas (*loc. cit.*). However, the problem of the attribution of the sculptures from Halikarnassos cannot be placed in the foreground of this discussion (see below, p. 247). For relevant discussion of the style of the friezes from the Mausoleum, see Brown, *op. cit.*, pp. 17 ff.; Ashmole, pp. 147 ff.; Ridgway, pp. 201 ff.

tial problem posed by the frieze—that of integrating the successive elements of a long horizontal composition—is solved by establishing a three-dimensional space, the product of the actions of the figures, and ensuring its unity by means of the "chain" effect just observed. This creates a precarious harmony between the two inherently discordant components of the relief, the illusionistically conceived figure groups and the flat surface they adorn; indeed, the instability of this tour-de-force solution of the design problem is suggested by the new, more "archaic" solution that is found in the single surviving block of the Centauromachy frieze from the same monument (fig. 205).[215] Here the "chain" composition is more clearly avowed and more explicit connections with the frieze of the Propylon become apparent at the same time. The groups are now relinquished, and the figures are instead spread out as single units against the face of the block (even though arrangement in two- or three-figure groups is traditional for this subject). The figures are linked together, as before, by marginal overlappings, but they are related to the background in a new way, being extended in frontal, profile, and rear views which give the maximum orientation to the two-dimensional plane. Foreshortening and disengagement from the background are minimal: "one has the feeling . . . that the figure has been sliced in half and placed against the background."[216] Setting aside differences of scale and content, the elements of the Samothracian solution of the problem of frieze design may be seen to emerge clearly in this block from Halikarnassos if it is compared with *F(S)1* (fig. 147): repetition of equivalent single-figure units; linkage of these units by overlapping of extremities; use of postures adjusted to the two-dimensional surface of the background; imposition of isocephaly on all figures. Some more precise points of similarity may be noted between the two friezes, somewhat to the disparagement of both, to be sure. The figures of the Centauromachy block, which lack the technical bravura of most of the surviving portions of the other Halikarnassos friezes, show an ineptitude in the realization of anatomical structure that is particularly apparent in the carving of the legs of the central Lapith woman. Something very like this uncertainty of execution afflicts the handling of the legs of the dancers of the Propylon, although here crudeness of form is accepted by the viewer as a simplification appropriate to the spirited archaizing manner. Indeed, the limitations of technique apparent in the Centauromachy block, which extend to the meager modeling of the Lapith woman's torso, the crabbed flatness of the handling of drapery and the angularity of the poses, become the virtues of the Samothracian frieze's archaism. Retaining and accentuating the isocephaly, the low relief, and the limited range of postures used for the Centauromachy, the designer of the Samothracian frieze employs the clasping of hands upon wrists as a linkage motif in place of the linkage secured mainly by the crossing of lower limbs, and he transforms the space-filling streams and tatters of drapery and centaurs' tails into the flat, wispy flounces which decorate the scarfs of alternating dancers and project from the lower edge of the apoptygma of each figure. Finally,

215. On British Museum 1032, see Ashmole, pp. 162 ff. Additional fragments of this frieze which are preserved in the storerooms of the British Museum inform us that the "horses" visible on slab 1032 are indeed centaurs.

216. *Ibid.*, p. 164.

the similarities between the two works may be pursued to the figures' long necks and, in particular, to such a detail as the attenuated outspread hand that occurs once on the Centauromachy block and repeatedly on the frieze of the Propylon (the dancer to the right of the kithara player on *F(S)1* shows this clearly).

The problem of the identification of the various masters of the Halikarnassos reliefs cannot be confronted here,[217] so we may simply stress the position of the Centauromachy block as an intermediary between the early Skopaic style found in some parts of the Amazonomachy and the style of the frieze of the Propylon, and turn to a consideration of Skopaic traits in the frieze itself. Recalling our detail from *F(S)1* (fig. 148), the dancers are small in scale and sketchily handled, qualities dependent on the architectural function of the frieze that separate them from all the sculptures ascribed to Skopas; but I would suggest that the supple body structure and expressive gestures that underlie their stylized pose point quite directly toward his art. This is the art, not of the Skopas of the warrior heads from the Temple of Athena Alea at Tegea,[218] but the creator of those "fluttery females in action"[219] who are best known from some recently found sculptures from the site, notably the beautiful akroterion shown in figure 206.[220] This Skopas is a master of the contrapuntal manipulation of a vulnerable feminine anatomy and its many-textured garments. The movement of the figure, especially of the upper torso, is fluent and subtly complicated, involving many changes of direction, both internally and in the gestures of the arms. The drapery is equally complex, in the diversity of its directional lines and in its contrasts of substance, which range from filmy transparency to heavily clustered folds, sometimes adherant, sometimes all but autonomously active. Allowing for the translation of these stylistic concepts into the new archaizing vocabulary, it seems conceivable that the Samothracian frieze could have originated, at least as a design, with the master of the Tegea akroterion.

A more explicit connection between the frieze of the Propylon and the art of Skopas occurs as an expression of the designer's wit, an unexpected quality in a Skopaic work, over which we may pause. The irony that colors the intercommunication taking place within the chain of dancers is evident in the courtly gesture with which alternating figures turn to invite the (inescapable) company of their neighbors to the rear, in the empty and implicitly reproachful mimicry of this gesture by the figure leading the musician, in the resourceful grasping of a rear flounce of drapery by the musician's follower (see *F(S)1*, fig. 147). The dancers' facial expressions are sometimes bland (frontispiece), but they are also sometimes inscrutibly animated (fig. 160): does not this liveliness mockingly evoke

217. See Stewart, pp. 95 ff., for a recent review of the problem, with bibliography.

218. *Ibid.*, pls. 7a-d, 8a,b.

219. M. Comstock and Cornelius Vermeule, *Greek, Etruscan and Roman Bronzes in the Boston Museum of Fine Arts*, Greenwich (Conn.), 1971, p. 74.

220. On this sculpture, see Stewart, pp. 49 f., pls. 1a-d, 2a-c. Stewart surveys the evidence concerning the date of the Temple of Athena Alea at Tegea and concludes that, while the building itself was perhaps completed by 355 B.C., its sculptures may not have been finished before 340 (*ibid.*, pp. 47, 67 ff., 80). The akroterion under discussion (my fig. 206) may therefore have been close in date to the frieze of the Propylon.

206. Akroterion attributed to the east pediment of the Temple of Athena Alea at Tegea. Piali Museum.

the archaic smile? The costume, as we have analyzed it,[221] must be seen as a playful confection, "antique-ing" a ceremonial form of dress by means of allusions, both correct and bogus, to the conventions of the past. I have remarked that the fractional pose is caricaturistic in the vehemence with which front and profile views collide:[222] surely one is justified in recognizing in the silhouetted buttock and leg that are thus accentuated a sly quotation from a work universally ascribed to Skopas, the Maenad in Dresden (fig. 203).[223]

221. See above, pp. 211 ff.

222. See above, p. 234.

223. Not only does the Maenad appear to be the model for the rear profile of the dancers of the frieze, but she may also, like them, have moved on tiptoes: see H. Protzmann, "Zum Verständnis des Bewegungsmotiv des Dresdener Mänade," *Dresdener Kunstblätter*, 16 (1972), pp. 17 f. Stewart dates the Maenad late in the decade 370-360 B.C. (p. 93, pl. 1b); relevant to the question of its influence on the frieze of the Propylon is his conclusion that it was intended to be seen from the left side (p. 92). A similar accentuation of the profile in Skopas' *oeuvre* occurs in the akroteria from Tegea (p. 49).

The humor of this touch is of course heightened by the multiplication of the familiar profile in the long line of dancers.[224]

It will be useful at this point to summarize the conclusions to be drawn from the foregoing comparisons, which were intended to provide the frieze of the Propylon with a receptive context in the art of the fourth century B.C., and to identify its Skopaic features. We have seen distinct signs of a preparation for the frieze's spatial and compositional characteristics in an evolution that took place among the reliefs of the Mausoleum at Halikarnassos, and have discovered some specific ties linking it to the most "advanced" of the Mausoleum slabs, that of the Centauromachy. The Samothracian work then appears to constitute a bridge to the Attic friezes of the Erotes type, conservative in their use of naturalistic figures but "advanced" in the exact duplication of these figures, just as it points in a longer perspective to the emblematic Ionic friezes of the next century. It emerges, moreover, as a critical monument in the development of archaistic art—a seemingly tentative and personal improvisation which, somewhat unexpectedly, may be shown to have supplied to the more familiar archaism of the Hellenistic and Roman periods some of its most characteristic motifs.[225] Skopas, as its designer, makes a surprising appearance as an innovator in this first extensive use of archaistic features in a major sculptural composition.

The span of his active life having encompassed the years ca. 375-330 B.C., the work on the Samothracian Propylon must have fallen near the end of Skopas' career.[226] Without entering into the details of the still unresolved discussion of the chronological relations among the works attributed to him, it may be worth remarking that this attribution lends support to the suggestion that Skopas' development moved not in a crescendo toward fuller articulation of the expressive power seen in his earlier sculptures, but rather in a diminuendo from the more robust statements of his youth to a drying and hardening of forms anticipatory of the last phase of fourth-century art.[227] The attribution, moreover, would give clearer definition to an aspect of Skopas' art that has stood in puzzling relationship to the heroic expressiveness of the long familiar Tegea warrior heads and the sensuous abandon of the Maenad in Dresden—namely an elegant, fragile grace that is to some extent shared by the akroterion from Tegea—making him an altogether more complex and

224. The humorous caricaturing of traditionally solemn subjects is frequently encountered in the art of the fourth century B.C., and may be documented by reference, for example, to the Dolon Painter (Krater in the British Museum, London, no. F157); for this painter, and for further remarks about the comic in fourth-century painting, see Martin Robertson, *Greek Painting*, Geneva, 1959, pp. 156 ff., pl. 159. Of more immediate relevance to the Samothracian frieze, however, is a skyphos from Thebes showing a satyric cult scene in which dancing female musicians approach the Mother Goddess accompanied by Hermes and Pan (see Ch[arles] P[icard], "Sur un skyphos du Cabiron," *RA*, ser. 6, 18 [1941], pp. 264 ff. and fig. 2, p. 265).

225. See App. II, pp. 304 ff., for the initial phases of this afterlife.

226. See Stewart, p. 1, for a summary of the documentation for Skopas' chronology.

227. This has been suggested by Brown (*op. cit.*, p. 31).

contradictory figure than previously imagined. This delicacy is strongly felt in the coffer heads of the Propylon; in the frieze it frosts toward a playfully brittle rococo, mannered and subtle in its effects, and eminently suitable as adornment of a brilliant miniature Ionic structure.

The following analysis of the styles of carving distinguishable in the frieze of the Propylon takes it for granted that one style, that of a designer who, it is suggested, was Skopas, guided all the hands that worked here.[228] Models must have been issued from his workshop, but the craftsmen charged with carrying them out did their work in accordance with a wide range of technical competence and understanding, as will be shown.

From the fact that the foregoing discussion of the frieze has dealt almost exclusively with two blocks, *F(S)1* and *F(S)12*, it may be inferred that these are in some way representative of the sculpture as a whole. They are, indeed, much the best of all the surviving portions in quality of execution, sharing a clarity and refinement of form that is absent elsewhere; the impression which they provide of the precision of the workmanship at its best can be sharpened only by recalling the prismatic cutting of drapery details that is preserved in two minute fragments, *F(S)5* and *F(S)26* (figs. 154, 174). The proportion of surviving pieces to the total original length of the frieze, which is less than one-third,[229] does not permit a secure judgment on whether *F(S)1* and *F(S)12* are, in fact, likely to represent the highest quality of workmanship originally present in the frieze. However, common sense would question whether greater technical refinement could well have been lavished on a project of this kind, especially in view of the extremely poor quality of many sections that were deemed acceptable.

The low proportion of survivals again urges caution in responding to the question whether *F(S)1* and *F(S)12* should be ascribed to the same hand. But repetition of a given figure type in a decorative scheme like the frieze of the Propylon would have been especially encouraging to the development by individual executing sculptors of fairly rigid formulae for the rendering of certain forms, and on this test it is doubtful that the same hand carved these two blocks. For example, in *F(S)1* the design of the apoptygma, as seen most clearly in the dancer to the right of the kitharist (fig. 210), is elaborated through a multiplication of the small vertical folds which descend in line with the advancing left leg, while a bolder and simpler rendering is provided at the corresponding point in the central figure of *F(S)12* (fig. 160). This heavier hand can be recognized as it draws the figure a little larger and traces a thicker groove around its outer contours; it also defines the main parts of the anatomy in an additive manner that produces a jerky, disjointed movement which is not found in the dancers of *F(S)1*, still faintly reflecting the organic coherence of the classical period. Thus, if Hand A carved *F(S)1*, Hand B, a competent, even

228. See Alan J. B. Wace's clarifying remarks about the distinction that is to be made between the "hands" active in the execution of a major architectural decoration and the master responsible for the general design ("Design and Execution," *Annuario*, p. 113; see above n. 49).

229. See above, p. 201.

enterprising imitator, executed *F(S)12*. Hand A, producing a subtler version of the figure, may be assumed to more adequately transmit the characteristics of the original models from which all the executants worked.[230] Hand A may also have been responsible for *F(S)2* and *F(S)7* (figs. 149, 156), fragments seeming to show traces of the refined, detailed execution that typifies his work.

The process of imitation by less skilled and perceptive assistants would account for the differences observable among those of the remaining blocks and fragments whose condition permits any assessment of style. The "Louvre" blocks, *F(S)10* and *F(S)11* (figs. 157, 158), may have been executed by the same hand: the surface of the latter block is too battered to allow certainty on this point, but the two pieces seem not to be incongruous in style, and their proximity in the Gattilusi tower invites the supposition that they were found together before being placed there, and may even have been broken from the same long block. I shall assign them to Hand C, noting that they present a loosened and softened version of Hand A's manner: the figures are taller and fuller in their proportions, the legs (the best preserved feature) are carelessly articulated, with thicker, more irregular strokes of the chisel. *F(S)3* (fig. 150) might be by the same hand. A peculiarity of this sculptor's work which associates it with additional pieces is the handling of the bottom of the central fold of the lower mantle and its juncture with the chiton below: the central fold ends at a point quite high above the level of the ankles, making room for exposure of a bigger patch of the crinkled surface of the chiton than is found on the other blocks we have examined. This detail, together with the clumsily drawn legs, links Hand C's work with the fragmentary corner block, *F(S)4* (figs. 151, 152), and with two smaller pieces, *F(S)19* and *F(S)22* (figs. 167, 170).

An even more exaggerated shortening of the central fold of the mantle, with corresponding extension of the portion of the chiton shown beneath, coupled with more delicacy of form and texture than Hand C's reliefs can boast, are to be found in three fragments, *F(S)24, F(V)31* and *F(V)32* (figs. 172, 176, 177), which therefore may be ascribed to Hand D.

This exercise in attribution is useful first of all in confirming what might anyhow have been predicted, that the execution of the frieze was the task of one or more leading sculptors (Hands A and B) and perhaps as many less competent assistants (Hands C and D). The most notable result of this inquiry is its evidence of the range of abilities that is displayed by the participants. The difference in quality between the work of Hand A and that of Hand C, for instance, is extremely marked. Special circumstances may have influenced this outcome; one wonders whether external pressure, such as the need to complete the work in readiness for a particular occasion, may have determined it. Another interesting product of the study of the executants' styles is the discovery that the archaizing fantasy of the frieze's designer had little viability in the hands of the available assistants. The complex blend of artistic resources that stood behind the creation of the

230. See above, n. 88.

207. Detail of an Attic calyx krater. Rome, Museo di Villa Giulia.

figures displayed on *F(S)1* (fig. 147), and the sophisticated imagination that brought them together to create this delightful design, can only have been dimly grasped by the lesser craftsmen delineated in our group.

M. L. H.

It has been pointed out that one of the most characteristic stylistic features of the frieze of the Propylon is the organization, the rhythm, of its dancing figures. The long chain of dancers is regularly subdivided into pairs of figures, for, apart from the figures who precede and follow the musicians, every second dancer turns to regard the figure following her (figs. 147, 157, 158, 210). The figure following each musician is clearly the leader of the chorus and, as such, faces toward her. The figure preceding each musician looks back toward her and, as a result, another symmetrical triad of figures is introduced into the long line of dancers. The frieze, therefore, is composed of two motifs: pairs of confronting dancers punctuated, as it were, by the recurrent triad of figures of which the musician is the center. It is this compositional movement and the related variation in spacing (the dancers facing each other are more widely spaced than those who do not) that imparts such life to what would otherwise be an intolerable length of identical sculptured figures—intolerable, at least, to Greek eyes.

How characteristic this aesthetic device is will be apparent if we compare the dancers of the frieze with the dancing figures we have earlier seen on Corinthian pots (figs. 191-193) which, as on innumerable other ceramic examples, invariably form a line of identical figures. Very rare exceptions to the standard line of identical dancing figures do occur in vase painting, as on an early classical calyx krater in the Villa Giulia (fig. 207),[231] where an occasional figure turns to regard a companion or to look out at the spectator. But here, there is no recurrent rhythm, no ornamental system.

Far closer to the design of the frieze is the group of dancers on the interior of an unusual white ground phiale in the Museum of Fine Arts in Boston (fig. 208).[232] Seven dancers wearing chiton and himation, preceded by a musician playing the double flute dance around a flaming altar.[233] Here, as on the frieze, the dancers clasp each other at the wrists, ἐπὶ καρπῷ. Four figures, the two behind the musician and two others look forward toward her; but, on each side of the fifth dancer, a pair of dancers face each other as do the confronting pairs on the frieze. Clearly, this is a ritual dance, although the nature of the divinity honored is not evident.[234] On the lid of a slightly later black-figure pyxis in the National Archaeological Museum in Athens a similar scene appears (fig. 209).[235] Here two pairs of confronting dancers follow a leader as they move swiftly toward an altar. On the related lid of a lekane from Taman,[236] one pair of the five dancers face each other. The implication of these lids is that there existed a kind of dance in which women held hands and periodically faced each other. Very likely, this was the form of the Samothracian dance, a liturgical dance in which the votaries of the Great Goddess wore her ceremonial attire. It is by no means impossible that Skopas, who as we know had been in Samo-

231. No. 909. Furtwängler-Reichhold, ser. I, pp. 80 f., pls. 17, 18; *CVA*, Italia, fasc. II, G. Q. Giglioli, Museo Nazionale di Villa Giulia a Roma, fasc. II, p. 12, pls. 21, 22; J. D. Beazley, *Attic Red-Figure Vase-Painting*, 2d edn., Oxford, 1963, I, p. 619. Attributed to the Villa Giulia Painter. It is assumed that this chorus of maidens performs the Parthenion, a venerable, ritual dance-song, in a sanctuary.

232. For this vase, see above, nn. 210-211 (the caption in Truitt, *op. cit.*, pp. 72 ff., fig. 20, is mistakenly labeled exterior view). Acc. no. 65.908; attributed to the Painter of London D12 in the Penthesilean workshop. Vessel pierced by two holes visible above the altar for suspension when not in use. I am indebted to Mrs. Hadzi for having called this vase to my attention.

233. The author, *ibid.*, p. 86, assumes that this is an out-of-doors scene. But the presence of a basket of wool with distaff and spindle and the fringed scarf suspended above it could as well imply that the scene is an interior one. Cf. the lid of the pyxis mentioned in n. 235.

234. The author, *ibid.*, p. 87, suggests that the divinity was Artemis.

235. No. 14909. André Dessenne, "Pyxis à figures noires du Musée National d'Athènes," *RA*, ser. 6, 36 (1950), pp. 40 ff., has dated it *ca.* 440 B.C. and interpreted the figures as participants in the Thesmophoria, a festival in honor of Demeter. A similar scene on the lid of a lekane from Taman (*ibid.*, pp. 73 ff., pl. IV, fig. 14) includes two musicians playing the kithara and double flutes—two of the instruments preserved on the extant portion of the frieze of the Propylon. Picard, *ibid.*, p. 159, n. 5, citing this article and referring to the Taman vase, commented that this dance was identical with the dance performed by the maidens on the frieze of the Propylon and that, among the new fragments in Samothrace, there might turn up a flute player—unaware of the existence of such a musician on a block at that time in the Louvre!

236. Dessenne, *ibid.*, p. 74, pl. IV, fig. 14.

208. Interior of a white ground phiale. Boston, Museum of Fine Arts.

209. Lid of a black-figure pyxis. Athens, National Archaeological Museum.

thrace,[237] had seen this very dance.[238] And wanting to allude to and emphasize the venerable character of this dance and rite, he cast his figures in an archaistic style.

Two features of the frieze remain curious: the length of the procession and the device selected to enliven it, the grouping of the dancers in confronting pairs (figs. 147, 157, 158, 210). Far the closest to this motif and to the composition of the frieze as a whole are certain sections of the sculptured friezes at Persepolis.[239] In these rare portions of the frieze, particularly on the east stairway of the apadana, the normal rhythm of endlessly repeated Medes and Persians on the dadoes and stairways of the royal audience halls is animated by the same device—by causing an occasional figure to look backward to the figure following him in the representation of the long New Year's Day procession (figs. 211, 212).[240] At Persepolis, the figures in the single units or zones of the frieze invariably move in one direction as do those on the Propylon. Thus, in the rare instances where two adjacent pairs confront each other, the effect is startlingly similar to the underlying organization of our frieze. The fact that these sculptures are archaic, that the Persians wear garments shaped according to the conventions of late sixth-century Greek art makes the analogy still more striking.[241] The so-called "stacked folds" of the Persians symmetrically flanking the conspicuous central pleat and the use of this frontal convention on figures seen in profile recurs in related form in the folds of the maidens' mantles. There, too, the central fold is emphasized within the narrower, flanking folds, and the frontal convention is used for figures that, from the waist down, are seen in profile. To be sure, both friezes go back to genuine archaic art, each, in their different ways, shaped under its influence.

Either Skopas devised this entire scheme independently or he must have seen it either at Persepolis or the presumably more accessible sites of Susa or Ecbatana.[242] The latter

237. See below Chap. IV, p. 276.

238. Interestingly enough, Dessenne, without having specified a particular artist, made this same suggestion, *op. cit.*, p. 72.

239. For this royal monument, begun by Darius I in 518 B.C. and carried on through the reigns of Xerxes and Artaxerxes I till ca. 460 B.C., see Erich F. Schmidt, *Persepolis I. Structures, Reliefs, Inscriptions*, Chicago, 1953, especially pls. 19, 22-26, 50, 52, 57, 58, 67, 69, 70, 72-74, views and details of the northern and eastern stairways of the apadana and the so-called Council Hall or Triple Portal; Donald N. Wilbur, *Persepolis*, New York, 1969, pp. 20, 50, 53, 58; Ann Farkas, *Achaemenid Sculpture* (Uitgaven van het Nederlands Historisch-Archaeologisch Instituut te Istanbul, XXXIII), Istanbul, 1974, pp. 46 ff.; and, for brief comment on the variations on the basic processional types, Henri Frankfort, "Achaemenian Sculpture," *AJA*, 50 (1946), p. 12.

240. This royal structure was not a residence but a ritual center reserved for the ceremonies of the festival of the Nauruz on New Year's Day. See Arthur Upham Pope, "Persepolis as a Ritual City," *Archaeology*, 19 (1957), pp. 123-130; Kurt Erdmann, "Persepolis: Daten und Deutungen," *Mitteilungen der deutschen Orient-Gesellschaft zu Berlin*, 92 (1960), pp. 38 ff., 45.

241. For analysis of these sculptures and their relationship to late archaic Greek art and the presence at Persepolis of Ionian craftsmen, see Frankfort, pp. 225 ff.; Gisela M. A. Richter, "Greeks in Persia," *AJA*, 50 (1940), pp. 15-30; Farkas, *op. cit.*, pp. 83 ff.; and for concise summaries of certain debated issues, including the relationship between Persepolis, Pasargadae, and Susa: Kurt Erdmann, "Griechische und achaemenidische Plastik," *Forschungen und Fortschritte*, 26 (1950), pp. 150 ff.; and Carl Nylander, *Ionians in Pasargadae* (Acta Universitatis Upsaliensis, *Boreas*, Uppsala Studies in Ancient Mediterranean and Near Eastern Civilizations, I), Uppsala, 1970, pp. 13 ff., 132 ff.

242. It is very possible that the royal monuments of these cities were provided with sculptured friezes similar in theme and aesthetic character to those at Persepolis. Cf. Erdmann, *op. cit.*, p. 151.

210. Detail from the frieze of dancing maidens. Samothrace Museum.

alternative is far more likely, especially since there appears to be no precedent in Greek monumental architectual sculpture for the use or design of a long procession of identical figures. Faced with the problem of representing a continuous line of ceremonial figures—now not archaic, like their Persian forebears, but archaistic—can he have recalled the simple but effective device at Persepolis whereby the introduction of a few pairs of confronting figures added so intensely to the life of an otherwise monotonous chain of repeated, often identical figures? Is this the source of his regular pairing of confronted figures? It is tempting to think so, especially if one recalls how widely Skopas had traveled and worked, not only in mainland Greece but also in Asia Minor, at Ephesos, Halikarnassos, Knidos, in the Troad, and in distant Bithynia.[243]

Under Artaxerxes III (359-338 B.C.) work was resumed at Persepolis.[244] In those years, Maussollos and Idrieus were his allies. The generals who led Idrieus' troops against the Cypriote kings on Artaxerxes' behalf were Greek.[245] Is it not conceivable that a Greek artist in the employ of the Carian dynasty, as Skopas was, would be given access to any of the

243. See above, Chap. II, n. 206, for the ancient sources documenting Skopas' work at these far-flung sites.

Frankfort, p. 231, comments: "Repetition is of the essence of Achaemenian art. . . ." The only variation within the strict scheme, he continues, is achieved by a turned head, a hand laid on a shoulder to prevent monotony. These two aspects of Achaemenid art are present in the frieze of the Propylon.

244. See Frankfort, p. 218; Wilbur, *op. cit.*, pp. 67 f.

245. Diodorus 16.42.7. He also reports on the friendly relations between the Athenians and the Macedonians and Persia at this time (16.43.1).

In connection with the artistic interrelationships between Persia and Greece in this very period, it is worth recalling that the well-known mid-fourth century capital from Salamis (Cyprus) in the British Museum on which an (archaistic?) goddess appears between bull protomes indubitably reflects Greek adoption and adaptation of a Persian prototype. See, in particular, Eugen von Mercklin, "Antike Stier-

211. Detail of the eastern stairway of the apadana at Persepolis.

212. Detail of the eastern stairway of the apadana at Persepolis.

legendary cities or monuments of Persia that interested him? Or did similar sculptured friezes exist in the more accessible region of coastal Asia Minor at the courts of such satraps as Maussollos and Idrieus?[246] It is not possible to decide among these alternatives. But the likelihood remains that Skopas had seen and been impressed by some such extraordinary monument and that he drew on this visual memory in designing the frieze of the Propylon.[247]

If, as I propose, Skopas was the designing architect-sculptor of this building, he then played a significant role in the formulation and use of the archaistic style. It is pertinent to recall that, according to Strabo, Skopas made a cult image of Apollo Smintheus for his sanctuary at Chryse in the Troad. He reports:

> In this Chryse is also the temple of Sminthian Apollo; and the symbol which preserves the etymology of the name, I mean the mouse, lies beneath the foot of his image. These are the works of Skopas of Paros.[248]

---

kapitelle," *RömMitt*, 60-61 (1953-54), pp. 184 ff.; *idem, Antike Figuralkapitelle*, Berlin, 1962, p. 29, no. 86; Carol La Branche, "The Greek Figural Capital," *Berytos*, 16 (1966), p. 77. The implication of this capital is that other, presumably, Greek artists were going to Persia at this time.

Previously, as Pliny reports (*N.H.* 34.19.68), the sculptor Telephanes of Phokaia worked for Xerxes and Darius, and it will be recalled that the statue once called Penelope, I believe now convincingly identified as a Mourning Aphrodite, a Greek original dating ca. 400 B.C., was found in the ruins of Persepolis after its destruction in 331 B.C. See Ernst Langlotz, "Zur Deutung der 'Penelope,'" *JdI*, 76 (1961), pp. 72-99. For a different view, see Brunilde Sismondo Ridgway, *The Severe Style in Greek Sculpture*, Princeton, 1970, pp. 101 ff., where the statue is related to other replicas of the type and dated in the traditional period, ca. 460-450 B.C. Mrs. Ridgway does not discuss the identity of the figure found in Persepolis.

246. Brian Cook has drawn my attention to the fact that on the Chariot Frieze from the Mausoleum at Halikarnassos, both the charioteers and their horses are also presented with slight variations in posture to avoid monotony in a repetitive composition.

247. If Skopas actually had seen Persepolis itself, it is interesting to recall that the theme of its sculptures was analogous to that of the Panathenaic frieze on the Parthenon. In each case, a contemporary and recurrent festival is the subject. A. W. Lawrence, "The Akropolis and Persepolis," *JHS*, 71 (1951), pp. 111-19, has made an eloquent and convincing case for the conscious Greek emulation of Persepolis in the Periklean rebuilding of the Akropolis. His comments on the Panathenaic frieze, in particular, on certain aspects of its style and its theme —the hitherto unknown use of a subject drawn from contemporary life rather than the customary mythological subject matter of Greek architectural sculpture—as inspired by the friezes of Persepolis, on which the participants in the procession to the Great King on the occasion of the New Year's Festival are depicted, again, in the very locale of the actual ceremonial event, are of special interest in the present discussion. Ashmole, p. 117, has made the same point. In depicting on the Propylon an actual rite performed in the Sanctuary, Skopas would have been influenced thematically by the friezes of both the Parthenon and Persepolis—revealing a process of assimilation and creation similar to what we have found to be his architectural procedure.

In a recent article, Elizabeth G. Pemberton, "The Gods of the East Frieze of the Parthenon," *AJA*, 80 (1976), pp. 123 f., has, again, drawn attention to the relationship between Persepolis and the Panathenaic frieze, unaware of the existence of Lawrence's much earlier and more detailed article.

A sorely damaged frieze has been attributed to a related position on the cella wall of the late archaic Temple of Hera at Samos: Ernest Buschor, "Altsamischer Bauschmuck," *AthMitt*, 72 (1957), pp. 32 ff.; Berve-Gruber-Hirmer, *op. cit.*, p. 455.

248. 13.1.48; Ἐν δὲ τῇ Χρύσῃ ταύτῃ καὶ τὸ τοῦ Σμινθέως Ἀπόλλωνός ἐστιν ἱερὸν καὶ τὸ σύμβολον τὸ τὴν

This famous statue appeared on the coinage of nearby Alexandreia Troas from the end of the fourth century B.C. far into Imperial times. On certain tetradrachms which show the statue particularly clearly, there is an unmistakably archaistic image of Apollo (fig. 213)[249]—witness the figure's archaizing, flat-footed stance and the zigzag folds of his himation coupled with the more naturalistic rendering of the head and body. Surely this is Skopas' celebrated statue. The fact that on the coin type the mouse has not been shown, and that the statue is obviously archaistic has led many critics to doubt the correctness of this identification,[250] since, hitherto, Skopas has not been associated with the archaistic style. Yet the mouse may have been omitted because of the impossibility of making this small creature visible and intelligible within the inscribed coin type. More likely, on the actual statue, the mouse appeared in relief on a sculptured base.[251] Indeed, on other simplified, later issues reproducing the statue, its high base is notable (fig. 214).[252] Both the Geographer's phrase, "lies at the foot of his image" and his use of ἔργα, referring to both statue and base, may thus be explained.[253]

ἐτυμότητα τοῦ ὀνόματος σῶζον, ὁ μῦς, ὑπόκειται τῷ ποδὶ τοῦ ξοάνου. Σκόπα δ'ἐστὶν ἔργα τοῦ Παρίου. The translation is that of H. L. Jones, *The Geography of Strabo* (Loeb edn.), New York, 1929, VI, pp. 93 ff. See, too, Herakleides of Pontus: καὶ ξόανον οὕτω κατασκευασθῆναι βεβηκὸς ἐπὶ τῶι μυΐ. Quoted *ibid.*

249. Warwick Wroth, *Catalogue of the Greek Coins of Troas, Aeolis, and Lesbos*, London, 1894, pp. XVI ff., 11, nos. 22-24, pls. IV, 1, 2; V, 4, 13; H. von Fritze, "Aufgaben der griechischen Münzwissenschaft," *Nomisma*, 6 (1911), pp. 27 ff., pl. III, 1, 2; Sidney P. Noe, "Greek Coins Acquired by The American Numismatic Society in 1947," *The American Numismatic Society, Museum Notes*, 3 (1948), pp. 10 ff., pl. III A, B, C, 12; Lacroix, pp. 14, 76 f., 80 ff., pl. IV, 2. The example illustrated above in the collection of the Fitzwilliam Museum, Cambridge (see von Fritze, *op. cit.*, pl. III, 2; *Sylloge Nummorum Graecorum*, London, 1940, IV, Fitzwilliam Museum, pt. V-VII, pl. LXXXI, no. 4253; Alfred R. Bellinger, *Troy, The Coins*, Supplementary Monograph 2, Princeton, 1961, p. 95, A 135) is dated 160 B.C. (PMA, 141). I am indebted to Graham Pollard, Keeper of the Department of Coins and Medals, for this information.

250. On this long-disputed issue, see, for example, the statements of Bieber, *op. cit.*, p. 117, Lacroix, *loc. cit.*, Arias, pp. 110 f., and Picard, *Manuel*, vols. III, pp. 691 f., 697 ff., IV, 1, pp. 145 ff., who prefer to accept a suggestion made by Adolf Furtwängler, *Masterpieces of Greek Sculpture*, London, 1895, p 303 and n. 2, that another coin type on which a nude Apollo bends forward, holding a branch in one hand, and rests one raised bent leg on a base reflects the statue by Skopas. But this type occurs on the coinage of other cities as well as on that of Alexandreia Troas, as Wroth, *op. cit.*, p. XVII, and Lacroix, p. 85, have observed. More important, the creature on whom the god gazes is not the obligatory mouse of Strabo's text but a bird, presumably Apollo's raven, as Wroth, *op. cit.*, p. XIII, and Walter Leaf, *Strabo on the Troad*, Cambridge, 1923, p. 242, have pointed out.

Lacroix, p. 83, n. 1, was correct in rejecting the thesis of V. R. Grace, "Scopas in Chryse," *JHS*, 52 (1932), pp. 231 f., that Skopas was responsible only for the mouse, pointing out that both Strabo and Herakleides clearly state that the mouse appeared beneath the feet of the figure, i.e., as part of the statue. Other scholars, for example, Wroth, *op. cit.*, p. XVII, have assumed that Skopas was obliged to reproduce "an older temple-statue, to the general character of which he was compelled to adhere," i.e., that for "religious reasons," Skopas was obliged to give his statue an archaizing appearance.

251. As Karl Lehmann had observed in his notes on this problem.

252. Lacroix, pl. IV, 4, 5, 8, 10, 11. On the latter example, the base shows some form of relief sculpture.

253. Leaf's effort, *op. cit.*, p. 242, to explain this plural form as an oblique reference to the fact that Skopas not only made the cult image but designed the temple is not persuasive.

The present temple at Chryse is Hellenistic. Hans Weber, "Zum Apollon Smintheus-Tempel in der Troas," *IstMitt*, 16 (1966), p. 114, has dated it toward the end of the third century B.C. It was my

213. Reverse of a tetradrachm of Alexandreia Troas. Cambridge, Fitzwilliam Museum.

214. Reverse of an Imperial bronze coin of Alexandreia Troas. London, The British Museum.

In view of the cult legends regarding the sanctuary at Chryse and the legendary discovery of the god's cult image,[254] it is reasonable to assume that Skopas intentionally cast this statue in archaistic form to allude to the legendary past and to emphasize the antiquity of the original image. The overtones of the new image thus evoked the venerable past.

Given the cult image of Apollo Smintheus and the frieze of the Propylon, it is evident that one aspect of Skopas' style was, in fact, an archaizing current.[255] And if one of the major artists of the fourth century B.C. played an important role in establishing that current, its growing popularity in the last quarter of the century[256] and the appearance of other archaistic cult statues, to judge from their numismatic reproductions,[257] would be very understandable. Surely no minor artist was responsible for this trend.

Apart from the almost contemporary frieze of the Corinthian Monument of Lysikrates in Athens, the frieze of the Propylon is the last figural frieze in Greek architecture until the classical revival of the second century B.C.[258] In a curious way, its regular sequence of alternating figures anticipates the rhythm of alternating motifs of bucranes and rosette-

---

impression after examining the few marbles in *situ* in May, 1953, and considering the implications of R. P. Pullan's publication of the building, *Antiquities of Ionia*, IV, London, 1881, pp. 40-47, pls. XXVI-XXX; V, London, 1915, pp. 30-34, that it might be still later, in the mid-second century B.C. Occasional discrepancies exist between Pullan's text and drawings and his original sketches as W. R. Lethaby, *ibid.*, V, pp. 32 f., has pointed out.

In any case, the Skopaic statue that Strabo saw had been placed in a new, Hellenistic temple. Originally, in Skopas' lifetime, the statue must have stood either in a predecessor of that temple or, conceivably, in a precinct or temenos in honor of the Sminthian Apollo.

254. See Menander Rhetor, Περὶ Σμινθιακοῦ in *Rhetores Graeci* (ed. Spengal), III, p. 445; Leaf, *op. cit.*, pp. 243 f., and a coin illustrating and commemorating this legend: Wroth, *op. cit.*, pl. V, 14; Lacroix, p. 80, pl. IV, 13.

255. Hence, Picard's complaint, *Manuel*, IV, 1, p. 145, n. 1, that "nous n'avons aucune sculpture archaïsante de Skopas" is no longer a cogent argument for rejecting this aspect of the master's style. On the contrary, Charbonneaux's characterization, *op. cit.*, pp. 86 f., that one aspect of Skopas' art was "la retour aux sources" is more to the point and applies admirably both to this archaizing statue and to the Samothracian frieze.

256. Harrison, p. 64.

257. E.g., the Athena Alkidemos type on the tetradrachms of Alexandria issued by Ptolemy I, as governor of Egypt, in 315-314 B.C. Agnes Baldwin Brett, "Athena ΑΛΚΙΔΗΜΟΣ of Pella," *American Numismatic Society, Museum Notes*, 4 (1950), pp. 55 ff., pl. XI, no. 5; Orestes H. Zervos, "Early Tetradrachms of Ptolemy I," *ibid.*, 13 (1967), pp. 1 ff., pls. III, 20, IV, 21-26. For other related statues erected by the Successors in other capitals, see Brett, *op. cit.*, pp. 58 f.

Mrs. Brett has suggested that this coin type is a faithful copy of the statue of Athena Alkidemos that stood in her temple in Pella (*ibid.*, pp. 58, 60, 63, 67, 70). The statue also appears as a magistrate's symbol on coins struck by Alexander at Amphipolis in 326-325 (p. 59, pl. X, 1, 2), hence it must have existed at least by that time. If Skopas was commissioned by Philip II of Macedon to design the Propylon in Samothrace ca. 340 B.C. (see below, p. 273), one wonders whether he might not have made this cult image for the Macedonian capital. Despite the differences in costume between the goddess and the dancing maidens, which preclude many comparisons, the gait, the shape of the curving legs and feet, as well as the character of the folds between the legs are very analogous. See, now, P. W. Lehmann, "New Light on Skopas," *Bulletin of the American Society of Papyrologists*, 15 (1978), pp. 67-71.

258. Even in Doric architecture, figural sculpture disappeared after the metopes of the early third-century Temple of Athena at Ilion, for which see Beatrice Mills Holden, *The Metopes of the Temple of Athena at Ilion*, Northampton, 1964.

215. Detail from the frieze of the Propylon of Ptolemy II. Vienna, Ephesos-Museum.

paterae that were to follow in Ionic architecture in the coming century and of which the Propylon of Ptolemy II in Samothrace is a typical example (fig. 215).[259]

THE PEDIMENTS AND AKROTERIA

We have seen that the pediments of the Propylon were once adorned with sculpture, although no trace of this decoration has been preserved.[260] Whether that decoration took the form of thin carved blocks attached to the tympanum wall, that is, relief sculpture, or separately applied decoration is unknown. And whether any such applied decoration was made of marble or bronze is, again, unknown. But the fact that all the sculptures of the Propylon—the coffers, the frieze, the sima, and, probably, the ornamental drums—were painted makes it likely that any applied ornament was of painted marble.

The height of the pediments in relation to the height of the frieze, as we have again seen, precludes figural decoration.[261] Hence it must have been floral or foliate. On the fragmentary Gnathian krater that has proved to be so illuminating in connection with the two-winged ground plan of the Propylon (fig. 59),[262] the analogous small pediment has been ornamented with a palmette springing from a pair of tendrils that curl into the narrow corners of the pediment. Other motifs, doubtless flowers, flank the central palmette.

That some such scheme must have been used in the pediments of the Propylon is made abundantly clear by three sarcophagi found in the same chamber as the so-called Alexander Sarcophagus in the royal nekropolis at Sidon.[263] The lids of all three are in the

259. As Karl Lehmann noted in *Hesperia*, 20 (1951), p. 18. Schmidt, p. 40, quoting Friedrich Hauser, *Die neuattischen Reliefs*, Stuttgart, 1889, p. 175, agreed that, from the distance, the frieze of the Propylon was not characteristically different "von einen Palmetten- und Lotusband." See, too, Ridgway, p. 203.

For the Propylon of Ptolemy II, see Alfred K. Frazer, *The Propylon of Ptolemy II* (*Samothrace*, Vol. 10, forthcoming).

260. See above, pp. 138 f.

261. Height of the tympanum wall: 0.28 m.; height of the frieze: 0.324 m.

262. See above, pp. 87 f.

263. O. Hamdy Bey and Theodore Reinach, *Une Nécropole royale à Sidon*, Paris, 1892, pp. 48 ff., pl. XL, nos. 4-6. All four were made of Pentelic marble, and evidently produced by one workshop. Traces of color were preserved on the akroteria, antefixes, sima, and frieze, but only a bud or floral form in the corners of the pediment of no. 6 retained its blue (see n. 264).

216. Sarcophagus No. 5 from the Royal Nekropolis at Sidon. Istanbul, Archaeological Museums.

217. Detail of Sarcophagus No. 5 from the Royal Nekropolis at Sidon. Istanbul, Archaeological Museums.

form of architectural gables complete with pediments, akroteria, roof tiles, antefixes, ridge antefixes, and lion's head waterspouts, and the order, with its continuous frieze carved with a grapevine and its dentils, is Ionic (figs. 216, 217). All three have at the center of the pediment an open lotus flower rising from an acanthus calyx. On each side, an acanthus tendril curls into the wings of the pediment. Its shape recalls the tendrils of the sima of the Propylon: each ribbed stalk forks into a tendril and a lesser stalk from which, again, a pair of tendrils emerges, one curling upward, one hanging downward and, on Sarcophagus No. 6, the last tendrils sprout a singular floral form that shoots into the corners of the pediment (cf. figs. 95, 217).[264] The lids of these architectural sarcophagi provide a vivid sense of the luxuriant leafy forms, the cursive rhythm that, in all probability, characterized the sculptures of the pediments of the Propylon. Their date, late in the fourth century B.C., is an appropriate one.[265]

Another later monument is of interest in this connection. An ancient pedimental relief adorned with floral reliefs has been reused in a very appropriate position as the crowning motif in the gable of the west façade of the Panagia Gorgoepikoos in Athens (fig. 218).[266] It appears to be Roman (post-Trajanic?) and shows what seems to be a schematic basket and lid above a simplified leafy calyx in the center of the pediment. From the calyx tendrils coil into each side of the gable and terminate in leaves.

No trace of the akroteria that once crowned the pediments is preserved.[267] Hence,

---

See, too, Mendel, *op. cit.*, I, pp. 200-208, Nos. 72-74; and Hans Möbius, *Die Ornamente der griechischen Grabstelen*, Berlin-Wilmersdorf, 1929, p. 40, pl. 25 a, b.

The excellent recent publication of these sarcophagi by Volkmar von Graeve, *Der Alexandersarcophag und seine Werkstaat* (Istanbuler Forschungen, 28), Berlin, 1970, contains a full bibliography on these much discussed monuments.

264. Hamdy Bey, *op. cit.*, pp. 53 f., describes this form as a flower bud, Mendel, *op. cit.*, p. 207, as an *épi de blé*.

According to Von Graeve, *op. cit.*, pp. 10, 159 f., this sarcophagus was the work of the same designing master as the Alexander sarcophagus, while the other two "Ranken" sarcophagi are attributed to a second designing master.

265. Dated by Reinach, *op. cit.*, p. 343, ca. 330-320 B.C., on the basis of the "Alexander Sarcophagus"; by Karl Schefold, *Der Alexander-Sarcophag*, Berlin, 1968, pp. 7, 11, 28, between the Battle of Issus (333 B.C.) and the death of Alexander (323 B.C.), i.e., before the death, in 311 B.C., of Abdalonymos, the last king of Sidon, for whom the sarcophagus was made. Von Graeve, *op. cit.*, pp. 13, 168, dates the entire group in 312 B.C.

As Möbius, *op. cit.*, p. 40, noted, the pediments of these sarcophagi are closely related to the triangular fields between the coffers in the outer ceiling of the Tholos at Epidauros (Roux, pl. 51, figs. 1, 2). These luxuriant acanthus tendrils, unfolding in the narrow fields, terminate in a spiral flower, and, again, suggest how the wings of the Propylon's pediments may have looked. Von Graeve, *op. cit.*, pp. 10, 160, 165, too, has emphasized the relationship between these sarcophagi and the Tholos.

266. Oddly enough, no specific comment is made regarding this monument by Karl Michel and Adolf Struck, "Die mittelbyzantischen Kirchen Athens," *AthMitt*, 31 (1906), pp. 294 ff. or Paul Steiner, "Antike Skulpturen an der Panagia Gorgoepikoos zu Athen," *ibid.*, pp. 325 ff., although the diagram, pl. XXI, 1 and Beilage, fig. 7, illustrate its positon. It is simply reported, p. 301, as an ancient piece. I am grateful to Alison Frantz for the detail reproduced in fig. 218.

267. See above, p. 139. In Vol. 3, text I, pp. 359 f., it was stated that fragments of a floral akroterion attributable to the Propylon existed and one such fragment was illustrated in Fig. 310. Reexamination of these fragments and of the numerous additional akroterial fragments in the storeroom of the Antikensammlung of the Kunsthistorisches Museum in Vienna has indicated that the scale of all these

218. Detail of the west façade of the Panagia Gorgoepikoos in Athens.

we have restored conventional floral akroteria over both pediments and above the rear corners of the building.[268]

The last two ornamental features of the Propylon, its akroteria and pedimental sculptures, have been restored theoretically. So, too, were the coffers before the main door and in the wings of the porch. Yet we have had good reason to believe that these three units of the building were carved with floral and leafy forms. Such forms fit the character of the sculptured bolster of the capital, of the ornamental drum with its luxuriant palmettes, and of the exuberant sima with its flowers and rinceaux of acanthus.[269] Surely, this is a sculptor's building, with its sculptured coffers and frieze, its drums and sima, its pediments and akroteria.

Taken as a whole, there is a strong emphasis on floral, foliate forms in the ornament of the Propylon. It is tempting to regard this emphasis as a symbolic and meaningful

---

fragments is far too large for the small-scale pediments of the Propylon to the Temenos and that they must come from another building in the Sanctuary, probably the Propylon of Ptolemy II or a building on the Western Hill donated by a Milesian lady.

268. In restoring these akroteria, we have followed the prescription of Vitruvius 3.5.12, who states that lateral akroteria should equal the height of the tympanum and that the central akroterion should exceed them in height. The central akroteria are slightly less than one-third higher than the lateral akroteria, a proportion close to that of the Temple of Asklepios at Epidauros, the Temple of the Athenians at Delos, and the Hieron in Samothrace. See Vol. 3, text I, p. 386, n. 235, for the specific figures and appropriate references to these buildings.

269. According to Roux, pp. 365 ff., the definitive form of the Corinthian capital is Skopas' creation, in particular, the naturalistic character of its "décoration végétale," the new sense of living plant forms. The common denominator between the Corinthian capitals at Tegea and the sima of the Propylon is precisely this luxuriance of plant forms.

Charbonneaux, too, *La Sculpture grecque classique*, II, pp. 93 f., has stressed Skopas' passionate observation of nature and the important place that plants occupy in his *oeuvre*.

allusion to the flourishing of life, to the hope for eternal life that the divine images in the ceiling had the power to bestow.[270]

Analysis of the architectural features of the Propylon has yielded a date in the decades between 350-330 B.C. or soon after the buildings commissioned by Maussollos and Idrieus (353-344 B.C.).[271] Parallels for the style of the frieze imply a date of 340-330 B.C.[272] The style of the coffers is clearly Skopaic and has proved closely related to the most advanced heads from Tegea dated toward 340 B.C.[273] Around 350 B.C., Skopas was working at Halikarnassos. Theoretically, his activity in Samothrace should probably be connected with the years when he worked at a number of places in Anatolia and the Troad, again, doubtless, after his work at Halikarnassos. The more precise suggestion that the Propylon was built ca. 340 B.C. must await consideration of the biography of an historical personality: Philip II of Macedon.[274]

P. W. L.

270. As I have previously remarked, Vol. 3, text I, p. 387, n. 237. Roux, pp. 195 ff., in discussing the Tholos at Epidauros, has interpreted its ornamental forms in meaningful fashion and seen in the acanthus scrolls of its ceiling and its crowning floral akroterion symbols of immortality. In his discussion of the Alexander sarcophagus, Von Graeve, *op. cit.*, pp. 42 ff., has also emphasized the concrete symbols of a belief in immortality implicit in the imagery of the figural forms of its lid.

Elizabeth Jastrow, in an interesting article on a large group of small altars or supports for votive offerings found in sanctuaries of certain great goddesses of nature or in tombs, has pointed out the similar meaningful content of their iconography. They regularly show a female head seen *en face* emerging from an acanthus calyx and surrounded or framed by its tendrils, the foliate ornament of these images clearly being symbolic of the flourishing of life and the hope for immortality ("Two Terracotta Reliefs in American Museums," *AJA*, 50 [1946], pp. 67-80). The related heads on the South Italian vessels illustrated above, figs. 111 A, B, have the same meaning, as she has also seen.

For the meaningful character of floral ornament see, too, Konrad Schauenburg, "Zur Symbolik unteritalischer Rankenmotive," *RomMitt*, 64 (1957), pp. 198 ff.

271. See above, p. 144.

272. See above, pp. 235, 239, 241.

273. Stewart, pp. 73, 75. Regarding Stewart's lower limit, see below, Chap. IV, n. 28.

274. See below, pp. 273 f.

219. Air view of the Sanctuary, 1957.

IV. The History of the Temenos and the Propylon

A primitive hearth attests the earliest activity in the Sanctuary of the Great Gods. Set on natural soil 2.26 m. below the floor level of the fourth-century Temenos, it consisted of a pavement of small stones framed by boulders, the largest of which, 1.75 m. long and 0.70 m. high, was placed close to the northwestern foundation of the later precinct wall (figs. 220-221).[1] Horseshoe in shape, it suggests the type of simple fireplace that campers might

1. It lay 1.00 m. to the south of that foundation and 1.50 m. to the east of the sub-foundation of the later southwestern wall. Marked traces of fire are visible on its inner face.

The present account of the two earliest periods in the area of the later Temenos is based on the notes and diagrams of Karl Lehmann. They, in turn, are extracts from the excavation diary for the 1950 campaign which served as the basis of his own report in *Hesperia*, 21 (1952), pp. 34 ff.

220. Primitive hearth beneath the Temenos.

build. Earth, ashes, fragments of charcoal and a few burned bones of pigs and lambs[2]—one cut for the extraction of marrow[3]—were found on its floor.

Over this hearth, itself undatable, lay a second stratum, 0.65 m. in height, from a succeeding period. It consisted of a dense accumulation of burned bones and ceramic fragments which originally had been surrounded by a curving frame of stones encircling an area ca. 3.50 m. in diameter—evidently, a shallow pit over the initial hearth into which the debris of sacrifices was thrown. At its center, this heap of debris rose to a height 0.91 m. beneath the floor of the later precinct. The stone frame of the pit was surrounded by a stamped earth floor, itself 1.26 m. below the level of the same later floor.

Quantities of animal bones were found in this deposit. Again they were of the same variety as those found in the earlier hearth, consisting of the bones of lambs and especially of pigs, and indicate the same chthonic sacrifices.[4] The ceremonies performed here now included sacramental drinking, and evidently the vessels employed for this purpose were ritually broken up after use and deposited in a pit made for this purpose.[5]

2. We are indebted to Dr. Edwin Colbert of the American Museum of Natural History in New York City for examining the animal bones found during the campaign of 1950.

3. As remarked in *Hesperia*, 20 (1951), p. 10, the eating of marrow was a Homeric practice. Cf. *Odyssey* 9.293 and *Iliad* 22.500.

4. Pigs, in particular, were sacrificed to chthonic divinities. See *RE, s.v. Schwein*, cols. 812 f.

5. The ritual breaking of vessels in Samothrace persisted into the Hellenistic period, where it was characteristic of the potsherds found in the fill of the pronaos of the Hieron. See *Hesperia*, 19 (1950), p. 16.

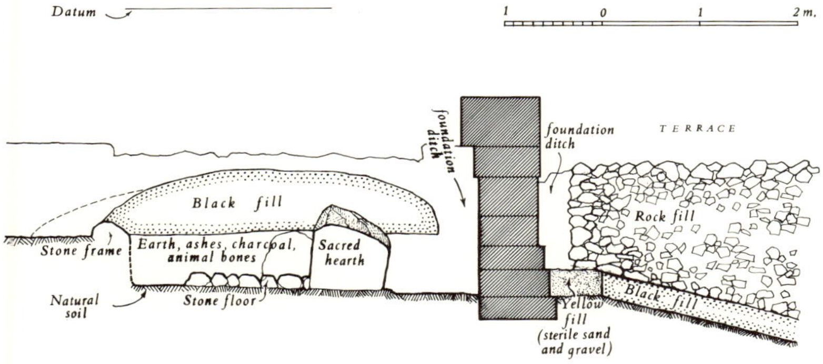

221. Schematic section showing primitive hearth and later black layer interrupted by limestone sub-foundation of the northern wall of the Temenos.

The pottery found in this burned, black layer ranged from fine subgeometric ware of the first half of the seventh century B.C. to coarse, handmade vessels.[6] The contrast between the elegant, wheelmade kantharoi with their thin fabric and restrained decoration and the crude, undecorated handmade cups found in this stratum suggests that it was at this period that Greek-speaking settlers came to Samothrace and mingled and worshiped with the native, Thracian-speaking inhabitants.[7]

Among the objects found in this deposit were two seashells pierced for suspension, one blackened on both sides by the burned material in which it was found (fig. 222).[8] They must have been either amulets or votive gifts and, as such, they imply the worship of Aphrodite.[9] The fact that in this early stratum there is evidence of the cult of Aphrodite will prove of the highest interest in connection with the function of the later precinct.

6. See the Catalogue of Finds, **1-82**. Although the pottery of this layer contained a concentration of subgeometric ware, it also included fragments of sixth-, fifth-, and fourth-century black-glazed vessels that reflect the later disturbance of the area that resulted from the building of two subsequent precincts, the last one dating ca. 340 B.C., and the previous faulty excavation of the Temenos, for which see the Introduction, p. 26.

The very extensive black layer, itself, contained a hole of yellowish earth filled with ashes, burned sheep and ram's bones, and ceramic fragments, an intrusion that may reflect a single later sacrifice.

7. For documents of the use of Thracian as a living language in Samothrace and for parallel dedications in Greek, see Karl Lehmann, *Samothrace*, Vol. 2, pt. II.

8. 50.209. Pierced by one hole. Size ca. 0.04 m. by 0.04 m. 50.221, pierced by two holes. Same size.

9. For shells as votive gifts to Aphrodite, see Maria Bratschkova, "Die Muschel in der antiken Kunst," *Bulletin de l'Institut archéologique bulgare*, 12 (1938), pp. 1 ff. Pierced shells, presumably votive gifts, were also found in the Mycenaean sanctuary in the Marmaria at Delphi (R. Demangel, *Le Sanctuaire d'Athèna Pronaia (Marmaria)* [*Fouilles de Delphes*, II C], Paris, 1926, p. 11, fig. 13). See, too, Dorothy Burr Thompson, "Three Centuries of Hellenistic Terracottas," *Hesperia*, 21 (1952), p. 149, for the further implication that such gifts signify (the hope for?) immortality.

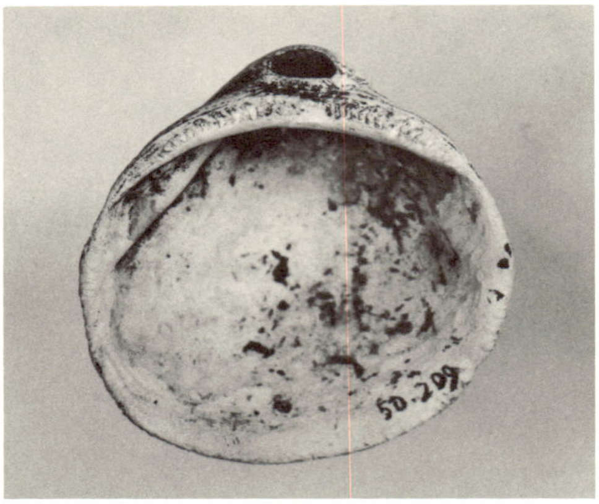

222. Sea shell. Samothrace Museum.

223. Foreground: view of the outer face of the northern sub-foundation of the Temenos; background: the Hieron.

224. View of the inner face of the northern sub-foundation of the Temenos, the primitive hearth seen against it.

225. View of the eschara in the Hieron.

Beween these earliest phases of worship in the Sanctuary and the later mid-fourth-century B.C. Temenos and terrace, there is evidence of another period, whether archaic or classical, it is impossible to say. The sub-foundation of the short, northwestern wall of the later Temenos is composed of two sections: an earlier limestone foundation toward the west and a later, sloppily built foundation of coarser limestone that overlaps it (Pl. III.3; figs. 30, 223, 224). Its courses are irregular and its blocks differ in size and shape but they clearly are adjusted to the previous fragment. This poorer foundation forms part of the foundation of the mid-fourth-century Temenos, being linked with an extension to the northwest, the short fragment of the original wall on this side of the precinct (Pl. I). The construction of these two sections of foundation cut through the black layer causing it and its contents to spill out to the north in the area of the later terrace (fig. 221).

Beneath the marble floor of the later Temenos, our Austrian predecessors found two, as they believed, bothroi (figs. 13-16).[10] Their *Opfergrube* A (fig. 14), with its stone frame presumably resting on natural soil and broken stones was clearly an eschara, its limestone border evidently framing a fire-resistant stone floor of the same type as the eschara found in the cella of the Hieron (fig. 225).[11] Their marble-framed *Opfergrube* B (fig. 15), however, was a bothros. Inasmuch as the marble floor of the later Temenos also contained an eschara and a bothros (Pl. LIX), it is reasonable to assume that eschara A and bothros B were forebears of the later ritual installation. Repeatedly, in the Samothracian Sanctuary, such a renewal of ritual installations occurred in successive chronological periods within a building or a structure—witness the Hieron and the Altar Court.[12] Hence it is plausible to suggest that the earlier section of the northwestern foundation is a remnant of the wall of an earlier Temenos or precinct that contained eschara A and bothros B. If so, it determined the orientation of the later Temenos and, conceivably, the line of its northern foundation.

10. *S,II*, p. 15, pls. V, VII.

11. Vol. 3, text I, pp. 128 f.

12. Cf. the successive apses of the Hieron (Vol. 3, text I, pp. 129 ff; text II, pp. 51 f., 59 ff.) and its *bathra* (text II, pp. 54 ff.). The Altar Court replaced an archaic rock altar (see Vol. 4, pt. II, pp. 109 ff.).

226. Detail of the outer face of the northern subfoundation of the Temenos.

When that later Temenos was built, the long southwestern foundation was linked with the earlier remnant by a makeshift device. Five courses of masonry were stuffed into the interval between these foundations (Pls. I, III.3; figs. 30, 226). They are spoils,[13] and differ both in material and size, and the height of each course is markedly lower than that of the blocks to which they have been adjusted.[14]

13. E.g., the western block of course three has a dowel hole at its western end where it abuts a fieldstone; the top course has a pry hole on its outer face.

14. In his report in *Hesperia*, 21 (1952), pp. 31 ff., Professor Lehmann proposed another explanation for these facts. He believed that the top blocks of this "stuffing" were the remnants of an entrance and that that entrance (1.18 m. below the floor of the later precinct) led into a terrace which extended to the west, toward the river valley. Presumably, altars flanked the interior of this door and Bothros B lay on this terrace which was dated ca. 400 B.C. by the ceramic finds in the foundation ditches and inner fill behind the earlier, fragmentary "wall." Final examination of this fill indicates that no date can be attached to it, that it was disturbed by the later activity of the Temenos builders, and that its sherds range from the seventh to the fourth centuries B.C. The foundations for the preserved altars (one of which was hypothetical) were removed in the course of excavation to allow for the ultimate uncovering of the black layer and hearth. Hence I have been unable to check on the nature of this "fieldstone foundation."

This theoretically late fifth-century period was preceded by an archaic period. The different technique used in laying the foundation of the long southwestern wall (for which see above, pp. 44 f.) was interpreted as implying another period and explained as evidence of an earlier structure or platform ca. 8.50 m. square in the southern part of the present Temenos. Eschara A went with and lay to the north of this high platform, and on it, it was suggested, there might have been the statue of an enthroned figure. But the difference in level between Eschara A and Bothros B was 0.21 m., judging by the Austrians' section—of no consequence beneath a floor shaken by repeated earthquakes. In the meantime, the "archaic hand" that was the basis of the archaic statue (along with fragments of a presumed throne found near the archaic altar north of the Hieron) has proved to belong to the northwestern corner akroterion of the Hieron—the hand holding a patera into which one of the pair of Hellenistic Victories above the façade poured a libation (see "Addendum to *Samothrace*, Vol. 3: The Lateral Akroteria," *Hesperia*, 41 (1972), pp. 463 ff.).

Thus I believe that Professor Lehmann's archaic period did not exist. The fact remains that an intermediate period did exist between the seventh-century B.C. cult area and the mid-fourth-century B.C. Temenos.

Thus, in traditional Samothracian fashion, this earlier precinct incorporated within its area the ritual places of the past—the hearth and the later sacrificial deposit. And it, in turn, was succeeded by the extant Temenos which, once again, contained an eschara and a bothros sunk in its marble floor.

The new elements in this ensemble were the Propylon and the marble-paved terrace to which it also gave access. Consideration of the architectural features of the Propylon has indicated that it must be dated between 350 and 330 B.C.[15] Examination of the pottery has also indicated that no fragment is later than the third quarter of the fourth century B.C.[16] Can an even more precise date be determined for the Propylon?

The Propylon was the first building in the Sanctuary to be built of marble, the first of a rapid succession of splendid marble buildings dedicated in the Sanctuary by members of the Macedonian royal house and the Diadochs: the Altar Court, the dedication of Philip III Arrhidaios and Alexander IV, the Rotunda of Arsinoe, the Propylon of Ptolemy II, and conceivably the Hieron, buildings dating between ca. 340-330 B.C. and ca. 280 B.C.[17] The fact that the first two or three of these buildings were dedications of Arrhidaios, one after he assumed his father's name on ascent to the throne, would in itself suggest that the Propylon was a dedication to the Great Gods by Philip II, and that Arrhidaios intentionally chose to link himself with his father's action and policy in this regard.

Philip II's special allegiance to the Sanctuary of the Great Gods is well known.[18] As a youth, he had been initiated in Samothrace.[19] Indeed, it was on that occasion that he had met and fallen in love with Olympias, Alexander's mother, as, in the legendary past, the initiate Kadmos had met and married Harmonia.[20] We have seen that according to the contemporary fourth-century historian Ephoros, a sacred drama involving Kadmos and Harmonia was performed in the Samothracian festivals,[21] a δρώμενον in all likelihood performed in the predecessor of the fourth-century Temenos.[22] Commemoration of his own initiation, meeting, and marriage by the donation of a new temenos and, attached to it, a splendid propylon designed by a famous artist would fit what is known of Philip's actions and policies.[23] His taste for lavish festivals in honor of the gods to commemorate the events of his own life culminated in the ill-fated celebration in which he lost his own life, when he appeared as σύνθρονος of the gods, his own image being carried in the procession along

15. See above, Chap. II.

16. See the Catalogue of Finds, **83-107**.

17. For these buildings, see *Samothrace*, Vol. 4, pt. II, pp. 164 ff., *Samothrace*, Vol. 3, text II, pp. 74 f.; *Hesperia*, 37 (1968), pp. 222 ff.; *Guide*[4], pp. 18, 54 ff., 88 ff., 91.

For Macedonian allegiance to Samothrace, see Rubensohn, pp. 143 ff.

18. Quintus Curtius, *Historia Alexandri* 8.1.26 (*Samothrace*, Vol. 1, **195**).

19. Plutarch, *Alexander* 2.2; Himerius *Orationes* 9.12 (*Samothrace*, Vol. 1, **193**, **194**).

20. See, in particular, Scholia to Euripides *Phoenissae* 7 and Diodorus 5.48.5 (*Samothrace*, Vol. 1, **75**, **142**).

21. Scholia to Euripides *Phoenissae* 7 (*Samothrace*, Vol. 1, **75**).

22. See below, p. 288.

23. Among those who have pointed out the parallelism of these historical and legendary events are Otto Rubensohn, p. 133; Otto Kern in *RE*, X, *s.v.* *Kabeiros, Kaberioi*, col. 1428 f.; Karl Lehmann, *Hesperia*, 21 (1952), p. 38; and C. Kerényi, *The Heroes of the Greeks*, London, 1959, p. 28.

with statues of the Twelve Gods.[24] Equation of himself and his own marriage with the person and life of a legendary hero in a cult of special significance in his life would seem altogether in character with his mentality.[25] At Olympia, too, he had dedicated another Ionic building, the Philippeion, that served as a dynastic monument to himself, Olympias, and Alexander in which Leochares' family group was made of chryselephantine,[26] the materials normally used for statues of divinity. Both donations, therefore, must antedate his last marriage in 337 B.C. and his subsequent estrangement from Olympias and Alexander.[27] The events of Philip's life as well as the varied archaeological evidence provided by the Propylon and the Temenos suggest that this act took place ca. 340 B.C. It may well have been in 338 B.C.[28]

In 340 B.C., Alexander was a precocious youth of sixteen. Yet the following year, when Philip was besieging Byzantium,[29] Alexander was left in complete control of Macedonia. Under the circumstances, the striking formal analogy between the profile head of a young man from the coffered ceiling of the Propylon (fig. 227) and a portrait of the youthful Alexander found on the Akropolis at Athens (fig. 228) is of more than stylistic interest.[30] Plausibly considered an original by Leochares,[31] the master responsible for the chrysele-

24. Diodorus 16.55.1-2; 91.3-6; 92.5.

25. It is especially interesting to note that Diodorus, one of the most important and reliable ancient writers on Samothrace, stresses Philip's piety (εὐσέβεια), using the specific technical term for initiates in the Samothracian mysteries, who were described as μύσται εὐσεβεῖς or *mystae piei* (16.60.4-5; 64.3). I doubt that this is a coincidence.

26. Pausanias 5.20.10. For the Philippeion, built after the battle of Chaeroneia, see Schleif-Zschietzschmann.

27. See J. R. Ellis, *Philip II and Macedonian Imperialism*, London, 1976, pp. 211 ff.

28. Stewart, p. 108, noting the relationship between the lion's head waterspouts on the Propylon and those of the Temple of Zeus at Nemea, for which he assumes a final date of 320 B.C., believes that the date of the Propylon should be lowered. On historical grounds (cf. the arguments adduced on pp. 274 ff.), a date in the 320s is impossible. The Temple at Nemea is clearly dependent on the Skopaic temple at Tegea dated ca. 360 B.C. (cf. Chap. II, n. 207). If, as appears likely, the Propylon was designed by Skopas ca. 340 B.C., or more precisely, ca. 338 B.C., the waterspouts and sima at Nemea may well reflect the ornamental forms of the two earlier Skopaic buildings. Both the waterspouts on the Propylon and at Nemea stem from lion's head spouts on the Temple of Asklepios at Epidauros (cf. above, pp. 121 ff.). Hence, it is of interest to note Stewart's very credible hypothesis (p. 90) that Skopas served as apprentice at precisely that Temple.

29. Plutarch, *Alexander* 9.1.

30. Akropolis Museum, no. 1331, found near the Erechtheum. Pentelic marble. Preserved height: 0.35 m.; width: 0.23 m. Stanley Casson, *Catalogue of the Akropolis Museum*, II, Cambridge, 1921, pp. 232 ff.; I. Miliades, *Guide sommaire du Musée de l'Akropole*, Athens, 1968, p. 63, no. 1331; Maria S. Brouskari, *The Akropolis Museum, A Descriptive Catalogue*, Athens, 1974, pp. 166 f., figs. 352-353.

31. See, in particular, Bernard Ashmole, "Demeter of Cnidus," *JHS*, 71 (1951), pp. 15 ff., pls. XI, fig. a, XII, figs. a, c, and his recent article, "Solvitur Disputando," *Festschrift für Frank Brommer*, Mainz/Rhein, 1977, p. 15, as well as Miliades, Casson and Brouskari, *loc. cit.*

This famous head, the earliest portrait of Alexander, figures in all the legion discussions of Alexander portraits. Two replicas of the head exist, one in Schloss Erbach, one in Berlin. For a recent discussion of all three, see Volkmar von Graeve, "Zum Herrscherbild Philipps II. und Philipps III. von Makedonien," *AA*, 1973, pp. 244 ff., who does not consider the Akropolis head an original by Leochares. Indeed, the issue has been hotly disputed. The likelihood that the head is a replica of Leochares' chryselephantine portrait of Alexander in the Philippeion has been pointed out by numerous writers, including Ashmole and Brouskari. It is a logical conclusion. I, too, consider the Akropolis head an original. Seen from the front, the head is decidedly youthful, as

227. *C(V)2.*

228. Portrait of Alexander the Great. Athens, Akropolis Museum.

phantine group of family portraits in the Philippeion, this portrait must have been erected after Alexander's first and last visit to Athens in 338 B.C., when he was a young man of eighteen.[32] It is characterized by the same rare hairdo[33] and forceful, regular features as the relief: the luxuriant hair covering the ears and falling on the nape of the neck; the short upper lip, the shape of the mouth, the contour of the chin, and the similar modeling of the cheeks. Obviously, these portraits are the work of different masters.[34] Whether the relief is the work of Skopas himself or his shop, one cannot say, but it is of special interest as the first indication that Skopas made any portrait. None is mentioned in the literary sources on the master.

The program of the coffered ceiling, it will be recalled, seems to have included the representation of divinities, legendary figures, and heroic initiates (fig. 139 B).[35] Was Alexander here equated with a legendary, heroic initiate, for example, the youthful Jason, leader of the Argonauts?[36] It is tempting to think so.

Analysis of the architectural and sculptural style of the Propylon has led to the conclusion that the *designing* master of the Propylon was Skopas of Paros.[37] To what extent the sculpture and architectural ornament of the building reflects his own hand, it is difficult to say. But that he created for the Samothracian Sanctuary a group of Aphrodite and Pothos which was worshiped with the most sacred ceremonies is known from the Elder Pliny.[38] Indeed, it is the first work of Skopas mentioned by Pliny in his thumbnail account of the master.

---

has been pointed out repeatedly by Margarete Bieber, the last time in "The Portraits of Alexander," *Greece and Rome*, 2nd ser., 12 (1965), p. 183. But her date, ca. 340 B.C., is historically impossible. It probably dates ca. 338 B.C.

32. Justin 9.4.5. Ellis, *op. cit.*, pp. 199 f.

33. For discussion of this hairdo and its heroic connotations, see Tonio Hölscher, *Ideal und Wirklichkeit in den Bildnissen Alexanders des Grossen* (Abhandlungen der Heidelberger Akademie der Wissenschaften, Phil.-hist. Kl.), Heidelberg, 1971, pp. 26 ff.

34. In connection with Skopas' relationship to his contemporaries, it is worth recalling that he, Leochares, and Timotheus worked together at the Mausoleum. Indeed, it has been suggested by Barbara Schlörb, *Timotheus* (*JdI*, 22. Ergänzungsheft), Berlin, 1965, p. 58, n. 150, that, at one point, the young Skopas worked under Timotheus.

35. See above, pp. 164 ff.

36. Jason as heroic initiate in Samothrace: Apollonios Rhodius *Argonautica* ll.915-21; Diodorus 5.49.6 (*Samothrace*, Vol. 1, **229**, **142**). His youth: Apollonios Rhodius *Argonautica* 1.972: "As with Jason, the soft down was just blooming on his chin." Unfortunately, there seems to be no sure representation of Jason as an independent statuary type.

37. Above, pp. 144 ff., 170 ff., 266. According to the most recent investigation of the Mausoleum at Halikarnassos by Kristian Jeppesen and Ian Zahle ("Investigations on the Site of the Mausoleum 1970/1973," *AJA*, 79 [1975], pp. 67-79), work on the monument was finally suspended ca. 340 B.C. Skopas, then, would have been free to accept another commission.

38. *Naturalis historia* 36.5.25: *Is fecit Venerem et Pothon qui Samothrace sanctissimis caerimoniis coluntur.* "He [Skopas] made the [statues of] Venus and Pothos that are worshiped at Samothrace with the most sacred ceremonies" (the translation of Naphtali Lewis, *Samothrace*, Vol. 1, **160**. I question whether [statues of] might not be [group of]).

Karl Kerényi, "Das Werk des Skopas für Samothrace," *Symbolae Osloenses*, 31 (1955), pp. 141 ff., has pointed out the fact the best manuscript of this portion of Pliny in Bamberg, Codex Bambergensis M.V. 10, uses the words *Venerem et Pothon*, while the less good Codex Parisinus 6801 says *Venerem et Phaethontem* (written phetontem) and that early nineteenth-century editions combine the two to read

The original work has not been preserved nor are there any copies of it. Some thirty copies or variants of what must have been a famous original by Skopas have been identified as the figure of Pothos on the basis of a gem in Berlin which shows a winged boy attended by Aphrodite's goose (figs. 229, 230).[39] He stands cross-legged, supports himself on a staff, and looks up with longing.

Although this type has been construed by many to reflect the Pothos of the Samothracian group (one example of the type is illustrated in fig. 231),[40] it is far more likely that

---

Venerem et Pothon et Phaethontem. Ludwig Urlichs, *Skopas, Leben und Werke,* Greifswald, 1863, pp. 99 f., discarded Phaethon as a worthless reading as have later editions. Nevertheless, Kerényi preferred to retain the latter reading and assumed (p. 152) that the group represented all three figures, Venus flanked by Pothos and Phaethon, on the far-fetched theory that, in Samothrace, two forms always flank a third (e.g. the snakes flanking the kerykeion on the Anaktoron stele!). The fact is that, in Samothrace, the Megaloi Theoi are four!

Unfortunately, Stewart, pp. 109 f., has accepted this faulty text tradition (without pointing out to the reader the correct text or, in his collection of the literary sources on Skopas, p. 127, indicating the precise manuscript tradition as Kerényi did). For further comment on Stewart's reconstruction of the lost Samothracian group see below note 39.

39. Adolf Furtwängler, *Die antiken Gemmen,* Leipzig and Berlin, 1900, II, pp. 208 f., pl. XLIII, no. 52, first identified the figure on this gem as Pothos, linked it with the Skopasian copies, and pronounced this type to be the Pothos of the Samothracian group.

For a convenient list of these copies, see Giovanni Becatti, "Il Pothos di Scopa," *Le Arti,* 3 (1941), pp. 401 ff., where the extensive bibliography on the type, discussed repeatedly from the eighteenth century on, is cited. Becatti lists twenty-seven copies; Stewart, pp. 144-146, lists over forty copies, variants, and versions. The difference between the two figures results primarily from Stewart's inclusion of a series of reflections on gems.

As remarked in the preceding note, Stewart, pp. 109 f., has accepted the faulty text tradition proposed by Kerényi. Retaining the established statuary type of Pothos, he has devised a balancing figure of Phaethon and used the youths to flank a hypothetical figure of Aphrodite. The incomplete statue of "Phaethon," found at Salamis in Cyprus, probably is a statue of Phaethon, judging by a sarcophagus in Copenhagen in which the figure occurs in a totally alien context unconnected with either Pothos or Aphrodite (see his pl. 45, figs. b, d). Aphrodite herself, the main figure of the Samothracian group, is never mentioned in Stewart's text, and the reader, therefore, has no clue as to why the restoration drawing of the group, Fig. 7, shows the goddess as a seated figure, since no analogy is cited by the author for either a seated or a standing figure—hence the main figure of the group is simply invented. On p. 173, n. 75, Stewart lamely repeats Kerényi's explanation "that the Aphrodite was not copied owing to a religious prohibition stemming from the secret nature of the Mysteries," the implication being that although it was legitimate to copy the subordinate image, the main figure could not be copied, and that the group itself must have been exhibited in a cult building, i.e., the Anaktoron or the Hieron, neither of which had cult images. On the contrary, the group must have been exposed in an area accessible to both initiate and non-initiate but, unfortunately, no replica of it exists. (See below, regarding the related group from Megara.) Lesser features of Stewart's triad (p. 110) are also non-Samothracian: e.g., the interpretation of Pothos' mantle as a veil, the *porphyris* of the Samothracian initiate, for which see Vol. 3, text II, pp. 26 ff., and the *altar* encircled by snakes adjacent to Phaethon. Stewart mentions no analogy for such altars or monuments in Samothrace and I, myself, am unaware of any. The main point, however, is that the best manuscript of this portion of Pliny precludes a triad for the Samothracian group. It is a pity that this otherwise splendid volume on Skopas is marred not only by an incorrect and misleading reconstruction drawing of the group but that, unfortunately, this reconstruction was selected by the publisher (without the author's knowledge or permission) to adorn the cover of the volume.

40. Among those who have accepted Furtwängler's thesis, none has been more enthusiastic

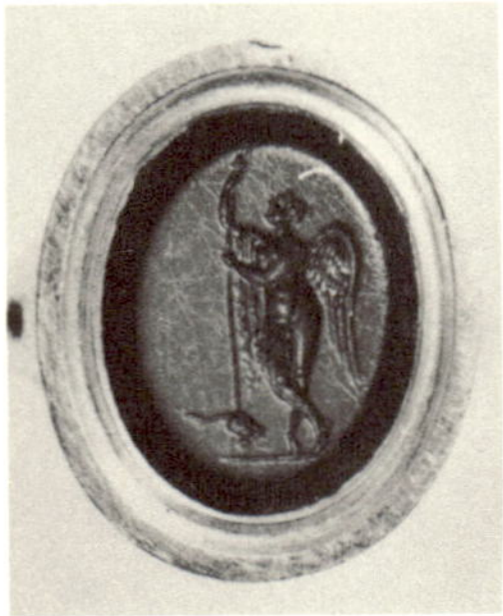

229. Nicolo. Berlin. Staatliche Museen.

230. Enlarged cast of Fig. 229.

231. Statue of Pothos. Rome, Palazzo dei Conservatori, Braccio Nuovo.

this statue reproduces another figure of Pothos, one of a triad of figures that Skopas made for the Temple of Aphrodite at Megara.[41] The main figure in the Samothracian group was clearly Aphrodite. Surely no copy of this group would omit her and reproduce only the subordinate image.[42] But the triad at Megara must have been composed of almost identical figures. According to Pausanias, "By Skopas are Love and Desire and Yearning, if indeed their functions are as different as their names."[43] The implication of these words is that these

---

than Heinrich Bulle, who insisted that both ends of the staff terminated in phalloi and drew far-reaching implications about the Samothracian cult from this assumption. See "Zum Pothos des Skopas," *JdI*, 56 (1941), pp. 121-150, and the posthumously published article "Skopas und die Persönlichkeitfragen in griechischen Plastik," *JdI*, 37 (1948), pp. 1-42. The latter article is largely an attempt to refute another by Walter Müller, "Zum Pothos des Skopas," *JdI*, 58 (1943), pp. 153-182, who believed that the copies reflected a lost bronze original of Eros supported by a torch made by a sculptor influenced by Skopas and Praxiteles in the time of Alexander—i.e., Müller did not accept Furtwängler's attribution. Nor did Rhys Carpenter, "Two Postscripts to the Hermes Controversy," *AJA*, 58 (1954), pp. 9 f., who maintained that the object held on the gem was a distaff and that the figure drew out a long thread of flax or wool on a spindle placed above the ground line—hence that the figure was a spinning Eros. This far-fetched interpretation is best forgotten.

The statue illustrated above is one of a pair of Pothoi found in an incompletely excavated Hadrianic villa in Rome. It is now in the Braccio Nuovo of the Palazzo dei Conservatori in Rome. See Wolfgang Helbig, *Führer durch die öffentlichen Sammlungen klassischer Altertümer in Rom* (4th edn., rev., ed. by Hermione Speier), II, Tübingen, 1966, pp. 436 f., no. 1644, inv. no. 2417, and A. M. Colini, "Scoperta di un gruppo di statue sulla pendice del Crispo," *Capitolium*, 18 (1940), pp. 861 ff. This author is among the many who have accepted Furtwängler's thesis; however, the author of the catalogue entry, Hans von Steuben, has rejected any connection between this pair of statues and the art of Skopas, as has Erika Simon, "Neuerwerbungen des Martin von Wagner-Museums Würzburg 1965-68," *AA*, 1968, p. 148, who considers this statue a later Hellenistic classicistic or Imperial Roman work. She, too, has accepted Kerényi's thesis regarding a Samothracian cult group of three figures (see above, n. 38), presumably unaware of the faulty text tradition on which it rests.

41. As Becatti, *op. cit.*, p. 410, and Arias, pp. 131 ff., have already seen. It is a singular fact that Stewart, p. 109, has refused to accept this logical explanation on the basis that more Romans are known to have visited Samothrace than the Temple at Megara, hence the abundance of copies of Pothos (although not of Aphrodite!). It is singular because Stewart makes a great point of the mutual influence on each other of Skopas and Praxiteles and exemplifies this influence, in particular, by the stylistic analogy between Skopas' Pothos and Praxiteles' Apollo Sauroktonos (pp. 104, 113 f., 170, nn. 1-3). He predicates a meeting between the artists in Asia ca. 360 B.C. But, as Pausanias 1.43.6 reports, *both* Skopas and Praxiteles made groups for the Temple of Aphrodite at Megara. No wonder Skopas' Pothos is Praxitelean in its dependence on a support and its bodily form! This obvious and fundamental literary text is not mentioned by Stewart.

42. A point noted by Kerényi, *op. cit.*, p. 150.

43. 1.43.6 Σκόπα δὲ Ἔρως καὶ Ἵμερος καὶ Πόθος, εἰ δὴ διάφορά ἐστι κατὰ ταὐτὸ τοῖς ὀνόμασι καὶ τὰ ἔργα σφίσι. The translation is that of W. H. S. Jones, *The Loeb Classical Library*, I, 233 ff.

It is a striking fact that in the Megara group, Skopas must have given visual, plastic form to the philosophical, literary imagery of Platonic thought. In the *Cratylos*, 419e-420b ἵμερος (longing), πόθος (yearning), and ἔρως (love) are defined and differentiated. Similar phrases and concepts occur in the *Symposium*, 197D, and *Phaedrus*, 251. See the remarks of Urlichs, *op. cit.*, pp. 91 ff., who has made the persuasive suggestion that Skopas had read Plato and endeavored to give tangible shape to his concepts. Cf., too, the remarks of Becatti, *op. cit.*, p. 407.

Behind the Megara group, there probably lay another, this time figural, tradition. On certain red-figured Attic vases, triads of identical winged youths occur. On a well-known stamnos in London, one is inscribed Himeros, and on a hydria in Berlin, the three bear the names Pothos, Himeros, and Eros. The Megara group appears to reflect knowledge of this iconological type and the shaping of it according to the subtle terms of Platonic concepts. For the personifications of different forms or phases of love—Eros, Himeros, and Pothos—were exceedingly similar in appearance, distinguishable, probably, through their attributes, attitudes, or inscribed base or bases.[44] For the Pothos of this group of closely related figures to be repeatedly copied is understandable; to omit Aphrodite and copy only the Pothos of the Samothracian group is highly unlikely.[45]

It may be worth speculating on the appearance of this lost group. Some light may be shed on the problem by a large terracotta group of Aphrodite and Pothos from Corinth dating from the mid-fourth century B.C. which appears to reflect a cult image (figs. 232 A, B, C).[46] The goddess wears a chiton, which has slipped off one shoulder, and a himation

---

London stamnos, British Museum E440, dated ca. 480 B.C., and attributed to the Siren Painter, see Friedrich Hauser in Furtwängler-Reichhold, ser. III, pp. 25 f., pl. 124; *Kleine Schriften von Adolf Furtwängler* (ed. by Johannes Sieveking and Ludwig Curtius), Munich, 1912, I, p. 7; J. D. Beazley, *Attic Red Figure Vase-Painting*, 2nd edn., Oxford, 1963, I, p. 289, no. 1; Barbara Philippaki, *The Attic Stamnos*, Oxford, 1967, p. 98; for the hydria, Berlin Antiquarium, no. 2633, attributed to the Kadmos Painter, a late fifth-century painter: Beazley, *op. cit.*, p. 1187, no. 32; Karl Anton Neugebauer, *Staatliche Museen zu Berlin, Führer durch das Antiquarium, Vasen*, II, Berlin, 1932, p. 128, pl. 66; G. E. Rizzo, "Vasi greci della Sicilia," *Monumenti antichi*, 14 (1904), cols. 18, 39-42, pl. 2; *Kleine Schriften*, pp. 13 f. Here, discussing this scene of the Judgment of Paris in an essay written in 1874, "Eros in der Vasenmalerei," Furtwängler, too, suggested that Skopas was the first to have created the plastic type of Eros, Himeros, and Pothos and cited the previous passages in Plato.

On another vase attributed to the Kadmos Painter, a volute krater in the Jatta Collection in Ruvo, no. 1093, the winged youths Eros, Himeros, Pothos appear in a scene of Dionysos and his thiasos. Here, however, Aphrodite is missing. See Beazley, *op. cit.*, p. 1184, no. 1; Heinrich Heydemann, "Satyr- und Bakchennamen," *Fünftes Hallisches Winckelsmannsprogramm*, 1880, pp. 5-10, 17 f., plate; Hellmut Sichtermann, *Griechische Vasen in Unteritalien aus der Sammlung Jatta in Ruvo*, Tübingen, 1966, pp. 20 f., no. 10, pls. 12, 17.

44. One thinks of other virtually identical triads like the Graces and the Seasons. Here, however, these personifications have been subtly differentiated. See above, n. 43.

One of the replicas of the Pothos-type faces left and is one of the five extant copies provided with wings or having traces of them. (It is in the Palazzo Vecchio in Florence; see Becatti, *op. cit.*, pl. CXLVI, figs. 11, 12, where it is incorrectly labeled Museo Archeologico.) A similar painted figure, facing left and wearing an identical melon coiffure, occurs in the Villa of the Mysteries at Pompeii (see Amadeo Maiuri, *La villa dei misteri*, Rome, 1931, pl. XIV). Reinhard Herbig, *Neue Beobachtungen am Fries der Mysterien-Villa in Pompeji* (*Deutsche Beiträge zur Altertumswissenschaft*, no. 10), Baden-Baden, 1958, p. 38, has noted that this cross-legged boy is related to the Florentine copy of Skopas' Pothos. (Otto Brendel, "Der grosse Fries in der Villa dei misteri," *JdI*, [1966], p. 242, followed Herbig in pointing out that the position and mood of this painted Eros reflect the statuary type of Pothos.) The attribute of the painted figure is a bow and he is, obviously, an Eros. The arms of the Florentine figure are restored. Are these variations on the Eros of Skopas' group?

45. The discovery of the previously mentioned pair of replicas in a very incompletely excavated Roman villa would seem to bear out this point. The third statue of the triad may have existed in a third room. The two statues in the Uffizi came from the Villa Medici in Rome in 1780, where a third replica, now in the Palazzo Vecchio, existed. (See Guido A. Mansuelli, *Galleria degli Uffizi, Le sculture*, Rome, I, 1958, pp. 53 ff., **31**, **32**.) Did they, too, come from one villa or site?

46. In the National Archaeological Museum, Athens, no. 4160. Height: 0.28 m. Semni Papaspyridi-Karouzou, *Ἑλληνιστικὰ ἀντίγραφα καὶ ἐπαναλήψεις ἀρχαίων ἔργωη*, *Ἀρχαιολογικὴ Ἐφημερίς*, 1956, pp. 175 ff., figs. 7-10, pl. 6. Previously published by Franz Winter, *Die Typenfigürlichen Terrakotten* (*Die antiken Terrakotten*, III²), II, Berlin and Stuttgart, 1903, p. 6, no. 5; Wolfgang Züchner, *Griechische Klappspiegel* (*JdI*, suppl. vol. 14), Berlin, 1942, pp. 177, 188, fig. 90; G. Kleiner, *Tanagrafiguren* (*JdI*, suppl. vol. 15), Berlin, 1942, pp. 168

232. Terracotta group of Aphrodite and Pothos from Corinth. Athens, National Archaeological Museum.

drawn over the low polos that rests on her long tresses. She stands at ease, one hand braced against her hip, the other clasping the winged boy, who clings to her arm and stands cross-legged—in the very posture of the Pothos from the Skopaic group at Megara.

This draped goddess wearing a polos is not the normal nude Aphrodite of later Greek art. Clearly, she is a form of the Great Mother and, as such, wears the costume and headgear of that all-powerful divinity who presided over the fertility of life.[47] She is the Aphrodite of the Homeric *Hymn to Aphrodite* equated with the Meter Theron on Mt. Ida, "the mother of wild creatures."[48] In Corinth, as in Samothrace, she was a mountain goddess. There she was worshiped on the summit of Acrocorinth,[49] "the sacred hill-city of Aphrodite,"[50] where many terracotta figurines of draped figures of the goddess or her votaries wearing chiton, himation, and often, too, a polos have been found.[51] In Samothrace, as we have seen, the Great Mother appears on Hellenistic coins similarly clad and wearing a polos (fig. 189).[52]

Although one can only speculate on the appearance of Skopas' Samothracian Aphrodite, the fact that the Great Mother worshiped in the Sanctuary under varied names, including that of Aphrodite, was shown on the city's coinage in this guise makes it tempting to suggest that it may have been this particular form of the Great Goddess-Aphrodite that Skopas represented in his group—that she appeared in the form of the Great Mother. If so, the contemporary terracotta group from Corinth in which Aphrodite wears the garments and headgear of the Great Mother may afford some insight into the generic character of that lost group. The previously mentioned terracotta head of a veiled female divinity or votary wearing a low polos above her long tresses (figs. 190, 233) seems to bear out this point.[53] This head, it will be recalled, is a fragment of a dedication found in the Samothracian Sanctuary. It bears a marked resemblance to the Aphrodite of the Corinthian group. Hence, it is tempting to regard it as a contemporary, if simplified, replica of

---

f., pl. 37c. Mrs. Karouzou had suggested in this article that the group reflected a cult statue of Aphrodite and Eros that stood in this city especially devoted to her worship. I am glad to report that in the course of valuable conversations with Mrs. Karouzou early in the winter of 1970, she agreed that the cross-legged, winged boy accompanying the goddess could as well be Pothos as Eros.

47. For the interrelationship between the Anatolian Great Mother and the Greek Aphrodite (herself of Semitic origin), see Nilsson, I, pp. 489 ff. For Aphrodite, W. H. Roscher and Adolf Furtwängler in Roscher, I[1], *s.v. Aphrodite*, cols. 390-419; F. Dümmler in *RE*, I, Stuttgart, 1894, *s.v. Aphrodite*, cols. 2729-2787. For the polos, see above, Chap. III, p. 221 and nn. 129, 131.

48. 5, lines 68 ff. Cf., too, Hesychius, *Lexicon*, *s.v.* Κυβήβη. *ἡ μήτηρ τῶν θεῶν. καὶ ἡ* Ἀφροδίτην . . .

49. Strabo 8.6.21; Pausanias 2.5.1. See, too, *RE*, *s.v. Korinthos*, suppl. vol. IV, Stuttgart, 1924, col. 1006.

50. Euripides, frg. 1084.

51. Agnes M. Stillwell, *The Potter's Quarter, The Terracottas* (*Corinth*, XV, 2), Princeton, 1952, pp. 7 f., pls. 3, I, 32, 40, 41; 16, X, 27, 34, for a few examples, and Gladys R. Davidson, "A Hellenistic Deposit at Corinth" *Hesperia*, 11 (1942), especially pp. 113 ff.

52. See above, p. 221.

53. See above, Chap. III, n. 133.

233. Terracotta head from the Sanctuary. Samothrace Museum.

the lost figure of Aphrodite.[54] Is the terracotta group from Corinth a very general replica of Skopas' lost group? Neither the Samothracian head nor the Corinthian group is Skopaic in style. But the stance of Pothos and the raiment and headgear of Aphrodite in the Corinthian group provide a clue to basic features of that lost group.[55] Indeed this terracotta group may provide more than a clue.

Pausanias reports that the Temple of Aphrodite at Elis contained a chryselephantine cult statue of Aphrodite Ourania by Pheidias. Adjacent to it was "a temenos . . . surrounded by a wall, and within the temenos has been made a base, and on this base there sits a bronze statue of Aphrodite on a bronze he-goat. This is a work of Skopas, and the Aphrodite is named Pandemos."[56] Once again, this is a lost work of the master. But this evidently

54. One other terracotta fragment of a female figure, a head wearing a polos over her long tresses, was found to the east of the Propylon of Ptolemy II. This fragment was one of scores of terracotta figures or fragments discovered in this area that seem to have come from an unexcavated sanctuary lying outside the main Sanctuary. They were unearthed in an effort to follow the line of the processional road leading from the city to the Sanctuary. The head, apparently Hellenistic in date, comes from a group of as yet incompletely accessioned figurines, Acc. No. 70.648, which included a quantity of hydrophoroi dating from the late sixth century to the early Roman period. I am indebted to Elsbeth B. Dusenbery for this information.

For hydrophoroi, a type of figurine connected primarily with the cult of Demeter, see J. N. Coldstream, *Knossos, The Sanctuary of Demeter* (*BSA*, suppl. vol. 8), London, 1973, pp. 68-70, nos. 61-70. I am indebted to Nancy Bookidis for this reference. In the present context, it is especially interesting to note that hydrophoroi have also been found in the Sanctuary of Aphrodite Euploia at Knidos. See Iris Cornelia Love, "Excavations at Knidos 1972," *Türk Arkeologi Dergisi*, 21, 2 (1974), p. 901, figs. 71-73.

55. Picard, *op. cit.*, III, p. 694, has suggested that the Pothos of the Samothracian group must have been similar to the Pothos of the group at Megara. More than a hundred years ago, Urlichs, *op. cit.*, pp. 101 ff., suggested that the Aphrodite of Skopas' group at Samothrace was equivalent to Kybele or Rhea and at least partially clad.

The interpretation of Skopas' group by C. Fredrich, "Lemnos," *AthMitt*, 31 (1906), p. 79, as Axieros and *Axiokersa* is totally confused. Arias, p. 62, n. 2, should have equated Aphrodite with Axieros not Axiokersa.

56. Pausanias 6.25.1. *τῆς δὲ περιέχεται μὲν τὸ τέμενος θριγκῷ, κρηπὶς δὲ ἐντὸς τοῦ τεμένους πεποίηται καὶ ἐπὶ τῇ κρηπῖδι ἄγαλμα Ἀφροδίτης χαλκοῦν ἐπὶ τράγῳ κάθηται χαλκῷ. Σκόπα τοῦτο ἔργον, Ἀφροδίτην δὲ Πάνδημον ὀνομάξουσι.*

famous statue was used as a coin type on the imperial coinage of Elis (fig. 234).[57] Like the Samothracian goddess, this Aphrodite is fully clad. Over her chiton, she wears a himation drawn up to serve as a veil that billows about her as she rides her leaping beast. Although no statuary replicas of the group exist, there are reflections of it in a wide variety of media.[58] None is more beautiful than a fine fourth-century mirror cover in the Louvre (fig. 235).[59] In Athens, too, there was a Sanctuary of Aphrodite Pandemos south of the bastion of the Temple of Athena Nike.[60] There her image seems to have been identical in type with the group in Elis, to judge by marble reliefs found in the vicinity.[61] Presumably the Athenian statue was not the work of Skopas.[62]

The implication of these analogous fourth-century types in Elis and Athens is that the groups in Samothrace and Corinth may also have been identical in type, and that the terracotta group from Corinth may well preserve both the type and the appearance of Skopas' lost group of Aphrodite and Pothos.

In his group of Aphrodite and Pothos, Skopas seems to have created a new statuary

57. First observed by Rudolf Weil, "Olympische Miscellen," *Historische und philosophische Aufsätze Ernst Curtius*, Berlin, 1884, pp. 134 f., pl. 3, fig. 8; F. Imhoof-Blumer and Percy Gardner, "A Numismatic Commentary on Pausanias," *JHS*, 7 (1886), pp. 76 f., fig. on p. 73, pl. P, XXIV; Lacroix, pp. 316 f., pl. XXVIII, 5. The type occurs on bronze coins of Hadrian, Septimius Severus, and Caracalla.

58. E.g., among others, on Kertsch hydrias dating from ca. 370-320 B.C.: Karl Schefold, *Untersuchungen zu den Kertscher Vasen*, Berlin and Leipzig, 1934, p. 17, **142**, p. 25, **195**, pl. 10, 1, fig. 29, pl. 139, figs. 4, 5; as a terracotta figurine type: Edmond Pottier and Salomon Reinach, *La Nécropole de Myrina*, Paris, 1887, pp. 293 ff., pl. VI, 2; on a lead tessera: *Monumenti inediti*, 8 (1864-1868), pl. 52, no. 304.

On this statue, its meaning, and reflections, see Adolf Furtwängler, *Kleine Schriften*, Munich, 1913, II, p. 475 ff. The date of this group has been disputed. But Urlichs, *op. cit.*, pp. 5 ff., was probably correct in assuming that it was an early work because of its material, pointing out that Skopas normally worked in marble and that this bronze group may have been executed while he was under the influence of his father, the sculptor Aristandros, whose reported work was of bronze. The earliest reflection of this group may be its appearance on the Berlin hydria, now dated ca. 370 B.C. Stewart, p. 93, dates the group ca. 370 and Schlörb, *op. cit.*, p. 59, and n. 182, has also dated it in the seventies.

59. No. 1707. First published by Maxime Collignon, "Aphrodite Pandémos," *MonPiot*, 1 (1894), pp. 143-150, pl. XX, who has discussed the entire problem of Skopas' group and its reflections. For a more recent reference: Züchner, *op. cit.*, pp. 7 f., KS 4, pl. 6, who considers it Corinthian and to be dated ca. 375 B.C.

See, too, the related image on a gold-plated silver medallion found in a grave at Beroia dating from the second century B.C. now in the Archaeological Museum at Thessaloniki. *Treasures of Ancient Macedonia, Athens* [1979], p. 43, no. 55, pl. 12.

60. R. E. Wycherley, "Achaia Agora," *Phoenix*, 20 (1966), pp. 286 ff.; Luigi Beschi, "Contributi di topografia ateniese," *Annuario*, 29-30 (1967-68), pp. 522 ff.; A. N. Oikonomides, *The Two Agoras in Ancient Athens*, Chicago, 1964, pp. 2 ff.; Ida Thallon Hill, *The Ancient City of Athens*, London, 1953, pp. 131 f.; Jane E. Harrison, *The Mythology and Monuments of Ancient Athens*, London, 1890, pp. 331 ff. An inscribed lintel dating in the third quarter of the fourth century B.C. from the chapel of the goddess refers to her as "great and holy."

61. I.N. *Σβορῶνος, Τό ἐν 'Αθήναις, 'Εθνικόν Μουσεῖον*, Athens, 1903, pl. CLVII, no. 2422, found on the south slope of the Akropolis. See F. von Duhn, "Griechische Reliefs," *AZ*, 35 (1877), p. 158, no. 58. A second relief, now in the Louvre, evidently has a similar provenance. See Collignon, *op. cit.*, pp. 147 ff., fig. 2. See addendum, p. 302.

62. Pausanias 1.22.3 comments that the statues of Aphrodite Pandemos and Peitho "were the work of no inferior artists."

234. Reverse of a bronze coin of Elis. Berlin, Staatliche Museen.

235. Bronze mirror cover. Paris, Musée du Louvre.

236. Detail from the east frieze of the Parthenon (restored cast by J. E. Platt). London, The British Museum.

type.[63] Previously, Aphrodite had been represented as an independent figure. Now a type earlier known in relief, the goddess with a winged boy familiar from the east frieze of the Parthenon (fig. 236), has been shaped into a free-standing statuary group. The maternal overtones of Aphrodite's relationship to Eros on the frieze must have been altered in Skopas' group, since the goddess was probably a standing figure. Yet on the frieze, too, the boy is supported by the goddess, and there, too, his legs appear to be slightly crossed. Conceivably, in the Samothracian group, the figure of Pothos regarded Aphrodite with the ardent longing of the Pothos of the Megara group. Thus in Samothrace, as in his even more complex group of Eros, Pothos, and Himeros in Megara, Skopas appears to have created another, new statuary type.[64]

63. As Urlichs, *op. cit.*, p. 102, had noted.

64. The relief form continued, too, witness a fine mirror in the British Museum, acc. no. 292, dating from the third quarter of the fourth century B.C., which shows on its cover Aphrodite and a figure who is probably Pothos not Eros as he has been generally called. For a recent discussion of this mirror, see Züchner, *op. cit.*, KS 14, pp. 13 f., pls. 24, 25. As Becatti has pointed out, "Il Pothos di Scopa," p. 410, the cast of a relief on the cheekpiece of a helmet in

Where did the group stand in the Samothracian Sanctuary? The cult buildings in Samothrace, the Anaktoron and the Hieron, were not temples but buildings for congregational worship. Hence they lacked cult images. The only logical place for the group to stand was in the Temenos,[65] an open precinct surrounded by a wall analogous to the Temenos of Aphrodite Pandemos in Elis within which stood Skopas' statue of Aphrodite mounted on a goat. And if Skopas was designing architect-sculptor of the Propylon to the Temenos, as there is reason to assume, the suggestion that his group once stood in this precinct gains in credibility. At Tegea, too, in addition to having been designing architect-sculptor of the temple, he made the cult statues of Asklepios and Hygeia flanking the older ivory image of Athena Alea by Endoios.[66]

Given the date of the Propylon and the Temenos, it is reasonable to assume that Skopas' group of Aphrodite and Pothos dated from the same time, ca. 340 B.C., although, theoretically, it could have been a later addition to the Temenos.[67]

---

a private collection in Berlin (Gerhart Rodenwaldt, *Die Kunst der Antike*, Berlin, 1927, p. 348) presents Aphrodite and Eros in a more romantic fashion than that of the figures on the Panathenaic frieze that is a prelude to the emotional character of Skopas' Pothos. For a splendid characterization of this cheekpiece, see Bernard Ashmole, "Some Nameless Sculptors of the Fifth Century B.C.," *Proceedings of the British Academy*, 48 (1962), pp. 232 f.

65. As was suggested by Karl Lehmann, *Hesperia*, 21 (1952), p. 29, and *Guide*⁴, p. 64. The earlier suggestion that Skopas' group was the cult image in the "Old Temple," that is, stood in the building assumed to have occupied the area that has proved to be an open precinct, was not far removed from this hypothesis. See, for example, Otto Benndorf in *S,II*, p. 101; Rubensohn, pp. 141 f.; and Bieber, *Skopas*, p. 118 (above, Chap. II, n. 206).

66. Pausanias 8.46.1-47-1. See A. Delivorrias, "News from Arcadia and Laconia," *AAA*, 1 (1968), pp. 121 f., fig. 1 on p. 118, for a newly found torso that may be a fragment of the statue of Hygeia.

In *Hesperia*, 21 (1952), p. 29, fig. 1 and Pl. 6A, right background, Professor Lehmann reported the existence of a fieldstone foundation which he interpreted as a support for the base of Skopas' group. After this foundation had been recorded and photographed, it was removed in the interest of further excavation in this area of the Temenos adjacent to the north wall of the precinct. Hence I have found it impossible to check on the character of this foundation. From the evidence dictated into the daily diaries for the relevant days in June and July of 1950 and the available photographs, I, myself, do not believe that this foundation was a support for the group of Aphrodite and Pothos. I interpret it as part of the fieldstone packing that supported the marble floor and porous limestone underpavement of the Temenos. It should be pointed out that this section of the fieldstone packing does *not* appear in Pl. I, the plan of the extant Temenos, Propylon, and terrace. Stewart, p. 172, n. 73, was unaware of this fact.

67. Pierre Devambez, "Sculptures thasiennes," *BCH*, 66-67 (1942-43), pp. 204 ff., figs. 2, 3, pl. X, has drawn attention to a Skopaic head found in the Agora of Thasos that he suggested was executed by one of Skopas' best pupils, who had accompanied the master to Samothrace to finish or install the group of Aphrodite and Pothos there and, under the influence of Pothos, went to Thasos to create a stylistically related statue. Stewart, p. 115, pl. 47b,c, has accepted Devambez's statement. Devambez assumed that the figure in the Conservatori Museum (above, fig. 231) was a copy of the Samothracian group rather than of the group in Megara. But inasmuch as the Samothracian and Megarian Pothoi appear to have been related, his comparison is understandable. In any case, he assumed that Skopas was physically present simply to work on the sculptured group.

One other head found in the Samothracian Sanctuary is Skopaic in style. Inasmuch as it was not found in the Temenos, it should not be included in this chapter. Yet, since it may be useful to have all Skopaic sculptures found in Samothrace dealt with in this volume, it is included in a short Appendix, for which see below, p. 303.

What was the function of the Temenos? First of all, ceremonies connected with the ritual installations in the precinct clearly took place there, rites celebrated at the bothros and eschara involving sacrifices to the chthonic divinities and to the hero-founder of the cult.[68] Secondly, a ritual drama was doubtless performed there since, as yet, no theater existed in the Sanctuary.[69] As we have seen, according to the fourth-century historian Ephoros, a contemporary of Philip II, whose history of Macedon reached the year 340 B.C., a sacred drama connected with Kadmos and Harmonia was performed at the Samothracian festivals, in all likelihood in this very precinct accessible to initiate and uninitiate alike. He states: "Kadmos carried her [that is, Harmonia] off when he sailed by Samothrace. . . . And even now in Samothrace they go in quest of her in their festivals."[70] Presumably, this search was followed by the ensuing episode, the wedding, for which the gods provided the marriage feast, as Diodorus so graphically reports.[71] As we have seen, the Wedding of Kadmos and Harmonia would have been an appropriate theme for the lost central portion of the frieze of the Propylon.[72]

What more appropriate place for Skopas' group of Aphrodite and Pothos to stand, Aphrodite Zerynthia, goddess of fertility, than in this Temenos?[73] Aphrodite, Kybele, the Magna Mater—by whatever name she was "worshiped at Samothrace with the most sacred ceremonies"[74]—in whose rites the choruses of maidens danced clad, like the goddess, in chiton, mantle, and polos, those dancing maidens seemingly echoed on the frieze of the Propylon.[75] According to the majority of ancient authors, Harmonia was the daughter of Aphrodite.[76] A few believed that Elektra was her mother.[77] Nonnus, evidently attempting

68. See above, p. 82.

69. For the theater, dated in the second century B.C., see Fernand Chapouthier, Antoine Salač, François Salviat, "Le Théâtre de Samothrace," *BCH*, 80 (1956), pp. 118 ff.; *Guide*[4], p. 77.

70. Scholia to Euripides *Phoenissae* 7 (*Samothrace*, Vol. 1, **75**).

71. See above, Chap. III, p. 231 f. and n. 165. The assumption that the Wedding was also included in the dramatic performances of the festival is an old one. Cf. Kern, *RE, s.v. Kabeiros, Kaberioi*, col. 1428 f.

72. See above, pp. 232 f.

73. In Samothrace, the epithet Zerynthia was applied to Aphrodite. See Suidas, *s.v.* *Ζηρυνθία. ἡ Ἀφροδίτη* and Etymologicum Magnum *s.v.* *Ζηρυνθία: Ἀφροδίτη ἐν Θρᾴκῃ* (*Samothrace*, Vol. 1, **155**, **155a**). Zerynthus was also the cave of Hekate (Vol. 1, **53**, **152-154**, **156**, **226a**), for whom the same epithet might be appropriate. For Aphrodite in Samothrace, see Hemberg, pp. 85 f., 120 f.

The connection between Aphrodite and weddings is obvious. Pausanias 3.13.9 refers to an old wooden statue of Aphrodite Hera in Sparta and comments: "A mother is wont to sacrifice to the goddess when a daughter is married."

For Aphrodite as a goddess of fertility, presiding not only over the fruitfulness of people and animals but also over the fruitfulness of plants, see Roscher, I[1], *s.v. Aphrodite*, cols. 392 f. The luxuriant plant motifs in the sculptural and ornamental decoration of the Propylon may reflect this concept.

74. Pliny *Naturalis historia* 36.5.25 (*Samothrace*, Vol. 1, **160**).

75. The reader will recall the analogous dances performed to Hera in her temenos in Lesbos documented by the *Anthologia Palatina* 9.189 and Schol. A D to *Iliad* I, 129.

76. The normal antique tradition. Cf. *RE, s.v. Harmonia*, vol. VIII, Stuttgart, 1912, cols. 2379 ff. In the Samothracian sources, Euripides (Vol. 1, **75**).

77. Among the Samothracian sources, Vol. 1, **32**, **67**, **70**, **70a**.

to bridge the two traditions, speaks of Harmonia as a "maiden immigrant from heaven, whom Aphrodite . . . carried, a suckling lying in her arms, to the fostering house of Elektra."[78] Aphrodite, goddess of the Moon,[79] Elektra, the Shining One, are they not one and the same? Whoever has seen the full moon rise over the mountain and shine over the open Temenos in the Sanctuary of the Great Gods will understand this mystery.

Thus the relationship between Aphrodite and Harmonia, of Aphrodite, goddess of fertility, and her child Pothos, implies, once again, that the presence of Skopas' group in the precinct where the Wedding of Harmonia to Kadmos seems to have been performed was an appropriate one.[80] The cult of Aphrodite attested in the earliest dedications in the depths below the later Temenos[81] has proved to be a significant feature in the history and function of the precinct.

Finally, if Philip II of Macedon was, indeed, the donor of the Propylon, it probably was he, rather than Skopas, who selected the theme of the frieze to emphasize the parallelism between his own life and that of the heroic past.

237. View of the terrace wall from the northeast.

From the northern wing of the Propylon, one might pass to a broad, open terrace retained by a lofty, pseudopolygonal terrace wall rising high above the river to its west (figs. 34-38, 237).[82] Like the Temenos, this terrace was paved with marble, and from it, one might look

78. Vol. 1, 74.

79. See Roscher, I^1, *s.v. Aphrodite*, col. 391. Regarding Aphrodite in Samothrace, it is significant that, as Elsbeth B. Dusenbery informs me, among all the terracotta figurines found in the nekropoleis associated with the Sanctuary of the Great Gods, the only types representing a divinity are various forms of Aphrodite, together with other subordinate or ritual figures connected with her circle.

80. Regarding the significance of Aphrodite, a passage in Aeschylos' *Suppliants*, lines 1034 ff., is of interest: "for she [Kypris], together with Hera, hath power most near to Zeus, and for her august rites (ἔργοις ἐπὶ σεμνοῖς) the goddess of varied wiles is held in honor. And in the train of their mother are Desire (or Yearning, Πόθος) and she to whom nothing is denied, ever winning Persuasion (Πειθώ); and to Harmonia hath been given a share of Aphrodite" (translation by H. W. Smyth, Loeb Classical Library, I, pp. 101 ff.).

81. Above, p. 269.

82. The platform or terrace wall for the late

northward toward the sea and the distant coast of Thrace. At least from the late Hellenistic period on, the terrace was provided with benches. The elegant marble supports for these benches were inserted into thin marble containers let into the pavement (Pl. LIV.2; figs. 238 A, B).[83] Each side of the support is carved with an identical pattern. The presumably wooden seat rested on two large volutes rising from lion's paws. Above the paws, the legs are subdivided or paneled by sharply defined vertical fillets. At the bottom, above the paws, the legs are decorated with three, tiny patera-like studs. Between each volute and the lateral face of each leg, an arrow-shaped shoot emerges. Together, they point toward the central motif of the support: a great upside-down or hanging lotus flower. Two crisp, curving petals on each side flank another arrow-shaped central petal. The acanthus calyx is composed of two fluent, curling leaves whose lobes are separated by deeply drilled holes. The motif is closely related to the upright lotus flowers on the raking sima of the late fourth-century Hieron (fig. 239)[84] but the style of the calyx is closer to the acanthus calyx of the second-century floral akroterion of the Hieron.[85] The effect of this composition is abstract, linear, and calligraphic. The visible portion of the supports ends in a horizontal fillet below which a roughly cut tang projects for insertion into its container. On a second fragment of such a support, the resting surface for the wooden bench is partially preserved (figs. 240 A, B).[86] It confirms the existence of this feature on the complete support. Today,

---

fourth-century Temple of Hemithea at Kastabos is somewhat related in construction to the terrace wall before the Temenos. In both, roughly shaped ashlar blocks of various sizes are combined with polygonal blocks, creating a somewhat disorderly effect. See Cook-Plommer, pl. IV, 2-5.

83. 49.412. Height: 0.455 m.; width, 0.695 m.; width of leg: 0.16 m. The actual seat must have been of wood, judging by the character of the upper surface of this marble support and the fact that it lacks any dowel hole for the attachment of a marble seat.

This support, seen by the Austrians in the school in Chora, where it was correctly reported to have come from Palaiopolis, had passed into the collection of marbles in Hagios Demetrios in that village before we transported it to the Museum in Palaiopolis. Conze (*S.I.*, pp. 23, 76 and pl. 47) had ascribed it to the pronaos of the "Dorischer Marmortempel," because of the discovery of related feet and volutes north of that building. In *Hesperia*, 20 (1951), p. 25, pl. 13d, it was tentatively attributed to the installation of the southern part of the cella, because of the recovery of related fragments in that part of the building. Later, when it was observed that the feet found in or near the Hieron lacked the lower tang characteristic of this example, and that the bases standing on the terrace were equipped with such tangs for insertion into separate bases, it became clear that this particular support belonged to the category of bench located on this terrace. Three such containers or bases were found on the terrace (see Pl. LIV.2). This bench support was later mounted in one of these bases and is, at present, in the center of Hall C. See *Guide*, p. 80; *Guide*^{2}, p. 83, *Guide*^{3}, p. 87; *Guide*^{4}, p. 109. Although the specific base in which it stands does not fit to a centimeter (i.e., it was not made for this particular support), in type, the two belong together. Previously published in Vol. 3, text I, pp. 148 ff., figs. 101, 102.

84. *Ibid.*, p. 77, fig. 131.

85. *Ibid.*, figs. 282, 302.

86. Acc. No. 53.465. In storage. Broken at top, rear, and bottom. Preserved height: 0.195 m.; preserved width: 0.33 m.; width of upper leg: 0.135 m. Found east of the porch of the Hieron. In view of post-antique activity in the area of the Temenos, and of the previous excavations and dumps left in this vicinity by our predecessors, this fact is of no significance. Another fragmentary support of this variety, No. 49.386, was discovered north of the terrace wall next to the best-preserved Ionic column shaft of the Propylon. An unnumbered fragmentary lion's foot in the storeroom of the Kunsthistorisches Museum in Vienna belongs to this same group.

238. A, B. Late Hellenistic bench support. Samothrace Museum.

239. Fragment of the southern raking sima of the Hieron. Samothrace Museum.

240. A, B. Fragment of a bench support. Samothrace Museum.

241. A, B. Fragmentary statue base.

it is no longer present, but in the nineteenth century, when it was drawn by Hauser, it existed.[87]

At the foot of the grey crystalline porphyry terrace wall and posed on bedrock, there is a remnant of what seems to have been a base for a statue (Pls. I, II.4; figs. 241 A, B).[88] Originally longer than it is today, its oblong shape suggests, even now, that it may have supported an equestrian figure. The bedrock on which the terrace wall, too, was built has

87. See *S,I*, pl. 47.

88. Width: 1.35 m.; preserved length: 3.40 m. The anathyrosis on the last block on the eastern face indicates that the base must have been at least one block longer. The extant base is two courses high at its southern end and its eastern face reaches in 0.15 m. behind the face of the terrace wall—an indication that base and wall were probably contemporary. The base is composed of two faces separated by a rubble fill that has been divided into compartments by thin transverse blocks. According to Professor Lawrence Majewski of the Institute of Fine Arts, the technical name for this stone is amygdaloidal basalt (lava).

A number of additional blocks from this base that were not found *in situ* have been assembled nearby, close to the modern river retaining wall.

In the last edition of the *Guide*[4], p. 66, and in the article on Samothrace in *The Princeton Encyclopedia of Classical Sites*, Princeton, 1976, p. 804, I have mistakenly suggested that this fragmentary base might be a section of "wall" and reflect an earlier, seventh-century temenos or sanctuary. This was clearly an error. The "wall" has no foundation nor is there adequate space between it and the river to allow for however small a precinct.

been cut back to receive this base which must have been ca. 1.50 m. high. Built of local red porphyry, its ashlar masonry contrasted vividly with the grey pseudopolygonal terrace wall.

Slightly to the east of this wall and roughly aligned with it is a conspicuous rock altar (Pls. I, III.4; figs. 242, 243).[89] The carefully dressed bedrock on which the main blocks of the altar stood is approximately level with the line of the bedrock beneath the terrace wall (figs. 237, 242). To erect this altar, the rocky cliff to its east that curves northward toward the Rotunda of Arsinoe and rises ca. 4 m. higher than this lowest level has been pared back.

The major block of this rock altar is of crystalline porphyry related to the stone of the terrace wall. This huge boulder has been carefully trimmed so that its sides are roughly parallel and its top and bottom approximately level. Adjacent to it at the west and south were two smaller boulders, each of which has fallen out of position, but the dressing of their surfaces indicates their original application to the major boulder. Other smaller stones were fitted in between the main triad and the latter once stood on the dressed down bedrock that served as a platform for the altar. This platform was once framed by a marine limestone step resting on a single foundation course. Today only one block of the step is *in situ* at the northeastern corner of the altar, and the lower foundation course is preserved only along the eastern side and partially at the south, where, originally, a double width formed a *prothysis* on which the priest stood. The shattered fragments at present visible beneath the western boulder would have been invisible when the western step was in place.[90]

When the altar was excavated, the lead swallowtailed clamps that originally linked the foundation course beneath the step were *in situ* (fig. 244).[91] This form of clamp, particularly characteristic of archaic architecture, continued in use through the fourth century B.C. and even later.[92] It is especially interesting that in the pavement slabs of the South

89. Found in 1950. Published by Karl Lehmann in *Hesperia*, 21 (1952), p. 33, pl. 76; *ibid.*, 22 (1953), pp. 22 ff., pl. 8e,f.

90. Length of original altar: ca. 1.75 m.; height of main boulder: 0 58 m. above step; average width of foundation course below step: 0.43 m. One block of this foundation course is of yellow tufa and was evidently a spoil. Thus this rock altar included a variety of materials: the porphyry boulder, the marine limestone steps and foundation course, and the tufa spoil.

The severely damaged state of this rock altar reflects the post-antique chaos in this area of the excavation, for which see below, pp. 299 f., and the fact that in 1956, after the torrential rains of November 1955, we found that one of the lesser boulders at the southwest had been dislodged and splintered. It was repaired at the time.

91. Stolen by local vandals some time after 1954, when the photographs illustrated above were made. As a result of this theft, it appears that the cuttings for these clamps are singular. The lead clamps were equipped with the customary iron pins. The cutting on one block was normal: a shallow swallowtail cutting with a deeper rectangular hole for the iron Π-clamp; for its mate, in which the other side of the clamp was fastened, only the rectangular cutting for the Π-clamp was made—that is, it lacks the usual shallow, swallowtailed cutting on the matching block.

92. Roland Martin, *Manuel d'architecture grecque*, I, Paris, 1965, pp. 238-254; Ejnar Dyggve and Frederik Poulsen, *Das Laphrion, Der Tempelbezirk von Kalydon*, Copenhagen, 1948, pp. 260-262. In the fabric of the nearly contemporary fourth-century Hieron, very slightly flaring swallowtailed clamps were used to link the marble blocks to their porous backers (see Vol. 3, text I, pp. 46 ff.). Here, however, no additional iron Π-clamp was used.

242. Rock altar, seen from the northeast.

243. Rock altar, seen from the southwest.

244. Detail of lost swallow-tailed clamps on foundation for step of Rock Altar.

Propylaea at Labraunda, a building that has proved so relevant to the architectural discussion of the Propylon to the Temenos, precisely this form of clamp was used.[93] The foundation course was set in a fill of black mud containing a sparse amount of black-glazed sherds dating from the fourth century B.C.[94] The altar, therefore, was contemporary with the Temenos and terrace.[95] Again, fragments of lamb bones were found in the fill of this altar.[96]

Rock altars are characteristic of the Samothracian Sanctuary. The great archaic rock altar that preceded the Altar Court,[97] the Sacred Rock to the southwest of the Rotunda of Arsinoe,[98] the altar in the Double Precinct,[99] all testify to this fact. Even the natural porphyry rock on which libations were poured in the bothros of the Hieron[100] reflects the same practice. But these altars were outcroppings of natural rock, whereas the altar to the east of the terrace was man-made.

To what divinity or divinities was this rock altar dedicated? The others, especially the predecessor of the Altar Court, seem to have been dedicated to the collective Great Gods. Yet it is conceivable that this altar was dedicated to the divinity seemingly honored in the Temenos adjacent to it—the Great Goddess-Kybele-Axieros, in the form of Aphrodite Zerynthia.[101]

93. *Labraunda*, pp. 8 f., fig. 5 B.

94. Insufficiently preserved to be catalogued. See general statement, p. 383.

95. In his discussions of this rock altar (above, n. 89), Professor Lehmann dated it in the sixth century B.C. and, considering that only the largest boulder belonged to the original period, assumed that the other boulders were additions intended to support a later, hypothetical altar at a higher level contemporary with the fourth-century Propylon. This theory involved the assumption that in the fourth century B.C., access to this lowest level of the central sanctuary was no longer possible. This assumption, as we now know, was incorrect (see below, p. 296). Although swallowtailed clamps were standard in the archaic period, they also occur in other surely dated fourth-century buildings (above, nn. 92, 93), and the few, undecorated black-glazed potsherds, once considered archaic in character, proved in 1974 to be fourth century B.C. in date. Hence the altar is clearly fourth century in date and contemporary with the Propylon. This in itself—quite apart from the fact that it would have been necessary to reach other monuments at this low level of the Sanctuary before the construction of the Rotunda and the radical changes of level that this construction entailed—means that it was still essential in the fourth century B.C. to descend to this lower level from the Eastern Hill. For the further implications of these facts in regard to the presumed spring theoretically adjacent to this rock altar, see below, n. 104.

96. Again, we are indebted to Dr. Edwin Colbert of the American Museum of Natural History in New York City for having examined and identified these bones.

97. Vol. 4, pt. II, p. 109.

98. *Hesperia*, 20 (1951), pp. 3 f.

99. *Ibid.*, 19 (1950), p. 8; 20 (1951), p. 2.

100. Vol. 3, text I, pp. 131 ff., text II, p. 44.

101. Professor Lehmann believed that this was an altar to Hekate (*Hesperia*, 22 [1953], pp. 23 f.; *Guide*, pp. 55 f.; *Guide*², *Guide*³, pp. 56 f.; *Guide* ⁴, pp. 60 f.). He interpreted the rocky cliff and bedrock in the area of the altar as a half-natural, half-artificial "cave" of Hekate and linked it with the legendary Zerynthian Cave of Hekate attested by the literary sources on Samothrace (Vol. 1, **53**, **152**, **153**, **154**, **155**, **156**, **226e**). The discovery of what appeared to be a pyramid-like object near the altar that was interpreted as an aniconic symbol of Hekate (*Hesperia*, 22 [1953], p. 24, pl. 6f.) seemed to bear out this view. In the meantime, this object has been recognized as a fragment of a marble building block (Theodor Kraus, *Hekate*, Heidelberg, 1960, p. 68, n. 332, was correct in doubting the previous interpretation). The later discovery of a Hellenistic marble head belonging to a triple Hekateion (57.555) again lent support to this theory. The head was a chance find in the river valley south of the modern culvert in the theater, hence unconnected with the altar. Nevertheless, it does indicate that there was a Samothracian cult of Hekate as the literary sources

In the fourth century B.C., the processional road leading across and down the Eastern Hill of the Sanctuary descended to a point directly above this rock altar (fig. 1).[102] It must have turned sharply to the southeast and, at some now unknown point, led to the Propylon and to the early classical Hieron to its south.[103] Thence, it must have descended past the Propylon to the narrow interval between the terrace and the rock altar.[104] To the north lay another altar, the Sacred Rock,[105] and the structures that preceded the Rotunda of Arsinoe.[106] From this lowest level of the Sanctuary, the visitor ascended to the Western Hill to the fourth-century dining rooms on the far side of the central river.[107] When the Rotunda was built early in the third century B.C.,[108] the level of this central area of the Sanctuary was drastically altered. A gigantic earth fill was poured into the area between the Eastern Hill, the terrace north of the Temenos, the Rotunda, the now high retaining walls of the river and, to the south, between the Eastern Hill and the region of the Propylon-Temenos. One uniform level extended from the euthynteria of the Rotunda to a high point on the terrace wall concealing the huge, high limestone foundation of the Rotunda and burying the old altars below it. Whether the rock altar was replaced at this new high level is unknown. Given the religious conservatism of the Samothracian Sanctuary, it may have been replaced; but no trace of it has survived. Nor is this surprising in view of the severe damage to this area of the Sanctuary in post-antique times. With the creation of this new, high level early in the third century B.C., the processional road descended the Eastern Hill to a fork level with the entrances of both the Rotunda and the Propylon-terrace.

At this same period, after the construction of the Rotunda, monuments seem to have been erected against the polygonal terrace wall retaining the terrace. Whether these monuments were new or simply the reinstallation of monuments previously placed at the foot of the terrace wall is uncertain. The northwest corner of the terrace wall was now sheathed at its base by a limestone foundation preserved to a height of three courses at the west (Pls. I, II.1, 2; figs. 19, 33, 35, 37).[109] Once the high, earth fill had been poured into the

---

had attested. I, myself, do not believe that this was an altar to Hekate, but the fact remains that the epithet Zerynthia was applied both to Aphrodite and to Hekate (Vol. 1, **155**, **155a**).

102. For this stepped ramp, see James R. McCredie, "Samothrace: Preliminary Report on the Campaigns of 1965-67," *Hesperia*, 37 (1968), p. 231 and *idem*, "Samothrace: Supplementary Investigations, 1967-1977," *Hesperia*, 48 (1979), p. 7.

103. Vol. 3, text II, pp. 59 ff.

104. The fourth-century date of the rock altar, the necessity, at this period, for the Sacred Rock and the structures antedating the Rotunda of Arsinoe to be accessible precludes the suggestion of Professor Lehmann (*Hesperia*, 22 [1953], pp. 23 f., *Guide*, pp. 55 f.; *Guide*², *Guide*³, pp. 56 f.; *Guide*⁴, pp. 60 f.), that a perennial spring was associated with this altar. The water found here in the campaign of 1951 must have been a form of ground water.

105. Above, n. 98.

106. For the time being, see *Guide*⁴, pp. 8, 58 f.

107. *Guide*⁴, p. 79.

108. Pending the appearance of *Samothrace*, Vol. 7, *The Rotunda of Arsinoe*, see *Guide, Guide*², *Guide*³, pp. 49 ff.; *Guide*⁴, pp. 54 ff.

109. It extends ca. 7.00 m. east of the original corner and its present west face runs ca. 4.00 m. toward the southwest. The northern face projects ca. 1.50 m. beyond the wall, the western, at its greatest

area between the Rotunda, the terrace, and the retaining walls of the river, it was no longer possible to found monuments (or structures) by erecting them on bedrock—the normal procedure in the Sanctuary. This limestone foundation, itself laid on bedrock, appears to be a remnant of the lowest section of such an artificial support. For the most part, its ashlar blocks, evidently spoils from other structures, have been clamped together to strengthen them for this purpose.[110] The missing, upper section of this outer sheath-foundation must have been loosely adjusted to the face of the polygonal wall, since only three of its uppermost boulders have been dressed down, indicating both the new ground line in this area between the Terrace and the Rotunda, and the fact that the monuments (or objects) were set directly against the polygonal wall at the new, high level.[111] Conceivably, the monument previously supported on the porphyry base to the east was also reinstalled at the new level.

Once in later antiquity, centuries after its construction in the fourth century B.C., the Propylon required minor repair, doubtless as the result of a slight earthquake that affected a section of its roof. Two of the extant geison-sima blocks show traces of a crude repair (Pls. XXVII, XXVIII.2; figs. 49, 50).[112] The jaws of the lions' head waterspouts had originally overlapped the fillet of the sima, but on this pair of blocks, a semicircular hole has been cut into both the fillet of the sima and the corona of the geison. The jaws were evidently damaged, as they had been on the nearby Hieron.[113] There, new muzzles were carved and attached to the original spouts. Here, the damage must have been slighter. The newly cut holes allowed rainwater to pour through the spouts and dribble down the geison drip instead of having been spilled beyond the building as traces on the drip attest.

---

width, ca. 0.60 m.

110. Π-shaped iron clamps set in lead. Four blocks of this limestone sheathing, originally found in fallen position, that is not *in situ*, were inserted into a gap at its center during the excavation of 1949 in order to suggest its original line. They do not join precisely and, unfortunately, create the impression that this sheathing was more sloppily laid than it actually was.

111. The quantities of small fragments of molded bases and of marbles sculpture (too fragmentary and unintelligible to be included in the Catalogue of Finds) recovered in the accumulation of blocks in front of the terrace wall attest the existence of such monuments. See *Hesperia*, 20 (1951), p. 14.

The original explanation of this limestone foundation was that it was a "monument terrace," i.e., a base for monuments placed at this low level in front of the polygonal terrace wall and that it might have been "a later addition" to that wall. See *Hesperia*, 20 (1951), p. 14, pl. 7b. Subsequently, it was mistakenly interpreted as the incomplete section of an outer limestone facing for the inner polygonal wall, because it had been noted that the polygonal wall had been dressed back to receive another "face" (*Hesperia*, 21 [1952], p. 24, pl. 5c). Actually, only three of the uppermost row of boulders have been dressed back, the entire remainder of this lofty wall lacking any trace of such tooling. No example exists in the Sanctuary of the sheathing of a polygonal wall by a limestone ashlar facing—much less the use of a "sheath" itself made of two irregular faces. This incorrect explanation appears in all editions of the *Guide*, including the fourth (there, on p. 65).

I have greatly benefited from discussing the problem of this limestone facing with Ioannis Akamatis in late August 1976.

112. ++5, ++14.

113. Vol. 3, text II, pp. 79 ff., figs. 387, 388.

245. Antefix I, 423 B. Vienna, Ephesos-Museum.

Evidently, some tiles and timbers of the roof were also damaged. Resting upon or notched into the sima blocks (Pl. XLIX; fig. 90), harm to such members could easily be transmitted to the separately-laid coffer lids. One such lid, presumably to be associated with damage to the gutter, was knocked out of place and found its way into a fill used in a revision of one of the dining rooms below the Stoa.[114]

Presumably also to be associated with this damage, is the existence of a second antefix (Pl. XXXIII.1; fig. 245).[115] Identical with the original antefix (fig. 113) in basic type, it

114. 70.848. Found in a fill containing architectural fragments from other buildings in the Sanctuary that, in itself, attested earthquake damage. See above, pp. 157 f., *C(S)4*.

115. Although this antefix is neither mentioned nor illustrated in either *S,I* or *S,II*, its accession number, I, 423 B, indicates that it must have been associated with the solitary other antefix connected with the building—I, 423 A. In both Vol. 3, text I, fig. 136, and Vol. 4, pt. II, fig. 94, this antefix, Vienna I, 423 B, was illustrated as the presumably sole antefix from the Propylon.

It is conceivable that the central petal of this antefix was flanked by another pair of petals in lower relief than the other petals. At times, one seems to see other traces lower down that might imply a double palmette. But the rear member of such a double palmette is always taller than the front, superimposed palmette (see Vol. 3, text I, fig. 308, pls. CXII, CXVI). The worn state of this antefix, too, makes it difficult to determine its original character with certainty.

is cruder in execution. Its petals are deeply grooved; its V-shaped tendrils coarsely carved; their overhanging leaves crudely simplified, the perspective view so characteristic of both the original antefix and the sima having been eliminated; and the general form of the flower itself is wider and less elegant. In all likelihood, it was a repair. The date of this damage is uncertain. There is no evidence that this small building suffered the more extensive damage that the Hieron did in the Augustan-Tiberian period, when several sections of its roof were harmed and its original, fragile akroteria shattered.[116] Nor is this shock necessarily to be connected with the widespread damage to the Sanctuary in the period of Constantine.[117] In this earthquake-prone Sanctuary, lesser, erratic tremors must have been frequent.

Even before the violent earthquake that destroyed the Sanctuary in the mid-sixth century A.D.,[118] the area between the terrace and the Rotunda began to be severely molested. Soon after the Edict of Theodosius, the first of a series of limekilns was dug to the south of the Rotunda.[119] The floor of this deep kiln rested on natural soil slightly above the level of the riverbed. The old rocky slope southeast of the Rotunda formed a portion of its wall.[120] The earth fill before the terrace wall and to the east of the Propylon must have been dug away to the same low level, since when the last fearful earthquake demolished the Propylon, its blocks crashed not only on the terrace but pitched far below to the north and northwest of the terrace wall and to the east, between the building and the Eastern Hill, even falling below the level of the old fourth-century altar. [121] Spewed out in a wide arc, they fell on bedrock in the old ravine, reaching as far as the riverbed to the west and the limekiln to the east.[122] To the south, blocks and fragments of the pedimental sculptures of the Hieron were thrown down into the Temenos and outside its southwestern corner.[123]

After this catastrophe, vandals dug a road through the southeastern area of the Temenos, linking the limekiln to the east of the porch of the Hieron with the kiln to the north, in the process destroying most of the southeastern and northeastern foundations of the Temenos and the projecting southern wing of the Propylon (Pl. I; figs. 1, 13).[124] Subsequently, this valley road was transformed into a stream, doubtless caused by the over-

116. Vol. 3, text II, pp. 79-123.

117. *Ibid.*, p. 127, nn. 167-169.

118. For the date, see Glanville Downey, "Note on a Samothracian Inscription," *Hesperia*, 19 (1950), pp. 21 f.; vol. 4, pt. I, p. 108.

119. Accounts of the successive limekilns appear in Professor Lehmann's reports in *Hesperia*, 20 (1950), p. 12, and *ibid.*, 21 (1952), pp. 41 f.

120. The kiln was ca. 5 m. in diameter. In a second phase of the kiln, its floor was raised 1.50 m. to a level 3.50 m. beneath the euthynteria of the Rotunda.

121. For the location and discovery of key blocks of the Propylon, see the Introduction, pp. 23 f., 27 f., 31.

122. Large parts of the superstructure of the Rotunda also fell on the washed away slopes to its southwest and on the limekiln itself.

123. Vol. 3, text I, pp. 24, 270.

124. In *Hesperia*, 21 (1952), p. 41, there is reference to "a coin of Justinian found in the road among the debris of smashed building blocks" as a document of this destruction. I have been unable to find this coin, hence am unable to describe and date it precisely.

246. Fragmentary bronze Byzantine votive cross. Samothrace Museum.

flow of the river south of the Hieron in the now neglected Sanctuary. Gravel and sand to the east of the Temenos and terrace attested its existence. In the Byzantine Middle Ages, when lime burners were again at work, the stream was converted into a road or path and debris from the fallen buildings was dragged along it. It was here, over the southeastern corner of the old Temenos, that a series of column drums from the Hieron had been assembled[125]—whether to be shipped away for reuse or to be reduced to lime, for in the same period, a new, somewhat smaller kiln rose above the Early Christian kiln.[126] A portion of this Byzantine limekiln had been visible from the beginning of our work in the Sanctuary in 1938.[127] Indeed, it had already been noted by both our Austrian forebears and their own predecessors, Deville and Coquart.[128] In its vicinity, there had been assembled a collection of marbles intended for burning but abandoned.[129]

It is conceivable that the date of this activity may be provided by a chance find discovered to the west of the porphyry base: the upper arm of a fragmentary, bronze Byzantine votive cross (fig. 246).[130] Flaring in outline, pierced by a hole, and rough on its reverse, it must have been applied to a surface, whether to a wall or an architectural member.[131]

125. *Hesperia*, 21 (1952), p. 42.

126. Ca. 4 m. in diameter. An accumulation of ca. 1 m. height of fallen blocks separated the pre- from the post-earthquake kilns.

127. *AJA*, 43 (1939), p. 136, fig. 2.

128. S,*I*, pl. 1; II, pl. 1; Deville-Coquart, pl. 1.

129. Including the fragmentary pedimental figure of Harmonia from the Hieron: Vol. 3, text I, pp. 274 f., fig. 240.

130. 54.164. On exhibition in the Samothrace Museum, Hall C, Case 12, top shelf. Above the head, at the left, traces (?) of what may be IN. Preserved height: 0.0254 m.; preserved width at top: 0.0184 m.; at bottom: 0.0135 m.; thickness: 0.0021 m. Found on the surface of the bedrock to the west of the porphyry base.

131. See a fragmentary column that may have come from a ciborium showing cuttings for the insertion of such crosses from a tomb near the Church of St. Dionysos the Areopagite in Athens published by John Travlos and Alison Frantz, "The Church of St. Dionysos the Areopagite and the Palace of the

It bears the head of a beardless Christ depicted in crude, schematic, linear fashion. In its simple, angular, curving outlines, its style is related to the heads on an enamel medallion adorning an onyx paten in the Stoclet Collection in Brussels that dates from the tenth or eleventh centuries after Christ.[132] In function and style, it recalls the incised figures on a group of bronze reliquary crosses that may date from this same period.[133]

More important for the history of the Propylon was the existence of yet another large limekiln on the Eastern Hill.[134] An immense collection of marbles from the destroyed buildings in the Sanctuary had been assembled in a dump in its vicinity, including both a small fragment of the frieze of dancing maidens and the coffer lid that has proved such a crucial piece of evidence in the attribution to Skopas of the role of designing architect-sculptor of the building.[135]

The Propylon is unique among the buildings in the Sanctuary in the degree to which its blocks were reused in post-antique structures. Crucial, again, for its reconstruction was the recovery of all the ornamental drums from a tenth-century Byzantine fort on the lower, northern terrace of the Western Hill.[136] Built of spoils plundered from the destroyed buildings in the Sanctuary, it contained, too, the fragments of the all-important corner frieze block that ultimately established the correct reconstruction of the Propylon.[137] Centuries later, two blocks of the frieze of dancing maidens were carried away from the region of the shattered building to adorn one of the towers in the Gattilusi citadel in the ancient city, there to be sketched by Cyriacus of Ancona in October 1444.[138] Here or there, in the ancient city[139] or in a remote chapel near the northeast coast of the island,[140] other ornamental fragments of the building have been found.

As the centuries passed, all trace of the Propylon vanished. Once again, earth was washed down into the ravine and trees and shrubs sprang up over the Temenos and terrace. By the sixties of the nineteenth century, the explorers Deville and Coquart recorded this area as an island framed by a stream,[141] and still in the mid-twentieth century, river sand lay to the north of the terrace wall. Once again, this stream must have emanated

---

Archbishop of Athens in the 16th Century," *Hesperia*, 34 (1965), pp. 179 ff.; Tomb 10 on 181 f. and fig. 6. I am indebted to Alison Frantz for this and the following references.

132. Louis Bréhier, *La Sculpture et les arts mineurs byzantins*, Paris, 1936, p. 90, pl. LXIII.

133. E. S. King, "The Date and Provenance of a Bronze Reliquary Cross in the Museo Cristiano," *Memorie della Pontificia Accademia Romana di Archeologia*, 2 (1928), pp. 200 ff., pl. XXVIII, 13, 14. On p. 203, n. 71, these crosses are said to have been produced from the seventh century *onward*—i.e., no specific date was suggested. The Brussel paten may provide a clue to their date.

134. *Hesperia*, 37 (1968), p. 234.

135. Nos. 65.1146 and 66.611, figs. 150, 130, 142.

136. For brief reference to this fortress, see the *Guide*[4], pp. 20, 81. For the best preserved drum, 49.985, see above, pp. 106 f. Like 52.215, actually retrieved from the Church of Hagios Stephanos in Chora, it presumably came from this post-antique structure. The third fragmentary drum, 70.939, was found in the excavation of the fort.

137. Nos. 67.32 and 65.999. See above, pp. 34 ff.

138. See above, pp. 5 ff., figs. 4, 5.

139. No. 55.149. See above, p. 154, fig. 128.

140. No. 63.144. See above, pp. 191 f., fig. 164.

141. Deville-Coquart, p. 276, pl. 1.

from the region to the east of the Hieron and, pouring over the foundation of the Temenos, contributed to the devastation of the old precinct.

Most damaged and dispersed of all the major buildings in the Samothracian Sanctuary, the Propylon has been reborn in text and plates.

Addendum

For additional medallions, pendants, and a bronze mirror cover reflecting Skopas' lost group of Aphrodite Pandemos, see now Stella G. Miller, *Two Groups of Thessalian Gold* (University of California Publications in Classical Studies, 18), Berkeley and Los Angeles, 1979, pp. 38 ff., pls. 22 f., published after the present volume had been submitted to the Press.

Appendix I

48.289 (Fig. 247).[1] Female head; sporadic find, found between the Rotunda of Arsinoe and the Sacristy outside section G of the foundation of the Rotunda. Preserved height: 0.153 m.; preserved width: 0.11 m. Thasian marble. Broken on right of skull and temple; sheared off on top and at rear of head. Nose and center of mouth destroyed; exterior of eyes damaged. Severely weathered. Low, broad forehead; broad, fleshy face; slight protuberance on each side of mouth. Traces of small ear and strands of loose hair.

When compared with the two female heads from the coffered ceiling of the Propylon *C(S)1, 4* and the fragmentary akroterial head from Tegea (figs. 128, 131, 145), as well as with the male head *C(S)3* (fig. 130), this head is clearly Skopaic, characterized by the deepset eyes, double contour of the lids, broad full-cheeked face, and rounded chin typical of the master's style.

A Greek original that is either another badly damaged work by Skopas or by a member of his shop.

247. Fragmentary female head. Samothrace Museum.

1. Previously published by Karl Lehmann, "Excavations in Samothrace. Summer 1948," *Archaeology*, 2 (1949), pp. 40 f., no. 6; *idem*, "Samothrace: Third Preliminary Report," *Hesperia*, 19 (1950), pp. 18 f., pl. 12, and characterized as "a fourth century B.C. Greek original of Skopasian style." Mentioned by Hemberg, p. 69.

Appendix II

A NOTE ON THE FRIEZE OF THE PROPYLON AND ARCHAISTIC ART

I HAVE suggested that a study of the Hellenistic and Roman archaistic reliefs depicting dancing figures could prove rewarding to an effort to reconstruct motifs missing from the frieze of the Propylon.[1] This suggestion presumes that the frieze played an important role in the formation of the imagery to be employed subsequently in works in this vein. It would not be appropriate here to explore this hypothesis at length; however, a necessary preliminary step can be taken, by examining a few archaistic designs originating in the period of the Propylon and the succeeding generations, to determine the extent of its immediate influence. Indeed, this inquiry might seem a worthwhile test of the validity of some of the basic theses of our study of the Propylon, insofar as the creation by a celebrated artist of so original a work, under royal patronage, at a great religious center, could hardly have passed unnoticed in the wider world of Greek art, where evidence of its influence should almost certainly be attested.[2]

In order to assess this impact, we must recall an image which played a fundamental role in shaping the archaizing drapery formulae that were to be used in Attica from the late fifth century B.C. onward. This is the three-sided Hekataion that Alkamenes designed for the Akropolis in Athens, a monument which is reflected in numerous modest sculptures of Hellenistic date. Among these, the example in the British School in Athens has long been assumed to follow most closely the appearance of Alkamenes' original (fig. 188).[3] Characteristically, the Hekataia of this type use figures wearing the girded peplos with small neck opening, symmetrically divided overfall with long V-shaped pattern at the lower edge, and vertical folds at the center of the skirt.[4] During the Hellenistic period, many changes were rung upon the Alkamenian pattern, with respect both to the form of the monument and to its iconographic details. One of the new types, illustrated by a sculpture in Vienna, which is apparently an Attic work dating from the third century B.C. (fig. 248),[5] unmistakably betrays the influence of the Samothracian dancers—too unmis-

1. See above, Chap. III, n. 78.

2. The attribution of the frieze to Skopas is discussed above, pp. 233 ff.

3. See above, Chap. III, p. 219, n. 115; see also Harrison, pp. 62 f.

4. On the Hekataia, see Theodor Kraus, *Hekate, Studien zu Wesen und Bild der Gottin in Kleinasien und Griechenland*, Heidelberg, 1960. The "Minerva" of Poitiers may reflect an earlier version of the divided overfall and skirt seen in the Alkamenian Hekataion, but the date of the original is uncertain (see Herdejürgen, *op. cit.*, pp. 74 f., pl. 13a, who suggests ca. 475-450 B.C. above, Chap. III, n. 63).

5. Kraus, *op. cit.*, no. 14, pp. 129 f., pls. 7, 2;

248. Hekateion. Vienna, Kunsthistorisches Museum.

takably to require analysis; we may note, however, that the drapery is a hybrid, retaining the overfall with long V pattern typical of the fifth-century Hekataia, while incorporating such details as the mantle with diagonal diploidion, the lower garment with repeated vertical folds and pleats (here doubled to agree with the treatment of the apoptygma), and the chiton which emerges conspicuously below the skirt as well as on the torso. The figures again wear the polos, and the dance ἐπὶ καρπῷ is adapted to the columnar form of the monument, with the heads in alternating positions.[6]

The Attic votive reliefs which show Hermes and the Nymphs in the grotto of Pan bear witness to the intrusion of the Samothracian dancers at an appropriate moment. Most of these reliefs were made during the Hellenistic age, and since most seem to recapitulate earlier models, they are, on the whole, imprecisely dated.[7] Two types of Nymphs reliefs appear to have originated in the late fifth century B.C. The first, showing three dancing Nymphs moving to the left and led by Hermes, is exemplified by a late fifth-century relief in Berlin (fig. 202).[8] Fuchs has noted that this design depends on a well-known model of late archaic date.[9] In the second type of relief, the Nymphs are stationary, clustered together in classically composed overlapping positions—unmistakably the descendants of similar Pheidian groups.[10] It is this classical type of Nymphs relief that dominates the first half of the fourth century B.C., to which, indeed, no examples using dancing figures have been assigned. The type is well illustrated by a relief of exceptional quality from Mount Pentelikon (fig. 249).[11] In several examples assigned to the later fourth century, however,

---

8, 1-2. On the date of this Hekataion, see Schmidt, p. 38, who places it in the second half of the fourth century B.C. In this section of his book (*ibid.*, pp. 36 ff.), Schmidt discusses the interrelations among several of the archaistic works to be considered here, including the Samothracian frieze itself (see note 12, below, and bibliographies for *F(S)10* and *F(S)11*; however, his ordering of their chronology differs from mine, depending as it does on his dating of the frieze in the early third century B.C.

6. A figure similarly dressed appears on a small wooden Hekataion of ca. 300 B.C., which is in the Metropolitan Museum of Art, New York (acc. no. 39.11.3).

7. On the votive reliefs, see Fuchs, "Attische Nymphenreliefs," pp. 242 ff., with earlier bibliography; more recently, Willers has contributed to the discussion of this topic (*Zu den Anfängen der archaistischen Plastik in Griechenland*, pp. 28 ff.).

8. See above, Chap. III, p. 244.

9. See above, Chap. III, n. 208.

10. Such compositions are exemplified by a Nymphs relief from Enkali (National Archaeological Museum, Athens, no. 3874), which Fuchs has identified as a work of ca. 300 B.C. imitating an original of the late fifth century ("Attische Nymphenreliefs," p. 246, Beilage 66, 1; above Chap. III, n. 78), and the Archandros relief (National Archaeological Museum, Athens, no. 1329), which has been dated by Renate Feubel at ca. 415 B.C. (*Die attischen Nymphenreliefs und ihre Vorbilder*, Diss. Heidelberg, 1935, pp. 1 ff., pl. III, 1).

11. National Archaeological Museum, Athens, no. 4465: a date of ca. 350 B.C. has been suggested for this relief by Fuchs ("Attische Nymphenreliefs," pp. 246 ff., Beilage 68). A similar relief, also from Mount Pentelikon (National Archaeological Museum, Athens, no. 4466), has been dated by Fuchs in the last quarter of the fourth century (*ibid.*, p. 248 f., Beilage 69, 2); however, the plasticity of these figures, among other characteristics, forbids, in my opinion, a date so late in the century: indeed, the complexity of the groups of interacting and overlapping figures suggests a date *earlier* than that of no. 4465. On the other hand, the relief of Pan and the Nymphs in the Agora Museum, Athens (no. I 7154), whose inscription indicates a date around 330 B.C., shows that classically inspired compositions persisted in this genre into the second half of the

249. Nymphs Relief from Mount Pentelikon. Athens, National Archaeological Museum, no. 4465.

250. Nymphs Relief. Rome, Museo Barracco, no. 176.

the Nymphs, again becoming dancers, are shown spread out in a row and clasping hands. There is considerable diversity in the portrayal of these figures; it is the evidence which they supply of the influence of two particular models that is of interest in the present context. In one of these variants, exemplified by a relief in the Museo Barracco, Rome (fig. 250), the dancers move purposefully forward, heads turning to right and left; their archaized costume combines an overfall imitative of that of the Hekataion of Alkamenes with a chiton and mantle clearly based on the Samothracian formula.[12] In other examples, the Nymphs assume a more static, frontal pose (see fig. 179), which, as noted, resembles that of the type of dancer occurring in a drawing of a lost block of the frieze of the Propylon, *Fa* (fig. 178).[13] It seems reasonable to conclude that the Samothracian frieze provided two patterns among the many that were employed in these modest reliefs—both dancers, one the familiar active, fractionally viewed figure of the preserved reliefs, the other frontally posed, as in *Fa*.

The Attic votive reliefs illustrate the usefulness of the frieze of the Propylon as a compendium of new motifs available to the archaizing trend that became increasingly popular in the religious art of the late classical and Hellenistic ages; they also serve to increase our understanding of the meaning and purpose of archaism in its early stages of development. It should be emphasized that, in the votive reliefs, the element of archaism is limited to the dancing Nymphs, who appear within a setting that is often as naturalistic as those of the earlier members of the series (compare figs. 250 and 249). Archaism is thought of, then, not as a mode of representation enveloping the whole composition, but as an attribute identifying and determining the meaning of particular figures. Its function here is symbolic, extending the range of content accessible to an artist who remains essentially faithful to the naturalistic mode developed within the classical tradition. By means of pose, gesture and surface detail, that tradition by the mid-fourth century B.C. had infused its supernatural images with a "portrait"-like abundance of sensual and emotional life:[14] what breaks through in the tentative archaisms of this period is a recognition that the ancient values inherent in a permanent supernatural order are not encompassed by a style of subtle

---

century, in spite of the introduction of the files of dancers to which attention is drawn here: the sacrificial iconography of this relief may account for the compositional solution that has been chosen (see T. Leslie Shear, Jr., "A Votive Relief from the Athenian Agora," *Opuscula Romana*, IX:22 [1962], pp. 183 ff.). Other reliefs, probably to be dated in the early fourth century, which show classically grouped Nymphs, are: an example from Megara in the Sabouroff Collection (Adolf Furtwängler, *Die Sammlung Sabouroff*, I, Berlin, 1883, pl. XXVIII), and a relief of Dionysos and the Nymphs in the Collection Calvet, Avignon, which is dated ca. 400-375 B.C. (Müthmann, *op. cit.*, p. 33, pl. 12, 2; above, Chap. III, n. 83).

12. For the relief in the Museo Barracco, Rome (no. 176), see Chap. III, n. 209, and Carlo Pietrangeli, *Museo Barracco di scultura antica*, Rome, 1963, p. 111, pl. XVII, where it is dated at the beginning of the third century B.C. The similarity between these figures and the Samothracian dancers has been noted by Schmidt (p. 39), who also links these reliefs to an example in the Louvre, no. 36 (p. 36, pl. XVII, 2). Havelock points to the inscription as evidence that the relief in the Museo Barracco dates from the first century B.C. (*op. cit.*, p. 45, n. 9); but it could be a late version of a work of ca. 300 B.C.

13. See above, Chap. III, pp. 204 f., and n. 83.

14. See above, Chap. III, n. 187.

naturalism, but must in some cases be evoked by a symbolic use of imitative pose and costume. Willers has shown that the symbolic display of archaizing costume details begins within the late archaic period itself.[15] Early classical art continued this practice (cf. the Locrian pinax, fig. 184; above, p. 214 and expanded it to include other features, as illustrated by the hair of the Apollo from the western pediment of the Temple of Zeus at Olympia.[16] During the later fifth century B.C., the archaizing of certain individual images became stabilized as a result of the inventiveness of one artist: these are the Hekataion and Hermes Propylaios by Alkamenes.[17] This kind of archaism occurs in several fourth-century images, including that which is reflected in the statuette of Artemis from Paros (fig. 251), which imitates the drapery of the Hekataion (fig. 188).[18] Meanwhile we have seen that the

15. Willers, *op. cit.*, p. 55 (see above, Chap. III, n. 83); see also Folman, *op. cit.*, pp. 9 f. Herdejürgen places the earliest phase of archaism in the years immediately following 480 B.C.: see Chap. III, n. 63, above.

16. See Bernard Ashmole, *The Sculptures of the Temple of Zeus*, London, 1967, frontispiece; for fourth-century examples of the archaizing treatment of the hair, see the statue of "Artemisia" from Halikarnassos (*The Mausoleum and Sculptures from Halicarnassos and Priene in the British Museum*, no. 1001, pl. XVI), and two female portraits from Priene, which are in Berlin (Blumel, *op. cit.*, no. 104, p. 86, figs. 138, 159; no. 105, p. 87, figs. 140, 141).

17. On the Hekataion, see Chap. III, n. 115, with reference to Willers; on the Hermes Propylaios, see Willers, "Zum Hermes Propylaios des Alkamenes," pp. 37 ff.

18. On this statuette, see above, Chap. III, n. 177, where an amplified view of Skopas' activity as an archaistic artist is sketched.

A discussion of archaism in the fourth century B.C. should not neglect the statue-supports associated with certain Praxitelean types, e.g. the Lycian Apollo (Charles Picard, *Manuel d'archéologie grecque, La Sculpture*, IV, 1, Paris, 1954, figs. 151, 152, p. 353) and the Artemis from Kition (*ibid.*, fig. 156, p. 359). These supports are respectively statuettes of Artemis and, presumably, a votary: the former exhibits the drapery formula employed for the Samothracian dancers (see above, pp. 211 ff.), the latter a variant closer to the model of Alkamenes' Hekataion (see above, p. 304). An Attic reflection of the Samothracian drapery is to be found in a pair of basin-bearing korai in Eleusis: these statues are dated by Harrison in the late fourth or early third century B.C. (Harrison, p. 56; see Richter, *Korai*, figs. 683-685; Mylonas, *op. cit.*, p. 202, fig. 77).

The image of the divinity with attendant votary occurs in two archaized versions evidently datable in the fourth century B.C. These are the relief decorating the "Porte de Zeus" at Thasos (perhaps to be recognized as Hera, see Charles Picard, *Études Thasiennes*, VII, Paris, 1962, pp. 149 ff.; Georges Daux, "Chronique des fouilles et découvertes archéologiques en Grèce en 1961," *BCH*, 86 [1962-II], p. 945; Herdejürgen, *op. cit.*, p. 78, n. 479, with further bibliography), and a stele of Demeter and Hekate in Eleusis, assumed by Mylonas to belong to the archaic period, but belonging, in my opinion, to the late classical age (see Mylonas, *op. cit.*, p. 191, fig. 67; above, Chap. III, n. 181).

The archaism of the caryatids from the funerary monument of King Perikles at Limyra in Lycia refers not to a Greek model, but to a Persian one (see William A. P. Childs, *AJA*, 81 [1977], reviewing Jürgen Borchardt, *Die Bauskulpturen des Heroens von Limyra*, Berlin, 1976; see also Sybille Haynes, *Land of the Chimaera*, New York, 1974, pp. 110 ff.). But Persian models may have played a role at Samothrace, too (see above, pp. 255 ff.). R. Ross Holloway has commented on the influence of the taste of the Asiatic satraps on late classical art (*A View of Greek Art*, Providence [R.I.], 1973, pp. 162 ff.).

Archaism in the portraiture of the fourth century B.C. has been discussed by Breckenridge (*op. cit.*, p. 131), and Heinz Luschey has drawn attention to the use of archaic motifs in certain funerary stelai of the period ("Zur Wiederkehr archaischer Bildgedanken in der attischen Grabmalkunst des 4. Jahrhunderts v. Chr.," *Neue Beiträge zur klassischen Altertumswissenschaft* [Festschrift zum 60. Geburtstag von Bernhard Schweitzer, edited by Reinhard Lullies], Stuttgart, 1954, 22, 243 ff.). Herdejürgen assembles additional archaistic sculptures for her discussion of the "Schrägmantel" in the fourth century B.C. (*op. cit.*, pp. 78 ff.).

251. Statuette of Artemis. Paros, The Archaeological Museum.

252. "Base" from Epidauros (right side). Athens, National Archaeological Museum.

naturalistic art of the same period, as illustrated by the Centauromachy relief from Halikarnassos (fig. 205), was turning toward an abstraction of space and pose which prepared the way for the partial revival of archaic forms that is evident in the frieze of the Propylon and works dependent upon it.[19] This frieze and its reflections in the Attic votive reliefs, thus, belong to a new phase in the development of archaism, in which archaizing figures or groups, joined to naturalistic motifs in varying combinations, merge with the abstract current already in existence. A conspicuous member of this group is the so-called Epidauros Base in the National Archaeological Museum, Athens, a work that, in my opinion, is to be dated about a decade later than the frieze (fig. 252).[20] Here an archaizing figure identified as Hebe appears on the right flank of the block, approaching a divine assemblage on the front face, which is portrayed naturalistically. I would argue, indeed, that this monument in conjunction with the votive reliefs, indicates that the frieze of the Propylon may also have combined archaizing with naturalistic figures, and that those participating in the ritual which we suppose occupied the center of the façade may thus have been quite different from the dancers on the preserved blocks, who approached them from both sides.[21] In fact, recalling *Fa* (fig. 178), we have seen that this variety of treatment was probably present among the dancers themselves.[22]

19. See above, pp. 240 ff.

20. Svoronos, *op. cit.*, III, no. 1425, pp. 418 ff., pls. LXVIII, CXXVI. Harrison has noted the similarity between the dress of this figure and that of the Samothracian dancers (Harrison, p. 55), and finds other support for a date in the late fourth century B.C. (p. 67). Schmidt (pp. 28 ff.) and Fuchs (p. 53) date the "Base" ca. 350 B.C., and Semni Karouzou, calling it a plaque, dates it ca. 370 B.C. (p. 101).

21. See above, pp. 250 ff., 231 f.

22. See above, pp. 203 ff.

CATALOGUE OF FINDS

1. Ceramics

by Mary B. Moore

The scale of all profiles for Section I is 1:2;
for Section II, 1:1, unless otherwise stated.

I. The Fill of the Temenos and the Terrace

INTRODUCTION

The fill of the Temenos has yielded only a limited quantity of pottery, owing in part to the use of a stony packing instead of an earth fill in much of the terrace.[1] In the southeastern area of the precinct and in the eastern part of the terrace (Pl. I), much of the fill has been washed out by a stream, which, in post-antique times, poured over the ruins. In the southern half of the precinct, the context was disturbed. Thus, the areas of undisturbed fill are located in the northwestern half of the Temenos, the area up to five meters south of it,[2] and the area of the terrace, particularly along the north wall of the Temenos.

The pottery of the fill ranges in date from the first half of the seventh century to the third quarter of the fourth century B.C., and it is comprised of both local and imported wares. Among these there are only a small number of fragments with black glaze, all, but one,[3] from drinking vessels and small bowls. Most interesting of the various wares is a large quantity of a seventh-century B.C. fabric with subgeometric decoration that is called G 2-3 ware after the section in Settlement VIII at Troy, which yielded the most substantial quantity of this fabric.[4] At Samothrace, fragments of this fabric were found in all areas of the precinct and terrace fill, and even in the surface layers,[5] but the densest concentration of them came from a black layer of burned earth on each side of the north wall of the Temenos (Pl. I).[6] This black earth was not, however, a closed deposit, for it contained some fragments with black glaze, probably from an intrusion that occurred when some of the black earth was removed to allow construction of the precinct wall and the Propylon. Throughout the fill, but especially in the black layer, there was a considerable quantity of coarse handmade local ware with traces of burning on both inside and outside. The significance for the history of the sanctuary of these two wares, the fine wheelmade G 2-3 ware and the coarse local ware, both from a sacrificial deposit, is discussed above.[7] There were also a

1. Cf., above, p. 50.
2. I.e., up to the hole made by Salač in a previous excavation. See above, p. 26.
3. See below, **101**.
4. C. Boulter in *Troy*, p. 253. See also the discussion below, pp. 318 ff.
5. For example, nos. **5**, **49**, and some of the fragments of **50**.
6. See above, pp. 268 f.
7. See above, p. 269.

few fragments of "karchesia," and a very small quantity of gray ware, almost all of the latter too fragmentary for inclusion here.[8]

The arrangement of the various sections of the catalogue is chronological, and within each section, the restored vessels or fragments are grouped according to shape. For the description of the color of the clay included in each entry of the fine wares, we have relied on the Munsell Soil Color Charts.[9] For all fabrics, except for the G 2-3 ware, the gray bucchero, and the "karchesia," only pieces from undisturbed contexts are included. Owing to the special quality of the subgeometric ware, we have decided to include all fragments that contribute to the knowledge of this somewhat enigmatic fabric, whether they come from the fill or not. Those from the surface or from unstratified contexts are so designated in the catalogue entry.

G 2-3 WARE (**1-58**)

The G 2-3 ware, found in substantial quantity in Samothrace, considerably enlarges our knowledge of this fine fabric already acquired from study of the fragments found at other sites in the northeastern Aegean. Some of this ware was first found at Troy by Wilhelm Dörpfeld and was published in 1902 by Hubert Schmidt.[1] Many of these pieces were illustrated in small photographs and the significant profiles were printed in line drawings. The Cincinnati Expedition to Troy from 1932 to 1938 unearthed a large amount of G 2-3 ware in Settlement VIII and its publication in 1958 offered, up to that time, the most systematic and complete study of this fabric with reference to similar fragments from the earlier excavation.[2] In 1960 and 1961, excavation on Thasos yielded a considerable quantity of this pottery and its publication in 1964 presents the fullest account to date.[3] Elsewhere, a few fragments of G 2-3 ware have been found at Antissa on Lesbos,[4] at Clazomenae,[5] and at Lemnos, where three sites seem to have produced a Lemnian imitation of this fabric.[6]

8. See below, p. 375.

9. 1954 edition. Published by the Munsell Color Company, Inc., Baltimore, Maryland, 21218. The number following the color description of the clay in each entry of the catalogue below refers to the Munsell standard color chip that most closely approximates the color of the clay of the vessel.

1. Wilhelm Dörpfeld, *Troja und Ilion: Ergebnisse der Ausgrabungen in der vorhistorischen und historischen Schichten von Ilion, 1870-1894*, Athens, 1902, pp. 304 ff. (H. Schmidt); Hubert Schmidt, *Heinrich Schliemann's Sammlung trojanischer Altertümer*, Berlin, 1902, nos. 3650-3753.

2. Cedric Boulter in *Troy*, pp. 251 ff., especially pp. 253-255 and pp. 277 ff.

3. Paul Bernard, "Céramique de la première moitié du VIIe siècle à Thasos," *BCH*, 88 (1964), pp. 77 ff., especially pp. 88-104; also discussed recently by A. J. Graham, "The Foundations of Thasos," *BSA*, 73 (1978), pp. 61-98, especially pp. 67-69. I am indebted to James R. McCredie for drawing my attention to this reference.

4. Winifred Lamb, "Antissa," *BSA*, 32 (1931-32), pp. 41 ff., especially p. 56, pl. 23, nos. 6 and 8.

5. Unpublished. These fragments are mentioned by Vasilios Kallipolitis in *Αἰολικὰ Γράμματα*, 4 (1974), p. 203, where publication of them is promised. For the complete title of this article, see below, n. 12.

6. Bernard, *op. cit.*, pp. 88-90 for a complete bibliography and summary of the character of this pottery.

Thus far, only sites in the northeastern Aegean, specifically Troy, Clazomenae, Lesbos, Thasos, Samothrace, and perhaps Lemnos, have yielded examples of G 2-3 ware. The contexts of this material at Troy and at Thasos appear to belong, for the most part, to the first half of the seventh century,[7] a date already suggested for the material from Samothrace in the preliminary report of 1952.[8]

The place of origin and manufacture of G 2-3 ware presents a perplexing problem. At each site, neither the shapes nor the decoration of these vessels seems to show an internal development, as one would expect. Among the various find-spots, Lemnos should probably be eliminated as a candidate, for its material seems to represent a local imitation.[9] On historical grounds, the excavators of the two areas at Thasos have concluded that G 2-3 ware did not originate in Thasian workshops, but was probably brought to the island by settlers in the first half of the seventh century.[10] Two times Lesbos has been offered as the place of manufacture. In the early publication of the fragments from Troy, Schmidt suggested that the ware had been imported to Troy from Lesbos, which in the seventh century B.C. controlled the Trojan coast.[11] Recently, V. Kallipolitis, in a brief paper that deals with the problem of the lack of early pottery on Lesbos, has tried to show that this island was the home of the G 2-3 ware.[12] He bases his theory on the following: as Lesbos was a flourishing cultural center, famous for its school of epic poetry, it would seem peculiar if the well-known gray ware comprised the island's only ceramic fabric, while neighboring cities produced a variety of more colorful wares; the fragments of G 2-3 ware found on Lesbos form a unit with those from other sites, specifically Troy, Clazomenae, and Samothrace;[13] the latter island was probably settled by colonists from Lesbos who brought the vessels with them. Much of this theory might be acceptable were it not for the fact that among the sites that have yielded G 2-3 ware, Lesbos has produced the smallest quantity (only the few sherds discussed in the 1932 publication), a fact that Kallipolitis himself mentions,[14] but without further comment. Such a limited quantity, it would seem, almost automatically excludes Lesbos as a candidate, and until future excavation on this island yields a richer quantity of G 2-3 ware, it is perhaps best to eliminate Lesbos as its home. At the moment, too little is known about the unpublished fragments from Clazomenae to consider whether this city was the producer of these vessels or not.

Thus, the choice for the place of manufacture of G 2-3 ware, based on the evidence

7. Boulter in *Troy*, p. 254; Bernard, *op. cit.*, pp. 80 ff., especially pp. 87 and 92.

8. Cf. Karl Lehmann, "Samothrace: Fifth Preliminary Report," *Hesperia*, 21 (1952), pp. 19 ff., especially p. 35.

9. See above, n. 6.

10. Bernard, *op. cit.*, pp. 91 f.

11. Schmidt in Dörpfeld, *Troja und Ilion*, p. 309.

12. Kallipolitis, 'Η *ἀρχαϊκὴ κεραμικὴ τῆς Λέσβου: ἐνα πρόβλημα,*" Αἰολικὰ *Γράμματα*, 4 (1974), pp. 199 ff. I am indebted to James R. McCredie for drawing my attention to this reference. Karl Lehmann (*op. cit.*, p. 36) recognized the analogy between the Samothracian vessels and the fragments from Lesbos, but refrained from drawing further conclusions.

13. The examples from Thasos are not mentioned in this discussion.

14. Kallipolitis, *op. cit.*, p. 201. Lamb, *op. cit.*, p. 56 had reached the opposite conclusion, that the ware was imported.

available at present, seems to lie between Samothrace and Troy. Neither, however, seems to be a suitable candidate, and no scholar has opted for either site. At Samothrace, so far, G 2-3 ware has been found in one part of the sanctuary only.[15] At Troy, on the other hand, this pottery has been found in various areas of Settlement VIII,[16] and this evidence might tend to tip the scale in favor of Troy, were it not for one important consideration. Comparison of the examples from Samothrace with those from Troy, and also from Thasos, reveals some similarity of shapes and decoration, as will be shown in the catalogue below, but comparison also reveals such significant differences, particularly in the choice of ornamental patterns,[17] that one is tempted to conclude that either each site produced its own version of this ware or that each site selected and imported it from a location not yet known to us, that is, that the variations from place to place reflect the taste of the people who used these vessels. Of these alternatives, the latter seems a possibility, though by no means is it demonstrable. In spite of the quality and quantity of the G 2-3 ware from Samothrace, there is not enough evidence to claim this island as its place of manufacture. Until the time when the matter may be settled conclusively, it is more prudent to retain the name G 2-3 ware for this fabric.[18]

The G 2-3 ware from Samothrace consists mainly of drinking vessels, specifically a variety of kantharos with very thin walls. Fragments of kraters, jugs, amphorae, and other large vessels were also found, but in a very limited quantity. Of the various shapes, only the kantharoi provided enough fragments of any one vessel to allow complete restoration. For the larger vessels, only general characteristics, not even a complete profile, may be ascertained.

The clay of this fabric is fine and many of the pieces have fired very hard, so that they have an almost metallic quality. The color of the clay is various hues of reddish-yellow. Many of the vessels are covered with a cream-colored slip on the outside, with the decoration applied to the light surface in a glaze that varies in color from brownish-red to black. The decoration is limited to areas of the vase that articulate one part from another, chiefly lips, handles, and bases. The result is a handsome vessel with simple, neat decoration that does not detract from the elegance of the shape. Many of these subgeometric patterns, in particular the dot-rosette and the zetoid pattern, are well known from other fabrics of the seventh century B.C. Other patterns appear to be reserved for pottery manufactured in the northeastern Aegean, mainly for G 2-3 ware. Each ornament is described in the catalogue entry and is illustrated. Following p. 382 there is a chart that shows the various patterns that occur on G 2-3 ware from Samothrace, arranged according to location on the pot. In the right column of the chart, the occurrence of each pattern on G 2-3 ware from other sites is noted. From this it is clear that very few of the ornamental patterns found on

15. Recently a few fragments were recovered by chance from the Akropolis at Palaeopolis. One of the fragments is of particular interest because of its decoration and is included below (ad **23**).

16. *Troy*, pp. 275 ff.

17. See the chart of ornamental patterns following p. 382.

18. A similar conclusion had been reached independently by Bernard, *op. cit.*, p. 92.

the Samothracian pottery recur on the G 2-3 ware excavated at other sites, thus strengthening the suggestion made above that the origin of this fabric is still unknown.

The catalogue below includes every restored vessel and all fragments that contribute to our knowledge of this fabric. Each entry contains a description of the piece, the character of its decoration, its measurements, and, when relevant, comparison with material from other sites. For the restored vessels, the major areas of restoration are also noted. The illustrations and drawings round out the picture given by the descriptive text.

KANTHAROI

A. Flaring wall, offset lip, strap handles, and flaring foot with curved underside

1. Restored vessels

1. 50.614. (See figs.)[1]

Mended from twenty fragments with missing pieces restored in plaster and painted. Reddish-yellow clay (7.5 YR 6/6). Thin brown glaze inside. Outside unglazed except for decoration.

Restored: all of base, cul, and one handle; most of one side below lip (not illustrated); upper right section of other side; top of preserved handle.

Decoration. Lip: horizontal line top and bottom; in center of one side and to right of center of the other, a dotted rectangle with a large central dot, framed at each side by two parallel lines. Handle: line at each vertical edge; two transverse lines just above attachment at rim; line at root that continued round the vase.

Dimensions. Restored height at rim 16.5 cm.; at handle 18.0 cm.; diameter of rim front to back 14.2 cm.; restored width at handles 22.6 cm.; height of lip 3.2 cm.; width of handle 3.2 cm.

For two transverse lines on handle above rim, cf. the fragment from Thasos, H 108 (*BCH* 88 [1964], p. 97, no. 21 and p. 103, fig. 18).

1. *Hesperia*, 21 (1952), pl. 9 e.

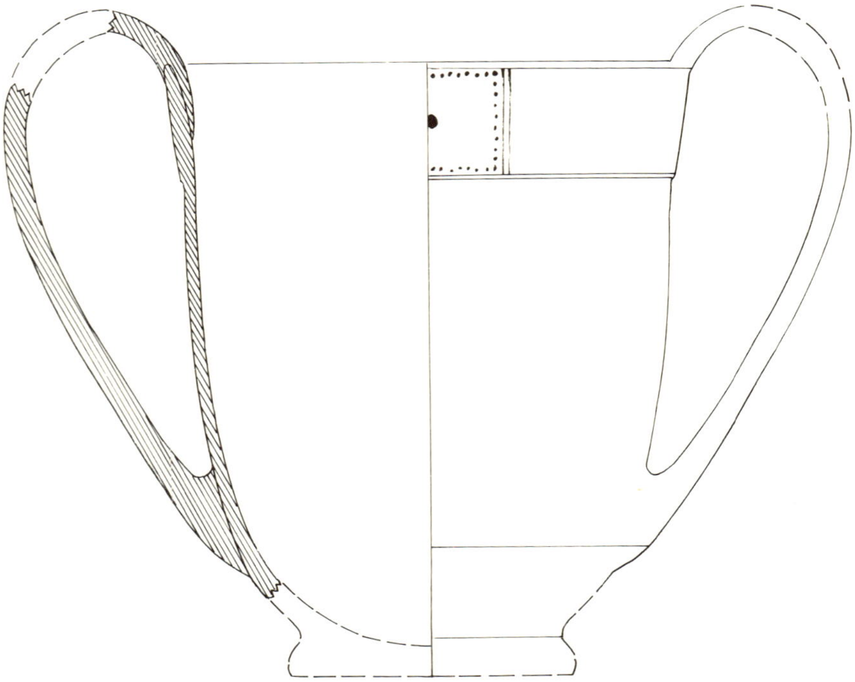

1

1

2. 51.145. (See figs.)
Mended from eleven fragments with missing pieces restored in plaster and painted. Reddish-yellow clay (5 YR 6/6). Thin reddish-brown glaze on inside. Outside unglazed except for decoration, some of it very faint.

Restored: base; all of body on one side, part on the other; one handle.

Decoration. Lip: line top and bottom, stopped at handles by a vertical line; two dot rosettes near center of lip. Line at each edge of handle. Line at handle root that continued round the vase.

Dimensions. Restored height at rim 17.5 cm.; at handles 19.4 cm.; restored diameter front to back 13.2 cm.; restored width at handles 23.6 cm.; height of lip 4.0 cm.; width of handles 3.1 cm.

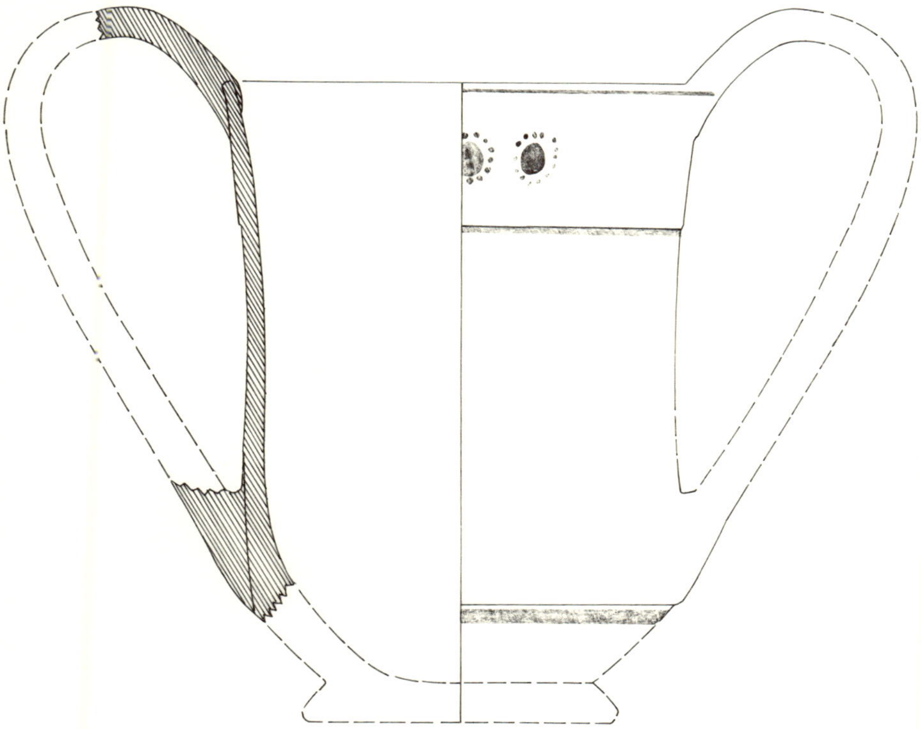

2

2

3. 50.567. (See figs.)[1]

Mended from ten fragments with missing pieces restored in plaster and painted. Light reddish-brown clay (5 YR 6/4). Reddish-brown glaze inside. Outside unglazed except for decoration.

Restored: base; both handles; all of one side, part of other side near right handle.

Decoration. Lip: two lines just below rim; three lines above junction of body. In middle of lip, zetoid pattern to right stopped at handle by a vertical line. To right of center on body, just below lip, three inverted triangles. Line at cul, line below that, then a band.

Dimensions. Restored height at rim 17.1 cm.; restored diameter front to back 13.3 cm.; height of lip 2.5 cm.

For the combination of the zetoid pattern and inverted triangles, cf., Troy G 63 and G 38 (*Troy*, fig. 304, nos. 1-2). These fragments come from a krater or a dinos. The zetoid pattern is bordered top and bottom by one line.

1. *Hesperia*, 21 (1952), pl. 9 f.

3

3

4. 51.80. (See figs.)
Mended from twenty-four fragments with missing pieces restored in plaster and painted. Light pinkish clay (7.5 YR 7/2). Thin glaze inside. Outside unglazed except for decoration, which is very faint.

Restored: most of cul; all of one handle; most of one side, part of rim and body on other side.

Decoration. Lip: line top and bottom; near the middle, portions of two rectangles each divided by two diagonals with dots in the interstices. It is not certain whether this pattern was repeated along the lip from handle to handle or not. At one handle, a vertical row of three small dots. Handle: line at each edge; transverse line just above attachment at rim; two more lines just above middle; line at handle root, which continues round the vase at the junction of the cul and body.

Dimensions. Restored height at rim 16.0 cm.; at handle 16.4 cm.; restored diameter front to back 14.0 cm.; restored width at handles 20.8 cm.; diameter of base 8.5 cm.; width of resting surface 0.2 cm.; height of lip 2.1 cm.; width of handle 2.5 cm.

For similar handle decoration, cf. Troy VIII.115, VIII,266, and VIII.267 (*Troy*, p. 277, fig. 303, 2 and p. 300, fig. 314, nos. 15, 16).

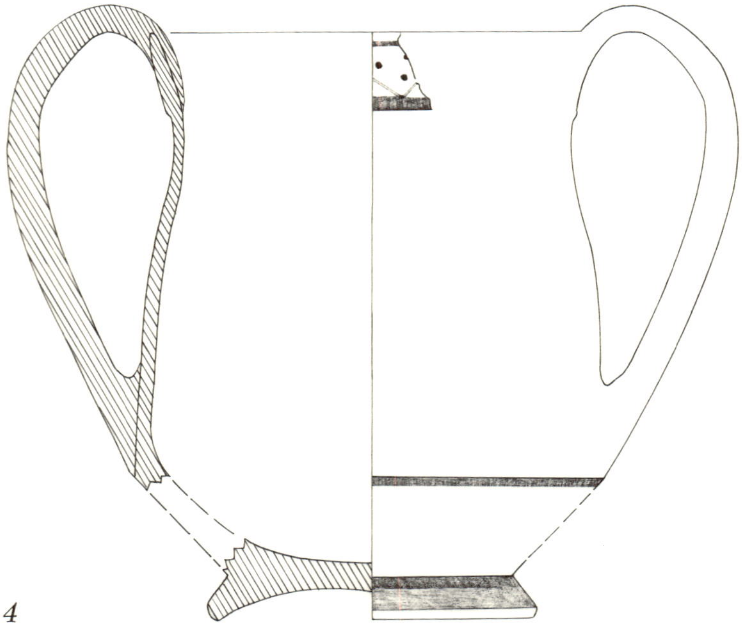

4

4

2. Fragments

5. (See figs.)

Four fragments of one vessel. Pink clay (7.5 YR 7/4). Black glaze inside, cracked near rim. Slip on outside. Glaze decoration.

50.489. Part of lip and wall. On lip, a line below rim, two lines at junction, part of a dotted rectangle with a dot in the center and two framing lines.

Preserved height 5.2 cm.; preserved width 4.2 cm.; height of lip 2.4 cm.

50.195 A. Fragment of lip and wall. Preserves some of horizontal lines at junction, the lower left corner of a dotted rectangle, and two framing lines.

Preserved height 2.7 cm.; preserved width 2.8 cm.

Surface find.

50.203 C. Fragment of strap handle at rim. Line at each edge of handle. On handle, just above rim, a large X, then parts of three transverse lines.

Width of handle 2.7 cm.

50.203 C 1. Fragment of strap handle and lip. On outside of lip, two vertical lines that separate decoration on lip from handle zone. Line at each edge of handle. On handle at rim, part of large X.

Width of handle 2.7 cm.

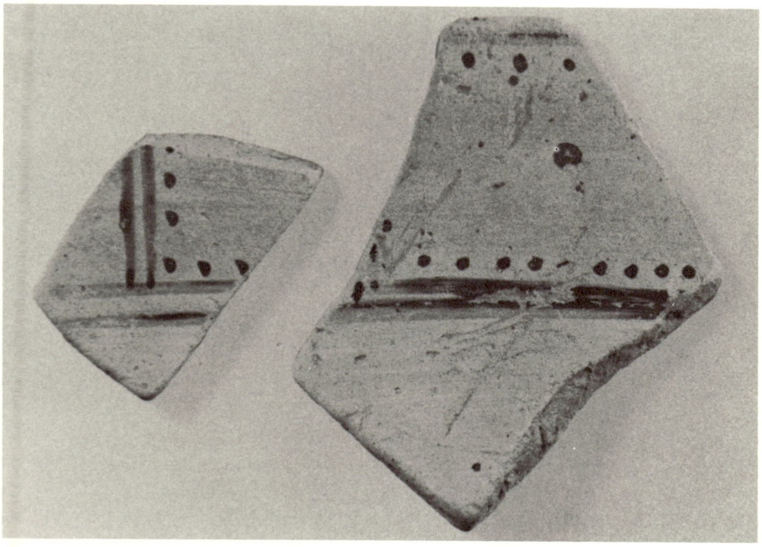

5

5

6.

Two fragments of one vessel. Pink clay (5 YR 7/4). Thin reddish-brown glaze on inside. Slip on outside. Glaze decoration.

53.129 A. (See fig.). Three joining fragments of lip and body. On lip, two lines below rim and one at junction. Two horizontal rows of six dots each framed right and left by two vertical lines, the whole ornament probably painted midway between the two handles.

Preserved height 9.4 cm.; diameter of rim 13.0 cm.; height of lip 2.5 cm.

53.129 B. Fragment of lip from near center, preserving horizontal lines, one pair of vertical lines, and two dots from each row.

Preserved height 4.4 cm.; diameter of rim 13.0 cm.; height of lip 2.5 cm.

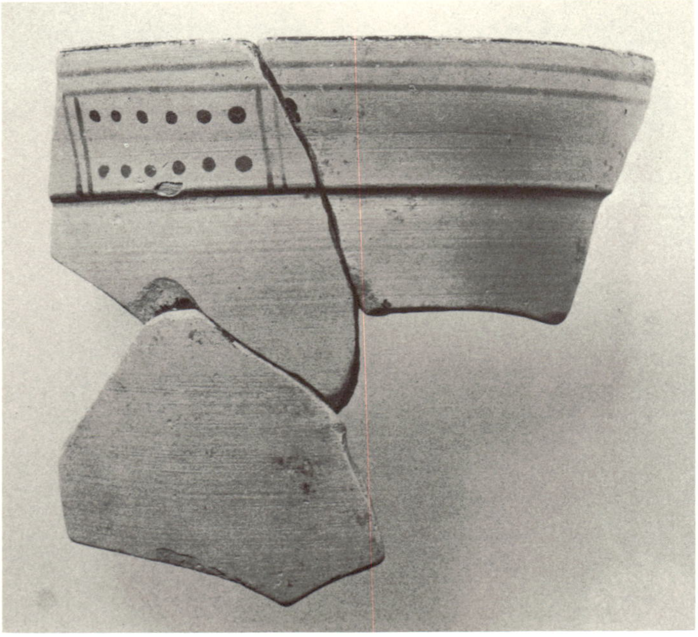

6

7.

Four fragments of one vessel. Reddish-yellow clay (5 YR 7/6). Glazed inside, ranging in color from reddish-brown to brownish-black. Unglazed outside, except for decoration.

53.128 A. (See fig.) Three joining fragments of offset lip and wall. On lip, below rim, row of dots, then a line, below that zetoid pattern to right, and two more lines.

Preserved height 9.7 cm.; preserved width 7.1 cm.; height of lip 2.3 cm.

50.203 E. (See fig.) Small fragment preserving part of lip with decoration as above. Below lip, inverted triangle.

Preserved height 3.1 cm.; preserved width 2.8 cm.; height of lip 2.3 cm.

50.487 B. Small fragment preserving part of lip with decoration as above.

Preserved height 2.6 cm.; preserved width 3.9 cm.; height of lip 2.3 cm.

53.128 B. Strap handle and small portion of rim and of wall near root, mended from four joining fragments. Line at each edge. Three transverse lines above attachment at rim; one line just below cul that presumably continued round the vase.

Preserved height 18.3 cm.; width of handle 2.5-2.9 cm.

This kantharos is similar in shape and decoration to no. **1**.

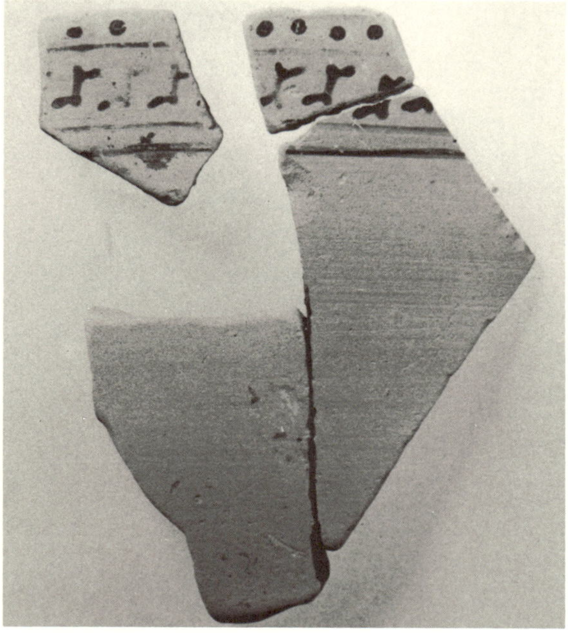

7

8. (See fig.)

Two fragments of one vessel. Reddish-yellow clay (7.5 YR 7/6). Black glaze inside. Slip on outside. Glaze decoration.

50.495. Two joining fragments of lip. Line at junction of lip and body. On lip, two inverted triangles and part of a third.

Preserved height 2.1 cm.; preserved width 3.4 cm.; height of lip 1.5 cm.

50.492. Fragment of handle at rim. Line at each edge of handle mostly flaked. On handle, just above rim, three triangles, then two tranverse lines of glaze, all partly flaked.

Width of handle 3.2 cm.

8

9.

Four fragments of one vessel. Light red clay (2.5 YR 6/8). Thin reddish glaze on inside. Slip on outside. Glaze decoration, very faintly preserved.

50.490. (See fig.) Three joining fragments of lip and wall. On lip, between line top and bottom, five-stroke step pattern to right.

Preserved height 8.8 cm.; preserved width 4.9 cm.; height of lip 2.3 cm.

50.490.2. Fragment of handle from area near rim, preserving some of the glaze inside rim. Line at each edge of handle; three transverse lines above attachment to rim.

Maximum preserved dimension 4.0 cm.; width of handle 2.4 cm.

50.490.1. Fragment of wall, cul, and handle root. Line at each edge of handle. Line at cul, another line 0.5 cm. below it, then a band of glaze.

Preserved height 8.6 cm.; preserved width 9.0 cm.; width of handle 2.3 cm.

50.133. Fragment of wall, cul and handle root.

Preserved height 4.3 cm.; preserved width 4.2 cm.

For the decoration and profile of the handle of this kantharos, cf. no. **1**.

9

10. (See fig.)
Two fragments of one vessel. Red clay (2.5 YR 6/8). Reddish-brown glaze on inside. Slip on outside. Glaze decoration.

50.498. Fragment preserving lip and small portion of wall from near handle zone. On lip, line below rim, another at junction, two vertical lines near left break. Vertical line near right edge indicates decoration interrupted by handle (as, e.g., nos. **2**, **21**, and **22**).

Preserved height 2.8 cm.; preserved width 3.9 cm.; height of lip 2.2 cm.

54.75. Fragment of lip preserving line top and bottom, part of dotted rectangle with dot in center, and small portion of framing line on right.

Preserved height 2.5 cm.; preserved width 3.2 cm.; height of lip 2.2 cm.

Same decoration as no. **22**, below.

11. 50.503. (See fig.)
Fragment of lip. Pink clay (7.5 YR 7/4). The thickening of the rim at the upper left indicates the beginning of the handle. Reddish-brown glaze on inside. Slip on outside. Glaze decoration. Line below rim, another near junction of body. Vertical line on left to separate decoration on lip from handle zone.

Preserved height 4.2 cm.; preserved width 3.0 cm.

10

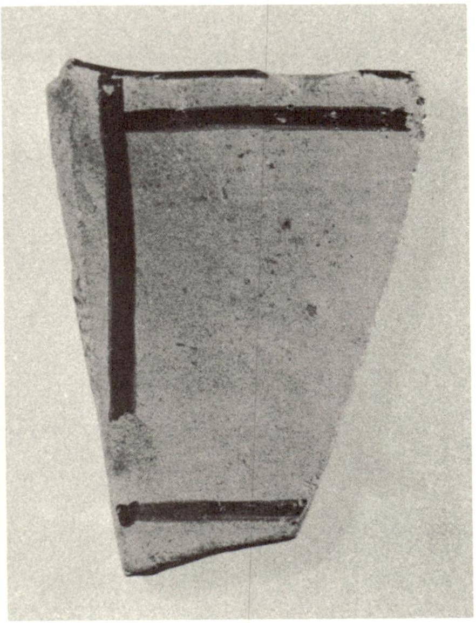

11

12. 50.499. (See fig.)
Fragment of lip and wall. Reddish-yellow clay (5 YR 6/6). Black glaze inside. On lip, line below rim, another just above junction. Part of dotted rectangle with large dot in the center, flanked by two vertical lines, presumably painted midway between handles (as no. **1**).

Preserved height 5.4 cm.; preserved width 4.5 cm.; height of lip 3.3 cm.

13. 50.195 B. (See fig.)
Fragment of lip. Pink clay (7.5 YR 7/4). Black glaze inside. Outside unglazed except for decoration which has mostly flaked. Between a line top and bottom, an X framed on the left hand side by parts of two lines, on the right by one.

Preserved height 2.9 cm.; preserved width 2.3 cm.

Surface find.

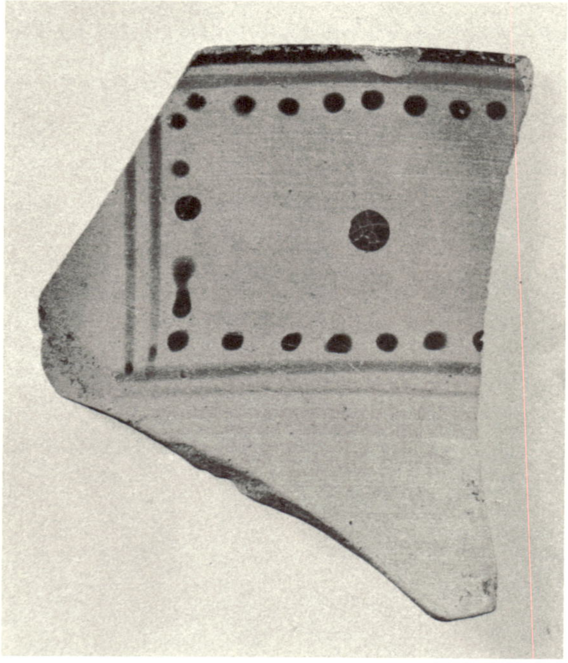

12

13

14. 50.488. (See fig.)
Fragment of lip. Reddish-yellow clay (5 YR 6/6). Reddish-brown glaze on inside. Slip on outside. Glaze decoration. Between line top and bottom, two compass-drawn circles.

Preserved height 3.2 cm.; preserved width 3.0 cm.

15. 50.200. (See fig.)

Fragment of lip. Reddish-yellow clay (5 YR 6/6). Thin reddish-brown glaze on inside. Outside unglazed except for decoration. Preserves two lines at rim, a dot below, and two vertical lines.

Preserved height 2.1 cm.; preserved width 2.0 cm.

14

15

3. Variants

The next two restored vessels appear to be variants of this shape of kantharos. The basic difference is that the lip is not offset, but forms a continuous curve with the body.

16. 50.398. (See figs.)[1]

Mended from eighteen fragments with missing pieces restored in plaster and painted. Reddish-yellow clay (5 YR 7/6). Thin reddish-brown glaze on inside. Outside unglazed except for decoration.

Restored: rim and most of body except at handles; part of cul on one side.

Decoration. Two lines below rim, 1.3 cm. apart, stopped at handle by a vertical line. Between two horizontal lines, a dot or part of linear pattern. Handles: line at each edge; three slightly oblique lines above attachment at rim; three more lines above middle of handle; two lines above handle root. Thick line at cul that continues round the vessel. Band of glaze 1.8 cm. above base; glazed base.

Dimensions. Height at rim 12.2 cm.; at handle 13.3 cm.; restored diameter back to front 13.3 cm.; width with handles 19.0 cm.; diameter of base 6.8 cm.; width of handles 2.3-2.5 cm.

Surface find.

For similar handle decoration, cf. no. **4** and the comparisons cited at the end of its description. For the shape, cf. Troy 32.29 (*Troy*, p. 299, figs. 306 a and 318 b and c).

1. *Hesperia*, 21 (1952), pl. 10 a; Iris C. Love, "Kantharos or Karcheseion? A Samothracian Contribution," *Essays in Memory of Karl Lehmann* (New York, 1964), fig. 15.

16

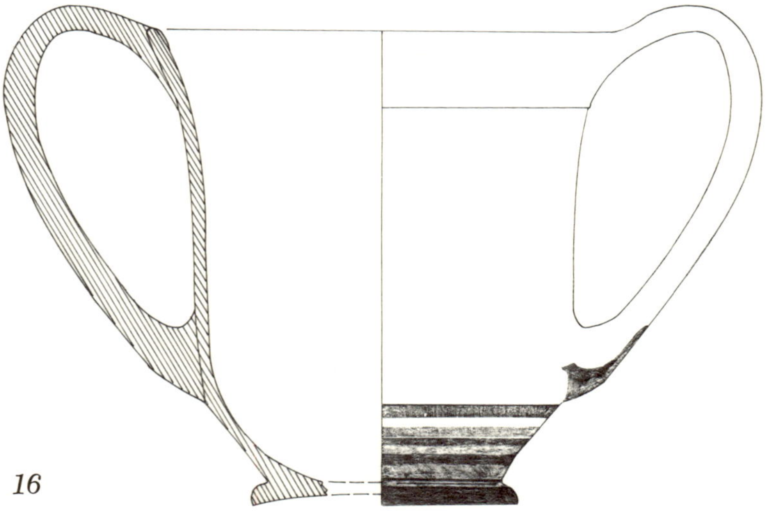

16

16

17. 51.73. (See figs.)
Mended from sixteen fragments with missing pieces restored in plaster and painted. Reddish-yellow clay (7.5 YR 7/6). Thin blackish-brown glaze on inside. Glaze decoration on outside. Surface worn.

Restored: most of one side except for area near one handle and just above base; lower part of other side, one handle except for attachment at rim.

Decoration. Line at each edge of handle. Base.

Dimensions. Height at rim 11.1 cm.; restored diameter of rim 10.8 cm.; restored width with handles 18.2 cm.; diameter of base 6.1 cm.; width of handles 2.3 cm.

The shape is similar to Troy 32.29 (*Troy*, fig. 306 a, fig. 317, no. 12 and fig. 318 b and c; also p. 299, where it is compared with no. **16**).

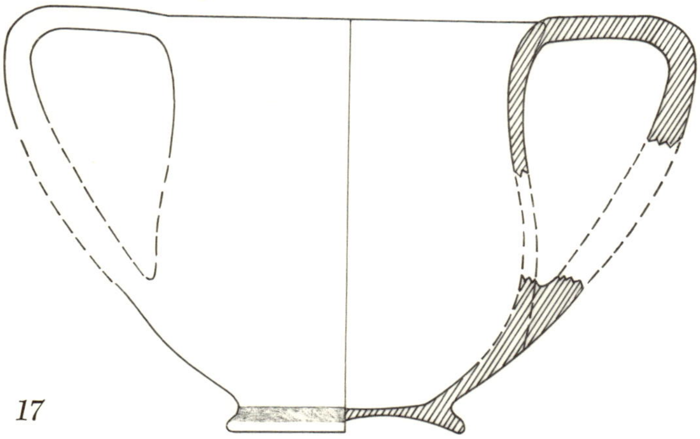

17

17

B. *Globular body, inset rim, strap handles and flaring foot with straight or curving underside;*[1] *on one example* (**24**), *the resting surface tapers to an edge.*

1. The question whether this shape should be called a kantharos or not has been raised by Paul Courbin in "Les origines du canthare attique archaïque," *BCH*, 77 (1953), pp. 322 ff. Although the name kantharos is the one normally given to geometric examples of this shape, this scholar contends that it is not really a kantharos, nor is it the direct ancestor of the Attic kantharos. But, since this shape bears more similarities to the kantharos than it does to any other known shape, in this study, for convenience, we shall retain the name kantharos.

1. Restored vessels

18. 50.125. (See figs.)[1]

Mended from twenty-eight fragments, with missing pieces restored in plaster and painted. Reddish-yellow clay (5 YR 6/6). Reddish-brown glaze on inside. Slip on outside. Very faint glaze decoration. Surface worn in many places.

Restored: some of rim and upper part of body on one side, part of the other; all of one handle, part of the other; part of body below handle zone; part of base under restored handle.

Decoration. Lip: between a line top and bottom, two dot-rosettes, one in the middle, the other near the handle (a third near the opposite handle is missing on each side); vertical line on each side of handle. Handle: line at each edge; two transverse lines just above attachment at rim; two lines below handle root that continue round the vase. Traces of glaze on base.

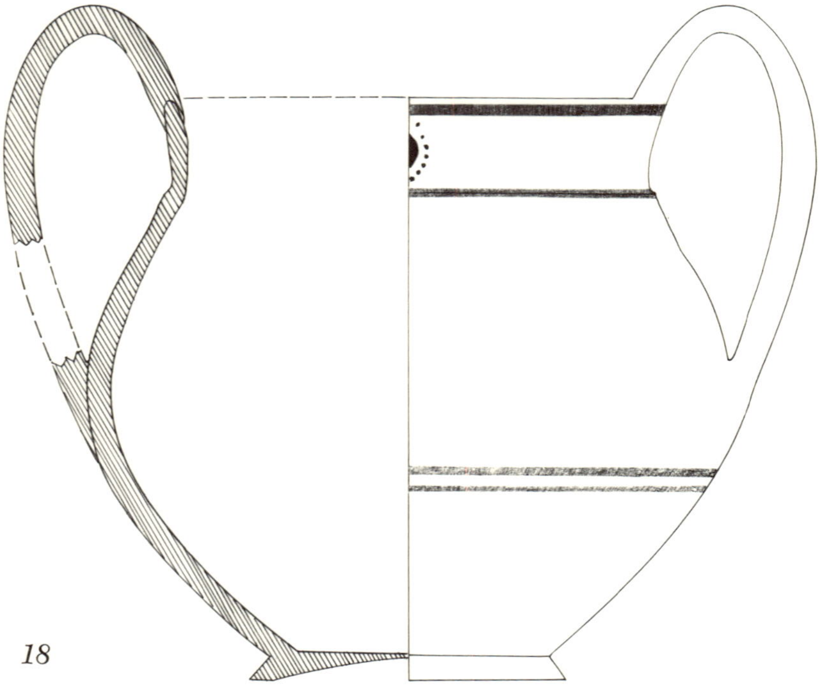

18

Dimensions. Height at rim 16.2 cm.; at handle 18.0 cm.; restored diameter of rim front to back 13.4 cm.; restored width at handles 21.0 cm.; diameter of base 7.9 cm.; width of resting surface 0.5 cm.; height of lip 2.7 cm.; width of handle 3.3 cm.

1. *Hesperia*, 21 (1952), pl. 10b.

18

19. 51.76. (See figs.)
Mended from sixteen fragments with missing pieces restored in plaster and painted. Reddish-yellow clay (5 YR 6/6). Thin reddish-brown glaze on inside. Outside unglazed except for decoration, which has flaked in places. Worn surface.

Restored: one side, except for small fragments near left handle root; small portion of lip and body on other side; one handle, most of other except for root and attachment at rim.

Decoration. Lip: between line top and bottom, zetoid pattern to right; line just above ring. Handle: line at each edge, two transverse lines above attachment at rim. Band of glaze 1.8 cm. wide below handle and another 1.0 cm. wide above the base. Glazed base.

Dimensions. Height at rim 14.2 cm.; at handle 17.0 cm.; restored diameter front to back 13.2 cm.; restored width with handles 21.4 cm.; diameter of base 8.5 cm.; width of resting surface 0.3 cm.; height of lip 2.3 cm.

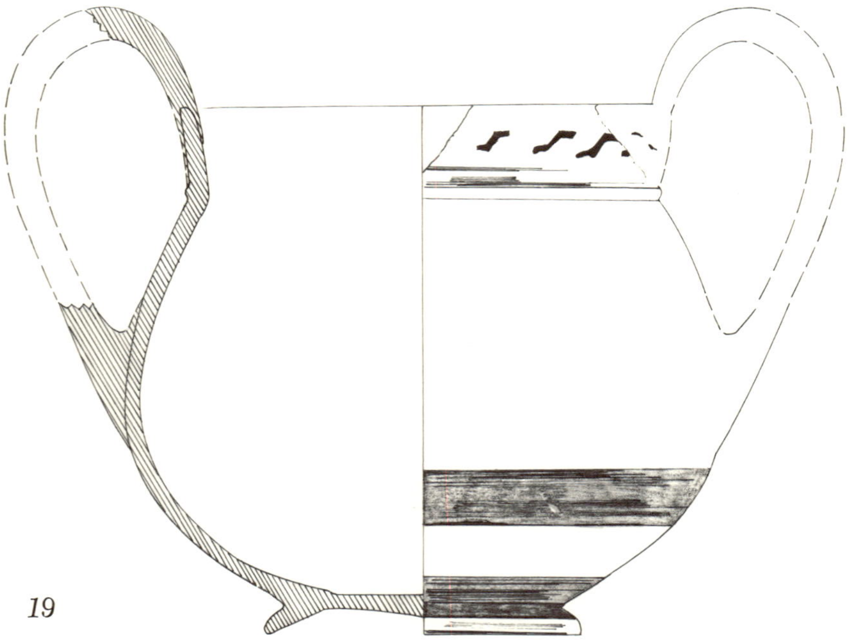

19

19

20. 51.78. (See figs.)
Mended from fourteen fragments with missing pieces restored in plaster and painted. Light yellowish-brown clay (10 YR 6/4). Traces of black glaze inside. Outside unglazed except for decoration, which is very faint. Worn surface.

Restored: base; one handle; all of one side, half of the other.

Decoration. Lip: line below rim, two lines above junction; in middle, zetoid pattern to right. In the center, on body, just below lip, short vertical line flanked right and left by a four-stroke zigzag line. Handle: line at each edge; two transverse lines above attachment at rim, then two units of a pattern, each comprised of a large X separated by two lines top and bottom.

Dimensions. Restored height at rim 13.0 cm.; at handle 16.0 cm.; restored diameter front to back 15.0 cm.; restored width with handles 22.5 cm.; height of lip 2.5 cm.; width of handle 3.5 cm.

For the lip pattern, cf. Troy G.56 and F.283 (*Troy*, p. 282 and fig. 305, no. 6; p. 295 and fig. 311, no. 1) and Thasos H 111 (*BCH*, 88 [1964], p. 97, no. 22 and fig. 13); for a handle fragment decorated with an X and two transverse lines, cf. Troy G.78 (*Troy*, p. 282 and fig. 305, no. 15); from Thasos there is a handle fragment (D 103) that preserves an X just above the rim, then six transverse lines and part of another X (*BCH*, 88 [1964], p. 97, no. 20 and p. 103, fig. 18).

20

20

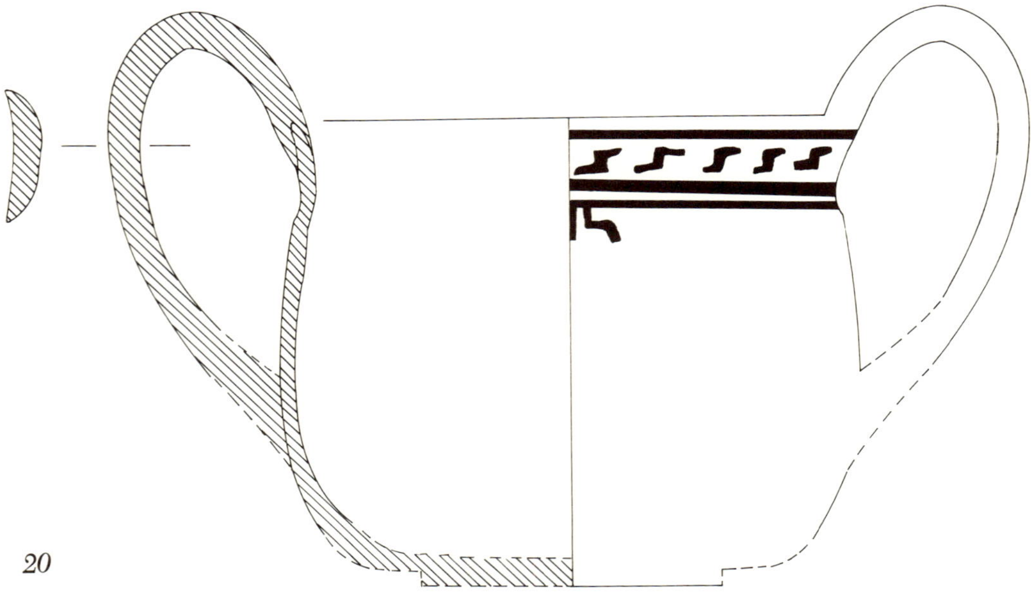

20

21. 51.86. (See figs.)
Mended from twenty-five fragments with the missing pieces restored in plaster and painted. Reddish-yellow clay (5 YR 6/6). Thin black glaze on inside. Slip on outside. Glaze decoration. Surface worn.

Restored: much of one side, including part of the lip; part of other side, particularly below the lip.

Decoration. Lip: between a line top and bottom, three rectangles comprised of four horizontal rows of seven dots each, the decoration stopped at handles by a vertical line. Handles: line at each edge; three transverse lines above attachment at rim (one handle only); three more lines near top of handle, and again near the middle; line at handle root continuing round the vase. Each group of transverse lines on both handles is connected by two diagonal parallel lines drawn from the upper left to lower right. Above base, a wide band of glaze (4.0 cm.), mostly flaked.

Dimensions. Height at rim 10.8 cm.; at handles 14.0 cm.; diameter of rim front to back 12.9 cm.; width at handles 20.9 cm.; diameter of base 6.7 cm.; width of resting surface 0.3 cm.; height of lip 1.9 cm.; width of handles 2.3 cm.

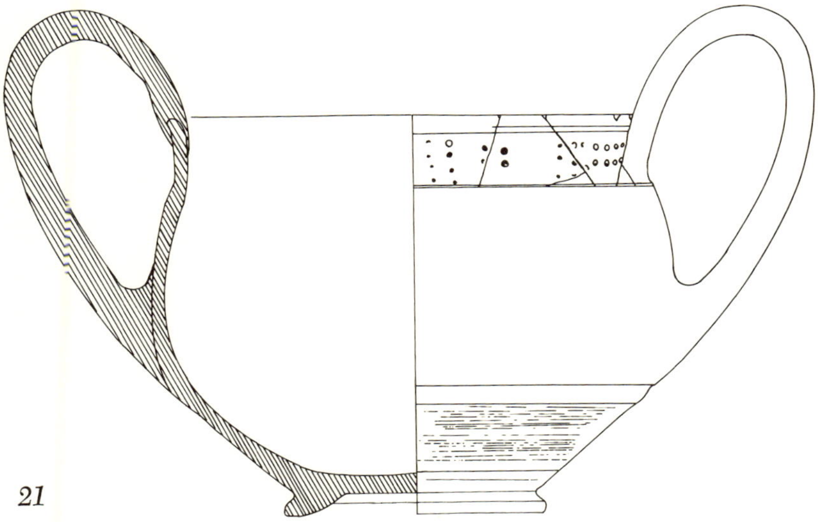

21

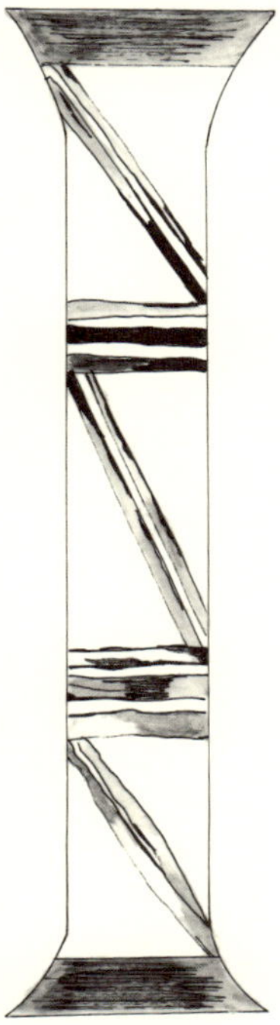

21

21

22. 51.370. (See figs.)
Mended from fourteen fragments with missing pieces restored in plaster and painted. Traces of reddish-brown glaze on inside. Reddish-yellow clay (5 YR 6/6). Outside unglazed except for decoration. Very worn surface.

Restored: base; one handle; most of one side, part of the other.

Decoration. Lip: line top and bottom, stopped at handle by a vertical line. Near center of lip, two dotted rectangles with a larger dot in the center, each framed by two vertical lines. Handle: line at each edge, mostly flaked; three transverse lines above attachment at rim.

Dimensions. Restored height at rim 10.5 cm.; at handle 14.0 cm.; restored diameter front to back 13.4 cm.; restored width at handles 19.1 cm.; height of lip 2.0 cm.; width of handle 2.7 cm.

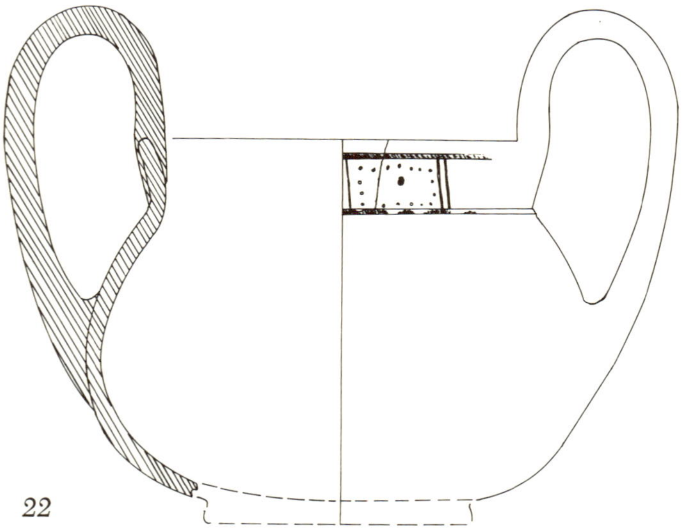

22

22

23. 51.77. (See figs.)
Mended from seventeen fragments with missing pieces restored in plaster and painted. Light red clay (2.5 YR 6/6). A few traces of reddish glaze on inside. Outside unglazed except for decoration, which is very faint. Very worn surface.

Restored: all of base; one handle; lower part of one side, right half of other.

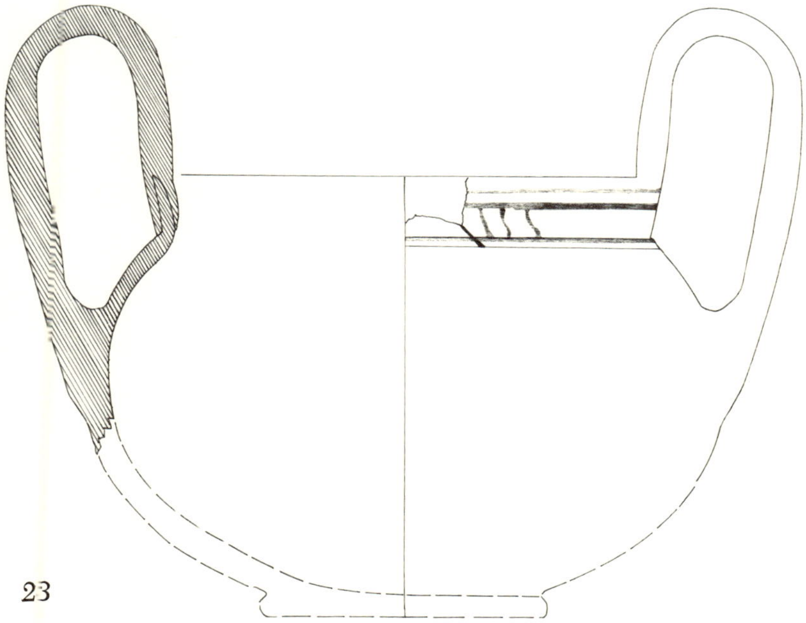

23

23

Decoration. Lip: two lines below rim, line at junction; near middle of one side, part of a netlike pattern. A nonjoining fragment (see below) also preserves part of this pattern, which does not occur elsewhere on the preserved fragments of this subgeometric pottery from the Temenos, but which does occur on a fragment recently found on the Akropolis at Palaeopolis and discussed below (ad **23**). Handle: line at each edge, preserved only at handle root; two transverse lines above attachment at rim.

Dimensions. Restored height at rim 12.4 cm.; at handle 16.6 cm.; restored diameter front to back 15.9 cm.; diameter of body 17.9 cm.; width of handle 2.9 cm.; height of lip 1.9 cm.

X. 51.309. (See fig.)
Nonjoining fragment of lip and body preserving part of pattern on lip.

Preserved height 6.0 cm.; preserved width 6.4 cm.

23

ad **23.** (See figs.)
Fragment of lip and body of a globular kantharos recovered from the Akropolis at Palaeopolis.[1] Reddish-yellow clay (5 YR 6/6). A few traces of reddish glaze on inside. Outside unglazed except for decoration. On lip, netlike pattern. Below the lip, there are two long inverted triangles.

Preserved height 4.4 cm.; preserved width 5.1 cm.; height of lip 1.4 cm.

For the lip pattern, cf. Troy G.48 (*Troy*, p. 282 and fig. 305, no. 13) where it is part of the vertical decoration of a cup or a bowl.

1. Above, p. 320, n. 15.

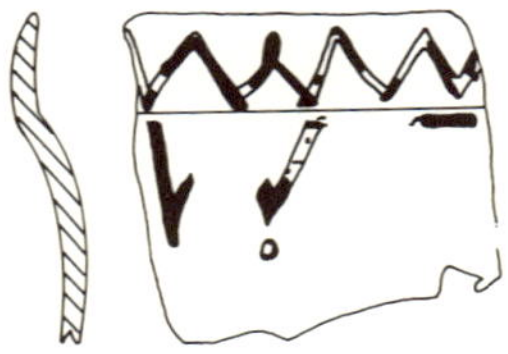

ad23

ad23

24. 51.88. (See figs.)
Mended from eleven fragments with missing pieces restored in plaster and painted. Unglazed except for decoration which has mostly flaked. The clay is grayish-brown in color and appears to have been burned.

Restored: most of one side, including lip, some of lower wall and lip of other side; part of handle root.

Decoration. Lip glazed inside. Circle of glaze on floor. Line at each edge of handle; two transverse lines above attachment at rim.

Dimensions. Height at rim 10.3 cm.; at handle 12.7 cm.; restored diameter of rim front to back 10.2 cm.; width with handle 14.7 cm.; diameter of base 6.7 cm.; height of lip 1.2 cm.; width of handle 2.8 cm.

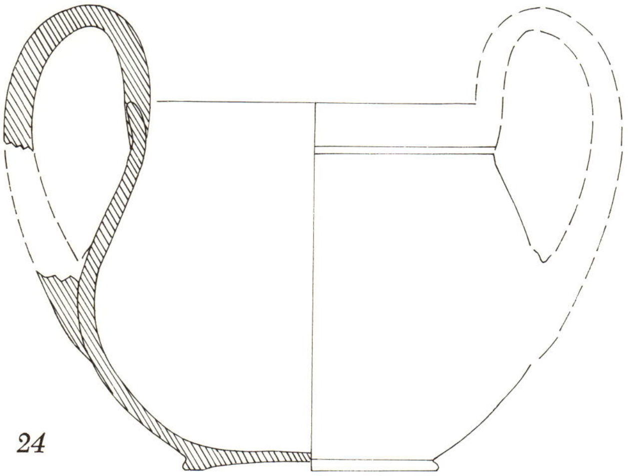

24

24

25. 51.79. (See figs.)
Mended from nineteen fragments with missing pieces restored in plaster and painted. Light red clay (2.5 YR 6/6). Traces of reddish-brown glaze on inside and at junction of foot and body. Very worn surface.

Restored: most of one side, except for area just above base; one handle except for portion attached to rim; part of one side from area just above foot to rim.

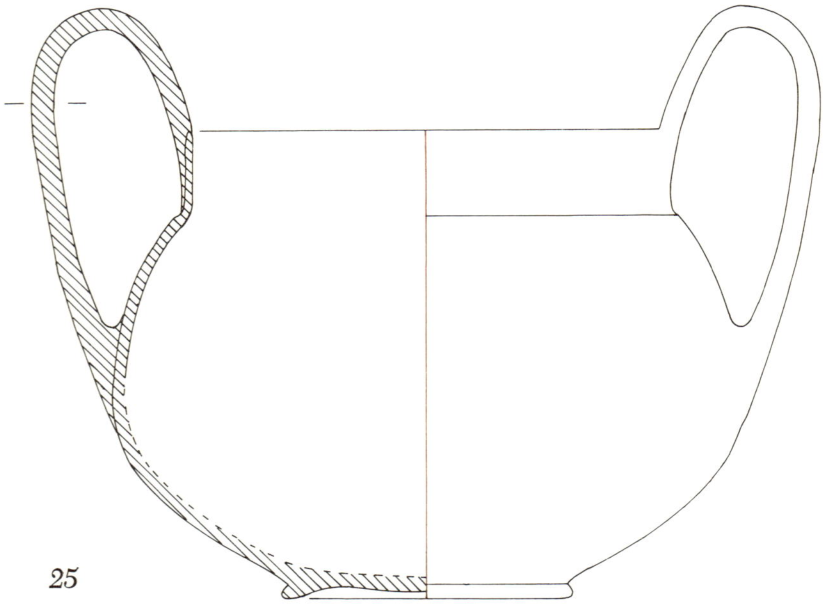

25

25

No preserved decoration.

Dimensions. Height at rim 12.9 cm.; at handle 16.4 cm.; restored diameter front to back 15.5 cm.; width with handles 21.4 cm.; diameter of base 7.6 cm.; width of resting surface 0.3 cm.; height of lip 2.1 cm.; width of handle 3.3 cm.

2. Fragments

26. (See figs.)

Two fragments of one vessel. Brownish-black glaze inside. Outside unglazed except for decoration.

74.1. Four joining fragments preserving part of lip and body, and all of one strap handle. Reddish-yellow clay (5 YR 6/6). On lip, zetoid pattern to right between one line at the top and two at the bottom, stopped at handle by a diagonal line terminating below

26

26

the lip in a spiral. Small portion of similar line on other side of handle. Handle: line at each edge; top glazed with root of knob preserved that served as a thumb rest. Below this glazed area, three transverse lines.

Preserved height 11.8 cm.; diameter of rim 16.0 cm.; height of lip 1.7 cm.

50.491. Three joining fragments of lip preserving zetoid pattern and lines. Below lip, in what may be the center, a hanging triangular ornament.

Preserved height 2.7 cm.; diameter of rim 16.0 cm.; height of lip 1.7 cm.

For the spiral on the body below the lip, cf. Troy VIII.263 (*Troy*, p. 300, and fig. 314, no. 12) and Troy no. 3677 (Schmidt, *Heinrich Schliemann's Sammlung trojanischer Altertümer*, p. 182, no. 3677). Both of these Trojan fragments have horizontal lines on the lip instead of a zetoid pattern. Troy no. 3657 shows a spiral below two friezes of zetoid pattern (*ibid.*, p. 181, no. 3657). This latter fragment comes from a krater or a dinos. For the knob on the handle, cf. a fragment from Troy (Dörpfeld, *Troja und Ilion*, p. 311, fig. 240), and no. **40** below.

27.

Two fragments of one vessel. Reddish-yellow clay (5 YR 7/6). Brownish-black glaze on inside. Outside unglazed except for decoration.

50.505. (See fig.) Fragment of lip and body. On lip, line at rim, another at junction. Between them, probably midway between handles, two dot-rosettes.

Preserved height 7.2 cm.; diameter of rim 12.2 cm.; height of lip 1.9 cm.

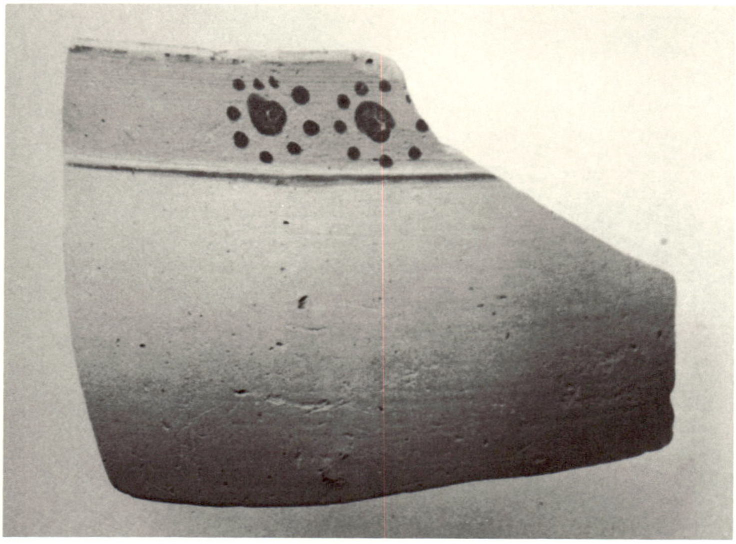

27

51.288. Two joining fragments of lip and body, preserving two horizontal lines and part of one dot-rosette.

Preserved height 4.3 cm.; height of lip 1.9 cm.

28. 50.150 B. (See figs.)

Five joining fragments preserving part of rim and body. Reddish-yellow clay (5 YR 6/6). A few traces of reddish-brown glaze on inside. Slip on outside. Glaze decoration. Surface very worn. On lip, zetoid pattern to left. Traces of a band of glaze (0.7 cm.) 8.0 cm. below lip.

Preserved height 11.0 cm.; preserved width 16.5 cm.; height of lip 2.1 cm.

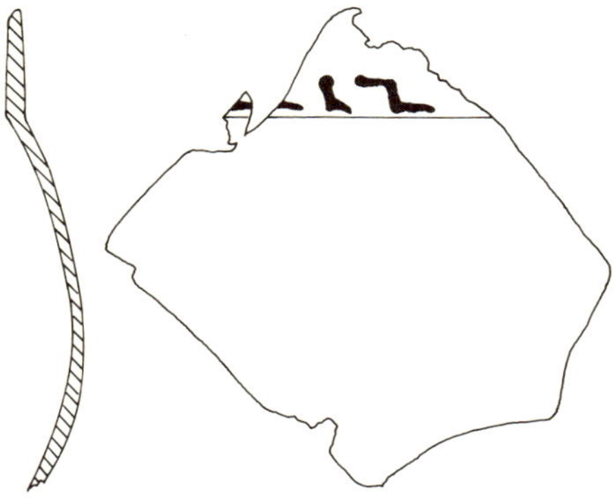

28

28

29. 53.126. (See fig.)
Eight joining fragments preserving part of lip, body, and strap handle. Reddish-yellow clay (5 YR 6/6). Traces of brownish glaze inside. Slip on outside. Decoration in glaze, faint in places. On lip, four horizontal lines, stopped at handle by a vertical line.

Preserved height 10.6 cm.; diameter of rim 11.0 cm.; height of lip 2.0 cm.

For three lines on the lip, cf. Troy G.40 (*Troy*, p. 282 and fig. 305, no. 4). This fragment is not from a globular kantharos, but from a cup.

29

30. 51.291. (See fig.)
Fragment of lip. Pink clay (7.5 YR 7/4). Traces of brownish-black glaze on inside. Outside unglazed except for decoration. Preserves part of dotted rectangle (three rows of two dots each) and three surrounding lines.

Preserved height 2.9 cm.; preserved width 1.8 cm.; height of lip 2.1 cm.

31. 50.493. (See fig.)
Fragment of lip. Reddish-yellow clay (5 YR 6/6). Thin blackish-brown glaze on inside. Outside unglazed except for decoration. Line at junction of lip and body. Small cross on lip.

Preserved height 2.7 cm.; preserved width 4.6 cm.; height of lip 2.0 cm.

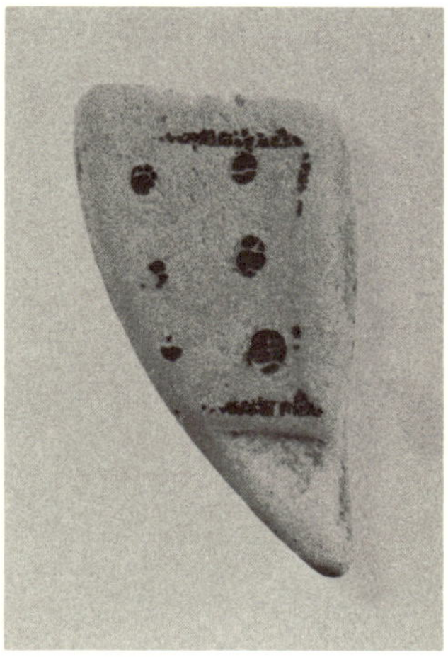

30

31

3. Variants

The following five restored vessels seem to be variants of the globular kantharos. The first four (nos. **32-35**) differ mainly by having a lip that forms a continuous curve with the body. The fifth (no. **36**) retains the inset lip, but is less tall. Its body does not curve inward as sharply toward the lip, and the handles are correspondingly shorter. The two fragments (no. **37**) are closest in shape to no. **32**.

A. RESTORED VESSELS

32. 51.74. (See figs.)
Mended from thirty-seven fragments with missing pieces restored in plaster and painted. Reddish-yellow clay (5 YR 6/6). Brownish-black glaze on inside. Outside unglazed except for decoration, which has almost completely flaked off.

Restored: most of one side; small portions of the other.

Decoration. Line at rim and on each edge of handles. Band of glaze on base.

Dimensions. Height at rim 17.3 cm.; at handle 18.9 cm.; restored diameter front to back 13.0 cm.; width with handles 19.8 cm.; diameter of base 7.3 cm.; width of handle 3.0 cm.

Unstratified find.

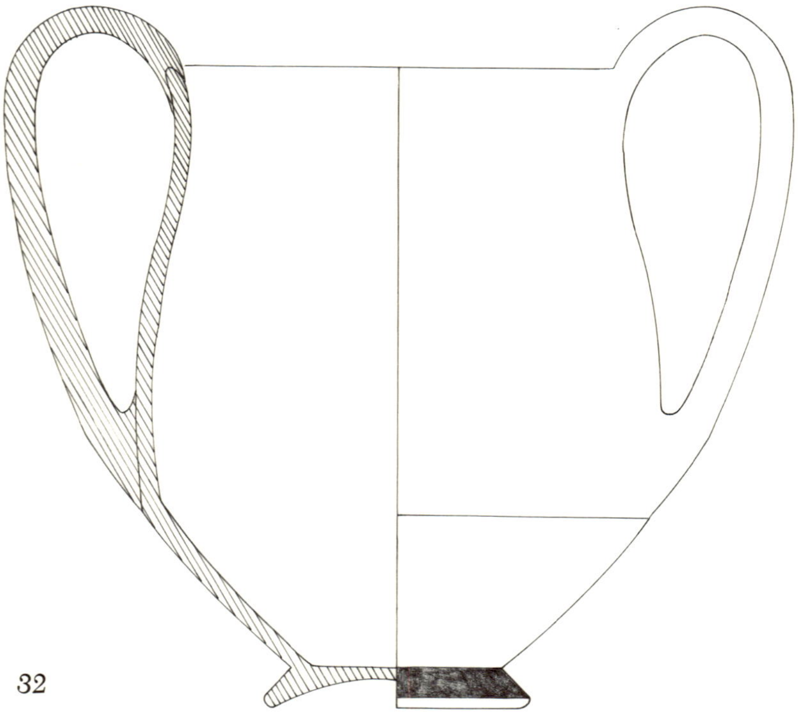

32

32

33. 51.75. (See figs.)
Mended from thirty-two fragments with missing pieces restored in plaster and painted. Reddish-yellow clay (5 YR 6/6). Reddish-brown glaze on inside. Outside unglazed except for lower half of base.

Restored: upper part of body including all of rim, one handle except for root, part of other handle.

Dimensions. Restored height at rim 14.2 cm.; at handle 15.0 cm.; restored diameter of mouth front to back 10.2 cm.; restored width with handles 18.8 cm.; diameter of base 6.6 cm.

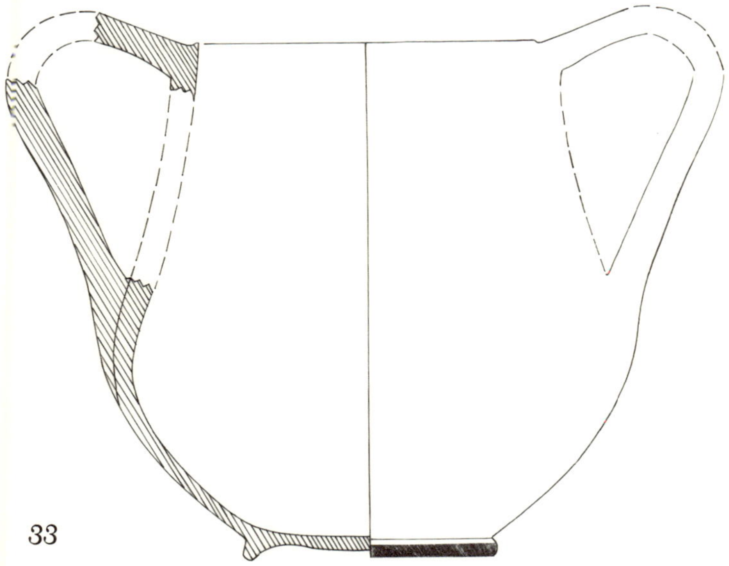

33

33

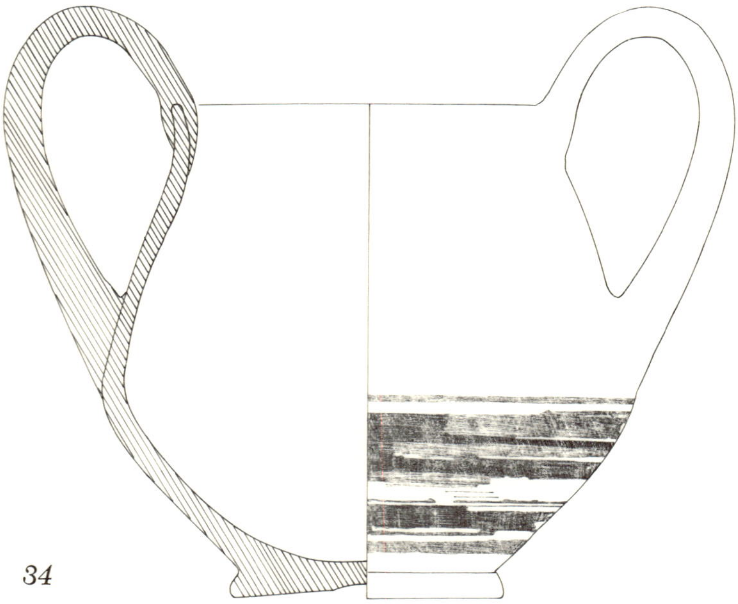

34

34

34. 50.597. (See figs.)
Mended from five fragments with missing pieces restored in plaster and painted. Reddish-yellow clay (7.5 YR 7/6). Black glaze inside. Outside unglazed except for decoration. Very worn surface.

Restored: most of one side from rim to just above foot; all of rim and part of body on other side; upper part of one handle.

Decoration. Handle: line at each edge; transverse line above attachment at rim. Band of glaze 5.0 cm. wide below handle.

Dimensions. Height at rim 13.2 cm.; at handle 16.0 cm.; diameter at rim front to back 14.4 cm.; width including handles 19.8 cm.; diameter of base 7.2 cm.; width of resting surface 0.3 cm.

35. 51.85. (See fig.)
Mended from eight fragments with missing pieces restored in plaster and painted. Light brown clay (7.5 YR 6/4). Reddish-brown glaze on inside, very worn. Outside unglazed except for decoration which is very faint.

Restored: most of one side above base; one handle except for attachment at rim.

Decoration. Line on lip 2.0 cm. below rim.

Dimensions. Height at rim 8.2 cm.; restored diameter of mouth 8.9 cm.; of body 10.1 cm.; diameter of base 5.5 cm.

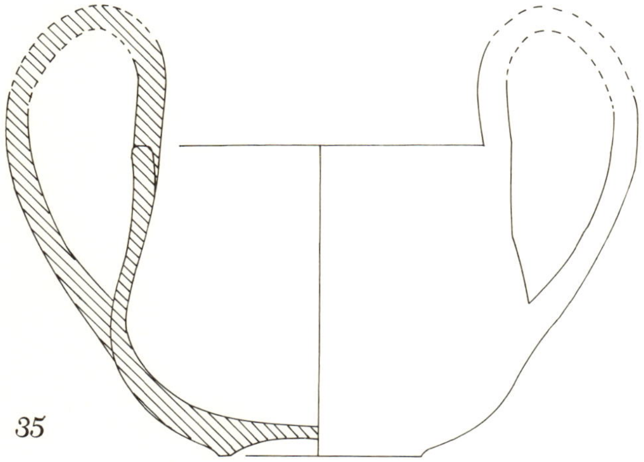

35

36. 50.563. (See figs.)[1]
Mended from ten fragments with missing pieces restored in plaster and painted. Reddish-yellow clay (5 YR 6/6). A few traces of reddish-brown glaze on inside. Outside unglazed except for decoration which is very faint. Worn surface.

Restored: all of one side; lower right portion of other side; one handle; most of base.

Decoration. Lip: line top and bottom. Handle: transverse line above attachment to rim; line down center from rim to root.

Dimensions. Height at rim 8.2 cm.; at handle 9.0 cm.; restored diameter front to back 15.4 cm.; restored width at handles 21.9 cm.; restored diameter of base 6.3 cm.; width of resting surface 0.2 cm.; height of lip 1.5 cm.; width of handle 3.0 cm.

For the median line on top of handle, cf. Troy G.3 (*Troy*, p. 282 and fig. 305, no. 14 and fig. 318, no. 7), and Thasos H 148 (*BCH*, 88 [1964], p. 93, no. 4, p. 94, fig. 11).

1. *Hesperia*, 21 (1952), pl. 10c.

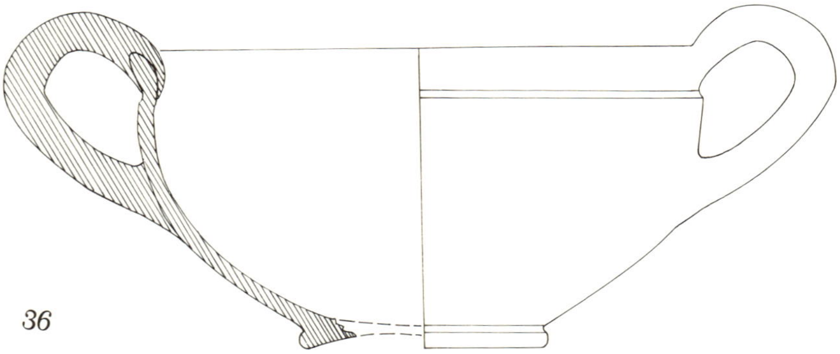

36

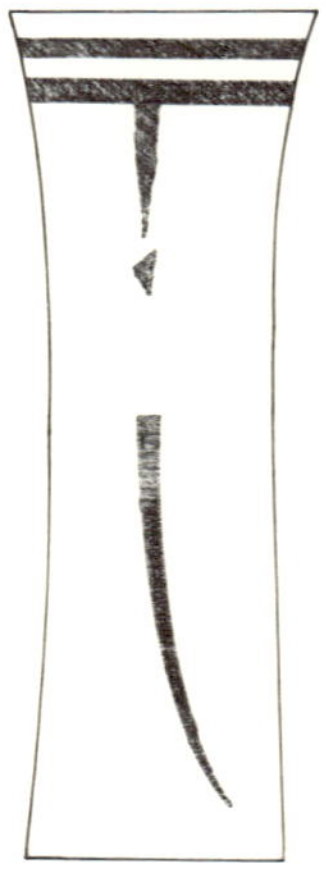

36

36

B. FRAGMENTS

37.

Two fragments of one vessel. Light brown clay (7.5 YR 6/4). Grayish-brown glaze on inside. Outside unglazed except for decoration.

53.127 A. (See fig.) Six joining fragments of lip and body. Below rim, row of dots. Preserved height 7.8 cm.; diameter of rim 12.0 cm.

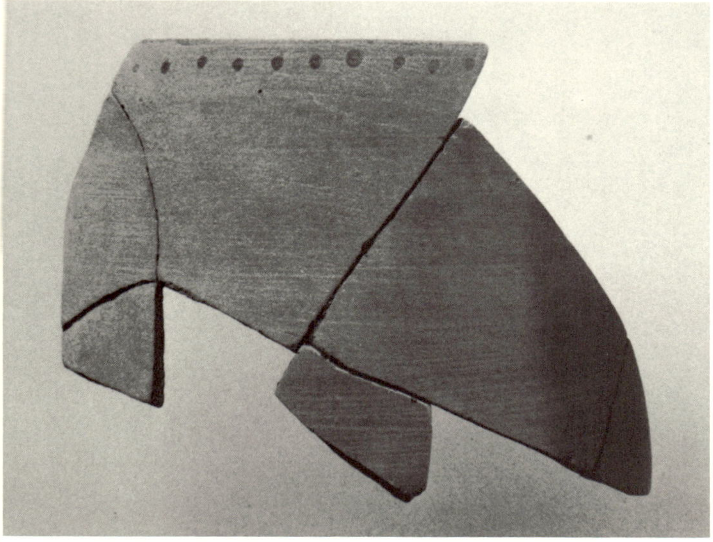

53.127A

53.127 B. Lower part of handle including root and part of wall. Line at each edge of handle. Preserved height 7.2 cm.; preserved width 5.6 cm.; width of handle 2.5 cm.

Close in shape to no. **32**.

C. *Fragments of kantharoi: exact shape uncertain.*

38. (See fig.)

Two fragments of one vessel. Reddish-yellow clay (7.5 YR 7/6). Lip separated from body by two incised parallel lines. Reddish-brown glaze on inside. Slip on outside.

x.50.65. Four joining fragments of lip and body.

Preserved height 6.9 cm.; preserved width 7.8 cm.

x.50.65.1. Fragment of lip and body.

Preserved height 4.9 cm.; preserved width 5.7 cm.

39. 50.131. (See fig.)

Fragment of lip and body separated by two incised parallel lines. Red clay (2.5 YR 5/6). Reddish glaze inside. Slip on outside. Surface flaked.

Preserved height 5.1 cm.; preserved width 5.3 cm.; height of lip 3.5 cm.

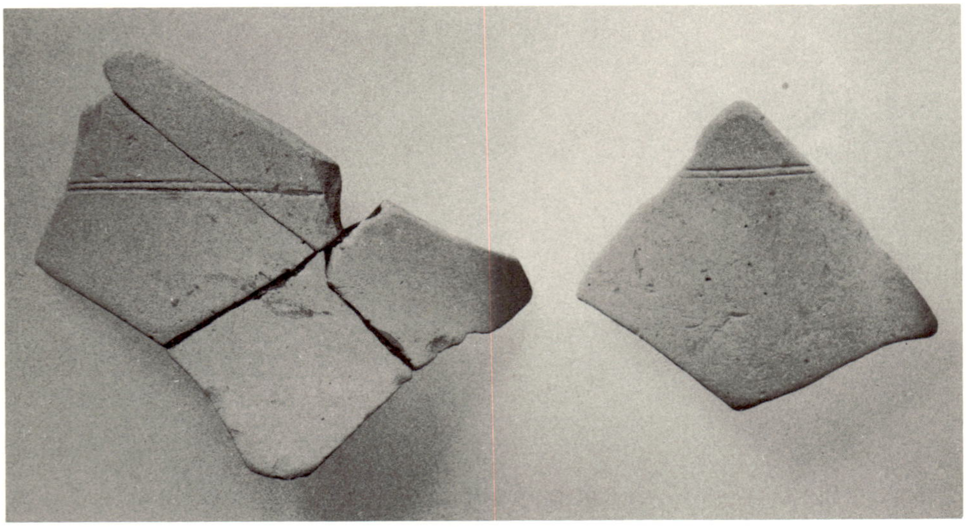

38

39

40. 50.62. (See fig.)
Fragment of strap handle from near top just above rim. Light brown clay (7.5 YR 6/4). Traces of burning. At top, break preserves root of thumb rest similar to that of no. **26**. Line at each edge of handle. On top, two transverse lines below a large X.

Width 3.0 cm.

A handle fragment from Antissa has the same linear decoration and may preserve the root of a knob (*BSA*, 32 [1931-32], pl. 23, 6). Cf. also a handle fragment from Thasos (D 103) that shows several lines between each X (*BCH*, 88 [1964], p. 97, no. 20 and p. 103, fig. 18).

40

41. 54.53. (See figs.)
Fragment of inset lip and body of open vessel, perhaps from a globular kantharos. Reddish-yellow clay (5 YR 6/6). Surface inside very worn. Outside unglazed except for decoration in red glaze. Line at junction. On body, below lip, four vertical lines.

Preserved height 5.4 cm.; preserved width 6.0 cm.

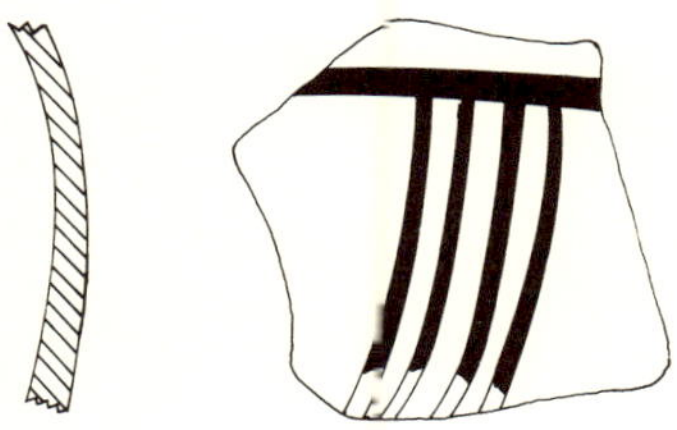

41 *41*

42. 54.54. (See figs.)
Four joining fragments of base and lower wall. Light reddish-brown clay (5 YR 6/4). Underside of base tapers to an edge. Unglazed inside and outside, except for decoration. Base glazed. Above base, three lines.

Preserved height 3.6 cm.; diameter of base 6.0 cm.

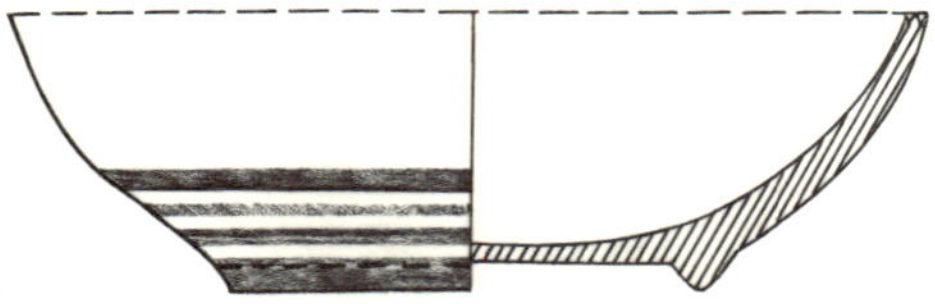

42

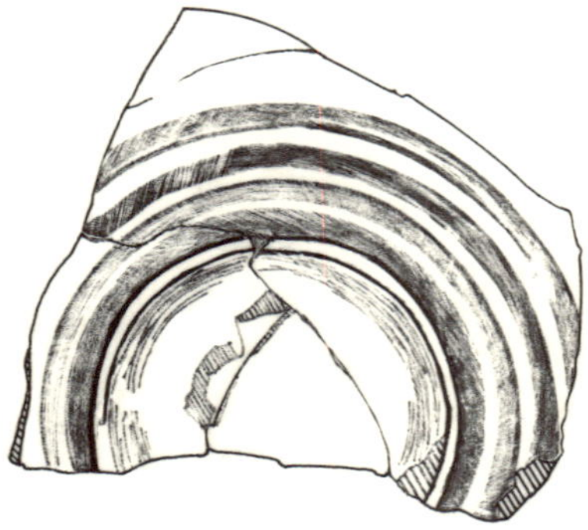

42

43. 50.166.
Two joining fragments of flaring ring base that tapers to an edge. Light brown clay (7.5 YR 6/4). Blackish-brown glaze inside except for reserved circle on center of floor, the only example on this ware from Samothrace. Slip on outside. Top of base glazed. Glaze has flaked in places.

Preserved height 2.8 cm.; diameter of base 7.4 cm.

Profile of base similar to nos. **4**, **17**, and **32**.

44. 50.203 D. (See fig.)
Two joining fragments of base of kantharos. Reddish-yellow clay (5 YR 7/6). A few traces of glaze on inside. Slip on outside. Band of glaze 0.6 cm. at base, then a line.

Preserved height 1.7 cm.; diameter of base 6.0 cm.

45. 54.50. (See fig.)
Two joining fragments preserving base, lower part of wall and handle root. Reddish-yellow clay (7.5 YR 7/6). Unglazed except for decoration. Circle painted on floor. Line down center of handle. Band of glaze 0.5 cm. wide at base.

Preserved height 4.0 cm.; diameter of base 6.6 cm.

For the profile of the base, cf. no. **36**.

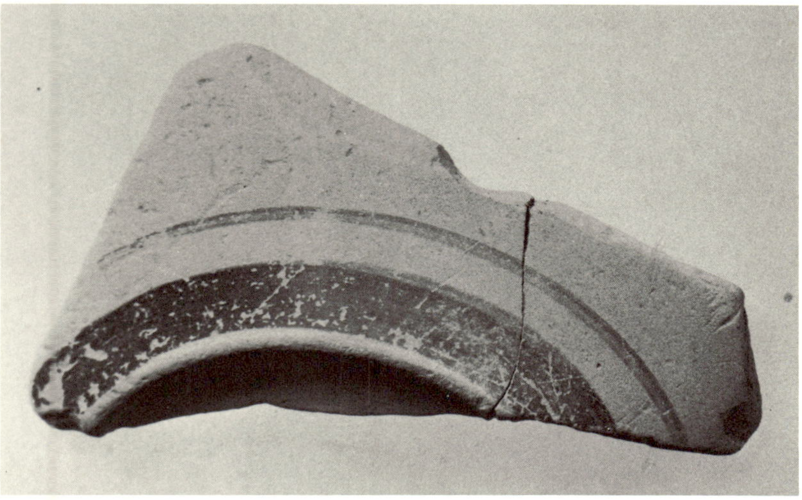

44

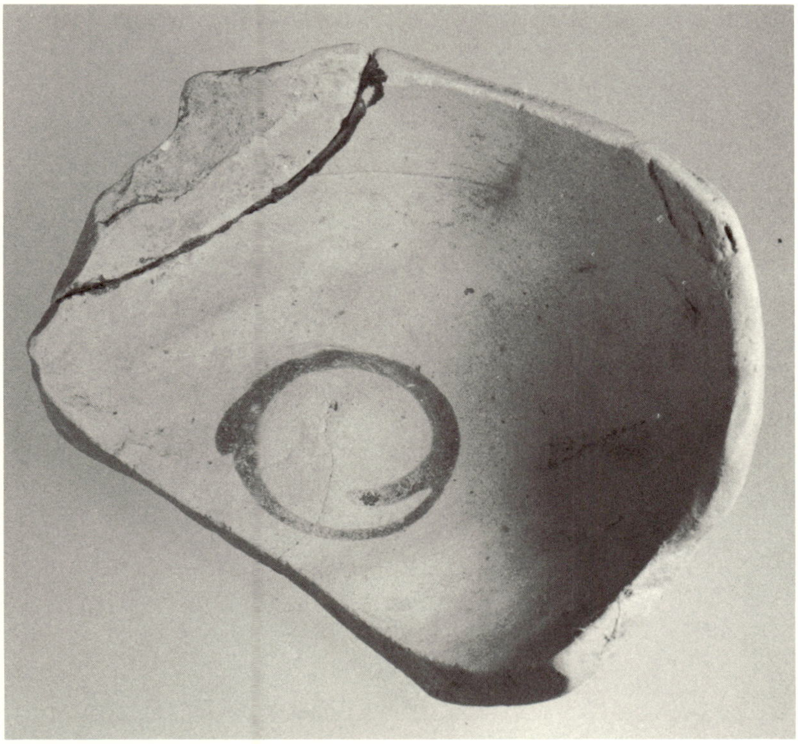

45

46

46. 50.148. (See fig.)
Fragment of floor. Reddish-yellow clay (5 YR 6/6). Red glaze on inside. Slip on outside except for glaze decoration. On underside of floor, circle.

Preserved height 3.3 cm.; preserved width 3.1 cm.

KRATERS

47. 51.41 B. (See fig.)

Two joining fragments of rim of large krater. Light brown clay (7.5 YR 6/4). Rim flat on top with convex overhang. Near the right of the fragment is the beginning of the handle root. Blackish-brown glaze on inside and on surface of rim. Slip on outside.

Preserved height 4.7 cm.; preserved width 16.8 cm.

Unstratified find.

48. 51.43. (See fig.)

Fragment of rim of large krater, perhaps from a vessel similar to no. **47**. Light brown clay (7.5 YR 6/4). Rim flat on top with convex overhang. Traces of blackish-brown glaze inside and on rim. Slip on outside. Glaze at bottom of fragment just above break.

Preserved height 6.8 cm.; maximum preserved width 8.2 cm.

Unstratified find.

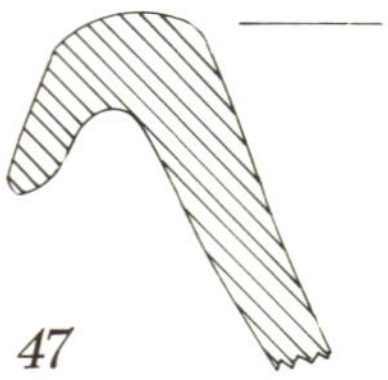

47

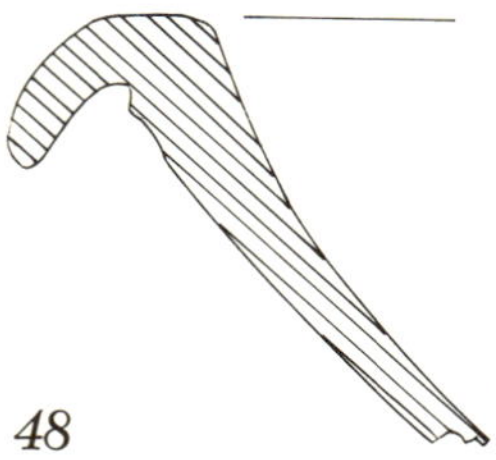

48

AMPHORAE

49. (See figs.)

Five fragments of a large amphora with flaring mouth, handles with central rib, and torus foot. Light reddish-brown clay (5 YR 6/4). Slip on outside and on inside of neck. Glaze decoration flaked in many places.

50.159. Fragment of neck and mouth. Outer edge of mouth badly chipped. Cross on neck.

Preserved height 7.2 cm.; preserved width 10.2 cm.

Unstratified find.

50.203 F and 50.217. Three joining fragments of lower part of handle and adjoining wall. Line at each edge of handle and on central rib. Three lines below handle root that continued round the vase.

Preserved height 14.0 cm.; preserved width 10.0 cm.

50.217 was an unstratified find.

50.449 and 50.247. Four joining fragments of lower part of handle and adjoining wall. Decoration as before.

Preserved height 7.1 cm.; preserved width 10.9 cm.

51.148 and 50.202 A. Three joining fragments from wall at level of handle root preserving three lines.

Preserved height 4.5 cm.; preserved width 10.6 cm.

50.202 A was an unstratified find.

51.150. Four joining fragments of lower wall and torus foot. Torus glazed on outside.

Preserved height 6.3 cm.; preserved width 13.6 cm.; width of resting surface 0.8 cm.

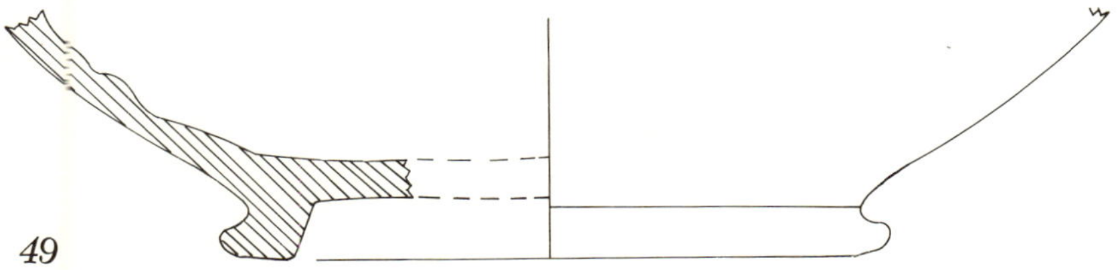

49

49

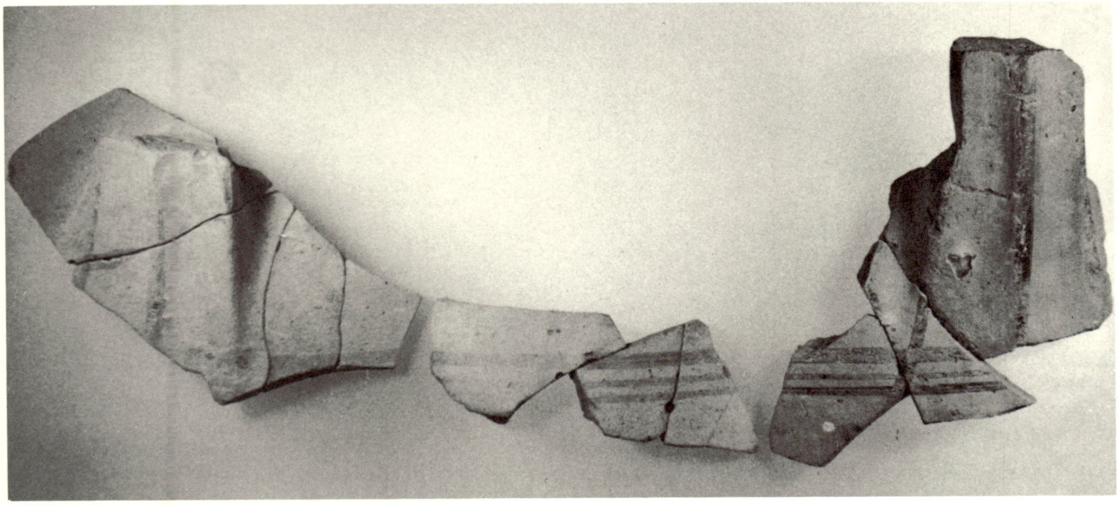

49

50. (See figs.)
Five fragments of a large amphora with strap handle and a circular decoration on the shoulder. Reddish-yellow clay (5 YR 7/6). Slip on outside. Glaze decoration.

51.154 A. Three joining fragments of a strap handle and part of neck and shoulder. Line on neck above junction of shoulder. Line on each side of handle. On top of handle, transverse line at junction of neck, three closely spaced oblique lines near middle of handle. Band 0.9 cm. wide at handle root that probably continued round the pot. Below this, at the break, a line. Part of the surface is gray from burning.

Preserved height 18.7 cm.; preserved width 7.5 cm.; width of handle 4.2 cm.

50.201 A and 50.171. Two joining fragments of strap handle. Decoration as before.

Preserved height 16.9 cm.; width of handle 4.3 cm.

50.171 was an unstratified find.

50.160 and 54.395. Two joining fragments of neck and shoulder, preserving the line at the junction and part of the circular decoration on shoulder.

Preserved height 5.0 cm.; preserved width 9.4 cm.

50.160 was an unstratified find.

50.154 B. Fragment of neck and shoulder preserving line at junction.

Preserved height 3.1 cm.; preserved width 7.6 cm.

50.201 E. Fragment of neck and shoulder, preserving line at junction and part of circular decoration on shoulder.

Preserved height 6.0 cm.; preserved width 7.0 cm.

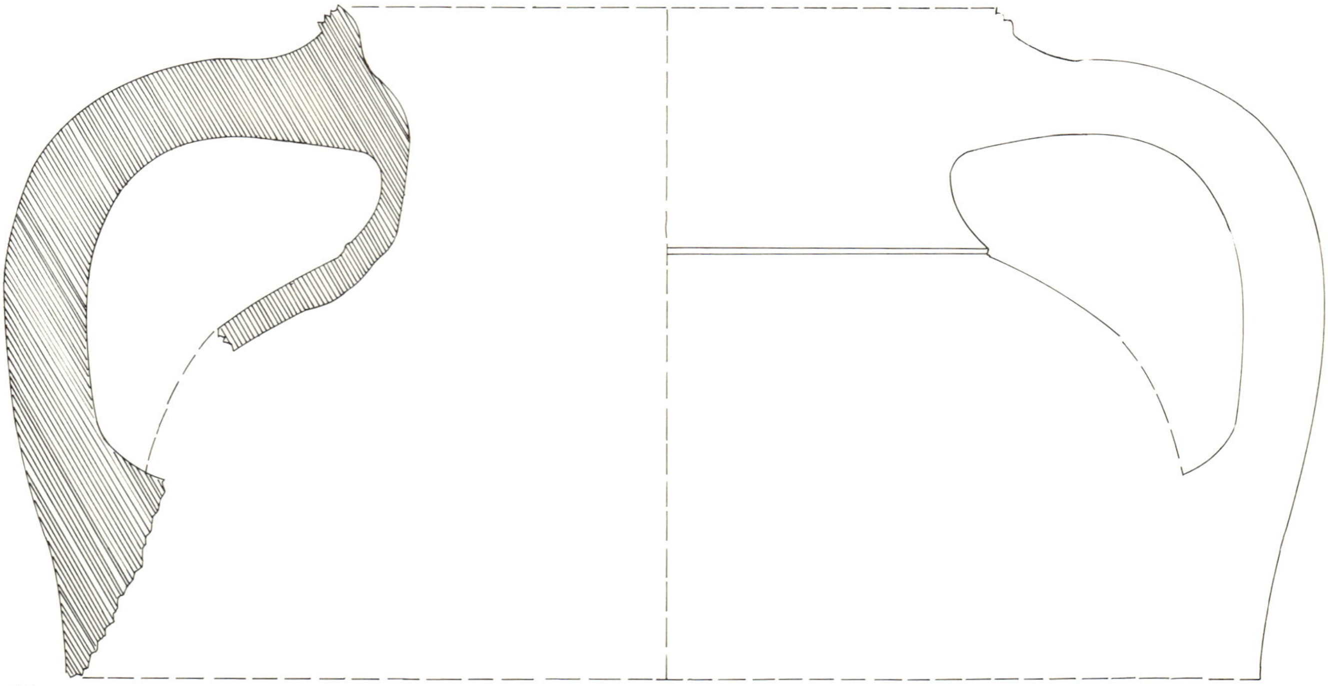

50

50

50

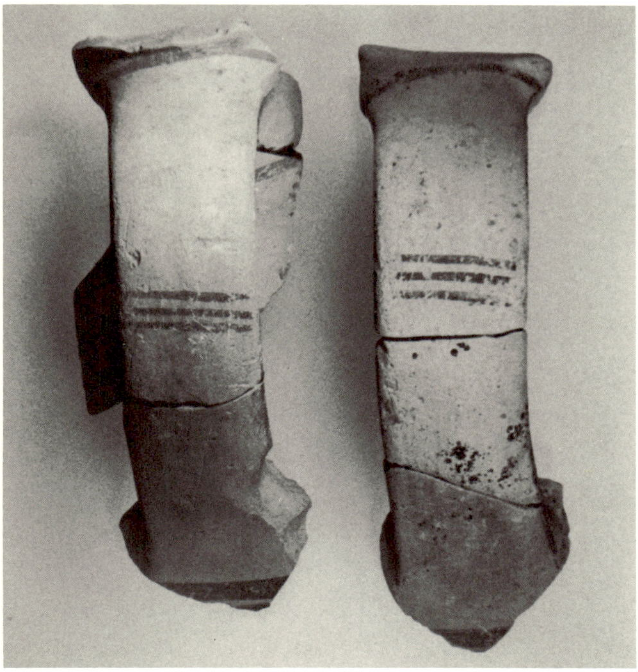

50

JUGS

51. 51.155 E. (See fig.)
Four joining fragments of neck and shoulder. Light brown clay (7.5 YR 6/4). Flaring mouth separated from neck by ring. Ring at junction of neck and shoulder. Slip on outside. Glaze decoration. Lip glazed on inside. Ring glazed. Band of glaze 4.0 cm. wide on neck just above junction.

Preserved height 10.4 cm.; maximum preserved width 12.2 cm.; height of neck 8.0 cm.

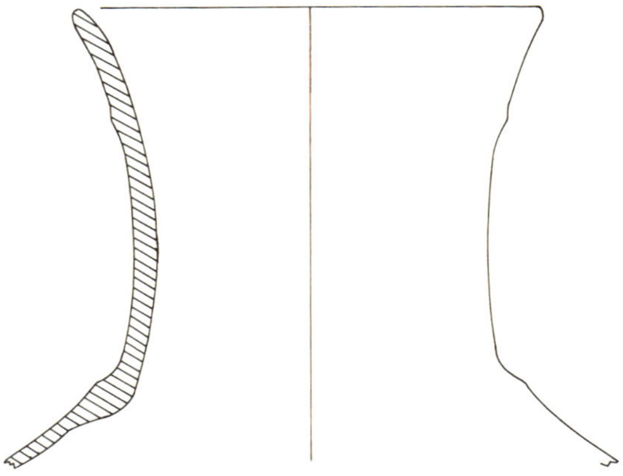

51

52. 50.219. (See fig.)
Seventeen joining fragments preserving part of mouth, neck, and body. Light brown clay (7.5 YR 6/4). Shoulder and part of neck restored in plaster and painted. Horizontal rib on neck at level of handle. Traces of glaze decoration on outside. Surface worn. Mouth glazed inside to a depth of 1.0 cm.; glazed on outside. Rib on neck, glazed. Line of glaze on each side of handle. Below handle, three lines that continue round the vase.

Preserved height 24.0 cm.; diameter of mouth 13.0 cm.; maximum preserved width 21.0 cm.; height of mouth 2.5 cm.; restored height of neck 10.5 cm.; width of handle 3.9 cm.

53. 50.598. (See figs.)
Fragmentary jug with flaring neck and strap handle. Reddish-yellow clay (5 YR 6/6). Mended from seven fragments with missing pieces restored in plaster and painted. Unglazed except for decoration.

Restored: half of neck, much of body except for area at handle zone.

Decoration. Neck glazed inside to a depth of 1.1 cm.; thick line 0.8 cm. below lip continuing along the top of handle near each edge to below root. Line at junction. Line at handle root continuing round the vase.

Dimensions. Preserved height 14.7 cm.; diameter of mouth 6.3 cm.; greatest restored diameter of body 17.1 cm.; width of handle 2.4 cm.

Compare a fragmentary jug from Troy (37.972), which looks like a slightly more developed version of the Samothracian piece (*Troy*, p. 277 and fig. 302 a-b). The Trojan jug is a little larger than the Samothracian one; it has a more flaring neck with a horizontal rib, and has more linear decoration on both its shoulder and neck.

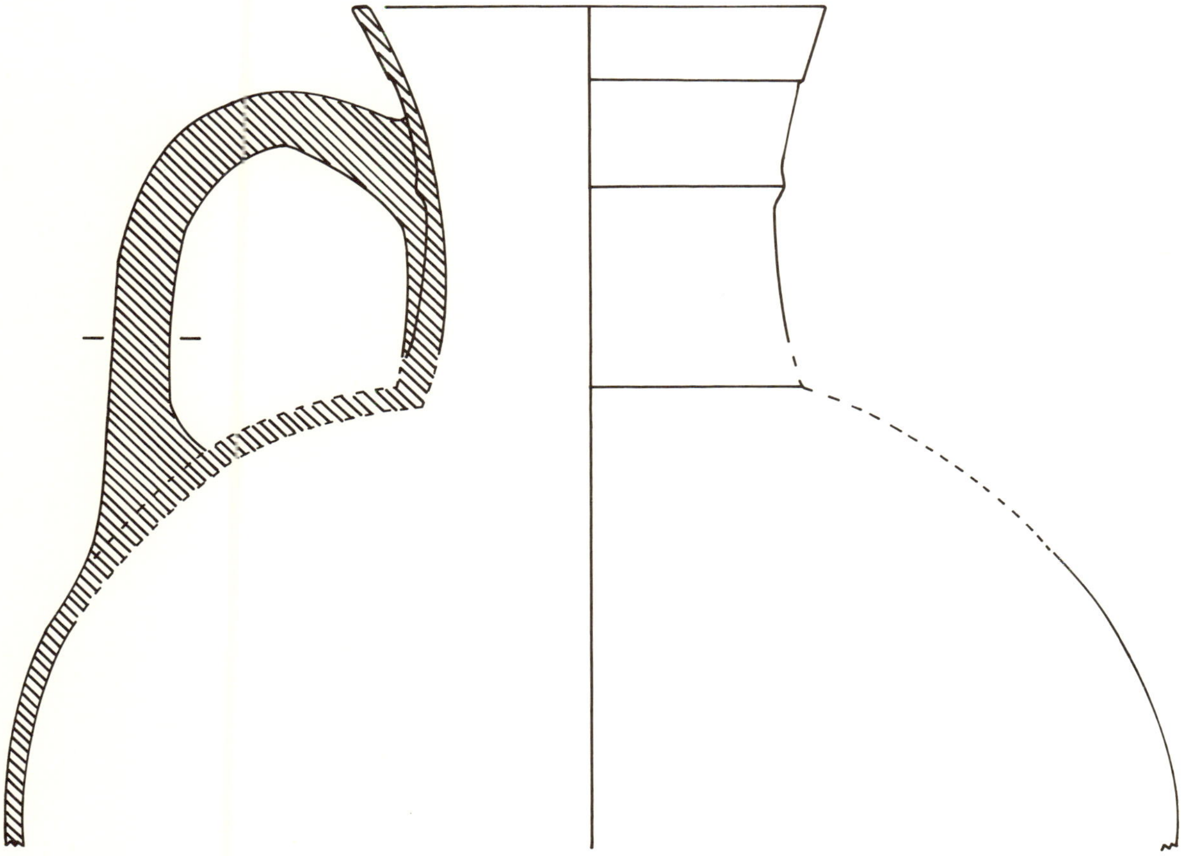

52

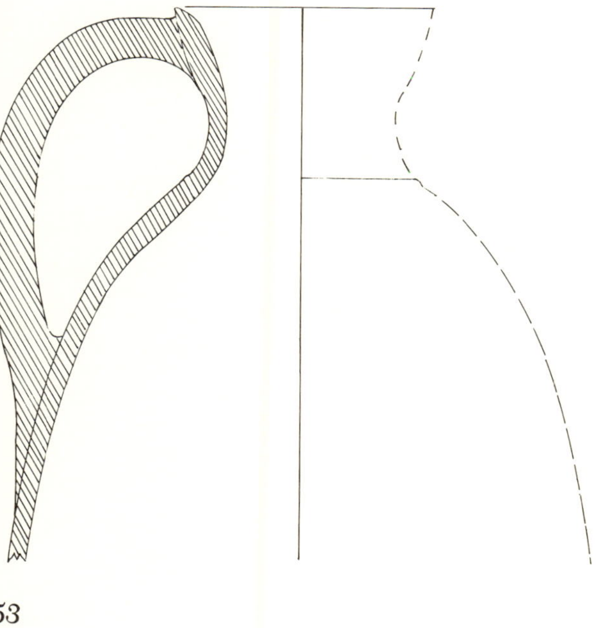

53

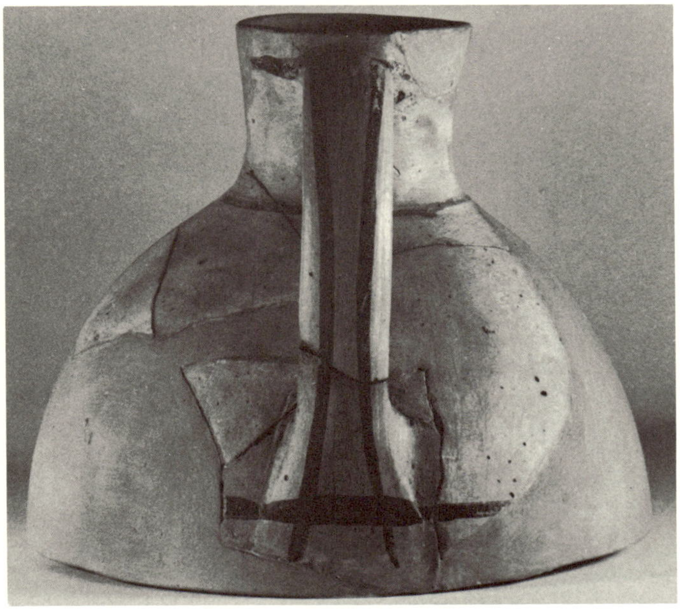

53

FRAGMENTS OF CLOSED VASES; SHAPE UNCERTAIN

54. 50.199. (See fig.)

Fragment of closed-mouth pot (jug?) preserving part of slightly offset lip and beginning of handle attached 1.6 cm. below rim. Pink clay (7.5 YR 7/4). Slip on outside. Lip glazed to a depth of 0.7 cm. on inside below rim. Band 0.9-1.2 cm. wide below rim, then two horizontal lines stopped at handle by a vertical line. Two lines on handle at lip.

Preserved height 5.2 cm.; preserved with 6.5 cm.

Similar to nos. **51** and **52**.

54

55. x.50.89. (See fig.)

Two nonjoining fragments of neck of closed-mouth pot. Reddish-yellow clay (5 YR 6/6). Beginning of handle root near right break. Horizontal rib at level of handle. Slip on outside. Blackish-brown glaze for decoration. Band of glaze below rim. Rib glazed. Line above and below it stopped at handle by a vertical line.

Preserved height 6.1 cm.; preserved width 4.5 cm.

56. 54.51. (See fig.)

Fragment of flaring lip. Reddish-yellow clay (5 YR 6/6). Slip on outside and on inside. Glazed inside to a depth of 0.7 cm. below rim. On outside, a band of glaze 1.2 cm. at rim, a line 2.3 cm. below band. Glaze on inside is a blackish-brown; on outside as decoration, a reddish-brown.

Preserved height 4.8 cm.; preserved width 5.0 cm.

55

56

57. 50.162. (See figs.)
Fragment from shoulder or body preserving portions of four concentric circles of varying thicknesses. Light brown clay (7.5 YR 6/4).

Preserved height 4.4 cm.; preserved width 3.5 cm.

Perhaps from the same vessel as no. **50**.

Unstratified find.

57

57

58. 50.203 B. (See figs.)
Fragment from shoulder or body preserving portions of three concentric circles of varying thicknesses. Light brown clay (7.5 YR 6/4). Slip on outside.

Preserved height 4.8 cm.; preserved width 2.8 cm.

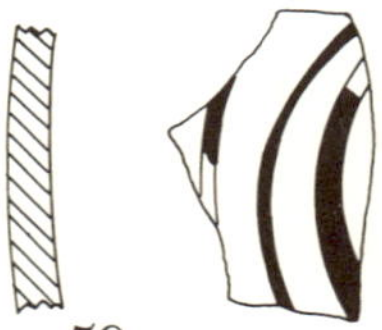

58

58

MISCELLANEOUS (59-67)

The following restored vessels and fragments do not appear to be examples of G 2-3 ware, yet their character suggests that they are contemporary with this material. The clay is fine or semifine and generally very hard. Some of the pieces have slip on the outside.

59. 51.87. (See fig.)
Cup with molded rim, strap handle, and flaring foot with the resting surface reduced to an edge. Light red clay (2.5 YR 6/8). Mended from eleven fragments with missing pieces restored in plaster and painted. Traces of reddish-brown glaze on inside. Outside appears to be unglazed except for area below handle and top surface of foot. Surface very worn.

Restored: one side except for small area above base; handle at attachment to rim.

No preserved decoration.

Dimensions. Height at rim 11.7 cm.; at handle 13.4 cm.; restored diameter of lip 15.0 cm.; width at handle 20.6 cm.; diameter of foot 7.1 cm.; height of rim 0.9 cm.; width of handle 3.0-3.5 cm.

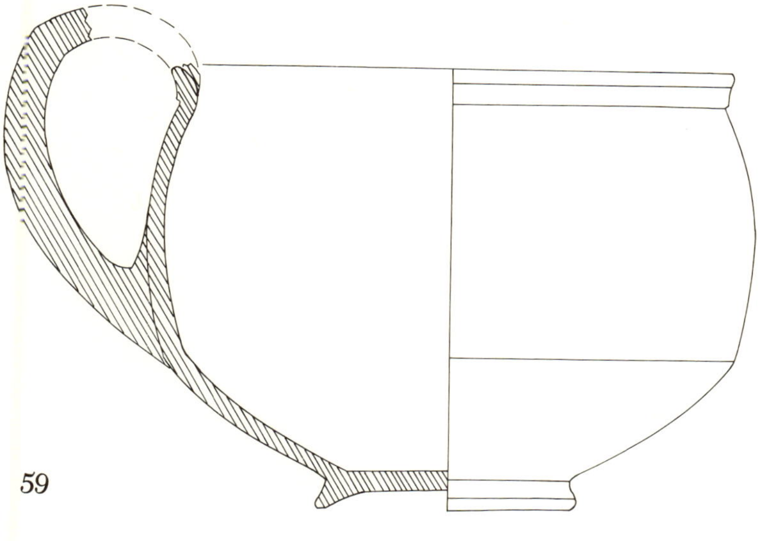

59

60. 50.446. (See fig.)
Cup with flaring rim and strap handle. Reddish-yellow clay (5 YR 6/6). Mended from four fragments with missing pieces restored in plaster and painted. Glaze decoration on outside. Surface very worn.

Restored: all of base; most of one side and about half of the other. It is not possible to determine whether the vessel had a second handle or not.

Decoration. Band of glaze 0.7 cm. wide at rim, another of the same width below the handle, a third 1.0 cm. wide above base. Line at each edge of handle.

Dimensions. Height 5.3 cm.; restored diameter 15.6 cm.; width of handle 2.2 cm. Unstratified find.

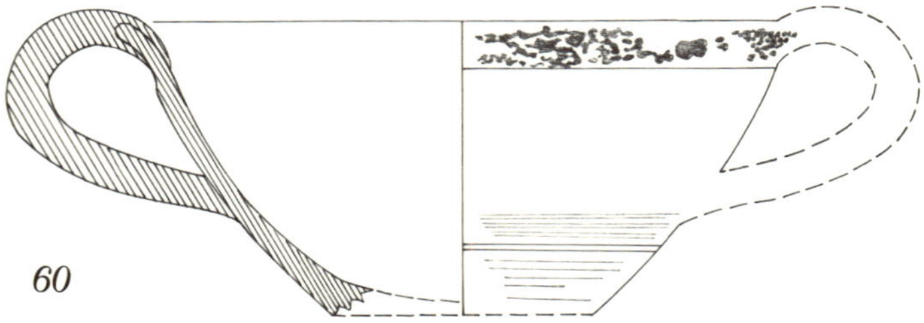

60

61. 50.562 (See fig.)
Cup with flaring wall and horizontal handle level with rim. Pinkish-gray clay (7.5 YR 6/2). Six joining fragments with missing pieces restored in plaster and painted. Glazed inside and outside.

Restored height at rim 5.6 cm.; restored diameter 19.0 cm.

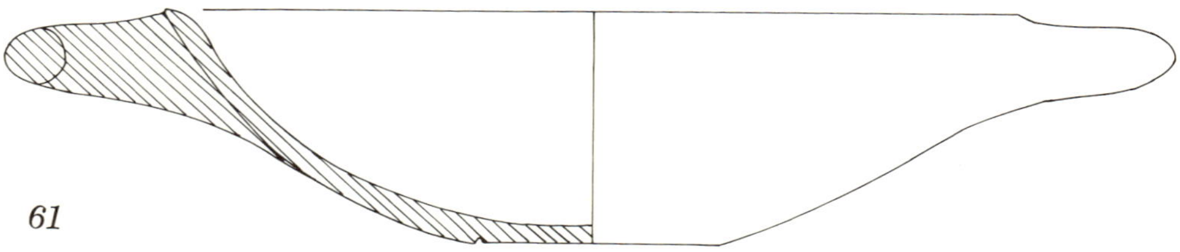

61

62. (See fig.)
Two nonjoining fragments of a cup with molded rim, as no. **59**. Reddish-yellow clay (5 YR 6/6). Faint traces of glaze on inside. Outside unglazed except for decoration.

50.154. Fragment of rim and body. Horizontal line on rim. Below rim, three vertical lines.

Preserved height 3.5 cm.; preserved width 2.6 cm.; height of rim 0.7 cm.

51.309. Fragment of rim and body.

Preserved height 2.9 cm.; preserved width 2.9 cm.; height of rim 0.7 cm.

62

63.

Two nonjoining fragments of a closed-mouth vessel with offset lip. Unstratified find.

50.196. (See fig.). Two joining fragments of lip and neck. Light brown clay (7.5 YR 6/4). Brownish-black glaze on outside of lip, and on inside to a depth of 1.2 cm. below rim.

Preserved height 4.1 cm.; diameter at rim 13.0 cm.; height of lip 2.3 cm.

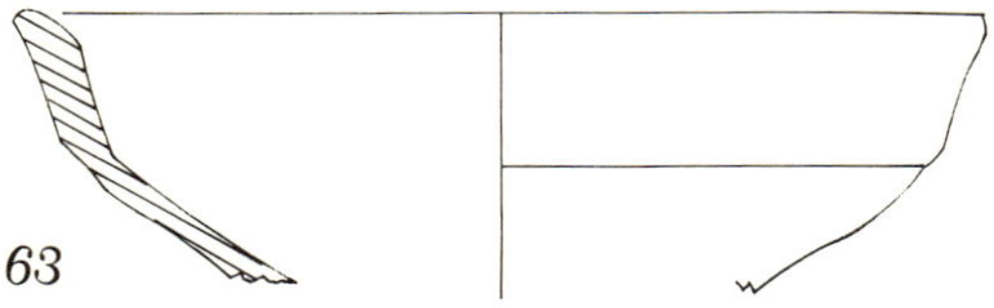

63

50.108. Fragment of lip and neck. At break, below lip, beginning of handle.

Preserved height 4.1 cm.; preserved width 3.8 cm.

64.

Two nonjoining fragments of a closed-mouth vessel with offset lip. Light brown clay (7.5 YR 6/4). Glazed inside to a depth of 0.9 cm. below rim. Band of glaze on lip 2.1 cm. wide.

50.201 D. Preserved height 4.0 cm.; preserved width 3.9 cm.

50.201 D 1. Preserved height 4.5 cm.; preserved width 5.6 cm.

Similar to no. **63**, except that the lip on this latter vessel is more offset than the one in this entry.

65. (See fig.)
Two nonjoining fragments of a closed-mouth vessel with offset lip and horizontal rib on neck 4.3 cm. below rim. Reddish-yellow clay (5 YR 7/6).

x.50.172. Fragment of lip and neck. Glazed inside to a depth of 0.9 cm. Lip and lower part of neck glazed.

Preserved height 5.2 cm.; preserved width 5.6 cm.; height of lip 2.0 cm.

x.50.351. Fragment of rib and lower part of neck. Small amount of glaze (a line?) above rib.

Preserved height 4.6 cm.; preserved width 3.5 cm.

65

66. 51.307. (See fig.)
Fragment of a closed-mouth vessel with torus mouth and horizontal rib on neck. Burned. Mouth and rib glazed.

Preserved height 6.7 cm.; preserved width 4.7 cm.

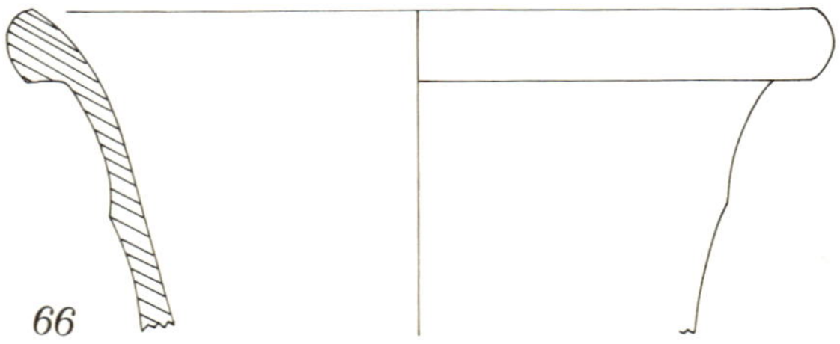
66

67. (See fig.)
Two nonjoining fragments of a large open vessel. Pink clay (5 YR 7/4). Glazed inside to a depth of 1.4 cm. below rim and on vertical outer surface. Reddish-brown glaze. Slip on inside and outside.

50.96. Preserved height 3.0 cm.; preserved length 5.7 cm.

50.203 H. Preserved height 3.4 cm; preserved width 4.7 cm.

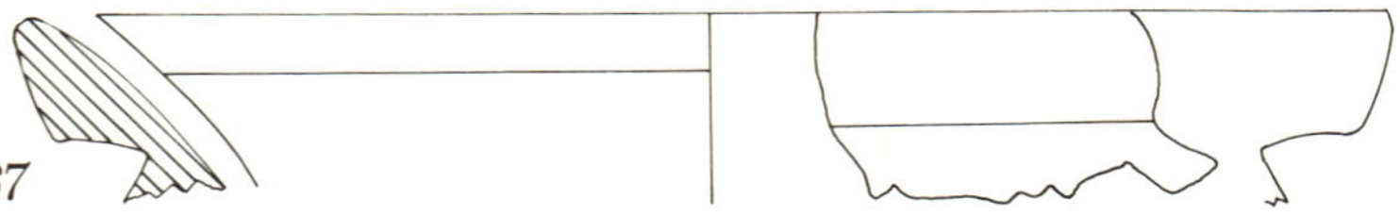
67

GRAY WARE AND GRAY BUCCHERO (**68-69**)

The fill of the Temenos and terrace yielded a very small quantity of gray ware, all fragmentary and all, except one fragment (no. **68**), from globular kantharoi of the type discussed above (nos. **18-37**). These fragments are very worn, but appear to be slipped instead of glazed, much in the manner of vessels from Thasos, Troy, and Lemnos.[1] Unfortunately, the Samothracian fragments are not well enough preserved to allow restoration of any one vessel, and only one fragment possesses enough character to merit inclusion in the catalogue.

We have also decided to include one fragment of gray bucchero, even though this piece comes from an unstratified context, since it is the only one found in the excavation of the Temenos and terrace. The fragment preserves part of the rim and one handle of a globular kantharos. The clay is hard, very fine, and covered with dull black glaze. The character of the piece and the use of glaze instead of slip suggest that the vessel may have been imported from Lesbos,[2] and if so, it offers further evidence of connections between these two islands in the seventh century B.C.

1. The most recent discussion of this ware is by Bernard, *op. cit.*, pp. 109 ff. (with bibliography). Here, the finds from Thasos, both imported and local, are presented, and comparisons made between them and examples from other sites.

2. For the connection of this technique with Lesbos, cf., *ibid.*, p. 110.

GRAY WARE

68. 51.161. (See fig.)

Fragment of offset lip and neck of closed-mouth vessel. Rather coarse gray clay (10 YR 5/1). Slip on outside.

Preserved height 5.4 cm.; diameter of rim 12.0 cm.; height of lip 2.1 cm.

GRAY BUCCHERO

69. 50.197. (See fig.)

Two joining fragments of rim and handle. Gray clay (10 YR 6/1).

Preserved height 6.8 cm.; preserved width 7.5 cm.; height of lip 2.0 cm.

Unstratified find.

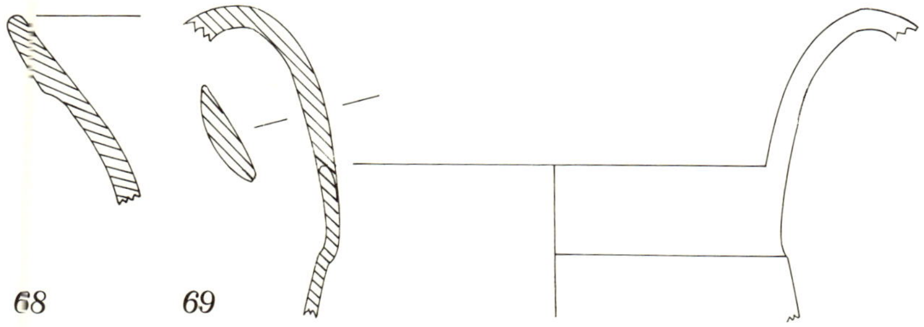

68 *69*

KARCHESIA OR KANTHAROI (70-72)[1]

The fill of the Temenos and terrace produced a few fragments of a rare variety of drinking vessel characterized by a flat base, concave walls, and two handles that reach from the base to the rim. Two of the fragments in the short catalogue below add to our knowledge of the decoration of this shape, for they preserve a linear pattern painted as a vertical panel on the surface of the vase. The other two fragments are from unstratified contexts, but because of the rarity of this shape, they are included here.

1. The identification of this shape as a karchesion was suggested by Iris C. Love in a previous volume of the Samothrace publications (Vol. 4, pt. II, p. 151), and was the subject of her contribution to the *Essays in Memory of Karl Lehmann*, New York, 1964, pp. 204 ff. ("Kantharos or Karchesion? A Samothracian Contribution"). In this essay she presents the visual evidence for this identification and discusses the history of the shape and its use. Most recently, the shape has been studied by J. W. Salomonson, "Ein 'samothrakischer' Kantharos in Utrecht," *Festoen. Opgedragen aan A. N. Zadoks-Josephus-Jitta bij haar seventigste verjaardag [Scripta Archaeologica Groningen 6]*, Groningen, 1977, pp. 509 ff.

70. (See fig.)

Two nonjoining fragments of one vessel. Reddish-yellow clay (5 YR 6/6). Reddish-brown glaze on inside. Outside unglazed except for decoration: a vertical pattern comprised of two parallel lines 1.0 cm. apart; between them a zigzag line with dots in the interstices.

50.497. Part of wall preserving portion of vertical pattern.

Preserved height 3.6 cm.; preserved width 2.5 cm.

x.50.86. Fragment of base and lower wall with some of the pattern.

Preserved height 2.3 cm.; diameter of base 5.0 cm.

71. 50.66 A. (See fig.)

Two joining fragments of lower wall and base. Reddish-yellow clay (5 YR 6/6). Traces of red glaze inside and outside.

Preserved height 3.2 cm.; diameter of base 11.5 cm.

Unstratified find.

72. 51.54. (See fig.)

Three joining fragments of lower wall and handle root. Light brown clay (7.5 YR 6/4). Black glaze inside, much flaked. Slip on outside.

Preserved height 2.0 cm.; diameter of base 9.0 cm.

Unstratified find.

70

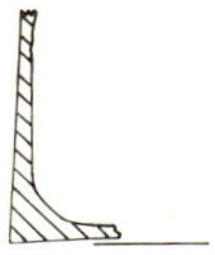

71

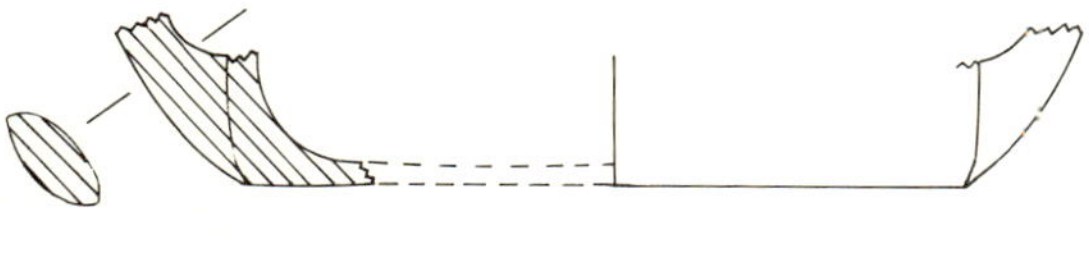

72

COARSE WARE (**73-82**)

The fill of the Temenos and terrace has produced a large quantity of very fragmentary, handmade vessels. The few pieces that permitted restoration consist mainly of unglazed cups and small bowls made from coarse, gritty clay that ranges in color from reddish-brown to grayish-black. Among the pieces is one rim fragment of a large vessel with molded or applied vertical rib (no. **81**). Of particular interest are three nonjoining fragments of a large pot (no. **82**), perhaps a pithos, with incised decoration. Some of these coarse fragments show traces of burning.

1. Restored vessels

73. 50.557. (See fig.)[1]

One-handled cup mended from two joining fragments with missing portions restored in plaster and painted.

Restored: most of bowl except for area below handle; part of floor.

Dimensions. Restored height at rim 8.2 cm.; height at handle 11.0 cm.; restored diameter of rim front to back 8.0 cm.

1. *Hesperia,* 21 (1952), pl. 9d.

74. 51.81. (See fig.)

Cup mended from fifteen fragments with missing pieces restored in plaster and painted.

Restored: handle except for root and attachment to rim; most of one side.

Dimensions. Height 7.0-7.5 cm.; restored diameter of rim front to back 13.2 cm.

73

74

75. 51.83. (See fig.)
Cup mended from fourteen joining fragments with missing pieces restored in plaster and painted.

Restored: much of one side; all of bottom.

Dimensions. Height at rim 6.4-7.0 cm.; at handle 10.0 cm.; restored diameter front to back 13.2 cm.; width including handle 16.2 cm.

75

76. 51.84. (See fig.)
Cup mended from eight joining fragments with missing pieces restored in plaster and painted.

Restored: most of one side; all of bottom; wall under handle.

Dimensions. Restored height at rim 7.7 cm.; at handle 9.4 cm.; restored diameter front to back 4.5 cm.; restored width at handle 18.0 cm.

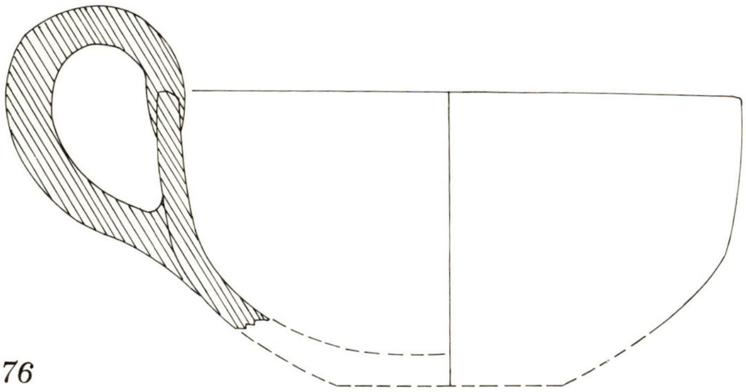

76

77. 50.558. (See fig.)[1]
One-handled cup mended from five joining fragments with missing pieces restored in plaster and painted. Unglazed inside and outside. Grayish-brown clay with traces of burning.

Restored: all of one side; top of handle.

Dimensions. Height at rim 7.0 cm.; restored diameter of rim front to back 11.2 cm.; width of handle 2.3 cm.

1. *Hesperia*, 21 (1952), pl. 9a.

77

78. 50.561. (See fig.)[1]
Cup with horizontal handles attached below rim. Mended from ten fragments with missing pieces restored in plaster and painted. Unglazed.

Restored: most of one side and handles except for roots; part of other side.

Dimensions. Height 7.0 cm.; restored diameter front to back 14.3 cm.

1. *Hesperia*, 21 (1952), pl. 9c.

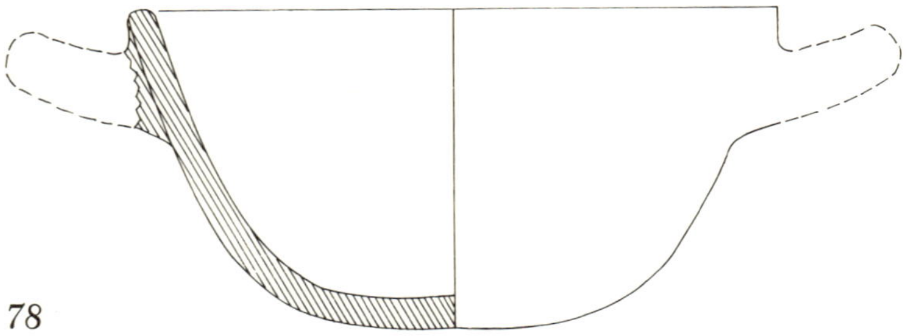

78

79. 50.560. (See fig.)[1]
Tumbler? Mended from five joining fragments with missing pieces restored in plaster and painted.

Restored: much of upper part of wall including all of rim.

Dimensions. Restored height 8.8 cm.; restored diameter at rim 9.0 cm.

1. *Hesperia*, 21 (1952), pl. 9b.

80. 50.559. (See fig.)
Bowl with missing portions restored in plaster and painted. About three-quarters of side restored.

Dimensions. Height at rim 7.5 cm.; restored diameter 13.7 cm.

79

80

2. Fragments.

81. 54.73. (See fig.)
Fragment of neck and rim of coarse vessel. Rounded rim. Vertical rib attached 1.7 cm. below top of rim. Unglazed. Surface burned.

Preserved height 4.8 cm.; preserved width 4.4 cm.

81

82. 54.72. (See fig.)

Three nonjoining fragments of a large coarse vessel with incised linear decoration. Unglazed. Traces of burning on outer surface.

A. Fragment preserving part of vertical zetoid pattern near left break. On lower right, part of rectangular decoration. Incision of upper right comprised of zigzag lines.

Preserved height 5.6 cm.; preserved width 5.6 cm.

B. Preserves part of zetoid pattern and to left, a spiral.

Preserved height 4.0 cm.; preserved width 5.2 cm.

C. Small fragment preserving a few lines, two of them parallel.

Preserved height 3.6 cm.; preserved width 2.0 cm.

The decoration on these fragments recalls that on some fragments of cinerary amphorae found on Lemnos in the Nekropolis of Hephaistia. Cf. *Annuario* 15-16 (1932-33), p. 81, fig. 131.

82

II. Black-Glazed Ware

THE black-glazed ware[1] comprises a very small proportion of the pottery from the Temenos and terrace, especially when it is compared with the large quantity of subgeometric material. In the catalogue below, the black-glazed fragments from the terrace fill have been separated from those found in the fill of the precinct itself. Although the former area has yielded by far the greater number of fragments and different shapes, the dates of the vessels from both fills are contemporary and in one case, a fragment from the fill of the terrace joins one found in that of the precinct (no. **92**).

These black-glazed fragments come mainly from small open vessels that range in date from the first half of the sixth century to the third quarter of the fourth century B.C. No vessel may be fully restored, nor may the complete profile of any be reconstructed. Many of the fragments are clearly of Attic manufacture, several appear to be of Samothracian origin, and one looks Ionian. For many, it is difficult to be certain of origin. The glaze ranges from a hard glossy black on some fragments to a dull brownish-black on others. On a few fragments, the glaze has misfired; on many it has flaked and abraded in places. One fragment has stamped decoration (no. **107**). One small bowl is hand-dipped instead of glazed on the wheel, and probably is a local piece (no. **95**).

1. The publication of the black-glazed material from the Athenian Agora (B. Sparkes and L. Talcott, *Black and Plain Pottery of the Sixth, Fifth, and Fourth Centuries B.C.* [*The Athenian Agora XII*], Princeton, 1970) has considerably lightened our task in determining shapes and variations in shapes for the Attic as well as for the non-Attic material. Thus, the comparisons and discussions are reduced to a minimum and the reader is referred to the appropriate section of the Agora publication.

FRAGMENTS OF BLACK-GLAZED POTTERY FROM THE FILL OF THE TERRACE (83-101)

CUPS

A. *Type* C[1]

1. Cf. *Agora XII*, p. 91.

83. 50.85 A. (See fig.)
Fragment of inset lip, gently concave, thickened slightly at rim. Reddish-yellow clay (5 YR 6/6). Broken at junction of lip and bowl. Hard black glaze on outside; misfired reddish-brown on inside.

Height 2.2 cm.; preserved length 5.4 cm.

Closest to Agora P 8826 (unpublished), dated late sixth-early fifth century B.C.

Attic. Late sixth century B.C.

B. *Vicup*[1]

1. Cf. *Agora XII*, p. 93.

84. 50.74 D. (See fig.)
Fragment of inset lip with very straight profile, tapering toward edge. Reddish-yellow clay (5 YR 6/6). Hard black glaze.

Preserved height 2.1 cm.; height of lip 1.8 cm.; preserved width 2.0 cm.

Perhaps from the same cup as no. **86** below.

The outer profile of this fragment is similar to Vicups from the Agora, but its inner profile curves considerably; those from the Agora have lips that are of about the same thickness throughout. Our fragment is closest to Agora P 25521 (*Agora XII*, p. 265, no. 434).

Attic. Second quarter of the fifth century B.C.

85. 50.65 N. (See fig.)
Fragment of bowl and inset lip. Light brown clay (7.5 YR 6/4). Portion of lip that is preserved indicates that it was rather straight in profile with very little flare. Black glaze that has misfired to a dark brown.

Preserved height 2.3 cm.; preserved width 3.7 cm.

Very little of this vessel is preserved, but the straight lip suggests that the fragment belongs to a Vicup rather than a Type C cup, which has a lip with a distinctive flare. Cf. *Agora XII*, pp. 91 f. for the Type C cup and p. 93 for the Vicup, especially no. 434 (Agora P 25521).

Attic. Ca. 475 B.C.

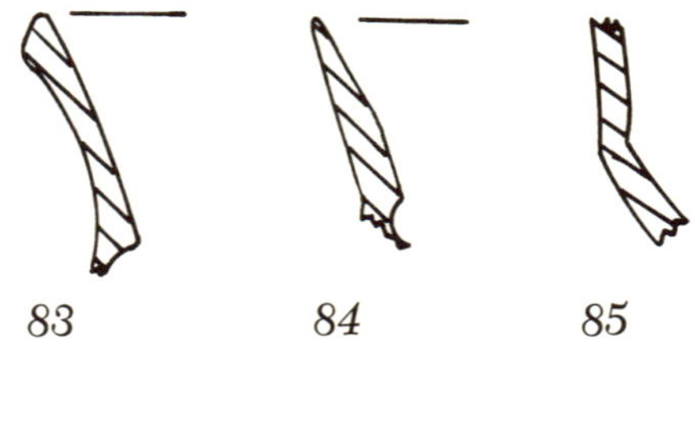

83 *84* *85*

86. 50.40 A. (See fig.)
Fragment of foot preserving part of stem and resting surface. Reddish-brown clay (5 YR 7/6). Foot in two degrees with a concave molding above a glazed torus. Two incised lines on top surface, one 1.0 cm., the other 1.5 cm. from the edge. The latter line is more deeply incised than the former. Reserved resting surface. Hard black glaze.

Preserved height 0.8 cm.; restored diameter 7.0 cm.; width of resting surface 0.5 cm.

Close to Agora P 10812 and P 5126 (*Agora XII*, nos. 436 and 437). The two incised lines on the top surface of the foot recur on Agora P 25521 (*Agora XII*, No. 434); here, however, the more deeply incised line is the inner one.

Attic. Second quarter of the fifth century B.C.

86

C. *Ionian Cup*

87. 50.65. I. (See fig.) Scale 1:2.
Two fragments of one vessel. Reddish-yellow clay (5 YR 6/6).

a. Fragment of deep bowl and sharply out-turned reserved lip. Reserved band on bowl 0.3 cm. wide just below lip and 0.65 cm. below it, another 0.65 cm. wide. Dull black glaze with a greenish cast.

Preserved height 4.5 cm.; preserved width 4.0 cm.

b. Fragment of conical flaring foot, reserved on underside and on resting surface. Glaze as before.

Preserved height 1.0 cm.; restored diameter 6.0 cm.

The sharply out-turned lip and the reserved bands on the outside suggest that this cup is of Ionian manufacture. For Ionian cups, cf. most recently *Agora XII*, p. 89, n. 6. Among the varieties of Ionian cups, this fragment seems closest to Rhodian Type IX (cf. J. Boardman and J. Hayes, *Excavations at Tocra 1963-1965. The Archaic Deposits I*, Oxford, 1966,

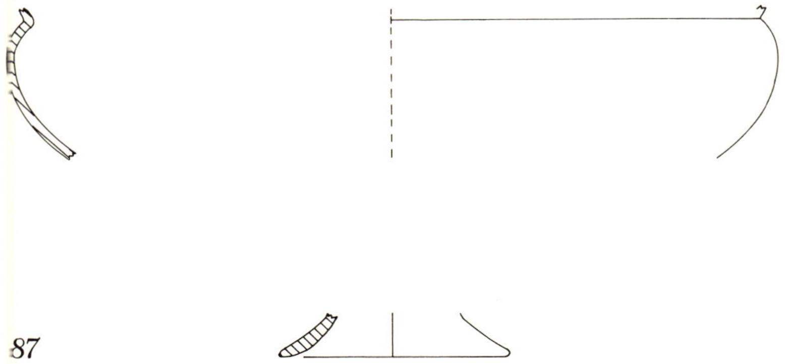

87

p. 113), which is characterized by an offset rim and conical foot with a flat resting surface. The inside is completely glazed except for a reserved line at the lip; the outside is glazed and reserved like no. **87**. Compare, especially, Tocra no. 1217 (*Tocra I*, p. 120 and II, p. 57, fig. 23); also Megara 10807 (*Mélanges d'archéologie et d' histoire de l' Ecole française de Rome,* 67 [1955], p. 25, fig. 4 c and pl. 10 b); Taranto inv. 4910 and inv. 20536 (*Annuario*, 37-38, n.s. 21-22 [1959-60], p. 61, no. 32, 1 and p. 62, fig. 45 a, p. 102, fig. 79 and p. 103, no. 50, 3).

First half of the sixth century.

BOLSAL[1]

1. Cf. *Agora XII*, pp. 107 ff.

88. 50.65 H. (See fig.)

Foot fragment. Reddish-yellow clay (5 YR 7/6). Flaring ring foot; reserved resting surface. Underside of bowl reserved and separated from the rest of the foot by a molding. On outside, groove between foot and bowl. Glaze has a greenish cast and has flaked in many places.

Preserved height 0.8 cm.; restored diameter 5.9 cm.

Compare Agora P 3904 (*Agora XII*, no. 538).

Attic? Late fifth century B.C.

88
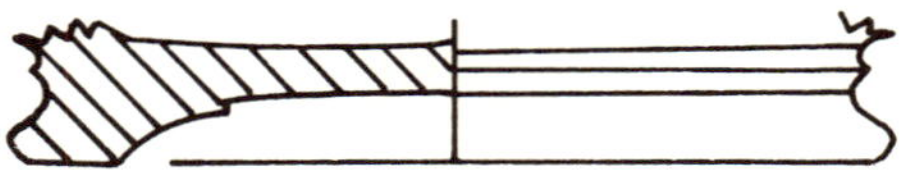

KANTHAROI[1]

1. For kantharoi of the fourth century B.C., cf. *Agora XII*, pp. 117 ff.

89. 50.74 A. (See figs.)

Fragment preserving spur, part of vertical member of handle and rim. Reddish-yellow clay (5 YR 6/6). Spur level with rim and tapers to a blunt end. Plain rim. Dull black glaze, flaked in many places.

Preserved height 2.4 cm.; restored diameter 9.5 cm.

Compare Agora P 12698, P 1828, and P 4442 (*Agora XII*, nos. 708-710).

Attic? Third quarter of the fourth century B.C.

90. 50.85 C. (See figs.)

Fragment preserving spur and part of vertical member of handle. Reddish-yellow clay (5 YR 7/6). Spur level with rim; tapers to a blunt end. Dull black glaze, misfired in places, flaked in others.

Preserved height 1.2 cm.; maximum preserved length 3.2 cm.

This fragment is similar in size and character to no. **89**, and the two may be from the same vessel. Compare Agora P 12698 (*Agora XII*, no. 708).

Attic? Third quarter of the fourth century B.C.

91. 50.74 C (See fig.)
Fragment of molded rim. Reddish-yellow clay (7.5 YR 6/6). Traces of dull black glaze on outside; brown glaze inside.

Preserved height 2.3 cm.; diameter 10.0 cm.

For fourth-century B.C. kantharoi with molded rims, cf. *Agora XII*, p. 122, nos. 696-704. No. **91** appears to be straighter and plainer in profile than those from the Agora, which have a ring at the lip.

Local ware. First half of the fourth century B.C.

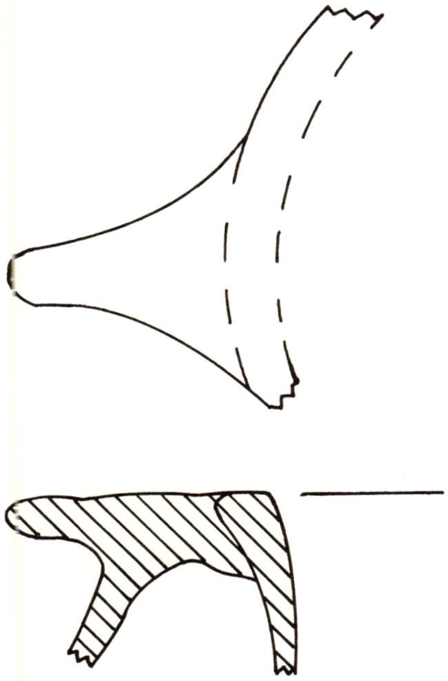

89

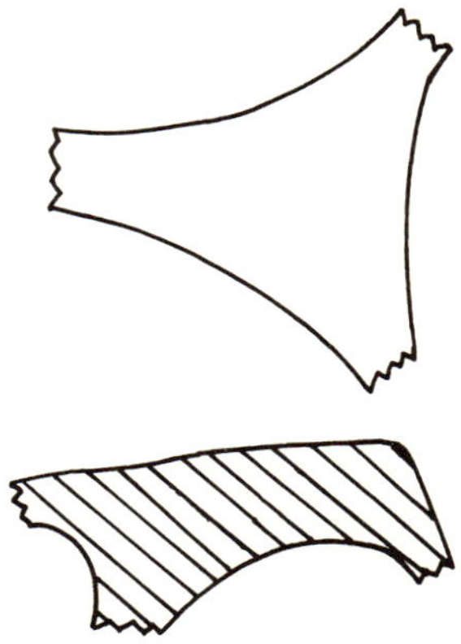

90

91

92. 50.41 A and 50.158 A. (See fig.)
Two joining fragments of foot and convex lower wall. Reddish-yellow clay (5 YR 6/6). Molded foot in two degrees with a grooved resting surface. Inner portion of resting surface glazed, outer part reserved. Groove between two moldings on outside of foot. Underside of bowl glazed, with central nipple. Hard black glaze.

Preserved height 4.0 cm.; diameter of foot 4.8 cm.; width of resting surface 0.8 cm.

Local ware? Third quarter of the fourth century B.C.

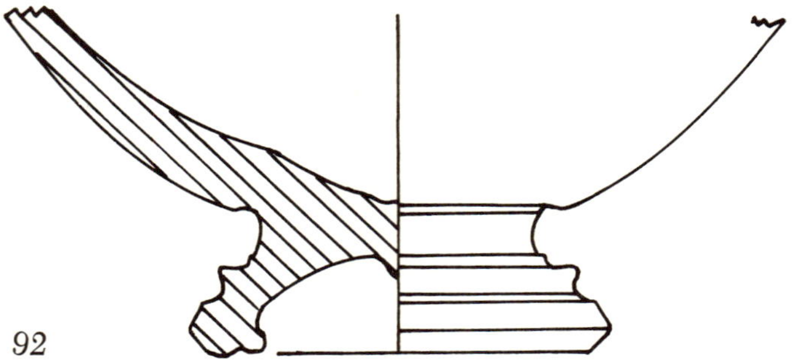

92

ONE-HANDLER[1]

1. For black one-handlers, cf. *Agora XII*, pp. 126 ff.

93. 50.65 F. (See fig.)
Fragment of lip and beginning of handle root, attached just below the rim. Light brown clay (7.5 YR 6/4). The wall flares slightly toward the rim, which is flat on top. Hard black glaze with a slightly greenish cast on the outside; flaked in several places.

Preserved height 3.2 cm.; restored diameter 16.0 cm.

Compare Agora P 16937, P 11800, P 11798, and P 7596 (*Agora XII*, nos. 753, 758-760).

Attic. Second quarter of the fourth century B.C.

93

BOWLS[1]

1. For black bowls, cf. *Agora XII*, pp. 128 ff.

94. 50.87 B. (See fig.)
Fragment preserving part of wall and out-turned rim. Reddish-yellow clay (5 YR 7/6). Dull black glaze, applied thinly, flaked in places. Some misfiring.

Preserved height 3.3 cm.; restored diameter 11.0 cm.

Similar to Agora P 5194 (*Agora XII*, no. 782).

Local ware? Late fifth century B.C.

94

95. 50.98, 50.99, and 50.103. (See fig.)
Five joining fragments of small bowl with incurving rim, preserving complete profile, except for foot, which is missing. Reddish-yellow clay (5 YR 7/6). The vessel was a hand-dipped one, as revealed by the irregular area with finger or thumb print of the potter just above the junction of the foot. The glaze has run sloppily over the surface after the bowl was righted.

Preserved height 3.2 cm.; restored diameter 12.0 cm.

Local ware. Fourth century B.C.

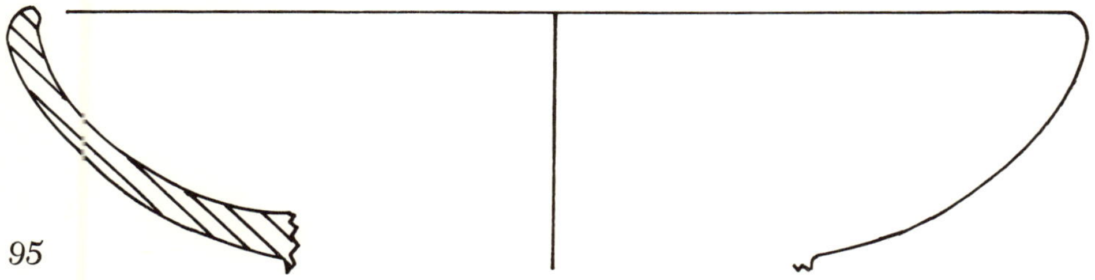

95

96. 50.87 C. (See fig.)
Fragment of small bowl with incurving rim, preserving part of wall and rim. Reddish-yellow clay (5 YR 6/6). Hard black glaze, flaked in many places, especially on lip.

Preserved height 1.9 cm.; restored diameter 9.0 cm.

Local ware? Fourth century B.C.

97. 50.65 G. (See fig.)

Fragment of small bowl with incurving rim, preserving part of wall and rim. Light brown clay (7.5 YR 6/4). Dull black glaze with a greenish cast. Flaked in many places. Lip worn.

Preserved height 1.8 cm.; diameter 8.5 cm.

Local ware. Fourth century B.C.

96 97

98. 50.87 A. (See fig.)

Base of small bowl with glazed underside and broad resting surface, which is reserved except for a line at inner edge and a band 0.4 cm. wide at outer edge. Light brown clay (7.5 YR 6/4). Reserved line on outside above and below junction of bowl and base. Hard black glaze.

Preserved height 0.6 cm.; diameter of base 6.5 cm.; width of resting surface 1.3 cm.

For this type of bowl, cf. *Agora XII*, p. 135, nos. 882-889.

Attic? First half of the fourth century B.C.

99. 50.74 E. (See fig.)

Fragment of ring foot with resting surface and curved underside reserved. Light brown clay (7.5 YR 6/4). Brownish-black glaze, flaked in many places.

Preserved height 1.1 cm.; width of resting surface 0.3 cm.; diameter 6.3 cm.

Local ware. Fourth century B.C.

100. 50.65 J. (See fig.)

Fragment of ring foot with resting surface and underside reserved. Reddish-yellow clay (5 YR 6/6). Brownish-black glaze, flaked in many places.

Preserved height 1.1 cm.; restored diameter 6.0 cm.; width of resting surface 0.5 cm.

Local ware. Fourth century B.C.

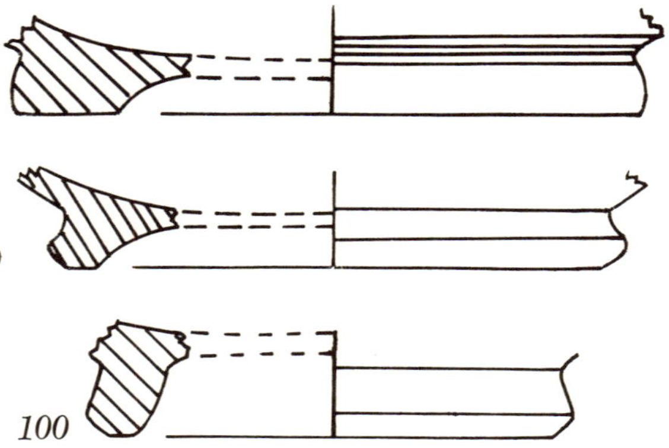

98 99 100

ASKOS[1]

1. For black askoi, cf. *Agora XII*, pp. 157 ff.

101. 50.74 B. (See fig.)
Fragment of spout, neck and handle of askos. Light brown clay (7.5 YR 6/4). Flaring mouth, overarching strap handle. Glazed inside to a depth of 1.2 cm. below rim. Hard black glaze, misfired brown in part, flaked in some places.

Preserved height 2.6 cm.; diameter of mouth 2.3 cm.

Not enough of this askos is preserved to be certain whether it had a deep or a shallow body. Compare Agora P 16457, P 4739, and P 20093 (*Agora XII*, nos. 1166, 1171, and 1176).

Attic? Fifth century B.C.

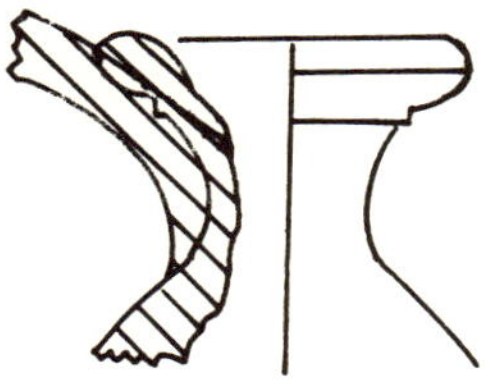

101

FRAGMENTS OF BLACK-GLAZED POTTERY FROM THE FILL OF THE TEMENOS (**102-107**)

CUPS

Type C[1]

1. For the shape, cf., above, p. 383.

102. 50.250 A. (See fig.)
Two joining fragments preserving part of bowl and concave lip with sharp incurve below. Light brown clay (7.5 YR 6/4). Hard black glaze, flaked and abraded in places.

Preserved height 3.7 cm.; restored diameter 18.0 cm.

The profile is similar to three fragments from the Altar Court: cf. Vol. 4, pt. II, p. 170, no. 52, p. 207, A 1, and p. 212, A 10. Cf. also, Agora P 24597 and P 24596 (*Agora XII*, nos. 408 and 410); also London E 66, an early classical red-figure cup by the Clinic Painter, a follower of Makron (*ARV*[2] 808, 2; H. Bloesch, *Formen attischer Schalen*, Berne, 1940, pl. 36, 4 c).

Attic. First quarter of the fifth century B.C.

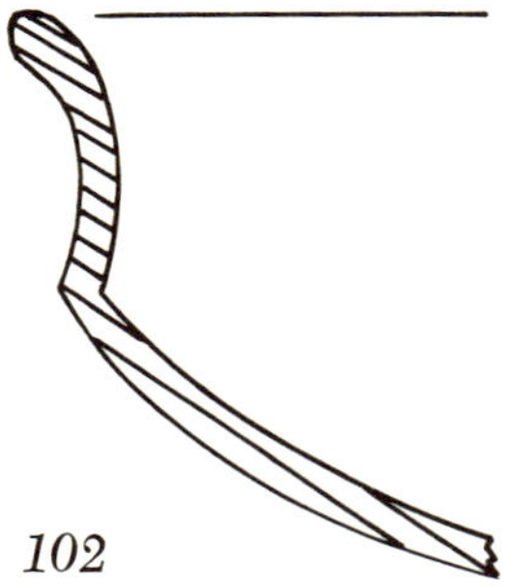

102

103. 50.250 B. (See fig.)
Fragment of concave lip, broken at junction of bowl. Light brown glaze (7.5 YR 6/4).

Preserved height 1.9 cm.; preserved width 2.5 cm.

Close to no. **83**, but less straight. Compare two with a similar profile found in the Altar Court: cf. Vol. 4, pt. II, p. 211, A 9 and p. 227, A 36; also Agora P 20757 and P 25276 (*Agora XII*, no. 404).

Attic? Late sixth-early fifth century B.C.

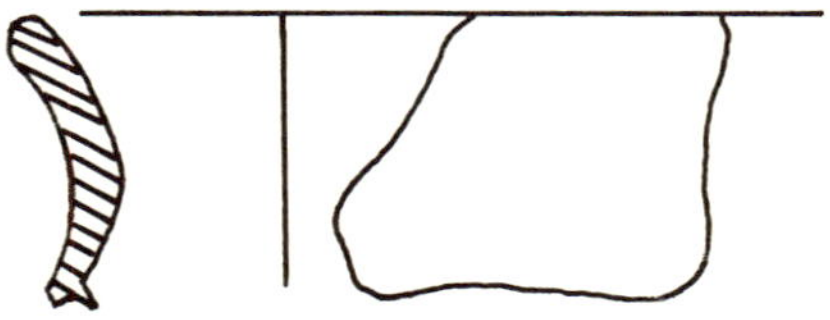

103

KANTHAROI[1]

1. For kantharoi of the fourth century, cf. above, p. 386.

104. 50.172 C. (See figs.)
Spur and beginning of vertical member of handle. Reddish-yellow clay (7.5 YR 7/6). Spur is narrow and tapering without flaring sides. Dull, brownish-black glaze, much of it flaked.

Preserved height 1.2 cm.; preserved length 3.2 cm.

Local ware. Ca. 350 B.C.

105. 50.172 B. (See figs.)
Spur and part of vertical member of handle. Reddish-yellow clay (7.5 YR 6/6). Spur tapers to a blunt end. Black glaze that has misfired in places to a dark brown.

Preserved height 2.6 cm.; preserved length 3.1 cm.

Compare Agora P 6935 (*Agora XII*, no. 712).

Local ware? Third quarter of the fourth century B.C.

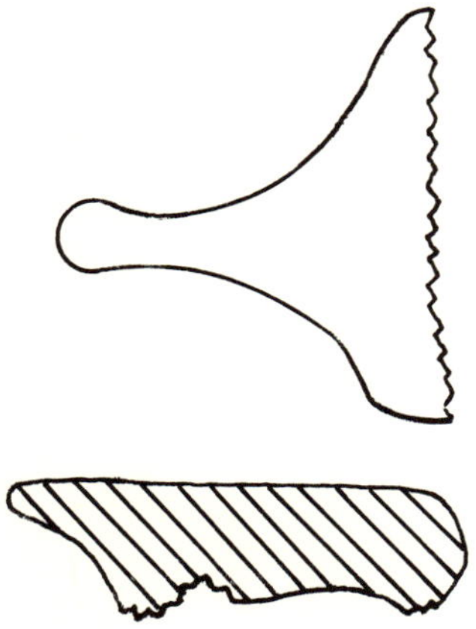

104

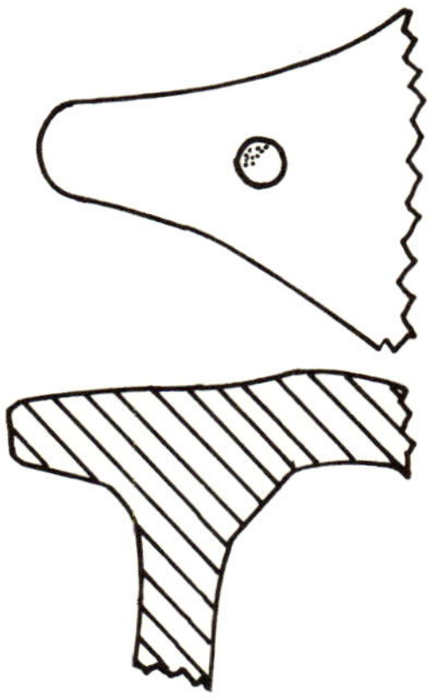

105

106. 50.172 A. (See fig.)
Molded foot in several degrees, with grooved resting surface that is reserved except for a line at inner edge. Reddish-yellow clay (5 YR 6/6). Grooves between moldings on outside. Underside of bowl and central nipple glazed. Hard black glaze, flaked in places.

Preserved height 2.3 cm.; restored diameter 5.3 cm.; width of resting surface 0.5 cm.

Compare Agora P 6935 and P 6680 (*Agora XII*, no. 712).

Local ware? Third quarter of the fourth century B.C.

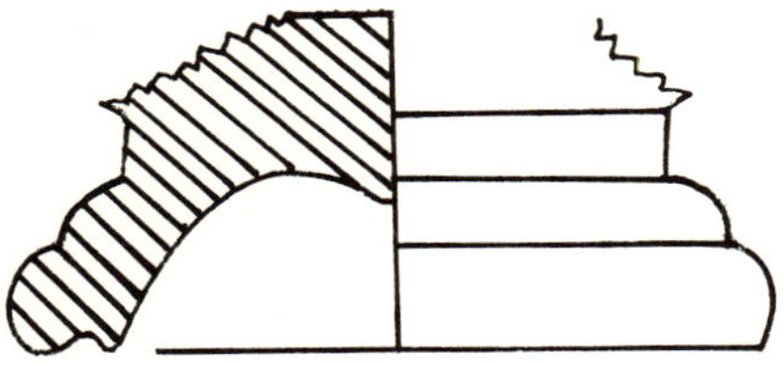

106

BOWL[1]

1. For black bowls, cf. above, p. 389.

107. 50.399. (See figs.)
Three joining fragments of small bowl with broad resting surface, which is reserved except for a line at the inner edge. Light brown clay (7.5 YR 6/4). Underside of floor and central nipple glazed. Outside of foot completely glazed, including groove at junction of bowl. On floor of bowl, part of four stamped palmettes, badly preserved. Hard black glaze that has a greenish cast on inside.

Preserved height 3.6 cm.; diameter of base 6.6 cm.

This piece is very similar to Agora P 23752 (unpublished): brownish-black glaze, abraded in places; resting surface of foot reserved except for a line of glaze at inner edge. On stamping, cf. most recently, *Agora XII*, p. 22, with bibliography.

Local ware? First half of the fourth century B.C.

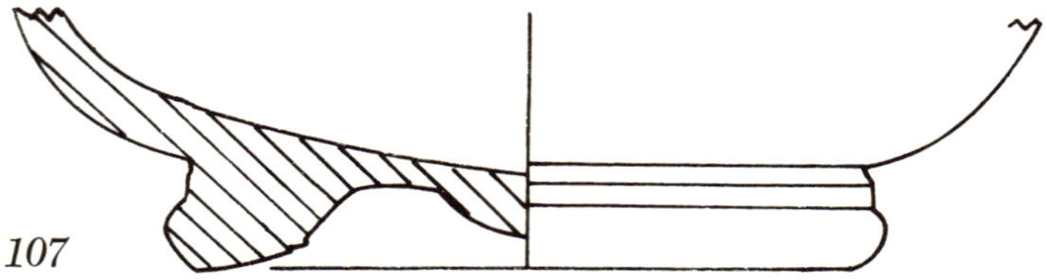

107

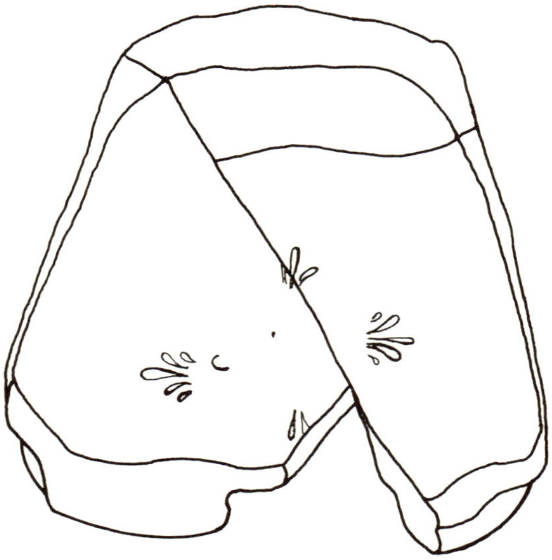

107

2. Sculptures

by Martha Leeb Hadzi

Sculptures

108. 50.452. (See figs.)
Small female marble torso. Although previously published as a male torso, and indeed identified in the *Guide* as a Pan or Satyr, this fragment must have belonged to a female figure, as the explicit depiction of its bust clearly indicates. The torso is preserved from neck to abdomen; the right shoulder and arm are missing, but the upper left arm remains intact. In front view, the neck opening of a light garment, probably a chiton, is seen to curve from the right shoulder down toward a point below the left shoulder; the edge of this garment can then be seen to enclose the left shoulder and, in the rear, to encounter the lower contour of the long hair which descends upon the figure's neck and upper back. Save for these details, the rear of the torso is weathered and broken in such a way that all other features are obliterated. What remains of the neck shows that the head turned toward the figure's right. On this side, to judge from the slanting line of the shoulders, the arm must have been raised. At the point where it would have been attached to the shoulder, there is a small dowel hole (0.0025 m. in depth); below this, at the level of the bust, there is a somewhat larger dowel hole (0.008 m. in depth), which must have served for the attachment of another compositional element—another figure, or the drapery or other attribute of this one?

108

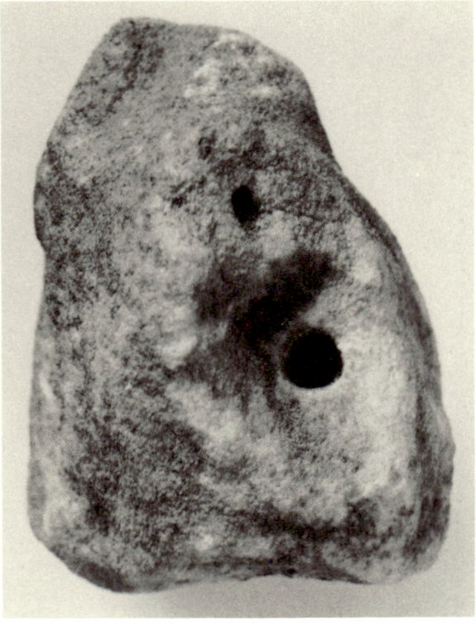

108

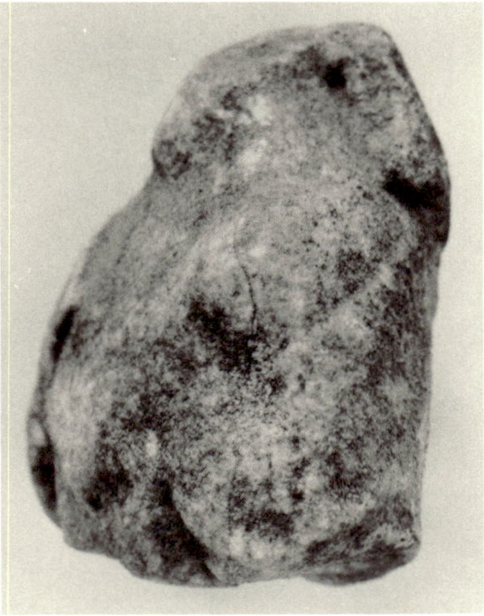

108

Preserved height 0.078 m.; preserved width ca. 0.073 m.; preserved thickness 0.053 m.

Found on the terrace adjoining the Temenos.

Hesperia, 21 (1952), p. 42; *Guide*[1], p. 87; *Guide*[2], p. 90; *Guide*[3], p. 95; *Guide*[4], p. 108.

Altogether, the décolletée arrangement of the chiton, the active pose, and the open design that is implied by the presence of the dowel holes, bespeak a sculpture of mature Hellenistic style.

109. 50.218 (See figs.)

Marble forelegs of a horse. This diminutive sculptured fragment represents a horse's front legs, extended toward the right. One leg, which terminates in a break just below the fetlock, is unfinished on the side that is hidden from view in the illustration; the other leg, terminating in a hoof, is roughly finished on its lower surface, hence must have been partially hidden by another superimposed form. A dowel hole in the hoof (0.0035 m. in depth) served for the attachment of that form, which was perhaps one of the legs of a second horse.

Preserved length 0.067 m.; greatest preserved width ca. 0.031 m.; greatest preserved thickness 0.022 m.

Found on the terrace adjoining the Temenos.

Hesperia, 21 (1952), p. 42; *Guide*[1], p. 87; *Guide*[2], p. 90; *Guide*[3], p. 95; *Guide*[4], p. 108.

The sculpture may be the remnant of a quadriga. It appears to have been part of a high relief of very small scale, perhaps decorating a stele, statue base or altar. It illustrates

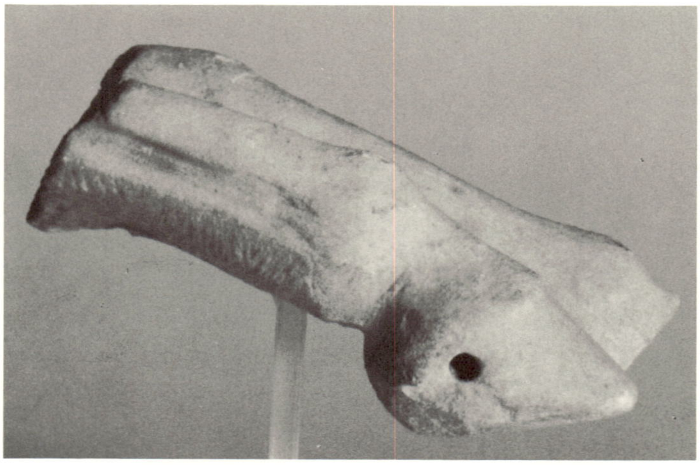

109

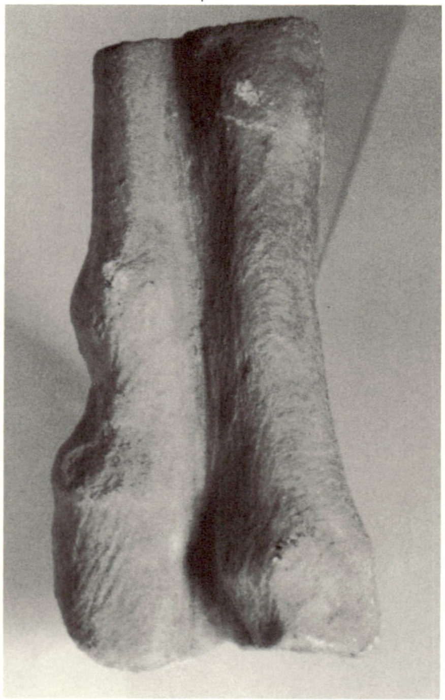

109

a relief style employing a daring projection of deeply undercut forms, with doweled additions of great fragility, technical features that are common in the later Imperial period. The *Decursio* reliefs from the base of the Column of Marcus Aurelius in the Vatican, for example, afford a parallel in style, in spite of the difference in scale.[1]

1. Lise Vogel, *The Column of Antoninus Pius*, Cambridge, 1973, pls. 9-15.

110. 49.247 (See figs.)

Fragmentary Thasian marble head of a veiled woman, the left half of which is broken away diagonally, so that a portion of the right side, including the veil and parts of the right eye and cheek, the chin and the lower left jaw and veil, are preserved. The neck terminates in a horizontal break, and the head is tipped upward and toward its right. Flesh surfaces are softly rounded, and details of hair, ear, and veil are delicately modeled; the channel separating the neck from the veil is deeply cut, suggesting a pictorial use of light and shade.

Preserved height 0.065 m.; preserved width ca. 0.05 m.; thickness ca. 0.046-0.05 m.

Found immediately northwest of the terrace adjoining the Temenos.

The work is certainly post-Praxitelean: this particular form of closely adhering veil, exposing the ear and a narrow band of hair, is found in late Hellenistic representations, as seen in a second-century statue of a woman in the Louvre.[1]

1. Margarete Bieber, *The Sculpture of the Hellenistic Age*, rev. edn., New York, 1961, p. 132, fig. 524.

110

110

3. Varia

by Elsbeth B. Dusenbery

Iron Ring

111

111. 50.81 (see fig.)

Circular iron finger ring. Mended from two fragments. Heavily corroded. Overlapping ends, inner surface flattened. No trace of bezel or ornament.

Outer diameter 0.024 m.; inner diameter 0.018 m.

Surface find from behind the north wall of the Temenos.

Previously published by Karl Lehmann, "The Mystery Cult of Samothrace: Excavations in 1953," *Archaeology*, 7 (1954), p. 94 and fig.

Iron rings apparently had a special magical importance involving magnetism in the Samothracian cult.[1] It has been suggested that iron rings may have been made inside the Sanctuary, where at least one piece of partly smelted ore (hematite) was found.[2] Unfortunately, except for this example and one other,[3] few possible traces of iron rings have been found during the excavation of the sacred area. Given the perishable nature of iron buried in damp soil and the power seemingly ascribed to the rings, which surely made them carefully guarded possessions, this is not entirely surprising.

Iron rings were not unusual in antiquity, although relatively few have resisted destruction by corrosion. They were commonly worn by the austere Spartans and Republican Romans, and they are recorded in considerable numbers in the inventories of votive gifts in Greek temples.[4] During the Roman Imperial period, it was chiefly slaves who wore iron rings, and evidently they often had the rings plated with gold to hide the base metal. Pliny

1. Vol. I, **212**; *Guide*⁴, pp. 25, 32.
2. *Guide*⁴, p. 102.
3. 64.765, from the foundation fill of the Stoa. This ring has a broad, undecorated oval bezel. It will be published in Volume 8 of this series.
4. For the history and use of iron rings in ancient times: F. H. Marshall, *Catalogue of the Finger Rings, Greek, Etruscan and Roman in the Departments of Antiquities, British Museum*, London, 1907, pp. XXXIV-XXXV.

wrote that such gilded iron rings were called Samothracian.[5] This suggests that, at least in Roman times, iron rings belonging to Samothracian initiates were frequently gilded. However, there are no traces of gold preserved on this example.

Such plain annular bands, usually made of bronze, sometimes with overlapping ends and sometimes flattened on the inner side, are frequently found in excavations. They come from contexts dating from many centuries.[6] These circles were obviously simple to make from prepared bar stock, and, without supporting evidence, they are impossible to date.

It cannot be assumed with so little evidence that this was in truth one of the famous Samothracian iron rings, though it seems very possible, nor that a simple hoop was the canonical shape of such rings. The ring from the foundation fill of the Stoa is different from this and the five rings recovered from burials in the Samothracian nekropoleis vary greatly in form. The two earliest date from the beginning of the fifth century B.C. and belong to Boardman's Group N, a widespread type.[7] The latest is the ring illustrated in the Samothrace *Guide* which has a Roman shape of the second or third century A.D.[8] We cannot be certain that these iron rings, even from graves just outside the Sanctuary, were the rings of initiates, but the possibility suggests itself that the special rings were available in various fashionable styles of their eras as well as in the, surely less costly, simple hoop.

5. Vol. I, **213**; see also **30**.

6. For example: John Boardman, *Greek Emporio*, Oxford, 1967, nos. 242-251, pp. 211-212, fig. 139, examples of the seventh and sixth centuries B.C.; David M. Robinson, *Excavations at Olynthus; Part X, Metal and Minor Miscellaneous Finds*, Baltimore, 1941, Nos. 496-502, pp. 155-156, pl. 27, examples of the fifth and fourth centuries B.C.

7. John Boardman, "Archaic Finger Rings," *Antike Kunst*, 10 (1967), pp. 25-27, pl. 7.

8. *Guide*[4], fig. 8; Marshall, *op. cit.*, nos. 202, 483.

INDEXES

1. TOPOGRAPHICAL INDEX OF ARCHITECTURAL MONUMENTS

A. OUTSIDE SAMOTHRACE

For additional references, see Index 4.

B. SAMOTHRACE

(I) THE TEMENOS

For additional references, see Index 4.

(II) THE TERRACE

For additional references, see Index 4.

(III) THE PROPYLON TO THE TEMENOS

For additional references, see Index 4.

(IV) OTHER STRUCTURES IN OR NEAR THE SANCTUARY

2. ANCIENT AUTHORS

3. PRINCIPAL GREEK AND LATIN WORDS

A. GREEK

This index does not include the article, common conjunctions, or prepositions.

B. LATIN

4. GENERAL INDEX

For specific references to the Temenos, Terrace, and Propylon, see Index 1 B (I-III). For other structures in Samothrace, see Index 1 B (IV); for the major references to monuments outside Samothrace, see Index 1 A.

BOLLINGEN SERIES LX

SAMOTHRACE

EXCAVATIONS CONDUCTED BY THE
INSTITUTE OF FINE ARTS, NEW YORK UNIVERSITY

KARL LEHMANN
PHYLLIS WILLIAMS LEHMANN
Editors

Library of Congress Cataloging in Publication Data

Lehmann, Karl, 1894-1960, ed.
Samothrace.

(Bollingen series, 60,)
Each vol. has also special t.p.
Vols. 3- edited by K. Lehmann and P. W. Lehmann.
Published since 1969 by Princeton University Press, Princeton, N.J., for Bollingen Foundation, New York.
Bibliography: v. 1, p.
CONTENTS: v. 1. The ancient literary sources, edited and translated by N. Lewis.—v. 2, pt. 1. The inscriptions on stone, by P. M. Fraser.—[etc.]—v. 5, pt. 1. The Temenos, by P. W. Lehmann and D. Spittle.
1. Samothrace—Antiquities—Collected works. 2. Excavations (Archaeology)—Greece, Modern—Samothrace—Collected works. 3. Greece, Modern—Antiquities—Collected works. I. Lehmann, Phyllis Lourene Williams, 1912, joint ed. II. New York University. Institute of Fine Arts. III. Series.
DF261.S3L38 939.1'1 58-8985
ISBN 0-691-09917-0 (v. 5)